REDRESSING FUNDAMENTAL RIGHTS VIOLATIONS BY THE EU

The EU prides itself on having created a legal system that puts the individual at its centre. Individuals benefit from a broad range of fundamental rights that protect them against EU power. However, to vindicate their rights against the EU, they have to make use of a remedies system as old as the EU itself. Unsurprisingly, with EU power growing and evolving, it also is increasingly difficult to challenge. This book critically examines the EU's remedies system from a fundamental rights perspective, focusing on the EU's activities outside the realm of lawmaking. It maps the existing mechanisms private parties can avail themselves of to enforce their fundamental rights against the EU and discovers their unused potential. In doing so, it offers an important synthesis of the state of play and directions for reform in areas where the EU falls short of its promise to provide a 'complete system of remedies'. This title is also available as Open Access on Cambridge Core.

Melanie Fink is Assistant Professor of European Law at Leiden University and APART-GSK Fellow of the Austrian Academy of Sciences at the Central European University. She researches and publishes in the areas of EU and public international law, with a focus on human rights and access to justice, the EU's role in border control, and accountability in the context of administrative cooperation, including through the use of artificial intelligence systems.

Redressing Fundamental Rights Violations by the EU

THE PROMISE OF THE 'COMPLETE SYSTEM OF REMEDIES'

Edited by
MELANIE FINK
Leiden University and Central European University

CAMBRIDGE
UNIVERSITY PRESS

CAMBRIDGE
UNIVERSITY PRESS

Shaftesbury Road, Cambridge CB2 8EA, United Kingdom

One Liberty Plaza, 20th Floor, New York, NY 10006, USA

477 Williamstown Road, Port Melbourne, VIC 3207, Australia

314–321, 3rd Floor, Plot 3, Splendor Forum, Jasola District Centre, New Delhi – 110025, India

103 Penang Road, #05–06/07, Visioncrest Commercial, Singapore 238467

Cambridge University Press is part of Cambridge University Press & Assessment, a department of the University of Cambridge.

We share the University's mission to contribute to society through the pursuit of education, learning and research at the highest international levels of excellence.

www.cambridge.org
Information on this title: www.cambridge.org/9781009373807

DOI: 10.1017/9781009373814

First published 2024

A catalogue record for this publication is available from the British Library

Library of Congress Cataloging-in-Publication Data
NAMES: Fink, Melanie, author.
TITLE: Redressing fundamental rights violations by the EU : the promise of the 'complete system of remedies' / edited by Melanie Fink.
DESCRIPTION: Cambridge, United Kingdom ; New York, NY : Cambridge University Press, 2024. | Includes bibliographical references and index.
IDENTIFIERS: LCCN 2024013532 (print) | LCCN 2024013533 (ebook) | ISBN 9781009373807 (hardback) | ISBN 9781009373821 (paperback) | ISBN 9781009373814 (epub)
SUBJECTS: LCSH: Civil rights–European Union countries. | Remedies (Law)–European Union countries. | Civil rights–European Union countries–Criminal provisions.
CLASSIFICATION: LCC KJE5132 .R43 2024 (print) | LCC KJE5132 (ebook) | DDC 342.2408/5–dc23/eng/20240412
LC record available at https://lccn.loc.gov/2024013532
LC ebook record available at https://lccn.loc.gov/2024013533

ISBN 978-1-009-37380-7 Hardback

This Edited Volume is part of the project 'No Right Without a Remedy' (Dr Melanie Fink), funded by the Austrian Academy of Sciences under the APART-GSK grant scheme.

Contents

Figures and Tables

FIGURES

TABLE

Contributors

Editor

Melanie Fink
Assistant Professor of European Law, Leiden University, and APART-GSK Fellow of the Austrian Academy of Sciences, Central European University

Authors

Koen Bovend'Eerdt
Scientific Bureau of the Dutch Supreme Court, Criminal Law Division (Wetenschappelijk Bureau van de Hoge Raad, sector straf)

Merijn Chamon
Associate Professor of EU Law, Maastricht University

Florin Coman-Kund
Associate Professor of European Union Law, Erasmus School of Law, Erasmus University Rotterdam, and Senior Expert in EU Governance, European Institute of Public Administration (EIPA) Maastricht

Joyce De Coninck
FWO Postdoctoral Researcher, Department of European, Public and International Law, Ghent University

Simona Demková
Assistant Professor of European Law, Europa Institute, Leiden University

Mariolina Eliantonio
Professor of European and Comparative Administrative Law and Procedure, Maastricht University

Giulia Gentile
Lecturer in Law, Essex Law School

Ljupcho Grozdanovski
Research Associate/Chercheur Qualifié, Fonds National de la Recherche Scientifique, University of Liège

Andreas Hofmann
Assistant Professor in European Union Studies, Leiden University

Argyro Karagianni
Assistant Professor of EU Public Economic Law, Utrecht University

Jasper Krommendijk
Professor of Human Rights Law, Radboud University Nijmegen

Lucía López Zurita
Postdoctoral Researcher, Center for Global Mobility Law, University of Copenhagen

Kris van der Pas
PhD candidate, Centre for Migration Law and Department of International and European Law, Radboud University Nijmegen

Clara Rauchegger
Senior Assistant Professor, Department of Legal Theory and Future of Law, University of Innsbruck

Maria José Schmidt-Kessen
Assistant Professor of International Business Law, Central European University

Miroslava Scholten
Associate Professor of EU Law Enforcement, Utrecht Centre for Regulation and Enforcement in Europe (RENFORCE), Utrecht University

Moritz Schramm
Adjunct Professor of Law, New York University; Affiliated Postdoctoral Researcher, Humboldt-University of Berlin; law clerk, Higher Regional Court of Berlin

Veronika Yefremova
PhD candidate, Leiden University

Table of Cases

COURT OF JUSTICE OF THE EUROPEAN UNION (CJEU)

Court of Justice

Case C-26/62 *Van Gend en Loos* [1963] ECLI:EU:C:1963:1
Case C-25/62 *Plaumann v Commission* [1963] ECLI:EU:C:1963:17
Case C-6/64 *Flaminio Costa v E.N.E.L.* [1964] ECLI:EU:C:1964:66
Joined Cases C-5/66, 7/66, 13/66–24/66 *Kampffmeyer and Others v Commission* [1967] EU:C:1967:31
Case C-30/66 *Becher v Commission* [1967] ECLI:EU:C:1967:44
Case C-29/69 *Stauder v Ulm* [1969] ECLI:EU:C:1969:57
Case C-11/70 *Internationale Handelsgesellschaft mbH v Einfuhr- und Vorratsstelle für Getreide und Futtermittel* [1970] ECLI:EU:C:1970:114
Case C-22/70 *Commission v Council. European Agreement on Road Transport (ERTA)* [1971] ECLI:EU:C:1971:32
Joined Cases C-41/70 to 44/70 *International Fruit Co. et al. v Commission* [1971] ECLI:EU:C:1971:53
Case C-4/69 *Lütticke v Commission* [1971] ECLI:EU:C:1971:40
Case C-17/74 *Transocean Marine Paint v Commission* [1974] ECLI:EU:C:1974:106
Case C-33/76 *Rewe* [1976] ECLI:EU:C:1976:188
Case C-101/76 *Koninklijke Scholten Honig NV* [1977] ECLI:EU:C:1977:70
Case C-123/77 *UNICME et al. v Council* [1978] ECLI:EU:C:1978:73
Case C-86/76 *Hoffmann-La Roche v Commission* [1979] ECLI:EU:C:1979:36
Case C-92/78 *Simmenthal v Commission* [1979] ECLI:EU:C:1979:53

Joined Cases C-64/76 and C-113/76 *Dumortier v Council* [1979] ECLI:EU:C:1979:223
Case C-44/79 *Liselotte Hauer v Land Rheinland-Pfalz* [1979] ECLI:EU:C:1979:290
Case C-136/79 *National Panasonic v Commission* [1980] ECLI:EU:C:1980:169
Case C-60/81 *IBM v Commission* [1981] ECLI:EU:C:1981:264
Case C-126/81 *Wünsche Handelsgesellschaft v Federal Republic of Germany* [1982] ECLI:EU:C:1982:144
Case C-155/79 *AM & S v* Commission [1982] ECLI:EU:C:1982:157
Case C-96/81 *Commission v Netherlands* [1982] ECLI:EU:C:1982:192
Case C-283/81 *Cilfit* [1982] ECLI:EU:C:1982:335
Case C-249/81 *Commission v Ireland* [1982] ECLI:EU:C:1982:402
Case C-199/82 *San Giorgio* [1983] ECLI:EU:C:1983:318
Joined Cases C-177/82 and C-178/82 *Van de Haar* [1984] ECLI:EU:C:1984:144
Case C-59/83 *Biovilac v EEC* [1984] ECLI:EU:C:1984:380
Case C-294/83 *Les Verts v Parliament* [1986] ECLI:EU:C:1986:166
Case C-222/84 *Johnston* [1986] ECLI:EU:C:1986:206
Case C-53/85 *AKZO Chemie BV and AKZO Chemie UK Ltd v Commission* [1986] ECLI:EU:C:1986:256
Case C-281/84 *Zuckerfabrik v Commission* [1987] ECLI:EU:C:1987:3
Case C-45/86 *Commission v Council* [1987] ECLI:EU:C:1987:163
Joined Cases C-89/86 and C-91/86 *Étoile commerciale and CNTA* v *Commission* [1987] EU:C:1987:337
Case C-314/85 *Foto-Frost* v *Hauptzollamt Lübeck-Ost* [1987] ECLI:EU:C:1987:452
Case C-92/88 *Assider v Commission* [1988] ECLI:EU:C:1988:222
Case C-148/88 R *Albani v Commission* [1988] ECLI:EU:C:1988:334
Case C-191/88 *Co-Frutta v Commission* [1988] ECLI:EU:C:1988:418
Case C-128/87 *Commission v Greece* [1989] ECLI:EU:C:1989:7
Case C-85/87 *Dow Benelux NV v Commission* [1989] ECLI:EU:C:1989:379
Case C-374/87 *Orkem v Commission* [1989] ECLI:EU:C:1989:387
Case C-322/88 *Salvatore Grimaldi v Fonds des maladies professionnelles* [1989] ECLI:EU:C:1989:646
Case C-308/87 *Grifoni v EAEC* [1990] ECLI:EU:C:1990:134
Case C-213/89 *Factortame* [1990] ECLI:EU:C:1990:257
Case C-16/90 *Nölle v Hauptzollamt Bremen-Freihafen* [1991] ECLI:EU:C:1991:402

Joined Cases C-6/90 and C-9/90, *Francovich/Bonifaci* [1991] ECLI:EU: C:1991:428
Case C-269/90 *TUM* [1991] ECLI:EU:C:1991:438
Case *Opinion 1/91 - Draft agreement between the Community, on the one hand, and the countries of the European Free Trade Association, on the other, relating to the creation of the European Economic Area* [1991] ECLI:EU:C:1991:490
Case C-97/91 *Oleificio Borelli SpA v Commission* [1992] ECLI:EU: C:1992:491
Case C-309/89 *Codorníu* [1994] ECLI:EU:C:1994:197
Case C-466/93 *Atlanta Fruchthandelsgesellschaft mbH and Others v Bundesamt für Ernährung und Forstwirtschaft* [1995] ECLI:EU: C:1995:370
Joined Cases C-46/93 and C-48/93 *Brasserie du Pêcheur* [1996] ECLI:EU: C:1996:79
Case C-392/93 *The Queen v H.M. Treasury, ex parte British Telecommunications* [1996] ECLI:EU:C:1996:131
Case C-283/94 *Denkavit Internationaal and Others v Bundesamt für Finanzen* [1996] ECLI:EU:C:1996:387
Case C-32/95 P *Commission v Lisrestal* [1996] ECLI:EU:C:1996:402
Case C-321/95 P *Stichting Greenpeace Council and Others v Commission of the European Communities* [1998] ECLI:EU:C:1998:153
Case C-386/96 P *Dreyfus* [1998] ECLI:EU:C:1998:193
Case C-185/95 *Baustahlgewebe v Commission* [1998] ECLI:EU: C:1998:608
Case C-6/99 *Association Greenpeace France and Others v Ministère de l'Agriculture et de la Pêche and Others* [1999] ECLI:EU:C:1999:587
Case C-198/98 P *Everson/Barras* [1999] ECLI:EU:C:1999:617
Joined Cases C-174/98 P and C-189/98 P *van der Wal v Commission* [2000] ECLI:EU:C:2000:1
Case C-17/98 *Emesa Sugar* [2000] ECLI:EU:C:2000:70
Case C-7/98 *Krombach* [2000] ECLI:EU:C:2000:164
Case C-352/98 P *Bergaderm and Goupil v Commission* [2000] ECLI:EU: C:2000:361
Case C-462/98 P *Mediocurso v Commission* [2000] ECLI:EU:C:2000:480
Case C-300/99 P *Area Cova and Others v Council* [2001] ECLI:EU: C:2001:71
Case C-274/99 P *Bernard Connolly v Commission of the European Communities* [2001] ECLI:EU:C:2001:127
Case C-120/99 *Italy v Council* [2001] ECLI:EU:C:2001:567

Case C-269/99 *Carl Kühne GmbH & Co. KG and Others v Jütro Konservenfabrik GmbH & Co. KG* [2001] ECLI:EU:C:2001:659

Case *Opinion 1/00 - Proposed agreement between the European Community and non-Member States on the establishment of a European Common Aviation Area* [2002] ECLI:EU:C:2002:231

Case C-50/00 P *Unión de Pequeños Agricultores* (UPA) [2002] ECLI:EU:C:2002:462

Case C-94/00 *Roquette Frères* [2002] ECLI:EU:C:2002:603

Case C-276/01 *Steffensen* [2003] ECLI:EU:C:2003:228

Case C-122/01 P *T.Port v Commission* [2003] ECLI:EU:C:2003:259

Case C-224/01 *Köbler* [2003] ECLI:EU:C:2003:513

Case C-234/ 02 P *Mediator v Lamberts* [2004] ECLI:EU:C:2004:174

Case C-263/02 P *Commission v Jégo-Quéré* [2004] ECLI:EU:C:2004:210

Case C-521/04 P(R) *Hans-Martin Tillack v Commission* [2005] ECLI:EU:C:2005:240

Joined Cases C-189/02 P, C-202/02 P, C-205/02 P to C-208/02 P and C-213/02 P *Dansk Rørindustri and Others v Commission* [2005] ECLI:EU:C:2005:408

Case C-198/03 P *Commission v CEVA and Pfizer* [2005] ECLI:EU:C:2005:445

Case C-341/04 *Eurofood IFSC Ltd.* [2006] ECLI:EU:C:2006:281

Case C-168/05 *Mostaza Claro v Centro Móvil Milenium SL* [2006] ECLI:EU:C:2006:675

Case C-292/05 *Erini Lechouritou and Others v Dimosio tis Omospondiakis* [2007] ECLI:EU:C:2007:102

Case C-432/05 *Unibet* [2007] ECLI:EU:C:2007:163

Case C-282/05 P *Holcim (Deutschland) v Commission* [2007] ECLI:EU:C:2007:226

Case C-438/05 *International Transport Workers' Federation and The Finnish Seamen's Union v Viking Line ABP and OÜ Viking Line Eesti* [2007] ECLI:EU:C:2007:772

Case C-64/05 P *Sweden v Commission*, [2007] ECLI:EU:C:2007:802

Case C-341/05 *Laval un Partneri* [2007] ECLI:EU:C:2007:809

Case C-227/06 *Commission v Belgium* [2008] ECLI:EU:C:2008:160

Case C-212/06 *Flemish care insurance* [2008] ECLI:EU:C:2008:178

Joined Cases C-402/05 P and C-415/05 P *Kadi Al Barakaat* [2008] ECLI:EU:C:2008:461

Joined Cases C-120/06 P and 121/06 P *FIAMM and Others v Council and Commission* [2008] ECLI:EU:C:2008:476

Case C-394/07 *Gambazzi* [2009] ECLI:EU:C:2009:219

Case C-343/07 *Bavaria NV and Bavaria Italia Srl v Bayerischer Brauerbund eV* [2009] ECLI:EU:C:2009:415
Case C-440/07 P *Commission v Schneider Electric* [2009] ECLI:EU: C:2009:459
Case C-425/08 *Enviro Tech (Europe) v Belgian State* [2009] ECLI:EU: C:2009:635
Joined Cases C 399/06 P and C-403/06 P *Hassan and Ayadi v Council and Commission* [2009] ECLI:EU:C:2009:748
Case C-419/08 P *Trubowest* [2010] ECLI:EU:C:2010:147
Case C-550/07 P *Akzo Nobel Chemicals and Akcros Chemicals* v *Commission* [2010] ECLI:EU:C:2010:512
Case C-306/09 *B.* [2010] ECLI:EU:C:2010:626
Case C-92/09 *Volker und Markus Schecke* [2010] ECLI:EU:C:2010:662
Case C-93/11 P *Verein Deutsche Sprache* [2011] ECLI:EU:C:2011:429
Case C-548/09 P *Bank Melli Iran v Council* [2011] ECLI:EU:C:2011:735
Case C-434/11 *Corpul Naţional al Poliţiştilor* [2011] ECLI:EU: C:2011:830
Case C-462/11 *Victor Cozman v Teatrul Municipal Târgovişte* [2011] ECLI:EU:C:2011:831
Case C-27/09 P *France v People's Mojahedin Organization of Iran* [2011] ECLI:EU:C:2011:853
Joined Cases C-411/10 and C-493/10 *N.S. v Secretary of State for the Home Department and M.E. and Others v Refugee Applications Commissioner and Minister for Justice, Equality and Law Reform* [2011] ECLI:EU: C:2011:865
Case C-134/12 *Corpul Naţional al Poliţiştilor* [2012] ECLI:EU: C:2012:288
Case C-135/11 P *Internationaler Tierschutz-Fonds gGmbH* [2012] ECLI: EU:C:2012:376
Case C-544/10 *Deutsches Weintor* [2012] ECLI:EU:C:2012:526
Case C-433/11 *SKP* [2012] ECLI:EU:C:2012:702
Case C-539/10 P *Al-Aqsa v Council and Pays-Bas / Al-Aqsa* [2012] ECLI: EU:C:2012:711
Case C-417/11P *Council v Bamba* [2012] ECLI:EU:C:2012:718
Case C-277/11 *M* [2012] ECLI:EU:C:2012:744
Case C-370/12 *Pringle* [2012] ECLI:EU:C:2012:756
Case C-12/11 *McDonagh* [2013] ECLI:EU:C:2013:43
Case C-300/11 *ZZ v Secretary of State for the Home Department* [2013] ECLI:EU:C:2013:36
Case C-399/11 *Melloni* [2013] ECLI:EU:C:2013:107

Case C-128/12 *Sindicato dos Bancários do Norte and Others* [2013] ECLI:EU:C:2013:149

Case C-58/12 P *Groupe Gascogne v Commission* [2013] ECLI:EU:C:2013:360

Case C-501/11 P *Schindler Holding Ltd vs European Commission* [2013] ECLI:EU:C:2013:522

Case C 583/11 P *Inuit Tapiriit Kanatami and Others v Parliament and Council* [2013] ECLI:EU:C:2013:625

Case C-101/12 *Schaible* [2013] ECLI:EU:C:2013:661

Case C-184/12 *United Antwerp Maritime Agencies (Unamar) NV v Navigation Maritime Bulgare* [2013] ECLI:EU:C:2013:663

Case C-291/12 *Schwarz* [2013] ECLI:EU:C:2013:670

Case C-4/11 *Bundesrepublik Deutschland v Kaveh Puid* [2013] ECLI:EU:C:2013:740

Case C-40/12 P *Gascogne Sack Deutschland v Commission* [2013] ECLI:EU:C:2013:768

Case C-50/12 P *Kendrion v Commission* [2013] ECLI:EU:C:2013:771

Case C-274/12 P *Telefónica v Commission* [2013] ECLI:EU:C:2013:852

Case C-363/12 Z [2014] ECLI:EU:C:2014:159

Joined Cases C-293/12 and C-594/12 *Digital Rights Ireland* [2014] ECLI:EU:C:2014:238

Case C-604/12 N [2014] ECLI:EU:C:2014:302

Case C-356/12 *Glatzel* [2014] ECLI:EU:C:2014:350

Case C-658/11 *Parliament v Council* [2014] ECLI:EU:C:2014:2025

Case C-264/12 *Sindicato Nacional dos Profissionais de Seguros e Afins* [2014] ECLI:EU:C:2014:2036

Case C-19/13 *Fastweb* [2014] ECLI:EU:C:2014:2194

Case C-3/13 *Baltic Agro* [2014] ECLI:EU:C:2014:2227

Case C-166/13 *Mukarubega v Seine-Saint-Denis* [2014] ECLI:EU:C:2014:2336

Case *Opinion 2/13 – Accession of the EU to the ECHR* [2014] ECLI:EU:C:2014:2454

Case C-404/12 P and 405/12 P *Council and Commission v Stichting Natuur en Milieu and Pesticide Action Network Europe* [2015] ECLI:EU:C:2015:5

Case C-456/13 P *Sugars v Commission* [2015] ECLI:EU:C:2015:284

Case C-546/12 P *Schräder v CPVO* [2015] ECLI:EU:C:2015:332

Case C-1/14 *Base Company and Mobistar* [2015] ECLI:EU:C:2015:378

Case C-583/13 P *Deutsche Bahn AG and Others v Commission* [2015] ECLI:EU:C:2015:404

Case C-362/14 *Schrems v Data Protection Commissioner* [2015] ECLI:EU:C:2015:650
Case C-439/13 P *Elitaliana* v *Eulex Kosovo* [2015] ECLI:EU:C:2015:753
Case C-603/13 P *Galp Energia España* [2016] ECLI:EU:C:2016:38
Case C-601/15 N [2016] ECLI:EU:C:2016:84
Case C-49/14 *Finanmadrid* [2016] ECLI:EU:C:2016:98
Joined Cases C-404/15 and C-659/15 PPU *Aranyosi and Căldăraru* [2016] ECLI:EU:C:2016:198
Case C-200/13 P *Council v Bank Saderat Iran* [2016] ECLI:EU:C:2016:284
Case C-191/14 *Borealis Polyolefine* [2016] ECLI:EU:C:2016:311
Case C-477/14 *Pillbox 38* [2016] ECLI:EU:C:2016:324
Case C-547/14 *Philipp Morris Brands and Others* [2016] ECLI:EU:C:2016:325
Case C-559/14 *Meroni* [2016] ECLI:EU:C:2016:349
Case C-78/16 *Pesce and Others* [2016] ECLI:EU:C:2016:428
Case C-134/15 *Lidl* [2016] ECLI:EU:C:2016:498
Case C-455/14 P *H v Council and Commission* [2016] ECLI:EU:C:2016:569
Case C-526/14 *Kotnik and Others* [2016] ECLI:EU:C:2016:570
Case C-543/14 *Ordre des barreaux francophones and germanophone and Others* [2016] ECLI:EU:C:2016:605
Joined Cases C-439/14 and C-488/14 *Star Storage et al.* [2016] ECLI:EU:C:2016:688
Joined Cases C-8/15 P to C-10/15 P *Ledra Advertising e.a. v Commission & ECB* [2016] ECLI:EU:C:2016:701
Joined Cases C-105/15 P to C-109/15 P *Mallis e.a. v Commission & ECB* [2016] ECLI:EU:C:2016:702
Case C-673/13 P *European Commission v Stichting Greenpeace Nederland & Pesticide Action Network Europe* [2016] ECLI:EU:C:2016:889
Case C-76/15 *Vervloet and Others* [2016] ECLI:EU:C:2016:975
Case C-444/15 *Associazione Italia Nostra Onlus* [2016] ECLI:EU:C:2016:978
Case C-272/15 *Swiss International Air Lines* [2016] ECLI:EU:C:2016:993
Case C-604/13 P *Dornbracht* [2017] ECLI:EU:C:2017:45
Case C-390/15 *RPO* [2017] ECLI:EU:C:2017:174
Case C-141/15 *Doux* [2017] ECLI:EU:C:2017:188
Case C-158/14 A *and Others* [2017] ECLI:EU:C:2017:202
Case C-157/15 *Samira Achbita v G4S Secure Solutions* [2017] ECLI:EU:C:2017:203

Case C-72/15 *Rosneft* [2017] ECLI:EU:C:2017:236
Case C-337/15 P *European Ombudsman v Staelen* [2017] ECLI:EU:C:2017:256
Case C-45/15 P *Safa Nicu Sepahan v Council* [2017] ECLI:EU:C:2017:402
Case C-258/14 *Florescu* [2017] ECLI:EU:C:2017:448
Case C-190/16 *Fries* [2017] ECLI:EU:C:2017:513
Case C348/16 *Sacko* [2017] ECLI:EU:C:2017:591
Case C-18/16 *K* [2017] ECLI:EU:C:2017:680
Case C-89/15 P *Riva Fire v Commission* [2017] ECLI:EU:C:2017:713
Case C-73/16 *Puškár* [2017] ECLI:EU:C:2017:725
Case C-531/15 *Otero Ramos* [2017] ECLI:EU:C:2017:789
Case C-599/15 *Romania* v *Commission* [2017] ECLI:EU:C:2017:801
Case C-521/15 *Spain v Council* [2017] ECLI:EU:C:2017:982
Case C-322/16 *Global Starnet* [2017] ECLI:EU:C:2017:985
Case C-102/16 *Vaditrans* [2017] ECLI:EU:C:2017:1012
Case C-473/16 *F v Bevándorlási és Állampolgársági Hivatal* [2018] ECLI:EU:C:2018:36
Case C-176/17 *Credit Polska* [2018] ECLI:EU:C:2018:71
Case C-16/16 P *Belgium v Commission* [2018] ECLI:EU:C:2018:79
Case C-64/16 *Associação Sindical dos Juízes Portugueses* [2018] ECLI:EU:C:2018:117
Case C-284/16 *Slowakische Republik (Slovak Republic) v Achmea BV* [2018] ECLI:EU:C:2018:158
Case C-152/17 *Consorzio Italian Management e Catania Multiservizi* [2018] ECLI:EU:C:2018:264
Case C-426/16 *Liga van Moskeeën en Islamitische Organisaties Provincie Antwerpen and Others* [2018] ECLI:EU:C:2018:335
Case C-238/18 *ECB v Latvia* [2018] ECLI: EU:C:2018:581
Case C-216/18 PPU *Minister for Justice and Equality (Deficiencies in the system of justice)* [2018] ECLI:EU:C:2018:586
Joined Cases C-622/16 P to C-624/16 P *Scuola Elementare Maria Montessori Srl v Commission* [2018] ECLI:EU:C:2018:873
Case C-151/17 *Swedish Match* [2018] ECLI:EU:C:2018:938
Case C-138/17 P *EU v Gascogne Sack Deutschland and Gascogne* [2018] ECLI:EU:C:2018:1013
Case C-150/17 P *EU v Kendrion* [2018] ECLI:EU:C:2018:1014
Case C-219/17 *Berlusconi and Fininvest* [2018] ECLI:EU:C:2018:1023
Case C-220/17 *Planta Tabak* [2019] ECLI:EU:C:2019:76
CaseC-266/18 *Aqua Med* [2019] ECLI:EU:C:2019:282

Case *Opinion 1/17* [2019] ECLI:EU:C:2019:341
Case C-391/16 *M (Révocation du statut de réfugié)* [2019] ECLI:EU:C:2019:403
Case C-644/17 *Eurobolt* [2019] ECLI:EU:C:2019:555
Joined Cases C-447/17 P and C-479/17 P *EU v Guardian Europe & Guardian Europe v EU* [2019] ECLI:EU:C:2019:672
Case C-284/19 P *Clarke v Commission* [2019] ECLI:EU:C:2019:799
Case C-616/17 *Blaise and Others* [2019] ECLI:EU:C:2019:800
Case C-453/18 *Bondora* [2019] ECLI:EU:C:2019:1118
Case C-785/18 *GAEC Jeanningros v Institut national de l'origine et de la qualité (INAO) and Others* [2020] ECLI:EU:C:2020:46
Case C-454/18 *Baltic Cable* [2020] ECLI:EU:C:2020:189
Case C-612/18 P *ClientEarth v Commission* [2020] ECLI:EU:C:2020:223
Case C-14/19 P *CSUE v KF* [2020] ECLI:EU:C:2020:492
Case C-311/18 *Data Protection Commissioner v Facebook Ireland Ltd & Maximilian Schrems* [2020] ECLI:EU:C:2020:559
Case C-517/17 *Addis* [2020] ECLI:EU:C:2020:579
Case C-784/18 P Mellifera v Commission [2020] ECLI:EU:C:2020:630
Case C-511/18 *La Quadrature du Net and Others* [2020] ECLI:EU:C:2020:791
Case C-134/19 P *Bank Refah Kargaran* [2020] ECLI:EU:C:2020:793
Joined Cases C-225/19 and C-226/19 *R.N.N.S., K.A. v Minister van Buitenlandse Zaken* [2020] ECLI:EU:C:2020:951
Case C-336/19 *Centraal Israëlitisch Consistorie van België and Others* [2020] ECLI:EU:C:2020:1031
Case C-258/20 *Klymenko* v *Council* [2021] ECLI:EU:T:2021:52
Case C-649/19 *Spetsializirana prokuratura (Déclaration des droits)* [2021] ECLI:EU:C:2021:75
Case C-481/19 *Consob* [2021] ECLI:EU:C:2021:84
Case C-193/19 A *v Migrationsverket* [2021] ECLI:EU:C:2021:168
Case C-501/18 *BT v Balgarska Narodna Banka* [2021] ECLI:EU:C:2021:249
Case C-565/19 P *Carvalho and Others v Parliament and Council* [2021] ECLI:EU:C:2021:252
Case C-572/18 P *ThyssenKrupp v Commission* [2021] ECLI:EU:C:2021:317
Case C-142/20 *Analisi G. Caracciolo* [2021] ECLI:EU:C:2021:368
Case C-685/20 P *Sharpston v Council and Representatives of the Member States* [2021] ECLI:EU:C:2021:485

Case C-911/19 *Fédération bancaire française (FBF) v Autorité de contrôle prudentiel et de résolution (ACPR)* [2021] ECLI:EU:C:2021:599
Case C-741/19 *Republic of Moldova v Komstroy LLC* [2021] ECLI:EU:C:2021:655
Case C-930/19 *Belgian State (Droit de séjour en cas de violence domestique)* [2021] ECLI:EU:C:2021:657
Case C-458/19 P *ClientEarth v Commission* [2021] ECLI:EU:C:2021:802
Case C-497/20 *Ranstadt Italia* [2021] ECLI:EU:C:2021:1037
Case C-156/21 *Hungary v European Parliament and Council of the European Union* [2022] ECLI:EU:C:2022:97
Case C-157/21 *Poland v European Parliament and Council of the European Union* [2022] ECLI:EU:C:2022:98
Case C-160/20 *Stichting Rookpreventie Jeugd and Others* [2022] ECLI:EU:C:2022:101
Case C-673/20 *Préfet du Gers and Institut national de la statistique and des études économiques* [2022] ECLI:EU:C:2022:449
Case C-817/19 *Ligue des droits humains* [2022] ECLI:EU:C:2022:491
Case C-203/21 *Delta Stroy 2003* [2022] ECLI:EU:C:2022:865
Case C-37/20 *Luxembourg Business Register* [2022] ECLI:EU:C:2022:912
Case C-69/21 *Staatssecretaris van Justitie en Veiligheid (Éloignement – Cannabis thérapeutique)* [2022] ECLI:EU:C:2022:913
Case C-694/20 *Orde van Vlaamse Balies and Others* [2022] ECLI:EU:C:2022:963
Case C-158/21 *Puig Gordi and Others* [2023] ECLI:EU:C:2023:57
Case C-626/21 *Funke Sp. z o.o. v Landespolizeidirektion Wien* [2023] ECLI:EU:C:2023:412
Case C-351/22 *Neves 77 Solutions* [case in progress]
Case C-755/21 P *Kočner v EUROPOL* [2024] ECLI:EU:C:2024:202.

General Court

Case T-116/89 *Prodifarma e.a. v Commission* [1990] ECLI:EU:T:1990:85
Case T-85/94 *Branco I* [1995] ECLI:EU:T:1995:4
Case T-346/94 *France-Aviation v Commission* [1995] ECLI:EU:T:1995:187
Joined Cases T-134/94, T-136/94, T-137/94, T-138/94, T-141/94, T-145/94, T-147/94, T-148/94, T-151/94, T-156/94 and T-157/94 *NMH Stahlwerke GmbH* [1996] ECLI:EU:T:1996:85
Case T-42/96 *Eyckeler & Malt AG v Commission* [1998] ECLI:EU:T:1998:40

Case T-54/96 *Oleifici Italiani and Fratelli Rubino v Commission* [1998] ECLI:EU:T:1998:204
Case T-50/96 *Primex Produkte Import-Export GmbH & Co. KG, Gebr. Kruse GmbH, Interporc Im- und Export GmbH v Commission* [1998] ECLI:EU:T:1998:223
Joined Cases T-34/96 and 163/96 *Bernard Connolly v Commission of the European Communities* [1999] ECLI:EU:T:1999:102
Case T-277/97 *Ismeri Europa v Court of Auditors* [1999] ECLI:EU:T:1999:124
Case T-14/98 *Hautala v Council* [1999] ECLI:EU:T:1999:157
Case T-182/96 *Partex v Commission* [1999] ECLI:EU:T:1999:171
Case T-290/97 *Mehibas Dordtselaan BV v Commission* [2000] ECLI:EU:T:2000:8
Joined Cases T-172/98 and T-175/98 to T-177/98 *Salamander et al.* [2000] ECLI:EU:T:2000:168
Case T-178/98 *Fresh Marine v Commission* [2000] ECLI:EU:T:2000:240
Case T-1/99 *T.Port* [2001] ECLI:EU:T:2001:36
Case T-186/97 *Wilson Holland and Others v Commission* [2001] ECLI:EU:T:2001:133
Case T-191/00 *Edinger* [2001] ECLI:EU:T:2001:183
Case T-120/99 *Kik v OHIM* [2001] ECLI:EU:T:2001:189
Case T-9/98 *Mitteldeutsche ErdölRaffinerie* [2001] ECLI:EU:T:2001:271
Case T-241/00 *Azienda Agricola "Le Canne" Srl v Commission* [2002] ECLI:EU:T:2002:57
Case T-177/01 *Jégo-Quéré v Commission* [2002] ECLI:EU:T:2002:112
Case T-223/01 *Japan Tobacco and JT International v Parliament and Council* [2002] ECLI:EU:T:2002:205
Case T-199/99 *Sgaravatti v Commission* [2002] ECLI:EU:T:2002:228
Joined Cases T-377/00, 379/00, 380/00, T-260/01 and 272/01 *Philip Morris and Others v Commission* [2003] ECLI:EU:T:2003:6
Case T-56/00 *Dole Fresh Fruit International LTd v Council and Commission* [2003] ECLI:EU:T:2003:58
Case T-102/00 *Vlaams Fonds v Commission* [2003] ECLI:EU:T:2003:192
Case T-215/02 *Gomez Reino* [2003] ECLI:EU:T:2003:352
Case T-177/02 *Malagutti-Vezinhet v Commission* [2004] ECLI:EU:T:2004:72
Case T-139/02 *Idiotiko Institouto v Commission* [2004] ECLI:EU:T:2004:75
Case T-341/02 *Regione Siciliana v Commission* [2004] ECLI:EU:T:2004:228

Joined Cases T-110/03, T-150/03 and T-405/03 *Sison* [2005] ECLI:EU:T:2005:143
Case T-250/02 *Autosalone Ispra v EAEC* [2005] ECLI:EU:T:2005:432
Case T-69/00 *FIAMM* [2005] ECLI:EU:T:2005:449
Case T-210/01 *General Electric Co. v Commission* [2005] ECLI:EU:T:2005:456
Case T-364/03 *Medici Grimm KG v Council of the European Union* [2006] ECLI:EU:T:2006:28
Case T-279/03 *Galileo International Technology and Others v Commission* [2006] ECLI:EU:T:2006:121
Case T-395/04 *Air One v Commission* [2006] ECLI:EU:T:2006:123
Case T-193/04 *Tillack v Commission* [2006] ECLI:EU:T:2006:292
Case T-138/03 *É.R. and Others v Council and Commission* [2006] ECLI:EU:T:2006:390
Case T-351/03 *Schneider Electric SA v Commission of the European Communities* [2007] ECLI:EU:T:2007:212
Case T-259/03 *Nikolaou v Commission* [2007] ECLI:EU:T:2007:254
Joined Cases T-125/03 and T-253/03 *Akzo Nobel Chemicals Ltd, and Akcros Chemicals Ltd v Commission* [2007] ECLI:EU:T:2007:287
Case T-48/05 *Franchet and Byk v Commission* [2008] ECLI:EU:T:2008:257
Case T-212/03 *My Travel Group v Commission* [2008] ECLI:EU:T:2008:315
Case T-437/05 Brink's Security Luxembourg v Commission [2009] ECLI:EU:T:2009:318
Case T-212/06 *Bowland Dairy Products v Commission* [2009] ECLI:EU:T:2009:419
Case T-158/07 *Cofac v Commission* [2009] ECLI:EU:T:2009:489
Case T-189/02 *Ente per le Ville vesuviane v Commission* [2009] ECLI:EU:C:2009:529
Case T-429/05 *Artedogan v Commission* [2010] ECLI:EU:T:2010:60
Case T-74/08 *Now Pharm v Commission* [2010] ECLI:EU:T:2010:376
Case T-117/07 *Areva and Others v Commission* [2011] ECLI:EU:T:2011:69
Case T-369/07 *Latvia v Commission* [2011] ECLI:EU:T:2011:103
Case T-144/07 *ThyssenKrupp Liften Ascenseurs v Commission* [2011] ECLI:EU:T:2011:364
Case T-19/06 *Mindo v Commission* [2011] ECLI:EU:T:2011:561
Case T-262/10 *Microban v Commission* [2011] ECLI:EU:T:2011:623

Case T-88/09 *Idromacchine Srl, Alessandro Capuzzo and Roberto Capuzzo v European Commission* [2011] ECLI:EU:T:2011:641
Case T-341/07 Sison v Council [2011] ECLI:EU:T:2011:687
Case T-514/09 *bpost NV v Commission* [2011] ECLI:EU:T:2011:689
Case T-133/08 *Schräder v CP VO* [2012] ECLI:EU:T:2012:430
Case T-63/10 *Jurašinović v Council* [2012] ECLI:EU:T:2012:516
Case T-541/10 *ADEDY and Others v Council* [2012] ECLI:EU:T:2012:626
Case T-215/11 *ADEDY and Others v Council* [2012] ECLI:EU:T:2012:627
Case T-56/09 *Saint-Gobain Glass France and Others v Commission* [2014] ECLI:EU:T:2014:160
Case T-447/11 *Catinis v Commission* [2014] ECLI:EU:T:2014:267
Case T-317/12 *Holcim (Romania) v Commission* [2014] ECLI:EU:T:2014:782
Case T-384/11 *Safa Nicu Sepahan v Council* [2014] ECLI:EU:T:2014:986
Case T-217/11 *Staelen v European Ombudsman* [2015] ECLI:EU:T:2015:238
Case T-536/11 *European Dynamics Luxembourg* [2015] ECLI:EU:T:2015:476
Case T-721/14 Belgium v Commission [2015] ECLI:EU:T:2015:829
Case T-138/14 *Chart v EEAS* [2015] ECLI:EU:T:2015:981
Case T-381/14 *Pshonka v Council* [2016] ECLI:EU:T:2016:361
Case T-26/15 P *Commission v Hristov* [2016] ECLI:EU:T:2016:390
Case T-577/14 *Gascogne Sack Deutschland and Gascogne v EU* [2017] ECLI:EU:T:2017:1
Case T-189/14 *Deza v ECHA* [2017] ECLI:EU:C:2017:4
Case T-479/14 *Kendrion v EU* [2017] ECLI:EU:T:2017:48
Case T-40/15 *ASPLA and Armando Álvarez v EU* [2017] ECLI:EU:T:2017:105
Case T-344/15 *France v Commission* [2017] ECLI:EU:T:2017:250
Case T-63/16 E-Control v ACER [2017] ECLI:EU:T:2017:456
Case T-704/14 *Marine Harvest* v *Commission* [2017] ECLI:EU:T:2017:753
Case T-653/16 R *Malta v Commission* [2018] ECLI:EU:T:2018:241
Case T-577/17 ThyssenKrupp v Commission [2018] ECLI:EU:T:2018:411
Case T-786/14 *Bourdouvali v Council* [2018] ECLI:EU:T:2018:487
Case T-603/16 *Brahma v Court of Justice of the European Union* [2018] ECLI:EU:T:2018:820
Case T-433/15 *Bank Saderat v Commission* [2019] ECLI:EU:T:2019:374

Case T-399/17 *Dalli v Commission* [2019] ECLI:EU:T:2019:384
Case T-406/15 *Mahmoudian v Council* [2019] ECLI:EU:T:2019:468
Case T-405/15 *Fulmen v Council* [2019] ECLI:EU:T:2019:469
Case T-274/18 *Klymenko v Council* [2019] ECLI:EU:T:2019:509
Case T-755/17 *Germany v ECHA* [2019] ECLI:EU:T:2019:647
Case T-48/17 *ADDE v Parliament* [2019] ECLI:EU:T:2019:780
Case T-323/16 *Banco Cooperativo Español* [2019] ECLI:EU:T:2019:822
Case T-365/16 *Portigon AG* [2019] ECLI:EU:T:2019:824
Case T-526/19 *Nord Stream 2* [2020] ECLI:EU:T:2020:210
Case T-105/19 *Louis Vuitton Malletier v EUIPO - Wisniewski (Représentation d'un motif à damier)* [2020] ECLI:EU:T:2020:258.
Case T-295/19 *Klymenko v Council* [2020] ECLI:EU:T:2020:287
Case T-437/16 *Italy v Commission* [2020] ECLI:EU:T:2020:410
Case T-594/18 *Pharma Mar v Commission* [2020] ECLI:EU:T:2020:512
Case T-322/19 *El-Qaddafi v Council* [2021] ECLI:EU:T:2021:206
Case T-302/19 *Yanukovych v Council* [2021] ECLI:EU:T:2021:333
Case T-303/19 *Yanukovych v Council* [2021] ECLI:EU:T:2021:334
Case T-517/19 *Homoki v Commission* [2021] ECLI:EU:T:2021:529
Case T-528/20 *Kočner v EUROPOL* [2021] ECLI:EU:T:2021:631
Cases T-351/18 and T-584/18 *Ukrselhosprom PCF LLC and Versobank AS, established in Tallinn (Estonia) v European Central Bank (ECB)* [2021] ECLI:EU:T:2021:669
Case T-771/20 *KS and KD v Council and Others* [2021] ECLI:EU:T:2021:798
Case T-195/21 *Klymenko v Council* [2021] ECLI:EU:T:2021:925
Case T-791/19 *Sped-Pro S.A. v Commission* [2022] ECLI:EU:T:2022:67
Case T-151/20 *Czech Republic v European Commission* [2022] ECLI:EU:T:2022:281
Case T-698/16 *Trasta Komercbanka and Others v ECB* [2022] ECLI:EU:T:2022:737
Case T-330/19 *PNB Banka AS* [2022] ECLI:EU:T:2022:775
Case T-282/21 *SS and ST v Frontex* [2022] ECLI:EU:T:2022:235
Case T-426/21 *Nizar Assad* [2023] ECLI:EU:T:2023:114
Case T-379/21 *Vendrame v Commission* [2023] ECLI:EU:T:2023:399
Case T-600/21 *WS and Others v Frontex* [2023] ECLI:EU:T:2023:492

Civil Service Tribunal

Case F-50/09 *Missir Mamachi di Lusignano v Commission* [2011] ECLI:EU:F:2011:55

Opinions of Advocates General

Opinion of AG Roemer in Case C-25/62 *Plaumann v Commission* [1963] ECLI:EU:C:1963:7

Opinion of AG Tesauro in Case 55/88 *Katsoufros* [1989] ECLI:EU: C:1989:364

Opinion of AG Lenz in Case C-73/95 P *Viho Europe BV v Commission* [1996] ECLI:EU:C:1996:164

Opinion of AG Ruiz-Jarabo Colomer in Case C-427/00 *Commission v UK* [2001] ECLI:EU:C:2001:396

Opinion of AG Jacobs in Case C-50/00 P *Unión de Pequeños Agricultores* (UPA) [2002] ECLI:EU:C:2002:197

Opinion of AG Geelhoed in Case C-234/02 P *Mediator v Lamberts* [2003] ECLI:EU:2003:394

Opinion of AG Sharpston in Cases C-92/09 and C-93/02, Volker und Markus Schecke [2010] ECLI:EU:C:2010:353

Opinion of AG Kokott in Case C-416/10 *Križan* [2012] ECLI:EU: C:2012:218

Opinion of AG Cruz Villalón in Case C-617/10 *Åkerberg Fransson* [2013] ECLI:EU:C:2012:340

Opinion of AG Cruz Villalón in Case C-176/ 12 *Association de médiation sociale* [2013] ECLI:EU:C:2013:491

Opinion of AG Bot in Case C-511/13 P *Philips Lighting Poland and Philips Lighting v Council* [2015] ECLI:EU:C:2015:206

Opinion of AG Wahl in Joined Cases C-8/15 P to C-10/15 P *Ledra Advertising e.a. v Commission & ECB* [2016] ECLI:EU: C:2016:290

Opinion of AG Wathelet in Joined Cases C-105/15 P to C-109/15 P *Mallis e.a. v Commission & ECB* [2016] ECLI:EU:C:2016:294

Opinion of AG Bot in Case C-258/14 *Florescu* [2016] ECLI:EU: C:2016:995

Opinion of AG Bot in Case C-612/15 *Kolev* [2017] ECLI:EU:C:2017:257

Opinion of AG Saugmandsgaard Øe in Case C-64/16 *Associação Sindical dos Juízes Portugueses* [2017] ECLI:EU:C:2017:395

Opinion of AG Bobek in Case C-16/16 P *Belgium v Commission* [2017] ECLI:EU:C:2017:959

Opinion of AG Kokott in C-176/17 *Profi Credit Polska* [2018] ECLI:EU: C:2018:711

Opinion of AG Mengozzi in Case C-279-09 *DEB* [2020] ECLI:EU: C:2010:489

Opinion of AG De La Tour in Case C-193/19 A v *Migrationsverket* [2020] ECLI:EU:C:2020:594

Opinion of AG Campos Sánchez-Bordona in Case C-501/18 *BT* [2020] ECLI:EU:C:2020:729

Opinion of AG Bobek in Case C-911/19 Fédération bancaire française (FBF) v Autorité de contrôle prudentiel et de résolution (ACPR) [2021] ECLI:EU:C:2021:294

Opinion of AG Hogan in Case C-497/20 *Ranstadt Italia* [2021] ECLI:EU:C:2021:725

Opinion of AG Bobek in Case C-348/20 P *Nord Stream 2* [2022] ECLI:EU:C:2021:831

Opinion of AG Rantos in Case C-755/21 P *Kočner v EUROPOL* [2023] ECLI:EU:C:2023:481

Opinion of AG Kokott in Cases C-750/21 P and C-256/22 P *Pilatus Bank plc v ECB* [2023] ECLI:EU:C:2023:431

EUROPEAN COURT OF HUMAN RIGHTS (ECTHR)

De Wilde, Ooms and Versyp v Belgium App nos 2832/66, 2835/66 and 2899/66 (ECtHR, 18 June 1971)

Confédération française démocratique du travail v the European Communities, alternatively: their Member States a) jointly and b) severally (dec.) App no. 8030/77 (ECtHR, 10 July 1978)

M. & Co v Germany (dec.) App no 13258/8 (ECtHR, 9 February 1990)

Kruslin v France App no 11801/85 (ECtHR, 24 April 1990)

Imbrioscia v Switzerland App no 13972/88 (ECtHR, 24 November 1993)

Saunders v United Kingdom App no 19187/91 (ECtHR, 17 December 1996)

Matthews v United Kingdom App no 24833/94 (ECtHR, 18 February 1999)

Cha'are Shalom Ve Tsedek v France App no 27417/95 (ECtHR, 27 June 2000)

Dangeville v France App no 36677/97 (ECtHR, 16 April 2002)

Posti and Rahko v Finland App no 27824/95 (ECtHR, 24 September 2002)

Phull v France App no 35753/03 (ECtHR, 11 January 2005)

Bosphorus v *Ireland* App no 45036/98 (ECtHR, 30 June 2005)

Behrami and Behrami v France and Saramati v France, Germany and Norway (dec.) App no 71412/01 (ECtHR, 2 May 2007)

Connolly v 15 Member States of the European Union (dec.) App no 73274/01 (ECtHR, 9 December 2008)

Hickey v the UK App no 39492/07 (ECtHR, 4 May 2010)

A, B and C v Ireland App no 25579/05 (ECtHR, 16 December 2010)
Al-Jedda v United Kingdom App no 27021/08 (ECtHR, 7 July 2011)
Menarini Diagnostics Srl v Italy App No 43509/08 (ECtHR, 27 September 2011)
Eweida and Others v United Kingdom App nos 48420/10, 36516/10, 51671/10 et al. (ECtHR, 15 January 2013)
Dhahbi v Italy App no 17120/09 (ECtHR, 8 April 2014)
Ibrahim and Others v the United Kingdom App nos 50541/08, 50571/08, 50573/08 and 40351/09 (ECtHR, 13 September 2016)
Lozovyye v Russia App no 4587/09 (ECtHR, 24 April 2018)
Sanofi Pasteur v France App no 25137/16 (ECtHR, 13 February 2020)
Bivolaru and Moldovan v France App no 40324/16 and 12623/17 (ECtHR, 25 March 2021)
Case of Norwegian Confederation of Trade Unions (LO) and Norwegian Transport Workers' Union (Ntf) v Norway App no. 45487/17 (ECtHR, 10 June 2021)
Lee v the UK App no 18860/19 (ECtHR, 7 December 2021)
A.D. *v Greece* App no 55363/19 (ECtHR, 4 April 2023)

NATIONAL COURTS

Belgium

Court Constitutionelle [Belgium] 33/2012

Germany

Bundesverfassungsgericht [Germany], 29 May 1974, BVerfGE 37, 271 *Solange I*
Bundesverfassungsgericht [Germany], 22 October 1986, BVerfGE 73, 339 *Solange II*
Bundesverfassungsgericht [Germany], 31 March 1998, BVerfGE 97, 350 *Euro*
Bundesverfassungsgericht [Germany], 7 June 2000, BVerfGE 102, 147 *Bananenmarktordnung*
Bundesverfassungsgericht [Germany], 7 June 2000, BVerfGE 89, 155 *Maastricht*
Bundesverfassungsgericht [Germany], 30 June 2009, BVerfGE 123, 267 *Lissabon*
Bundesverfassungsgericht [Germany], 22 June 2011, 2 BvR 1219/10

Bundesverfassungsgericht [Germany], 7 December 2011, BVerfGE 129, 124 *EFS*
Bundesverfassungsgericht [Germany], 12 September 2012, 2 BvR 1824/12
Bundesverfassungsgericht [Germany], 12 September 2012, 2 BvR 1438/12
Bundesverfassungsgericht [Germany], 12 December 2012, BVerfGE 132, 195 *Europäischer Stabilitätsmechanismus*
Bundesverfassungsgericht [Germany], 14 January 2014, BVerfGE 134, 366 *OMT-Beschluss*
Bundesverfassungsgericht [Germany], 21 June 2016, 2 BvR 2731/13
Bundesverfassungsgericht [Germany], 13 October 2016, 2 BvR 1823/16
Bundesverfassungsgericht [Germany], 13 October 2016, 2 BvR 1444/16
Bundesverfassungsgericht [Germany], 30 July 2019, BVerfGE 151, 202 *Europäische Bankenunion*
Bundesverfassungsgericht [Germany], 5 May 2020, 2 BvR 980/16
Bundesverfassungsgericht [Germany], 5 May 2020, 2 BvR 1651/15
Bundesverfassungsgericht [Germany], 5 May 2020, BVerfGE 154, 17 *PSPP-Programm der EZB*
Bundesverfassungsgericht [Germany], 15 June 2020, 2 BvR 71/20
Bundesverfassungsgericht [Germany], 15 April 2021, BVerfGE 157, 332 *Eigenmittelbeschluss-Ratifizierungsgesetz*
Bundesverfassungsgericht [Germany], 6 December 2022, 2 BvR 547/21

Greece

Symvoulio tis Epikrateias [Greece] 668/2012
Symvoulio tis Epikrateias [Greece] 2307/2014

Latvia

Satversmes tiesa [Latvia] 2009-43-01 Ilmārs Drēziņš et al. v the Parliament
Satversmes tiesa [Latvia] 2009-44-01 Raimonds Priede-Baņģieris et al. v the Parliament
Satversmes tiesa [Latvia] 2009-76-01 Uldis Mugurevičs v the Parliament
Satversmes tiesa [Latvia] 2009-88-01 Vēsma Vilka v the Parliament
Satversmes tiesa [Latvia] 2009-111-01 Dace Ābele et al. v the Parliament
Satversmes tiesa [Latvia] 2010-21-01 Eduards Ikvilds v the Parliament

Netherlands

Rechtbank Den Haag [Netherlands] *Stichting Urgenda v State of the Netherlands* nr. 19/00135, ECLI:NL:RBDHA:2015:7145

United Kingdom

England and Wales High Court [UK] *Tomanović et.al. v the European Union et.al.* [2019] EWHC 263 (QB)

Table of Legislation

EUROPEAN UNION LAW

Treaty establishing the European Economic Community [1957] OJ C340/173

Council Directive 85/374/EEC of 25 July 1985 on the approximation of the laws, regulations and administrative provisions of the Member States concerning liability for defective products [1985] OJ L210/29

Council Directive 89/397/EEC of 14 June 1989 on the official control of foodstuffs [1989] OJ L186/23

Council Directive 2000/78/EC of 27 November 2000 establishing a general framework for equal treatment in employment and occupation [2000] OJ L303/16

Regulation (EC) No 1049/2001 of the European Parliament and of the Council of 30 May 2001 regarding public access to European Parliament, Council and Commission documents [2001] OJ L145/43

Directive 2001/83/EC of the European Parliament and of the Council of 6 November 2001 on the Community code relating to medicinal products for human use [2001] OJ L311/67

Consolidated Version of the Treaty establishing the European Community [2002] OJ C325/33

Directive 2001/95/EC of the European Parliament and of the Council of 3 December 2001 on general product safety [2002] OJ L11/4

Council Framework Decision of 13 June 2002 on the European arrest warrant and the surrender procedures between Member States [2002] OJ L190/1

Directive 2002/58/EC of the European Parliament and of the Council of 12 July 2002 concerning the processing of personal data and the protection of privacy in the electronic communications sector (Directive on privacy and electronic communications) [2002] OJ L201/37

Council Regulation (EC) No 1/2003 of 16 December 2002 on the implementation of the rules on competition laid down in Articles 81 and 82 of the Treaty [2003] OJ L1/1

Council Regulation (EC) No 58/2003 of 19 December 2002 laying down the statute for executive agencies to be entrusted with certain tasks in the management of Community programmes [2003] OJ L11/1

Regulation (EC) No 1829/2003 of the European Parliament and of the Council of 22 September 2003 on genetically modified food and feed [2003] OJ L268/1

Council Directive 2004/113/EC of 13 December 2004 implementing the principle of equal treatment between men and women in the access to and supply of goods and services [2004] OJ L373/37

Commission Regulation (EC) No 773/2004 of 7 April 2004 relating to the conduct of proceedings by the Commission pursuant to Articles 81 and 82 of the EC Treaty [2004] OJ L123/18

Directive 2006/54/EC of the European Parliament and of the Council of 5 July 2006 on the implementation of the principle of equal opportunities and equal treatment of men and women in matters of employment and occupation (recast) [2006] OJ L204/23

Regulation (EC) No 593/2008 of the European Parliament and of the Council of 17 June 2008 on the law applicable to contractual obligations (Rome I) [2008] OJ L177/6

Directive 2009/22/EC of the European Parliament and of the Council of 23 April 2009 on injunctions for the protection of consumers' interests (Codified version) Text with EEA relevance [2009] OJ L110/30

Commission Directive 2009/37/EC of 23 April 2009 amending Council Directive 91/414/EEC to include chlormequat, copper compounds, propaquizafop, quizalofop-P, teflubenzuron and zeta-cypermethrin as active substances [2009] OJ L211/23

Regulation (EC) 810/2009 of the European Parliament and of the Council of 13 July 2009 establishing a Community Code on Visas (Visa Code) [2009] OJ L243/1

Regulation (EU) No 1093/2010 of the European Parliament and of the Council of 24 November 2010 establishing a European Supervisory Authority (European Banking Authority) [2010] OJ L 331/12

Regulation (EU) No 1094/2010 of the European Parliament and of the Council of 24 November 2010 establishing a European Supervisory

Authority (European Insurance and Occupational Pensions Authority) [2010] OJ L 331/48.

Regulation (EU) No 1095/2010 of the European Parliament and of the Council of 24 November 2010 establishing a European Supervisory Authority (European Securities and Markets Authority) [2010] OJ L 331/84

Decision 2011/695 of the President of the European Commission of 13 October 2011 on the function and terms of reference of the hearing officer in certain competition proceedings [2011] OJ L275/29

Regulation (EU) No 1215/2012 of the European Parliament and of the Council of 12 December 2012 on jurisdiction and the recognition and enforcement of judgments in civil and commercial matters (recast) [2012] OJ L351/1

Regulation (EU, Euratom) No 883/2013 of the European Parliament and of the Council of 11 September 2013 concerning investigations conducted by the European Anti-Fraud Office (OLAF) [2013] OJ L248/1

Regulation (EU, Euratom) 2016/2030 of the European Parliament and of the Council of 26 October 2016 amending Regulation (EU, Euratom) No 883/2013, as regards the secretariat of the Supervisory Committee of the European Anti-Fraud Office (OLAF) [2016] OJ L317/1

Council Regulation (EU) No 1024/2013 of 15 October 2013 conferring specific tasks on the European Central Bank concerning policies relating to the prudential supervision of credit institutions [2013] OJ L287/63

Directive 2013/11/EU of the European Parliament and of the Council of 21 May 2013 on alternative dispute resolution for consumer disputes (Directive on consumer ADR) [2013] OJ L165/63

Directive 2013/11/EU of the European Parliament and of the Council of 21 May 2013 on alternative dispute resolution for consumer disputes (Directive on Consumer ADR) [2013] OJ L165/63

Regulation (EU) No 524/2013 of the European Parliament and of the Council of 21 May 2013 on online dispute resolution for consumer disputes and amending Regulation (EC) No 2006/2004 and Directive 2009/22/EC (Regulation on consumer ODR) [2013] OJ L165/1

Directive (EU) 2013/32 of the European Parliament and of the Council of 26 June 2013 on common procedures for granting and withdrawing international protection [2013] OJ L180/60

Regulation (EU) No 952/2013 of the European Parliament and of the Council of 9 October 2013 laying down the Union Customs Code (recast) [2013] OJ L269/1

Regulation (EU) No 1052/2013 of the European Parliament and of the Council of 22 October 2013 establishing the European Border Surveillance System (EUROSUR) [2013] OJ L295/11

Directive 2014/65/EU of the European Parliament and of the Council of 15 May 2014 on markets in financial instruments and amending Directive 2002/92/EC and Directive 2011/61/EU [2014] OJ L173/349

Regulation (EU) No 806/2014 of the European Parliament and of the Council of 15 July 2014 establishing uniform rules and a uniform procedure for the resolution of credit institutions and certain investment firms in the framework of a Single Resolution Mechanism and a Single Resolution Fund and amending Regulation (EU) No 1093/2010 [2014] OJ L225/1

Directive 2016/343 of the European Parliament and of the Council of 9 March 2016 on the strengthening of certain aspects of the presumption of innocence and of the right to be present at the trial in criminal proceedings [2016] OJ L65/1

Regulation (EU) 2016/679 of the European Parliament and of the Council of 27 April 2016 on the protection of natural persons with regard to the processing of personal data and on the free movement of such data, and repealing Directive 95/46/EC (General Data Protection Regulation) [2016] OJ L119/1 (GDPR)

Directive (EU) 2016/680 of the European Parliament and of the Council of 27 April 2016 on the protection of natural persons with regard to the processing of personal data by competent authorities for the purposes of the prevention, investigation, detection or prosecution of criminal offences or the execution of criminal penalties, and on the free movement of such data, and repealing Council Framework Decision 2008/977/JHA [2016] OJ L119/89

Directive (EU) 2016/681 of the European Parliament and of the Council of 27 April 2016 on the use of passenger name record (PNR) data for the prevention, detection, investigation and prosecution of terrorist offences and serious crime [2016] OJ L119/132

Regulation (EU) 2016/794 of the European Parliament and of the Council of 11 May 2016 on the European Union Agency for Law Enforcement Cooperation (Europol) [2016] OJ L135/53

Regulation (EU) 2016/1036 of the European Parliament and of the Council of 8 June 2016 on protection against dumped imports from countries not members of the European Union (codification) [2016] OJ L176/21

Consolidated Version of the Treaty on European Union [2016] OJ C202/13 (TEU)

Consolidated Version of the Treaty on the Functioning of the European Union [2016] OJ C202/47 (TFEU)

Charter of Fundamental Rights of the European Union [2016] OJ C202/389 (CFR)

Council Regulation (EU) 2017/1939 of 12 October 2017 implementing enhanced cooperation on the establishment of the European Public Prosecutor's Office ('the EPPO') [2017] OJ L283/1

Regulation (EU) 2018/1139 of the European Parliament and of the Council of 4 July 2018 on common rules in the field of civil aviation and establishing a European Union Aviation Safety Agency, and amending Regulations (EC) No 2111/2005, (EC) No 1008/2008, (EU) No 996/2010, (EU) No 376/2014 and Directives 2014/30/EU and 2014/53/EU of the European Parliament and of the Council, and repealing Regulations (EC) No 552/2004 and (EC) No 216/2008 of the European Parliament and of the Council and Council Regulation (EEC) No 3922/91[2018] OJ L212/1

Regulation (EU) 2018/1240 of the European Parliament and of the Council of 12 September 2018 establishing a European Travel Information and Authorisation System (ETIAS) and amending Regulations (EU) No 1077/2011, (EU) No 515/2014, (EU) 2016/399, (EU) 2016/1624 and (EU) 2017/2226, OJ L236/1

Regulation (EU) 2018/1726 of 14 November 2018 and amending Regulation (EC) No 1987/2006 and Council Decision 2007/533/JHA and repealing Regulation (EU) No 1077/2011 [2018] OJ L295/99

Regulation (EU) 2018/1725 of the European Parliament and of the Council of 23 October 2018 on the protection of natural persons with regard to the processing of personal data by the Union institutions, bodies, offices and agencies and on the free movement of such data, and repealing Regulation (EC) No 45/2001 and Decision No 1247/2002/EC [2018] OJ L295/39

Regulation (EU) 2018/1806 of the European Parliament and of the Council of 14 November 2018 listing the third countries whose nationals must be in possession of visas when crossing the external borders and those whose nationals are exempt from that requirement [2018] OJ L303/39

Regulation (EU) 2018/1861 of the European Parliament and of the Council of 28 November 2018 on the establishment, operation and use of the Schengen Information System (SIS) in the field of border checks, and amending the Convention implementing the Schengen Agreement, and amending and repealing Regulation (EC) 1987/2006 [2018] OJ L312/56

Directive (EU) 2018/1972 of the European Parliament and of the Council of 11 December 2018 establishing the European Electronic Communications Code (Recast), [2018] OJ L321/36

Directive (EU) 2019/1 of the European Parliament and of the Council of 11 December 2018 to empower the competition authorities of the Member States to be more effective enforcers and to ensure the proper functioning of the internal market [2019] OJ L11/3

Regulation (EU) 2019/817 of the European Parliament and of the Council of 20 May 2019 on establishing a framework for interoperability between EU information systems in the field of borders and visa [2019] OJ L135/27

Regulation (EU) 2019/818 of the European Parliament and of the Council of 20 May 2019 on establishing a framework for interoperability between EU information systems in the field of police and judicial cooperation, asylum and migration [2019] OJ L135/85

Regulation (EU) 2019/1896 of the European Parliament and of the Council of 13 November 2019 on the European Border and Coast Guard and repealing Regulations (EU) No 1052/2013 and (EU) 2016/1624 [2019] OJ L295/1

Regulation (EU) 2020/2092 of the European Parliament and of the Council of 16 December 2020 on a general regime of conditionality for the protection of the Union budget [2020] OJ L 433/1 (Euratom)

Regulation (EU, Euratom) 2021/1163 of the European Parliament of 24 June 2021 laying down the regulations and general conditions governing the performance of the Ombudsman's duties (Statute of the European Ombudsman) and repealing Decision 94/262/ECSC, EC, Euratom [2021] OJ L 253/1

Regulation (EU) 2021/2303 of the European Parliament and of the Council of 15 December 2021 on the European Union Agency for Asylum and repealing Regulation (EU) No 439/2010 [2021] OJ L468/1

Regulation (EU) 2022/868 of the European Parliament and of the Council of 30 May 2022 on European data governance [2022] OJ L152/1

Council Decision (EU) 2022/1500 of 9 September 2022 on the suspension in whole of the application of the Agreement between the European Community and the Russian Federation on the facilitation of the issuance of visas to the citizens of the European Union and the Russian Federation [2022] OJ L234/1

Regulation (EU) 2022/2065 of the European Parliament and of the Council of 19 October 2022 on a Single Market For Digital Services and amending Directive 2000/31/EC (Digital Services Act) [2022] OJ L277/1

Regulation (EU) 2022/2370 of the European Parliament and of the Council of 23 November 2022 amending Regulation (EC) No 851/2004 establishing a European centre for disease prevention and control [2022] OJ L314/1

Decision of the Controller of Procedural Guarantees Adopting Implementing Provisions for the Handling of Complaints [2022] OJ C494/17

INTERNATIONAL LAW

European Convention for the Protection of Human Rights and Fundamental Freedoms, as amended by Protocols Nos. 11 and 14, 4 November 1950

International Law Commission, Report of the Fifty- Third Session: Articles on Responsibility of States for Internationally Wrongful Acts, UN Doc A/56/ 10, 2001

Basic Principles and Guidelines on the Right to a Remedy and Reparation for Victims of Gross Violations of International Human Rights Law and Serious Violations of International Humanitarian Law, UNGA Resolution 60/147 of 16 December 2005, UN Doc A/RES/60/147, 21 March 2006

International Law Commission, Report of the Sixty-Third Session: Articles on the Responsibility of International Organizations, UN Doc A/66/10, 2011

UN Huma Rights Office of the High Commission, Guiding Principles on Business and Human Rights (2011) HR/PUB/11/04

Introduction

MELANIE FINK*

The EU prides itself on having created a legal system that puts the individual at its centre. So much so that this is what the Court of Justice of the EU (CJEU) has identified as the core of what distinguishes the EU from other international organisations.[1] Yet, the 1957 Treaties of Rome, setting up the European Economic Community, a predecessor of the EU, included no general fundamental rights protection regime.[2] A community with a primarily economic scope was not considered to be in need of one.[3] However, as the EU evolved, so did the role and place of fundamental rights in its legal system. Over the course of several decades, the CJEU developed the contours of an EU-specific fundamental rights protection regime that culminated in the adoption of a legally binding Charter of Fundamental Rights of the EU (CFR, 'the Charter').[4] Initially, this fundamental rights protection regime may have emerged from a need for 'self-preservation'.[5] But over time, it has evolved to become a core aspect of the EU's identity and self-perception,

* I would like to thank Tessa ter Avest for her excellent research assistance throughout this project.

1 Case C-26/62 *Van Gend en Loos* [1963] ECLI:EU:C:1963:1, 12; see also Charter of Fundamental Rights of the European Union [2016] OJ C202/389 (CFR), preamble.

2 Treaty establishing the European Economic Community (Rome, 25 March 1957) (TEEC).

3 Nanette A Neuwahl, 'The Treaty on European Union: A Step Forward in the Protection of Human Rights?' in Nanette A Neuwahl and Allan Rosas (eds), *The European Union and human rights* (Martinus Nijhoff 1995) 1–2; Sionaidh Douglas-Scott, 'The European Union and Fundamental Rights' in Robert Schütze and Takis Tridimas (eds), *Oxford Principles of European Union Law: The European Union Legal Order: Volume I* (Oxford University Press 2018) 384–385.

4 One of the first mentions of 'fundamental human rights' was made in Case C-f29/69 *Stauder v Ulm* [1969] ECLI:EU:C:1969:57. While the CFR was signed in Nice on 7 December 2000, it only became legally binding with the entry into force of the Treaty of Lisbon [2007] OJ C306/1.

5 For a concise account of the '*Solange* saga' see Neuwahl (n 3) 3–6; Douglas-Scott (n 3) 383–384.

featuring as a founding value in Article 2 of the Treaty on European Union (TEU).[6]

There is no doubt that today individuals benefit from a broad range of fundamental rights that protect them against EU power. Yet, as Cappelletti and Garth noted in their seminal work on access to justice back in 1978, 'the possession of rights is meaningless without mechanisms for their effective vindication'.[7] For that very reason, Article 47 CFR guarantees everyone whose rights have been violated the right to an effective remedy. This includes a right to access procedures before a tribunal within the context of which an individual can obtain relief for fundamental rights violations that have occurred.[8] From this perspective, the right to an effective remedy is not just any right but the prerequisite for the effective enjoyment of all other rights and 'one of the foundations of a European Union based on the values of the rule of law'.[9]

Nonetheless, the remarkable rise of fundamental rights protection in the EU has remained almost entirely limited to the substantive sphere and was not accompanied by any major procedural reform. The formal incorporation of the Charter into the EU legal system at primary law level resulted in individuals being able to make use of the generally available EU remedies system to vindicate their Charter rights, even though this possibility had in any case already existed for those rights also recognised as general principles of Union law. But this remedies system has significant limits.

At its centre is the action for annulment under Article 263 Treaty on the Functioning of the EU (TFEU), within the context of which EU legal acts can be reviewed and, if in conflict with higher-ranking law, annulled.[10] Individuals are, quite tellingly, 'non-privileged applicants'. Although they have the possibility to file actions for annulment, the standing requirements are so stringent that they are rarely met in practice.[11] Under similar conditions,

[6] Consolidated Version of the Treaty on European Union [2016] OJ C202/13 (TEU), art 2.

[7] Mauro Cappelletti and Bryant Garth, *Access to Justice: Vol. I A World Survey* (Book I, Sijthoff; Giuffrè 1978) 8.

[8] Herwig C Hofmann, 'Article 47: Specific Provisions (Meaning)' in Steve Peers and Others (eds), *The EU Charter of Fundamental Rights: A Commentary* (2nd edn, Hart 2021) 1285; Kathleen Gutman, 'The Essence of the Fundamental Right to an Effective Remedy and to a Fair Trial in the Case-Law of the Court of Justice of the European Union: The Best Is Yet to Come' (2019) 20 German Law Journal 884, 886–889.

[9] Opinion of AG Bot in Case C-511/13 P *Philips Lighting Poland and Philips Lighting v Council* [2015] ECLI:EU:C:2015:206, para 88. See also Case C-311/18 *Data Protection Commissioner v Facebook Ireland Ltd & Maximilian Schrems* [2020] ECLI:EU:C:2020:559, para 187.

[10] Consolidated Version of the Treaty on the Functioning of the European Union [2016] OJ C202/47 (TFEU), art 263. Under similar conditions, individuals can make use of the action for failure to act under Article 265 TFEU.

[11] TFEU, art 263(4).

individuals can challenge inactivity of an EU body by lodging an action for failure to act, but the mechanism is geared towards making EU bodies act, rather than ensuring the action they take is lawful.[12] The only more broadly accessible procedure is the action for damages under Articles 268 and 340 TFEU in order to claim compensation for damage caused by the EU. However, the threshold for liability to arise is notoriously high, limiting chances of success.[13]

The essence of this remedies system was designed and drafted in 1957, with the creation of the European Economic Community, and has not undergone substantial reform since then.[14] While the Charter became legally binding with the Lisbon Treaty, a deliberate choice was made then not to add a dedicated fundamental rights complaints procedure, built on national examples such as the German *Verfassungsbeschwerde* or the Spanish *recurso de amparo*, to the EU remedies system.[15] Instead, some 'tweaks' were made to the standing requirements of Article 263(4) TFEU. Predominantly, this served the purpose of accounting for the very specific case of otherwise unchallengeable self-executing EU acts of general application and thus had only limited effect.[16] Other gaps in the EU's remedies system were left unaddressed. The potential of mechanisms other than the action for annulment to close these remained underexplored.

In the meantime, EU power has continued to evolve, exposing ever deeper gaps in the EU's remedies system. The EU has gained competences in more inherently fundamental rights sensitive areas, such as immigration and asylum law or crime prevention. It has expanded its activities from lawmaking to executive powers, the impact of which is more immediately felt by individuals. And it has set up large administrative agencies reaching into all corners of bureaucratic activity.

[12] TFEU, art 265. Once the EU body in question has acted, the legality of that action can be reviewed in the context of Article 263 TFEU. See Case T-282/21 *SS and ST v Frontex* [2022] ECLI:EU:T:2022:235, paras 31–33.

[13] To claim compensation from the EU, applicants *inter alia* have to show that the breach complained of is 'sufficiently serious', Case C-352/98 P *Bergaderm and Goupil v Commission* [2000] ECLI:EU:C:2000:361, para 42.

[14] See TEEC, arts 173, 175, 178, 215.

[15] See the recommendations by the European Convention, which drafted the (failed) Constitutional Treaty that was later adopted with some alterations as the Lisbon Treaty: The European Convention, Final Report of Working Group II, 22 October 2002, CONV 354/02, 15.

[16] Angela Ward, 'Article 47: The Right to an Effective Remedy under the First Paragraph of Article 47 and Challenge to EU Measure' in Steve Peers and Others (eds), *The EU Charter of Fundamental Rights: A Commentary* (2nd edn, Hart 2021) 1329–1331.

The effect of these factors on the right to an effective remedy is most evident in relation to the EU agency Frontex.[17] Deploying the EU's first ever armed force is one of the most striking examples of how significantly the EU has evolved.[18] At the same time, it exposes how ill-equipped the remedies system seems to be to deal with this evolution: for years, the fundamental rights violations Frontex has been involved in have been well documented. Yet, the first ever case where the legality of Frontex's activities in this respect were substantively assessed by a competent court was brought in September 2021 before the CJEU under an action for damages, the only judicial action available to the applicants. It was dismissed on 6 September 2023 by the CJEU without any substantial discussion of the fundamental rights dimension of the case.[19]

This raises the question: Is a remedies system designed for an EU that adopts laws with a predominantly economic scope still capable of effectively protecting against an actor with a much more diverse mandate and toolbox? Or has the EU outgrown its own remedies system?

1.1 THE AIM OF THIS BOOK

Ever since the 1986 case of *Les Verts*, the CJEU has consistently held that the Treaties on which the EU is based (in the following, 'the Treaties') have established a 'complete system of remedies', even in the face of challenges by its own Advocates Generals.[20] This book critically examines this claim from a fundamental rights perspective, taking into account actions beyond annulment and the EU's activities outside the realm of lawmaking.

The book follows three lines of enquiry. First, how can private parties vindicate their fundamental rights within the current EU remedies system? This volume maps the existing mechanisms private parties can avail themselves of to enforce their fundamental rights against the EU and identifies

[17] Regulation (EU) 2019/1896 of the European Parliament and of the Council of 13 November 2019 on the European Border and Coast Guard and repealing Regulations (EU) No 1052/2013 and (EU) 2016/1624 [2019] OJ L295/1 (EBCG Regulation).

[18] EBCG Regulation, art 82 and Annex V.

[19] Case T-600/21 *WS and Others v Frontex* [2023] ECLI:EU:T:2023:492.

[20] Case C-294/83 *Les Verts v Parliament* [1986] EU:C:1986:166, para 23; more recently Case C-72/15 *Rosneft* [2017] ECLI:EU:C:2017:236, para 66. A powerful critique was offered by AG Jacobs, who argued that the limited access of private parties to the Court to challenge the validity of Union measures 'is incompatible with the principle of effective judicial protection', Opinion of AG Jacobs in Case C-50/00 P *Unión de Pequeños Agricultores v Council* [2002] ECLI:EU:C:2002:197, para 49.

their strengths and weaknesses, with particular regard to the requirements that follow from the right to an effective remedy. In doing so, it specifically focuses on the EU's role beyond an economically oriented lawmaker to account for the changes EU power has undergone and the challenges this raises from a remedies perspective.

Second, is there unused potential within the remedies system to enable individuals to vindicate their fundamental rights? The general wisdom is that the EU's remedies system offers only very limited possibilities for private applicants to hold the EU accountable. While this is certainly true, many of the limitations are only sketched out in very general terms in the Treaties and ultimately stem from the strict interpretation thereof by the CJEU. This means that the remedies system as we find it in the Treaties might harbour untapped potential to accommodate fundamental rights complaints. This volume explores how that potential may be exploited.

Third, should infringements of rights be treated differently from other breaches of EU law in terms of how they can be addressed from a remedies perspective? Article 47 CFR grants everyone whose rights may have been violated a right to an effective remedy, which might form a legal basis to afford individuals a more central position in the enforcement of obligations that confer rights on them. Yet, in a complex judicial system like the EU's, where alongside the CJEU national judges play a crucial role in the enforcement of EU law, it is not always self-evident how exactly the right to an effective remedy should be given concrete shape. This volume enquires whether rights generally, fundamental rights specifically, or even just some fundamental rights require a tailor-made remedies mechanism and, if so, what this could look like.

I.2 THE SCOPE OF THIS BOOK

Three notions are central to this book: the remedies system, EU authorities, and fundamental rights.

I.2.1 *The Remedies System*

The notion of 'remedies system' is understood in this book to cover every mechanism that (potentially) offers individuals the possibility to vindicate their rights against the EU. Much of the discussion to date has focused on the action for annulment as the primary means of judicial control and, to some degree, the preliminary reference procedure. However, the argument surrounding the 'completeness' of the EU's remedies system builds on the idea of the complementarity of the mechanisms provided.[21] No mechanism is 'complete' on its own, but together they are. Thus, to assess 'completeness', it is essential to look at the remedies system as a whole. This book does so, covering in particular judicial remedies before the CJEU, national courts, and the European Court of Human Rights.

While the focus is on judicial mechanisms – ultimately being what the right to an effective remedy requires – this volume also takes into account non-judicial mechanisms. The latter have largely been neglected in legal scholarship, even though they have significant potential, especially in a system where judicial remedies may be scarce or difficult to access.[22] This book thus also explores where and how non-judicial mechanisms can complement – or even outperform – court-centred forms of dispute resolution.

I.2.2 *EU Authorities*

The notion of 'EU authorities' is understood both narrowly and broadly. It is narrow in that Member State authorities are excluded from the enquiry. From the outset, the remedies system was primarily designed with the non-compliant Member State in mind. This book changes the perspective, investigating the degree to which the remedies system can also effectively respond to fundamental rights violations committed by the EU itself.

Within this setting, the notion of 'EU authorities' is understood broadly. It covers all types of EU bodies, be they institutions, offices, or agencies, and all types of conduct these authorities may engage in. While the book covers law-making as an important way in which the Union acts, its focus is on executive and operational activities, as well as those types of conduct that are in the grey zone in between, such as soft law or support and guidance to Member State authorities. The reason is not that these activities are per se more fundamental rights sensitive but rather that the remedies system was 'not made for them'. For obvious historical reasons, the EU's own breaches of EU law were – if at all – imagined to be committed through EU legislation. In light of the evolution of the EU, this book explores how flexible the remedies system is to accommodate today's EU in all its dimensions.

It is worth noting that the enquiry is therefore not limited to a particular EU body or EU bodies in a particular policy area. Having said this, it is in fact

[21] E.g., *Rosneft* (n 20) para 66.

[22] Notable exceptions, for example: Michal Krajewski, *Relative Authority of Judicial and Extra-Judicial Review: EU Courts, Boards of Appeal, Ombudsman* (Hart 2021); Moritz Schramm, 'Emulated Guardians: Practice, Politics, and Performativity of the DSA and the Oversight Board' (PhD Thesis, HU Berlin, June 2023).

inspired by the EU's activities in the area of migration and asylum law and, more specifically, the EU agency Frontex, which illustrates the gaps in the current remedies system remarkably well. However, many of the challenges that obstruct individual access to justice are of a more general nature, which is why this book is too: the 'non-privileged' access of private parties to the remedies system, the focus in the remedies system on the EU as a lawmaker, and the lack of a common forum to lodge complaints against the EU and one or more Member States, to name but a few. To achieve a remedies system that stands the test of time, it is important to look beyond the current activities of a single agency and the problems these may raise. This book thus takes a forward-looking approach, striving to offer an analysis that is of broader relevance today and in a continuously evolving Union.

I.2.3 *Fundamental Rights*

Finally, the notion of fundamental rights. Fundamental rights as protected by the CFR form the very core of this book. The question at the heart of all chapters in this volume is how private parties, and individuals more specifically, may vindicate their fundamental rights against the EU. While this is related to the more general issue of effective enforcement of EU law, the discussion in this book is limited to only those mechanisms that in one way or another allow individuals themselves to take an active role in the enforcement of their own rights.

The reason for the focus on fundamental rights is simple: The promise of rights for individuals entails a promise that these can be enforced. Rights are – to quote Cappelleti and Garth a second time – 'meaningless if they cannot be enforced'. To put it differently, the true strength of rights protection within a legal order becomes apparent when we understand the extent of individuals' power in situations where they cannot rely on public authorities to willingly uphold their rights.

But the reasons for the focus on fundamental rights go deeper. It is remarkable that something that was not even worth mentioning back when the EU's predecessor was created is a cornerstone of its legal system today. In many ways, the rise of fundamental rights protection within the EU legal order is intimately connected with the changes in the breadth and nature of EU power, infusing it with legitimacy. Yet the substantive rise of fundamental rights protection was not accompanied by the creation of strong enforcement tools for the beneficiaries of this protection. The rights on paper thus risk raising expectations that the EU is not always able to meet, which in turn may feed into growing disillusionment with the EU but also a certain loss of credibility on the world stage.

Ultimately, this book seeks to contribute to a vision on how to 'complete' the project of bringing fundamental rights to the core of the EU's legal system, not just substantively but also through procedural mechanisms that are available and accessible to individuals, thus truly living up to the promise of the 'complete system of remedies'.

1.3 THE STRUCTURE OF THIS BOOK

The book is structured into four parts. Part I delves into judicial mechanisms before the CJEU. Its aim is to take stock of the CJEU's approach to fundamental rights complaints in direct and indirect actions and explore the room these procedures provide to accommodate these types of complaints. It starts with the two main mechanisms through which individuals may directly access the Court: Chapter 1 on the action for annulment (Giulia Gentile) and Chapter 2 on the action for damages (Melanie Fink, Clara Rauchegger, Joyce De Coninck). This is followed by a closer look at evidence rules and how they enable (or not) effective judicial protection in Chapter 3 (Ljupcho Grozdanovski). Concluding Part I is an empirical study of the role of fundamental rights complaints against the EU within the context of the preliminary reference procedure in Chapter 4 (Lucía López Zurita).

Part II investigates how remedies beyond the CJEU may accommodate fundamental rights–based complaints against the EU. It starts with an assessment of EU review bodies beyond the judiciary in Chapter 5 (Moritz Schramm). This is followed by a look at the role of national courts in Chapter 6 (Andreas Hofmann) and the European Court of Human Rights in Chapter 7 (Jasper Krommendijk) in offering remedies to individuals whose rights may have been violated by an EU body.

Part III explores ways to push the boundaries of the EU's remedies system. Chapter 8 (Kris van der Pas) takes a look at the existing mechanisms through the lens of strategic litigation, enquiring what room there might be to exploit their full potential. The two remaining chapters in this part step outside the current form the remedies system takes. Chapters 9 and 10 explore the benefits that fundamental rights–specific alternative dispute resolution (Veronika Yefremova) or online dispute resolution (Maria José Schmidt-Kessen) might yield, respectively.

Part IV delves deeper into the limits and potential of the remedies system. Each chapter takes as a starting point a type of activity that the remedies system prima facie struggles to accommodate. The chapters in this part are organised according to the degree to which the activity in question entails direct contact with the private party potentially harmed. In this vein, it starts with a discussion of the remedies individuals have against EU law enforcement in Chapter 11 (Koen Bovend'Eerdt, Argyro Karagianni, Miroslava Scholten) and more generally factual conduct by an EU body in Chapter 12 (Florin Coman-Kund), both of which are likely to entail some form of direct interaction between the EU body and a private party. Both types of conduct challenge the remedies system because they were simply less common in the EU's early days, which is why devising remedies against them may not have seemed a priority.

Chapter 13 then takes a closer look at so-called composite procedures (Mariolina Eliantonio), understood as administrative procedures where both an EU body and a Member State authority formally cooperate in reaching a decision. The specific complexity here is that the many actors involved may blur not only the lines of substantive responsibility but also the lines of competence of national courts on the one hand and the CJEU on the other. In Chapter 14, the book zooms in on soft law (Merijn Chamon) with which the EU shapes outcomes in a way that may be hard to grasp within a remedies system that is focused on ensuring the legality of legally binding acts. Finally, Chapter 15 considers the newly emerging reliance by the EU on artificial intelligence (Simona Demková) and the suitability of the remedies system to accommodate this type of activity when it impacts the fundamental rights of individuals.

In Part IV, the fundamental rights perspective runs as a common thread through all the chapters at three levels. As a preliminary question, the chapters discuss how each type of activity may interfere with fundamental rights. The main question then is how infringements of fundamental rights through these types of conduct can be challenged by private parties. Finally, each chapter assesses how this relates to the promise of an effective remedy or access to justice more broadly, formulating recommendations on that basis.

PART I

Remedies before the CJEU

1

The Power of Procedure

Fundamental Rights in the Action for Annulment before EU Courts

GIULIA GENTILE

1.1 INTRODUCTION

As an order construed on compliance with fundamental rights, the EU has a specific interest in upholding fundamental rights: on the one hand, respect of fundamental rights enhances the EU's moral aspirations and legitimacy in the face of Member States' claim to supremacy over fundamental rights protection; on the other hand, compliance with fundamental rights by the EU sets the standards for Member States that are deviating from those guarantees.[1] The action for annulment before the EU Courts has a central role to play in this context. All EU acts should respect EU fundamental rights as higher law of the EU.[2] Through the action for annulment, applicants may challenge EU law on grounds of breaches of fundamental rights and achieve one of the following outcomes. First, an EU act may be found to be compatible with EU fundamental rights. Alternatively, EU acts may be declared as incompatible with EU fundamental rights and thus annulled.

Compliance with fundamental rights can be assessed with reference to issues of substance or procedure: for instance, the content of an EU act may breach an EU fundamental right (substantive compliance); similarly, respect of fundamental rights should occur with reference to the procedures used to adopt EU acts (procedural compliance).[3] Accordingly, different fundamental rights of a more substantive (e.g., privacy, freedom of expression) or procedural

[1] This becomes especially relevant following the rule of law backsliding in some EU Member States.

[2] Consolidated Version of the Treaty on European Union [2016] OJ C202/13 (TEU), art 6.

[3] See Darren Harvey, 'Process-oriented federalism in the EU: A (partial) response to critiques of process review advocacy in the EU' (2021) 46(4) European Law Review 460.

(right to an effective remedy, good administration, etc.) nature may be invoked to contest EU law.[4] In conjunction with the annulment, EU courts signal to EU institutions the obligations they must follow to respect fundamental rights, concerning both the procedure for the adoption of EU acts as well as their content.[5] Therefore, the annulment review has both a cathartic and a regulatory function. It is cathartic insofar as it can expunge from the EU legal order EU acts that are unlawful because they are non-compliant with EU fundamental rights. It is also regulatory insofar as it determines the obligations of EU institutions that are to be respected to honour compliance with fundamental rights.

This chapter investigates the approach of the EU judicature to the protection of fundamental rights through the action for annulment. After providing an overview of the EU model of judicial review (Section 1.2) and the rules governing the action for annulment (Section 1.3), the chapter delves into the case law and sheds light on the limits surrounding the protection of fundamental rights in the context of the action for annulment. Due to the division of competences between the General Court and the Court of Justice to review EU acts, the chapter explores the case law of these two courts separately, in Sections 1.4 and 1.5, respectively. The analysis showcases the influence of EU procedural fundamental rights in shaping the procedural duties of EU institutions.

This finding highlights the power of procedure in the EU constitutional architecture. By moulding the procedural obligations of EU institutions in the adoption of EU measures, the EU courts have enhanced the rule of law pedigree of the EU and ensured the respect of individual fundamental entitlements in the adoption of EU measures. The centrality of procedural fundamental rights issues in the judicial review of EU law is a direct reflection and consequence of the plethora of procedures that constellate the EU governance. Applicants have used the action for annulment to contest the procedures used by EU institutions to adopt EU measures and, more rarely, their substance. A shift in such a procedure-focused paradigm may occur if a more *substantive* contestation of EU law, based on fundamental rights pleas that do not focus on procedure, emerges.

4 However, procedural fundamental rights can also be relied upon to challenge the content of an act, rather than its adoption. For instance, an EU act laying down procedural rules may be found to contravene the right to a fair trial.

5 Malu Beijer, 'Procedural Fundamental Rights Review by the Court of Justice of the European Union' in Janneke Gerards and E Brems (eds), *Procedural Review in European Fundamental Rights Cases* (Cambridge University Press 2017).

1.2 THE EU JUDICIAL REVIEW MODEL: AN OVERVIEW

Across Europe and beyond, courts have become guardians of the law. They have been entrusted with the duty to scrutinise measures adopted by regulators and legislators and to ensure compliance with the Kelsenian pyramid of legal sources. The core values dominating this model are those of coherence and hierarchy. Coherence of legal orders derives from the compatibility of all secondary measures (or *praemissa minor*) with higher law (*praemissa maior*). Describing this phenomenon, Lustig and Weiler wrote, 'It is hard to find a constitution drafted in the last century that has not adopted some variant of this model [i.e. judicial review].'[6] They observed that a judicial review–centric model 'was conquering the democratic world . . . becoming part of democratic ontology – what it is to be a democracy'. Judicial review has been defined as an 'unqualified public good' based on a 'double faith': first, the faith in a 'higher law' composed of norms protecting individual rights and liberties against tyrannies – including tyrannies of democratic majorities – and binding legislatures; second, the faith in courts as the most efficient guarantee for the effectiveness and enforcement of such higher law.[7]

Among the 'higher law' sources, fundamental rights have progressively acquired an increasing importance.[8] Fundamental rights protection is one of the elements of the constitutionalism born out of the conflicts affecting the world in the last century. Fundamental rights express the essential values of a society.[9] Not all societies will necessarily protect the same fundamental rights and thus values, meaning that varying protections accordingly emerge. Hence, scrutinising public bodies' actions and measures in light of fundamental rights contributes towards ensuring that those entities comply with the essential choices on which the social contract is built.[10] No less important is an additional function of fundamental rights–based judicial review: it contributes towards fighting abuses of power by public authorities. This latter function translates into the imposition of negative and positive duties on public bodies, a list of 'dos and don'ts' that are compatible with the enjoyment of essential

[6] D Lustig and Joseph H H Weiler, 'Judicial review in the contemporary world – retrospective and prospective' (2018) 16(2) International Journal of Constitutional Law 315, 316.

[7] Ibid 316.

[8] See, for instance, David Bilchitz, *Poverty and Fundamental Rights: The Justification and Enforcement of Socio-economic Rights* (Oxford University Press 2007) 102.

[9] See, for instance, Martha Nussbaum, *Women and Human Development: The Capabilities Approach* (Cambridge University Press 2000) 83. Similarly, Raz states that 'the specific role of rights in practical thinking is . . . the grounding of duties in the interests of other beings'; Joseph Raz, *The morality of freedom* (Clarendon Press 1986) 180.

[10] Bilchitz (n 8).

legal entitlements. The idea that fundamental rights impose limits on the action of public authorities is a crucial manifestation of the rule of law.[11] As rightly remarked by Lustig and Weiler, 'judicial review became a hallmark of the very notion of the rule of law...'.[12]

This judicial review model based on the centrality of courts, fundamental rights, and the protection of the rule of law also applies to the EU. First, courts are of the essence in the EU legal order: they have a specific constitutional role linked to the effective application of EU law. Under the combined reading of Article 19 TEU and Articles 263 and 267 TFEU,[13] the Treaties set out a system of 'complete remedies' according to the EU courts that entrust national and EU courts with effective application of EU law. As explained in *Opinion 1/17*,

> In order to ensure that those specific characteristics and the autonomy of the legal order thus created are preserved, the Treaties have established a judicial system intended to ensure consistency and uniformity in the interpretation of EU law ... it is for the national courts and tribunals and the Court to ensure the full application of that law in all the Member States and to ensure effective judicial protection, the Court having exclusive jurisdiction to give the definitive interpretation of that law.[14]

The jewels in the crown of the EU remedies system are the preliminary reference procedure,[15] which allows the Court of Justice of the EU (CJEU) a form of indirect review of national law against EU law, and the action for annulment, which empowers EU institutions and bodies, Member States, and individuals to challenge the legality of EU law before the CJEU,[16] including its compliance with EU fundamental rights.

Second, while the founding Treaties did not contain any specific protection for fundamental rights, the centrality of these rights in the EU legal architecture currently stems from several provisions. For instance, Article 2 TEU recognises that the respect of fundamental rights is one of the founding values of the EU, while Article 6 TEU acknowledges the binding nature of the

[11] Neil MacCormick, *Institutions of Law: An Essay in Legal Theory* (Oxford University Press 2007) 187 and ff.
[12] Lustig and Weiler (n 6) 316.
[13] Consolidated Version of the Treaty on the Functioning of the European Union [2016] OJ C202/47 (TFEU); Case C-50/00 P *Unión de Pequeños Agricultores* [2002] ECLI:EU:C:2002:462, para 40.
[14] Case *Opinion 1/17* [2019] ECLI:EU:C:2019:341, para 111, emphasis added.
[15] TFEU, art 267.
[16] The General Court operates as a court of first instance; its judgments can be appealed against before the Court of Justice.

Charter of Fundamental Rights of the European Union (the Charter)[17] and attributes the status of general principles of EU law to the rights guaranteed by the European Convention of Human Rights (ECHR). Additionally, Article 51 of the Charter indicates that the EU institutions, bodies, offices, and agencies of the Union are subject to compliance with the Charter, with due regard for the principle of subsidiarity. But the impact of EU fundamental rights goes as far as shaping even traditionally inter-governmental areas of law, such as EU foreign policy. As an example, the declaration on Articles 75 and 215 TFEU establishes that 'the respect for fundamental rights and freedoms implies, in particular, that proper attention is given to the protection and observance of the due process rights of the individuals or entities' concerned by EU foreign policy measures.

Third, the connection between judicial review and the rule of law in the EU legal order can be traced from the seminal *Les Verts* judgment.[18] In that case, the CJEU held that the 'European Economic Community is a community based on the rule of law, inasmuch as neither its member states nor its institutions can avoid a review of the question whether the measures adopted by them are in conformity with the basic constitutional charter, the Treaties'. It follows that the judicial scrutiny over EU measures in light of EU fundamental rights via the action for annulment is a manifestation of the EU understanding of the rule of law.

1.3 THE ACTION FOR ANNULMENT IN EU LAW

1.3.1 *Pleas*

The action for annulment is governed by several rules. Five are grounds for judicial review before the EU judicature: lack of competence, infringement of an essential procedural requirement, infringement of the Treaties or of any rule of law relating to their application, and misuse of powers.[19] These grounds reflect a Kelsenian model of hierarchy of norms, where EU secondary measures can be scrutinised against higher norms, including EU fundamental rights. They also indicate that the invalidity of EU law in light of EU fundamental rights can emerge in the context of the adoption or the application of EU measures. Hence, fundamental rights–based judicial review in the EU has a clear potential to significantly influence the conduct of EU institutions.

[17] Charter of Fundamental Rights of the European Union [2016] OJ C202/389 (CFR).

[18] Case C-294/83 *Les Verts v Parliament* [1986] ECLI:EU:C:1986:166.

[19] TFEU, art 263.

1.3.2 *Standing*

Applicants are divided into three categories: privileged, semi-privileged, and non-privileged.[20] The privileged applicants – being the Member States, the European Parliament, the Council, and the Commission – are allowed to bring an action for annulment without proving any interest on their side (they can do it simply in the interests of legality).[21] Other institutions such as the Court of Auditors, the European Central Bank, and the European Committee of the Regions have limited power to bring an action for annulment, 'for the purpose of protecting their prerogatives'.[22] One may wonder whether EU institutions or Member States should be able to challenge EU law in light of EU fundamental rights. Member States and EU institutions may in principle invoke fundamental rights protection in the absence of indications to the negative in the Treaties. However, criticisms have been raised.[23] Finally, natural and legal persons – the most likely applicants to allege violations of fundamental rights – are non-privileged applicants subject to rather stringent admissibility conditions. In particular, they can challenge (a) acts addressed to them, (b) acts not addressed to them but of direct and individual concern, and (c) regulatory acts of direct concern to them that do not entail implementing measures. In addition, Article 275 TFEU specifies that the addressees of restrictive measures adopted by the Council on the basis of Title V, Chapter 2 TEU can challenge those measures through the action for annulment.

The classification of applicants and the relevant standing rules reflect the peculiar function of the action for annulment in the EU legal order. The broader leeway given to the EU institutions and Member States to challenge EU law is linked to the role of these entities to represent the public interest. It is for this reason that individuals have more stringent standing requirements; in turn, these settings allow the *general* interest enshrined in EU legislation to prevail over *individual* claims. Such standing rules have implications on the ability to challenge EU law in light of EU fundamental rights. Fundamental rights are conceptualised by many authors first and foremost as individual

[20] Ibid

[21] See Case C-45/86 *Commission v Council* [1987] ECLI:EU:C:1987:163, para 3; Case T-369/07 *Latvia v Commission* [2011] ECLI:EU:T:2011:103, para 33.

[22] TFEU, art 263.

[23] Sara Poli, 'The right to effective judicial protection with respect to acts imposing restrictive measures and its transformative force for the Common Foreign and Security Policy' (2022) 59 (4) Common Market Law Review 1045.

entitlements,[24] building on the idea that individuals have some fundamental protection against abuses. Hence, while it may be possible that public bodies seek to protect fundamental rights because they are connected to a collective interest or general policy, individuals remain the most likely parties to complain about fundamental rights violations. While the EU has not expressly espoused this theory, the Charter of Fundamental Rights indicates that Charter rights are individual rights.[25] It follows that the restrictive standing rules for natural and legal persons inevitably limit the ability of those applicants to pursue fundamental rights claims against EU institutions.

In particular, as correctly observed by Krajewski,[26] the standing system before EU courts favours the ability of economic operators, who are often the addressees of individual decisions adopted by the EU institutions, to challenge EU measures. By contrast, NGOs or individuals who may be interested in protecting fundamental rights that are not directly connected to economic interests de facto have a harder time proving their standing requirements under Article 263 TFEU.[27] It follows that the litigation brought before the EU courts through the action for annulment may consider fundamental rights issues but mainly those that are invoked by economic operators. As will be illustrated in Section 1.4, most of the EU fundamental rights pleas are indeed raised in the context of challenges against EU sanctions.[28] The mismatch between standing rules and the strengthened role of individuals – not just economic actors – in the EU law governance appears as the reflection of the path dependency between the original structure of the Treaties, the focus on economic freedoms, and the more limited EU competences. Under the founding Treaties, the enhanced role of the Member States to contest Community measures reflected the more circumscribed areas in which Community law operated. Yet with the advancement of EU legislation and the broader impact that EU measures have on individuals' interests, the question is whether reform of standing rules is necessary to reflect this transformation in the EU governance.

[24] See, among others, Aileen McHard, 'Reconciling Human Rights and the Public Interest' (1999) 62 Modern Law Review 671; Denise Meyerson, 'Why Courts Should not Balance Rights Against the Public Interest' (2007) Melbourne University Law Review 873, 874.

[25] The Preamble of the Charter states '[The Union] places the individual at the heart of its activities, by establishing the citizenship of the Union and by creating an area of freedom, security and justice'.

[26] Michał Krajewski, *Relative Authority of Judicial and Extra-Judicial Review: EU Courts, Boards of Appeal, Ombudsman* (Hart 2021).

[27] Ibid 77.

[28] See Section 1.4.2.

There is also another constraint to the protection of EU fundamental rights through the action for annulment. Only EU acts provided with legal effects 'vis-à-vis third parties' can be reviewed by EU courts. The EU judicature has recently interpreted this concept in a rather stringent way, meaning that only acts that are legally binding according to the intentions of their authors can be challenged.[29] This latest jurisprudence seems to restrict the ability to challenge EU law.[30] In previous cases, the EU courts had indeed repeatedly established that any provisions adopted by the institutions, whatever their form, which are intended to have binding legal effects are regarded as 'challengeable acts' for the purposes of Article 263 TFEU.[31]

It is clear that the action for annulment could be a crucial instrument to review the lawfulness of EU action in light of EU fundamental rights. However, it is also evident that many of the procedural rules governing this action constrain the ability to review EU law in light of EU fundamental rights. These settings raise questions about the ability of EU Courts to effectively patrol the protection of fundamental rights in EU governance. In order to assess how fundamental rights are applied in the context of this action, several parameters need to be considered. First, there is a dialectic relationship between the General Court and the Court of Justice. While at first instance the former has competence to review pleas based on facts and law, on appeal the latter can only review pleas of law and cannot engage in complex factual assessments.[32] As a result, the General Court is in charge of interpreting most of the cases against EU institutions involving pleas based on breaches of fundamental rights, the Court of Justice hearing only a narrower fraction of appealed cases.

Second, the fundamental rights pleas raised by the parties before the EU judicature shape the ways in which EU courts use EU fundamental rights in the action for annulment. Whether applicants tend to raise complaints about the procedures followed by the EU institutions, or instead the substance of EU acts, moulds the nature of the EU jurisprudence and the role of fundamental rights in the judicial review of EU law.

[29] Giulia Gentile, 'Ensuring Effective Judicial Review of EU Soft Law via the Action for Annulment before the EU Courts: A Plea for a Liberal-Constitutional Approach' (2020) 16 European Constitutional Law Review 466

[30] See also Merijn Chamon in this volume, Chapter 14.

[31] See, to that effect, Case C-22/70 *Commission v Council. European Agreement on Road Transport (ERTA)* [1971] ECLI:EU:C:1971:32, paras 39 and 42, and Case C-599/15 *Romania* v *Commission* [2017] ECLI:EU:C:2017:801, para 47 and the case law cited.

[32] Giulia Gentile, The ECJ as the EU Court of Appeal (2020) 13(1) Review of European Administrative Law 73, 76.

Third, there is another parameter worth mentioning: due to its competence to review both facts and law, the General Court can more easily identify violations of EU fundamental rights. That court can verify the factual background to cases and can therefore assess, for instance, whether the procedures followed by EU institutions to adopt EU measures are compliant with fundamental rights. By contrast, as mentioned, the Court of Justice's competence is limited to pleas of law, and it therefore may need to develop more sophisticated legal tests to assess compliance with fundamental rights. How the two courts establish violations and apply the relevant judicial tests determines the power of fundamental rights review in the EU. An exploration of the jurisprudence of these two courts is therefore necessary to assess how EU fundamental rights are protected through the action for annulment.

1.4 THE GENERAL COURT

This section analyses the case law of the General Court. It first provides some numerical evidence on the actions for annulment involving fundamental rights, such as their admissibility and the extent of annulment of EU acts before the General Court (Section 1.4.1). The analysis then progresses with a study of the case law and demonstrates the centrality of procedural fundamental rights in the actions for annulment before the General Court.

1.4.1 *Some Numerical Evidence*

According to Curia, between 1 December 2009 and 31 December 2022, the total number of actions for annulment brought before the General Court amounted to 7,586.[33] Of those actions, 1,307[34] led to the annulment of EU acts, while 1,100 cases were dismissed on inadmissibility grounds.[35] The number of annulment actions brought in the same period that involved

33 Search terms used on InfoCuria: Court = 'General Court'; Period or date = 'Date of delivery'; period = 'from 01/12/2009 to 31/12/2022'; Procedure and result = 'Actions for annulment'; Documents = Documents published in the ECR: Judgments – Orders; Documents not published in the ECR: Judgments – Orders (All); Period from 01/12/2009 to 31/12/2022.

34 Search terms used on InfoCuria: Court = 'General Court'; Period or date = 'Date of delivery'; period = 'from 01/12/2009 to 31/12/2022'; Procedure and result = 'Actions for annulment'; Documents = Documents published in the ECR: Judgments – Orders; Documents not published in the ECR: Judgments – Orders (All); Period from 01/12/2009 to 31/12/2022.

35 Search terms used on InfoCuria: Court = 'General Court'; Period or date = 'Date of delivery'; period = 'from 01/12/2009 to 31/12/2022'; Procedure and result = 'Actions for annulment'; Documents = Documents published in the ECR: Judgments – Orders; Documents not published in the ECR: Judgments – Orders (All); Period from 01/12/2009 to 31/12/2022.

fundamental rights pleas was around 830 cases,[36] while those that included mentions of a general principle of EU law totalled 582;[37] 130 actions for annulment that included mentions of 'fundamental rights' were dismissed.[38] In the same period, the General Court granted the annulment of EU law in 312 cases involving fundamental rights arguments, either raised by the parties or by the General Court.[39] Therefore, the percentage of cases involving fundamental rights and entailing an annulment (partial or total) equates to 4.1% of the total number of cases initiated in the relevant period and 64% of the total number of annulment decisions. It may be comfortably stated that the quantitative influence of EU fundamental rights in the jurisprudence of the General Court is relatively limited compared to the total number of annulment cases initiated before the General Court. Yet most of the annulment decisions appear to include pleas based on fundamental rights.

Interestingly, effective judicial protection is one of the central fundamental rights in the EU case law. A rough estimate indicates that about 30% of the cases leading to annulment of EU measures before the General Court included a plea based on effective judicial protection. The dominance of this general principle of EU law and its relevant Charter provisions reflects the constitutional ethos of the EU, according to which access to courts to enforce EU law is one of the pillars of the EU version of the rule of law.

Other fundamental rights that have received special attention in the jurisprudence of the General Court are the right to good administration, the right

[36] Search terms used on InfoCuria: Court = 'General Court'; Period or date = 'Date of delivery'; period = 'from 01/12/2009 to 31/12/2022'; Procedure and result = 'Actions for annulment'; Documents = Documents published in the ECR: Judgments – Orders; Documents not published in the ECR: Judgments – Orders (All); Period from 01/12/2009 to 31/12/2022; Text = 'fundamental rights'.

[37] Search terms used on InfoCuria: Court = 'General Court'; Period or date = 'Date of delivery'; period = 'from 01/12/2009 to 31/12/2022'; Procedure and result = 'Actions for annulment'; Documents = Documents published in the ECR: Judgments – Orders; Documents not published in the ECR: Judgments – Orders (All); Period from 01/12/2009 to 31/12/2022; Text = 'general principle'.

[38] Search terms used on InfoCuria: Court = 'General Court'; Period or date = 'Date of delivery'; period = 'from 01/12/2009 to 31/12/2022'; Procedure and result = 'Actions for annulment'; Documents = Documents published in the ECR: Judgments – Orders; Documents not published in the ECR: Judgments – Orders (All); Period from 01/12/2009 to 31/12/2022; Text = 'fundamental rights'.

[39] Search terms used on InfoCuria: Court = 'General Court'; Period or date = 'Date of delivery'; period = 'from 01/12/2009 to 31/12/2022'; Procedure and result = 'Actions for annulment'; Documents = Documents published in the ECR: Judgments – Orders; Documents not published in the ECR: Judgments – Orders (All); Period from 01/12/2009 to 31/12/2022; Text = 'fundamental rights'. This number also includes cases that involved pleas based on 'general principles of EU law'.

to property,[40] the right of defence,[41] the presumption of innocence,[42] the proportionality of penalties,[43] and the *ne bis in idem*.[44] In several cases, the General Court has raised fundamental rights pleas of its own motion.[45] The rights to privacy, data protection, equal treatment, access to documents, and non-discrimination have appeared in a handful of cases.

Overall, the most invoked and cited fundamental rights are those relating to procedural issues. This distribution of fundamental rights–based pleas influences the General Court's case law and the type of positive and negative obligations it imposes on EU institutions: procedure triumphs in the action for annulment. This finding leads to two observations. First, justice in EU litigation is shaped via procedural arguments; second, private applicants do not tend to contest EU measures on their substance but rather on issues of procedure. The focus on procedural matters is a symptom of a justice culture concentrating on procedural fairness, which demands opportunities for participation from the parties involved in procedures.[46]

The influence of procedural fundamental rights in reviewing EU measures emerges even more clearly from a qualitative perspective. Indeed, the General Court's case law suggests that the influence of fundamental rights in the action for annulment can be incisive and bear significant consequences for the EU institutions.

1.4.2 *The Influence of Procedural Rights in the General Court's Jurisprudence*

The weight of procedure emerges powerfully from the General Court's case law in a number of areas. First and foremost, EU procedural fundamental rights shape the very duties of EU courts. For instance, the EU courts are themselves required to comply with the principle of effective judicial protection, meaning that the action for annulment should offer an effective

40 Case T-302/19 *Yanukovych v Council* [2021] ECLI:EU:T:2021:333.

41 Case T-105/19 *Louis Vuitton Malletier v EUIPO – Wisniewski (Représentation d'un motif à damier)* [2020] ECLI:EU:T:2020:258.

42 Case T-381/14 *Pshonka v Council* [2016] ECLI:EU:T:2016:361.

43 Case T-56/09 *Saint-Gobain Glass France and Others v Commission* [2014] ECLI:EU:T:2014:160.

44 Case T-144/07 *ThyssenKrupp Liften Ascenseurs v Commission* [2011] ECLI:EU:T:2011:364.

45 Case T-117/07 *Areva and Others v Commission* [2011] ECLI:EU:T:2011:69.

46 Joel Brockner and Others, 'Culture and Procedural Fairness: When the Effects of What You Do Depend on How You Do It' (2000) 45(1) Administrative Science Quarterly 138; K van den Bos, H A M Wilke, E A Lind, 'When Do We Need Procedural Fairness? The Role of Trust in Authority' 75(6) Journal of Personality and Social Psychology 1449.

remedy to scrutinise the action of the EU.[47] This protection, however, does not entail that the limitation to standing deriving from the presence of a legal interest in bringing proceedings against an EU act should be disapplied. On the contrary, the General Court clarified that the standing rules are instrumental in ensuring access to court and the proper administration of justice.[48]

Another area in which the right to effective judicial protection is extensively invoked and applied is the review of EU sanctions. Restrictive measures or 'sanctions' are an essential tool of the EU's Common Foreign and Security Policy. They are used by the EU as part of an integrated and comprehensive policy approach, involving political dialogue, complementary efforts, and the use of other instruments at its disposal. Addressees of these measures are entitled to challenge them through the action for annulment via the combined reading of Articles 275 and 263 TFEU.

The approach to the judicial review of sanctions was drastically transformed with the *Kadi* judgment issued by the Court of Justice, further discussed below. In that decision, the Court of Justice established two principles:[49] first, that the EU legal order is bound to respect EU fundamental rights in its external policies, even when implementing UN resolutions imposing sanctions;[50] second, the EU judicature should carry out a full judicial review of the ways in which the EU institutions, and especially the Council, draw up lists including the addressees of sanctions.[51] These principles have profoundly shaped the praxis of the General Court in its review of EU sanctions. Since that judgment, the General Court has consistently held that it must ensure effective judicial review concerning these measures.[52]

The judicial review of EU sanctions especially focuses on the procedure followed to adopt these measures. In this context, the General Court evaluates the statement of reasons and the evidence provided by the Council. In the *Aisha Muammer*[53] case, the General Court clarified that the question of the appropriateness of the statement of reasons is different from whether the evidence used by the Council is correct.[54] The appropriateness of the

[47] CFR, art 1; See, by analogy, Case T-437/05 *Brink's Security Luxembourg v Commission* [2009] ECLI:EU:T:2009:318, para 71 and the case law cited.

[48] Case T-19/06 *Mindo v Commission* [2011] ECLI:EU:T:2011:561, paras 97 and 98.

[49] Case C-402/05 P and C-415/05 P *Kadi Al Barakaat* [2008] ECLI:EU:C:2008:461.

[50] Ibid paras 281 to 284.

[51] Ibid para 326.

[52] See, for instance, Case T-426/21 *Nizar Assad* [2023] ECLI:EU:T:2023:114, para 70.

[53] Case T-322/19 *El-Qaddafi v Council* [2021] ECLI:EU:T:2021:206.

[54] Case C-417/11P *Council v Bamba* [2012] ECLI:EU:C:2012:718.

statement of reasons is measured against several requirements. First, the statement cannot be a general stereotypical formulation.[55] Second, it must be appropriate to the act at issue and the context in which it was adopted. It must be appraised by reference to the circumstances of each case, in particular the content of the measure in question, the nature of the reasons given, and the interest that the addressees of the measure, or other parties to whom it is of direct and individual concern, may have in obtaining explanations.[56] Third, the reasons given for a measure adversely affecting a person are sufficient if that measure was adopted in a context that was known to that person and which enables them to understand the scope of the measure.[57] Hence, whether the addressee of EU sanctions had the genuine opportunity to learn the reasons underpinning the adoption of those measures is crucial in the assessment of the lawfulness of the statement of reasons.

Separate from the assessment of the appropriateness of the statement of reasons is the judicial review of the factual basis on which the sanctions were imposed. The EU standard of effective judicial protection entails a verification of the factual allegations in the summary of reasons underpinning that decision, with the consequence that judicial review cannot be restricted to an assessment of the cogency in the abstract of the reasons relied on but must concern whether those reasons, or, at the very least, one of those reasons, deemed sufficient in itself to support that decision, is substantiated.[58] The scrutiny of the evidence used allows the General Court to exercise an extensive review of the material used by the Council to impose sanctions. In so doing, the General Court is able to ensure procedural fairness and ultimately avoids the creation of a hyper-securitised approach to the sanction regime that disregards fundamental rights entitlements.

Compliance with fundamental rights in the area of EU sanctions goes as far as demanding that the Council verify that third countries in support of which sanctions are imposed have complied with fundamental rights, and especially guarantees of effective judicial protection. In *Klymenko v Council*,[59] the General Court held that the Council cannot conclude that the adoption or maintenance of sanctions against individuals rests on a sufficiently solid factual basis before having itself verified whether the rights of defence and the right to effective judicial protection were observed at the time of the

[55] Ibid para 82.
[56] Ibid para 83.
[57] Ibid para 84.
[58] Ibid para 102. See also Case T-303/19 *Yanukovych* [2021] ECLI:EU:T:2021:334; Case T-295/19 *Klymenko v Council* [2020] ECLI:EU:T:2020:287.
[59] Case T-274/18 *Klymenko v Council* [2019] ECLI:EU:T:2019:509.

adoption of the decision by the third state in question on which it intends to rely.[60] Namely, mere reliance on documents provided by the third state that illustrate compliance with fundamental rights is not sufficient to discharge the duty to verify compliance with effective judicial protection by the third country. This means that even when the information on the basis of which sanctions are imposed is provided by a member of the Council of Europe, EU institutions have to conduct an ad hoc verification of compliance with EU fundamental rights by that state. Moreover, through its statement of reasons, the Council must clearly identify the grounds on which it considers that the third country has complied with the fundamental right in question.[61] It follows that effective judicial protection requires the Council to engage in a thorough analysis of the evidence submitted to it as a legal basis for the adoption of sanctions to be included in the statement of reasons to the addressees.

The General Court has also detailed the obligations stemming from the principle of effective judicial protection for EU and national institutions in other fields of law. As an example, effective judicial protection imposes specific duties on EU institutions in the field of competition. These obligations go as far as requiring the EU Commission to examine whether the national authorities involved in competition proceedings may be in breach of the rule of law due to a lack of independence. In *Sped-Pro S.A.*,[62] the General Court held that the Commission is required to verify compliance with the right to an effective remedy by Polish national authorities in the context of competition investigations in light of the *Minister for Justice and Equality case*.[63] The General Court's reasoning was as follows. Since the relationship between national and EU authorities in the competition field is governed by the principles of sincere and loyal cooperation and mutual trust, similarly to the EU and national authorities operating in the field of the EU Area of Freedom, Security and Justice, it follows that in the competition law field as well there is a presumption of compliance with EU law and especially fundamental rights by national institutions, except in extraordinary circumstances.[64] When a case falls within the competence of national authorities, the Commission should assess whether the interests of the complainants can be

60 See Case C-258/20 *Klymenko* v *Council* [2021] ECLI:EU:T:2021:52, para 68 and the case law cited; Case T-195/21 *Klymenko v Council* [2021] ECLI:EU:T:2021:925, para 70.

61 *Klymenko* v *Council* (n 59) paras 70 and 73.

62 Case T-791/19 *Sped-Pro S.A. v Commission* [2022] ECLI:EU:T:2022:67.

63 Case C-216/18 PPU *Minister for Justice and Equality (Deficiencies in the system of justice)* [2018] ECLI:EU:C:2018:586.

64 Ibid para 88.

effectively safeguarded by national authorities[65] in compliance with the principle of effective judicial protection and therefore the rule of law.[66] This assessment is to be carried out especially in jurisdictions where the EU judicature has identified a breach of the rule of law.

Another procedural fundamental right extensively considered in the General Court's case law is the right to good administration enshrined in Article 41 of the Charter. This provision gives rise to several sub-rights, such as the right to be heard,[67] the right of access to personal files,[68] the obligation to give reasons,[69] and the right to damages for losses caused by EU institutions,[70] among others. The General Court has moulded these sub-rights to enhance fairness in the EU administration's operations. The *ADDE v Parliament*[71] case offers a valuable illustration of this point. The General Court established that the principle of impartiality deriving from Article 41 of the Charter requires members of the Bureau of the European Parliament, a body responsible for matters relating to the European Parliament's budget, administration, and organisation, to ensure an appearance of impartiality.[72] Hence, the expression of comments on social media against a specific party would undermine the impartiality guarantees of the Bureau and breaches Article 41 of the Charter. Similarly, in the context of the procedures for the marketing of new pharmaceutical products, the experts hired by the Commission should be impartial and not display any conflict of interest. As held in *Pharma Mar v Commission*,[73] the requirement of impartiality to which the EU institutions, bodies, offices, and agencies are subject also extends to experts consulted in that regard.[74] In order to show that the organisation of an administrative

[65] Ibid para 89.

[66] Accordingly, the General Court evaluated whether the Commission had carried out a detailed scrutiny of the evidence submitted by the complainant and held that the Commission had only carefully considered one of the arguments presented by the complainant. The conclusion of the Court was that the Commission had failed to comply with the duty to state reasons under EU law. Ibid para 130 and ff.

[67] CFR, art 41(2)(a).

[68] Ibid art 41(2)(b).

[69] Ibid art 41(2)(c).

[70] Ibid art 41(3).

[71] Case T-48/17 *ADDE v Parliament* [2019] ECLI:EU:T:2019:780.

[72] Ibid para 58 and ff.

[73] T-594/18 *Pharma Mar v Commission* [2020] ECLI:EU:T:2020:512.

[74] See Case T-74/08 *Now Pharm v Commission* [2010] ECLI:EU:T:2010:376, para 88 and the case law cited; see also Case T-603/16 *Brahma v Court of Justice of the European Union* [2018] ECLI:EU:T:2018:820, para 149. Accordingly, the fact that the opinion issued is not binding on the authority responsible for adopting the decision is not in itself such as to relieve the body that issued the opinion from its obligation to observe the principle of impartiality (see, to that effect, Case T-26/15 P *Commission v Hristov* [2016] EU:T:2016:390, para 46).

procedure does not ensure sufficient guarantees to exclude any legitimate doubt as to possible bias, it is not necessary to prove lack of impartiality. A legitimate doubt which cannot be dispelled is sufficient in that respect.[75] In that case, the General Court further established that the right to be heard in advance of any decision adversely affecting the interests of a party must be ensured even where the applicable rules do not expressly provide for such a formality.[76] The right to be heard is thus a general obligation to be ensured in all fields of EU law where EU institutions adopt decisions having adverse implications on the addressees, regardless of the presence of EU secondary rules detailing the relevant procedures.

Beyond rights of a procedural nature, the General Court has on occasion heard cases alleging the breach of more substantive rights, such as the principle of equal treatment. A notable case on this principle is *Italian Republic v European Commission*.[77] In that case, the principle was interpreted to require the European Commission to ensure equal treatment of candidates from a linguistic standpoint in selection procedures. This means that limitations of the choice of the second language used in competitions are discriminatory.[78]

All in all, the General Court has offered a remarkable contribution to the interpretation of fundamental rights in the EU while enhancing procedural fairness in the EU. The significant role of the General Court in the interpretation and application of EU fundamental rights is further strengthened by comparison with the jurisprudence of the Court of Justice.

1.5 THE COURT OF JUSTICE

This section analyses the case law of the Court of Justice. It first provides some numerical evidence on the actions for annulment involving fundamental rights, such as their admissibility and the extent of annulment of EU acts before the Court of Justice, as well as the fundamental rights used to challenge any EU measures and first instance decisions (Section 1.5.1). The analysis then progresses with a study of the case law and summarises the approach to fundamental rights protection adopted by the Court of Justice on appeal.[79]

[75] *Pharma Mar v Commission* (n 73) para 68.

[76] See, to that effect, Case C-277/11 *M* [2012] ECLI:EU:C:2012:744, para 86, and Case T-48/17 *ADDE v Parliament* [2019] ECLI:EU:T:2019:780, para 89 and the case-law cited.

[77] Case T-437/16 *Italy v Commission* [2020] ECLI:EU:T:2020:410.

[78] Ibid para 88.

[79] Search terms used on InfoCuria: Court = 'Court of Justice'; Period or date = 'Date of delivery'; period = 'from 01/12/2009 to 31/12/2022'; Procedure and result = 'Actions for annulment';

1.5.1 *Some Numerical Evidence*

Moving on to the Court of Justice, in the same period of reference (1 December 2009 and 31 December 2022) the Court delivered 1,761 decisions[80] in the form of judgments or orders on appeal against General Court's decisions in actions for annulment. Of those, around 230 orders and judgments include references to 'fundamental rights'[81] or 'general principle'.[82] Only 17 appeals were successful, either totally or partially;[83] 13 appeals involving fundamental rights pleas were successful, corresponding to 0.6% of all appeals against an order or a judgment issued in an action for annulment and 76% of the total number of successful appeal decisions issued by the Court of Justice. Three cases including pleas based on fundamental rights were dismissed on admissibility grounds.[84] Hence, the Court of Justice has, in most cases, tended to side with the interpretations of EU fundamental rights provided by the General Court. Such an alignment further means that it is virtually impossible to win an appeal before the Court of Justice. Overall, the

Case status = 'Cases closed'; Documents = Documents published in the ECR: Judgments – Orders; Documents not published in the ECR: Judgments – Orders (All); Period from 01/12/2009 to 31/12/2022; Text = 'fundamental rights'.

80 Search terms used on InfoCuria: Court = 'Court of Justice'; Period or date = 'Date of delivery'; period = 'from 01/12/2009 to 31/12/2022'; Procedure and result = 'Actions for annulment', 'Appeals'; Case status = 'Cases closed'; Documents = Documents published in the ECR: Judgments – Orders; Documents not published in the ECR: Judgments – Orders (All); Period from 01/12/2009 to 31/12/2022.

81 Search terms used on InfoCuria: Court = 'Court of Justice'; Period or date = 'Date of delivery'; period = 'from 01/12/2009 to 31/12/2022'; Procedure and result = 'Actions for annulment'; Case status = 'Cases closed'; Documents = Documents published in the ECR: Judgments – Orders; Text = 'fundamental rights'. It should be noted that not all first instance decisions delivered by the General Court were appealed against.

82 Search terms used on InfoCuria: Court = 'Court of Justice'; Period or date = 'Date of delivery'; period = 'from 01/12/2009 to 31/12/2022'; Procedure and result = 'Actions for annulment', 'Appeals'; Case status = 'Cases closed'; Documents = Documents published in the ECR: Judgments – Orders; Documents not published in the ECR: Judgments – Orders (All); Period from 01/12/2009 to 31/12/2022; Text = 'general principle'.

83 Search terms used on InfoCuria: Court = 'Court of Justice'; Period or date = 'Date of delivery'; period = 'from 01/12/2009 to 31/12/2022'; Procedure and result = 'Actions for annulment'; Case status = 'Cases closed'; Documents = Documents published in the ECR: Judgments – Orders; Documents not published in the ECR: Judgments – Orders (All); Period from 01/12/2009 to 31/12/2022; Text = 'fundamental rights'.

84 Search terms used on InfoCuria: Court = 'Court of Justice'; Period or date = 'Date of delivery'; period = 'from 01/12/2009 to 31/12/2022'; Procedure and result = 'Actions for annulment'; Case status = 'Cases closed'; Documents = Documents published in the ECR: Judgments – Orders; Documents not published in the ECR: Judgments – Orders (All); Period from 01/12/2009 to 31/12/2022; Text = 'fundamental rights'.

quantitative presence of fundamental rights in the Court of justice's jurisprudence on appeal appears even less substantive than in the General Court's case law. Yet the Court of Justice has made powerful use of fundamental rights in specific circumstances. What is more, recent rule of law saga cases signal a potential new direction towards more substantive pleas (and therefore contestation) of EU law.

1.5.2 *Circumscribed, Yet Not Inconsequential: Procedural Fundamental Rights Reviews before the Court of Justice*

As already mentioned, *Kadi*[85] is an example of the transformative power of procedural fundamental rights in the context of the judicial review of EU measures. In that case, the Court of Justice established that it is the duty of the EU judicature, in accordance with the powers conferred by the Treaties, to ensure the full review of the lawfulness of all Union acts in the light of the fundamental rights forming an integral part of the European Union legal order. The scope of the judicial review before the EU judicature also covers EU measures designed to give effect to resolutions adopted by the Security Council under Chapter VII of the Charter of the United Nations.[86] In particular, effective judicial review allows the EU courts to exercise oversight of the action of EU institutions in the adoption of sanctions and thus to accordingly identify duties for those bodies to ensure compliance with fundamental rights. It follows from *Kadi* that compliance with EU fundamental rights is a requirement of the EU constitutional arrangement and binds the action of EU institutions even in the field of foreign policy.[87] The protection of fundamental rights in the EU via judicial review is linked to the autonomy of EU law.[88]

Since the seminal *Kadi* saga, the Court of Justice has further detailed the procedural obligations deriving from the EU fundamental rights in the adoption of EU sanctions. On the one hand, the Court of Justice has delineated the scope of the judicial review to be carried out by EU courts; on the other hand, it has also identified the duties imposed on other EU institutions when adopting EU sanctions. For example, in the appeal in *French Republic v*

85 Case C-399/06 P and C-403/06 P *Hassan and Ayadi v Council and Commission* [2009] ECLI:EU:C:2009:748.

86 See also, to that effect, Case C-548/09 P *Bank Melli Iran v Council* [2011] ECLI:EU:C:2011:735, para 105.

87 *Kadi* (n 49).

88 Ibid.

People's Mojahedin Organization of Iran (PMOI),[89] the question was whether the General Court had committed an error in law by holding that the Council had not established that the contested decision had to be adopted urgently. Such evidence would have exempted the Council from the obligation to notify the addressee of the measure, PMOI, of the new evidence adduced against it. Consequently, the exercise of the right to be heard was also excluded. Therefore, the case concerned both the way in which the General Court had conducted its review at first instance, as well as the evidentiary requirements imposed on the Council to support the exemption from a novel notification to the addressee of a sanction.

The Court of Justice recalled that the requirement to notify the addressee of the sanction before the imposition of the measure derives from the right of defence as protected under Article 41 of the Charter.[90] It then distinguished two scenarios: the adoption of an initial decision to include an individual in a sanction list and the decision to maintain an individual on such a list. In the case of an initial decision to freeze funds, the Council is not obliged to inform the person or entity concerned beforehand of the grounds on which that institution intends to rely to include that person or entity's name in the sanction list. The Council can notify the person or entity concerned of the grounds and afford the right to be heard at the same time as, or immediately after, the decision is adopted.[91] The absence of a duty to notify before the adoption of a sanction list is an exception to the fundamental right of defence that is justified by the need to ensure that the freezing measures are effective. However, this situation is to be distinguished from the adoption of a decision maintaining an individual in a sanction list. In this latter case, the surprise effect is no longer necessary to preserve the effectiveness of the sanction regime. Therefore, the adoption of such a measure must, in principle, be preceded by notification of the incriminating evidence to allow the person or entity concerned an opportunity of being heard. These principles were applied at first instance by the General Court, which found that the Council had violated the right of defence of the addressee of the measure extending the inclusion in the sanction list. The Court of Justice thus confirmed the assessment carried out by the General Court and concluded that the latter had not committed an error in law in stating that the Council had not proved the urgency of the

[89] Case C-27/09 P France v People's Mojahedin Organization of Iran [2011] ECLI:EU:C:2011:853.
[90] Ibid para 66.
[91] Ibid para 61.

situation as a justification not to notify the new material and evidence to the addressee of the sanction.

But the relevance of effective judicial protection in the EU judicial review of EU law encounters a limit when confronted with the wording of Article 263 TFEU, which refers only to acts adopted by EU bodies in a broad sense. The latest decision on the tensions between the reviewability of EU acts and the individual right to effective judicial protection is the *Sharpston* case.[92] Following the withdrawal of the UK from the EU, former Advocate General Sharpston saw her role terminated. She later challenged decision (EU) 2020/1251 of the Representatives of the Governments of the Member States of 2 September 2020 appointing Advocate General Rantos to replace her at the Court. One of the arguments submitted by Ms Sharpston was that the impossibility of challenging the measure at stake deprived her of the right to effective judicial protection enshrined in Article 47 of the Charter. Having lost at first instance before the General Court, she appealed before the Court of Justice, which agreed with the General Court and confirmed the inadmissibility of the action because the decision to nominate a new Advocate General was not an EU act but rather an act of the Member States. For the purposes of our analysis, we can therefore observe that the Court of Justice, like the General Court, is reluctant to broaden the scope of Article 263 TFEU under the aegis of effective judicial protection.

Due to the Court of Justice's competence in reviewing pleas of law, the impression emerging from its jurisprudence is that breaches of fundamental rights are subject to more legally structured tests compared to the review carried by the General Court. In this context, Article 52 of the Charter is of relevance. This provision articulates a multi-layered assessment to evaluate the lawfulness of limitations to fundamental rights in the EU. Limitations are lawful under a fourfold requirement: first, restrictions to fundamental rights should be provided for by law; second, they should respect the essence of Charter rights; third, they should respect proportionality; fourth, they should be necessary and genuinely meet objectives of general interest recognised by the Union or the need to protect the rights and freedoms of others. But the application of this provision in the action for annulment is still under development. For instance, the relationship between the protection of the essence and principle of proportionality is unclear and not rigidly drawn in the EU case law, although a trend seems to emerge whereby the two assessments appear separate, as per the wording of Article 52 of the Charter.

[92] Case C-685/20 P *Sharpston v Council and Representatives of the Member States* [2021] ECLI:EU:C:2021:485.

Proportionality still has a dominant place due to case law path-dependencies and the influence of the Strasbourg case law.[93]

An example in point is *Stichting Al-Aqsa*.[94] In that case, the applicant appealed against the General Court's judgment confirming the lawfulness of restrictive measures. One of the pleas raised concerned an alleged violation of the fundamental right to property due to the asset freeze entailed by the restrictive measure. After the Court of Justice recalled that the right to property under European Union law does not enjoy absolute protection, it also stated that the exercise of that right may be restricted, provided that those restrictions correspond to objectives of public interest pursued by the European Union and do not constitute, in relation to the aim pursued, a disproportionate and intolerable interference, impairing the very substance (or essence)[95] of the right so guaranteed. In its assessment, the court followed a proportionality assessment. First, it evaluated the presence of an objective of general interest[96] and, subsequently, its legitimacy.[97] It next assessed the necessity of the asset freeze and then the proportionality of the maintenance of the appellant on the list at issue. Concerning this latter issue, the court held that this measure was proportionate due to the presence of a periodic review.[98] Proportionality can therefore take over the evaluation of the protection of the essence, which loses its autonomy as a legal test.

Moreover, cases such as *Schindler Holding Ltd*[99] further showcase that, in parallel to EU standards of protection, the ECHR is still exercising significant influence, even after the entry into force of the Charter. In that judgment, the Court of Justice recalled that, while the rights protected by the Convention constitute general principles of EU law, and Article 52(3) of the Charter requires rights contained in the Charter that correspond to rights guaranteed by the ECHR to be given the same meaning and scope as those laid down by the ECHR, the Convention does not bind the EU until its accession. The fundamental right issue raised in the case concerned whether the imposition of criminal penalties in the context of competition proceedings by the European Commission was incompatible with Article 6 ECHR. Recalling

93 Takis Tridimas and Giulia Gentile, 'The Essence of Rights: An Unreliable Boundary?' (2019) 20 German Law Journal 794.

94 Case C-539/10 P *Al-Aqsa v Council and Pays-Bas* [2012] ECLI:EU:C:2012:711.

95 Tridimas and Gentile (n 93).

96 *Al-Aqsa v Council and Pays-Bas* (n 94) para 123.

97 Ibid para 124.

98 Ibid para 129.

99 Case C-501/11 P *Schindler Holding Ltd vs European Commission* [2013] ECLI:EU:C:2013:522.

the *Menarini* judgment,[100] the Court of Justice held that 'entrusting the prosecution and punishment of breaches of the competition rules to administrative authorities is not inconsistent with the ECHR in so far as the person concerned has an opportunity to challenge any decision made against him before a tribunal that offers the guarantees provided for in Article 6 of the ECHR'.[101] Hence, the Court of Justice seeks alignment with the Strasbourg court as far as possible while retaining the autonomous interpretation of EU fundamental rights.

Remarkably, the rule of law saga has, to a certain extent, allowed for a more substantive contestation of EU measures. Article 2 TEU creates a web of fundamental principles that constitute the backbone of the EU legal order. They are the principle of non-discrimination, pluralism, and the rule of law, among others. They are all directly or indirectly linked to fundamental rights. In *Hungary v European Parliament and Council of the EU*[102] and *Poland v European Parliament and Council of the EU*,[103] Hungary and Poland challenged the Rule of Law Conditionality Framework, which connects the disbursement of the EU budget in favour of Member States to the respect of the rule of law. In addition to pleas concerning the division of competences, the Member States challenged the notion of rule of law used by the EU institution in the Conditionality Framework.[104] In particular, it was argued that the contested regulation breaches the principles of legal certainty and legislative clarity on the ground that the concepts in that regulation, on the basis of which a Member State may be found to have breached the principles of the rule of law, have no uniform definition in the Member States. Therefore, the case required the Court of Justice to articulate the EU notion of the rule of law and not merely to assess whether the procedures followed by EU institutions to adopt the Rule of Law Conditionality Framework complied with procedural rights. The Court observed that the Commission had relied on a variety of reports and that the framework included an evidence-based approach. Additionally, the States affected by the framework can initiate dialogue

[100] *Menarini Diagnostics Srl v Italy* App No 43509/08 (ECtHR, 27 September 2011).

[101] Ibid para 34.

[102] Case C-156/21 *Hungary v European Parliament and Council of the European Union* [2022] ECLI:EU:C:2022:97.

[103] Case C-157/21 *Poland v European Parliament and Council of the European Union* [2022] ECLI:EU:C:2022:98.

[104] Regulation (EU, Euratom) 2020/2092 of the European Parliament and of the Council of 16 December 2020 on a general regime of conditionality for the protection of the Union budget OJ L 433I (Rule of Law Conditionality Framework).

and cooperation with the Commission. All these factors meant that the notion of rule of law used in the framework did not breach the principle of legal certainty.

All in all, the Court of Justice has exercised a central role in ensuring that EU measures comply with EU fundamental rights, by complementing the jurisprudence of the General Court. Also before the Court of Justice procedure triumphs. Whether more substantive contestation of EU law in light of EU fundamental rights emerges remains to be seen. A step in that direction are the cases initiated by Hungary and Poland concerning the Rule of Law Conditionality Framework.

1.6 PROCEDURE OVER SUBSTANCE (THUS FAR): CONCLUDING REMARKS

The chapter has undertaken a journey through the jurisprudence of EU courts delivered in the context of actions for annulment. First, it has highlighted the strengths and the weaknesses of the action for annulment to protect fundamental rights. Limitations to the ability to ensure the full potential of fundamental rights judicial review in the EU are the stringent standing requirements for individuals and narrow notion of reviewable acts. Second, the chapter has observed that procedural fundamental rights dominate the EU case law. This is because parties have invoked procedural fundamental rights to challenge EU law but also due to the inclination of the EU judicature to rely on those fundamental rights. The centrality of procedure gives rise to observations concerning the areas of contestation of EU measures: parties mainly criticise the procedures followed by EU institutions in adopting EU measures and whether the latter afford any form of procedural guarantees. Hence, what applicants seem to be interested in is the ability to engage in participatory dynamics that can shape the adoption of EU law. A step towards more substantive contestation of EU measures appears in the recent *Hungary v European Parliament and Council of the EU* and *Poland v European Parliament and Council of the EU* cases. In these cases, the substantive contestation stems from different visions of the meaning and implications of the rule of law in the EU. Substantive contestation of EU measures is welcome and reflects the maturity of the EU legal order, where pluralism of fundamental rights inevitably creates debates as to what EU fundamental rights mean.

2

The Action for Damages as a Fundamental Rights Remedy

MELANIE FINK, CLARA RAUCHEGGER,
AND JOYCE DE CONINCK

2.1 INTRODUCTION

The EU has traditionally distinguished itself from international law by according the individual a central role within its legal system.[1] It is considered one of the idiosyncrasies of the EU that individuals can directly rely on provisions of EU law before domestic and EU courts and are protected through an extensive and, in many ways, progressive catalogue of fundamental rights – the Charter of Fundamental Rights of the EU (CFR, 'the Charter').[2] The protection offered through this catalogue of fundamental rights is reinforced by the right to an effective remedy guaranteed by Article 47 of the Charter. Yet, despite these legal safeguards, strong mechanisms to ensure effective protection of such rights vis-à-vis the EU remain elusive to individuals.

There are, in essence, three direct avenues for individuals to access the Court of Justice of the EU (CJEU, 'the Court'): the action for annulment (see Chapter 1), the action for failure to act, and the action for damages. Legal scholarship has focused on the downsides and promises of the action for annulment as the primary avenue to ensure remedies for fundamental rights violations in the EU legal order.[3] The action for damages has received much

[1] Sionaidh Douglas-Scott, 'The European Union and Fundamental Rights' in Robert Schütze and Takis Tridimas (eds), *Oxford Principles Of European Union Law: The European Union Legal Order: Volume I* (Oxford University Press 2018) 384. On the status of individuals in international (human rights) law more generally: Anne Peters, *Beyond Human Rights: The Legal Status of the Individual in International Law* (Cambridge University Press 2016) 644.

[2] Charter of Fundamental Rights of the European Union [2016] OJ C202/389 (CFR).

[3] For an overview of literature on the topic, see Chapter 1 of this volume.

less attention.[4] In part, this is because it has often been perceived as a vehicle to recover economic loss and has thus been used predominantly by companies and other economic operators. Yet, the action for damages might prove essential to ensure full compliance with the right to an effective remedy within the EU legal order, especially considering the shortcomings of the other direct avenues to the CJEU.

This chapter explores the potential of the action for damages to offer a remedy for fundamental rights violations committed by the EU. While the action for damages is easily accessible to individuals, the conditions under which compensation is granted are strict. This chapter assesses how these conditions are, could be, and should be applied by the CJEU in the fundamental rights context.

First, the chapter explores the main functions of liability law in the context of fundamental rights protection (Section 2.2). Next, the chapter provides a quantitative perspective on the CJEU's case law involving fundamental rights in action for damages proceedings (Section 2.3). This is followed by a critical analysis of the particular challenges posed by the CJEU's strict interpretation of the condition of unlawfulness – a requirement for liability to arise – when applied to breaches of fundamental rights (Section 2.4). Finally, the chapter zooms in on the obstacles to establishing joint liability between the EU and its Member States for joint fundamental rights violations (Section 2.5). The chapter concludes by reflecting on the possibilities for better utilising the potential of the action for damages for fundamental rights protection in the EU, while remaining within the limits of the current constitutional framework set out in the Treaties (Section 2.6).

[4] Literature on the action for damages in the fundamental rights context: Clara Rauchegger, 'Article 47: Damages for Breach of the Charter as a Remedy under the First Paragraph of Article 47' in Steve Peers and Others (eds), *The EU Charter of Fundamental Rights: A Commentary* (2nd edn, Hart 2021); Melanie Fink, 'The Action for Damages as a Fundamental Rights Remedy: Holding Frontex Liable' (2020) 21 German Law Journal 532; Joyce De Coninck, 'Catch-22 in the Law of Responsibility of International Organizations: Systemic Deficiencies in the EU Responsibility Paradigm for Unlawful Human Rights Conduct in Integrated Border Management' (PhD Thesis, Ghent University 2020); Melanie Fink, *Frontex and Human Rights: Responsibility in 'Multi-Actor Situations' under the ECHR and EU Public Liability Law* (Oxford University Press 2018); Nina Półtorak, 'Action for Damages in the Case of Infringement of Fundamental Rights by the European Union' in Ewa Bagińska (ed), *Damages for Violations of Human Rights: A Comparative Study of Domestic Legal Systems* (Springer 2016); Angela Ward, 'Damages under the EU Charter of Fundamental Rights' (2012) 12 ERA Forum 589.

2.2 DAMAGES LIABILITY AS A REMEDY FOR FUNDAMENTAL RIGHTS VIOLATIONS

This section examines the general functions of liability law[5] to explore its potential as a remedy for fundamental rights violations. It draws on domestic private law and public international law with the aim of gaining a better understanding of the role that damages liability can play as a vehicle for fundamental rights protection in the EU law context. The section is structured around the three core aims of liability law: compensating harm (Section 2.2.1), preventing undesired behaviour (Section 2.2.2), and vindicating rights (Section 2.2.3).

2.2.1 *Compensating Harm Caused by Fundamental Rights Violations*

The main function of liability law is to provide compensation for harm.[6] Harm arising from fundamental rights violations can be of a pecuniary (monetary, economic, financial) or non-pecuniary nature. Violations of the right to property are the most straightforward example of a fundamental rights violation leading to an economic loss. Other examples of pecuniary harm caused by fundamental rights violations include costs of medical treatment or loss of income because of a violation of the right to physical integrity. However, it is characteristic of fundamental rights violations that in many cases the non-pecuniary harm they cause is more significant than any immediate financial consequences. Non-pecuniary harm may consist of, for instance, physical or psychological pain, loss of dignity, embarrassment, or fear.

In EU liability law, the principle of full compensation suggests that non-pecuniary harm is generally recoverable.[7] Accordingly, the CJEU awards damages for both pecuniary and non-pecuniary harm arising from fundamental rights violations and it does so even when the victims are legal persons.[8]

[5] It is typically referred to as 'tort law' in common law jurisdictions and 'delict law' in civil law jurisdictions. For the purposes of this chapter, the broader term 'liability law' is used.

[6] Walter van Gerven, Jeremy Lever, and Pierre Larouche, *Cases, Materials and Text on National, Supranational and International Tort Law* (Hart 2000) 69; Carol Harlow, *State Liability: Tort Law and Beyond* (Oxford University Press 2004); Dorota Leczykiewicz, 'Compensatory Remedies in EU Law: The Relationship Between EU Law and National Law' in Paula Giliker (ed), *Research Handbook on EU Tort Law* (Edward Elgar 2017) 63.

[7] Katri A Havu, 'Damages Liability for Non-material Harm in EU Case Law' (2019) 44 European Law Review 492, 494.

[8] For example: Case C-50/12 P *Kendrion v Commission* [2013] ECLI:EU:C:2013:771, para 100; Case C-40/12 P *Gascogne Sack Deutschland v Commission* [2013] ECLI:EU:C:2013:768,

The notion of non-pecuniary harm in EU liability law is broad, covering pain or physical suffering, harm to emotional well-being, or psychological suffering, reputational damage or other harm to personality rights as well as harm arising from a state of uncertainty.[9]

Like harm, compensation can be of a pecuniary or non-pecuniary nature. In modern liability regimes at the domestic level, both types of harm, pecuniary and non-pecuniary, tend to be compensated with money, typically ruling out other forms of substantive remedy, such as apologies or physical retaliation ('an eye for an eye').[10]

Beyond the national private law context, there is room for substantive remedies of a non-pecuniary nature. In public international law, suffering a wrong entitles the injured state to engage in conduct that would otherwise be wrongful.[11] In addition, non-pecuniary harm on the part of the state (as opposed to an individual) is generally considered not to be 'financially assessable' and is made good through 'satisfaction', such as an acknowledgement of the breach, an expression of regret, or a formal apology.[12]

In the international human rights context, the UN Basic Principles and Guidelines on the Right to a Remedy and Reparation for Victims of Gross Violations of International Human Rights Law and Serious Violations of International Humanitarian Law specify that 'full and effective reparation' includes restitution, compensation, rehabilitation, satisfaction, and guarantees of non-repetition.[13] Whereas 'compensation' is understood narrowly to mean only pecuniary compensation, satisfaction is much broader and includes remedies such as verification and publication of the truth, an official declaration restoring dignity or reputation, a public apology, or sanctioning perpetrators.[14]

para 95; Case C-58/12 P *Groupe Gascogne v Commission* [2013] ECLI:EU:C:2013:360, para 89; Case T-577/14 *Gascogne Sack Deutschland and Gascogne v EU* [2017] ECLI:EU:T:2017:1, paras 144–165; Case T-479/14 *Kendrion v EU* [2017] ECLI:EU:T:2017:48, paras 67–135.

9 Havu (n 7) 495–496.

10 Stephen D Sugarman, 'Tort Damages for Non-Economic Loss: Personal Injury' in Mauro Bussani and Anthony J Sebok (eds), *Comparative Tort Law: Global Perspectives* (Edward Elgar 2015) 324–325.

11 See especially International Law Commission, Report of the Fifty-Third Session: Articles on Responsibility of States for Internationally Wrongful Acts, UN Doc A/ 56/ 10, 2001 (ASR), art 22 (countermeasures).

12 Ibid art 37 (satisfaction).

13 UN General Assembly, Basic Principles and Guidelines on the Right to a Remedy and Reparation for Victims of Gross Violations of International Human Rights Law and Serious Violations of International Humanitarian Law, 21 March 2006, UN Doc A/RES/60/147, principles 19–235.

14 Ibid principle 22.

Likewise, compensation for violations of the International Covenant on Civil and Political Rights can involve measures of satisfaction, such as public apologies, public memorials, or guarantees of non-repetition.[15]

Regionally, violations of the European Convention on Human Rights (ECHR) can also be remedied by affording 'just satisfaction'.[16] This means that remedies other than pecuniary ones can be awarded. Yet pecuniary compensation is the most common remedy for the European Court of Human Rights (ECtHR).[17] A quantitative analysis of the case law shows that the ECtHR has made monetary awards in 94% of all the cases in which it found a violation. In most of the cases in which no monetary award was made, the ECtHR held that a finding of a violation was sufficient to redress the breach. The award of other non-monetary remedies is extremely rare and only awarded in pilot judgments under Article 46 ECHR.[18]

In EU liability law, compensation can be of a pecuniary or non-pecuniary nature, including compensation in kind, if necessary in the form of injunctions to do or not to do something (Figure 2.1).[19] In cases concerning non-pecuniary harm, the CJEU frequently finds that the harm is sufficiently compensated without monetary reparation.[20] In particular, the CJEU often finds that the annulment or finding of illegality of the unlawful measure is sufficient to remedy non-pecuniary harm.[21] For instance, in the sanctions case *Abdulrahim*, the Court of Justice stated that the recognition of unlawfulness of the contested measure could constitute 'a form of reparation for the non-material harm'.[22] In other cases, the particular circumstances justified pecuniary reparation.[23]

[15] International Covenant on Civil and Political Rights, UNGA Resolution 2200A (XXI) of 16 December 1966, UN Doc A/6316, 999 UNTS 171 (ICCPR); Dinah Shelton, 'Reparations in Human Rights Law' in Rachel Murray and Debra Long (eds), *Research Handbook on Implementation of Human Rights in Practice* (Edward Elgar 2022) 36–58.

[16] European Convention for the Protection of Human Rights and Fundamental Freedoms, as amended by Protocols Nos. 11 and 14, 4 November 1950 (ECHR), Article 41.

[17] This is different for the Inter-American Court of Human Rights, where emphasis is given to other remedies as opposed to pecuniary remedies. Veronika Fikfak, 'Compliance and Compensation: Money as a Currency of Human Rights' in Rachel Murray and Debra Long (eds), *Research Handbook on Implementation of Human Rights in Practice* (Edward Elgar 2022) 115.

[18] Ibid 103.

[19] Case T-279/03 *Galileo International Technology and Others v Commission* [2011] ECLI:EU:T:2006:121, para 63. Confirmed by Case T-19/07 *Systran and Systran Luxembourg v Commission* [2010] ECLI:EU:T:2010:526, para 121; Case T-88/09 *Idromacchine and Others v Commission* [2011] ECLI:EU:T:2011:641, para 81.

[20] Havu (n 7) 501.

[21] Ibid 501–502.

[22] Ibid 502. See Case C-239/12 P *Abdulrahim v Rat und Kommission* [2013] ECLI:EU:C:2013:331, paras 71-72.

[23] For an overview of the case law: Havu (n 7) 502.

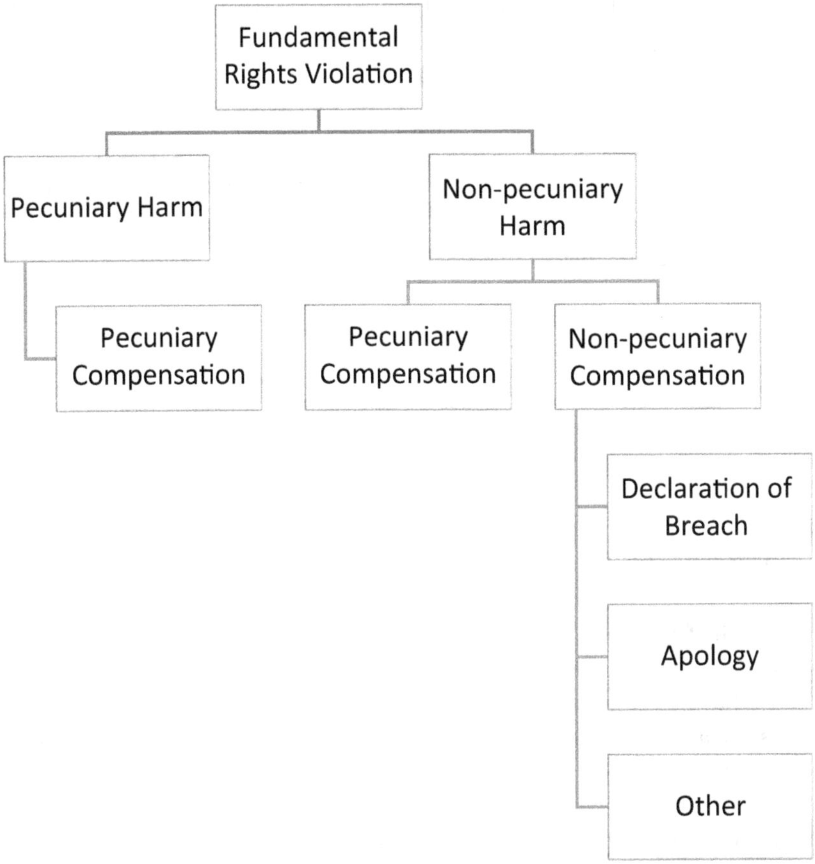

FIGURE 2.1 Types of harm and compensation

2.2.2 *Condemning and Preventing Undesired Behaviour*

Domestic liability law is primarily reactionary and focused on remedying past wrongs, whereas public law is concerned with improving the machinery of government.[24] Nevertheless, the impact of liability law goes beyond merely compensating harm. On the one hand, both victims and society more generally may perceive compensation, especially when it goes beyond the actual financial loss, as a form of condemnation or even punishment of the

[24] Ekaterina Aristova and Ugljesa Grusic, 'Introduction: Civil Remedies and Human Rights in Flux' in Ekaterina Aristova and Ugljesa Grusic (eds), *Civil Remedies and Human Rights in Flux: Key Legal Developments in Selected Jurisdictions* (Hart 2022) 21.

wrongdoer, even when it is – from a legal point of view – still strictly compensatory rather than punitive.[25]

On the other hand, damages liability may serve to deter wrongful conduct.[26] The preventive function of liability regimes is particularly important in the fundamental rights context. Harm arising from a fundamental rights violation can, by its very nature, often not be made good by financial means or indeed remedied at all.[27] For this reason, changing state behaviour to prevent future violations is important in international human rights law.[28]

2.2.3 *Vindicating Rights*

Beyond providing substantive remedies for fundamental rights violations, liability law is generally considered instrumental for states to comply with their obligations under the right to an effective remedy.[29] This is particularly the case for the EU. Under certain circumstances, especially when EU conduct under scrutiny is informal, factual, or preparatory in nature (see Chapters 12–14), the action for damages may be the only judicial mechanism available to individuals to challenge it. The requirement in Article 47 of the Charter that an effective judicial remedy must be available suggests that some form of compensation (pecuniary or non-pecuniary) should be provided under the action for damages, at least where other remedies are not available. Thus, the action for damages is instrumental for the EU to meet its obligations under Article 47 of the Charter.[30]

In this vein, the right to compensation has been qualified as a fundamental principle of EU law and the 'necessary extension of the principle of effective judicial protection and access to the courts'.[31] As held by Advocate General Mengozzi, 'the right to reparation of persons harmed by an infringement of

[25] Sugarman (n 10) 325.

[26] Ibid 325–326; Leczykiewicz (n 6) 63; Jason N E Varuhas, *Damages and Human Rights* (Hart 2016) 14–21; van Gerven, Lever, and Larouche (n 6) 69; Harlow (n 6) 10–41.

[27] Lewis A Kornhauser, 'Incentives, Compensation, and Irreparable Harm' in André Nollkaemper, Dov Jacobs, and Jessica N M Schechinger (eds), *Distribution of Responsibilities in International Law* (Cambridge University Press 2015) 121–123.

[28] Dinah Shelton, *Remedies in International Human Rights Law* (3rd edn, Oxford University Press 2015) 2, 22.

[29] Cees van Dam, *European Tort Law* (Oxford University Press 2013) 23.

[30] Rauchegger (n 4) 1316; Fink, 'The Action for Damages as a Fundamental Rights Remedy' (n 4) 536. See also: Case C-93/11 P *Verein Deutsche Sprache* [2011] ECLI:EU:C:2011:429, para 30; Opinion of AG Geelhoed in Case C-234/02 P *Mediator v Lamberts* [2003] ECLI: EU:3003:394, para 107.

[31] Case C-234/02 P *Mediator v Lamberts* [2004] ECLI:EU:C:2004:174, paras 82–83. See also: Case C-224/01 *Köbler* [2003] ECLI:EU:C:2003:513, para 33.

EU law is a specific variation on the principle of effective judicial protection', which is now enshrined in Article 47 of the Charter.[32]

The importance of the action for damages in remedying breaches of EU law is also recognised in Article 41(3) of the Charter by virtue of which the right to have the Union make good any damage it caused is a fundamental right in itself.[33] While Article 41(3) of the Charter only reproduces Article 340 (2) TFEU and does not modify the conditions under which liability arises,[34] it may form the basis for the CJEU to develop the conditions for liability in line with the requirements of fundamental rights law.[35] Section 2.6 makes suggestions as to what this development could and should entail.

2.3 A QUANTITATIVE GLANCE AT FUNDAMENTAL RIGHTS IN CJEU DAMAGES CASE LAW

Article 340(2) TFEU holds that the EU must make good any damage caused by its institutions or by its servants in the performance of their duties. The procedure that serves to establish whether the conditions for liability are met and award compensation is the action for damages, which the CJEU is exclusively competent to hear.[36] Within the CJEU, Article 256(1) TFEU allocates the competence to hear actions for damages at first instance to the General Court, with the Court of Justice hearing actions for damages only in the case of appeals on points of law.[37] In what follows, the action for damages will be analysed from a quantitative perspective, focusing on cases in which the Charter was mentioned.

Up to 2014, the action for damages had given rise to 39 successful cases in which the CJEU granted compensation to applicants.[38] Between 2015 and 2023, the body of case law grew incrementally, but rather slowly, amounting

32 Opinion of AG Mengozzi in Case C-279-09 *DEB* [2020] ECLI:EU:C:2010:489, para 46.

33 Kathleen Gutman, 'The Non-Contractual Liability of the European Union: Principle, Practice and Promise' in Paula Giliker (ed), *Research Handbook on EU Tort Law* (Edward Elgar 2017) 47.

34 Explanation accompanying the Charter; art 52(2); Paul Craig, 'Article 41: The Right to Good Administration' in Steve Peers and Others (eds), *The EU Charter of Fundamental Rights: A Commentary* (2nd edn, Hart 2021) 1130.

35 Similarly Pekka Aalto, *Public Liability in EU law: Brasserie, Bergaderm and Beyond* (Hart 2011) 125; Gutman (n 33) 47.

36 Consolidated Version of the Treaty on the Functioning of the European Union [2016] OJ C202/47 (TFEU) arts 268, 274.

37 This excludes disputes between the Union and its servants.

38 Rafał Mańko, 'Action for Damages against the EU: European Parliament Briefing' (*European Parliamentary Research Service*, December 2018) 1 <www.europarl.europa.eu/RegData/etudes/BRIE/2018/630333/EPRS_BRI(2018)630333_EN.pdf>.

to a total of 54 cases with a successful outcome during this period,[39] of which all but one judgment were delivered by the General Court.[40] The overall number of cases of damages proceedings during this period, that is, including successful and unsuccessful ones, is 172 for the Court of Justice and 745 for the General Court.[41] It is a common outcome of action for damages proceedings that no damages are awarded since most often claims are either not sufficiently substantiated with evidentiary support, or the conditions for liability, which will be discussed in Section 2.4, are simply not met.[42]

Out of the fifty-four successful damages cases since 2015, more than 80% included references to the Charter in the grounds of judgment. In these forty-five cases, the Charter rights that were most frequently mentioned were those enshrined in Articles 41 and 47.[43] This is not surprising as Article 41 guarantees good administration rights binding on the EU institutions, bodies, offices and agencies, including the right to have the Union make good any damage it has caused (see Section 2.2.3). Article 47 is closely related to Article 41. It guarantees general fair trial rights that are also binding on the Member States. These two rights provide for partly overlapping protection.[44] This protection is furthermore complemented by Article 48 of the Charter, which has also appeared in several of the successful damages cases and guarantees respect for the rights of the defence for anyone who has been charged.[45]

Another Charter provision that plays a prominent role in damages cases that have yielded a successful outcome, albeit significantly less than Articles 41 and 47, is Article 31, which affords fair and just working conditions.[46] Further Charter provisions that are referred to in several successful damages cases are, in order of importance in numbers: Article 7 (Respect for private and family

39 These cases were found on the InfoCuria database of the CJEU, excluding the Civil Service Tribunal, using the search terms: Court = 'Court of Justice, General Court', Period = 'from 01/01/2015 to 01/06/2023', Procedure and result = 'Action for damages, Application granted'.

40 The sole judgment with a successful outcome delivered by the Court of Justice was Case C-89/15 P *Riva Fire v Commission* [2017] ECLI:EU:C:2017:713.

41 These cases were found on the InfoCuria database of the CJEU, excluding the Civil Service Tribunal, using the search terms: Court = 'Court of Justice, General Court', Period = 'from 01/01/2015 to 01/06/2023', Procedure = 'Action for damages'.

42 Havu (n 7) 500–501.

43 Article 41 of the Charter was referred to in 21 of the cases that were selected through the search described in n 39 and Article 47 of the Charter in 19 of these cases.

44 Angela Ward, 'Article 47: Interrelationship with Other Provisions of the Charter' in Steve Peers and Others (eds), *The EU Charter of Fundamental Rights: A Commentary* (2nd edn, Hart 2021) 1250.

45 Article 48 of the Charter was referred to in four of the cases that were selected through the search described in n 39.

46 Article 31 of the Charter was referred to in six of the cases that were selected through the search described in n 39.

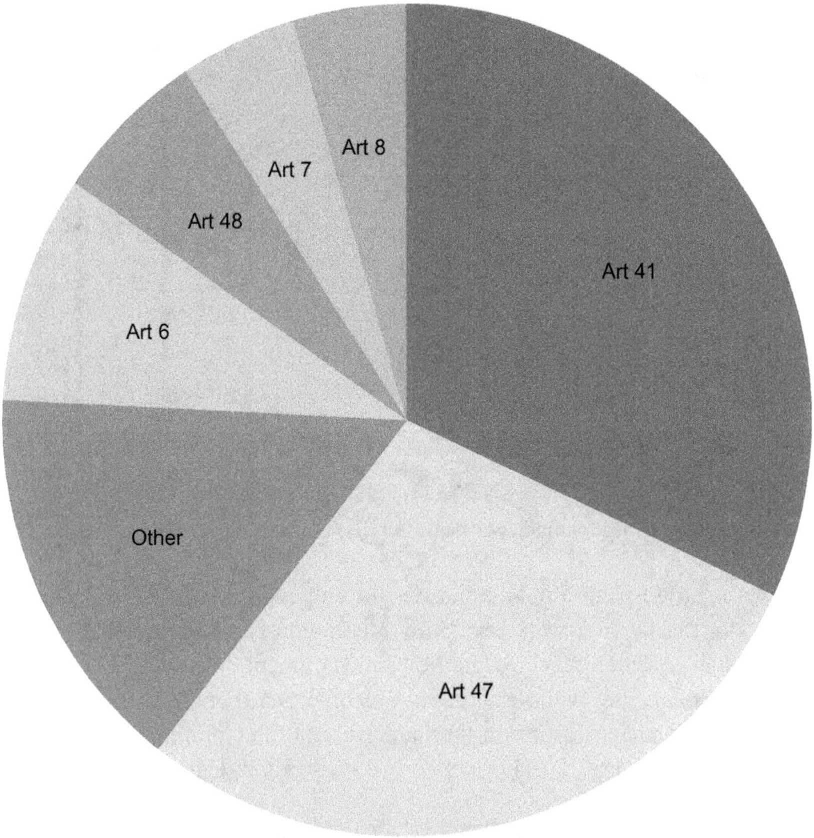

FIGURE 2.2 Charter rights in successful damages cases (1)

life), Article 8 (Protection of personal data), Article 21 (Non-discrimination), Article 16 (Freedom to conduct a business), and Article 17 (Right to property).[47] These are all fundamental rights that can effectively be claimed and enforced vis-à-vis the EU, by virtue of the EU's nature as a non-state actor and by virtue of the nature of the rights involved (Figures 2.2 and 2.3).

The large majority of the forty-five cases in which these Charter rights were applied concerned staff of the EU's civil service.[48] This explains the prominent role of the right to fair and just working conditions. Most of the remaining

[47] Articles 7 and 8 of the Charter were each referred to in three of the cases that were selected through the search described in n 39 and Articles 16, 17, and 21 of the Charter in two cases each.

[48] Thirty-three of the forty-five successful cases (see n 39) in which the Charter was mentioned were staff cases.

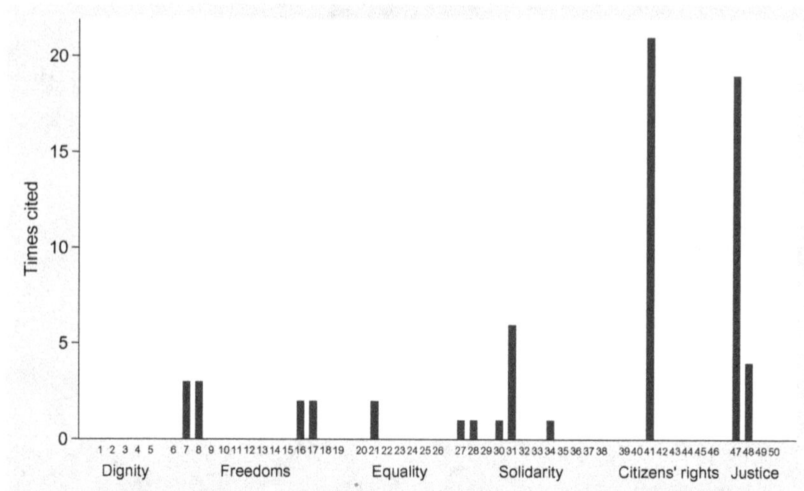

FIGURE 2.3 Charter rights in successful damages cases (2)

cases concerned either public procurement or competition law.[49] Articles 41 and 47 of the Charter were frequently mentioned in all three categories of case, that is, in staff, public procurement, and competition law cases. Only two of the damages cases with a successful outcome that mentioned the Charter regarded restrictive measures in the framework of the Common Foreign and Security Policy (CFSP).[50] They concerned the freedom to conduct a business and the right to property.

The Charter rights that were at issue in the aforementioned cases have overwhelmingly been clarified and concretised by the EU legislator in secondary legislation. This means that the abstract fundamental rights commitments found in the Charter had already been transposed into concrete and judiciable obligations for the EU through secondary legislation. Arguably the chances to hold the EU liable are greater where Charter rights have been concretised and articulated by the EU legislator in secondary legislation (see also Section 2.4.2).

Other cases concerned Charter rights that have not been fleshed out by the legislator. In these cases, the CJEU drew on its own previous case law and conducted a (more or less complete) fundamental rights balancing exercise in

49 Eight of the forty-five successful cases (see n 39) in which the Charter was mentioned concerned competition law, while six concerned the public procurement context.

50 Case T-405/15 *Fulmen v Council* [2019] ECLI:EU:T:2019:469; Case T-406/15 *Mahmoudian v Council* [2019] ECLI:EU:T:2019:468. In these cases, Articles 16 and 17 of the Charter were applied.

accordance with Article 52(1) of the Charter to determine whether a restriction to a fundamental right could be justified. In particular, a strand of case law has emerged assessing whether the Article 47 right to adjudication within a reasonable time was violated due to lengthy competition law proceedings before the General Court.[51] Furthermore, the CJEU balanced fundamental rights that were not substantiated through secondary legislation when determining whether CFSP restrictive measures violated the right to property and the freedom to conduct a business.[52]

However, none of the successful cases concerned interferences via omission, interferences in cases of shared (operational) conduct, or the positive (fundamental rights) obligations stemming from Charter provisions.

2.4 'UNLAWFULNESS' AS A CONDITION FOR EU FUNDAMENTAL RIGHTS LIABILITY

Article 340(2) TFEU does not define the conditions for EU liability but instead leaves it to the CJEU to do so. The Court has not developed an approach to the action for damages that is specific and tailored to fundamental rights violations but applies the same conditions as for any other breach of EU law.[53]

EU liability for fundamental rights violations is therefore subject to three explicit, cumulative conditions.[54] First, for EU damages liability to arise, there must be unlawful conduct on behalf of the EU. The condition of unlawfulness is qualified in two ways: the infringed rule must be intended to confer rights on individuals and the breach must be sufficiently serious. In addition, EU liability is predicated on the occurrence of damage on the part of the victim as a second condition and an uninterrupted causal relationship between the unlawful conduct and the damage as a third condition.

The particular challenges posed by the qualified condition of unlawfulness in establishing fundamental rights violations warrant further examination. This is why this section focuses on unlawfulness as a condition for EU

51 Especially: *Kendrion v Commission* (n 8); *Gascogne Sack Deutschland v Commission* (n 8); *Groupe Gascogne v Commission* (n 8); *Gascogne Sack Deutschland and Gascogne v EU* (n 8); *Kendrion v EU* (n 8); Case C-150/17 P *EU v Kendrion* [2018] ECLI:EU:C:2018:1014; Case C-138/17 P *EU v Gascogne Sack Deutschland and Gascogne* [2018] ECLI:EU:C:2018:1013.

52 *Fulmen v Council* (n 50); *Mahmoudian v Council* (n 50).

53 Piotr Machnikowski, 'European Union' in Ken Oliphant (ed), *The Liability of Public Authorities in Comparative Perspective* (Intersentia 2017) 574; Gutman (n 33) 47; Ward, 'Damages under the EU Charter of Fundamental Rights' (n 4) 590; Rauchegger (n 4) 1321; Fink, 'The Action for Damages as a Fundamental Rights Remedy' (n 4) 542.

54 Case C-352/98 P *Bergaderm and Goupil v Commission* [2000] ECLI:EU:C:2000:361, para 42.

fundamental rights liability. It first identifies the provisions of the Charter that are intended to confer rights on individuals (Section 2.4.1). It then turns to the sufficiently serious breach requirement, bringing forward three arguments against applying this requirement to fundamental rights violations (Section 2.4.2) and examining the CJEU's application of the requirement in its case law (Section 2.4.3).

2.4.1 *No Conferral of Rights by Charter Principles*

For EU liability to arise, there must be unlawful conduct on behalf of the EU in violation of a norm of EU law that is intended to confer rights on individuals. Whether an EU rule is intended to confer rights on individuals is to be determined in relation to whom the provision is addressed to or owed.[55] EU fundamental rights regulate the relationship between the Member States and the EU, on the one hand, and individuals, on the other hand, and have been developed first and foremost with the protection of the individual in mind.[56] This suggests that the fundamental rights enshrined in the Charter confer rights on individuals.

However, not all provisions of the Charter articulate rights. The Charter distinguishes between rights and principles and only violations of Charter rights engage the EU's damages liability. Article 52(5) of the Charter states that principles, as opposed to rights, require implementation by legislative or other acts taken by the EU or the Member States and 'shall be judicially cognisable only in the interpretation of such acts and in the ruling on their legality'.[57] According to Advocate General Cruz Villalón in *AMS*, where principles have not been given specific expression through legislation, 'the possibility of directly relying on a "principle" so as to exercise an individual right based upon that principle' is excluded.[58] What this means is that principles are not automatically justiciable; their justiciability requires their prior implementation.[59]

Yet Charter principles are not simply 'truncated rights' that turn into fully fledged rights through implementation.[60] Rather, they are structurally

55 Fink, *Frontex and Human Rights* (n 4) 200–202.
56 Ibid 203, 206.
57 The distinction between rights and principles is also mentioned in CFR, art 51(1).
58 Opinion of AG Cruz Villalón in Case C-176/ 12 *Association de médiation sociale* [2013] ECLI:EU:C:2013:491, para 68.
59 Tobias Lock, 'Rights and Principles in the EU Charter of Fundamental Rights' (2019) 56 Common Market Law Review, 1222.
60 Ibid 1218.

different from rights in that they merely entail duties but do not come with a corresponding claim right.[61] They impose a one-sided, non-relational duty on the EU or the Member States and therefore belong to the realm of objective law.[62] Rights, in contrast, are relational in that they provide subjective entitlements. Consequently, Charter rights fulfil the condition of conferring rights on individuals, whereas Charter principles do not.

Even though Charter principles can mainly be found in the broad domain of economic, social, and cultural rights, the characterisation of a Charter provision as belonging to this domain is not what determines its nature as a principle. To find out whether a Charter provision contains a right or a principle, one has to look at the wording of the provision. There are three types of wording that indicate Charter principles. First, the wording may be devoid of any rights language, as is the case for Articles 36 to 38 of the Charter. Second, the formulation 'the Union recognises and respects' seems determinative of a general principle. This formulation is found in Articles 25, 26, 34(1) and (3), and 36 of the Charter, all of which the Charter Explanations identify as principles. Third, Article 35 of the Charter only confers a right 'under the conditions established by national laws and practices'. Unlike the more general formulation 'in accordance with national laws and practices', the formulation of Article 35 indicates a principle.[63]

Following this approach in distinguishing between Charter rights and principles, all the Charter provisions that the CJEU has referred to in successful damages cases since 2015 contained Charter rights (see Section 2.3).[64] This further supports the argument that only Charter rights confer rights on individuals and can thus engage the EU's damages liability.

2.4.2 *Three Arguments against Applying the 'Sufficiently Serious Breach' Test to Fundamental Rights*

A breach of Union law does not lead to liability, 'however regrettable that unlawfulness may be', unless it qualifies as 'sufficiently serious'.[65] Thus, there is conduct of the EU that is unlawful and leads to damage but is not 'unlawful

[61] Ibid 1220.
[62] Ibid 1203.
[63] Ibid 1218–1219.
[64] The reference to Article 34(1) of the Charter in Case T-462/17 appears in the part of the judgment that relates to the action for annulment, Case T-462/17 *TO v EEA* [2019] ECLI:EU:T:2019:397, para 91.
[65] For example, Case T-384/ 11 *Safa Nicu Sepahan v Council* [2014] ECLI:EU:T:2014:986, para 50.

enough' for liability to arise. The decisive criterion is whether the Union body concerned 'manifestly and gravely disregarded the limits on its discretion'.[66] A number of factors are hence relevant to establish the seriousness of the breach: the extent of discretion the authority in question enjoys, the obviousness ('manifestly') of the breach, and the reprehensibility of committing it ('gravely').[67]

If this logic is translated to the fundamental rights context, it means that there are fundamental rights breaches that are unjustified under fundamental rights law yet are not obvious or reprehensible enough for liability to arise. The General Court implied this when it noted that neither the Charter nor the ECHR 'preclude that the Community's non-contractual liability be made subject ... to the finding of a sufficiently serious breach of the fundamental rights invoked by the applicant'.[68] However, applying the'sufficiently serious breach' test to the fundamental rights context may be problematic for three reasons.

The first reason concerns the right to an effective remedy (see Section 2.2.3). Article 47 of the Charter requires the Union to make a complaints mechanism available for any rights violation, regardless of whether it is 'simple' or 'serious'. In circumstances where the action for damages is the only possibility for individuals to seek redress for fundamental rights violations committed by an EU body, the right to an effective remedy may thus require the Court to refrain from applying the sufficiently serious breach requirement altogether. Given the CJEU's exclusive jurisdiction over EU unlawful conduct, there is otherwise no remedy available for cases concerning 'simple' breaches of fundamental rights by the EU.

A notable example where judicial remedies beyond the action for damages are virtually absent is so-called factual conduct (see also Chapter 12) or soft law (see also Chapter 14). Neither of these forms of administrative action are considered by the CJEU to have 'binding legal effect' and they therefore largely escape judicial review under Article 263 TFEU. In this context, Rademacher argues for a loosening of the conditions for the EU's damages liability on the basis of Article 47 of the Charter by refraining from applying the sufficiently serious breach requirements under certain circumstances.[69] If the sufficiently serious breach requirement is applied, factual conduct and

66 *Bergaderm* (n 54) para 43.

67 Discussing each in detail: Fink, *Frontex and Human Rights* (n 4) 207–228.

68 Case T-341/07 *Sison v Council* [2011] ECLI:EU:T:2011:687, para 81.

69 Timo Rademacher, 'Factual Administrative Conduct and Judicial Review in EU Law' (2017) 29 European Review of Public Law 399, 430–435.

soft law may escape judicial scrutiny altogether since they escape judicial review by the CJEU under alternative procedures.

Second, the overarching rationale for the 'sufficiently serious breach' requirement is unsuitable for the fundamental rights context. Making liability contingent on fault or a sufficiently serious breach requirement may be necessary to ensure that public authorities can exercise discretion in the public interest and to prevent them becoming 'overcautious'.[70] Indeed, in the CJEU's case law, the reason for the sufficiently serious breach requirement is tied to avoiding a 'chilling effect' on the exercise of discretion.[71] In the words of the Court, it serves the purpose of securing the 'room for manoeuvre and freedom of assessment' that public authorities need to fulfil their functions in the general interest whilst ensuring that third parties do not 'bear the consequences of flagrant and inexcusable misconduct'.[72]

Leaving aside whether these policy considerations against lowering the liability threshold are supported by empirical evidence,[73] they do not fit when fundamental rights are at issue. In the case of fundamental rights, the balance between the interests of the individual and society at large is already struck in the context of the determination of whether a breach of a fundamental right has effectively occurred. It forms not only part of the proportionality analysis for qualified fundamental rights[74] but is also taken into account in formulating the positive obligations public actors may incur to prevent breaches of fundamental rights.[75] Accordingly, the requirement of a sufficiently serious breach should not be applied in an action for damages when the rule of EU law that is breached is a fundamental right since this requirement

70 Van Dam (n 29) 531–532; Ken Oliphant, 'The Liability of Public Authorities in Comparative Perspective' in Ken Oliphant (ed), *The Liability of Public Authorities in Comparative Perspective* (Intersentia 2017) 860–863; Jane Wright, 'The Retreat from *Osman*: *Z v United Kingdom* in the European Court of Human Rights and Beyond' (2002) International & Comparative Law Quarterly 55, 56. More broadly: Jef de Mot and Michael Faure, 'The Liability of Public Authorities: An Economic Analysis' in Ken Oliphant (ed), *The Liability of Public Authorities in Comparative Perspective* (Intersentia 2017).

71 Rademacher (n 69) 431.

72 For instance Case T-351/03 *Schneider Electric SA v Commission of the European Communities* [2007] ECLI:EU:T:2007:212, para 125; similarly, Case C-392/93 *The Queen v H.M. Treasury, ex parte British Telecommunications* [1996] ECLI:EU:C:1996:131, para 40.

73 Wright (n 70) 56. See also (contrasting the English with the French approach): van Dam (n 29) 532.

74 For a discussion on different types of fundamental rights: Janneke Gerards, *General Principles of the European Convention on Human Rights* (Cambridge University Press 2023) 19–30.

75 CFR, art 52(1); Tom R Hickman, 'Tort Law, Public Authorities, and the Human Rights Act 1998' in Duncan Fairgrieve, Mads Andenas, and John Bell (eds), *Tort Liability of Public Authorities in Comparative Perspective* (The British Institute of International and Comparative Law 2002) 44.

unnecessarily replicates the balancing exercise that is inherent in the fundamental rights analysis.[76] Besides, if non-pecuniary forms of compensation are more extensively relied on by the CJEU than pecuniary ones, this also contributes to preventing a 'chilling effect' for public authorities (see Section 2.2.1).[77]

Third, the factors that the CJEU uses to determine a sufficiently serious breach are unsuitable when the rule of EU law that is violated is a fundamental right. In establishing a sufficiently serious breach, the CJEU considers a number of factors, including the discretion retained by the EU, the complexity of the case, the clarity of the (concrete) binding legal obligations on the EU, and the intentional character of the act or omission.[78] The clearer the rule that is violated, the more likely that a breach is considered sufficiently serious by the CJEU.

The requirement of clarity in particular poses a significant obstacle to EU liability for fundamental rights violations arising from EU conduct. To be applicable to concrete situations, abstract fundamental rights must generally be 'translated' into concrete negative or positive, procedural, or substantive fundamental rights obligations. This process of concretisation of abstract fundamental rights has largely taken place in relation to the Member States. The CJEU itself has predominantly interpreted EU fundamental rights in relation to the Member States as duty-bearers. Furthermore, the rich case law of the ECtHR on the interpretation of the ECHR, which is relevant for the Charter due to its Article 52(3), is currently exclusively concerned with Member State obligations. Similarly, also the case law of domestic (constitutional) courts that, by virtue of Article 52(4) of the Charter, can guide the interpretation of Charter rights that result from the constitutional traditions common to the Member States is also exclusively concerned with Member State obligations.

Some fundamental rights obligations, such as those resulting from the rights to good administration guaranteed by Article 41 of the Charter, can obviously be discharged by the EU's (administrative) bodies in the same way as they could be by Member State bodies. However, it is unclear whether this is the case for

[76] Fundamental rights that do not permit a balancing exercise on account of their absolute nature (e.g., the prohibition of torture) should in any case – by nature of the implicated right – automatically be considered sufficiently serious.

[77] Rademacher (n 69) 431.

[78] Concerning the clarity of the obligation: *The Queen v H.M. Treasury, ex parte British Telecommunications* (n 72) para 43. Case C-283/94 *Denkavit Internationaal and Others v Bundesamt für Finanzen* [1996] ECLI:EU:C:1996:387, paras 51–52. Concerning the complexity of the case and the intentional character of the breach: Case T-364/03 *Medici Grimm KG v Council of the European Union* [2006] ECLI:EU:T:2006:28, para 87; Case C-282/05 P *Holcim (Deutschland) v Commission* [2007] ECLI:EU:C:2007:226, para 50. See also (and sources cited therein): Koen Lenaerts and Others (eds), *EU Procedural Law* (Oxford University Press 2014) 11, 60.

other fundamental rights obligations too. The positive (substantive) obligation under the right to life, for example, requires action by states to prevent industrial and environmental disasters.[79] The EU simply does not always have the means or competences to meet such types of positive obligation, particularly where such competence is retained by or shared with Member States. As a functionally tailored non-state actor, the EU is thus constrained as to its competences, power, and budget in manners that Member States are not. Consequently, concrete obligations stemming from abstract fundamental rights commitments might differ between the EU and its Member States and there is a need for more conceptual clarity as regards the EU itself as a duty-bearer.[80]

To sum up, three arguments militate against applying the 'sufficiently serious breach' test to fundamental rights. First, where no alternative remedies are available to challenge EU action, excluding damages on the basis that the breach of EU law was not sufficiently serious can have the consequence that the breach of EU law escapes judicial review altogether, which is problematic from the perspective of the right to an effective remedy guaranteed by Article 47 of the Charter. Second, it is not necessary to apply this test to fundamental rights cases to ensure a degree of discretion for public authorities since a balancing exercise is already inherent in the fundamental rights analysis. Third, the criterion of clarity of the violated rule is generally at odds with the abstract formulation of fundamental rights and their need to be concretised by courts. More specifically, there is a lack of case law on the EU as a duty-bearer of Charter rights that could provide clarity.

2.4.3 *The CJEU's Approach to the 'Sufficiently Serious Breach' Test in Fundamental Rights Cases*

While the CJEU has never explicitly pronounced itself on the question whether the 'sufficiently serious breach' test applies to fundamental rights,[81] there is case law that suggests that it might not. In some cases, the Court seemed to base this approach on the lack of discretion enjoyed by public authorities when fundamental rights are at issue.[82]

79 For example: *Öneryildiz v Turkey*, App no 48939/99 (ECtHR, 30 November 2004); *Budayeva and Others v Russia*, App nos 15339/02, 21166/02, 20058/02, 11673/02 and 15343/02 (ECtHR, 20 March 2008).

80 Also arguing for a need for more conceptual clarity of EU fundamental rights law: Douglas-Scott (n 1) 386–387.

81 See also: Fink, 'The Action for Damages as a Fundamental Rights Remedy' (n 4) 542.

82 Case T-48/05 *Franchet and Byk v Commission* [2008] ECLI:EU:T:2008:257, para 219; Case T-138/14 *Chart v EEAS* [2015] ECLI:EU:T:2015:981, para 114. It should be noted, however,

In other cases, the CJEU, namely the Court of Justice, indicated that it would apply the test but then seemed to consider a breach of a qualified fundamental right as automatically meeting it. In these cases, the Court conducted a fundamental rights balancing exercise to determine whether the Charter right was infringed and stopped the analysis there. Although the Court noted in these cases that a serious breach of EU law was required, it did not actually examine the seriousness of the breach of the Charter right.[83] For instance, in *Kendrion*, *Gascogne Sack Deutschland*, and *Groupe Gascogne v Commission*, the Court examined the circumstances of the specific case, such as the complexity of the dispute and the conduct of the parties. Concluding that the right to adjudication within a reasonable time had been breached, it simply held that this constituted a sufficiently serious breach of a rule of law that is intended to confer rights on individuals.[84] It can be speculated that this approach indicates that any breach of a qualified Charter right – where the Court has already found the limitation to be disproportionate – is sufficiently serious to lead to the EU's damages liability.

Conversely, there is also case law of the General Court that suggests that fundamental rights violations falling below a threshold of 'seriousness' do not lead to liability. In *Sison*, for example, the General Court established that the sanctions imposed on the applicant were incompatible with EU law and thus illegal, but the breach did not qualify as sufficiently serious due to the complexity of the situation, the difficulties in interpreting and applying the relevant rules, and the lack of well-established precedent on the topic.[85] Next, the General Court turned to the question of whether the illegality of the sanctions breached Sison's fundamental rights in a manner capable of triggering EU liability, holding that the alleged breach of fundamental rights was

that the Court in these cases seems to (incorrectly) derive the lack of discretion from the obligation not to act in breach of fundamental rights. It is also unclear to what extent the Court of Justice would agree with the General Court on this aspect, see the discussion in Case T-217/11 *Staelen v European Ombudsman* [2015] ECLI:EU:T:2015:238, para 86; Case C-337/15 P *European Ombudsman v Staelen* [2017] ECLI:EU:C:2017:256, paras 31–45.

83 Indications of this approach may be found in cases dealing with the right to property and the freedom to conduct a business, where the Court held that disproportionate interferences with (i.e., violations of) fundamental rights, are 'intolerable', 'unacceptable', or otherwise equivalent to a sufficiently serious breach. For example, Joined Cases C-120/06 P and C-121/06 P *FIAMM and Others v Council and Commission* [2008] ECLI:EU:C:2008:476, paras 183–184.

84 *Kendrion v Commission* (n 8) para 106; *Gascogne Sack Deutschland v Commission* (n 8) para 102; *Groupe Gascogne v Commission* (n 8) para 96. See also: Case C-603/13P *Galp Energia España* [2016] ECLI:EU:C:2016:38, para 58; Case C-604/13P *Dornbracht* [2017] ECLI:EU:C:2017:45, paras 97–100; Case C-608/13 *CEPSA* [2016] ECLI:EU:C:2016:414, paras 67–68.

85 *Sison v Council* (n 68).

'inseparable' from the illegality previously established. For that reason, it concluded that even if a breach of fundamental rights existed, 'that breach is also not sufficiently serious, in the particular circumstances of the case, to incur the non-contractual liability of the Community'.[86] Similarly, in other cases, the General Court examined the obviousness and reprehensibility of the fundamental rights breaches alleged, which suggests that the relevant authorities would not have incurred liability for a 'simple' violation.[87]

The foregoing demonstrates that the CJEU is not explicit about whether the 'sufficiently serious breach' requirement applies to fundamental rights and that it is inconsistent in its approach. This has significant implications for the principles of legal certainty, legitimate expectations, and the effectiveness of EU fundamental rights law. In light of the concerns set out in Section 2.4.2, the Court should clarify that breaches of fundamental rights are not subject to the sufficiently serious breach test.

2.5 JOINT LIABILITY BETWEEN THE EU AND ITS MEMBER STATES

In the EU's multi-level administration, the EU and its Member States more often than not are jointly responsible for ensuring that fundamental rights are guaranteed. This joint responsibility can result from shared exercise of public power, for instance in joint decision-making procedures (see also Chapter 13), or from the parallel exercise of public power by the EU and one or more Member States over the same situation, for instance, in the context of operational cooperation. When fundamental rights are violated in the context of EU law, there is thus often a combined failure of several actors at the EU and Member State level.

The assumption may be that these types of failures lead to joint liability.[88] However, in the EU legal system, joint liability is the exception, rather than

[86] *Sison v Council* (n 68) para 80.

[87] *Schneider Electric SA v Commission of the European Communities* (n 72) paras 154–156. This was not objected to by the Court of Justice upon appeal: Case C-440/07 P *Commission v Schneider Electric* [2009] ECLI:EU:C:2009:459, para 173. See also: *Safa Nicu Sepahan* (n 65) paras 32–36, 60–67. This was upheld on appeal: Case C-45/15 P *Safa Nicu Sepahan v Council* [2017] ECLI:EU:C:2017:402, paras 29–42.

[88] For a discussion of different aspects of joint liability: Joyce De Coninck, 'Effective Remedies for Human Rights Violations in EU CSDP Military Missions: Smoke and Mirrors in Human Rights Adjudication?' (2023) 24 German Law Journal 342; De Coninck, 'Catch-22 in the Law of Responsibility of International Organizations' (n 4); Melanie Fink, 'EU Liability for Contributions to Member States' Breaches of EU Law' (2019) 56 Common Market Law Review 1227; Fink, *Frontex and Human Rights* (n 4); Peter Oliver, 'Joint Liability of the Community and the Member States' in Ton Heukels and Alison McDonnell (eds), *The Action for Damages in Community Law* (Kluwer Law International 1997); Wouter Wils, 'Concurrent

the rule. This section outlines the various factors that contribute to this reality, both in relation to the establishment (Section 2.5.1) and the implementation (Section 2.5.2) of joint liability.

2.5.1 *Establishing Joint Liability: Attribution and Causation*

When more than one actor is involved in causing damage, two concepts are used to determine whether one or all of them are liable: attribution and causation. The two concepts each fulfil different roles in the allocation of liability.

Attribution links the unlawful conduct to the responsible actor, that is, to its 'true author'. Only the entity considered the 'author' of a violation will incur liability for its consequences. For example, when a 'pushback' during a Frontex-coordinated joint border control operation violates fundamental rights, it might be difficult to establish the actual 'author' (or 'authors') of the violation since the actions of the EU and Member State authorities were intertwined.[89]

In contrast, causation is the link between the unlawful conduct and the damage that occurred. For example, when the EU has failed to prevent a fundamental rights violation by a Member State even though it would have been obliged to do so, the question arises whether this inaction was a sufficiently direct cause for the damage that occurred.

The questions of attribution and causation are sequential.[90] The 'true author' of an unlawful act must be identified before it can be assessed whether the unlawful conduct by this author was a sufficiently direct cause for the damage. At the CJEU, attribution and causation are assessed at different stages of liability proceedings. Attribution of conduct to either the EU or a Member State must occur at the admissibility stage of the proceedings, as the CJEU is only competent to rule on the liability of the Union. Attribution of the relevant unlawful conduct to the Union is thus a precondition for the competence of the Court to adjudicate on the substance of the case.[91] In contrast, it is to be determined at the merits stage of the proceedings whether or not unlawful conduct is causally linked to the damage that occurred.

Liability of the Community and a Member State' (1992) 17 European Law Review 191; Christopher Harding, 'The Choice of Court Problem in Cases of Non-Contractual Liability under E.E.C. Law' (1979) 16 Common Market Law Review 389.

89 Fink, *Frontex and Human Rights* (n 4).

90 In more detail: Fink, 'EU Liability for Contributions to Member States' Breaches of EU Law' (n 88) 1235–1237.

91 Explicitly: Case T-277/97 *Ismeri Europa v Court of Auditors* [1999] ECLI:EU:T:1999:124, para 49.

While attribution of conduct is a familiar concept in public international law, this is less so in EU law generally and EU liability law more specifically.[92] Accordingly, significant gaps exist in research regarding the role and interpretation of this concept in EU (liability) law.[93]

Furthermore, the CJEU has not developed a coherent approach to attribution in its case law. In some instances, the Court uses the concept in its damages case law, occasionally even listing it as a fourth condition for a successful claim.[94] However, the CJEU is inconsistent in its terminology. It uses 'attribution of conduct' interchangeably with 'attribution of damage' or 'imputation' and sometimes simply describes a specific course of conduct as being 'in fact the responsibility of [the Union]'.[95] More fundamentally, it sometimes conflates the meaning of attribution and causation.[96]

Apart from these terminological inconsistencies, the case law indicates that the CJEU uses multiple and sometimes overlapping tests of attribution, which are applied differently depending on the substantive area of EU law at stake, the implicated parties, and the applicable procedure.[97] While there is little case law on the issue and the terminological inconsistencies complicate a clear assessment, a rule appears to emerge in EU liability law whereby unlawful conduct is attributed to the authority competent to make legal

[92] See especially ASR, chapter II; International Law Commission, Report of the Sixty-Third Session: Articles on the Responsibility of International Organizations, UN Doc A/66/ 10, 2011 (ARIO), chapter II.

[93] For recent contributions to this field of study: Fink, 'EU Liability for Contributions to Member States' Breaches of EU Law' (n 88); De Coninck, 'Catch-22 in the Law of Responsibility of International Organizations' (n 4).

[94] For instance: Case T-317/12 *Holcim (Romania) v Commission* [2014] ECLI:EU:T:2014:782, para 86. In Case T-250/02 *Autosalone Ispra v EAEC* [2005] ECLI:EU:T:2005:432, paras 42, 68–98, the lack of attribution to the Community led to the dismissal of the action. See also: Joined Cases C-89/86 and C-91/86, *Étoile commerciale and CNTA v Commission* [1987] EU: C:1987:337, para 18; Case T-279/03 *Galileo International Technology and Others v Commission* [2006] ECLI:EU:T:2006:121, para 129. In literature: Lenaerts and Others (n 78) 11, 81; Alexander Türk, *Judicial review in EU law* (Edward Elgar 2009) 241; Francette Fines, 'A General Analytical Perspective on Community Liability' in Ton Heukels and Alison McDonnell (eds), *The Action for Damages in Community Law* (Kluwer Law International 1997) 16–18.

[95] Fink, 'EU Liability for Contributions to Member States' Breaches of EU Law' (n 88).

[96] Ibid 1238–1239.

[97] De Coninck, 'Catch-22 in the Law of Responsibility of International Organizations' (n 4) 154–167; Simone Vezzani, 'The International Responsibility of the European Union and of Its Member States for Breaches of Obligations Arising from Investment Agreements: Lex Specialis or European Exceptionalism?' in Mads Adenas and Others (eds), *EU External Action in International Economical Law: Recent Trends and Developements* (T. M. C. Asser Press/ Springer 2020) 314–315.

choices, that is, to the authority enjoying legal decision-making power.[98] This test seems to be applied relatively strictly, with very little margin to take into account other forms of influence, power, or pressure outside the ambit of the competence to act in a legally binding manner.[99]

As a result of the CJEU's incoherent approach to attribution, it is unclear how exactly EU liability law deals with situations where more than one actor may have been involved in fundamental rights violations. The ex post determination of attribution (explicit or implicit) without any ex ante clarification as to the applicable threshold is particularly detrimental to applicants, who need to decide on the forum for their claim for compensation (CJEU or national courts), since to date no forum exists that could allocate joint responsibility and the subsequent burden of compensation in tandem.

With respect to causation, the CJEU has repeatedly held that a causal link exists when an infringement of the law was a necessary and sufficiently direct condition for damage to occur.[100] A breach is too remote or indirect if an intervening event 'breaks' the chain of causation. This may be the occurrence of exceptional or unforeseeable events, or imprudent conduct by the applicant, but also imprudent conduct by other public (Member State) authorities, if that proves to be the determinant cause of the damage.[101] In some cases, the CJEU indicates that 'exclusive' causation might be required for liability to arise, thus excluding joint liability at the substantive level.[102] In other cases, however, the Court seemed more open to allowing for several determining causes that may all have contributed in a sufficiently decisive manner to the occurrence of the damage for liability to arise.[103] This particular question is one of the main points of contention in *Kočner v EUROPOL*, a case recently

[98] Fink, *Frontex and Human Rights* (n 4) 232–266, in particular 263–266; Fink, 'EU Liability for Contributions to Member States' Breaches of EU Law' (n 88) 1240–1244.

[99] Two notable exceptions in this respect are Case C-146/91 *KYDEP v Council and Commission* [1994] EU:C:1994:329, paras 24–27; Case T-786/14 *Bourdouvali and Others v Council and Others* [2018] EU:T:2018:487, para 99. In more detail: Fink, 'EU Liability for Contributions to Member States' Breaches of EU Law' (n 88) 1244–1245.

[100] On the threshold for causation: A G Toth, 'The Concepts of Damage and Causality as Elements of Non-contractual Liability' in Ton Heukels and Alison McDonnell (eds), *The Action for Damages in Community Law* (Kluwer Law International 1997) 192.

[101] Case C-419/08 P *Trubowest* [2010] ECLI:EU:C:2010:147, paras 59, 60–61; Joined Cases C-64 and C-113/76 *Dumortier v Council* [1979] ECLI:EU:C:1979:223, para 21.

[102] E.g., *Trubowest* (n 101) para 61.

[103] Case F-50/09 *Missir Mamachi di Lusignano v Commission* [2011] ECLI:EU:F:2011:55, para 181, citing in particular Case C-308/87 *Grifoni v EAEC* [1990] ECLI:EU:C:1990:134, paras 17–18; Case T-178/98 *Fresh Marine v Commission* [2000] ECLI:EU:T:2000:240 paras 135–136.

decided by the Court of Justice.[104] Whereas the General Court had dismissed the action due to the absence of an 'exclusive' causal link between Europol and the alleged damage,[105] the Court of Justice followed Advocate General Rantos' suggestions and held that Europol and the Member State jointly and severally incur liability for the non-material damage stemming from the violations of the applicant's fundamental rights.[106] While in the case of Europol, the founding regulation specifically envisages that the agency and national authorities can be jointly liable, the decision of the Court of Justice on this matter may have broader consequences for joint liability between the EU and its Member States more generally.

It is safe to conclude that joint conduct and subsequent joint responsibility of the EU and its Member States in safeguarding fundamental rights does not ipso facto translate into joint liability. If not excluded at the admissibility stage through the application of a high and uncertain attribution threshold, a strict causation test will often prevent joint liability at the merits stage of the proceedings.[107] In any event, joint liability – while theoretically possible – remains the exception to the rule.

2.5.2 *Implementing Joint Liability: Court Competence and Parallel Proceedings*

Even where the EU and a Member State are exceptionally jointly liable, the procedural implementation of this joint liability in the EU's remedies system presents a significant obstacle. In the case of *Kampffmeyer*, the Court had in principle recognised the Community's liability for the Commission's approval of an unlawful measure taken by Germany.[108] However, since the applicants had brought parallel actions against Germany concerning the same damage, the Court held that in order to 'avoid the applicants being insufficiently or excessively compensated for the same damage', it was 'necessary for the national court to have the opportunity to give judgment on any liability on

[104] Case C-755/21 P *Kočner v EUROPOL* [2024] ECLI:EU:C:2024:202.

[105] Case T-528/20 *Kočner v EUROPOL* [2021] ECLI:EU:T:2021:631.

[106] Opinion of AG Rantos in Case C-755/21 P *Kočner v EUROPOL* [2023] ECLI:EU:C:2023:481, para 55; *Kočner v EUROPOL* (n 104).

[107] De Coninck argues that in cases of joint conduct between the EU and its Member States resulting in fundamental rights violations, more often than not liability will be avoided altogether, leaving victims without access to an effective remedy vis-à-vis any of the implicated actors: Coninck, 'Catch-22 in the Law of Responsibility of International Organizations' (n 4); Coninck, 'Effective Remedies for Human Rights Violations in EU CSDP Military Missions' (n 88).

[108] Joined Cases C-5/66, 7/66, 13/66–24/66 *Kampffmeyer and Others v Commission* [1967] EU:C:1967:31, page 262.

the part of the Federal Republic of Germany' before the damage for which the Community should be held liable could be determined.[109] The Court thus stayed the proceedings awaiting the decision of the national court on the matter.[110]

This approach has been widely criticised.[111] First, it can make it particularly lengthy and complicated for applicants to obtain compensation when more than one actor is involved, which raises concerns from the perspective of the right to an effective remedy. In *Kampffmeyer*, for instance, the proceedings remained stayed for almost twenty years before they were removed from the Court's register.[112] Second, it renders EU liability substantively subsidiary to Member State liability. From a fundamental rights perspective especially, this is problematic. Given that many of the EU's activities require some form of participation by the Member States, this may significantly impact the chances of holding the EU liable for its contribution to fundamental rights violations that have directly been committed by Member State authorities.

In the absence of an adjudicatory mechanism to consider questions of joint fundamental rights responsibility between the EU and its Member States in tandem, the institutional design of the EU significantly complicates joint liability in practice. Hence, not only are there legal obstacles to establishing joint liability in substance, there are equally significant institutional obstacles to establishing joint liability in the procedural set up and practice.

2.6 CONCLUSION

The action for damages has the potential to provide redress to individuals who have experienced violations of their fundamental rights by an EU entity, thanks to several distinguishing characteristics it possesses. The admissibility threshold is significantly lower than with respect to the action for annulment. Obtaining a verdict on substance requires neither a particular form of EU conduct, such as a legally binding act, nor proof of a specific interest on the

[109] Ibid page 266.

[110] The same approach was followed in more recent cases: Case T-138/03 *É.R. and Others v Council and Commission* [2006] ECLI:EU:T:2006:390, para 42; *Holcim (Romania) v Commission* (n 94) paras 78–83.

[111] Oliver (n 88) 288; Uwe Säuberlich, *Die Außervertragliche Haftung im Gemeinschaftsrecht: Eine Untersuchung der Mehrpersonenverhältnisse* (Springer 2005) 242–243; Ulf F Renzenbrink, *Gemeinschaftshaftung und Mitgliedstaatliche Rechtsbehelfe: Vorrang, Subsidiarität oder Gleichstufigkeit?* (Peter Lang 2000) 161–162, 176–183; Harding (n 88) 403–405. See also: AG Darmon in Case C-55/90 *Cato* [1992] ECLI:EU:C:1992:52 (Opinion 2), para 18.

[112] Fink, 'EU Liability for Contributions to Member States' Breaches of EU Law' (n 88) 1262.

part of the applicant to have the EU measure assessed as to its legality.[113] Moreover, at the substantive level, the action for damages is exceptionally flexible.[114] Article 340 TFEU merely states that the EU is to make good damage it causes 'in accordance with the general principles common to the laws of the Member States', without specifying the precise conditions. This provides room for the CJEU to develop a liability regime suitable for the EU, including in relation to its commitments under fundamental rights law.[115]

Yet the action for damages is currently not very effective as an avenue for a fundamental rights remedy. As the analysis in this chapter has shown, this is largely due to two factors.

First, the core obstacle encountered by individual victims in lodging a successful action for damages concerns the Court's insistence on the 'sufficiently serious breach' test. This chapter has argued that it is problematic to apply this test to the fundamental rights context for three main reasons. The first reason is that it would be incompatible with the right to an effective remedy if no remedy were available for fundamental rights violations that do not meet this threshold. Given the CJEU's exclusive jurisdiction over EU bodies and the restrictions pertaining to other direct actions, there is EU conduct that can only be challenged through an action for damages. If such conduct violates fundamental rights in a manner that does not pass the 'sufficiently serious breach' threshold, there is no remedy at all for those affected. The second reason is that the balance between individual and societal interests that the 'sufficiently serious breach' test serves to strike by preserving a degree of discretion to public authorities is already built into the fundamental rights balancing exercise. The third reason why the 'sufficiently serious breach' test should not be applied to fundamental rights is that the criterion of clarity employed by the Court to establish whether the threshold is met proves near impossible to meet when fundamental rights violations by the EU are at issue. To date, there is a significant lack of certainty regarding the scope of concrete fundamental rights obligations as they apply to the EU specifically.

The second major obstacle is that the limits to the establishment and enforcement of joint liability sit uneasily with the fact that due to the EU's multi-level administration, safeguarding fundamental rights is in many situations a joint responsibility between the EU and its Member States. The

[113] Dominik Hanf, 'EU Liability Actions' in Robert Schütze and Takis Tridimas (eds), *Oxford Principles Of European Union Law: The European Union Legal Order: Volume I* (Oxford University Press 2018) 914–918.

[114] Ibid 911.

[115] Rademacher (n 69).

existing framework not only carries considerable uncertainty but also subjects applicants to prolonged litigation spanning years or even decades. It also risks making EU liability subsidiary to the liability of its Member States. In other words, despite the theoretical possibility to establish joint responsibility, substantive and institutional obstacles significantly prevent findings of joint responsibility in practice.

The first of these two obstacles, the 'sufficiently serious breach requirement', is not pre-determined by the Treaties but has been developed by the CJEU. It could thus in principle be dropped or reinterpreted, altogether or for specific areas, especially if there is evidence that national liability regimes do so too. Liability law is deeply embedded in the attitudes of a society towards the notions of injury, sanction, and conflict resolution.[116] As a result, national regimes for compensation of damages resulting from fundamental rights violations vary significantly.[117] While a comparative analysis of national fundamental rights liability regimes is beyond the scope of this chapter, research has shown that it is not uncommon among EU Member States to opt for special approaches to liability regarding fundamental rights, for instance, by reinterpreting the requirements of fault, causation, or damage in public liability regimes.[118]

To close the gap that arises in the EU's remedies system, especially when fundamental rights are violated through conduct that is not reviewable under Article 263 TFEU (see Chapter 1), the CJEU may rely on Article 47 of the Charter and the approaches adopted in national liability laws to develop a fundamental rights–specific regime for damages liability. This may involve disapplying the 'sufficiently serious breach' requirement altogether, establishing a (rebuttable) presumption of seriousness when (certain) fundamental rights are concerned, or applying criteria to establish seriousness that are better suited to the nature of and types of fundamental rights law as they apply to the EU. To accommodate concerns regarding any possible 'chilling effect' that more leniency might have, a distinction could be made between claims that involve monetary compensation and those that only seek termination, declarations, apologies, or other forms of non-monetary compensation.[119] As Section 2.2.1 has shown, the CJEU already grants non-monetary

[116] Mauro Bussani and Marta Infantino, 'The Many Cultures of Tort Liability' in Mauro Bussani and Anthony J Sebok (eds), *Comparative Tort Law: Global Perspectives* (Edward Elgar 2015).

[117] For a general overview: Ewa Bagińska (ed), *Damages for Violations of Human Rights: A Comparative Study of Domestic Legal Systems* (Springer 2016).

[118] Ibid.

[119] See also: Rademacher (n 69).

compensation under appropriate circumstances, so relying on these more extensively would not be a structural departure from existing case law.

Alternatively, a fundamental rights–specific liability regime may also be achieved through secondary legislation.[120] A recent example of such an approach is the 2022 Commission proposal for an Artificial Intelligence Liability Directive with the aim to adapt non-contractual liability rules to the specific challenges posed by AI.[121] Given that the EU has no general competence to adopt fundamental rights–specific legislation that would apply horizontally, it may be possible to develop such instruments for specific policy areas, particularly where the effective judicial protection gap is particularly obvious, such as in the Area of Freedom, Security and Justice. Notably, the founding regulation of the EU agency Europol envisages joint liability between the agency and national authorities.[122] In addition, in the realm of EU trade agreements, the absence of a horizontally applicable approach to fundamental rights clauses does not prevent convergence in the language, method, and objectives of fundamental rights clauses in different EU trade agreements. Hence, the absence of an overarching, horizontal competence to develop a fundamental rights liability framework that spans across various domains of substantive EU law in the interest of ensuring (individual) access to an effective remedy does not impede a common, albeit sectoral, approach to fundamental rights liability.

The second factor identified in this chapter that hampers effectiveness of the action for damages as a fundamental rights remedy concerns the limits to the establishment and enforcement of EU liability when the EU cooperates with Member States. This is more complex to resolve. The ideal solution is a combination of clear rules on attribution and causation that govern cooperative scenarios and a common forum to establish and enforce joint liability between the EU and its Member States. Given that the competences of the CJEU are delimited in the Treaties, the common forum is difficult to achieve. However, clear attribution and causation rules that reflect the respective fundamental rights obligations of the EU and its Member States and the interaction between them can, and should, be developed by the CJEU.

[120] A similar proposal is made in relation to the judicial protection gap arising with respect to factual conduct by ibid.

[121] Proposal for a Directive of the European Parliament and of the Council on adapting non-contractual liability rules to artificial intelligence (AI Liability Directive), 28 September 2022, COM(2022) 496 final.

[122] Regulation (EU) 2016/794 of the European Parliament and of the Council of 11 May 2016 on the European Union Agency for Law Enforcement Cooperation (Europol) [2016] OJ L135/53.

3

Evidence as Enabler – or Filter – of Actions Brought by Private Parties Directly before the EU Courts

LJUPCHO GROZDANOVSKI*

3.1 INTRODUCTION

Rarely has legal scholarship interpreted the Treaty provisions on the so-called direct actions through the lens of evidence.[1] And understandably so, as none of the relevant Treaty provisions – Articles 263, 265, and 340 of the Treaty on the Functioning of the European Union (TFEU)[2] – mention any specific conditions or modalities pertaining to the evidence required for the instituting of those actions. Yet evidence theory as a vantage point for the analysis of said provisions and corresponding case law may shed new light on the much-debated issue of whether, when applied, they afford a high standard of effective judicial protection to private parties.

Bearing in mind this volume's focus on fundamental rights, the present chapter will seek to critically analyse the rationale and design of the evidentiary requirements that private litigants must meet when launching direct actions. Our aim will be to determine if those requirements enable or hinder the exercise of the right to a legal remedy, pursuant to Article 47 of the Charter of Fundamental Rights of the European Union (CFR).[3] To conduct this analysis, a few preliminary, methodological observations should be made in

* The author thanks Professor Francesca Episcopo (UVA) for her input and comments on the analytical framework (effectiveness/evidence) of this study.

[1] The term 'evidence' will be understood as any knowable fact or group of facts, considered with a view to its being offered for the purpose of producing conviction as to the truth of a proposition. See John Henry Wigmore, A *Treatise on the Anglo-American System of Evidence in Trials at Common Law* (Little, Brown 1923) 1.

[2] Consolidated Version of the Treaty on the Functioning of the European Union [2016] OJ C202/47 (TFEU).

[3] Charter of Fundamental Rights of the European Union [2016] OJ C202/389 (CFR).

relation to (the concept and system of) evidence in EU law. Though much can be said in this regard, our analysis will take into account two opposed points of view: the one procedural, the other processual.

From a procedural perspective[4] (focused on the EU's normative power to codify evidence or any kind of procedural rules), evidence does not hold a prominent place in the EU procedural law jargon,[5] any allusion to the Union's 'general system' or law of evidence having historically been viewed as oxymoronic. According to Wróblewski, such a law is a body of (ideally codified) rules and principles that answer four essential questions: How does the law distinguish between facts that require evidence from those that do not? Which evidence is admissible? How is evidence assessed? What is the role of evidence in the performance of (judicial) review?[6] Under the guidance of Wróblewski's criteria, a law of evidence would ideally lay down principles that regulate key points of the process of accessing, adducing, and debating evidence. These typically include the distribution of the burdens of proof,[7] the criteria used to define relevant facts (*facti probandi*)[8] and admissibility,[9] the standards of proof,[10] and the benefit from presumptions.[11]

An overview of EU positive law reveals no trace of an instrument akin to the US Federal Rules of Evidence.[12] Indeed, the Treaties have never conferred a

4 In this chapter, we will distinguish the procedural (or proceduralist) view on evidence, which focuses on the enforcement and existence of prescriptive rules and principles that regulate the access, adducing, and debating of evidence. Under the processual view, the focus is on the process of giving evidence and the procedural guarantees afforded to private parties in view of enhancing their 'discursive' capacity.

5 Maria Fartunova, *La prevue dans le droit de l'Union européenne* (Bruylant 2013).

6 Jerzy Wróblewski, 'La preuve juridique: axiologie, logique et argumentation' in Chaïm Perelman and Paul Foriers (eds), *La preuve en droit: études* (Bruylant 1981) 331–355, 338.

7 The burden of proof translates to a distribution between the parties of the task to initiate the presentation of evidence that is necessary for the adjudicator to arrive at a conclusion with respect to the questions of fact raised. See, inter alia, Louis Kaplow, 'Burden of Proof'(2012) 121 The Yale Law Journal 738; Michelle T Grando, *Evidence, Proof, and Fact-Finding in WTO Dispute Settlement* (Oxford University Press 2009) 70.

8 Relevance is an exclusionary criterion applied to select the facts the proof of which is likely to affect the outcome of a dispute. See Evan Bell, 'An Introduction to Judicial Fact-Finding' (2013) 39 Commonwealth Law Bulletin (2013) 519, 521.

9 Admissibility is a selection criterion that applies to the litigants' evidence. It determines the evidence that, by virtue of a legal provision or a court decision, the parties in a trial may or may not present in support of their claims.

10 A standard of proof specifies 'a minimum threshold for asserting as proven some hypothesis'. See Larry Laudan, *Truth, Error and Criminal Law. An Essay in Legal Epistemology* (Cambridge University Press 2006) 64.

11 For a study on the types and effects of presumptions in EU law, see Ljupcho Grozdanovski, *La présomption en droit de l'Union européenne* (Anthémis 2019).

12 *Federal Rules of Evidence* (Michigan Legal 2021).

competence enabling the Union's legislature to enact a 'code' with evidentiary principles that would apply across the areas covered by those Treaties. True, there are examples of secondary law instruments that establish sectoral systems of evidence,[13] but those remain sporadic and minimally harmonising.[14] The leading principle in the field remains that of the residual priority (and discretion) that Member States have in applying their national rules on evidence in actions brought on the grounds of EU law.[15] In this context, the verdict seems clear: an EU law (or general system) of evidence does not and cannot exist.

This observation can, however, be nuanced from the second (processual) perspective, focused on the exercise, by private parties, of their so-called procedural abilities during the process of adjudication. In justice scholarship, the abilities doctrine emerged as a 'spin-off' from the capabilities strand, seminally developed by Nussbaum.[16] Taking a 'humanist approach' to the

[13] This view is supported by the way in which the Treaty provisions conferring competences to the Union are worded. Structurally speaking, those provisions include three types of indications: first, that the Union has a conferred competence in a given field (implying a transfer or limitation of national sovereignty), second, that the Union institutions have normative powers to exercise the conferred competence, third, the extent of the Member States' discretion, in the case of shared competences. Whenever procedures are mentioned, said provisions usually refer to procedures followed in the enactment of Union legislation, leaving out any useful mention on procedures followed in the context of adjudication and evidence assessment. See Grozdanovski (n 11) 78.

[14] For example, in the field of non-discrimination, see Council Directive 2000/78/EC of 27 November 2000 establishing a general framework for equal treatment in employment and occupation [2000] OJ L303/16, art 10; Council Directive 2004/113/EC of 13 December 2004 implementing the principle of equal treatment between men and women in the access to and supply of goods and services [2004] OJ L373/37, art 9; Directive 2006/54/EC of the European Parliament and of the Council of 5 July 2006 on the implementation of the principle of equal opportunities and equal treatment of men and women in matters of employment and occupation (recast) [2006] OJ L204/23, art 19; in the field of product liability, see Council Directive 85/374/EEC of 25 July 1985 on the approximation of the laws, regulations and administrative provisions of the Member States concerning liability for defective products [1985] OJ L210/29, arts 4 and 7; in the field of customs Union, see Regulation (EU) No 952/2013 of the European Parliament and of the Council of 9 October 2013 laying down the Union Customs Code (recast) [2013] OJ L269/1, art 61; in the field of anti-dumping see Regulation (EU) 2016/1036 of the European Parliament and of the Council of 8 June 2016 on protection against dumped imports from countries not members of the European Union (codification) [2016] OJ L176/21, art 5; in the field of competition law, see Council Regulation (EC) No 1/2003 of 16 December 2002 on the implementation of the rules on competition laid down in Articles 81 and 82 of the Treaty [2003] OJ L1/1, art 17.

[15] Sacha Prechal and Rob Widdershoven, 'Redefining the Relationship between Rewe-effectiveness and Effective Judicial Protection' (2011) 2 Review of European Administrative Law 31, 31.

[16] Martha C Nussbaum, *Creating Capabilities. The Human Development Approach* (Harvard University Press 2013).

concept of justice, the philosopher suggested a list of ten capabilities,[17] understood as basic entitlements that humans require for a thriving and meaningful life. Translated into procedure, those capabilities took the shape of procedural abilities, understood as entitlements that litigants ought to benefit from in order to make their views known (typically before a court) and effectively participate in the (fair) resolution of their disputes.[18]

Mirroring Nussbaum's capabilities list, Owusu-Bempah suggested a list of – also – ten fundamental procedural abilities: (a) understand the nature of the charge, (b) understand the evidence adduced, (c) understand the trial process and the consequences of being convicted, (d) give instructions to a legal representative, (e) make a decision about whether to plead guilty or not guilty, (f) make a decision about whether to give evidence, (g) make other decisions that might need to be made by the defendant in connection with the trial, (h) follow the proceedings in court on the offence, (i) give evidence, (j) any other ability that appears to the court to be relevant in the particular case.[19]

The abilities doctrine proposes a more 'organic', associative view of evidence and effective judicial protection. It perceives the administration of justice not only as a matter of machinal law-to-fact application but as a complex, multi-actor/stage process in which both courts and litigants participate in the fair resolution of disputes. In other words, the level of effectiveness of any system designed to afford judicial protection is largely dependent on the level of effectiveness of the parties' involvement in the process of adjudication. In the jargon of procedural justice scholarship, this involvement is qualified as effective or 'meaningful participation', that is, the exercise, in a context of procedural equality (or parity), of the abilities to present and refute arguments in a formalised discourse setting such as that of a trial.[20]

The association between evidence and effective judicial protection is not only supported by the procedural abilities scholarship but can also be inferred from the case law of the Court of Justice of the European Union (CJEU). In a legal order – like that of the EU – with a complex judiciary and system(s) of

[17] Nussbaum's capabilities include life, health, physical integrity, thought and imagination, emotions, practical reason, affiliation (or 'life in communities'), 'play' (essentially recreational activities), and political/material environment.

[18] Echoing Habermasian discursive ethics, Solum defined effective (or meaningful) participation as 'including the condition that all participants have an equal opportunity to engage in, advance, or refute arguments, question claims, and so forth'. See Lawrence B Solum,'Procedural Justice' (2004) 78 Southern California Law Review 181, 267.

[19] Abenaa Owusu-Bempah, 'The interpretation and application of the right to effective participation' (2018) 4 The International Journal of Evidence & Proof 321, 331.

[20] See Solum (n 18); Paul Stancil, 'Substantive Equality and Procedural Justice' (2016) 4 Iowa Law Review 1633, 1636.

legal remedies (ideally) aimed at upholding the interpretative uniformity of EU law, principles of evidence were bound to emerge as the CJEU gradually defined the basic features of private parties' effective participation in actions brought on the grounds of EU law (either before the national courts or before the Union Courts). From this perspective, the impossibility for a codified Union law of evidence was, in a way, compensated by principles that are functionally rooted in effectiveness and fairness and instrumentally meant to enhance the litigants' capacity to play an active role in trials. Though it is difficult to suggest a general, clear-cut taxonomy of those principles, the sectoral Union legislation as well as the CJEU's case law reveal roughly two families: principles that confer entitlements in support of the basic *ability to give evidence* and principles that regulate the *distribution of evidentiary duties*.

The main purpose of evidentiary entitlements is to enable litigants to gain access to relevant facts, acquire knowledge of the arguments and evidence presented by their adversaries, and have the possibility to rebut those arguments by adducing additional evidence. It is important to stress that the benefit from those entitlements should be such that any asymmetry in the parties' access to relevant information should be avoided. This rationale of fairness expressed in the fundamental condition of equality under which litigants should access and give evidence, allows us to explain why many of the procedural entitlements pertaining to evidence have emerged as expressions of the fair trial safeguards, in particular the right to access courts, the right to effective defence, the equality of arms principle,[21] and the principle of contradictory debate. The abilities that have thus been recognised by the CJEU include, namely, the right to unhindered access to facts[22] in view of exercising the right to be heard,[23] the right to respond to allegations by

[21] The equality of arms principle, qualified as 'corollary' to the right to a fair trial, is meant to create conditions that do not place a party at a substantial disadvantage vis-à-vis their opponent. The decisive point in that regard is whether the party to the proceedings is able to defend I effectively in the circumstances of the case. See Opinion of AG Ruiz-Jarabo Colomer in Case C-427/00 P *Commission v UK* [2001] ECLI:EU:C:2001:396, para 127.

[22] See namely case T-210/01 *General Electric Co. v Commission* [2005] ECLI:EU:T:2005:456, para 724; joined Cases T-110/03, T-150/03 and T-405/03 *Sison* [2005] ECLI:EU:T:2005:143, para 48; Case T-63/10 *Jurašinović v Council* [2012] ECLI:EU:T:2012:516, para 25; Case T-536/11 *bpost NV v Commission* [2015] ECLI:EU:T:2011:689, para 25; Case T-536/11 *European Dynamics Luxembourg* [2015] ECLI:EU:T:2015:476, para 50; Case C-174/98 P *Netherlands v Commission* [2000] ECLI:EU:C:2000:1, para 17; Case C-198/98 P *Everson/Barras* [1999] ECLI:EU:C:1999:617, para 17.

[23] See namely Case C-7/98 *Krombach* [2000] ECLI:EU:C:2000:164, para 27, 39 et seq.; Case C-341/04 *Eurofood IFSC Ltd.* [2006] ECLI:EU:C:2006:281, para 66; Case C-394/07 *Gambazzi* [2009] ECLI:EU:C:2009:219, para 28; Opinion of AG Kokott in Case C-416/10 *Križan* [2018] ECLI:EU:C:2012:218, para 175.

adducing the evidence allowing effective defence,[24] the right to impartial appraisal of evidence (consubstantial to the principle of impartiality of judges),[25] and, in criminal procedures, the right to benefit from the presumption of innocence.[26]

Regarding the distribution of evidentiary duties, the term 'distribution' should be understood as the placement, on the parties, of specific obligations to present or respond to evidentiary arguments, to adduce certain types of evidence, or to attain certain standards of proof and of persuasion. In the absence of positive law to say otherwise, the EU is a so-called free proof system,[27] that is, a system with no pre-established rules on who proves what, with which items of evidence, and to what extent. In this context, the basic distributary principle that regulates the allocation of burdens is *actori incumbit probatio* by virtue of which the initial burden to give evidence and to move forward falls on the claimant.[28]

However, allocating burdens is not everything, since their 'weight' (or feasibility) is determined by a series of additional requirements that regulate the probative value and admissibility of specific items of evidence, as well as the standards of proof (e.g., preponderance of evidence or 'beyond reasonable doubt'), which must be met for a contradictory debate to unfold based on concrete, evidence-based arguments as opposed to 'mere' assertions. In view of enhancing the ability of litigants to effectively present 'their versions' of the disputed facts,[29] the CJEU has established a series of requirements that define – albeit through broad brushstrokes – the 'weight' of the burdens of proof carried in actions brought on the grounds of EU law. The specificity of these principles is that they appear more as rational requirements rather than

24 Case C-200/13 P *Council v Bank Saderat Iran* [2016] ECLI:EU:C:2016:284, para 41; Case C-559/14 *Meroni* [2016] ECLI:EU:C:2016:349, para 33; Opinion of AG Bot in Case C-612/15 *Kolev* [2017] ECLI:EU:C:2017:257, para 101.

25 Joined Cases C-174/98 P and C-189/98 P *van der Wal v Commission* [2000] ECLI:EU:C:2000:1, para 17; Case C-64/16 *Associação Sindical dos Juízes Portugueses* [2018] ECLI:EU:C:2018:117, para 65; Case C-238/18 *ECB v Latvia* [2018] ECLI:EU:C:2018:581, para 108.

26 See CFR, art 48; Green Paper on the presumption of innocence, COM(2006) 174 final; Directive 2016/343 of the European Parliament and of the Council of 9 March 2016 on the strengthening of certain aspects of the presumption of innocence and of the right to be present at the trial in criminal proceedings [2016] OJ L65/1.

27 Free proof 'far from meaning that anything goes, refers to structured rational arguments based on ordinary practical reasoning'. See William Twining, 'Moving Beyond Law: Interdisciplinarity and the Study of Evidence' in Philip Dawid, William Twining, and Mimi Vasilaki (eds), *Evidence, Inference and Enquir* (British Academy 2011) 78.

28 See David Kenny,'Proportionality, the burden of proof, and some signs of reconsideration', [2014] 52 Irish Jurist 141, 143.

29 Opinion of AG Tesauro in Case C-55/88 *Katsoufros* [1989] ECLI:EU:C:1989:364, para 5.

detailed, checklist-type prescriptions on points like relevance, admissibility, probative value, and standards of proof. The Court and its Advocates General (AG) considered, for example, that *indicia* cannot be taken as conclusive evidence unless they are 'corroborated' by additional evidence:[30] that, specifically in competition law, parallel behaviour is 'strong evidence' of a concerted practice;[31] that any disturbance of the functioning of the Internal Market should be supported by objective[32] and cogent[33] evidence; that infringements (Article 258 TFEU) cannot be supported by presumptions of non-conformity with EU law provisions;[34] that requests for interim measures should not be supported by 'weak' indirect evidence (hearsay).[35]

This brief overview is, by no means, a detailed analysis but a canvassing of some of the key features of the 'general system of evidence' of the EU meant to set the stage for the remainder of this chapter. The key takeaway is the following: private parties' ability to give evidence ought to support their effective participation in a trial and in doing so allow them to claim the benefit from the judicial protection EU law promises to provide. In other words, evidence should be an enabler of effective judicial protection, regardless of whether judicial redress is sought before national courts or directly before the Union Courts. However – as will be argued – the evidentiary requirements that litigants must meet in direct actions do not seem to follow this justice-enabling trend.

In this context, the present chapter will first discuss the interrelationship between the right to a remedy and the effective ability to give evidence (Section 3.2). Against the backdrop of this discussion, it will, second, explore the various ways in which evidence can hinder the judicial protection provided by the Treaty provisions on direct actions. In this regard, we will conduct two analyses. Our first analysis will concern the direct actions where evidentiary requirements obstruct the access to a legal remedy. This is the case in annulment and failure to act proceedings, the admissibility of which depends on the adducing of specific (and often unrealistic) evidence by private parties (Section 3.3). Our second analysis will concern the direct actions where evidence requirements limit private parties' effective (or meaningful) participation and seeking of judicial redress. This is the case in actions for damages, which do not have clearly distinguished admissibility/substance

30 Case 128/87 *Commission v Greece* [1989], ECLI:EU:C:1989:7, para 24.

31 See, e.g., Case 374/87 *Orkem v Commission* [1989] ECLI:EU:C:1989:387.

32 Case 191/88 *Co-Frutta v Commission*, [1988] ECLI:EU:C:1988:418, para 21.

33 Case 92/88 *Assider v Commission*, [1988] ECLI:EU:C:1988:222, para 24.

34 Case 96/81 *Commission v Netherlands* [1982] ECLI:EU:C:1982:192, para 6.

35 Case 148/88 R *Albani v Commission* [1988] ECLI:EU:C:1988:334, para 18.

stages (like, say, annulment proceedings) but are characterised by evidentiary requirements that are such that private litigants often experience difficulty in arguing their cause and having the judicial redress they hope to have when seeking compensation for harm causally connected to the conduct of a Union institution (Section 3.4).

3.2 THE INTERRELATIONSHIP BETWEEN 'EFFECTIVE' JUDICIAL PROTECTION AND THE 'EFFECTIVE' ABILITY TO GIVE EVIDENCE

Notwithstanding the references to effectiveness in the Treaties and the CJEU's case law, a clear definition of this concept is lacking. In a generic sense, it can be understood as a standard[36] applied in the assessment of the capacity of national or Union measures to ensure the proper legislative, administrative, or judicial implementation of EU law. To further clarify the meaning of this standard and how it relates to 'effective' judicial protection, as well as to the ability to give evidence, we will address two questions. First, on the issue of scope: In a given procedure, does effectiveness apply only to the modalities that enable the access to a remedy, or does it also extend to the modalities according to which evidence is given and assessed? Second, on the issue of uniformity: Does the principle of effective judicial protection generate the same requirements of effectiveness for the systems of procedures of the Member States and that of the Union?

To answer these questions, a few preliminary observations should be made. A cursory overview of the CJEU's case law does not reveal rigid criteria that could be used to 'measure' the effectiveness of a national or Union measure implementing an EU law provision. It does seem, however, that effectiveness is an outcome-oriented notion: a measure is 'effective' so long as it does not compromise the attaining of the objectives the Treaties assign to the Union. *Prodifarma* (dealing with an issue of collective dominance) can be mentioned as an example of a case where the Member States' compliance with Article 102 TFEU (prohibition of abuse of dominance)[37] was interpreted as also implying their compliance with the Union's general objectives, in particular effective competition in the Internal Market. This approach of viewing specific Treaty provisions (such as Article 102 TFEU) as particularising general

[36] Our understanding of the notion of 'standard' is that proposed by Bernard who defined normative standards as referents for the interpretation of rules and the assessment of circumstances of fact, derived from selected principles, values, paradigms, or necessities. See Elsa Bernard, *La spécificité du standard juridique en droit communautaire* (Bruylant 2010) 37.

[37] Case T-116/89 *Prodifarma e.a. v Commission* [1990] ECLI:EU:T:1990:85.

Union objectives (listed in Article 3 TEU)[38] is, in a way, the Union Courts' 'signature reasoning' when it comes to ensuring the full *effet utile* (and by that, full effectiveness) of Union law.[39]

Scholarship has labelled this outcome-oriented notion of effectiveness as substantive, essentially translating to 'the capacity of chosen legislative patterns in obtaining results that are as close as possible to realizing the ideal expressed by the political actors, considering the context of operation'.[40] In the context of EU law, the *ultima ratio* of substantively effective EU law provisions is, of course, the full guarantee of entitlements (rights and duties) that private parties derive from those provisions. The reasoning behind this effectiveness–rights correlation is fairly straightforward: only when an EU law provision is 'effective' can the benefit from the rights it confers to individuals be 'effective' as well. It can even be argued that there is an 'in the law we trust' presumption by virtue of which Union law provisions invariably provide the most adequate possible safeguards to individuals. This is, arguably, why EU law provisions benefit from 'strong' (i.e., not easily rebuttable) presumptions of legality and validity:[41] because of those provisions' potential to be rights-giving, all subjects of Union law (including private parties) 'must acknowledge the full effectiveness of legislative acts of the institutions so long as neither the Court of Justice nor the [General Court] has found them to be illegal'.[42]

To concretely uphold substantive effectiveness, procedural means were, of course, needed, in order to allow individuals to practically (and effectively) claim the benefit from their rights. In *Van Gend & Loos*, the Court stressed that 'the vigilance of individuals concerned to protect their rights amounts to an effective supervision . . . of the Member States'.[43] The judicial protection afforded under Union law is usually considered as 'effective' if private parties have access to legal remedies that allow them to launch actions on the

[38] Consolidated Version of the Treaty of the European Union [2016] OJ C202/13.

[39] See Pierre Pescatore, 'Les objectifs de la Communautés européenne comme principes d'interprétation dans la jurisprudence de la Cour de justice' in *Etudes de droit européen 1962–2007* (Bruylant 2008) 385. In line with *Prodifarma*, in the *Viho* case (dealing with the compatibility with Article 101 TFEU of intra-group agreements) AG Lenz stressed that the prohibition in Article 81 TEC (Treaty Establishing the European Community) (Article 101 TFEU) gave a specific expression to Article 3(g) TEC which 'calls for a system ensuring that competition in the internal market is not distorted'. See Opinion of AG Lenz in Case C-73/95 P *Viho Europe BV v Commission* [1996] ECLI:EU:C:1996:405.

[40] Mauro Zamboni, 'Legislative Policy and Effectiveness: A (Small) Contribution from Legal Theory' [2018] 9 European Journal Risk Regulation 416, 420.

[41] See Grozdanovski (n 11) 147 seq.

[42] Case T-120/99 *Kik v OHIM* [2001] ECLI:EU:T:2001:189, para. 47.

[43] Case 26/62 *Van Gend en Loos* [1963] ECLI:EU:C:1963:1, ECR 13.

grounds of Union law provisions. Indeed, the access to a remedy has been historically considered as *the* procedural guarantee associated with the principle of effective judicial protection – a canon seminally given in Rewe[44] and Johnston.[45]

But from the perspective of procedural abilities – this chapter's theoretical vantage point – the Court's long-standing case law on the principle of effective judicial protection leaves open the first question this section seeks to answer: Does the standard of effectiveness in 'effective judicial protection' apply only to the access to remedies or does it also extend to the parties' ability to adduce evidence?

The standard view[46] has indeed been narrow: judicial protection has been thought to be 'effective' when (usually national) systems of procedures made remedies available for actions brought on the grounds of EU law. Seldom has effective judicial protection been connected, in any important way, to the private parties' abilities to give evidence. This is, namely, due to a dissociation between the right (to a remedy) and the entitlements and/or requirements to give evidence for the purpose of exercising that right. Take *Factortame*,[47] for instance. The CJEU stressed that UK law ought to make available interim measures for actions based on EU law because 'the full effectiveness of Community law would be ... impaired if a rule of national law could prevent a court seised of a dispute governed by Community law from granting interim relief in order to ensure the full effectiveness of the judgment to be given on the existence of the rights claimed under Community law'.[48] However, the 'full effectiveness' referred to in this case did not extend to requirements on evidence that the claimants were held to

44 Case 33/76 *Rewe* [1976] ECLI:EU:C:1976:188.

45 Case 222/84 *Johnston* [1986] ECLI:EU:C:1986:206. Typically, two canonical understandings of effectiveness result from the *Rewe/Johnston* cases. In *Rewe*, the legal protection of individuals under Union law was viewed as deriving from the latter's direct effect. In the absence of Union rules in the field of procedure, the Court considered that the Member States have discretion to 'determine the procedural conditions governing actions at law intended to ensure the protection of rights [derived from the direct effect of Union law, so long as those conditions] are not less favourable than those relating to similar actions of domestic nature' (cf. *Rewe* (n 44) para 5). Effectiveness in *Johnston*, no longer tied to the direct effect of Union law, resulted from the duty for the Member States to use 'measures which are sufficiently effective to achieve the aim [of Union law provisions] and that they must ensure that the rights thus confirmed may be effectively relied upon before the national courts by the persons concerned' (cf. *Johnston* (n 45) para 17).

46 See, e.g., Luis Arroyo Jiménez, 'Effective Judicial Protection and Mutual Recognition in the European Administrative Space' (2021) 22 German Law Journal 344, 358.

47 Case C-213/89 *Factortame* [1990] ECLI:EU:C:1990:257.

48 Ibid para 21.

meet, the assumption being that the 'evidentiary technicalities' would, in any case, be defined by national law.

Of course, there have been cases where rules on evidence were sanctioned by the CJEU for having failed the 'effectiveness test'. However, these are cases where said rules did not directly obstruct private parties' access to a remedy but restricted the benefit from rights *other than* the right to a remedy. Famously in *San Giorgio*, the Court rejected an Italian rule that made the repayment of charges levied contrary to Union law conditional on documentary evidence that those charges had been passed on to consumers.[49] The Court considered that 'any requirement of proof which has the effect of making it virtually impossible or excessively difficult to secure the repayment of charges levied contrary to Community law would be incompatible with Community law'.[50] Similarly, in *Otero Ramos*, the Court sanctioned an irrebuttable presumption of veracity of an employer's declaration on the working conditions of female workers, since that presumption deprived 'of all practical effect' the principle of equality between men and women.[51]

Based on these trends, two observations can be made. First – in a negative sense – cases like *San Giorgio* and *Otero Ramos* suggest that effectiveness limits the Member States' procedural autonomy in the field of evidence when national rules of evidence adversely affect the benefit from a subjective right conferred by a Union law provision. Second – in a positive sense – the implication from this case law is that a system of evidence ought to support (or enable) the benefit and exercise of *any* such right, including the right to access a remedy.

The abilities doctrine as a theoretical framework for this chapter supports this view: a rule of evidence that sets out, say, practically unfeasible admissibility conditions would – unsurprisingly – make a private party's access to a remedy difficult. The structure of Article 47 CFR also supports the association between the right to a remedy and the ability to give evidence as it seems to rely on a *holistic view* of the concept of 'procedure': the latter is not only limited to remedies *stricto sensu* but also includes procedural entitlements that allow litigants to access and participate in the proceedings those remedies give way to. As per Article 47(2) CFR, these entitlements are expressed in the fair trial safeguards, that is, fair and public hearing, reasonable time, independent and impartial tribunal, and the assistance of a legal counsel. As argued earlier,[52]

49 Case 199/82 *San Giorgio* [1983] ECLI:EU:C:1983:318.

50 Ibid para 14.

51 Case C-531/15 *Otero Ramos* [2017] ECLI:EU:C:2017:789.

52 See the Introduction to this volume.

most of the Union's 'general' entitlements (or procedural rights) in the field of evidence have been derived by the CJEU from the right to a fair trial. The merging of the right to a legal remedy (Article 47(1) CFR) with the fair trial safeguards (Article 47(2) CFR) in a single constitutional provision gives an important hint for the remainder of this chapter: it does matter if, in addition to having the legally recognised ability to access a remedy, private parties also have the necessary procedural abilities to practically access and exercise that remedy.

Though this holistic reading of the principle of effective judicial protection is unorthodox, it has been endorsed by a part of scholarship. Wildemeersch, for instance, suggested that effective judicial protection as a principle should be understood *lato sensu*, that is, not only as defining a standard of effectiveness for the right to access remedies and courts but also as defining all the components of systems of remedies,[53] including the procedures designed for the adducing of evidence. Alternatively, he interpreted the right to a legal remedy *stricto sensu* as referring 'only' to the right to access courts.[54] Recent case law also supports this 'holistic view'. In the *Steffensen*[55] case, for example, the issue addressed by the Court was whether the Foodstuff Directive[56] entitled a manufacturer to request a second opinion after an initial investigation procedure had taken place, during which samples had been collected from that manufacturer's retailers and found non-conforming with the German legislation. The claimant argued that the German fact-finding procedure was improper since it did not allow them to express their views or present their own evidence, thus infringing their right to a fair hearing. From the perspective of the CJEU's 'standard' case law on effectiveness, the Court's ruling was unsurprising: it stated that the Directive might (not 'should') provide the basis for a second evidence-gathering procedure, if the national court found that the German rules on evidence were incompatible with the principles of equivalence and effectiveness.[57] However, from the perspective of the procedural entitlements associated with effective judicial protection, the Court's reasoning is noteworthy because it seems to suggest that the availability of legal remedies is not the only such guarantee that stems from this principle. The latter also includes entitlements pertaining to evidence

53 Jonathan Wildemeersch, *Contentieux de la légalité des actes de l'Union eu opéenne: le mythe du droit à un recours effectif* (Buylant 2019) 68.

54 Ibid.

55 Case C-276/01 *Steffensen* [2003] ECLI:EU:C:2003:228.

56 Council Directive 89/397/EEC of 14 June 1989 on the official control of foodstuffs [1989] OJ L186/23.

57 *Steffensen* (n 55) para 79.

gathering and assessment, considering the importance – stressed by the Court itself – that private parties be given 'adequate opportunity to participate in the proceedings before the court',[58] these proceedings being 'considered as a whole, including the way in which evidence was taken'.[59]

Assuming – as we do – that the principle of effective judicial protection implies a holistic reading of the term 'procedure', the second question, raised in this section, remains yet to be answered. Indeed, the cases mentioned all deal with the effectiveness of *national* systems of procedures and remedies. This begs the question of whether the effectiveness requirements the Court has defined in connection to those systems do, or should also, apply to the system of remedies in the Treaties. In other words, is there a uniform standard of effectiveness that both the Member States' and the Union's systems of procedures should aspire to achieve?

With the entry into force of the Lisbon Treaty, Article 47 CFR – a primary law provision – was interpreted by the CJEU as 'a reaffirmation of the principle of effective judicial protection'.[60] Given the constitutional nature of this article, it is reasonable to assume that the standard of effectiveness it implies concerns the Member States' and Union's systems of procedure alike. This would suggest that, much like the requirements under national systems of remedies, the requirements framing private parties' access to the direct actions should not make that access 'virtually impossible or excessively difficult'. Article 47 CFR thus supports an argument in favour of uniformity.

In pre-Lisbon times, savant minds would presumably not view this argument as convincing, given that the contours of the principle under consideration have been canvassed in the Court's case law primarily dealing with the Member States' systems of legal remedies. Post-Lisbon, a subtle trend toward uniformity was detected by Wildemeersch,[61] who observed the Court's increasing tendency to rely on Article 47 CFR in lieu of the 'usual' effectiveness/equivalency test when seeking to determine if national systems of remedies succeeded in meeting the effectiveness requirement.[62] It is tempting to interpret this trend as a sign of standardisation (or standard-shifting) of the level of effectiveness associated with the judicial protection afforded by both

58 Ibid para 77.

59 Ibid (emphasis added).

60 After Lisbon, the Court has often stressed that Article 47 CFR constitutes 'a reaffirmation of the principle of effective judicial protection'. See, inter alia, Joined Cases C-439/14 and C-488/14 *Star Storage et al.* [2016] ECLI:EU:C:2016:688, para 46; Case C-348/16 *Sacko* [2017] ECLI:EU:C:2017:591, para 31; Case C-73/16 *Puškár* [2017] ECLI:EU:C:2017:725, para 59.

61 Wildemeersch (n 53).

62 Ibid 68 et seq; See also Prechal and Widdershoven (n 15).

national and the Union's systems of remedies. But this trend does not yet seem to be consolidated. In *Randstad Italia*,[63] for example – in essence, dealing with the availability of remedies enabling the Italian judiciary Supreme Court to review the decisions of the administrative Supreme Court – Advocate General (AG) Hogan[64] examined Italy's procedural autonomy under Article 47 ECFR, but the CJEU referred (back) to its tried-and-true effectiveness/equivalency test.[65]

The debate on the uniformity of the standard of effectiveness (stemming from the principle of judicial protection) is multi-faceted, complex, and beyond the scope of this chapter. May it suffice positing the following: rather than a proper (binding) constitutional requirement, this type of uniformity appears to be an aspirational ideal for the Members States' and Union's systems of remedies (and by extension, of evidence). It is reasonable to assume that the procedural abilities that private parties should have in national systems of procedure ought to be equivalent to those that are guaranteed in the context of direct actions. However, as our further discussion will show, though the national and Union's systems of remedies converge in their finality (i.e., affording judicial protection to individuals) they strongly diverge in the procedural means through which they seek to attain that finality. The result of this divergence is a selective, rather than uniform, application of the standard of effectiveness associated with the principle of effective judicial protection.

3.3 THE REQUIREMENTS ON EVIDENCE RESTRICTING THE EFFECTIVE ACCESS TO A REMEDY IN THE CONTEXT OF THE LEGALITY REVIEW

3.3.1 *The Heavy Burden of Proving Standing in Annulment and Failure to Act Proceedings*

If Article 263(4) TFEU was read as defining a system of evidence, the key point it would define – albeit broadly – would be that of relevance,[66] laying

63 Case C-497/20 *Ranstadt Italia* [2021] ECLI:EU:C:2021:1037.

64 Opinion of AG Hogan in Case C-497/20 *Ranstadt Italia* [2021] ECLI:EU:C:2021:725, paras 63 seq.

65 *Randstadt Italia* (n 63) paras 58 seq.

66 In general evidence scholarship, relevance can be defined as 'the capacity to make a positive or negative contribution to a practical verdict'. See Maria C Redondo, 'Legal Reasons: between Universalism and Particularism' (2005) 2-1 Journal of Moral Philosophy 47, 48. Its role is essentially exclusionary considering that it is 'and can only, be judged by reference to the issues which the court is called upon to decide'. See Bell (n 8) 521. Anderson et al. argue that the 'test of relevance' is 'not so much a rule of evidence as a presupposition involved in the very

down the basic criteria of the *factum probandum*, that is, the fact(s) for which evidence is sought for the action to be declared admissible. The admissibility *probandum* in annulment actions launched by private parties against Union acts not addressed to them consists of two relevant facts: direct and individual concern. As is well known, the CJEU clarified the features of those facts in the *Plaumann* case,[67] dealing with a German clementine importer who challenged the legality of a Commission decision addressed to Germany, allowing for the maintenance of import duties on clementines from non-Member States. The applicant considered that they met the direct/individual concern requirements because the total number of importers of clementines was small and easily ascertainable. In this case, the Court famously discussed only individual concern as, having found it lacking, it considered that there was no need to address the direct concern criterion. However, the latter was discussed by AG Roemer, who strongly criticised the applicants' views of directness 'as no more than a measure of the strength of the interest', frustrating the raison d'être of Article 263 TFEU, which – the AG argued – 'must be understood in a particular way from the system of the Treaty and the structure of the Community order ... [and its] organisation of legal protection'.

It is interesting to note that AG Roemer's reasoning on direct concern was developed against the backdrop of the Union's 'federal structure ... a situation in which the [Union] institutions are raised above national courts with powers which in part have direct effects in the sphere of the Member States but in part are limited and in realizing specific aims require cooperation of Member States'.[68] The reference in the AG's Opinion to the 'ontological grounds' of Article 173 of the Treaty Establishing the European Economic Community (TEEC, currently Article 263 TFEU) is telling since directness within the meaning of this article echoes the direct effect doctrine, established in *Van Gend & Loos*[69] a few months prior to the *Plaumann* ruling. Although direct concern and direct effect are separate concepts, they serve the same normative purpose, that is, the judicial protection of private parties before national courts, under the direct effect doctrine, and before the Union Courts, under the direct concern requirement. Because of this, they share a common evidentiary requirement: for either to be established, litigants are held to show the absence of mediation between themselves and the applicable EU law

conception of a rational system of evidence'. See Terence Anderson, David Schum, and William Twining, *Analysis of Evidence* (Cambridge University Press 2005) 290.

67 Case C-25/62 *Plaumann v Commission* [1963] ECLI:EU:C:1963:17.

68 Ibid 115.

69 *Van Gend en Loos* (n 43).

provisions. This 'absence of mediation' (or immediacy)[70] translates to proof of absence of discretion – namely from the Member States – in the implementation of EU law provisions.[71]

In this context, and considering that in *Plaumann* the implementation of the contested decision required that Germany take the necessary measures (and therefore exercise discretion), the direct concern leg of the *probandum* was ultimately not considered as established.[72] With this reading of Article 173 TEEC the canon was set: in its subsequent case law,[73] the CJEU would systematically seek to determine if a Union provision had, without any type of institutional or normative mediation, directly affected or altered the legal situation of the applicant. This 'test' of direct concern was applied *talis qualis* in failure to act proceedings. For example, the omission by the Commission to amend an approved national programme on vocational training was found not to directly affect the legal position of a private party applicant, considering the extent of national discretion in the implementation of that programme.[74] Similarly, given the level of discretion of the European Commission in the context of infringement proceedings, its refusal to respond favourably to an invitation to launch such proceedings could not provide sufficient grounds for the author of the invitation to establish direct concern.[75]

It was, however, on the proof of individual concern that the *Plaumann* case gave the apex evidentiary requirement in (and presumably the strongest procedural 'filter' of) annulment actions launched by private parties. In this regard, AG Roemer stressed – again, sharply – that the limited number of clementine importers 'cannot be decisive'[76] since individual concern does not

70 See Léontin-J Constantinesco, *L'applicabilité directe dans le droit de la CEE* (Bruylant 2006) 10.

71 Joined Cases 41 to 44/70 *International Fruit Co. et al. v Commission* [1971] ECLI:EU:C:1971:53, para 26; Joined Cases T-172/98 and T-175/98 to T-177/98 *Salamander et al.* [2000] ECLI:EU:T:2000:168, para 22.

72 Opinion of AG Roemer in Case C-25/62 *Plaumann v Commission* [1963] ECLI:EU:C:1963:7, 115.

73 See namely Case 101/76 *Koninklijke Scholten Honig NV* [1977] ECLI:EU:C:1977:70, para 23; Case 123/77 *UNICME et al. v Council* [1978] ECLI:EU:C:1978:73, para 16; Case C-386/96 P *Dreyfus* [1998] ECLI:EU:C:1998:193, para 43; Case T-54/96 *Oleifici Italiani and Fratelli Rubino v Commission* [1998] ECLI:EU:T:1998:204, para 56; Case T-9/98 *Mitteldeutsche Erdöl-Raffinerie* [2001] ECLI:EU:T:2001:271, para 47; Case T-223/01 *Japan Tobacco and JT International v Parliament and Council* [2002] EU:T:2002:205, para 45; Case T-314/02 *Regione Siciliana v Commission* [2004] ECLI:EU:T:2004:228, paras 53 seq.; Case T-323/16 *Banco Cooperativo Español* [2019] ECLI:EU:T:2019:822, para 49; Case T-365/16 *Portigon AG* [2019] ECLI:EU:T:2019:824, para 68 seq.

74 Case T-139/02 *Idiotiko Institouto v Commission* [2004] ECLI:EU:T:2004:75.

75 Case C-284/19 P *Clarke v Commission* [2019] ECLI:EU:C:2019:799.

76 *Plaumann* Opinion (n 72) 116.

arise from the individuality of particular persons but 'from membership of the abstractly defined group of all those who wished to import clementines during the period in question'.[77] The Court took an even stricter stance, asserting that a person is individually concerned by a decision not addressed to that person if it affects them 'by reason of certain attributes which are peculiar to them or by reason of circumstances in which they are differentiated from all other persons and by virtue of these factors distinguishes them individually just as in the case of the person addressed'.[78]

This interpretation provided the normative understanding of individual concern as being an extremely high level of individuation, the applicant's 'particular features' or 'circumstances' having become *facti probans* (facts that prove the *probandum*) necessary to establish that they are, in actuality, the addressees of a Union act formally not addressed to them. In this context, merely showcasing some distinguishing personal features (like a limited number of addressees) is not enough. A cursory overview of the CJEU's case law shows that the desired level of individuation is proven to the satisfaction of the Court when two criteria are met. First, the applicants must establish factual individuation: they must prove that in fact (i.e., by virtue of specific characteristics) the circle of addressees of a contested act is identified, identifiable, and closed. Second, this factual individuation is paired with – what can be qualified as – normative individuation: the applicant should be singled out by virtue of the legal effects produced by the contested act, not by the characteristics of the market concerned.[79] Needless to say, establishing these two versants of individuation has proven to be challenging.

What is more, those requirements were transposed to failure to act proceedings, though, in the latter, applicants face the added challenge of supporting, with evidence, an *ex hypothesi* argument. Namely, under Article 265 TFEU, they carry the (heavy) burden of proving that, had an act been adopted, it would have been of individual concern. For instance, the existence of a sufficient relationship of competition between an applicant and a recipient of State aid, which the former had invited the Commission to investigate, was viewed by the General Court as a circumstance warranting sufficient individuation.[80] In contrast, in *Edinger*,[81] the refusal by the Commission to request the withdrawal of bilateral measures taken by the EU Member States vis-à-vis

[77] Ibid.

[78] *Plaumann* (n 67) 107.

[79] Case C-348/20 P *Nord Stream 2* [2022] ECLI:EU:C:2022:548, para 159.

[80] Case T-395/04 *Air One v Commission* [2006] ECLI:EU:T:2006:123.

[81] Case T-191/00 *Edinger* [2001] ECLI:EU:T:2001:183, para 24.

Austria during its Haider episode did not, in any way, individualise the applicant.[82]

A common characteristic in the cited cases is the level of austerity on the part of the EU Courts in assessing the applicants' arguments of direct and individual concern: establishing the admissibility *probandum* under Article 263(4) TFEU and, by extension, Article 265 TFEU seems to be the exception rather than the rule. The question which then arises is whether, under those provisions, private parties are not required to adduce a so-called *probatio diabolica*: evidence that is formally admitted but practically difficult or impossible to adduce. For a legal order priding itself on its 'complete system of procedures' and its strong commitment to a high standard of judicial protection afforded to private parties, this is surprising. The surprise is even greater when one considers some of the CJEU's cases where the Court did not hesitate to sanction national rules on evidence that placed unrealistic burdens on private parties, thus restricting their ability to effectively benefit from the rights they derived from Union law. The abovementioned *San Giorgio*[83] and *Otero Ramos*[84] come to mind in this regard.

The CJEU's selective reading of private parties' evidentiary abilities afforded under national and Union systems of remedies is open to criticism. This reading is of course alarming, especially in cases where a claimant might argue that a Union act is illegal because it infringes on a fundamental right other than the right to a remedy. In *Jégo-Quéré*,[85] for instance, dealing with the annulment of a regulation defining the size of fishing boats and the types of fishing nets used for the fishing of juvenile hake, the applicant was – arguably – the only fishing company to have vessels and nets covered by the contested act. It had nevertheless failed to establish the specific ways in which that act individualised it from any economic operator actually or potentially in the same situation.[86] Bearing in mind the CJEU's case law on the effectiveness of national procedural rules, it is reasonable to assume that if said act was

[82] In this case, the Member States had agreed not to pursue commercial relations with Austria, so long as the government was formed by the Freiheitliche Partei Österreichs (FPÖ). The applicant in *Edinger* was an Austrian national who sent to a number of addressees, including a number of European Commission departments, 'an appeal to condemn publicly any premature judgment, any discrimination and any boycott of Austria, its representatives and citizens and holding them up to scorn, and to demand the immediate withdrawal of those measures, which are contrary to the European spirit'. See *Edinger* (n 81) para 3.

[83] *San Giorgio* (n 49).

[84] *Otero Ramos* (n 51).

[85] Case C-263/02 P *Commission v Jégo-Quéré* [2004] ECLI:EU:C:2004:210.

[86] Ibid para 46.

a national regulation, the Court would have no doubt found that it restricted, say, the applicant's right to conduct business, as guaranteed by Union law.

Of course, the CJEU's rigour in assessing the proof of individual concern has not always amounted to declarations of inadmissibility. In *Codorníu*,[87] for example, dealing with a regulation allowing only French and Luxembourg producers of sparkling wine to use the Grand Crémant label – the Court considered that the applicant, a Spanish producer of sparkling wine, had succeeded in establishing the existence of a situation that 'from the point of view of the contested provision differentiates [them] from all other traders'.[88] It remains, however, that, more often than not, private parties fail to pass the admissibility test of Article 263(4) TFEU because the burden they carry is simply too heavy. In reaction to this, pleas have been made to relax those evidentiary requirements and increase the effectiveness characterising private parties' access to a legality review. Alas, the protection of the right to a legal remedy, but also other fundamental rights, have often been the leitmotivs of these – often disregarded – pleas.

3.3.2 *Pleas to Lighten the Burden to Prove Standing in Annulment and Failure to Act Proceedings*

Chronologically, there have been two types of plea for the lightening of the admissibility burden in the context of the legality review. The plea based on the right to access a remedy came first and is procedural in nature (that is, pertains to the normative design of the system of evidence in annulment and failure to act proceedings). The criticism here was that the Court's austere application of the Plaumann criteria raised an almost insurmountable barrier obstructing private parties' direct access to the Union Courts.

The more recent, second plea is based on those parties' procedural abilities and is processual in nature (that is, pertains to the modalities according to which litigants give evidence in the context of the legality review). The criticism here is that the conduct of the Union institutions in making evidence unavailable to litigants restricts their ability to prove standing under Article 263 (and by extension, 265) TFEU.

Regarding the 'procedural' right to a remedy strand, the emblematic example is, of course, the *UPA* Opinion[89] in which AG Jacobs famously

[87] Case C-309/89 *Codorníu SA v Council* [1994] ECLI:EU:C:1994:197.

[88] Ibid para 23.

[89] Opinion of AG Jacobs in Case C-50/00 P *Unión de Pequeños Agricultores (UPA)* [2002] ECLI:EU:C:2002:197.

suggested a redefinition of the individual concern *probandum*: in lieu of proving the (excessively high) degree of individuation discussed earlier, the AG suggested that the applicant establish a 'substantial adverse effect on [their] interests' that the challenged measure has or is liable to have.[90] This Opinion was not followed by the CJEU who, in its ruling,[91] considered that the failure to meet the *Plaumann* criteria did not restrict the otherwise ample opportunity for litigants to seek judicial protection *via* other procedural routes.[92] But the Court missed the point of AG Jacobs' Opinion, which did not suggest altogether eliminating the individual concern *probandum* but to – merely – 'lighten' the burden it entails, in view of facilitating private applicants' effective access to a remedy.[93] True, Article 267(3) TFEU provides an alternative to Article 263 TFEU through the involvement of the Member States' courts, but the coexistence of two remedies conducive to the same type of review does not justify the fact that one of them is virtually impracticable.

A step toward the 'lightening' of the direct/individual concern burden was thought to be made with the entry into force of the Lisbon Treaty. Article 263 (4) TFEU eliminated the proof of individual concern in actions seeking the annulment of regulatory acts not requiring implementing measures. However, a reading of Article 263 TFEU from the perspective of evidence might suggest that it, in fact, created two burdens, corresponding to two distinct types of normative acts. For general legislative acts, claimants continue to carry the 'standard' *Plaumann* burden of proving direct and individual concern. For actions concerning self-executing regulatory acts, the duty to prove individual concern was indeed eliminated, though it is not certain that this translated into a considerable lightening of the overall burden to prove standing. Regulatory acts being a new category introduced with, but not defined in, the Lisbon Treaty, the launching of annulment proceedings against those would require proof that (i) an act is, indeed, regulatory (as opposed to legislative);[94] (ii) it does not require implementation measures; and (iii) it is

90 Ibid para 103.

91 *UPA* (n 89).

92 Ibid para 40 seq.

93 *UPA*, Opinion (n 89) para 98: 'Some commentators have contrasted the high standards which the Court's case-law imposes on national legal systems with the limited access for individuals to Community Courts. While it may be too harsh to speak of "double standards", in that respect, it cannot be denied that the strict rules on standing under [Article 263(4) TFEU] as currently interpreted by the Court . . . seem increasingly untenable in the light of the Court's case-law on the principle of effective judicial protection.'

94 The notion of regulatory act as a *probandum* for establishing *locus standi* was defined by the CJEU in the *Inuit* case in opposition to legislative acts, stating that 'the concept of "regulatory act" within the meaning of [Article 263(4) TFEU] refers to acts of general application other

of direct concern to the claimant. The possibility for litigants to avoid proving individual concern was understandably attractive, though in practice Article 263(4) TFEU was ultimately not the 'effectiveness booster' it was expected to be with the entry into force of the Lisbon Treaty. A cursory overview of the CJEU's case law reveals that the Court has seldom qualified an act as both regulatory and self-executing, often finding that the acts applicants argued were regulatory relied on implementing measures.[95]

Regarding the processual abilities strand, the recent *Nord Stream 2* case is a noteworthy example.[96] A Swiss gas company challenged a 2019 directive amending provisions of the 2009 so-called Gas Directive.[97] The applicant brought an annulment action against the 2019 act before the General Court,[98] which was dismissed for lack of proof of direct concern. The appeal before the Court of Justice included two grounds: first, the appellant argued direct concern although the directive had not yet been transposed, implying that it had not deployed its legal effects likely to 'directly' affect the applicant's situation. This of course raised the issue of the interpretation of the direct concern *probandum* when the contested act is a directive, by definition requiring the Member States' intervention to be transposed into national law.

than legislative acts'. See C-583/11 P *Inuit Tapiriit Kanatami and Others v Parliament and Council* [2013] ECLI:EU:C:2013:625, para 34. Though the Court seems to retain the enactment procedure as a defining factor in operating the distinction between legislative and regulatory acts, it remains that this 'clarification' opens more questions than it answers. As Werkmeister et al. noted, 'the legal term "regulatory" comprises a new *topos* of European legal acts that cannot be classified within the existing categories under Article 288 TFE'. See Christophe Werkmeister, Srephan Potters, and Johannes Traut, 'Regulatory Acts within Article 263(4) TFEU – A Dissonant Extension of *Locus Standi* for Private Applicants' [2010–2011] 13 Cambridge Yearbook of European Legal Studies 311, 319–320; See also Pieter-Augustijn Van Malleghem and Niels Baeten, 'Before the laws stands a gatekeeper – Or, what is a "regulatory act" in Article 263(4) TFEU?' (2014) 51 Common Market Law Review 1187. After the *Inuit* case, the CJEU had the opportunity to – somewhat – clarify the features of regulatory acts by focusing on two key elements (derived from *Inuit*): the procedure followed in their enactment and the discretion left to either Union or Member States' institutions in their implementation. For example, the General Court qualified as a regulatory act within the meaning of Article 263(4) TFEU, a Commission decision on the non-inclusion of an additive in the production of plastic materials. See Case T-262/10 *Microban v Commission* [2011] ECLI:EU:T:2011:623.

95 C-274/12 P *Telefónica v Commission* [2013] EU:C:2013:852, para 38; Case C-456/13 P *T&L Sugars v Commission* [2015] ECLI:EU:C:2015:284, para 46 seq.

96 Case C-348/20 P *Nord Stream 2* (n 79).

97 Commission Directive 2009/37/EC of 23 April 2009 amending Council Directive 91/414/EEC to include chlormequat, copper compounds, propaquizafop, quizalofop-P, teflubenzuron and zeta-cypermethrin as active substances [2009] OJ L211/23 (no longer in force).

98 Case T-526/19 *Nord Stream 2* [2020] ECLI:EU:T:2020:210.

The first ground of appeal raised a very clear issue in connection with the right to a remedy, the main question being whether annulment proceedings are, in practice, impossible to launch when they concern a directive (i.e., a general act) which – to further complicate matters – has not yet been transposed into national law. The obstruction to the right to a remedy in such a case is obvious: given the general nature of directives and the need for implementation measures, it is reasonable to assume (in light of the CJEU's case law) that, try as they might, private parties would never be able to establish direct concern.

The second ground of appeal raised an interesting evidentiary issue. Curiously, during the procedure before the General Court and based on Article 130(2) of the CJEU's Rules of procedure,[99] the Council withdrew three documents for which the appellant requested disclosure of their unredacted version. This raised the issue of the equality of arms principle – a fair trial safeguard – in the sense that the Council's withdrawal of items of evidence affected the appellant's knowledge of facts necessary to express their views throughout the procedure (i.e., admissibility and substance).

On the first point, AG Bobek virulently opposed the systematic inadmissibility of annulment proceedings brought against not-yet-transposed directives. He stressed that this can 'hardly be reconciled with the right to an effective remedy which Article 47 [ECFR] ensures to everyone … and with the freedom to conduct a business and the right to property, recognized in respectively 16 and 17 of the Charter'.[100] The CJEU followed the AG's Opinion, stating that for directives, the fact that transposition measures have not yet been adopted 'is not, in itself, relevant since they do not call into question the direct nature of the connection between that directive and its effects [on individuals]'.[101] The possibility to establish direct concern in such cases was laudably admitted in the name of effective judicial protection.

On the second point, the request to disclose evidence was examined through the prism of a right to access documents issued by the Union institutions, governed by Regulation 1049/2001.[102] Although the EU legal order is

99 In the 2022 version of the CJEU's Rules of procedure, the corresponding provision is Article 130(2), which allows for secret or confidential documents to be excluded from the official communication between the parties.

100 Opinion of AG Bobek in Case C-348/20 P *Nord Stream 2* [2022] ECLI:EU:C:2021:831, para 52.

101 Case C-348/20 P *Nord Stream 2* (n 79) para 74.

102 Regulation (EC) No 1049/2001 of the European Parliament and of the Council of 30 May 2001 regarding public access to European Parliament, Council and Commission documents [2001] OJ L145/43.

governed by the principle of freedom of proof, with no general rules on the admissibility of evidence,[103] AG Bobek cautioned against considering said regulation as a 'go-to' instrument when issues on the access to and admissibility of evidence in annulment proceedings arise. Instead, he suggested that those issues be addressed from the perspective of (here again) the right to effective judicial protection: '[T]he rules on evidence seek to ensure the proper administration of justice, enabling the [CJEU] to carry out its mission under Article 19 TEU. The overarching aim is to guarantee to everyone the right to an effective remedy enshrined in Article 47 of the Charter.'[104] Against this backdrop, the Court would need to assess how the admissibility or non-admissibility of certain types of evidence is likely to affect the economy of procedure, the fairness of the proceedings, and the respect for the rights of the defence.[105] Again, the CJEU's ruling converged with the AG's Opinion. The fundamental principles of evidence in EU law should be interpreted so as to allow the assessment of the 'reasonable opportunity' of the applicant to present their case 'including his or her evidence, under conditions that do not place him or her at a substantial disadvantage vis-à-vis his opponent'.[106]

In the context of the CJEU's standard case law on the direct and individual concern *probandum*, *Nord Stream 2* brings some hope. It seems to be in line with the broad understanding of effective judicial protection we suggested earlier in this chapter:[107] the effectiveness of the judicial redress offered to private litigants under Article 263 and Article 265 TFEU should go beyond the 'mere' issue of access to a legal remedy, extending to the (evidentiary) modalities according to which those remedies can, or should be accessed. This is an important point to stress because *Nord Stream 2* is one of the rare cases where the admissibility and substance of an action for annulment against a general Union act was assessed in connection with the applicant's ability to give evidence. This increased awareness of the importance of evidence might – dare we hope – trigger a more procedural abilities–oriented interpretation of Articles 263 and 265 TFEU.

Such a shift would be welcomed because it would allow applicants to argue that any restriction on their ability to give evidence might also restrict their right to a remedy, as well as other rights enshrined in the Charter. The interconnectedness between procedural abilities to give evidence and fundamental rights has been typically associated with the CJEU's economic

[103] Case C-348/20 P *Nord Stream 2*, Opinion (n 100) para 116 seq.
[104] Ibid para 130.
[105] Ibid para 138.
[106] Case C-348/20 P *Nord Stream 2* (79) para 128.
[107] See Section 3.2.

sanctions case law. In *Kadi*, for instance,[108] the contested measure instituted a freezing of funds that infringed the applicant's right to property. To establish that infringement, they of course required that evidence be disclosed (by the Council) on the reasons underlying that sanction. Similarly, in *Nord Stream 2*, the proof of the violation of the right to conduct business depended on the applicant's ability to both demonstrate standing and have access to the documents the Council had decided to withdraw. The analogy between *Nord Stream 2* and the *Kadi* case law is apparent: in both cases, it was the access to evidence that dictated, to a large extent, the success of the arguments pertaining to the violation of fundamental rights as the core issue of the debate on the substance of the proceedings. However, the specificity of *Nord Stream 2* is – again – that this access was recognised in relation to a *general* Union measure, as opposed to the individual acts instituting economic sanctions, by definition destined for specific groups of addressees.

It is too early to tell if *Nord Stream 2* will become a trend-setting case on the interrelationship between evidence and standing/substance in annulment actions brought against general Union acts. While we wait for new developments in the Court's case law, the *Plaumann* austerity does not seem to have been relaxed. The reason for this is – what can be seen as – the Court's (over) protective attitude toward secondary Union law, the rationale that emerges being that legality should be the norm, illegality the (rare) exception. If we were to place procedural entitlements (access to evidence, feasibility of evidence, equality of arms, contradictory debate) and the presumed legality of EU law on a balance, the scales would clearly tip in favour of the latter, which begs the question of whether direct actions are a notable exception to the standard of effectiveness that Article 47 CFR seems to uphold (in paragraphs 1 *and* 2). The answer seems to be 'yes' and our discussion of the system of evidence under Article 340 TFEU (non-contractual liability) gives additional confirmation of this.

3.4 THE REQUIREMENTS ON EVIDENCE RESTRICTING THE LITIGANTS' EFFECTIVE PARTICIPATION (AND ABILITY TO SEEK JUDICIAL REDRESS) IN ACTIONS FOR DAMAGES

Like the actions conducive to a legality review, the evidence in non-contractual liability proceedings seeks to establish unlawfulness in the conduct of a Union institution having resulted in the suffering of harm by a private party. However, unlike the Treaty provisions on illegal acts or

[108] Joined Cases C-402/05 P and C-415/05 P *Kadi Al Barakaat* [2008] ECLI:EU:C:2008:461.

omissions – which provide minimal information on the admissibility conditions (and corresponding burdens) applicants must satisfy – Article 340 TFEU[109] makes no mention of private parties nor of evidence but merely states that 'the Union shall, in accordance with the general principles common to the laws of the Member States, make good any damage caused by its institutions or by its servants in the performance of their duties'. Presumably, this Article would require some proof of causation,[110] but its wording alone does not allow us to clearly map out the relevant facts that litigants ought to establish in order to have standing when seeking compensation for a harm caused by a Union institution or civil servant.

Charged with the task of conceiving the overall design of the system of evidence in non-contractual liability actions, the CJEU drew a parallel with the system of evidence applied in the field of State liability. Referring to the conditions set out in *Francovich*[111] and consolidated in *Brasserie du Pêcheur*,[112] in *Bergaderm*,[113] the Court stressed the importance of – what can be qualified as – structural[114] uniformity of both the Union's and the Member States' liability regimes, by reiterating – as already stated in *Brasserie*[115] – that the conditions for non-contractual liability of both cannot differ.[116] In light of this, the system of evidence[117] applied in State liability provided the template for the system of evidence of the EU's non-contractual liability. However, the burdens and relevant facts for each leg of the facts to be proven (unlawful conduct, harm, causation) were yet to be defined.

Regarding the proof of sufficiently serious breach, applicants are required to establish a violation of a norm by a Union entity (institution, agency, civil servant, etc.) that can qualify as a rule of law intended to confer rights on

[109] Regarding the liability of the ECB, Article 288(3) TEC stated that it will make good any damage caused by it or its servants in the performance of their duties in the conditions for liability of the other institutions, listed in Art. 288(1) TEC. Article 340(3) TFEU specifies that the compensation of such a harm will be performed in accordance with the general principles common to the laws of the Member States.

[110] This presumption is warranted by an *argument of coherence* of sorts, since the Union may be viewed as 'an outgrowth of national systems – an order stemming from the legal traditions of the Member States and modelled on those traditions'. See Stefano Bertea,'Looking for Coherence within the European Community' (2005) 11 European Law Journal 154, 155.

[111] Joined cases C-6/90 and C-9/90 *Francovich/Bonifaci* [1991] ECLI:EU:C:1991:428.

[112] Joined Cases C-46/93 and C-48/93 *Brasserie du Pêcheur* [1996] ECLI:EU:C:1996:79.

[113] Case C-352/98 P *Bergaderm and Goupil v Commission* [2000] ECLI:EU:C:2000:361.

[114] By 'structural' we refer to the design of the systems of evidence in non-contractual liability.

[115] *Brasserie du Pêcheur* (n 112) para 28 seq.

[116] *Bergaderm and Goupil v Commission* (n 113) para 42.

[117] *Brasserie du Pêcheur* (n 112) para 72: 'A rule of Community law breached is intended to confer rights upon them, the breach is sufficiently serious and there is a direct causal link between the breach and the damage sustained by the individuals'.

individuals.[118] The practical issue of what exactly that evidence entailed was raised early on. An initial clarification was given in *Kampffmeyer*,[119] where the CJEU stressed that the claimants needed to establish a 'wrongful act or omission capable of giving rise to liability on the part of the [Union]'.[120] The concept of 'wrongful act' was to be understood as an 'unlawful act', not to be found 'in a mistaken evaluation of the facts but in [a] general conduct which is shown clearly by the improper use made of [an EU law provision]'.[121] In its subsequent case law, the Court further clarified the relevant facts that could establish an 'improper use of an EU law provision'. In *Bergaderm*,[122] it seminally considered that the 'decisive test'[123] for determining whether a breach of Union law was sufficiently serious required evidence that a Union institution had manifestly and gravely disregarded the limits on its discretion.[124] Where a Member State or a Union institution has only considerably reduced, or even no, discretion, the mere infringement of EU law may be sufficient to establish the existence of a sufficiently serious breach.[125]

By defining the features of the breach of Union law that was the original cause of a harm, the CJEU brought some clarity on the otherwise laconic wording of Article 340 TFEU. However, grey areas persisted in terms of the litigants' practical ability to adduce the evidence according to the Court's requirements. For example, the Court did not list the criteria that would allow litigants to distinguish cases where the Union enjoyed broad discretion from cases where this discretion was minimal or non-existent. It is in the case law following *Bergaderm* that we can discern certain criteria used by the Court in its appraisal of the manifest and grave disregard of the limits of an institution's discretion. The key criterion in this regard was the level of discretion warranted by the rule of law infringed,[126] along with the complexity of the

[118] See, inter alia, Case C-282/05 P *Holcim (Deutschland) v Commission* [2007] ECLI:EU:C:2007:226, para 47; Case T-786/14 *Bourdouvali v Council* [2018] ECLI:EU:T:2018:487, para 246; Case 399/17 *Dalli v Commission* [2019] ECLI:EU:T:2019:384, para 47.

[119] Joined Cases C-5/66, 7/66, 13/66–24/66 *Kampffmeyer and Others v Commission* [1967] EU:C:1967:31. In this case, the ECJ considered that the Commission had made an improper application of a 1962 Regulation, by authorising protective measures for the import, in Germany, of French maize, though economic actors having applied for import licences would suffer economic losses due to those measures.

[120] Ibid 262.

[121] Ibid (emphasis added).

[122] *Bergaderm and Goupil v Commission* (n 113).

[123] Ibid para 43.

[124] Ibid.

[125] Ibid para 44 (emphasis added).

[126] See Case C-198/03 P *Commission* v *CEVA and Pfizer* [2005] ECLI:EU:C:2005:445, para 66.

situation to be regulated, the difficulties in the application or interpretation of the legislation, the clarity and precision of the rule infringed, and whether the error of law made was inexcusable or intentional.[127]

The merit of these clarifications notwithstanding, it remains the case that in practice we detect a tendency by the Court to interpret the evidentiary requirements as filters rather than 'enablers' of actions for compensation brought by private parties. A key reason for this is the Court's limited review of the extent of the institutions' discretion. In general, the Union Courts have seldom considered there to be a 'manifest and grave disregard' of the limits of institutional discretion in liability claims, when those claims pertained to normative choices made for the purpose of implementing common policies.[128] The standard formula in such cases is that the EU legislature 'enjoy broad discretion in those cases in which it has to evaluate a complex economic situation', which is not limited solely to the nature and scope of the measures to be taken but also 'to the finding of basic facts'.[129] The implication from this limited judicial review is that, as a matter of principle, the institutions are – again – presumed to act within the limits of their powers, any disregard of those limits being perceived as a rare exception. However, the impact of this presumption on the claimants' procedural abilities under Article 340 TFEU is that they were and continue to carry a burden that is quite heavy, the proof of 'unlawful' exercise of normative discretion needing to be such that it strongly (and exceptionally) justifies the rebuttal of said presumption.

Similar observations can be made regarding the evidence of the harm suffered. In this regard, applicants are required to show that they were 'particularly harmed or harmed in a different way and much more seriously than all other economic operators'.[130] In other words, the harm should not be the result of risks that go beyond the normal hazards – whatever 'normal' is – in a given sector (say, international trade).[131] It goes without saying that proving the abnormality of a harm suffered is a difficult task, especially when a claimant seeks compensation for an imminent harm, which ought to be established with sufficient certainty.[132]

127 See, inter alia, Case T-429/05 *Artedogan v Commission* [2010] ECLI:EU:T:2010:60, para 62; Case T-341/07 *Sison v Council* [2011] ECLI:EU:T:2011:687, para 40; Case T-433/15 *Bank Saderat v Commission* [2019] ECLI:EU:T:2019:374, para 56.

128 See, inter alia, Case C-425/08 *Enviro Tech (Europe) v Belgian State* [2009] ECLI:EU:C:2009:635, para 47.

129 See, e.g., Case C-120/99 *Italy v Council* [2001] ECLI:EU:C:2001:567, para 44.

130 Ibid para 199; see also, Case C-59/83 *Biovilac v EEC* [1984] ECLI:EU:C:1984:380, para 28.

131 Ibid para 209.

132 Case 281/84 *Zuckerfabrik v Commission* [1987] ECLI:EU:C:1987:3, para 14.

But even for harm that has already materialised, proving its special or abnormal nature is far from reasonably feasible. The *T-Port* case[133] provides a telling example of this. Following a Regulation on the organisation of the banana market in the EU, a German importer sought compensation for the damage suffered by reason of their obligation to buy export licences in order to commercialise bananas from third countries in Germany. The General Court[134] declared the action inadmissible due to the lack of the 'indispensable evidence'[135] by which the applicant would prove the amount they actually paid in exporting bananas from certain third countries. As evidence of harm, the claimant had provided an auditor's certified statements, which the General Court viewed as inconclusive.[136] Moreover, the applicant ought to have taken greater care to communicate information on various points because 'the Commission expressly drew the applicant's attention to the fact that such information was essential if the existence and extent of the damage alleged were to be established'.[137] In the appeal brought before the CJEU, the Court's judgment was in line with that of the General Court, as far as evidence was concerned. The Court, indeed, stressed that by basing the action on the fact that costs were incurred, the applicant 'had not adduced sufficient proof of having actually sustained loss'.[138] Considering that the existence and extent of the alleged damage was not established, and given the lack of sufficient evidence to show any direct causal link between the unlawful conduct and the harm suffered, the action was dismissed.

Similarly, in *Dole Fresh Fruit International*,[139] an importer of fresh fruit brought an action for damages by reason of the adoption of a Council Decision and Regulation. The defendants argued that the applicant 'has not adduced sufficient evidence of the existence and extent of the alleged loss or the existence of the causal link between the unlawful conduct [and] that loss'.[140] However – and interestingly – the General Court defined those standards through the aptitude of the claimant's evidence to enable the exercise of the right to effective defence.[141] The Court required 'for the basic

[133] Case C-122/01 P *T.Port v Commission* [2003] ECLI:EU:C:2003:259.

[134] Case T-1/99 *T.Port v Commission* [2001] ECLI:EU:T:2001:36.

[135] Ibid para 60.

[136] Ibid para 61.

[137] Ibid para 62.

[138] Ibid para 67.

[139] Case T-56/00 *Dole Fresh Fruit International Ltd. v Council and Commission* [2003] ECLI: EU:T:2003:58.

[140] Ibid para 36 (emphasis added).

[141] Ibid para 39: '[The applicant's statement must be] sufficiently clear and precise to enable the defendant to prepare its defence and the Court to rule on the application.'

legal and factual particulars relied on to be indicated, at least in summary form, coherently and intelligibly in the application itself'.[142] To this end, the applicant must 'set out the evidence from which the [unlawful conduct] can be identified, the reasons for which the applicant considers that there is a causal link between the conduct and the damage it claims to have suffered and the nature and extent of that damage'.[143] In this case, the General Court considered that the applicant did provide a sufficient description of the nature and the extent of the alleged harm, the conduct that caused it, and the causal link between the two. But the action was ultimately dismissed because the applicant had – unsurprisingly – failed to establish the manifest and grave disregard of the limits of the discretion that the defendant institutions enjoyed.[144]

The practical difficulties in adducing the abovementioned evidence did not push the Court to reconsider the evidentiary requirements pertaining to the serious breach *probandum*. One might argue that claimants ought to have a right to compensation whenever they suffer a harm caused by an institution's conduct, be it legal or illegal. This issue was raised in *FIAMM*.[145] The applicants in this case suffered harm due to a lengthy dispute, within the WTO, between the United States and the EU, on the commercialisation of bananas. They stated that the infringed rule of law was not a Union provision but one of international law, in particular the *pacta sunt servanda* principle, arguing that, by violating this principle, the EU institutions had failed to comply with their obligations under the WTO agreement. Since the Union Courts do not have jurisdiction to assess the lawfulness of the institutions' conduct under WTO rules, and considering that the claimant had failed to prove the unlawfulness of said conduct under EU law, the action was prima facie inadmissible.

However, the General Court went on to determine if the harm suffered could be compensated in the absence of unlawful action, when there is evidence showing a causal link between that harm and the conduct of the Union institutions. The General Court thus stated that the absence of proof of unlawful conduct does not mean that undertakings that are required to bear a 'disproportionate part of the burden resulting from a restriction of access to export markets can in no circumstance obtain compensation by virtue of the [Union's] non-contractual liability'.[146] The General Court's daring attempt to

[142] Ibid.
[143] Ibid para 40.
[144] Ibid para 82.
[145] T-69/00 *FIAMM* [2005] EU:T:2005:449.
[146] Ibid para 157.

redesign the system of evidence in liability proceedings was justified by the general principles common to the laws of the Member States, which do not systematically require proof of unlawfulness as a determining cause of a given harm.[147]

Much like the *UPA* case[148] in annulment proceedings, *FIAMM* can be interpreted as a plea for the lightening of the burden of proof in actions for damages, by disregarding the requirement – resulting from the case law, not the wording of Article 340 TFEU – that unlawfulness is a mandatory *probandum* that applicants must establish. The analogy with *UPA* is of course not total. In *FIAMM*, the 'lightening' of the *onus probandi* was not directly motivated by the right to access a remedy. It was, however, indirectly so. Maintaining the condition to establish unlawful conduct, on the part of the EU's institutions, as the determining cause for a harm would mean that private parties do not have a legal remedy available to seek compensation for harm resulting from prima facie lawful conduct. The General Court's ruling in FIAMM would have been in line with the right to a remedy since it would have *broadened* the procedural abilities of litigants in seeking compensation for harm causally related to a Union institution (having acted lawfully or not).

However, in the appeal,[149] the Court marked a return to the *Brasserie du Pêcheur/Bergaderm* orthodoxy, (re)asserting that the proof of sufficiently serious breach invariably required the establishing of illegal conduct of a Union entity.[150] The Court's unwavering interpretative orthodoxy of claimants' evidentiary duties under Article 340 TFEU mirrors its 'clinging' to the *Plaumann* criteria in the context of annulment proceedings: notwithstanding the difficulty in attaining the standard of proof required in liability actions, the CJEU ultimately refused to lighten the burden of proving serious breach, thus confirming – as was the case in the context of the legality review – the 'filtering out' rationale underlying the system of evidence under consideration.

3.5 CONCLUSION

In light of the above, let us conclude by, first, commenting on the effectiveness of the procedural abilities conferred to private parties in the context of direct actions. Our analysis suggests that those abilities were neither designed to facilitate the access to a remedy (the seminal example being that of

[147] Ibid para 158.
[148] *UPA*, Opinion (n 89).
[149] Joined Cases C-120/06 P and C-121/06 P *FIAMM* [2008] ECLI:EU:C:2008:476.
[150] Ibid para 170 seq.

annulment proceedings), nor to support the parties' effective participation in the actions they launch before the Union's Courts (the seminal example being that of actions for compensation). With the abilities doctrine as the backdrop and based on our holistic reading of the term 'procedure'[151] – as including all the stages, components, and actors in a trial – it would follow that the (in) effectiveness of private parties' ability to meet the evidentiary requirements defined for said actions is, naturally, conducive to the (in)effectiveness of the judicial protection that the EU Courts are assumed to afford under the Treaty provisions examined in this chapter. As mentioned earlier, the CJEU does not seem to practise what it preaches where the principle of effective judicial protection is concerned: on the one hand, said principle had justified the Court's – not so uncommon – shaping of Member States' procedural laws and systems of remedies while, on the other hand, the Court seems to be far more tolerant toward the restrictive procedural requirements that it had, itself, raised as gatekeepers for access to the remedies enshrined in the Treaties.

This two-speed effective judicial protection allows us to, second, give some concluding remarks on the uniformity of the principle of effective judicial protection, discussed earlier in this chapter.[152] As we argued,[153] the wording and structure of Article 47 CFR prima facie support an argument of uniformity. Nothing in this Article gives the impression that it generates two standards of effectiveness, one that would apply to national systems of procedures, the other to the Union's. On the contrary, the fundamental right enshrined in its first paragraph implies – because it is a fundamental right – that both the Member States and the EU should exercise their procedural autonomy in a way that gives private parties if not equal, at least equivalent opportunity to seek judicial redress before national and Union Courts alike. This does not mean that the legal remedies and systems of evidence on the levels of the Member States and the EU should be harmonised, but they should ideally include conditions under which the access to courts is framed by evidentiary requirements that are, at the very least, feasible. In other words, Article 263(4) TFEU would be a decorative remedy if, in the face of the *Plaumann* criteria, private applicants were driven to challenge the legality of, say, a directive before a national court (taking the route of Article 267(3) TFEU) because the evidentiary requirements before that court are more realistic than those defined in *Plaumann*. Practice confirms that effective judicial protection is, indeed, applied selectively, depending on the system of remedies (national or

[151] See Section 3.2.
[152] Ibid.
[153] Ibid.

the Union's) called to provide judicial protection on the grounds of EU law. The 'big' question is, of course: Why? To sketch out an answer to this question, we should note the EU's judiciary machinery seems to run on a number of axiological (i.e., value-based) assumptions.

The first assumption is that private parties are, in any case, never left without a remedy, because they often have several procedural routes available for the claims they wish to make on the grounds of Union law. It is curious to observe that when the CJEU addresses the ethos of the Treaty provisions on direct actions, it does not qualify them as effective so much as it qualifies them as complete. Axiologically, the completeness principle is coherent with the aspiration toward unity and effectiveness of Union law[154] as well as with the latter's capacity to create rights in favour of private parties. We could even argue that the principles established in *Les Verts*[155] and *Rewe/Johnston* carry the imprint of *Van Gend & Loos.*[156] Inaugurating the direct effect doctrine in this case, the Court famously stressed that the rights that Union law confers upon individuals 'become part of their legal heritage'[157] and – as mentioned earlier[158] – called upon their vigilance to protect those rights. The effectiveness of that protection required a system of procedures that would providentially leave no lacuna in the procedural pathways that private litigants could follow in seeking judicial redress based on Union law. In other words, the completeness principle translates to a *choice* of procedures, the assumption being that effective judicial protection would, come what may, be afforded: if judicial redress could not be sought following one procedure (say, annulment proceedings), a claimant would in any case have alternative procedures to seek the same type of redress (say, the preliminary ruling procedure).

The trouble with that assumption is that it is not tenable in relation to the direct actions: the mere fact that individuals have ample choice of procedures is not a convincing justification for the fact that those actions are impracticable, as our analysis of the evidentiary requirements associated with those sought to show. So why is the Court so obstinately refusing to change those requirements?

Bentham may provide some food for thought on this point. For him, procedural law 'is good' if it supports substantive law[159] and procedural

[154] *Križan* (n 23) para 70.
[155] Case C-294/83 *Les Verts v Parliament* [1986] ECLI:EU:C:1986:166.
[156] *Van Gend & Loos* (n 43). This connection between effective judicial protection and direct effect was made in Wildemeersch (n 53) 46 seq.
[157] *Van Gend & Loos* (n 43) [ECR] 12.
[158] See Section 3.2.
[159] Jeremy Bentham, A *Treatise on Judicial Evidence* (Baldwin 1825) 3.

fairness (or justice)[160] is achieved if a dispute is resolved in conformity with the law. Bentham's assumption is that the law can – so to speak – 'do no wrong', his perception of justice being limited to the concept of legal justice, that is, adjudication that, in a given dispute, upholds the content and the authority of substantive law. In other words, the law itself cannot be presumed to be unfair or unjust.

The rationale underlying the design of the systems of evidence relies on a second axiological assumption similar to that expressed by Bentham. We alluded to this assumption in our discussion on substantive effectiveness:[161] the EU's legislature is (strongly) presumed to comply with the Treaties and, by doing so, it is assumed to enforce legislation that confers subjective rights that the objectives in those Treaties warrant. The effectiveness of the law is therefore the consequence of the effective (and again, providential and primary law-conforming) normative action of the EU institutions. The Union Courts have explicitly confirmed this. For example, in a case dealing with the confidentiality of the European Commission's documents,[162] the General Court stressed that the 'provisions of the Treaty may be interpreted only in the manner most favourable to the sound functioning of the [Union] institutions'.[163] With regard to the specific issue raised in this case (i.e., access to documents), the General Court considered that 'the possibility of an impairment of the sound functioning of the institutions, detrimental to the attainment of the objectives of [the Treaty], cannot be ruled out *a priori* in the event of their unconsidered disclosure of certain documents'.[164] The General Court's ruling is noteworthy and rather 'Benthamian': since the Union institutions' normative action (or conduct) is presumed to be lawful, the result of that action (say, secondary law act) cannot be considered as unlawful. In this context, the procedural restraints discussed in this chapter make sense: if the EU legislature 'can do no wrong', it is only logical that the occasions to challenge the lawfulness of that legislature's conduct be extremely limited. True, private parties who exceptionally succeed in meeting the Court's evidentiary requirements do, sometimes, succeed in rebutting that presumption. More often than not, however, the latter remains standing for the reasons discussed in the previous sections.

[160] There is a debate on whether fairness and justice are synonymous. This debate being beyond the scope of this chapter, we will not address it and will, for simplicity's sake, consider that procedural fairness and justice have equivalent meanings.

[161] See Section 3.2.

[162] Joined Cases T-134/94, T-136/94, T-137/94, T-138/94, T-141/94, T-145/94, T-147/94, T-148/94, T-151/94, T-156/94 and T-157/94 *NMH Stahlwerke GmbH* [1996] ECLI:EU:T:1996:85.

[163] Ibid pt 72 (emphasis added).

[164] Ibid pt 73.

Using evidence to 'manipulate' the access to and administration of justice is the oldest procedural trick in the book. In medieval times, defendants in criminal ordalian trials were required to prove their innocence through absurd modes of proof (say, plunging their hands in boiling water and hoping they would remain unharmed). Mind you, proof of innocence was admitted, perfectly legal only, it was a type of proof that virtually no one could succeed in providing. But the EU's direct actions are modern procedures committed to upholding a workable idea of the rule of law; after all, we now have Article 47 CFR. True as this may be, if the analogy with archaic proceedings and modes of evidence should be seen as irrelevant or untenable, the evidentiary shields raised around the Union's secondary law provisions should perhaps be placed a bit lower, so that private parties can effectively challenge those provisions and, in doing so, benefit from all the rights that EU law confers on them, including the right to effective judicial protection.

4

Fundamental Rights Complaints in the Preliminary Reference Procedure

LUCÍA LÓPEZ ZURITA

4.1 INTRODUCTION

The European Union legal order is, following the jurisprudence of the Court of Justice (the Court), a complete system of judicial protection.[1] In this system, the main direct way of access to the Court for individuals is the action for annulment in Article 263 Treaty on the Functioning of the European Union (TFEU). The Treaty grants *locus standi* to challenge the legality of EU acts to 'any natural or legal person against an act addressed to that person or which is of direct and individual concern to him'.[2] However, the narrow interpretation of these standing criteria leaves many individuals without any direct way to challenge EU acts before the Court.[3] The limitation is consequential for individual applicants unable to gain standing, for only the Court has the prerogative to rule on the validity and/or interpretation of EU acts.[4] This is how the procedure for a preliminary ruling in Article 267 TFEU came to the fore: it filled the gaps of access to the Court left by the interpretation of Article 263 TFEU.[5]

The drafting of Article 267 TFEU is minimalistic. It establishes that national courts and tribunals, in case of doubt about the validity or

[1] Case C-50/00 P *Unión de Pequeños Agricultores (UPA)* [2002] ECLI:EU:C:2002:462, para 40. Koen Lenaerts, 'The Rule of Law and the Coherence of the Judicial System of the European Union' (2007) 44 Common Market Law Review 1625.

[2] Consolidated Version of the Treaty on the Functioning of the European Union [2016] OJ C202/47, art 263.

[3] Case C-25/62 *Plaumann v Commission* [1963] ECLI:EU:C:1963:17.

[4] Case C-314/85 *Foto-Frost v Hauptzollamt Lübeck-Ost* [1987] ECLI:EU:C:1987:452.

[5] For a good summary, see Paul Craig and Gráinne de Búrca, *EU Law: Text, Cases, and Materials* (7th edn, Oxford University Press 2020).

interpretation of EU law, can refer a question to the Court. Preliminary references can question the validity of EU secondary law or seek the correct interpretation of any EU law provision, including primary law.[6] References on validity refer to conformity of EU acts with primary law, including the Charter of Fundamental Rights of the European Union (CFR, the Charter) and general principles, while references on the interpretation of EU law are more commonly questions concerning the compatibility of national law with EU law.[7] Therefore, the preliminary reference procedure offers the possibility to raise, albeit indirectly, breaches by both the Member States and the Union. Advocate General Jacobs in his Opinion on *Jégo Quéré* referred to the preliminary reference procedure as 'an alternative method of proceeding to Article [263]'.[8] The comparison has been amply criticised in the doctrine, and the narrow interpretation of Article 263 TFEU remains contested.[9]

Today, the preliminary reference procedure works for the most part as a decentralised infringement procedure, allowing individuals to challenge the compatibility of national law with EU law.[10] As famously put by Pescatore, the preliminary reference procedure is the 'infringement procedure of the EU citizen'.[11] Unarguably, the procedure has been central to the development of the EU legal order and the integration project.[12] Yet this role of the preliminary reference procedure might not be enough at present. The Union no longer *only produces* EU law but is increasingly involved in its *putting into practice*: the range of EU action is ever growing and so are EU organs and bodies, sometimes with very substantial executive functions. Therefore, the Union has more to say, and more ways to directly affect, via its actions, the lives and, by extension, the fundamental rights, of private persons, both natural and legal. This chapter explores whether the preliminary reference procedure

6 TFEU, art 267.

7 Charter of Fundamental Rights of the European Union [2016] OJ C202/389.

8 Case C-263/02 *Jégo Quéré* [2004] EU:C:2004:210.

9 For a critical analysis of this interpretation of the Court, see Henry G Schermers and Denis F Waelbroeck, *Judicial Protection in the European Union* (Kluwer Law International 2001); Hjalte Rasmussen, 'Why Is Article 173 Interpreted against Private Plaintiffs?' (1980) 5 European Law Review 112.

10 Rene Barents, 'EU Procedural Law and Effective Legal Protection' (2014) 51 Common Market Law Review 1437, 1455.

11 Pierre Pescatore, 'Van Gend En Loos, 3 February 1963 – A View from Within' in Miguel Poiares Maduro and Loïc Azoulai (eds), *The Past and Future of EU Law: The Classics of EU Law Revisited on the 50th Anniversary of the Rome Treaty* (Hart 2010).

12 Karen Alter, *Establishing the Supremacy of European Law: The Making of an International Rule of Law in Europe* (Oxford University Press 2001); Daniel Kelemen, *Eurolegalism: The Transformation of Law and Regulation in the European Union* (Harvard University Press 2011).

also works as a 'citizens' infringement' procedure against the Union and reflects on whether this is a possibility at all.

The chapter is structured as follows. Sections 4.2 and 4.3 present the possibilities and limitations in the use of the preliminary reference procedure for individuals to bring claims based on breaches of their fundamental rights against the Union. Section 4.4 maps all instances in which private natural and legal persons have used the procedure for a preliminary ruling to bring a claim against the Union for breaches of their fundamental rights since the coming into force of the Treaty of Lisbon.[13] The findings of the mapping are presented in Section 4.5. Section 4.6 identifies how the parties raise this type of claims in the preliminary reference procedure, discusses the accessibility of the procedure for applicants, and assesses the shortcomings of the procedure as a means to redress breaches of fundamental rights by the Union. It argues that these shortcomings have to do with the structure and design of the procedure itself. Section 4.7 concludes.

4.2 USING THE PRELIMINARY REFERENCE PROCEDURE AGAINST THE UNION

This section explores how the preliminary reference procedure might be used to challenge breaches of fundamental rights by the Union. It first describes the types of acts that can be challenged and the grounds that might be used against the Union within the framework of Article 267 TFEU to subsequently reflect on the concrete possibilities for individuals to bring this type of claim via the preliminary reference procedure.

4.2.1 *Challengeable Acts*

The Article includes no rules on standing, and applicants are fully dependent on the national rules for *locus standi*. The only EU limitation regarding standing in Article 267 TFEU is the *TWD* rule:[14] where the applicant unequivocally had or would have had standing to challenge the act with a direct action, the indirect challenge via the preliminary reference procedure is barred.[15] The Court has taken a relatively broad view on when standing for bringing an annulment action is unequivocal,[16] but, generally, this leaves out

[13] Treaty of Lisbon [2007] OJ C306/1.

[14] Case C-188/92 *TWD Textilwerke Deggendorf* [1994] ECLI:EU:C:1994:90.

[15] Koen Lenaerts and Others, *EU Procedural Law* (Oxford University Press 2014) 465–467.

[16] Morten Broberg and Niels Fenger, *Preliminary References to the European Court of Justice* (2nd edn, Oxford University Press 2014).

individually targeted acts (e.g., decisions). Therefore, the indirect challenge mostly refers to acts of general application affecting individuals.[17] Typically, the challenge will come through a preliminary reference on the validity of EU provisions, though the Chapter will discuss other possibilities below.

The acts that can be challenged under Article 267 TFEU are much broader than for Article 263 TFEU. The drafters of the Lisbon Treaty rewrote Article 267 TFEU, which now allows referral of questions on the 'validity and interpretation of acts of the institutions, bodies, offices and agencies'. The terms are intended to cover practically every EU act,[18] and so Article 267 TFEU also allows for the indirect challenge of all sorts of non-binding acts, including recommendations, statements, communications, and notices, regardless of whether they are directly applicable or have binding effect.[19] Theoretically, it could also open the way to challenge any action exercised directly by the Union on the ground. In those cases, however, there might be no written acts or implementing measures at the Member State level, so what concretely to challenge might be problematic.[20]

4.2.2 *Types of Questions*

How can private parties concretely challenge acts of the Union via the preliminary reference procedure? The obvious way to challenge EU acts is through references on validity. Preliminary references on validity are judicial review cases, in which the legality of an EU act, usually a piece of secondary legislation, is challenged on grounds of not complying with the provisions of primary law. As stated, with the exception of instances in which the private applicant would have had standing to challenge the EU measure under Article 263 TFEU,[21] Article 267 TFEU includes no limitations on who can challenge the EU act. This is similarliy the case when the act that is challenged is of no relevance, and the Court has no problem in examining questions of validity after one or more rulings on the interpretation of the EU provision.[22]

[17] Case C-583/11 P *Inuit Tapiriit Kanatami and Others v Parliament and Council* [2013] ECLI:EU:C:2013:625.

[18] Broberg and Fenger, *Preliminary References to the European Court of Justice* (n 16) 115.

[19] Ibid.

[20] For a good analysis of the question, see Melanie Fink, 'The Action for Damages as a Fundamental Rights Remedy: Holding Frontex Liable' (2020) 21 German Law Journal 532. She proposes the action for damages as an alternative.

[21] Lenaerts and Others (n 15) 465.

[22] See, for instance, case C-393/99 *Hervein and Others* [2002] ECLI:EU:C:2002:182. See further Morten Broberg and Niels Fenger, *The Procedure before the Court of Justice* (Oxford University Press 2021).

The Court generally tries to avoid the annulment of EU acts and particularly secondary legislation.[23] The Court prefers reading directives in a manner consistent with primary law and generally exercises restraint as per the political, economic, and social grounds behind the piece of legislation.[24] Indeed, the Court states that secondary legislation must be 'interpreted as to not affect its validity'.[25] It is therefore unsurprising that most validity challenges under Article 267 TFEU are generally unsuccessful.

Questions of validity frequently coexist with questions of interpretation in the same order for reference. It is possible for a national court to refer questions on interpretation that hint at a possible breach of primary law, including rights of the Charter, by a piece of secondary legislation, without directly questioning the validity of the provision. These references connect the interpretation of EU secondary legislation to primary law in a manner that questions EU legislation itself, thus coming close to a 'fake validity' question.[26] This ultimately relates to the relationship between primary and secondary law,[27] and the Court has two main ways of replying. It can reformulate the question to specifically acknowledge the validity issue underlying the reference, and thus give a validity ruling,[28] or leave the question as one of interpretation. In the latter case, the Court will try to interpret secondary law so as to fit within the limits of primary law. In *Sturgeon*, for instance, the Court read the regulation on compensation to passengers[29] in the light of primary law to find that passengers of delayed flights had the same right to compensation as passengers of cancelled flights.[30]

[23] Broberg and Fenger, *Preliminary References to the European Court of Justice* (n 16); Lenaerts and Others (n 15).

[24] Sacha Prechal, 'Individuals Challenging Directives in EU Courts' (2022) 59 Common Market Law Review 41, 48.

[25] Joined Cases C-402/07 and C-432/07 *Sturgeon* [2009] ECLI:EU:C:2009:716.

[26] The expression belongs to Michał Krajewski.

[27] Phil Syrpis, 'The Relationship between Primary and Secondary Law in the EU' (2015) 52 Common Market Law Review 461. See also Gareth Davies, 'Legislative Control of the European Court of Justice' (2014) 51 Common Market Law Review 1579.

[28] For instance, in Case C-300/07 *Hans & Christophorus Oymanns* [2009] ECLI:EU:C:2009:358. The national court had addressed several questions on interpretation, but the Court interpreted that the referring court 'raises, although not expressly, a question concerning the validity' and therefore 'wishes to ask the Court for a ruling on the validity'.

[29] Regulation (EC) No 261/2004 of the European Parliament and of the Council of 11 February 2004 establishing common rules on compensation and assistance to passengers in the event of denied boarding and of cancellation or long delay of flights, and repealing Regulation (EEC) No 295/91 [2004] OJ L46/1.

[30] Sacha Garben, 'Sky-High Controversy and High-Flying Claims? The *Sturgeon* Case Law in Light of Judicial Activism, Euroscepticism and Eurolegalism' (2013) 50 Common Market Law Review 15.

4.2.3 *Types of Grounds*

Article 267 TFEU allows private applicants to raise any infringement of their fundamental rights by the Union. Not only that, but breaches of fundamental rights are 'a favourite ground' to challenge the legality of directives and were already before the entry into force of the Charter.[31] As the duty for the Union to comply with the fundamental rights of the Charter is recognised in Article 51(1) CFR,[32] there is no need for applicants to prove any implementation of EU law under Article 51 CFR, for they are directly challenging an act of an institution.[33] Similarly, and at least theoretically, there is no need for questions on the compatibility of the Union act with national law, that is, there is in principle no need for any measures at the national level for the private applicant to be able to challenge the EU act,[34] though typically some sort of implementing measures are needed in the national legal orders to be able to bring a claim to a national court.

Moreover, it should be considered that the same claim can be framed in different ways for what concerns fundamental rights. For instance, in *Schecke*,[35] two applicants challenged the regulation obliging the disclosure of data on the recipients of EU funds, including recipients of Common Agricultural Policy funds, on grounds of their fundamental right to the protection of personal data. Nevertheless, they could have challenged it on grounds of a breach of their personal dignity, as their concern related more to the impact on their daily lives.[36] Similarly, a much older case like *Mulder*,[37] which deals with the protection of legitimate expectations for milk producers who wished to re-enter the market, clearly involves the freedom to conduct a business or property, even if the case does not use the language of fundamental rights.

4.3 INHERENT LIMITATIONS IN THE PROCEDURE

After reflecting on the concrete ways in which acts of the Union might be challenged using the preliminary reference procedure, this section reflects on

31 Prechal (n 24) 43.

32 Sonia Morano-Foadi and Stelios Andreadakis, 'Reflections on the Architecture of the EU after the Treaty of Lisbon: The European Judicial Approach to Fundamental Rights' (2011) 17 European Law Journal 595, 601.

33 Angela Ward, 'Article 51 – Field of Application' in Steve Peers and Others (eds), *The EU Charter of Fundamental Rights: a commentary* (2nd edn, Hart 2021) 1573.

34 Ibid 1574.

35 Case C-92/09 *Volker und Markus Schecke* [2010] ECLI:EU:C:2010:662.

36 Morano-Foadi and Andreadakis (n 30) 608–609.

37 Joined Cases C-104/89 and C-37/90 *Mulder (milk quotas)* [1992] ECLI:EU:C:1992:217.

the limitations inherent to it. These limitations go beyond a mere comparison with the direct action of Article 263 TFEU and look at how the structure, aims, and working of the procedure might constrain the position, capacity, and possibilities of private parties to challenge breaches of their fundamental rights. To be sure, these limitations are common to any kind of challenge under Article 267 TFEU but become particularly relevant when those challenges concern potential breaches by the Union.

This section takes the perspective of private applicants and examines three main groups of limitations. First, the preliminary reference procedure establishes a system of judicial cooperation in which private parties are entirely dependent on national law and the national courts for the indirect challenge of EU acts. This makes any challenge 'long and uncertain' for applicants.[38] Secondly, the preliminary reference procedure is not a 'real judicial remedy for the parties',[39] which seriously limits the possibilities of the parties within the procedure.[40] Thirdly, the procedure was conceived to ensure the uniformity of EU law[41] and plays a central role in EU integration,[42] which results in a central position of the Court within the procedure.

4.3.1 *First Limit: The Central Role of National Courts*

The first limitation faced by private parties in the procedure is that they are fully dependent on national law and procedures to bring such claims to the Court. Indeed, unlike Article 263 TFEU, Article 267 TFEU includes no rules on standing because those are national. Even when national law grants standing before the national court, private parties depend fully on national courts to decide that a reference is needed.

According to the Rules of Procedure of the Court,[43] national courts are not obliged to send a preliminary reference, but if they decide to do so, it is entirely up to them how to draft the preliminary questions and the rest of the elements in the order for reference.[44] Furthermore, the national courts can

[38] Schermers and Waelbroeck (n 9) 452.
[39] Ibid.
[40] Schermers and Waelbroeck (n 9).
[41] Pierre Pescatore, 'Les Travaux Du "Groupe Juridique" Dans La Négociation Des Traités de Rome' (1981) 34 (1/4) Studia Diplomatica 159, 159.
[42] Thomas de la Mare and Catherine Donnely, 'Preliminary Rulings and EU Legal Integration: Evolution and Stasis' in Paul P Craig and Grainne de Búrca (eds), *The evolution of EU law* (Oxford University Press 2011); Alter (n 12).
[43] Rules of Procedure of the Court of Justice [2012] OJ L265/1.
[44] According to Article 94 Rules of Procedure, the order for reference must contain the text of the questions, a summary of the subject matter of the dispute and the relevant facts, the relevant national law, and an account of the reasons justifying the referral.

also attach a pre-emptive opinion[45] or provisional answer,[46] that is, share their views as to how the question at issue should be resolved (e.g., whether the claim of the private party should be granted or if the secondary provision should be annulled).[47] However, the Court does not seem to be too interested in the opinions of its national counterparts, and the influence of these pre-emptive opinions seems rather modest.[48]

Finally, the influence of the parties in the drafting of the question differs greatly from one country to another: in some Member States, referring judges limit their intervention to the verification and submission of the questions, while others give the parties no real chance to influence the question.[49]

4.3.2 *Second Limit: The Reduced Role of the Parties in the Proceedings*

The preliminary reference procedure is a non-contentious,[50] 'special' procedure that aims to ensure the uniformity of EU law throughout the territory of the European Union.[51] To do so, it 'instituted direct cooperation between the Court of Justice and the national courts by means of a procedure which is completely independent of any initiative by the parties'.[52] Technically, there are no parties to the proceedings,[53] and the Court has stated that 'the parties in the main action are merely invited to state their case within the legal limits laid down by the national court'.[54] In this sense, Sarmiento writes that 'it could

45 Stacy A Nyikos, 'Strategic Interaction among Courts within the Preliminary Reference Process – Stage 1: National Court Preemptive Opinions' (2006) 45 European Journal of Political Research 527.

46 Rob van Gestel and Jurgen de Poorter, *In the Court We Trust: Cooperation, Coordination and Collaboration between the ECJ and Supreme Administrative Courts* (Cambridge University Press 2019).

47 Recommendations to national courts and tribunals in relation to the initiation of preliminary ruling proceedings [2019] OJ C380/1, art. 17 and Annex I. Compare to Rules of Procedure, art. 94.

48 Anna Wallerman Ghavanini, 'Mostly Harmless: The Referring Court in the Preliminary Reference Procedure' (2022) 47 European Law Review 310.

49 Morten Broberg, 'Preliminary References as a Means for Enforcing EU Law' in Andras Jakab and Dimitry Kochenov (eds), *The Enforcement of EU Law and Values: Ensuring Member States' Compliance* (Oxford University Press 2017) 105.

50 Barents (n 9) 1455. Lucía López Zurita, 'The Survival of the Fitted? Individual Protection in the European Court of Justice's Preliminary Ruling Procedure' (PhD thesis, European University Institute 2021).

51 Case C-6/64 *Costa Enel* [1964] ECLI:EU:C:1964:66.

52 Case C-210/06 *Cartesio* [2008] ECLI:EU:C:2008:294.

53 K P E Lasok, *Lasok's European Court Practice and Procedure* (3rd edn, Bloomsbury Professional 2017) 1258.

54 Case C-62/72 *Bollman* [1973] ECLI:EU:C:1973:24, para 4. The case is still quoted by the Court (for instance, see Case C-2/06 *Kempter* [2008] ECLI:EU:C:2008:78, para 41).

be said, quite radically, that the legal situation of the parties becomes a secondary concern for the ECJ'.[55]

The Rules of Procedure of the Court offer individuals who are a party in the main proceedings the possibility, not obligation, to intervene in defence of their position before the Court.[56] The parties might submit written observations[57] and oral pleadings (though these tend to be very brief),[58] explaining their legal arguments or their version of the facts submitted. According to Article 23 of the Statute and Article 96 of the Rules of Procedure of the Court, the Member States, the European Commission, the institution that adopted the act in dispute, and the parties to the main proceedings (determined by national law) can submit observations to the Court. Therefore, by the time the claim makes its way to Luxembourg, a whole new set of parties is added to the case.

Parties to the case are only allowed to submit observations regarding the reply to be given to the question, thus they are in the same position as the different Member States and other institutions that might intervene in the proceedings but without the knowledge and resources available to them.[59] The purpose of the observations is to clarify the scope of the dispute and the answers to be given to the questions.[60] There is only one round of written pleadings, and there is no opportunity to reply in writing to the submissions of the other parties.[61] Parties are not supposed to comment on the referred question itself, as this is part of the exclusive prerogative of the national court, nor can they change the content of the question.[62] The possibility that the parties could influence the Court to consider other arguments seems fairly limited.[63]

55 Daniel Sarmiento, 'Amending the Preliminary Reference Procedure for the Administrative Judge' (2009) 2 Review of European Administrative Law 29, 35.

56 It should be noted that the parties in the main proceedings are automatically parties in the procedure before the Court (Rules of Procedure, art. 23(2)), following the rules of representation and attendance in the national legal system (Rules of Procedure, art. 97).

57 Rules of Procedure of the Court, art 57(1).

58 Schermers and Waelbroeck (n 9) 649. They speak of an opportunity for 'extremely succinct oral comment'.

59 For instance, speaking of the Commission, Azoulai writes that it 'has appropriated for itself the language of jurisprudence'. Pascal Mbongo and Antoine Vauchez, *Dans La Fabrique Du Droit Européen: Scènes, Acteurs et Publics de La Cour de Justice Des Communautés Européennes* (Bruylant 2009) 158.

60 Practice Directions to the Parties Concerning Cases Brought Before the Court [2020] OJ L421/1, art 10.

61 Ibid art 33.

62 Broberg and Fenger, *Preliminary References to the European Court of Justice* (n 16) 359.

63 Jos Hoevenaars and Jasper Krommendijk, 'Black Box in Luxembourg: the Bewildering Experience of National Judges and Lawyers in the Context of the Preliminary Reference Procedure' (2021) 46 European Law Review 61.

4.3.3 *Third Limit: The Procedural Freedom of the Court*

The raison d'être of the preliminary reference procedure is ensuring the uniformity of EU law.[64] This function necessarily coexists with the other goals and roles that the procedure has come to fulfil within the EU legal order, notably providing the Court with a tool to carry out its judicial law-making and guaranteeing the effective judicial protection of individuals, even if in an indirect manner.[65] In other words, this is not a procedure primarily oriented to provide a remedy to the parties.

The consequence of the peculiar nature and divergent goals of the preliminary reference procedure is the central role of the Court within it. The Court enjoys a degree of control over the proceedings that is remarkable in comparison both to other proceedings before the Court and to other international courts. Such freedom becomes apparent when the broader framework of the procedure is explored. This includes the Rules of Procedure of the Court, which have been reformed following concrete proposals of the Court,[66] the non-public, internal guidelines of the Court,[67] and its case law.

Given the configuration of the procedure as a cooperation between courts and the limited role of the parties, the treatment of the concrete questions depends greatly on the Court. This concerns matters including the attribution of the case to a chamber and a judge rapporteur,[68] the interaction with the parties,[69] the capacity of the Court to change the scope of the questions,[70] or the extent to which it conducts a proportionality test or

[64] Pescatore (n 41); Van Gestel and De Poorter (n 46).

[65] Van Gestel and De Poorter (n 46) 156.

[66] Urška Šadl and Others, 'Law and Orders: The Orders of the European Court of Justice as a Window in the Judicial Process and Institutional Transformations' (2022) 1 European Law Open 549.

[67] Court of Justice of the European Union, 'Guide Pratique Relative Au Traitement Des Affaires Portées Devant La Cour de Justice' [2020] OJ L042I/1.

[68] Silje Synnøve Lyder Hermansen, 'Building Legitimacy: Strategic Case Allocations in the Court of Justice of the European Union' (2020) 27 Journal of European Public Policy 1127; Christoph Krenn, 'A Sense of Common Purpose: On the Role of Case Assignment and the Judge-Rapporteur at the European Court of Justice' in Mikael Rask Madsen, Fernanda Nicola, and Antoine Vauchez (eds), *Researching the European Court of Justice: methodological shifts and law's embeddedness* (Cambridge University Press 2022).

[69] Síofra O'Leary, *Employment Law at the European Court of Justice: Judicial Structures, Policies and Processes* (Hart 2002); Lenaerts and Others (n 15).

[70] Urška Šadl and Anna Wallerman Ghavanini, '"The Referring Court Asks, in Essence": Is Reformulation of Preliminary Questions by the Court of Justice a Decision Writing Fixture or a Decision-Making Approach?' (2019) 25 European Law Journal 416; Broberg and Fenger, *Preliminary References to the European Court of Justice* (n 16).

defers to the national courts.[71] An analysis of each procedural factor is beyond the scope of this chapter,[72] but some examples serve to show the extent of this procedural freedom. For instance, the allocation of cases at the Court to a *juge rapporteur* is an exclusive prerogative of the President, not subject to any sort of procedural constraint.[73] Similarly, none of the procedural instruments regulating the preliminary reference procedure mention reformulation, but the Court has coined the practice and reverts to it frequently. For the type of cases discussed in this chapter, the Court reformulates to turn questions of validity into questions of interpretation or vice versa. The latter is the most frequent scenario, but it is also the case, albeit less frequently, that the referring court sends questions exclusively on interpretation, which the Court reformulates as validity questions.[74] The Court might also reformulate the question to limit the review of the EU provision at stake or add other grounds to those submitted to review the legality of the EU act.[75]

The influence of the private parties in the procedural treatment of the case is limited. To continue with the examples above, Member States and other institutions might request that a Grand Chamber hear the case, but this possibility does not extend to other parties in the proceedings. As for reformulation, the submissions of the parties might influence the Court to reformulate the questions,[76] but they cannot force the Court to do so.[77]

[71] Jan Zglinski, 'The Rise of Deference: The Margin of Appreciation and Decentralized Judicial Review in EU Free Movement Law' (2018) 55 Common Market Law Review 1341; Lucía López Zurita and Stein Arne Brekke, 'A Spoonful of Sugar: Deference at the Court of Justice' (2023) *Journal of Common Market Studies*, available at https://doi.org/10.1111/jcms.13547 (last accessed May 2024).

[72] Many can be cited for a comprehensive analysis of the procedure. See among others Lenaerts and Others (n 15); Lasok (n 53); Broberg and Fenger, *Preliminary References to the European Court of Justice* (n 16); Christoph Krenn, *The Procedural and Organisational Law of the European Court of Justice: An Incomplete Transformation* (Cambridge University Press 2022); López Zurita, 'The Survival of the Fitted?' (n 50).

[73] Krenn, 'A Sense of Common Purpose' (n 68).

[74] Lenaerts and Others (n 15) 469.

[75] Ibid.

[76] Broberg (n 49). See also Ricardo García Antón, *La Cuestión Prejudicial y La Fiscalidad Directa* (European University Institute 2015); Ricardo García Antón, 'The Reformulation of the Questions Referred to the CJEU for a Preliminary Ruling in Direct Taxation: Towards a Constructive Cooperation Model' (2015) 24 EC Tax Review 258; David W K Anderson and Marie Demetriou, *References to the European Court* (2nd edn, Sweet & Maxwell 2002). Broberg and Fenger however state that the reformulation is rarely influenced by the submissions of the parties see Broberg (n 49) 106.

[77] Broberg and Fenger, *Preliminary References to the European Court of Justice* (n 16) 361.

4.4 EMPIRICAL MATERIAL AND RESEARCH PROCESS

This section explains the research process behind the mapping of the cases in this chapter. The process consists of two main steps: first, a search of all relevant cases and, secondly, the qualitative coding of those cases to gather information regarding the applicants, the framing of the claims, and the treatment of the fundamental rights. All of these are relevant to understand the actual and potential use of the preliminary reference procedure for challenging breaches of fundamental rights by the Union.

First, I collected all preliminary rulings containing the word *validity* and with a mention of the Charter of Fundamental Rights (in any part of the ruling) in the Curia database from the entry into force of the Treaty of Lisbon (1 December 2009) to the end of 2022.[78] I repeated the search in the dataset IUROPA to ensure that no ruling was missing.[79] After manually eliminating false positives,[80] the dataset contains fifty-four preliminary rulings on validity and validity and interpretation. The dataset includes any case in which validity was mentioned, even if the Court ended up not ruling on the validity of the EU provision.

A limitation of the study must be acknowledged. The analysis relies solely on the judgments of the Court, without considering the orders for reference of the national courts or the actual submissions of the parties, due to the fact that they are not publicly available. Yet those materials are analysed through their summaries in the judgment of the Court, which means that the analysis relies on the information provided by the Court and cannot take account of silences or omissions in the judgments.

The mapping relies on the close scrutiny of the decisions in the dataset to observe a series of factors. Each judgment of the dataset was hand-coded with the variables presented below. For clarity, the variables are separated into three different groups. Alongside the information described below, the mapping also takes into account the size of the chamber hearing the case and the EU institutions, organs, or bodies intervening before the Court, as well as elements related to the procedural treatment at the Court.

4.4.1 *Claimants*

The chapter is concerned solely with cases with private parties as applicants. The private applicants might be natural persons, private companies, or NGOs.

78 <www.curia.europa.eu>.

79 Stein Arne Brekke and Others, 'The CJEU Database Platform: Decisions and Decision-Makers' [2023] Journal of Law and Courts, 1. All data is available open-access in <www.iuropa.pol.gu.se>.

80 For instance, cases on the 'validity' of a European arrest warrant.

The information is collected from the section on the factual background of the case in the ruling.[81]

4.4.2 *Framing of the Claim*

The goal of this set of variables is to understand how the claim is framed by the applicants and/or the national court. First, I record whether the reference concerns solely the validity of an EU act or provision or also includes questions on interpretation.

Secondly, I record who brought the question of invalidity to the reference. Within the limitations acknowledged above, this might have been brought up by the applicants in the case or afterwards by the national court.

Thirdly, I record if the claim is framed as a breach of fundamental rights or the Charter is used as any other provision, without a specific fundamental rights framing. The difference is subtle, insofar as in both cases there is a link to fundamental rights. It mostly reflects a difference in the degree to which fundamental rights are central to the claim. For the former, the applicants argue that the breach affects one or more of their fundamental rights, whereas for the latter they mention provisions of the Charter but do not specifically argue that what is at stake is a violation of fundamental rights.

Finally, I record whether the referring court included a pre-emptive opinion on how the Court should reply to the question regarding the validity of the EU act or provision and the existence of a breach of fundamental rights and whether the use of fundamental rights can be traced back to the applicants or the referring court.

4.4.3 *Fundamental Rights Treatment*

The variables in this category focus on how the Court treats the fundamental rights component of the case (if applicable) in the ruling. I first record the extent to which the Court engages with the analysis of the fundamental rights at stake in the case. The Court might disregard completely the fundamental rights aspect of the case, engage minimally, or engage in a detailed or extensive manner.

Secondly, I record any mention of the Charter in the operative part of the ruling. The reason for this is that the operative part, or *dispositif*, sets the boundaries of the reply to the national court. It is nothing short of a

[81] Usually under the heading 'The dispute in the main proceedings and the questions referred for a preliminary ruling'.

prescription in which the Court establishes the binding interpretation of European Union law and incidentally decides, within the limits of Article 267 TFEU, on the compatibility of the national measure with European Union law.[82]

Finally, I record the final result in the case: whether the Court annuls the act completely or partially, does not give a ruling on the validity of the provision, or rejects the existence of a breach of fundamental rights.

4.5 PRIVATE APPLICANTS AND FUNDAMENTAL RIGHTS IN THE PRELIMINARY REFERENCE PROCEDURE: A MAPPING

The results of the mapping exercise are summarised in Table 4.1.

4.5.1 *Claimants*

Most of the applicants are individuals, that is, natural persons (48%), followed by private companies (39%), and NGOs (6%).[83] The latter usually bring the case to Court on behalf of a group of individuals. For instance, in *Centraal Israëlitisch Consistorie*, a Jewish association challenged the legality of measures restricting the ritual slaughter of animals on behalf of the Jewish community in Belgium.[84]

The variety in the individual applicants mirrors the diversity of policy areas displayed in Figure 4.1: alongside company owners and farmers,[85] we find asylum seekers,[86] or benefits recipients.[87] As for the claims, unsurprisingly, there is more variety in the claims coming from private applicants: challenges to European arrest warrants,[88] instances of discrimination because of disability or religion,[89] the possible invalidity of the asylum system,[90] etc. In the cases in which the applicant is a private company, the claims mostly concern exports,

[82] For the difference between grounds and operative part applied to a model see Kálmán Pócza, Gábor Dobos, and Attila Gyulai, 'How to Measure the Strength of Judicial Decisions: A Methodological Framework' (2017) 18 German Law Journal 1557.

[83] This seems consistent with previous studies, see Damian Chalmers and Mariana Chaves, 'The Reference Points of EU Judicial Politics' (2012) 19 Journal of European Public Policy 25; López Zurita 'The survival of the Fitted?' (n 50).

[84] Case C-336/19 *Centraal Israëlitisch Consistorie van België and Others* [2020] ECLI:EU:C:2020:1031.

[85] For instance, *Volker und Markus Schecke* (n 35).

[86] Case C-601/15 PPU N. [2016] ECLI:EU:C:2016:84.

[87] Case C-363/12 Z. [2014] ECLI:EU:C:2014:159.

[88] Case C-649/19 *Spetsializirana prokuratura* [2021] ECLI:EU:C:2021:75.

[89] Case C-356/12 *Glatzel* [2014] ECLI:EU:C:2014:350.

[90] Case C-601/15 PPU N. [2016] E CLI:EU:C:2016:84.

TABLE 4.1 *Private applicants and fundamental rights in the preliminary reference procedure*

VARIABLES	PERCENTAGE (%)
Claimants	
Individual applicants	48
Private companies	39
NGOs	6
Framing of the Claim	
Framed as validity and interpretation	65
Framed solely as validity	35
Validity raised by referring court	61
Validity raised by applicant	39
Preemptive opinion by referring court	35
Order for reference contains references to FRs	80
Claim framed in FRs terms	70
framed by the applicants	39
framed by the national court	61
Fundamental Rights Treatment	
FRs analysis by the CJEU	81
minimal analysis	34
extensive analysis	55
Mention of the Charter in operative part	44
Incompatibility with EU law	20
Invalidity of the EU act	15

The table summarises the findings. The findings are organised following Section 4.4. First, the variables referring to claimants, followed by those concerned with the framing of the claim, and finally the variables concerned with the treatment of the fundamental rights component of the case. The figures in the right-hand column indicate the percentage of the total of cases (n = 54), except where the variable is in italics, where the figure shown is a percentage of the subset of cases in which the main variable is recorded. For instance, for the variable 'FRs analysis by the CJEU', the figure of 81% relates to the total number of cases, whereas the 'minimal analysis' figure (34%) is the proportion of that 81% of cases.

taxes, and licences. This corresponds neatly to the policy areas described in the figure. The two most common policy areas are approximation of laws and fundamental rights, followed by freedom of establishment and services and the Area of Freedom, Security, and Justice. It is also interesting to note that many cases have 'agriculture and fisheries' as a policy area, which has to do with the many cases concerning the Common Agricultural Policy and other EU funds,

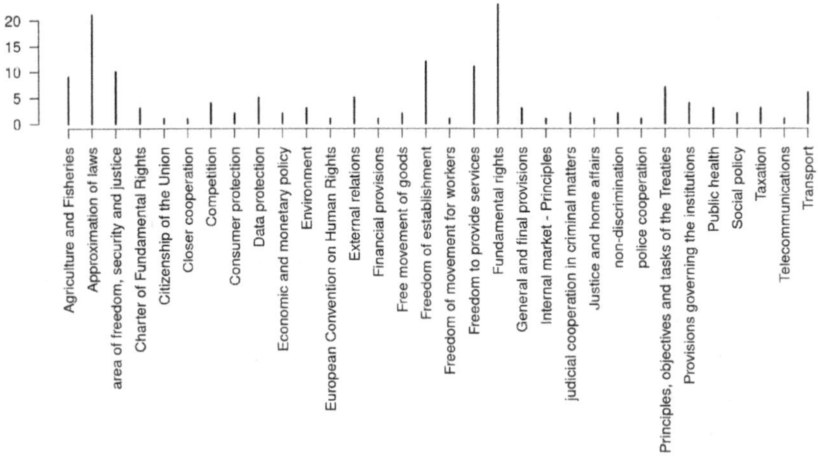

FIGURE 4.1 Policy areas of the cases in the dataset
This figure displays the policy areas of the cases in the dataset. It relies on the classification of the Court, which assigns one or more relevant policy areas to the case.

where EU decisions directly affect the legal position of the parties, including their fundamental rights.

4.5.2 *Framing of the Claim*

As for the framing, most of the references include questions on both validity and interpretation (65% compared with 5% on validity only). Issues of validity are predominantly raised by national courts (61%). Sometimes the applicant did not raise any issue of invalidity.[91] On other occasions, the applicant specifically signalled the national implementation as the origin of the breach in their fundamental rights[92] or expressly rejected the existence of any issue of validity.[93] Applicants less frequently raise the potential invalidity of the provision, and on occasion invalidity is raised as an alternative to considering the national measures compatible with EU legislation.[94]

The second aspect of the framing of the claim, as discussed in Section 4.4, concerns the use of fundamental rights, that is, whether the claim is framed as a breach of fundamental rights or the Charter is used as any other provision, without a specific fundamental rights framing. Table 4.1 shows that nearly all

91 Case C-362/14 *Schrems v Data Protection Commissioner* [2015] ECLI:EU:C:2015:650, specifically stating that the applicant did not raise invalidity.

92 Case C-1410/20 *Caracciollo* [2021] ECLI:EU:C:2021:368.

93 Case C-160/20 *Stichting Rookpreventie Jeugd*,[2022] ECLI:EU:C:2022:101.

94 Case C-336/19 *Centraal Israëlitisch Consistorie van België* [2020] ECLI:EU:C:2020:1031.

preliminary questions refer expressly to one or more provisions of the Charter (80% of cases), but a significantly lower number of claims are framed in fundamental rights terms (57%). For instance, in *Liga van Moskeeën*, the applicants do not merely refer to articles of the Charter but explicitly argue that the regulation they contest constitutes an infringement of their freedom of religion.[95]

As with invalidity arguments, national courts more frequently frame the claim as a fundamental rights breach (48% of those cases with a FRs framing) than applicants do. The right to an effective judicial remedy (Article 47 CFR) is the most referred provision in the questions, followed by the various provisions on equality and non-discrimination (Articles 20–23 CFR) and the right to the protection of personal life and data (Articles 7 and 8 CFR).

National courts include a pre-emptive opinion in 35% of cases. With few exceptions, the pre-emptive opinions argue in favour of the invalidity of the EU act and/or the existence of a breach of fundamental rights in the case. Pre-emptive opinions are overwhelmingly not followed.[96]

4.5.3 *Fundamental Rights Treatment by the Court*

Confirming previous literature in this regard,[97] the Court only exceptionally annuls the EU act (seven cases, including two of partial invalidity). For the most part, the Court annuls regulations. Moreover, in 18% of cases, the Court did not examine the validity of the EU act,[98] because it either considered that issue irrelevant or preferred to focus solely on interpretation.

With regard to the procedural treatment by the Court, some findings should be highlighted. First, and consistent with prior research,[99] stylistic reformulation is frequent in cases dealing with the validity of EU acts: the Court rewrites the questions in most cases.[100] Instances of substantive reformulation serve to consider provisions not mentioned by the national court in its order for reference,[101] reformulate questions on validity as questions on interpretation,[102] and limit the extent of the validity review conducted.[103] Secondly,

[95] Case C-426/16 *Liga van Moskeeën* [2018] ECLI:EU:C:2018:335, para 21.
[96] This is consistent with previous research, see Wallerman Ghavanini (n 48).
[97] Prechal (n 24); Lenaerts and Others (n 15); Broberg and Fenger, *Preliminary References to the European Court of Justice* (n 16).
[98] For example, in Case C-481/19 *Consob* [2021] ECLI:EU:C:2021:84.
[99] Šadl and Wallerman Ghavanini (n 70); López Zurita, 'Survival of the Fitted?' (n 50).
[100] An exception is Case C-102/16 *Vaditrans* [2017] ECLI:EU:C:2017:1012.
[101] Case C-390/15 *RPO* [2017] ECLI:EU:C:2017:174.
[102] Case C-142/20 *Caracciolo* [2021] ECLI:EU:C:2021:368.
[103] Case C-673/20 *Préfet du Gers* [2022] ECLI:EU:C:2022:449.

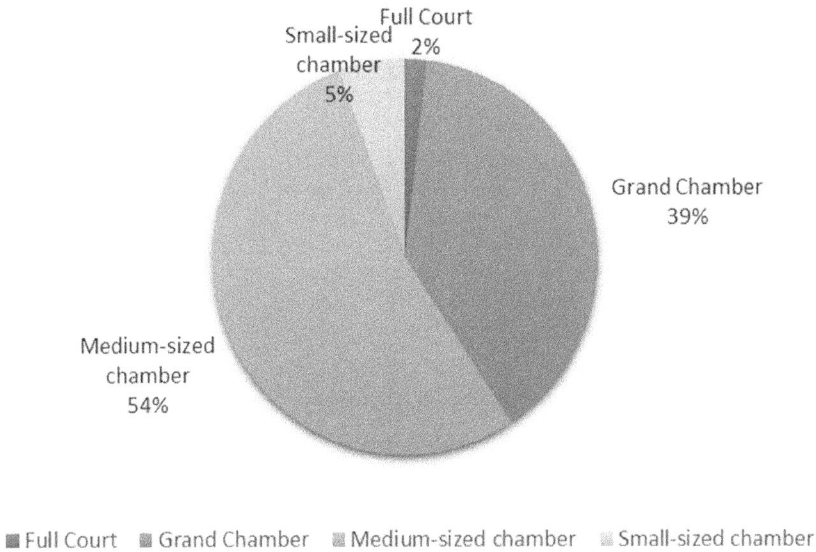

FIGURE 4.2 Case distribution among chambers
This figure shows how the cases are distributed among chambers, using the data of the Court. Over half of the cases are heard by medium-sized chambers (either five or seven judges). Nearly 40% of the cases were heard at the Grand Chamber, whereas only 2% were sent to the full court. Finally, only 5% of cases were heard by small chambers of three judges.

the Court reviews the proportionality in a little over 40% of cases. Thirdly, deference to the national courts is almost absent from the findings, and it is always part of the grounds. In other words, the Court never defers in the operative part.[104]

Finally, Figures 4.2 and 4.3 summarise some relevant information concerning the chambers in which these cases are heard and the EU institutions, organs, and bodies intervening in them. Even if the majority of cases (54%) are heard by medium-sized chambers of five or seven judges, nearly 40% of the cases are heard in the Grand Chamber. As there is no mention in those cases about any Member State's request to have the case sent to the Grand Chamber,[105] this distribution reflects the Court's own perception of the relevance of the case.[106]

[104] López Zurita and Brekke (n 71).

[105] The possibility is established in Rules of Procedure, art. 60. An analysis of the role of the Grand Chamber in Michal Bobek, 'What Are Grand Chambers For?' (2021) 23 Cambridge Yearbook of European Legal Studies 1.

[106] Hermansen (n 68).

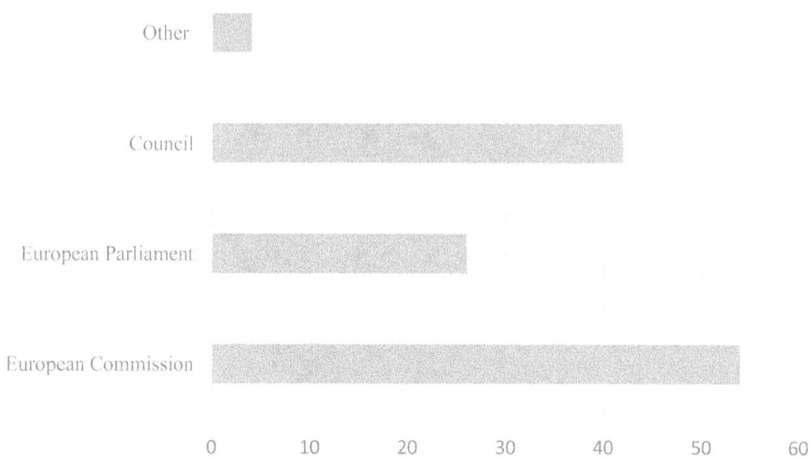

FIGURE 4.3 Intervention of EU institutions
This figure shows which EU institutions intervene in the cases in the dataset, which contains fifty-four cases. Unsurprisingly, the Commission intervenes in practically all cases. The Council intervene in over forty cases, whereas the European Parliament did the same in nearly thirty. Finally, other EU bodies and organs intervened in around five cases.

4.6 PRIVATE APPLICANTS AND FUNDAMENTAL RIGHTS IN THE PRELIMINARY REFERENCE PROCEDURE: AN ASSESSMENT

This section discusses the result of the findings in Section 4.5. As explained in Section 4.3, the focus is on private parties who bring potential breaches of their fundamental rights to the preliminary reference procedure. The section reflects, in the light of the mapping conducted above, on the possibilities, strengths, and shortcomings of the preliminary reference procedure as a means for the protection of fundamental rights that the European Union itself might have breached.

Beginning with the applicants, the findings suggest that the cases analysed concern individuals and legal persons in almost equal measure, with a slightly higher number of natural persons. It is perhaps surprising that only a very small number of cases were brought by NGOs, as it is thinkable that cases concerning the validity or compatibility of EU act are particularly prone to litigation by this type of applicant. Further research is needed to understand to what extent the individual applicants in the case may have been supported by NGOs.

The findings in Section 4.5 further suggest that private applicants, both natural and legal persons, are mostly focused on the national measures or the implementation of the EU provisions or acts at the national level. Comparatively, fewer applicants 'look behind' the implementing level and up to the EU act where the breach of their rights might have originated. National courts fill in this lacuna by pointing to the possible incompatibility of the EU act with norms of primary law, including the Charter, oftentimes with extensive pre-emptive opinions arguing the case. This happens in 61% of cases and highlights the central role of national courts within the model established by Article 267 TFEU.

The focus of private applicants on the implementing measures at the national level is entirely linked to the fact that the potential breaches concern measures of general application, most commonly secondary legislation, and particularly directives and regulations. The direct challenge of these measures is made difficult by the strict criteria of standing under Article 263 TFEU, and therefore it is only logical that the challenge comes via Article 267 TFEU.

The reliance on some sort of implementing or national measures would indicate that actions of the Union not accompanied by some sort of action at the Member State level are virtually unchallengeable via the preliminary reference procedure, and applicants would have to rely on direct actions. However, this also means that for most cases implementing measures are needed as they are the only way to gain standing to bring a case before a court under national procedural law. This indeed leaves the applicants entirely dependent on the national procedural rules to be able to eventually challenge the EU act itself.

When applicants succeed in getting a reference sent to the Court, the treatment of fundamental rights suggested by the findings is somehow puzzling. Most claims referred directly to provisions of the Charter, be it in the framing adopted by the applicants or later adopted by the referring court in its order for reference. However, fundamental rights are mostly added to the questions in the form of citations of provisions of the Charter. It is less common for the applicants to build their whole argument around a violation of their fundamental rights. What this means is that fundamental rights become a secondary part of the claim. Interestingly, the claims refer mostly to a handful of rights, which do not necessarily correspond to the areas in which the legislation of the Union, and generally acts of the Union, are expanding at present.[107] This indicates a temporal mismatch between the enactment of legislation at the EU level and its effects at the national level,

[107] Urška Šadl, Lucía López Zurita, and Sebastiano Piccolo, 'Route 66. Mutations of the Internal Market Explored through the Prism of Citation Networks' (2023) 21 International Journal of Constitutional Law 826.

which further points to the difficulties of challenging EU acts in the absence of any implementing measures.

Does the framing matter? The sample is too small to draw any definitive conclusion, but the findings suggest as much. It seems that where the claim is more clearly framed as a violation of fundamental rights, rather than just citing the Charter in the preliminary questions, the Court is more likely to declare the measure incompatible. Further research is needed to definitely establish whether this is the case and if it happens only in preliminary rulings concerned with the possible incompatibility of an EU act or provision. Furthermore, a framing of the claims in terms of fundamental rights corresponds to an extensive analysis of the fundamental rights component of the case by the Court, which is substantially less frequent where fundamental rights are not a central part of the reference.

Unsurprisingly, the Court is very reticent to annul EU acts and declared the invalidity of an EU provision only in a handful of cases. The Court prefers to focus on interpretation and measures at the national level. Generally, the findings suggest a high deference towards the EU legislator[108] where the compatibility of EU legislation with the Charter is questioned. Interestingly, the findings suggested that deference towards national courts was almost anecdotal, even when most of the cases included questions of both validity and interpretation that might have justified leaving a margin of manoeuvre to the national courts, which the Court is known to increasingly do.[109] The close connection of these cases, even if focused on interpretation, with the survival of EU acts might explain the reluctance of the Court to give any space to the national courts that might jeopardise it.

The preliminary reference procedure is not a remedy oriented to the redress of breaches suffered by private parties but rather a system of cooperation oriented towards the uniformity of the EU legal order. Section 4.3 argued that this substantially affects and (re)defines the position of the private parties in the proceedings. In cases where the compatibility of the EU legislation is at stake, this becomes particularly apparent. Two of the findings are noteworthy in this regard. First, in the vast majority of cases, at least the Commission and another institution submitted observations and participated in the oral hearings. This fact further points to the salience of the case but also highlights the secondary role of the parties once the case arrives before the Court. Indeed, the analysis of the potential breaches of fundamental rights by the Union before the Court necessarily focuses on the judicial review of legislation, and

[108] This confirms previous research on deference, see Zglinski (n 71).
[109] Ibid.

the concerns and specificities of the private parties' case become secondary. Even if this is certainly always the case in this procedure,[110] it is especially blatant when the validity of Union acts is at stake.

Secondly, almost 40% of the cases in the dataset were allocated to the Grand Chamber. This number is significant (by comparison in the whole of 2022, the Grand Chamber heard only forty-nine preliminary references). In the absence of any recorded request by the Member States to have the cases heard at the Grand Chamber, it is possible to conclude that it was a decision of the Court to hear many of these references in a Grand Chamber, which further suggests that the Court is conscious of the high salience of the cases. In other words, the Court does not perceive these cases as routine, even where the claims in most of them are fairly modest and the possible incompatibility of EU legislation with primary law only tangential to the main issue. Yet that possibility seems to be enough for the Court to allocate the cases in a high proportion to the Grand Chamber.

4.7 CONCLUSION

This chapter explored the possible use of the preliminary reference procedure as a means to challenge Union acts potentially breaching fundamental rights. It focused on the position of private applicants, both legal and natural persons. The chapter described the ways in which Article 267 TFEU allows for this type of challenge and then reflected on the limitations that the procedure poses to the legal position, capacity, and possibilities of the parties to bring forward these claims and obtain redress. It argued that these limitations are inherent to the procedure, and as such common to both preliminary references on interpretation and validity, but become particularly relevant for the latter.

Against this theoretical ground, the chapter mapped all preliminary references on validity and validity and interpretation brought by private applicants and gathered information regarding the applicants themselves, the framing of their claims, and the fundamental rights component of those references. The findings suggested that the preliminary reference procedure is, at least at present, only limitedly used to challenge Union acts for potential breaches of fundamental rights. Importantly, the findings indicate that the focus of the cases is almost always on implementing measures, however tenuous, which brings into question the feasibility of using the procedure to challenge a whole

[110] López Zurita, 'Survival of the Fitted?' (n 50).

array of cases in which measures at the national level have not yet taken place or might never occur.

At the end of the day, validity references turn into judicial review cases, in which the actual claim of the applicants becomes secondary to the check of compatibility of the EU measure against primary law. This seems inherent to the working of the procedure itself and consistent with its goal of ensuring the uniformity of the EU legal order. The context of extreme procedural freedom in which the Court operates in the preliminary reference procedure exacerbates the secondary role of the parties. However, where the action of the Union is growing, and with it its possibilities of encroaching on the lives of natural and legal persons and their fundamental rights, it is worth reflecting on whether the preliminary reference procedure can really complete the patchy system of judicial protection in the Union in this respect.

PART II

Remedies beyond the CJEU

5

Complementarity, Structure, and Ambivalence

Review Bodies' Role in Protecting Fundamental Rights

MORITZ SCHRAMM*

5.1 INTRODUCTION

Thinking about protecting fundamental rights often equals thinking about courts. Courts protect rights and are the most revered accountability forum vis-à-vis public power. This is especially so in the European Union, where fundamental rights norms and their accompanying institutions were first developed by the Court of Justice of the European Union (CJEU) and then expanded with the judicial process as the main avenue to justice in mind. However, in lockstep with the European Union's vast executive expansion since the 1990s, the EU offers much more than courts to protect fundamental rights today. In fact, a rich but underemphasised bouquet of mechanisms unfolds if one takes a closer look. Examples range from the European Ombudsman (the Ombudsman) and various Boards of Appeal (BoAs), to newly established 'Fundamental Rights Officers' (FROs) in the context of migration and asylum. Although all these bodies and mechanisms differ widely in their detail, they share a common mission: enabling – or at least pretending to enable – individuals to protect their fundamental rights. Most of their procedures are individualised and *ex post*. Typically, these bodies aim to remedy, in one form or another, fundamental rights violations attributable to the EU. Yet none of the bodies discussed here is formally a court. For lack of a better term, we may call these mechanisms *Review Bodies beyond Courts* or,

* I would like to thank Melanie Fink and Freya Schramm for their valuable feedback on earlier drafts of this chapter. Further, I benefitted from several background talks with officials working for Review Bodies who I would also like to thank for candid and illuminating conversations. Wherever the text directly reproduces information obtained in these conversations, I highlight that in a footnote. Apart from this, the usual disclaimers apply.

for short, *Review Bodies*. As an umbrella concept, Review Bodies includes all actors except courts that, upon individual petition, independently review potential fundamental rights violations by EU actors.

This chapter progresses in five steps. First, it contextualises Review Bodies as an entrenched but normatively ambivalent new normal in EU executive governance. Second, the chapter offers short portraits of each of the three types of body presented, namely the European Ombudsman, Boards of Appeal, and the newly established Fundamental Rights Officers. In general, the chapter puts particular emphasis on the FROs as these have not yet been subject to intense academic scrutiny. Third, the chapter offers a taxonomy of the Review Bodies. Structured along three axes, the section illuminates the interests the Review Bodies represent as well as their authority and expertise. Fourth, the chapter offers several possibilities for reform, most crucially that Review Bodies should team up with EU courts to combine their advantages in structure-focused expertise with the authority of the judicial process. Fifth, the chapter concludes by summarising the key takeaways.

5.2 AN AMBIVALENT NEW NORMAL

As already mentioned, thinking about fundamental rights protection and accountability often equals thinking about courts. Court-centred thinking is particularly prominent in EU law, a legal system shaped like few others by a single judicial institution.[1] Consequently, many EU lawyers might consider Review Bodies beyond the CJEU unimportant. Critics might then point either to Review Bodies' normative output, like Ombudsman reports or the FROs' recommendations, which are not legally binding. Others might dismiss Review Bodies as rather technical and specialised, like Boards of Appeal that control EU agencies' licensing of aeroplane parts, chemicals, or pharmaceuticals. Sometimes, one might even rightly say both, as, for example, the European

[1] The origins of said court-centricity might be found in Eric Stein, 'Lawyers, Judges, and the Making of a Transnational Constitution' (1981) 75 American Journal of International Law 1; but see in contrast Joseph H H Weiler, 'The Transformation of Europe' (1991) 100 The Yale Law Journal 2403, 2407. Recently, the seal might have been broken as scholars begin dragging actors beyond courts and judges into the spotlight, see Antoine Vauchez, 'The Force of a Weak Field: Law and Lawyers in the Government of the European Union (For a Renewed Research Agenda)' (2008) 2 International Political Sociology 128; Tommaso Pavone, *The Ghostwriters: Lawyers and the Politics behind the Judicial Construction of Europe* (Cambridge University Press 2022); from an international law perspective, see Fuad Zarbiyev, 'On the Judge Centredness of the International Legal Self' (2021) 32 European Journal of International Law 1139; Joost Pauwelyn and Krzysztof Pelc, 'Who Guards the "Guardians of the System"? The Role of the Secretariat in WTO Dispute Settlement' (2022) 116 American Journal of International Law 534.

Central Bank's Administrative Board of Review or the Frontex Fundamental Rights Officer cannot issue legally binding decisions but deal with highly complex and, sometimes, very fundamental rights–sensitive matters.[2]

In other words, although Review Bodies are sprinkled along the crucial junctures of EU executive power, they have a low public profile. Consequently, Review Bodies' downstream effects on the legitimacy of the Union executive are yet to be fully explored. Nonetheless, for several reasons outlined below, Review Bodies should be understood as the proliferated, important, and ambivalent new normal that they are.

5.2.1 *Complementarity and Structural Focus*

On the one hand, Review Bodies advance access to justice through two distinct features. Review Bodies *complement* but do not replace 'classic' judicial protection. Today, Review Bodies are a widespread albeit imperfect accountability mechanism complementary to actions in front of EU courts.[3] Review Bodies are complementary in the sense that formally they are neither courts nor block the path to judicial review.[4] Nonetheless, the practice of some Review Bodies, namely Boards of Appeal, could be described as adjudication, even though they are not 'courts' in the sense of EU constitutional law.[5] All Review Bodies are designed as 'independent' institutions yet belong, in one way or another, to the typical ecosystem of a contemporary administrative state.[6] Generally

[2] See Section 5.4.2.

[3] The typical judicial remedy against fundamental rights violations by EU actors is the action for annulment based on Article 263 TFEU. Further, individuals may seek damages according to Article 340 TFEU, Consolidated Version of The Treaty on the Functioning of the European Union [2016] OJ C202/47, arts 263 and 340. See further Melanie Fink, 'The Action for Damages as a Fundamental Rights Remedy: Holding Frontex Liable' (2020) 21 German Law Journal 532, 533 et seq.

[4] That aspect is emphasised by the recently reformed Article 58a(3) of the CJEU Statute, which restricted appeals from the General Court to the Court of Justice to cases that 'raise ... an issue that is significant with respect to the unity, consistency or development of Union law', Consolidated Version of the Treaty on the Functioning of the European Union Protocol (No3) on the Statute of the Court of Justice of the European Union [2016] OJ 202/210, art 58a (3). However, even though this limits review by the European Court of Justice, judicial review by the General Court is still guaranteed.

[5] The term 'adjudicate' is used here as it is understood in the United Kingdom, Canada, or Australia, i.e., referring to appellate review, not like in the United States, where adjudication may also refer to first instance decisions by administrative actors, see further Peter Cane, *Controlling Administrative Power: An Historical Comparison* (Cambridge University Press 2016) 325 et seq.

[6] See, for comparable debates in the United States, Jerry L Mashaw, *Bureaucratic Justice: Managing Social Security Disability Claims* (Yale University Press 1983).

speaking, Review Bodies have less formal authority than courts, meaning most of them cannot 'bindingly decide' or offer immediate 'relief'. This weaker formal authority then impairs Review Bodies' public authority (Boards of Appeal might be an exception here, see below). However, differences from the judicial process also offer advantages. Often, Review Bodies are specialised adjudicators, have, or at least claim to have, additional expertise compared to courts, and may entertain a more lenient standing regime than courts.[7]

Second, Review Bodies focus on *structure* and not (only) on legality.[8] Whereas courts often focus on the legality of specific executive actions in individual cases, Review Bodies have a broader, perhaps at times even better, perspective on the root causes of problematic executive behaviour. Although most Review Bodies respond to individualised complaints, their review often appears more focused on the structural practices, set-ups, and circumstances that lead to fundamental rights violations in the first place. This is important. Serious and repeated fundamental rights violations do not emerge primarily from isolated, unusual incidents. Rather, such offences reflect deeper-rooted problems entrenched in governance architectures, behavioural patterns, and organisational set-ups.[9] Against that backdrop, Review Bodies' focus on structure appears crucially important to improve EU executive governance. EU courts, aching under heavy caseloads, may, sometimes, underestimate how strongly the effective protection of fundamental rights depends on structural factors like organisation, personnel, and funding.

[7] However, the Frontex FRO's complaint mechanism highlights that a lenient standing regime does not necessarily equal broad accessibility. Access is not only a matter of legal standards but, far too often, mainly an issue of practical feasibility. See Section 5.4.2.

[8] The term 'structure' describes recurring and stabilised sets of practices within organisational contexts. These practices can be or touch upon anything from internal norms or formal rules to explicit and public procedures or institutions. For the sociological foundations, see Pierre Bourdieu, *Outline of a Theory of Practice* (Cambridge University Press 1977) 72 et seq; highlighting the difference of *formal* structures to internal practice, see John W Meyer and Brian Rowan, 'Institutionalized Organizations: Formal Structure as Myth and Ceremony' (1977) 83 American Journal of Sociology 340 (in that sense, many of the phenomena described here as 'structural root causes for fundamental rights violations' are 'practice' in the sense of Meyer and Rowan or, to borrow their words, '*informal* structures'); for a focus on 'structure' as root causes of fundamental rights violations, see, e.g., Daniel Halberstam and Sina von der Boegart, 'A Fresh Look at Judicial Remedies in EU Equality Law and Beyond: The Untapped Possibility of Structural Injunctions' [2023] Michigan Law Public Law and Legal Theory Research Paper Series 2–3.

[9] Insightful from a historical and comparative perspective: Lani Guinier, 'From Racial Liberalism to Racial Literacy: Brown v. Board of Education and the Interest-Divergence Dilemma' (2004) 91 Journal of American History 92.

5.2.2 *Functional Differentiation*

On the other hand, Review Bodies reflect the ongoing functional differentiation of EU law.[10] Europe faces inherently globalised and transnational challenges that cannot be effectively met domestically. Markets, digitisation, the climate crisis – the key to, somehow, successfully approaching these issues lies, also, in EU law. Thus, EU law will deal with more and more issues, each more complicated than the next. 'Dealing' with these issues then regularly spawns complex normative material and novel institutions.[11] Between the 1990s and the late 2010s, inspired by New Public Management and alongside the overall ascent of 'governance', these novel institutions were typically 'agencies'.[12] However, agencies still need accountability, especially when vested with the power to make legally binding decisions in highly complex and financially sensitive matters. Thus, to protect (fundamental) rights and control these agencies, Review Bodies beyond courts became, in one form or another, the 'tool of choice for European lawmakers'.[13] As a rule of thumb, Review Bodies emerge wherever the EU exerts administrative power over individuals or legal persons. The more specialised an area, the more likely we will encounter a Review Body.

[10] For a rich description of that process see Curtin, who, under the topos of 'fragmentation' highlights that EU law 'expands and diversifies in terms both of its objects and its techniques'; Deirdre Curtin, 'From a Europe of Bits and Pieces to a Union of Variegated Differentiation' in Paul P Craig and Gráinne De Búrca (eds), *The Evolution of EU Law* (Oxford University Press 2021) 373. For a critique of the concept of 'governance' in its European context, see Christoph Möllers, 'European Governance: Meaning and Value of a Concept' (2006) 43 Common Market Law Review 313.

[11] Typifying that normative material and the emerging institutions often operates on a rather coarse level. Regularly, novel EU norms and institutions reflect what is believed to be effective in a specific substantive area but not what would fit an overarching theoretical canon. In that sense, understanding how those diverse actors are structured and how they exercise power is even more crucial. For an illuminating and comprehensive analysis of the EU's burgeoning executive power, see Deirdre Curtin, *Executive Power of the European Union: Law, Practices, and the Living Constitution* (Oxford University Press 2009).

[12] On the historical context of the Union's 'agencification', see Merijn Chamon, *EU Agencies: Legal and Political Limits to the Transformation of the EU Administration* (Oxford University Press 2016) 45 et seq; Edoardo Chiti, 'The Agencification Process and the Evolution of the EU Administrative System' in Craig and De Búrca (eds), *The Evolution of EU Law* (Oxford University Press 2021) 123 et seq.

[13] Speaking of EU agencies regulating the financial sector: Marco Lamandini and David Ramos Muñoz, 'Law and Practice of Financial Appeal Bodies (ESAs' Board of Appeal, SRB Appeal Panel): A View from the Inside' (2020) 57 Common Market Law Review 119, 120. For a comprehensive overview of the genesis and current state of such Boards of Appeal, see Merijn Chamon, Annalisa Volpato, and Mariolina Eliantonio (eds), *Boards of Appeal of EU Agencies: Towards Judicialization of Administrative Review?* (Oxford University Press 2022).

In principle, that is a very positive development. The very existence of Review Bodies points to a crucial legitimacy asset of the European Union: self-control.[14] Even as the Union's administrative power diversifies and complicates, it does not do so in an 'uncontrolled' manner as some demagogues or critics might argue. In contrast, the Union's executive expansion remains chaperoned by various guardians, some in Luxembourg, others spread all over the continent.

5.2.3 *Tripartite Government*

Further, the functional differentiation of the Union's executive power has a crucial but undertheorised side effect: it challenges a traditional reading of the notion of tripartite government.[15] Most Review Bodies do not 'organically' fit into broad categories like executive or judicial. Expressed in the reverse, Review Bodies' low public profile is partly owing to the fact that they challenge these widespread 'organic' understandings of the separation of powers in

[14] See esp. Peter L Lindseth, *Power and Legitimacy: Reconciling Europe and the Nation-State* (Oxford University Press 2010) 253 et seq; see further recently Matthias Ruffert, *Law of Administrative Organization of the EU: A Comparative Approach* (Edward Elgar 2020). For the concept of 'legitimacy assets', see Ingo Venzke and Joana Mendes, 'The Idea of Relative Authority in European and International Law' (2018) 16 International Journal of Constitutional Law 75; Joana Mendes and Ingo Venzke (eds), *Allocating Authority: Who Should Do What in European and International Law?* (Hart 2018).

[15] In domestic (and international) contexts, some argue that such institutions should be understood as a new 'fourth branch' complementing the legislative, executive, and judicial branch. That fourth branch's distinctive characteristic would be its 'independence' from the political process and pro-active fostering of pre-set goals and values, e.g., protecting electoral fairness, the environment, or preventing maladministration. Although it is evident that many contemporary phenomena do not fit an organ-focused reading of Montesquieu, it seems unclear whether the idea of a 'fourth branch' easily fits the European Union. After all, the Union's level of democratic accountability lags behind that of most democratic states and, crucially, itself follows a somewhat value and goal-oriented trajectory ('an ever-closer Union'). In other words, squeezing the EU into an inherently state-centred model of three branches (and not, say, various balanced functions and institutions) risks overlooking its distinctive genealogy and mode of operation. The original notion can be found in Montesquieu, *The Spirit of the Laws* (1748) XI.6; See further Bruce Ackermann, 'Good-Bye, Montesquieu' in Susan Rose-Ackerman, Blake Emerson, and Peter L Lindseth (eds), *Comparative Administrative Law* (2nd edn, Edward Elgar 2017); Tarunabh Khaitan, 'Guarantor Institutions' (2021) 16 Asian Journal of Comparative Law 1; Mark V Tushnet, *The New Fourth Branch: Institutions for Protecting Constitutional Democracy* (Cambridge University Press 2021); Antoine Vauchez, 'The Genie of Independence and the European Bottle: How Independence Became Europe's Most Contentious Legal and Political Category' (2022) 20 International Journal of Constitutional Law 1; arguing for an updated understanding of the notion of tripartite government, see Christoph Möllers, *The Three Branches: A Comparative Model of Separation of Powers* (Oxford University Press 2013).

the European Union. This aspect is particularly relevant for Boards of Appeal. They adjudicate but are nonetheless not formal courts. Intuitively, many still conceptualise tripartite government, or, in other words, the separation of powers, as a distinct separation of institutions or, to borrow from Koen Lenaerts, 'organs' (i.e., parliament, ministerial bureaucracy, courts).[16] Review Bodies transgress such a model of distinct branches of government. For example, Review Bodies may be not formally judicial but nonetheless adjudicate. Equally, they may be 'organically' executive but (largely) independent of political control. However, as Lenaerts argued, 'an organic understanding of the separation of powers is not practicable in the European Community.... In view of this, the understanding of the separation of powers principle should not in the first place be an organic one, but a functional one'.[17] This is important. Review Bodies offer accountability and, at least in the case of Boards of Appeal, do so in a quintessentially adjudicative fashion. The fact that no BoA is considered a court under Union law seems therefore puzzling. Consequentially, many argue that BoAs would be 'administrative in nature' and are 'not judicial bodies' because, inter alia, many currently do not live up to the standards established by the right to an effective remedy as enshrined in Article 47 Charter of Fundamental Rights of the European Union (CFR).[18] From an institutionalist – or 'organic' to use Koen Lenaert's words – reading of the principle of tripartite government this makes sense.

However, simultaneously, the same string of literature considers BoAs increasingly 'judicialized'.[19] Only a functionalist perspective explains what otherwise appears to be a contradiction. On the one hand, judicial functions may very well be embedded into administrative organisational contexts. From a comparative and historical perspective, this is even the norm rather than the exception. Many legal regimes feature guardian institutions that are not part of the judiciary but nonetheless adjudicate executive power.[20] In turn, judicial

[16] Koen Lenaerts, 'Some Reflections on the Separation of Powers in the European Community' (1991) 28 Common Market Law Review 11, 12–13.

[17] Referring mainly to legislative and executive powers but the argument also works, mutatis mutandis, for the Union's judicial function (esp. regarding Boards of Appeal), see ibid.

[18] Charter of Fundamental Rights of the European Union [2016] OJ C202/389; see, e.g., Merijn Chamon, Annalisa Volpato, and Mariolina Eliantonio, 'Conclusion' in Merijn Chamon, Annalisa Volpato, and Mariolina Eliantonio (eds), *Boards of Appeal of EU Agencies: Towards Judicialization of Administrative Review?* (Oxford University Press 2022) 323–324.

[19] Ibid 323.

[20] Examples abound in many common law jurisdictions, such as so-called legislative courts or Article I tribunals in the United States or administrative tribunals in the United Kingdom or Australia. From the rich literature, see Cane *Controlling Administrative Power* (n 5) 325 et seq; Peter Cane, *Administrative Tribunals and Adjudication* (Hart 2010); Michael Asimov, 'Five Models of Administrative Adjudication' (2015) 63 The American Journal of Comparative Law

review of administrative action historically developed 'organically' (largely) out of the executive branch and not from courts or the judicial branch, the example of France being the most illustrious one.[21] Therefore, conceptualising the overall 'nature' of a phenomenon in stylised categories like 'administrative' or 'judicial' risks obscuring rather than elucidating the phenomenon's actual operation.[22] On the other hand, the argument that a Review Body cannot be 'judicial' because it does not sufficiently comply with (the CJEU's reading of) the criteria of effective remedies in Article 47 CFR can be turned on its head. Maybe BoAs indeed operate in quite a 'judicial' way – hence the inevitable discussions about 'judicialization' – but are imperfect and need reform to comply with their normative goal, that is, providing an effective remedy. Simply put, non-compliance with Article 47 CFR does not render BoAs 'administrative in nature' but imperfect to fulfil their adjudicative function.

5.2.4 *The Peril of Ceremony*

Lastly, Review Bodies are important yet ambivalent in terms of legitimacy as they cloak the Union's burgeoning transnational executive in publicly legitimising notions of accountability and rights protection. Review Bodies reflect increasingly institutionalised narratives of 'accountability', 'transparency', and 'good governance'.[23] Therefore, Review Bodies have diffused as a 'quick fix' to accountability deficits and, by extension, legitimacy deficits in the EU executive.[24]

3; for the US debate, see James E Pfander, 'Article I Tribunals, Article III Courts, and the Judicial Power of the United States' (2004) 118 Harvard Law Review 643; Richard H Fallon, 'Of Legislative Courts, Administrative Agencies, and Article III' (1988) 101 Harvard Law Review 915; William Baude, 'Adjudication Outside Article III' (2020) 133 Harvard Law Review 1511.

[21] See esp. France's strict reading of Montesquieu and the consequential narrow '*fonctions judicaires*', cf. John Bell and François Lichère, *Contemporary French Administrative Law* (Cambridge University Press 2022) 61 et seq.

[22] Further, notions like 'court' or 'judicial' are inherently context-dependent and multifaceted. See esp. Mauro Cappelletti, *The Judicial Process in Comparative Perspective* (Clarendon Press 1989) 217 et seq; see also famously Martin M Shapiro, *Courts, a Comparative and Political Analysis* (University of Chicago Press 1981).

[23] Seminal on the formative power of institutionalised practices and narratives for organisational structures: Meyer and Rowan (n 8). Critical of the narrative of 'governance': Möllers 'European Governance' (n 10).

[24] See the illuminating literature on policy diffusion started by D Eleanor Westney, *Imitation and Innovation The Transfer of Western Organizational Patterns to Meiji Japan* (Harvard University Press 1987); and later picked up by Beth A Simmons, Frank Dobbin, and Geoffrey Garrett (eds), *The Global Diffusion of Markets and Democracy* (Cambridge University Press 2008) (see

However, the extent to which Review Bodies indeed deliver on their promises of expertise, independence, and '(administrative) justice' is not always clear. Review Bodies' faint authority, reliance on non-binding measures, relatively scant funding, and low public profile might impede their ability to effectively identify and weigh into the root causes of recurring offences. Then, Review Bodies would not complement judicial accountability but remain timid bystanders. In such a case, the very existence of a Review Body might even thwart long-term improvement, as an existing but ultimately 'toothless' Review Body might bolster the false impression of accountability. Submitting complaints to a Review Body could then be understood as mere ceremony, without real-world effects.[25] Thereby, Review Bodies might disguise scarcely accountable, rights-endangering governance. For example, the recent trend to establish 'Fundamental Rights Officers' in the area of migration could be criticised as partly ceremonial. For more than a decade now, we have been aware of the 'systemic' problems in some Member States and, arguably, also the Union's own executive structures.[26] Establishing a new but rather weak institution, the FROs, to make serious and systemic fundamental rights abuses more transparent instead of overhauling the structures that lead to these offences, might have been the only politically feasible compromise. However, from a normative perspective, such Realpolitik may end up delivering only a ceremonial mimicry of justice but neither structural improvement nor effective remedy in individual cases.

The risks of that trend are palpable. Setting up new, perhaps merely ceremonial institutions instead of addressing deeper rooted governance problems perpetuates, rather than remedies structural flaws. Eventually, this may trade the public appearance of accountability and rights protection for the erosion of substantive legitimacy, which hinges upon effective – and not merely ceremonial – accountability and rights protection.

esp. the part about emulation at 31–40); Charles R Shipan and Craig Volden, 'The Mechanisms of Policy Diffusion' (2008) 52 American Journal of Political Science 840.

[25] I use the term 'ceremonial' as understood in neo-institutionalist organisation theory, see esp. the influential work by Meyer and Rowan (n 8).

[26] See, for various examples, Case C-4/11 *Bundesrepublik Deutschland v Kaveh Puid (Systemic Deficiencies in Greece)* [2013] ECLI:EU:C:2013:740; Nick Waters, Emmanuel Freudenthal, and Logan Williams, 'Frontex at Fault: European Border Force Complicit in "Illegal" Pushbacks' (*Bellingcat*, 23 October 2020) <www.bellingcat.com/news/2020/10/23/frontex-at-fault-european-border-force-complicit-in-illegal-pushbacks/>; Stefanos Levidis and Others, 'Drift-Backs in the Aegean Sea' (*Forensic Architecture*, 15 July 2022) <https://forensic-architecture.org/investigation/drift-backs-in-the-aegean-sea>; Melanie Fink and Jorrit J Rijpma, 'The Management of the European Union's External Borders' in Evangelina Tsourdi and Philippe De Bruycker (eds), *Research Handbook on EU Migration and Asylum Law* (Edward Elgar 2022).

5.2.5 *Interim Conclusion*

To summarise, Review Bodies exist in almost any administrative context. In court-focused systems like the EU, they reflect functional differentiation, complementing the accountability mechanisms provided by EU courts through offering more specialised, more structure-focused, or more accessible forums to challenge the Union's burgeoning executive power. Yet some Review Bodies may be more of a 'quick fix', responding to current discourses about transparency and accountability instead of establishing stringent protection of fundamental rights. Review Bodies with weak authority in particular risk remaining ceremonial actors advancing the perception but with no actual practice of legitimating accountability and rights protection. Today, Review Bodies are an ambivalent new normal in a Union that increasingly transcends its traditional executive federalism and incrementally morphs into a multifaceted administrative behemoth.

5.3 SHORT PORTRAITS

After that general context, we now briefly portray the three types of Review Bodies presented in this chapter. These bodies are, first, the European Ombudsman; second, specialised Review Bodies attached to agencies, typically called 'Boards of Appeal'; and third, the relatively novel Fundamental Rights Officers that, among other things, enable complaints about potential fundamental rights violations through EU agencies at the Union's borders.

5.3.1 *The European Ombudsman*

The European Ombudsman, established in 1995, follows the most generalist approach of all Review Bodies presented here.[27] According to Article 228(1) Treaty on the Functioning of the European Union (TFEU), the 'European Ombudsman' shall investigate and remedy 'maladministration' by the European Union. Individuals may file complaints with the Ombudsman to investigate specific administrative proceedings. Further, the Ombudsman may conduct investigations of its own, called 'own initiative inquiries' as well as

[27] From the rich literature on the European Ombudsman, see esp. Michał Krajewski, *Relative Authority of Judicial and Extra-Judicial Review: EU Courts, Boards of Appeal, Ombudsman* (Hart 2021) 139 et seq; Anne Peters, 'The European Ombudsman and the European Constitution' (2005) 42 Common Market Law Review 697; Anchrit Wille and Mark Bovens, 'Watching EU Watchdogs Assessing the Accountability Powers of the European Court of Auditors and the European Ombudsman' (2022) 44 Journal of European Integration 183.

'strategic inquiries'.[28] The latter two often focus on suspected structural problems such as Frontex's handling of transparency and accountability.[29] The Ombudsman's key advantage vis-à-vis most other Review Bodies is its welcoming standing regime.[30] While other Review Bodies require *Plaumann*-inspired, neatly individualised standing requirements, the Ombudsman is open to complaints from almost anyone dealing with the EU administration.[31] Further, the Ombudsman's mandate is also general in the temporal dimension. While most individual complaints seek to remedy past maladministration, the Ombudsman, ex officio, may also investigate more political, ongoing matters of general concern.[32]

5.3.2 *Boards of Appeal*

The biggest and most diverse group of Review Bodies beyond courts are Boards of Appeal (for short, as introduced above, 'BoAs').[33] Terminologically, 'Boards of Appeal' is an imperfect umbrella term as most but not all such bodies go by that name.[34] To avoid overly complicating things, we will however stick to the term. In a broad sense, Boards of Appeal are specialised, independent bodies that review agency actions vis-à-vis individual and legal persons.[35] Although

28 See further Wille and Bovens (n 27) 193–194.

29 For the former, see European Ombudsman Case OI/1/2021/KR *Revolving Door* (16 May 2022) <https://europa.eu/!c46qcF>; for the latter, see European Ombudsman Case OI/4/2021/MHZ *Frontex* (17 January 2022) <https://europa.eu/!3q7bvM>.

30 See, in that sense also, Krajewski, *Relative Authority of Judicial and Extra-Judicial Review* (n 27) 145.

31 See comprehensively ibid 163 et seq.

32 ibid 142 et seq.

33 See Chamon, Volpato, and Eliantonio (n 13); Krajewski, *Relative Authority of Judicial and Extra-Judicial Review* (n 27) 103 et seq; Paola Chirulli and Luca De Lucia, *Non-Judicial Remedies and EU Administration: Protection of Rights versus Preservation of Autonomy* (Routledge 2021) 103 et seq.

34 For example, the Single Resolution Board's board of appeal is called Appeal Panel, cf. Regulation (EU) 806/2014 of the European Parliament and of the Council of 15 July 2014 establishing uniform rules and a uniform procedure for the resolution of credit institutions and certain investment firms in the framework of a Single Resolution Mechanism and a Single Resolution Fund and amending Regulation (EU) No 1093/2010 [2014] OJ L225/1, art 85(1).

35 The first agency for which a Board of Appeal was created was the EU Intellectual Property Office (EUIPO) in 1994. Interestingly, that first board of appeal followed a private law arbitration model that can be traced back to a 1973 international convention on patents. The second agency to get its own board of appeal was the Community Plant Variety Office (CPVO), which was modelled on the EUIPO. Then, in a classic example of policy diffusion, other decision-making agencies followed suit – even though their practice and organisational set-ups differed fundamentally to the EUIPO and the CPVO. These agencies were the European Aviation Safety Agency (EASA); the European Chemicals Agency (ECHA); the

their precise authority, mandate, and institutional practices differ, all Boards of Appeal offer appellants an independent second look at the facts and law of each case.[36] Typically, BoA decisions are legally binding.[37]

Recent reforms of the statute of the Court of Justice elevated BoAs' institutional status. Since 2019, the Court of Justice does not hear cases reviewed already by the 'independent board(s) of appeal' of four specified agencies and the General Court, unless they touch upon foundational issues. Thereby, four BoAs – namely those attached to the European Union Intellectual Property Office, the Community Plant Variety Office, the European Chemicals Agency, and the European Union Aviation Safety Agency – effectively became first instance adjudicators below the General Court. However, for the time being, the EU has refrained from rebranding these BoAs as specialised courts according to Article 257 TFEU.[38] Much in the same vein, the General Court underscored the adjudicative function of BoAs in 2019, when it applied Article 47 CFR instead of the much lower standards of Article 41 CFR to a BoA for the first time.[39] In the medium term, this might trigger procedural reforms at the BoAs. Whether those will be for the better remains to be seen. Some BoAs follow an inquisitorial model, which is typical (and sensible) for adjudicative review of administrative actors but at odds with the otherwise adversarially structured EU judicial process.[40]

European Agency for the Cooperation of Energy Regulators (ACER); three agencies supervising financial and prudential services, the so-called European Supervisory Authorities (ESAs) with one joint board of appeal; the EU's central banking resolution authority; the Single Resolution Board (SRB), whose board of appeal is called 'Appeals Panel'; and the European Railways Authority (ERA). For the historical context, see Hanf, who rightly highlights that especially the first two boards of appeal were 'legal transplants' with a 'very particular nature' as they dealt with private parties and are thus structurally different to most other adjudicative guardians of public power, cf. Dominik Hanf, 'The Trailblazers: The Boards of Appeal of EUIPO and CPVO' in Merijn Chamon, Annalisa Volpato, and Mariolina Eliantonio (eds), *Boards of Appeal of EU Agencies: Towards Judicialization of Administrative Review?* (Oxford University Press 2022) 60, 78.

36 Cf. Merijn Chamon, Annalisa Volpato, and Mariolina Eliantonio, 'Introduction' in Merijn Chamon, Annalisa Volpato, and Mariolina Eliantonio (eds), *Boards of Appeal of EU Agencies* (Oxford University Press 2022) 3–4.

37 For the one exception, the European Central Bank's Administrative Board of Review, see Section 5.3.2.

38 See further Jacopo Alberti, 'The Position of Boards of Appeal: Between Functional Continuity and Independence' in Merijn Chamon and Mariolina Eliantonio (eds), *Boards of Appeal of EU Agencies* (Oxford University Press 2022).

39 See Case T-755/17 *Germany v ECHA* [2019] ECLI:EU:T:2019:647.

40 See, in that regard, also Krajewski, *Relative Authority of Judicial and Extra-Judicial Review* (n 27) 117 et seq.

5.3.3 *Fundamental Rights Officers*

The newest and perhaps most peculiar type of Review Bodies are Fundamental Rights Officers (for short, as introduced above, 'FROs'). FROs are attached to the two agencies dealing with migration, namely the European Border and Coast Guard Agency, commonly known as Frontex, and the European Union Agency for Asylum (EUAA), which is a vastly expanded version of the European Asylum Support Office.[41] Fundamental Rights Officers emerged as new institutions in the 2010s in response to increasing concerns about the fundamental rights record of the Union's border regime.[42] In the law and 'governance' of asylum in and migration to Europe, traditional 'executive federalism' gave way to ad hoc, make-shift arrangements veiled by diffused responsibilities, informality, and externalisation.[43] One

[41] See Regulation (EU) 2019/1896 of the European Parliament and of the Council of 13 November 2019 on the European Border and Coast Guard and repealing Regulations (EU) No 1052/2013 and (EU) 2016/1624 [2019] OJ L295/1 (EBCG Regulation), arts 109 and 111; Regulation (EU) 2021/2303 of the European Parliament and of the Council of 15 December 2021 on the European Union Agency for Asylum and repealing Regulation (EU) No 439/2010 [2021] OJ L468/1 (European Asylum Agency Regulation) arts 49 and 51.

[42] In fact, it was the European Ombudsman that recommended the establishment of individual review mechanisms to Frontex as early as 2013 (and again in 2015). However, the agency did not act upon these recommendations. Only the 2019 overhaul of the EBCG Regulation expanded the role of the already existing – but at that point entirely marginalised – FRO and introduced a complaint mechanism. These institutional reforms, albeit imperfect, can be seen as productive interplay of structure-focused review by the Ombudsman and mounting political outrage over apparent fundamental rights abuses. The reformed EBCG Regulation explicitly alludes to the agency's 'extended tasks' that 'should be balanced with strengthened fundamental rights safeguards' (recital 24) and that it was necessary to 'monitor ... the respect for fundamental rights in the border management and return activities of the agency' (recital 42), EBCG Regulation, recitals 24 and 42. For further historical context on FROs, see Marco Stefan and Leonhard den Hertog, 'Frontex: Great Powers but No Appeals' in Merijn Chamon, Annalisa Volpato, and Mariolina Eliantonio (eds), *Boards of Appeal of EU Agencies: Towards Judicialization of Administrative Review?* (Oxford University Press 2022) 151, 158–159.

[43] See, e.g., Loïc Azoulai and K M de Vries (eds), *EU Migration Law: Legal Complexities and Political Rationales* (Oxford University Press 2014); Violeta Moreno Lax, *Accessing Asylum in Europe: Extraterritorial Border Controls and Refugee Rights under EU Law* (Oxford University Press 2017); Melanie Fink, *Frontex and Human Rights: Responsibility in 'Multi-Actor Situations' under the ECHR and EU Public Liability Law* (Oxford University Press 2018); Juan Santos Vara and Laura Pascual Matellán, 'The Informalization of EU Return Policy: A Change of Paradigm in Migration Cooperation with Third Countries?' in Eva Kassoti and Narin Idriz (eds), *The Informalisation of the EU's External Action in the Field of Migration and Asylum* (Springer 2022) 37 et seq; Aysel Küçüksu, 'Adjudicating Asylum as a Technical Matter at the Court of Justice of the European Union: Neglecting Human Rights When the CEAS Appears to Be in Jeopardy?' in Eva Kassoti and Narin Idriz (eds), *The Informalisation of the EU's External Action in the Field of Migration and Asylum* (Springer 2022) 169 et seq. From a comparative and normative perspective, see already Thomas Gammeltoft-Hansen and James C Hathaway, 'Non-Refoulement in a World of Cooperative Deterrence' (2015) 53 Columbia Journal of Transnational Law 235.

result of these tendencies is an overall lack of properly working review mechanisms, especially at the EU border itself.[44]

FROs shall be 'independent in the performance of his or her duties' and 'shall be responsible for ensuring the Agency's compliance with fundamental rights in all its activities'.[45] FROs' existence reflects the – tacit – acknowledgement that there is a structural problem with fundamental rights abuses in European migration governance.

Apart from overseeing and advising their respective agencies in fundamental rights matters, FROs are 'responsible for handling' complaints by individuals who are adversely affected by the respective agency.[46] Remarkably, the Frontex FRO is even responsible for helping the agency to 'set up and further develop' its complaint mechanism.[47] That is potentially a significant divergence from common practice in other fields, where one would assume that procedures to protect fundamental rights are thoroughly detailed in law and not incrementally developed in internal rules, guidelines, and practices.

5.4 A TAXONOMY OF REVIEW BODIES' CHARACTERISTICS

As already mentioned, Review Bodies differ significantly in terms of their characteristics. Therefore, a taxonomy of these characteristics clarifies the strengths and weaknesses of each body. Three axes structure the taxonomy. The first axis marks what could be described as a Review Body's *orientation*. Does a Review Body focus on remedying individual grievances, like a court, or more on the public interest, like the European Ombudsman. The second axis is the most complex. It describes the reflexive interplay of a Review Body's legal and political *authority* with the kinds of *measures* it takes. Boards of Appeal, for example, are vested with the authority to bindingly adjudicate, a kind of measure the other Review Bodies lack. In turn, other bodies may operationalise other measures, such as public reports, political pressure, or internal discourse to influence the course of action of EU executive actors. Inevitably, authority beyond formal mechanisms like adjudication builds over

44 The European Court of Human Rights explicitly held that in Greek 'hot spots' for asylum seekers, Greece and, by implicit extension, the EU do not provide remedies that are 'available in theory and in practice . . . and capable of providing redress', *A.D. v Greece*, App no 55363/19 (ECtHR, 4 April 2023) paras 23–24.

45 European Asylum Agency Regulation, arts 49(2) and (3); see also, however with less emphasis on the officers' independence EBCG Regulation, art 109(4).

46 EBCG Regulation, art 111(4); European Asylum Agency Regulation, art 51(4).

47 EBCG Regulation, art 111(1); See further Sarah Tas, 'Frontex Actions: Out of Control?' 2020 TARN Working Paper 03/2020 11–15.

time and remains contingent on a wide range of contextual factors. Lastly, the third axis looks at the kind of *expertise* Review Bodies provide – here we can distinguish between substantive and organisational expertise – and their *financial resources*.

5.4.1 *Orientation towards Public or Individual Interest*

The first axis distinguishes between Review Bodies oriented mainly towards protecting individual interests and those looking out more for the public interest. Albeit remedying individual interests advances the rule of law and, thereby, also the public interest, distinguishing individual interest–oriented bodies from public interest–oriented bodies offers analytical value. In particular, variations in standing regimes are best understood as tailored towards the needs of reviewing public or individual interests.[48] For example, BoAs review individual agency decisions vis-à-vis individual natural or legal persons. In these procedures, BoAs may nullify the agency decision and, depending on the BoA's authority, even replace it with their own decision. Such a procedure serves, predominantly, individual interests, that is, the exercise of property rights. Because of this individual interest orientation, standing requirements before Boards of Appeal reflect those before formal EU courts.[49] In contrast, European Ombudsman proceedings, even when initiated by individual complaints, generally also look towards improving the administrative procedures that led to individual instances of maladministration in the first place. Since the European Ombudsman cannot nullify or otherwise bindingly interfere with the EU executive but seeks to generally advance good administration, standing requirements to file a complaint to the European Ombudsman are very lenient: any EU citizen or resident may file complaints about any 'instance of maladministration' by the EU.[50]

The Fundamental Rights Officers operate somewhere in between these two positions. On the one hand, FROs' main task is to advise and oversee their respective agency's fundamental rights track record. Their oversight is independent of individual petitions and is more reminiscent of the Fundamental

48 See in that sense also Krajewski, *Relative Authority of Judicial and Extra-Judicial Review* (n 27) 144 et seq passim.

49 Cf. ibid 125 et seq.

50 Regulation (EU, Euratom) 2021/1163 of the European Parliament of 24 June 2021 laying down the regulations and general conditions governing the performance of the Ombudsman's duties (Statute of the European Ombudsman) and repealing Decision 94/262/ECSC, EC, Euratom [2021] OJ L253/1 (Statute of the European Ombudsman), art 2(1).

Rights Agency's mandate.[51] On the other hand, Fundamental Rights Officers are also 'responsible for handling complaints' vis-à-vis the agencies.[52] Against Frontex, such complaints may be filed by 'anyone who is directly affected' by the 'actions or failure to act on the part of staff involved in [e.g.] a joint operation'.[53] Many such operations aim to remove or exclude individuals from EU territory. Although this might not formally exclude those individuals from EU jurisdiction, physical absence from EU territory complicates or practically prevents the exercise of EU fundamental rights.[54] Hence, the complaint mechanisms' practical feasibility remains questionable. In 2021, only twenty-seven complaints were filed, only six of which were deemed admissible.[55]

5.4.2 *Authority and Measures*

Perhaps the most decisive characteristic of each Review Body is its authority. Authority is important to effectively remedy fundamental rights violations and is closely related to the type of measures a Review Body takes. The introduction anticipated that, typically, we consider courts to be *the* guardians of fundamental rights. Consequently, the typical measure to remedy fundamental rights violations would be a judgment, that is, a legally binding normative act issued by a judicial institution to decide an individual case. However, courts already operate with various other normative tools, such as settlements or more structure-oriented forms of judicial control.[56] Since most Review Bodies cannot adjudicate, BoAs being again the exception, the European Ombudsman or Fundamental Rights Officers use various tools to exert oversight and (attempt to) remedy fundamental rights violations. Since the Review Bodies presented here complement the Union's judicial process, their measures are often distinctly different to those obtainable in court. Nevertheless, we

[51] In fact, there are even personal continuities from the Fundamental Rights Agency to Frontex's Fundamental Rights Officer, who formerly worked for the Fundamental Rights Agency.

[52] EBCG Regulation, art 111(4); European Asylum Agency Regulation, art 51(4).

[53] EBCG Regulation, art 111(2); mutatis mutandis, European Asylum Agency Regulation, art 51 (2) mirrors the EBCG Regulation's language.

[54] Territory and space are not the only denominators used to subtly govern migration flows. Another element is time. See Floris de Witte, 'Here Be Dragons: Legal Geography and EU Law' (2022) 1 European Law Open 113; Martijn Stronks, *Grasping Legal Time: Temporality and European Migration Law* (Cambridge University Press 2022).

[55] Frontex Fundamental Rights Officer, Annual Report 2021 (Frontex FRO 2021), 26.

[56] See foundationally Abram Chayes, 'The Role of the Judge in Public Law Litigation' (1976) 89 Harvard Law Review 1281; Judith Resnik, 'Managerial Judges' (1982) 96 Harvard Law Review 374; for EU law, see recently the proposal by Halberstam and von der Boegart (n 8).

shall use a court judgment as a reference point to illustrate the kinds of measures Review Bodies might take.

We begin with those bodies that appear like the EU courts' extended family: Boards of Appeal. BoAs share many characteristics with 'classic' (whatever that means) judicial institutions. Often conceptualised as 'quasi-judicial', many Boards of Appeal are vested with the authority to issue legally binding decisions.[57] Depending on the respective BoA's procedural framework, its decisions may nullify or entirely replace agency decisions. However, in practice, BoAs' authority varies greatly.[58] Although various specialised Review Bodies have emerged in EU governance, only some have generated meaningful amounts of case law over the years, while others show only a very marginal, perhaps even declining influx of cases.

One particularly peculiar member of that extended family is the 'Administrative Board of Review' that oversees the European Central Bank's supervisory function. Just like BoAs, the Administrative Board of Review offers independent, specialised review.[59] However, unlike 'classic' Boards of Appeal, the Administrative Board of Review only 'express[es] an opinion' that is not legally binding.[60] Nonetheless, one could argue that Administrative Board of Review decisions have normative influence as, on the one hand, the CJEU

57 What exactly 'quasi-judicial' means often remains unclear. Ultimately, the prefix 'quasi' only negatively distinguishes from a stylised image of courts and the judicial process but fails to positively establish the phenomenon's characteristics. For a, in my eyes convincing, function-oriented perspective that qualifies Boards of Appeal as functional adjudicators/courts, see Hannes Krämer, *Rechtsschutz im EG-Eigenverwaltungsrecht zwischen Einheitlichkeit und sektorieller Ausdifferenzierung: eine Untersuchung unter besonderer Berücksichtigung des Gemeinschaftsmarkenrechts* (Duncker & Humblot 2007) 90–93.

58 For an overview of the various boards of appeal, see Chamon, Volpato, and Eliantonio (n 13); Chirulli and De Lucia (n 33).

59 Council Regulation (EU) No 1024/2013 of 15 October 2013 conferring specific tasks on the European Central Bank concerning policies relating to the prudential supervision of credit institutions [2013] OJ L287/63 (SSM Regulation) art 24 paras 1, 2, 4 and 7.

60 SSM Regulation, art 24 para 7. This provokes the question whether one should refer to the Administrative Board of Review as a Board of Appeal. In a broader sense, that may be answered in the affirmative since also those specialised adjudicators that issue legally binding decisions are not uniformly labelled Board of Appeal (e.g., the Single Resolution Board's Appeal Panel). The fact that the Administrative Board of Review replaces agency decisions, does not publish its decisions, and deliberates confidentially also does not automatically render it 'administrative'. The first is something commonly done, in one way or the other, by administrative courts in some jurisdictions, the latter two are common phenomena in judicial proceedings concerning sensitive information. In other words, Board of Appeal can be understood as an umbrella term for the sum of those bodies, with inevitable deviations in some of its parts. Regarding the Administrative Board of Review, see Lamandini and Muñoz (n 13) 126–127; Matteo Arrigioni, 'The Administrative Board of Review of the European Central Bank: A Critical Analysis' [2020] Rivista Orizzonti del Diritto Commerciale 519.

relies on them in its decisions and, on the other hand, the expertise and independence of Administrative Board of Review members lends a certain authority even to non-binding 'opinions'.[61] Further, neither the Administrative Board of Review's deliberations nor its decisions are public.[62] These procedural and institutional arrangements again highlight the overall thrust towards functional differentiation – perhaps even fragmentation – in EU administrative law.[63] While confidentiality and non-bindingness appear questionable from an overarching rule of law perspective, they might be justified for practical necessity and the specific organisational requirements for effective financial oversight.[64]

Now we leave the extended family of courts. Except for BoAs, the Review Bodies presented here issue normative material that is formally non-binding. Hence, we leave the realm of adjudication behind us and leap towards the complex – some might say weaker – authority of recommendations, guidelines, reports, and the like. The other Review Bodies studied here, the Ombudsman and Fundamental Rights Officers, are more on this 'weaker' side of the axis. However, given their expertise, non-binding normative material may still have some degree of authority. That authority is best understood as 'relative' to the legitimacy assets (e.g., legal bindingness, expertise, publicity, etc.) each body mobilises.[65]

We start with Fundamental Rights Officers. FROs are relatively novel institutions, attached to the reformed and expanded Frontex as well as the EU Agency for Asylum.[66] FROs protect fundamental rights in the migration context. However, arguably inspired by the European Ombudsman and, perhaps, the Fundamental Rights Agency, FROs focus more on documenting structural governance problems than reviewing or remedying individual grievances. One key element of the Frontex FRO's practice is situational embeddedness. The FRO, represented by observing and advising staffers, the so-called Fundamental Rights Monitors, follows EU agencies and Member States to the

[61] In that sense also Arrigioni (n 60) 529 et seq.

[62] The Administrative Board of Review's confidentiality regime may be reasonably justified with the specifics of prudential supervision, see Concetta Brescia Morra, René Smits, and Andrea Magliari, 'The Administrative Board of Review of the European Central Bank: Experience After 2 Years' (2017) 18 European Business Organization Law Review 567, 580.

[63] See above at n 10.

[64] See further Konrad Vossen, *Rechtsschutz in Der Europäischen Bankenaufsicht* (Mohr Siebeck 2020) 233–245.

[65] See Joana Mendes and Ingo Venzke (eds), *Allocating Authority: Who Should Do What in European and International Law?* (Hart 2018) 77–78; for Review Bodies: Krajewski, *Relative Authority of Judicial and Extra-Judicial Review* (n 27) 1–2, 9–10.

[66] For historical context see above at n 42.

field.[67] Fundamental Rights Monitors could be described as the eyes and ears of the FRO and 'shall constantly assess the fundamental rights compliance of operational activities, provide advice and assistance in that regard and contribute to the promotion of fundamental rights' at the European borders.[68]

Although FROs form part of the agency's 'complaint handling mechanisms', they only review the 'admissibility' and not the merits of complaints against agency behaviour.[69] Admissible complaints are only 'forward[ed]' to the agency.[70] Instead of remedying complaints, FROs only 'register and ensure follow-up by the Agency'.[71] In essence, FROs' authority to 'handl[e]' individual complaints means to distribute but not to remedy complaints.[72] Further, the Frontex FRO at least faces continuing challenges in the field. For example, in one instance, Member State authorities simply deleted potentially incriminating camera recordings that the FRO had requested as evidence.[73] Thus, the FRO's slim operational authority might endanger the Frontex FRO, and their team's ability to fulfil their mandate, which is to 'be responsible for handling complaints … in accordance with the right to good administration'.[74]

Further, apart from complaints filed by affected individuals, the Frontex FRO also handles an internal complaint mechanism, called 'serious incident reporting'.[75] In simple terms, the serious incident reporting scheme enables people working for the participating actors – especially FRO staffers that observe agency and Member State action in the field, so-called fundamental rights monitors – to report fundamental rights violations committed by Frontex or co-operating state actors.[76] So far, roughly one serious incident per week is reported (sixty-two in 2021, a stark increase from only ten in 2020).[77] However, the serious incident reporting scheme's start has been bumpy. Several actors, especially Member States, flat-out rejected the

67 EBCG Regulation, art 110 but also arts 44(3)(b), 51(2), 60(3)(f).
68 For the quotes see ibid art 110(1).
69 European Asylum Agency Regulation, art 51(2); EBCG Regulation, art 111(2).
70 European Asylum Agency Regulation, art 51(4)(c); EBCG Regulation, art 111(4).
71 European Asylum Agency Regulation, art 51(4)(f); EBCG Regulation, art 111(4).
72 See also Stefan and Hertog (n 42) 163–165.
73 Frontex FRO2021 (n 55) 27 (see under the heading 'complaint No. 2020-00018'). At the time of writing in June 2023, the Frontex FRO had not yet published the annual reports for 2022 and 2023.
74 European Asylum Agency Regulation, art 51(4); EBCG Regulation, art 111(4).
75 For an overview, see Frontex FRO 2021 (n 55) 22–25. See further the Decision of the Executive Director, No R-ED-2021-51, Standard Operating Procedure (SOP) – Serious Incident Reporting of 19 April 2021, 3 et seq
76 See in detail Frontex FRO 2021 (n 55) 22 et seq.
77 Ibid 22.

accuracy of reported fundamental rights violations with the argument that said violations would be 'incompatible with applicable procedures governing their operational activities'.[78] Further, the FRO highlighted that Frontex's operational staff (border guards etc.) had an 'inhibition threshold' to report fundamental rights violations.[79]

Crucially, in the migration context, informalisation, tacit ignorance of fundamental rights abuses, and diffused responsibilities of Member States, EU actors, and, as the Frontex FRO ominously calls it, other 'assets', pose a challenge to fundamental rights of their own.[80] Any kind of review only works if practice – like a push-back – links to responsibility.[81] That link is not a legalist formality. As Melanie Fink showed in painstaking detail, EU agencies and Member States have 'far-reaching possibilities to influence the course of action' at the European borders.[82] Similar things could be said about the EUAA and its 'assistance' in status determination. Inevitably, this influence entails legal responsibility. Obscuring attribution and severing legal and political links between legitimised actors and, perhaps, illegitimate actions would be a dangerous experiment.

Fundamental Rights Officers are hardly the silver bullet against structural flaws nestled within the EU's migration regime. Quite the contrary, installing predominantly transparency-oriented bodies that lack the authority to grant relief only highlights that structural problems exist – not that a solution has been found. Therefore, that the EU decided to invest considerable funds (two million Euro in 2021) and personnel (between sixty and a hundred people) in the task of making Frontex more fundamental rights–sensitive invites simultaneously criticism and praise. It could be criticised as a mere ceremonial fig leaf, signalling that the problem is taken care of. While the actors who should take care of the problem, the FRO and its monitors, lack meaningful authority to remedy complaints or weigh into abusive practices.[83]

78 Ibid 23.

79 Ibid.

80 See Melanie Fink and Narin Idriz, 'Effective Judicial Protection in the External Dimension of the EU's Migration and Asylum Policies?' in Eva Kassoti and Narin Idriz (eds), *The Informalisation of the EU's External Action in the Field of Migration and Asylum* (Edward Elgar 2022) 124 et seq; Gaia Lisi and Mariolina Eliantonio, 'The Gaps in Judicial Accountability of EASO in the Processing of Asylum Requests in Hotspots' (2019) 4 European Papers 589, 590. For the other 'asset' quote, which apparently refers to personnel that are working for Frontex but are not 'Frontex staff', see Frontex FRO 2021 (n 55) 14.1.

81 See in that sense also the detailed analysis by Fink and Idriz (n 80) 124 et seq (esp. 141–142).

82 Cf. Fink *Frontex and Human Rights* (n 43) 332.

83 On the phenomenon of 'de-coupling', see Meyer and Rowan (n 8) 356 et seq (note that Meyer and Rowan refer to *formal* structures, which are something different from the 'structures' discussed here, see further n 8).

However, perhaps, a fault confessed is half redressed. FROs' potential lies in identifying structural problems that lead to repeated fundamental rights violations and recommending possible solutions. For example, in its 2021 annual report, the Frontex FRO assessed 'serious fundamental rights concerns' in six EU Member States and one co-operating state (Albania).[84] Further, the Frontex FRO identifies – in broad language, but nonetheless – structural practices that lead to repeated fundamental rights violations by the agency itself and Member States. Such structural practices range from 'a lack of female officers deployed in almost all areas', to a lack of translators, or 'limited visibility ... of the Complaints Mechanism'.[85] Further, the Frontex FRO explicitly criticises the 'risk' that 'Frontex staff and assets' are involved in 'illegal individual or collective expulsions of migrants', especially at the Greek and Bulgarian border.[86] Further, the FRO directly criticises 'collective expulsions of migrants and the violation of the non-refoulement principle by Lithuanian border guards'.[87] In that context, the body also laments that Frontex 'risk(s)' being complicit through a 'failure to act'.[88] None of this is news. Yet, as a much-needed, more fundamental rights–oriented overhaul of the EU asylum complex appears politically impossible, the FROs might offer bits and pieces of transparency and incentives for incremental reforms from within. Crucially – but from a transparency perspective perhaps problematically – the FRO's influence comes not via grand reports or naming and shaming. Instead, as the Frontex FRO put it in a conversation with the author, they seek to advance a fundamental rights–oriented 'trajectory of cultural changes' within Frontex.[89]

That being said, the European Agency for Asylum got its very own FRO as part of a major institutional reform in 2022. Once fully operational, the EUAA will be by far the largest EU agency in terms of workforce and, arguably, fundamental rights exposure. However, its FRO lacks many of the Frontex FRO's institutional abilities. The EUAA regulation does not explicitly provide for a serious incident reporting scheme, nor does it offer Fundamental Rights Monitors, i.e. 'eyes and ears' of the FRO on the ground. Presumably, the EUAA will not engage in physical border protection like Frontex. The EUAA focuses more on the bureaucratic side of handling asylum requests.[90]

84 Frontex FRO 2021 (n55) 7 and 11–17.
85 Ibid 17.7.
86 Ibid 14.
87 Ibid 12 (see at concern 12.1).
88 Ibid.
89 Background talk with Jonas Grimheden, Frontex Fundamental Rights Officer, 2 May 2023.
90 See esp. European Asylum Agency Regulation, art 16.

Therefore, the risk for fundamental rights violations like physical push-backs or collective expulsions may be smaller for the EUAA compared to Frontex. However, the EUAA's powers are only vaguely delineated. The agency shall provide 'operational and technical assistance' to the Member States to handle requests for 'international protection'.[91] How exactly the EUAA's 'operational and technical assistance' or 'facilitation' will manifest remains unclear.[92] Given the thrust towards informalisation and lack of transparency, such forms of administrative 'assistance' and 'facilitation' might risk eroding fundamental rights guarantees.[93] For example, we learned from Mariana Gkliati's empirical work that the Appeal Committees, which dealt with appeals by individuals stranded on Greek islands in 2016 and 2017, often transferred their reasoning 'word-by-word from one decision to [an]other, even when the committees are composed of different members'.[94] Such habits and shortcuts may be inevitable in large administrative and judicial operations (highlighting, again, how similar judicial and administrative practices often are).[95] However, review degenerating to mere rubber-stamping would violate the individual's fundamental rights to an *individual* status determination envisaged by Article 18 CFR and the 1951 Geneva convention and its 1967 protocol.[96] Such rubber-stamping practices would epitomise the kind of structural and organisational problems that Review Bodies can identify and, through expertise and advice, perhaps help remedying. That the EUAA FRO apparently lacks 'eyes and ears' might substantially undermine its capacity to do so.

[91] For the assistance provided by the EUAA see European Asylum Agency Regulation, art 16(2)(c).

[92] See European Asylum Agency Regulation, art 16(2).

[93] Cf. the comparable situation of 'team members' in the case of Frontex described by Fink, *Frontex and Human Rights* (n 43) 326 et seq; see in general Eva Kassoti and Narin Idriz (eds), *The Informalisation of the EU's External Action in the Field of Migration and Asylum* (Springer 2022).

[94] Mariana Gkliati, 'The Application of the EU-Turkey Agreement: A Critical Analysis of the Decisions of the Greek Appeals Committees' (2017) 10 European Journal of Legal Studies 81, 94.

[95] See, in that regard, also Resnik (n 56); Owen M Fiss, 'The Bureaucratization of the Judiciary' (1983) 92 The Yale Law Journal 1442.

[96] Even if one accepts current procedural backlog as an argument to introduce more group-oriented status determination procedures, such group-oriented determination procedures would require absolute transparency and effective accountability mechanisms. For a brief overview, see Bruce Burson, 'Refugee Status Determination' in Cathryn Costello, Michelle Foster, and Jane McAdam (eds), *The Oxford Handbook of International Refugee Law* (Oxford University Press 2021) 585 etc. For the Geneva Convention, see Convention Relating to the Status of Refugees, United Nations, Treaty Series, vol. 189, p. 137, signed 28 July 1951 (*1951 Geneva Convention*); and Protocol Relating to the Status of Refugees, United Nations, Treaty Series, vol. 606, p. 267, done at New York, on 31 January 1967 (*1967 Protocol to the Geneva Convention*).

Lastly, we turn to the authority of the Ombudsman. The Ombudsman's general mandate to 'uncover maladministration' comes with the authority to issue only non-binding decisions. In turn, the Ombudsman's decade-long presence, political gravitas, and discursive ability incrementally vested it with what could be described as *political* authority. In contrast to legal authority, which their recommendations lack, the Ombudsman builds largely on public pressure and strategically piggybacks political discourses. 'Own initiative inquiries' and 'special reports' in particular seldom occur in a political and discursive vacuum but reflect, lend weight to, and substantiate pre-existing concerns. Assessing the Ombudsman's authority, therefore, should not be reduced to that of its specific recommendations but also its ability to weigh into political debates and make informed calls for change.

Further, as Krajewski noted, the Ombudsman's non-binding and structure-focused approach constitutes perhaps the institution's 'greatest strength' as it reflexively allows for broad accessibility.[97] The Ombudsman seeks to remedy not only individual grievances but also to pierce the veil and help overcome the structural preconditions that lead to maladministration and, potentially, fundamental rights violations. To do so, the Ombudsman combines thorough legal analysis – like that exercised by EU courts – with predominantly process- and institution-focused advice.[98] For separation of powers reasons, many courts may be reluctant to spell out specific institutional or procedural measures that would improve administrative dealings. In contrast, the Ombudsman, which is not a judicial institution, brings the necessary expertise and authority to aid administrators in effectively operationalising legal requirements.

For example, circling back to the asylum complex, the Ombudsman's strategic inquiry into Frontex advised how Frontex should revise aspects of its organisational set-up.[99] Much in the same vein, that the 2019 overhaul of Frontex's founding regulation included a – however imperfect – complaint mechanism can be traced back to two strategic inquiries by the Ombudsman. Those inquiries investigate Frontex's lack of individualised accountability mechanisms in 2012 and 2014.[100] This struggle highlights both the potentials and the pitfalls of the Ombudsman's authority. Ultimately, it was the European legislator – especially the European Parliament – and not Frontex itself that

97 Krajewski, *Relative Authority of Judicial and Extra-Judicial Review* (n 27) 139.

98 Ibid.

99 See European Ombudsman *Frontex* (n 30) para 15 et seq; see also the four suggestions at 5–6, and Annex II.

100 European Ombudsman Case OI/5/2012/BEH-MHZ *Frontex* (12 November 2013) <https://europa.eu/!JknBXb>; European Ombudsman Case OI/9/2014/MHZ *Joint Return Operations* (4 May 2015) <https://europa.eu/!JknBXb>.

established the complaint mechanism. On its own, the Ombudsman could not 'implement' their recommendations. Yet, leveraging its political authority, the Ombudsman managed to infuse their ideas into the political process. Therefore, on the one hand, after several years and via the detour of the legislative overhaul, the Ombudsman's recommendation led to structural reform. On the other hand, the now implemented complaint mechanism is far from perfect and its use negligible. Further, that Frontex (and some Member States) would ignore the two Ombudsman recommendations and then, later, as described above, only grudgingly accommodate the Ombudsman's recommendations shows that structural change only through Review Bodies might often be an illusion. Review Bodies may be supporting actors in a broader play of accountability forums, as also including courts, parliaments, the press, and public discourse. However, as it will be argued in more detail below, Review Bodies are most efficient when teaming up with other accountability forums and contributing their specific substantive and organisational knowledge of structural governance problems.

In conclusion, we see that the legal authority of Review Bodies, except Boards of Appeal, is different – one could say weaker – than that of courts. All bodies analysed here, in one form or the other, respond to individual petitions. Yet neither the Ombudsman nor Fundamental Rights Officers can bindingly stop fundamental rights violations. However, if we take a more nuanced look, Review Bodies incrementally construe their very own authority relative to their organisational setting, public perception, and legal mandate. The measures Review Bodies use to operationalise their authority range from adjudication (BoAs) to non-binding normative material (FROs, Ombudsman), internal advice (FROs, presumably also the Ombudsman), and public pressure campaigns and political mingling (Ombudsman).

5.4.3 *Expertise and Funding*

The substantive and organisational knowledge of Review Bodies brings us to the last axis of this taxonomy. One of Review Bodies' key characteristics and – if used strategically – main advantages is their expertise. Unlike EU courts, which have general jurisdiction, Review Bodies often exercise specialised jurisdiction and, therefore, employ more specialised experts than EU courts. This has two downstream effects. On the one hand, many Review Bodies have, especially when compared to courts, extra knowledge in the substantive fields they oversee.[101] For example, BoAs are typically staffed with people who

[101] However, practically and financially enabling expertise is not always easy. See especially Krajewski, *Relative Authority of Judicial and Extra-Judicial Review* (n 27) 111.

have special knowledge of the specific regulatory field covered by their respective agency. Similarly, FROs are, at least partly, staffed with people who have a background in fundamental rights and asylum law. We may call this *substantive* expertise. On the other hand, Review Bodies accumulate expert knowledge about EU executive structures themselves. In other words, Review Bodies are also experts in the institutionalised practices and (in)formal habits entrenched into EU executive power. We may call this *organisational* expertise.

Although all Review Bodies entertain these two expertise dimensions, we may again distinguish among the actors presented here. BoAs are predominantly on the substantive expertise side of the spectrum. Even though their review also ventures into the organisational and structural aspects of their respective agencies, BoAs are designed as substantive experts in the regulatory area of their agencies.[102] Most founding regulations for agencies that feature a BoA state that board members and the, usually few, members of staff shall have the 'necessary expertise' to review the agency acts.[103] A paradigmatic example is the Joint Board of Appeal of the European Supervisory Authorities. It reviews agency action regulating financial services. According to Article 58 (2) of the three respective regulations, members of the Board of Appeal 'shall be individuals of high repute with a proven record of relevant knowledge of Union law and of having international professional experience, to a sufficiently high level in the fields of banking, insurance, occupational pensions, securities markets or other financial services'.[104] However, since many BoAs are rather small institutions with few (if any) full-time employees, safeguarding

[102] For a detailed analysis of the ECHA BoA's review, see Michał Krajewski, 'Judicial and Extra-Judicial Review: The Quest for Epistemic Certainty' in Merijn Chamon, Mariolina Eliantonio, and Annalisa Volpato (eds), *Boards of Appeal of EU Agencies* (Oxford University Press 2022) 289.

[103] For example, for the Joint Board of Appeal of the European Supervisory Authorities, the relevant clause reads '[t]he Board of Appeal shall have sufficient legal expertise to provide expert legal advice on the legality of the Authority's exercise of its powers', see Article 58(2) respectively in Regulation (EU) No 1095/2010 of the European Parliament and of the Council of 24 November 2010 establishing a European Supervisory Authority (European Securities and Markets Authority), amending Decision No 716/2009/EC and repealing Commission Decision 2009/77/EC [2010] *OJ L*331/84; Regulation (EU) No 1093/2010 of the European Parliament and of the Council of 24 November 2010 establishing a European Supervisory Authority (European Banking Authority), amending Decision No 716/2009/EC and repealing Commission Decision 2009/78/EC[2010] *OJ L*331/12; Regulation (EU) No 1094/2010 of the European Parliament and of the Council of 24 November 2010 establishing a European Supervisory Authority (European Insurance and Occupational Pensions Authority), amending Decision No 716/2009/EC and repealing Commission Decision 2009/79/EC [2010] *OJ L*331/48.

[104] Ibid.

that expertise might not always be easy. As Krajewski noted for at least one BoA, 'the Commission and co-legislators wrongly assumed that just *one* technically qualified member is capable of guaranteeing the necessary level of expertise'.[105] EU agencies deal with immensely complex regulatory matters. Therefore, offering high-quality review of these matters is complex in and of itself.[106] However, low funding and a small workforce might impair some BoAs' ability to offer comprehensive expertise-based review.

Picking up the thread of funding as a necessary prerequisite for expertise, the Frontex Fundamental Rights Officer and the European Ombudsman seem to have more robust funding than at least some BoAs. For example, Frontex allocated two million Euros to 'fundamental rights activities' in its 2022 budget.[107] According to Jonas Grimheden, then Frontex FRO, all or most of this money went to the FRO, which had a staff of roughly sixty-five people in spring 2023 but aimed at expanding to more than a hundred.[108] Remarkably, in 2020, Frontex allocated no funds to 'fundamental rights activities' and roughly 780,000 Euros in 2021.[109] That sharp increase in personnel and funding indicates at least some financial underpinning and, by extension, the workforce required to develop the Frontex FRO into a serious player for incremental improvements of European asylum governance.

Circling back to the two poles of substantive and organisational expertise, FROs are squarely in the centre. FROs intrinsically combine substantive and organisational expertise. FROs' substantive expertise is to understand the organisational practices (and problems) at Frontex and the new Asylum Agency.[110] On the one hand, FROs focus on how the respective agencies conduct their operations, which gives them a thorough understanding of the agencies' organisational practices. On the other hand, the Frontex FRO's 'monitors' in particular look at this practice from a substantive fundamental rights perspective. In general, however, FROs mainly seek to make Frontex actions more transparent and, by extension, more accountable.

[105] Krajewski, *Relative Authority of Judicial and Extra-Judicial Review* (n 27) 111.

[106] The various BoAs fare very differently in that regard. See, e.g., Carlo Tovo, 'The Boards of Appeal of Networked Services Agencies: Specialized Arbitrators of Transnational Regulatory Conflicts?' in Merijn Chamon, Annalisa Volpato, and Mariolina Eliantonio (eds), *Boards of Appeal of EU Agencies: Towards Judicialization of Administrative Review?* (Oxford University Press 2022) 50 et seq.

[107] Frontex Budget 2022, VOBU Ref FDS/FIN/NAAL/2022 <https://frontex.europa.eu/assets/Key_Documents/Budget/Frontex_VOBU_2022.pdf> 3.

[108] Background talk, Frontex FRO Grimheden (n 89).

[109] Frontex Budget 2022 (n 107) 3.

[110] See Section 5.3.2.

Lastly, the European Ombudsman leans strongly towards the organisational expertise pole. The Ombudsman's expertise focuses exclusively on organisational expertise as its mandate is to remedy maladministration.[111] The Ombudsman does not review the substantive accuracy of agency decisions but analyses the procedures through which decisions are made and, if needs be, whether a procedure might have endangered fundamental rights. With a budget of just over twelve million Euros and a staff of between seventy-three (permanent) and a little under a hundred (including trainees), the Ombudsman's budget is larger than that of the FRO and most to all BoAs.[112] However, mirroring the challenges of other Review Bodies, the Ombudsman's expertise, workforce, and funding must be seen in perspective. As mentioned above, the Ombudsman has a general mandate, spanning potential maladministration by any EU actor. That is a multitudinous and chaotic universe of actors with tens of thousands of employees. From that perspective, the Ombudsman's budget might be large relative to more specialised BoAs but still small relative to its humongous task.

Further, if the Frontex FRO expands as projected, the size of its workforce might eclipse that of the Ombudsman. This, again, provokes queries. If the workforce of the Frontex FRO and the Ombudsman are roughly the same (both between 50 and 100), and both review EU executive actors for maladministration or even fundamental rights violations, why is the Ombudsman's budget six times that of the Frontex FRO (more than twelve million Euros compared with two million Euros)? Vice versa, what does it tell us about the state of fundamental rights at one single agency if the office overseeing said agency's fundamental rights record employs as many people as the body overseeing the whole European Union for any kind of maladministration?

5.4.4 *Interim Conclusion*

The outlined taxonomy offers several key takeaways. On the one hand, Review Bodies' authority emerges only incrementally. While courts' authority rests on their legal power as well as their position at the cusp of our socio-cultural imaginary (remember Dworkin's Herculean judge?), Review Bodies must build their authority from scratch. Consequentially, they also use a broader panoply of measures to oversee and control executive behaviour. Many of these measures are indirect and certainly not 'binding' in a legalist sense of the

[111] Ibid.

[112] European Ombudsman, Annual Report 2022, 36 at 7.1 and 7.2.

word. However, indirect, non-binding measures may point to the structural root causes of fundamental rights violations. That would be a crucial factor in eventually fixing those structural errors.

On the other hand, none of the Review Bodies covered here is fully convincing from an access to justice perspective. The Ombudsman does important work but some of their recommendations are ignored or watered down in the political process. Fundamental Rights Officers highlight rather than solve the grave fundamental rights problems at the Union's governing of asylum and migration. That is not to say that FROs can do no good. Yet one cannot help but characterise FROs at least in part as ceremonial legitimation of otherwise structurally flawed practices at the Union's borders. BoAs offer a well-established and much needed extra layer of adjudication. Nonetheless, BoAs would require and, I would argue, deserve a more prominent place in discussions about the Union's administrative justice architecture. Lastly, all bodies appear to offer considerable expertise in their respective fields. Yet, to further advance that expertise, all bodies would arguably need more funding.

5.5 POSSIBILITIES FOR REFORM

We conclude with several possibilities for reform. This chapter presented three Review Bodies – the European Ombudsman, Boards of Appeal, and Fundamental Rights Officers – as complementary paths to justice in the EU. None of these Review Bodies can replace the judicial process, which arguably remains the most authoritative avenue to attain individual justice for fundamental rights violations. Yet, Review Bodies are here to stay. It is likely they will diffuse further, perhaps even beyond the classic realm of public executive power into the intricate spheres of public-private administrative–like governance mechanisms.[113] The governance of data and the digital economy especially have spawned a rich but ambivalent cluster of bodies that shall protect individual rights like the freedom of speech or privacy but lack meaningful enforcement capacities.[114]

5.5.1 *Teaming Up*

This chapter premised that recurring fundamental rights violations reflect structural problems nestled within organisational practice. Remedying

[113] Moritz Schramm, 'Administrification of Platform Governance: A New Role for the European Ombudsman in the DSA Framework?' in Deirdre Curtin (ed), *The Evolving Role of the European Ombudsman* (Hart, forthcoming 2024).

[114] See further Moritz Schramm, *The Emulation of Courts in the Digital World: Platforms, the Oversight Board, and the Digital Services Act* (Cambridge University Press, forthcoming 2025).

structural problems requires more than occasional judicial review. Courts focus mainly on reviewing the legality of individual acts and seldom focus on the structural forces that might drag organisations towards violating fundamental rights. Here, Review Bodies – despite their many shortcomings – have a crucial advantage. Because they are not bound by the judicial process' narrow focus on individual legality, Review Bodies may develop a more thorough understanding of the structural issues in each governance context. In other words, Review Bodies might help individual petitioners only mediately, for example, through recommendations, investigations, and public statements (BoAs are an exception here). However, Review Bodies may be crucial in identifying and eventually reforming the structural root causes that lead to fundamental rights violations. They can do so precisely *because* their normative output is, usually, non-binding.

Nonetheless, effectively implementing Review Bodies' often consultative and non-binding output hinges strongly on the goodwill of the EU institutions. Although internal communication, public recommendations, or naming and shaming may work to a degree, executive actors retain the last word over any bit of structural reform short of legislative overhaul. Yet structure-focused but non-binding review that merely seeks to 'gently civilise' recalcitrant offenders is not enough if those offenders – for whatever reason – simply do not wish to change.

This highlights a mismatch in the Union's access to justice architecture. On the one hand, Review Bodies might thoroughly understand what might go wrong in the Union's executive. Yet Review Bodies lack the authority to weigh in. On the other hand, those institutions that could weigh in, courts, mostly focus on vindicating individual grievances through individualised measures (reinstatement, financial compensation, etc.) instead of helping executive actors to remedy structural flaws that might lead to repeated fundamental rights violations. But how to reconcile these two strings of justice?

Therefore, the main take away from this chapter is that Review Bodies and other accountability forums should team up. Together, courts and Review Bodies would combine judicial authority with Review Bodies' structural and substantive expertise. Combining these two elements would advance justice in a more comprehensive way than either of those two mechanisms could on its own. Currently, complementarity too often translates to isolated attempts to remedy fundamental rights violations by courts and Review Bodies. Thus, a pragmatic path forward would be to combine the analytical and recommendatory capabilities of Review Bodies with binding, authoritative judicial review. On their own, neither judicial review nor structural but non-binding review can do away with the root causes nestled into problematic governance structures, internal cultures, and organisational habitus. However, if courts and other Review Bodies team up, both actors' capabilities increase significantly. Recently, Daniel Halberstam and Sina von der Boegart called on EU courts to begin issuing 'structural injunctions'.[115] Review Bodies could contribute crucial substantive and organisational expertise for these injunctions.

Teaming up could take various forms. For example, Review Bodies could be heard as experts (Article 25 CJEU Statute) or file third-party interventions (Article 42 CJEU Statute) in annulment proceedings. If the Court of Justice espouses the Review Bodies' recommendations, the Court could include them, in one way or the other, in its judgment.

Further, Review Bodies should also actively engage with political actors and leverage their expertise to push for structural improvements. A case in point is the Ombudsman's 'special report' to the European Parliament from 2013, after Frontex 'rejected' a recommendation by the Ombudsman. Crucially, the Ombudsman criticised the fact that the agency 'had no mechanism in place by which it could deal with individual incidents of breaches of fundamental rights alleged to have occurred in the course of its work. The Ombudsman saw the lack of an internal complaint mechanism as a significant gap in Frontex's arrangements'.[116] A decade later, an overhaul of the Frontex regulation introduced such a complaint mechanism – even though in a largely impractical form. This tells us two things. On the one hand, remedying structural flaws requires various fundamental rights-oriented players – courts, Review Bodies, parliamentarians, the Fundamental Rights Agency, NGOs, the press – to team up. On the other hand, at least in the asylum complex, access to justice hinges upon political will and not on idealised legal guarantees.

5.5.2 *More Money, More Wit*

One common thread running through this chapter is that Review Bodies need more funding and more publicity. Arguably, the latter depends on the former. If Review Bodies are better funded, they could invest further in their expertise, which would be a legitimacy asset and, if operationalised well, might make them more publicly known. Except for BoAs, the Review Bodies studied here will continue to have little or no authority to issue legally binding decisions. Apart from jumping, in one way or the other, onto the court's bandwagon, Review Bodies should leverage their role as guardians more confidently and,

[115] Halberstam and von der Boegart (n 8) 9–16.

[116] European Ombudsman, *Special Report of the European Ombudsman in own-initiative inquiry OI/5/2012/BEH-MHZ concerning Frontex* (7 December 2013) 1–2.

crucially, more publicly. Accountability and oversight are not only questions of formal mandates and dry reports but can be effectively orchestrated through public messaging.[117] Also courts construe(d) their authority through performative iterations of power. As a consequence, the public incrementally acquiesced to courts' pre-eminent role in guarding fundamental rights.[118] Mutatis mutandis, Review Bodies should learn from that example. Therefore, Review Bodies should engage more directly in the public discourse to ramp up public and political pressure wherever reasons for fundamental rights abuses occur. That is particularly important in front of the backdrop of the EU's still fragmented public sphere and independent executive actors' lack of electoral accountability.

5.6 CONCLUSION

This chapter presented Review Bodies as complementary avenues to justice vis-à-vis the EU's expanding executive power. Review Bodies are complementary in the sense that they add to but do not replace judicial review. Among their key characteristics is that Review Bodies (potentially) focus on structural root causes of fundamental rights violations instead of individualised questions of legality. Yet their authority is often faint and the measures at their disposal remain indirect and non-binding. Although such measures may be even more appropriate to tackle organisational and entrenched issues, success is not guaranteed. On the one hand, Review Bodies performatively play with notions of review and access to justice, although their practical ability to deliver such justice often remains underdeveloped. This may evoke falsely legitimising impressions of accountability, which would then stabilise normatively questionable executive regimes. Above, it is argued that Review Bodies are, in principle, a positive development as they emphasise the Union's ability to

[117] See, in that regard, also Deirdre Curtin and Linda Senden, 'Public Accountability of Transnational Private Regulation: Chimera or Reality?' (2011) 38 Journal of Law and Society 163.

[118] Examples abound, from *Marbury v Madison* to *van Gend & Loos* or the Bundesverfassungsgericht's famous *Statusschrift*. For illuminating analyses of these phenomena in an international and European context, see Ingo Venzke, *How Interpretation Makes International Law* (Oxford University Press 2012) 16 et seq, 135 et seq; Antonin Cohen and Antoine Vauchez, 'The Social Construction of Law: The European Court of Justice and Its Legal Revolution Revisited' (2011) 7 Annual Review of Law and Social Science 417; Martti Koskenniemi, 'Performing Legal Expertise: Reflections on the Construction of Transnational Authority' in Emilia Korkea-aho and Päivi Leino-Sandberg (eds), *Law, Legal Expertise and EU Policy-Making* (Cambridge University Press 2022) 19 et seq; Pavone (n 1).

self-control.[119] However, presently, some Review Bodies cannot deliver effective guardianship. On the other hand, Review Bodies indeed offer more than many commentators, practitioners, and individuals might expect. Therefore, to advance access to justice in the Union's executive dealings, Review Bodies should team up with other accountability forums like parliaments and, crucially, courts. This might reflexively elevate their authority and pave the way to further institutional reform.

[119] See Section 5.3.2.

6

The Role of National Courts in Redressing Fundamental Rights Violations by the EU

ANDREAS HOFMANN

6.1 INTRODUCTION

National courts are central actors in the EU legal system. In the vast majority of cases, they are the first port of call for litigants seeking to either question the validity of an EU act or to enforce it against national authorities or private actors. In a system of remedies against EU acts themselves, they take on a filtering function. Comparatively few civil society actors – individuals, groups, or companies – have direct access to the EU courts. Such access is strongly restricted by case law of the Court of Justice of the European Union (CJEU), most importantly by the *Plaumann* doctrine the court developed in 1963:[1] only claimants that are directly and individually concerned by an EU act have standing to address their claim to the EU courts. Over the last few years, the General Court has heard an average of just over 400 annulment cases per year, while annulment cases by non-institutional actors at the Court of Justice are exceedingly rare.[2] All claimants that do not meet the *Plaumann* criteria therefore have to address a national court to achieve redress.

This chapter focuses on how national courts fill this role. In the EU's system of indirect legal review of EU acts, national courts are expected to refer controversial cases to the CJEU for a judgment on the validity of such acts. Chapters 4 and 13 in this volume concentrate on the preliminary reference procedure as a remedy to EU rights violations and the problem posed by acts that are jointly carried out by EU and national agents respectively. I will not

[1] Case C-25/62 *Plaumann v Commission* [1963] ECLI:EU:C:1963:17.

[2] Christian Adam and Others, *Taking the EU to Court. Annulment Proceedings and Multilevel Judicial Conflict* (Palgrave 2020).

address such scenarios but rather emphasise the possible autonomous role that national courts can and do take on in addressing alleged rights violations by the EU. While the CJEU has claimed for itself the sole authority to review the validity of EU acts, the hierarchy both of judicial institutions and of legal norms in the EU is far from settled. National apex courts, in particular, have claimed for themselves the position of ultimate arbiter over legal conflicts between the EU and fundamental rights contained in national legal orders. This opens opportunities for civil society actors to seize on the ambiguities inherent in a multi-level jurisdiction with contested hierarchies. In focusing on such efforts, this chapter is less interested in doctrinal questions of how to resolve conflicts inherent in a pluralist legal order. Rather, it looks at the circumstances under which civil society litigants – individuals, groups, and companies – address a claim to a national court and where national courts have historically been open to such claims. At times, such efforts blur the line between the search for individual redress and mobilisation against an EU policy more broadly. This chapter can therefore also be read as an overview of the 'legal mobilisation' of national sources of rights against EU acts.

Evidently, this subject matter raises strong normative concerns. It is possible to regard autonomous national courts as a normatively desirable backstop to a European legal order of rights and remedies with blind spots. Much of the literature, on the other hand, treats this issue as a (largely normatively undesirable) challenge to a European legal order that has by and large accepted the primacy of EU law as the guiding principle. From this point of view, national courts asserting national fundamental rights over EU acts presents a problem. While there can be a legitimate debate between these points of view, the process of democratic backsliding and the crisis of the rule of law in some Member States constitutes a graver problem that changes the parameters of the debate. Any normatively desirable role of national courts rests on their good faith efforts to protect fundamental rights to the fullest extent against any public authority. Where this is not the case, very different standards apply. I will come back to this in the conclusion to this chapter.

The chapter proceeds as follows. First, I will take an abstract look at the conditions under which litigants can potentially mobilise rights against EU acts in national courts. This encompasses the existence of rights in the first place, access to courts, and characteristics of the litigants themselves. I will then present an overview of empirical instances where civil society actors – individuals, groups, and companies – have in fact claimed fundamental rights against EU acts in national courts. I organise this overview along four different types of rights that litigants have claimed: economic rights, such as the right to property or the freedom of occupation; social rights, such as rights to social security or health care; civil liberties, such as the right to life or freedom from harm; and political rights, such as the right to vote. A final section concludes.

6.2 LEGAL OPPORTUNITY STRUCTURES AND LITIGANT CHARACTERISTICS

The opportunity to address national courts with a rights claim against the EU is conditioned by what the literature has termed 'legal opportunity structures',[3] a close analogue to the somewhat older concept of a 'political opportunity structure',[4] which has been used to delineate access opportunities of civil society organisations to the political process. I will primarily discuss two elements that make up the structure of legal opportunity. First, potential litigants will need to identify a source of law that they can claim against an EU act. This essentially encompasses all sources of rights that can potentially be claimed in a national court. The second central element of legal opportunity is access to courts. This primarily comprises rules of legal standing and the availability of specific remedy procedures. While these factors tend to be fairly stable over time, other factors may be more contingent. Prime among these is the receptivity of national judges to rights claims against the EU. Such receptivity may vary from court to court or even judge to judge. Some of this is known in advance and litigants can strategically direct their claims to sympathetic venues. At other times, they may simply need to try their luck. Finally, characteristics of potential litigants themselves influence their likelihood to turn to the courts. The choice of courts as a venue for contestation necessitates an awareness of the opportunities offered by the legal system. Without such 'legal consciousness'[5], individuals with valid grievances may never consider the courts as a potential source of a remedy in the first place. Where they do, they will then have to mobilise legal expertise to properly address their claims to courts. If individuals, groups, or companies do not have this expertise themselves, they have to invest resources to acquire it. In particular, cases that litigants bring strategically against an EU policy – rather than an individual act – require planning, coordination, and fairly long time horizons that are probably beyond the capabilities of individual litigants and require the

3 Chris Hilson, 'New social movements: the role of legal opportunity' (2002) 9 Journal of European Public Policy 238.

4 Herbert P Kitschelt, 'Political Opportunity Structures and Political Protest: Anti- Nuclear Movements in Four Democracies' (1986) 16 British Journal of Political Science 57.

5 Susan S Silbey, 'After legal consciousness' (2005) 1 Annual Review of Law and Social Science 323; Marc Hertogh, 'A "European" conception of legal consciousness: rediscovering Eugen Ehrlich (2004) 31 Journal of Law and Society 457.

involvement of organised interests. Sections 6.2.1–6.2.3 will cover these aspects in more detail. Section 6.2.1 looks at the sources of law that litigants could rely on in national courts to challenge EU acts. Section 6.2.2 looks at access to courts. Section 6.2.3 in turn focuses on the characteristics that litigants will need to have in order to effectively claim rights against EU acts.

6.2.1 *The Availability of Rights to Challenge EU Acts*

The catalogue of rights that litigants could potentially claim against a violation by the EU is certainly not small. Citizens, groups, and companies can draw on national, EU, or international sources of rights. At the EU level, the primary source has been the Charter of Fundamental Rights since its entry into force in 2009 and, beyond the EU, the European Convention on Human Rights, the European Social Charter, and various international human rights treaties. In addition, individuals, groups, and companies could rely on rights derived from national law. Which of these sources would national courts be likely to enforce against an EU act? Of course, following the CJEU's understanding of the hierarchy of European legal norms, national courts should not have the power to review EU acts at all. This understanding is contested. However, there seems to be little evidence that national courts are open to claims against EU acts that rest on international, European, or higher EU legal norms. In this regard, national courts appear to follow the *Foto-Frost* doctrine that the CJEU established in 1987.[6] Following this doctrine, while national courts have some leeway to independently interpret EU law as a standard of review for *national* conduct,[7] the CJEU requires all national courts, including lower courts, to refer questions about the validity of EU law to the CJEU for a preliminary ruling, even where the CJEU's answer may be obvious. Chapter 4 in this volume deals with the opportunity for national courts to refer questions about the validity of an EU rule or act to the CJEU so I will not pursue this here.

The legal basis on which national courts have shown a willingness to review EU acts is national fundamental rights. Here, we move into the contested area of the hierarchy of legal norms in Europe. The CJEU takes the view that EU law has primacy over national law,[8] even national constitutional law.[9] National courts have not always reacted enthusiastically

6 Case C-314/85 *Foto-Frost v Hauptzollamt Lübeck-Ost* [1987] ECLI:EU:C:1987:452.

7 Under the CJEU's doctrines of *acte clair* and *acte eclaire*, national courts of last instance can apply EU law themselves where EU law is sufficiently clear (*acte clair*) or where a substantively similar question has already been answered by the CJEU (*acte eclaire*).

8 Case C-6/64 *Flaminio Costa v E.N.E.L.* [1964] ECLI:EU:C:1964:66.

9 Case C-11/70 *Internationale Handelsgesellschaft mbH v Einfuhr- und Vorratsstelle für Getreide und Futtermittel* [1970] ECLI:EU:C:1970:114.

to this doctrine. National apex courts, and constitutional courts in particular, have frequently reserved the final word for themselves.[10] The catalogue of rights that potential litigants could rely on to challenge EU acts therefore depends on which rights are protected by national law. Comparative constitutional scholarship has highlighted substantial variation in the catalogue of rights contained in national constitutional documents or bills of rights. Some of this is related to age: older constitutions primarily encompass 'first generation rights' – mainly civil and political rights – whereas newer, post-WWII constitutions often additionally contain 'second generation rights' of a socio-economic nature.[11] Whilst all EU Member State constitutional documents guarantee first generation rights such as freedom of expression, freedom of assembly, property rights, and the right to vote, only some contain second generation rights such as a right to housing, health-care, or work. A wider catalogue allows for greater creativity on the part of litigants challenging EU acts. In addition, national apex courts have developed new rights and procedures for national citizens especially in light of possible intrusions by the EU. Most prominent among these is '*ultra vires* control' – a legal review of whether the EU has overstepped its delegated competences, first developed by the German constitutional court in its ruling on the Treaty of Maastricht.[12] More recently, this court has additionally identified national 'constitutional identity' as a red line to the intrusion of EU law.[13] Litigants have since relied on these concepts to contest EU acts and other European apex courts have incorporated them into their own catalogues.[14] The development and acceptance of these doctrines, however, does not seem to follow a discernible logic and appears largely contingent on the idiosyncrasies of the national courts in question. Potential litigants in different Member States are thus faced not only with different catalogues of rights but also a varying responsiveness of national judiciaries to claiming these rights against EU acts. This structures the opportunities for judicial remedies against EU fundamental rights violations and offers potential explanations for cross-national patterns in rights claims.

[10] Anne Marie Slaughter, Alec Stone Sweet, and Joseph Weiler (eds), *The European Court and National Courts Doctrine & Jurisprudence: Legal Change in its Social Context* (Hart 1998).

[11] Dennis M. Davis, 'Socio-Economic Rights' in Michel Rosenfeld and András Sajó (eds), *The Oxford Handbook of Comparative Constitutional Law* (Oxford University Press 2012).

[12] Bundesverfassungsgericht [Germany] BVerfGE 89, 155 *Maastricht*.

[13] Bundesverfassungsgericht [Germany] BVerfGE 123, 267 *Lissabon*; Federico Fabbrini and András Sajó, 'The dangers of constitutional identity' (2019) 25 European Law Journal 457.

[14] Wojciech Sadurski, '*Solange, Chapter 3*': *Constitutional Courts in Central Europe* (EUI LAW Working Paper 40/2006).

6.2.2 *Access to Courts*

Where potential litigants have identified both a source of rights that they can claim against an EU act and a national court that may be open to accepting such a claim, they need to have standing in this court to pursue it. First, this requires that the EU act in question has a national component. This is usually the case – directives need to be transposed into national law, and even directly effective EU law gains life on the ground through the action of national bureaucracies. Nonetheless, national legal systems differ widely in the type of access they grant individuals, groups, and companies to their judicial system.

In ordinary courts, standing is generally not a problem if the plaintiff can demonstrate personal and immediate harm. Greater variance exists when it comes to public interests. The Scandinavian, German, and Austrian legal systems have traditionally been very restrictive towards public interest litigation, whereas countries such as the United Kingdom, Ireland, France, Spain, and Portugal have been more open.[15] However, ordinary courts are not generally in the habit of accepting rights claims against EU acts. Rather, this tends to be the remit of apex courts, and constitutional courts in particular. These courts have special jurisdiction in fundamental rights issues and special review powers. National variation in the exact combination of access and review powers is again large.[16] Crucial for the present purposes is access for civil society actors (citizens, groups, and companies). Some constitutional courts can only be accessed by political actors (office-holders, political parties, Members of Parliament) or review cases referred by ordinary courts. Other constitutional courts allow for citizen access but limit the degree of judicial review. Constitutional complaint procedures allow for the widest degree of citizen access.[17] Such procedures are available in Germany, Austria, and Spain and were adopted in some Central and Eastern European countries after democratic transition.

6.2.3 *Litigant Characteristics*

Even systems with very open legal opportunity structures need litigants to use these opportunities. Some of the factors that encourage citizens, groups, and companies to do so are idiosyncratic (like group resources or normative

[15] Michel Prieur, *Complaints and appeals in the area of environment in the member states of the European Union* (Study for the Commission of the European Community, DGXI 1998).

[16] John Ferejohn and Pasquale Pasquino, 'Constitutional Adjudication: Lessons from Europe' (2004) 82 Texas Law Review 1671.

[17] Gerhard Dannemann, 'Constitutional Complaints: The European Perspective' (1994) 43 The International and Comparative Law Quarterly 142.

dispositions towards courts as venues for political contestation), while others are more widely shared. Legal culture, while hard to quantify, plays a role in shared discourses about the role of law and its uses in society – how prevalent rights claims are in political discourse.[18] Potential litigants need to conceive of their grievance as a rights issue. The prominent role of the constitution in US political discourse, for example, increases the consciousness that rights exist and can be activated.[19] Next to venerated constitutions, legal systems with a prominent and respected apex court will probably create a greater shared sense of legal opportunity than systems without such courts. Where citizens conceive of their grievances as rights issues, they also need to believe that there can be judicial solutions. In places like Germany, where the constitutional court has a prominent place within the political system, a rights claim may seem like an obvious choice to potential litigants, whereas in places characterised by more judicial deference to political decisions, such as the Scandinavian countries,[20] this might be much less so. This kind of legal consciousness can also be triggered by focusing events, like prominent legal cases with unexpected outcomes – see the recent wave of climate litigation after a series of much discussed if largely symbolic legal victories by individuals and civil society organisations focused on the fight against climate change.[21]

Finally, given legal opportunity and legal consciousness, individuals, groups, and companies need to meet the resource demands of litigation. Even in legal systems with generous access to constitutional review and low cost barriers, the chances of a successful legal challenge will be all the greater the better the legal quality of the complaint. With regard to alleged rights violations by the EU, this requires particular expertise in EU law. The rise of multinational law firms specialising in EU law has made this expertise available to all with the means to hire such counsel, but historically 'Euro-lawyers' were far and between.[22] Potential litigants with lesser means have to rely on a different form of 'support structure'[23] – pro bono lawyers and legal clinics or

[18] David Nelken, 'Using The Concept of Legal Culture' (2004) 29 Australian Journal of Legal Philosophy 1.

[19] Stuart A Scheingold, *The Politics of Rights: Lawyers, Public Policy, and Political Change* (Yale University Press 1974).

[20] Marlene Wind, 'The Nordics, the EU and the Reluctance towards Supranational Judicial Review' (2010) 48 Journal of Common Market Studies 1039.

[21] Joana Setzer and Lisa C Vanhala, 'Climate change litigation: A review of research on courts and litigants in climate governance' (2019) 10 WIREs Climate Change e580.

[22] Tommaso Pavone, *The Ghostwriters: Lawyers and the Politics behind the Judicial Construction of Europe* (Cambridge University Press 2022).

[23] Charles R Epp, *The Rights Revolution: Lawyers, Activists, and Supreme Courts in Comparative Perspective* (University of Chicago Press 1998).

organised interests with either in-house expertise or the means to purchase it elsewhere. Broadly speaking, a more active, organised civil society is more likely to produce such a structure. More specifically, this support structure is likely larger where EU law is part of regular legal curricula, which produces a greater pool of knowledgeable legal activists.

The factors listed above are not randomly distributed. Rather, they cluster in some legal systems and are absent in others. The prominence of Germany in the discourse on the relationship between national and EU law, for example, is no coincidence. Several factors combine to provide fertile ground for the legal contestation of EU acts. A large and comprehensively educated legal profession combines with comparatively generous material resources, an organised civil society, prominence of the constitution and a strong constitutional court in political discourse, the receptivity of this court to rights-based arguments against the EU, and comparatively low barriers of access to constitutional review (while litigants need to demonstrate individual concern, the constitutional court has been open to receiving 'mass constitutional complaints' – bundles of individual complaints that can number in the hundreds of thousands).[24]

It is difficult to gauge which of these factors is individually most predictive of rights-based litigation against EU acts. Where a system of constitutional adjudication is missing (such as in the Netherlands), litigants will need to seek remedies through administrative courts on a narrower basis of available procedures and sources of law. An organised civil society with a strong support structure for rights claims, however, may partially compensate for this disadvantage. Member States on the EU's southern and eastern periphery may have comparatively favourable legal opportunity structures, but litigants may not find the same support structure or receptive national judges. Research has started to address such factors, but much remains to be learned.[25]

6.3 RIGHTS-BASED LITIGATION AGAINST EU ACTS IN PRACTICE: AN EMPIRICAL OVERVIEW

Section 6.3.1–6.3.4 use these theoretical concepts as a heuristic frame to review what we know about litigation against EU acts in national courts.

[24] Stefan Thierse, 'Mobilisierung des Rechts: Organisierte Interessen und Verfassungsbeschwerden vor dem Bundesverfassungsgericht' (2020) 61 Politische Vierteljahresschrift 553.

[25] Andreas Hofmann and Daniel Naurin, 'Explaining interest group litigation in Europe: Evidence from the comparative interest group survey' (2021) 34 Governance 1235; Lisa Vanhala, 'Is Legal Mobilization for the Birds? Legal Opportunity Structures and Environmental Nongovernmental Organizations in the United Kingdom, France, Finland, and Italy' (2018) 51 Comparative Political Studies 380.

This overview is necessarily impressionistic – a systematic review of all such attempts would require a much larger research programme – but it should cover the most prominent instances. There are several conceivable ways of structuring such an overview: chronologically, by Member State, by type of litigant or type of EU act, etc. This chapter will use the type of rights that have historically been claimed against EU acts as a structuring element.[26] Section 6.3.1 deals with economic rights that have been claimed against EU trade regulation – rights to property, occupational freedom, and the right to conduct a business. Important early waymarks, such as the German constitutional court's *Solange I* ruling,[27] fall into this category. It was also historically the first set of rights to be mobilised against the EU and its predecessors – unsurprisingly, since the economy was the major focus of European regulation in the first decades of its existence. Section 6.3.2 focuses on social rights as a corrective to market forces. Such rights were mobilised primarily in the context of the EU's response to the European sovereign debt crisis, and against austerity policies in particular. Section 6.3.3 looks at civil liberties, such as the right to life and freedom from harm. Section 6.3.4 looks at political rights. That section will cover the transformation of the right to free and fair elections into a 'right to democracy' as envisaged by the German constitutional court.

6.3.1 *Economic Rights: Challenges to EU Trade Regimes*

A story of national remedies against EU rights violations is necessarily also a story of EU violations of fundamental rights. The potential nature of such violations is closely tied to what the EU does. For the first four decades,[28] this has largely been the construction of a customs union and a common market for goods, labour, services, and capital. It follows that the first rights-based challenges against EU acts related to such efforts to build a common market, and in particular against rules that regulated and constrained market activity in ways not previously experienced under national rules. These challenges therefore had a market-liberal bent, and they were brought by companies and entrepreneurs. The first prominent example in this vein was litigation initiated by Internationale Handelsgesellschaft, a German import/export company. In the late 1960s, this company was in the business of exporting cereals to countries outside the EU (then the European Economic Community).

[26] I stress the idea of a structuring element – most typologies suffer from overlap and fuzzy boundaries.

[27] Bundesverfassungsgericht [Germany] BVerfGE 37, 271 *Solange I*.

[28] I use the term 'EU' in a broad sense to include its predecessors starting with the European Coal and Steel Community (ECSC).

In accordance with EU rules on the cereal market, companies wishing to do so needed to apply for export licences. In order to secure such licences, companies needed to pay a deposit to the national authority tasked with disbursing such licences. Internationale Handelsgesellschaft followed this procedure in order to export 20,000 tons of maize meal. The business paid the deposit but ended up unable to export the full 20,000 tons. The responsible German authority then declared part of the deposit (of about 17,000 Deutsche Mark) to be forfeited.[29]

What remedies would be available to Internationale Handelsgesellschaft in this situation? According to the *Plaumann* doctrine, which the CJEU developed in 1963, Internationale Handelsgesellschaft would not have standing to challenge the validity of the EU policy on export licences before the CJEU because they were not directly and individually concerned by the rule itself. They were directly and individually concerned by the forfeiture, but this decision was taken by a German authority. Internationale Handelsgesellschaft appealed this decision to an administrative court in Frankfurt. Since the German authority had merely followed the stipulations of the EU rules on cereal markets, Internationale Handelsgesellschaft could only argue that the EU rule breached a higher norm. In the event, they argued that the EU rule infringed on their economic rights guaranteed by the German constitution, in particular the right to conduct a business and the principle of proportionality that governs restrictions to this right. The administrative court referred the question of the validity of the EU rules on deposits and forfeiture to the CJEU, pointing out that such a rule likely ran counter to German constitutional law. The CJEU used this case to develop notions of EU fundamental rights but ultimately confirmed the validity of the EU norm and insisted on its supremacy over German constitutional law.[30] Back in Frankfurt, the administrative court then referred the case to the German constitutional court for its say on the constitutionality of deposits and forfeitures (ordinary courts in Germany cannot rule on constitutionality). The German constitutional court famously went on to admonish the solution found by the CJEU and to assert the German constitution as the higher standard against which it would measure EU law 'as long as' (*solange*, in German) the EU had no fundamental rights catalogue of its own that would be a worthy equivalent of the rights accorded by the German constitution.[31]

29 Bill Davies, *Resisting the European Court of Justice: West Germany's Confrontation with European Law, 1949–1979* (Cambridge University Press 2012) 160.

30 *Internationale Handelsgesellschaft mbH* (n 9).

31 Bundesverfassungsgericht [Germany] BVerfGE 37, 271 *Solange I* (n 27); Bill Davies, 'Internationale Handelsgesellschaft and the Miscalculation at the Inception of the ECJ's

This ruling significantly expanded the opportunity structure for constitutional rights claims against EU rules in Germany, but very few claims seem to have materialised. Perhaps this is a product of the somewhat restrictive procedure the German constitutional court had devised for such scenarios: a litigant would bring a claim to a lower German court, which would then have to refer the issue to the CJEU for a first ruling on validity. If the CJEU were to uphold the validity, the lower court could then refer the question to the German constitutional court for a final review. Internationale Handelsgesellschaft had lost its deposit in 1969, the German constitutional court issued its final decision five years later, and it went against Internationale Handelsgesellschaft in substance. While the *Solange* principle may have sounded favourable, it was probably of limited practical use as a remedy against contested administrative decisions in day-to-day business operations. Very few cases therefore followed this model.

One such case concerned a German authority's refusal to grant a property owner permission to plant vines, following EU rules aiming to cut excess capacities on the wine market. The property owner (Liselotte Hauer) objected to this decision claiming an infringement of her constitutional right to occupational freedom, in addition to her property rights (to the prospective vineyard). The administrative court of Neustadt an der Weinstraße followed the procedure mandated by the German constitutional court: it referred the question to the CJEU,[32] which upheld the validity of the EU rule.[33] Restrictive publication practices of the German constitutional court make it impossible to ascertain whether Mrs Hauer subsequently lodged a constitutional complaint. In any case, court records contain no such reference.

Another case led the German constitutional court to reverse its *Solange* doctrine. The plaintiff this time, Wünsche Handelsgesellschaft, was a company active in the import of agricultural products from third countries. At issue was a decision by a German authority to deny this company a licence to import preserved mushrooms from Taiwan, based on a Commission regulation protecting the European market in mushrooms. Wünsche first appealed the decision of the German authority to the Frankfurt administrative court on factual grounds. The first instance court confirmed the validity of the

Human Rights Jurisprudence' in Bill Davies and Fernanda Nicola (eds), *EU Law Stories: Contextual and Critical Histories of European Jurisprudence* (Cambridge University Press 2017) 163.

32 Case 44/79 *Liselotte Hauer v Land Rheinland-Pfalz* [1979] ECLI:EU:C:1979:290.

33 Gunnar Folke Schuppert, 'Public Law: Towards a Post-National Model' in Kenneth Dyson and Klaus Goetz (eds), *Germany, Europe, and the Politics of Constraint* (Oxford Academic, Oxford University Press 2003) 122.

Commission regulation without submitting questions to the CJEU and rejected Wünsche's claim. Wünsche appealed this ruling to the German federal administrative court, who in turn referred the question to the CJEU. The EU court confirmed the validity of the Commission regulation.[34] Unhappy with this outcome, Wünsche claimed that the CJEU had ignored important arguments and therefore deprived Wünsche of its right to a fair trial. In consequence, it asked the federal administrative court to either re-refer the issue to the CJEU or to refer the fundamental rights claims to the German constitutional court. When the federal administrative court refused both options and dismissed its appeal, Wünsche lodged a constitutional complaint with the German constitutional court, claiming this time that the federal administrative court had infringed its constitutional right to a fair trial. The German constitutional court accepted the case for decision but dismissed it on the merits.[35] In doing so, it reverted from the *Solange* doctrine and stated that it no longer reserved the right to review EU rules on the basis of the German constitution, as long as the EU upheld effective fundamental rights protection. This closed the opportunity for rights claims against EU rules in German courts for a number of years.

This new reading was tested a few years later in yet another case concerning trade in agricultural products. The import company this time was the Atlanta group, which did much of its business in the import of bananas. Its business model was affected by a reorganisation of the European market for bananas that gave preferential treatment to bananas produced in overseas territories of the Member States or African, Caribbean, and Pacific (ACP) countries that were party to EU partnership agreements. Germany had previously not had import restrictions, and the new rule set strict import quotas from third countries. Atlanta now had to apply for an import licence with the responsible German authority and the quota it was assigned was significantly lower than its imports of previous years. Atlanta challenged this decision before the Frankfurt administrative court. Like companies before it, Atlanta claimed a breach of its constitutional right to property and its occupational freedom. Its warehouses and ripening stations were running at reduced capacity, and it had to let go of workforce. The Frankfurt administrative court referred the question to the CJEU, which upheld the validity of the regulation.[36] Unhappy with this result, Atlanta requested a referral of the case to the German

34 Case 126/81 *Wünsche Handelsgesellschaft v Federal Republic of Germany* [1982] ECLI:EU:C:1982:144.

35 Bundesverfassungsgericht [Germany] BVerfGE 73, 339 *Solange II*.

36 Case C-466/93 *Atlanta Fruchthandelsgesellschaft mbH and Others v Bundesamt für Ernährung und Forstwirtschaft* [1995] ECLI:EU:C:1995:370.

constitutional court for a review of the validity of the EU regulation based on German constitutional principles. The German constitutional court rejected Atlanta's claims, reaffirming its revised *Solange* doctrine.[37]

6.3.2 *Social Rights: Challenges to EU-Induced Austerity*

Section 6.3.1 outlined how private litigants (companies and entrepreneurs) leveraged national economic rights against EU trade regulation that in some way restricted their economic activity. This section in turn deals with litigants that claim social rights – such as rights to social security, housing, or education – against EU-induced measures that limited welfare benefits and labour protections during the European sovereign debt crisis.[38] The EU's response to this crisis consisted of creative new legal instruments – 'new forms of law'[39] – that simultaneously existed outside the 'regular' legal order of the EU and had concrete and dire consequences in countries that had to make use of the EU's sovereign loan programmes. At the core of the legal challenges was the establishment of the European Stability Mechanism (ESM) and its predecessors, an embodiment of the EU's dual objective to extend fiscal solidarity and impose strict budgetary discipline. Governments of EU Member States set up the ESM as a facility to guarantee that distressed sovereign debt would be serviced and defaults prevented. In return, recipients of bailouts were required to sign Memoranda of Understanding (MoU) that outlined measures these governments committed to in order to regain creditworthiness. These were strictly focused on measures to reduce budget deficits and to deregulate labour markets. They included cuts to public pensions, welfare benefits, public sector pay and entitlements, and limits to employment protections and collective bargaining rights.[40]

Legal challenges against such measures faced two central obstacles: the unclear allocation of responsibility between the EU, the ESM, and the national level and the dearth of rights to claim against them. Both obstacles

37 Bundesverfassungsgericht [Germany] BVerfGE 102, 147 *Bananenmarktordnung*.

38 Alicia Hinarejos, *The Euro Area Crisis in Constitutional Perspective* (Oxford University Press 2015); Mark Dawson, Henrik Enderlein, and Christian Joerges (eds), *Beyond the Crisis: The Governance of Europe's Economic, Political and Legal Transformation* (Oxford University Press 2015); Thomas Beukers, Bruno de Witte, and Claire Kilpatrick (eds), *Constitutional Change through Euro-Crisis Law* (Cambridge University Press 2017).

39 Samo Bardutzky, 'Constitutional Courts, Preliminary Rulings and the "New Form of Law": The Adjudication of the European Stability Mechanism' (2015) 16 German Law Journal 1771.

40 Claire Kilpatrick, 'Are the Bailouts Immune to EU Social Challenge Because They Are Not EU Law?' (2014) 10 European Constitutional Law Review 393.

were intertwined: while the EU Charter of Fundamental Rights offers social and economic rights, the *Plaumann* doctrine restricts access to EU courts and the applicability of the Charter to MoUs rests on the question of whether these count as EU law in the first place. National constitutions, on the other hand, vary widely in the degree to which they grant social rights.[41] Legal challenges to MoU-induced austerity measures thus varied by access to courts and the availability of rights to draw upon. In November 2010 and April 2011, a Greek public sector union brought annulment actions before the General Court against measures contained in Council decisions within the Excessive Deficit Procedure that mandated cuts to holiday bonuses, increased the retirement age, and reduced pension levels.[42] The General Court found these actions inadmissible – it did not find the Council decisions of direct concern to the union. It instead pointed out the possibility of an indirect challenge via the preliminary reference procedure. However, in preliminary reference cases brought by a Romanian police union,[43] an employee of a Romanian municipal theater,[44] and Portuguese unions for employees of the banking[45] and insurance[46] sectors against cuts to pay and entitlements, the CJEU found that the measures in question, being national measures based on an MoU, lacked a direct connection to EU law and it therefore lacked jurisdiction. These judgments in effect cut off the option of a remedy in EU courts.

This left litigants with national courts and national sources of law. In Latvia, citizens made use of their access to constitutional complaint procedures against legal statutes to claim social rights contained in the Latvian constitution (such as a right to social security and children's rights). Several citizens brought such complaints against cuts to pensions,[47] parental benefits,[48] and

41 Claire Kilpatrick, 'Constitutions, Social Rights and Sovereign Debt States in Europe: A Challenging New Area of Constitutional Inquiry' in Bruno de Witte, Claire Kilpatrick, and Thomas Beukers (eds), *Constitutional Change through Euro-Crisis Law* (Cambridge University Press 2017).

42 Case T-541/10 *ADEDY and Others v Council* [2012] ECLI:EU:T:2012:626; Case T-215/11 *ADEDY and Others v Council* [2012] ECLI:EU:T:2012:627.

43 Case C-434/11 *Corpul Național al Polițiștilor* [2011] ECLI:EU:C:2011:830; Case C-134/12 *Corpul Național al Polițiștilor* [2012] ECLI:EU:C:2012:288.

44 Case C-462/11 *Victor Cozman v Teatrul Municipal Târgoviște* [2011] ECLI:EU:C:2011:831000.

45 Case C-128/12 *Sindicato dos Bancários do Norte and Others* [2013] ECLI:EU:C:2013:149.

46 Case C-264/12 *Sindicato Nacional dos Profissionais de Seguros e Afins* [2014] ECLI:EU:C:2014:2036.

47 Satversmes tiesa [Latvia] 2009-43-01 *Ilmārs Drēziņš et al. v the Parliament*; Satversmes tiesa [Latvia] 2009-76-01 *Uldis Mugurevičs v the Parliament*; Satversmes tiesa [Latvia] 2009-88-01 *Vēsma Vilka v the Parliament*; Satversmes tiesa [Latvia] 2010-21-01 *Eduards Ikvilds v the Parliament*.

48 Satversmes tiesa [Latvia] 2009-44-01 *Raimonds Priede-Baņģieris et al. v the Parliament*.

the salary of judges,[49] with some success in particular regarding pension cuts.[50] In Greece, civil society organisations (trade unions and professional associations) and individuals claimed their right to property (an economic right, here repurposed as a right to social entitlements) in litigation before the highest administrative court against Greek cuts to public pensions.[51] The court was not receptive to this claim but rather held that the right to property did not protect pension benefits of a specific amount and the cuts served the legitimate goal of shoring up Greek public finances.[52] Unions also challenged government measures that reduced minimum wage levels and labour protections,[53] claiming several social rights contained in the Greek constitution, such as a right to a decent living or the principle of collective autonomy.[54] Litigation in Greece did not include challenges against other cuts to welfare entitlements, such as housing or family support, a fact that observers attribute to the lack of civil society mobilisation in this field.[55] Similarly, the absence of rights-based litigation against austerity measures following bailout conditionality in Ireland has been linked to the lack of a culture of rights in economic and social issues.[56] In Portugal, despite a comparatively broad catalogue of social rights (the Portuguese constitution contains rights to social security, health care, decent housing, a safe environment, protection of the family, parenthood, and children's rights), litigation was largely brought by political actors (opposition MPs and the Portuguese president) in abstract review proceedings, to which civil society actors have no access.[57] Here, too,

49 Satversmes tiesa [Latvia] 2009-111-01 *Dace Ābele et al. v the Parliament.*

50 Zane Rasnača, *Constitutional Change through Eurocrisis Law: Latvia* (European University Institute 2014).

51 Symvoulio tis Epikrateias [Greece] 668/2012.

52 Evangelia Psychogiopoulou, 'Welfare rights in crisis in Greece: The role of fundamental rights challenges' in Claire Kilpatrick and Bruno de Witte (eds), *Social Rights in Times of Crisis in the Eurozone: The Role of Fundamental Rights' Challenges* (EUI Working papers LAW 05/2014).

53 Symvoulio tis Epikrateias [Greece] 2307/2014.

54 Matina Yannakourou, 'Challenging austerity measures affecting work rights at domestic and international level. The case of Greece' in Claire Kilpatrick and Bruno de Witte (eds), *Social Rights in Times of Crisis in the Eurozone: The Role of Fundamental Rights' Challenges* (EUI Working papers LAW 05/2014).

55 Psychogiopoulou (n 52).

56 Aoife Nolan, 'Welfare Rights in Crisis in the Eurozone: Ireland' in Claire Kilpatrick and Bruno de Witte (eds), *Social Rights in Times of Crisis in the Eurozone: The Role of Fundamental Rights' Challenges* (EUI Working papers LAW 05/2014).

57 Cristina Fasone, *Constitutional Courts Facing the Euro Crisis. Italy, Portugal and Spain in a Comparative Perspective* (EUI Working Papers MWP 25/ 2014); Kilpatrick (n 41); Miguel Nogueira de Brito, 'Putting Social Rights in Brackets? The Portuguese Experience with Welfare Challenges in Times of Crisis' in Claire Kilpatrick and Bruno de Witte (eds), *Social*

commentators have highlighted the absence of a culture of rights and litigation in civil society.[58] The Portuguese constitutional court, however, did prove responsive to some of the rights challenges brought by political actors, relying in particular on the principle of equality in invalidating austerity measures that – in the view of the litigants – placed an undue burden on the public sector.[59] The Romanian constitutional court, too, invalidated measures contained in the country's MoUs for breaches of fundamental rights. These cases were, as in Portugal, largely brought by opposition MPs in abstract judicial review cases, who had relied on social rights such as a right to a decent standard of living.[60]

6.3.3 *Civil Liberties: Challenges to EU Intrusions on Personal Liberties*

The EU's historic focus on market regulation did not give rise to many occasions where EU acts would intrude on civil liberties, such as the right to life, human dignity or privacy, or the freedom of expression or assembly. Economic actors (companies, mostly) affected by concrete EU acts, such as 'dawn raids' in anti-trust enforcement, usually had recourse to judicial review before EU courts. Such acts are of direct and individual concern to those targeted, which will grant standing under the *Plaumann* doctrine.[61] With the expansion of EU competences into policy fields beyond the common market, however, personal liberties became a more pressing issue. EU acts in areas of border control, migration, and defence are evidently more likely to cause immediate personal harm than trade regulation (and, arguably, austerity) – and are hence more likely to violate civil liberties. Claimants in these areas face multiple barriers. Unclear chains of delegation and allocation of responsibility make it harder for those affected to show direct and individual concern to gain standing before EU courts. Moreover, they are generally individuals of limited means and rely on legal aid from law clinics or organised civil society. They are often unaware of the opportunities offered by the legal system, and even where they are, such opportunities are narrow.

Rights in Times of Crisis in the Eurozone: The Role of Fundamental Rights' Challenges (EUI Working papers LAW 05/2014) 76.

58 Nogueira de Brito (n 57) 77.

59 Roberto Cisotta and Daniel Gallo, 'The Portuguese Constitutional Court Case Law on Austerity Measures: A Reappraisal' in Claire Kilpatrick and Bruno de Witte (eds), *Social Rights in Times of Crisis in the Eurozone: The Role of Fundamental Rights' Challenges* (EUI Working papers LAW 05/2014) 90.

60 Kilpatrick (n 41).

61 Miroslava Scholten and Alex Brenninkmeijer, *Controlling EU Agencies: The Rule of Law in a Multi-jurisdictional Legal Order* (Edward Elgar 2020).

The involvement of Frontex, the EU's border and coast guard agency, in maritime operations in the Mediterranean is one of the most vigorously debated instances of potential rights violations by EU agents. Frontex assists national border guards in their operations, mainly in the deterrence of undocumented migration. This scenario gives rise to many occasions in which the agency has been accused of infringing the personal liberties of migrants. The nature of the agency's cooperation with national agencies, however, diffuses accountability and makes it difficult to contest individual action.[62] While affected persons and their support network (mostly NGOs and pro bono legal clinics supporting migrants)[63] have addressed rights claims to national courts, they rarely challenge Frontex directly. Of the several cases that Pijnenburg and van der Pas report being brought in Italian courts, only one specifically included the conduct of EU officials in a shipwreck that resulted in a substantial number of fatalities.[64]

A similar scenario unfolds in the context of EU foreign missions. Potential claimants here face the additional hurdle that foreign policy in the EU – like in many national settings – is largely exempt from judicial review. Stian Øby Johansen describes litigation by the relatives of nine ethnic Serbs who were killed in Kosovo between 1999 and 2000.[65] The litigants targeted the EU mission in Kosovo for its failure to investigate these crimes, claiming an infringement of their right to life and the prohibition of torture and inhuman or degrading treatment or punishment under the EU Charter of Fundamental Rights. After several unsuccessful attempts in international legal fora, including the EU General Court, the claimants turned to British courts, where their action resulted in a noteworthy judgment by the English High Court.[66] However, they ultimately failed to overcome the obstacle of finding a national (in this case, English) source of rights to claim before an English court. Following the CJEU's *Foto-Frost* doctrine, the English High Court refrained from adjudicating on the conformity of an EU act with a higher EU legal norm.[67]

62 Melanie Fink, 'The Action for Damages as a Fundamental Rights Remedy: Holding Frontex Liable' (2020) 21 German Law Journal 532.

63 Annick Pijnenburg and Kris van der Pas, 'Strategic Litigation against European Migration Control Policies: The Legal Battleground of the Central Mediterranean Migration Route' (2022) 24 European Journal of Migration and Law 401.

64 Ibid 413.

65 Stian Øby Johansen, 'Suing the European Union in the UK: *Tomanovic et. al. v. the European Union et. al.*' (2019) 4 European Papers 345.

66 England and Wales High Court [UK] *Tomanović et.al. v the European Union et.al.* [2019] EWHC 263 (QB).

67 Johansen (n 65).

6.3.4 *Political Rights: Challenges to EU Policies and EU Integration as Such*

The final group of rights reviewed here that have been claimed by litigants against EU acts are political rights, here understood as rights to political participation, and in particular the right to vote. Litigation that relied on such rights generally did not target individual EU measures but rather broad EU policies, such as the EU's financial rescue mechanisms during the Eurozone crisis or EU integration as such. Cases again almost exclusively originated in constitutional complaints before the German constitutional court, which were brought by a comparatively small group of prominent repeat litigants. Such litigation has its origins in a prominent case concerning the German ratification of the Treaty of Maastricht. A former EU Commission official and a number of members of the German parliament for the party Bündnis 90/Die Grünen claimed that the ratification of this treaty entailed a transfer of legislative competences to the EU level that essentially rendered domestic elections meaningless. This, they claimed, constituted a violation of their constitutional right to free and fair parliamentary elections.[68]

The German constitutional court accepted this claim in principle, even if it did not invalidate the ratification as such. The German judges reserved for themselves the authority to review the conformity of EU acts with the principle of conferral. In this reading, the right to vote not only entails participation in universal, free, and fair election but also that elected representatives can make meaningful choices about public policy – it entails, in a sense, a right to democracy.[69] This ability would be impaired if an excess of essential legislative competences were transferred to the EU or if EU institutions were to take decisions outside of their mandate that could tie the hands of future legislators.[70] This interpretation gave creative litigants extensive leeway in challenging EU policies. Litigants could now employ constitutional complaints against EU acts that, in their view, were not covered by EU competences circumscribed by primary EU law. Such complaints have since become a regular feature of major EU projects: the introduction of the Euro,[71] the Treaty of Lisbon,[72] EU responses to the

[68] Bundesverfassungsgericht [Germany] BVerfGE 89, 155 *Maastricht* (n 12).

[69] Isabel Feichtner, 'The German Constitutional Court's PSPP Judgment: Impediment and Impetus for the Democratization of Europe' (2020) 21 German Law Journal 1090.

[70] Ibid 1091; Peter Hilpold, 'So Long Solange? The PSPP Judgment of the German Constitutional Court and the Conflict between the German and the European 'Popular Spirit'' (2021) 23 Cambridge Yearbook of European Legal Studies 159, 166.

[71] Bundesverfassungsgericht [Germany] BVerfGE 97, 350 *Euro*.

[72] Bundesverfassungsgericht [Germany] BVerfGE 123, 267 *Lissabon*.

Eurocrisis,[73] and the EU rescue mechanisms established in reaction to the COVID-19 pandemic.[74] Litigants not only challenged EU legislation but also acts of the Europan Central Bank (ECB) and judgments of the CJEU. So far, only the complaints against the ECB's public sector purchase programme (PSPP) have had – famously – some degree of success. The German court created deep controversy by rejecting a previous CJEU ruling and ordering the ECB to give reasons for its programme of quantitative easing that reflected potential negative socio-economic effects (such as a potential real estate bubble).[75] Compare this to a similar challenge by two Belgian activists before the Belgian constitutional court,[76] which that court rejected because the litigants could not show individual concern.[77]

Given the German constitutional court's openness to such broad challenges, organised interests have discovered the mobilising potential of filing 'mass constitutional complaints' against EU acts.[78] The group 'Europolis' around lawyer and academic Markus C. Kerber filed at least five complaints against various bailout measures.[79] 'Bündnis Bürgerwille', a group surrounding the AfD-founder Bernd Lucke, filed a constitutional complaint against the ECB's public sector purchasing programme in the name of some 1,700 applicants[80] and a complaint against the EU's pandemic recovery fund NextGenerationEU co-signed by 2,275 individuals.[81] Another group, 'Mehr Demokratie', committed to promoting direct democracy, brought together 11,718 individuals to challenge the ESM.[82] The largest single constitutional complaint to date was lodged in 2016 by 'Mehr Demokratie' in cooperation with the groups 'Campact' and 'Foodwatch', who assembled 125,000

[73] Bundesverfassungsgericht [Germany] BVerfGE 129, 124 *EFS*; Bundesverfassungsgericht [Germany] BVerfGE 132, 195 *Europäischer Stabilitätsmechanismus*; Bundesverfassungsgericht [Germany] BVerfGE 134, 366 *OMT-Beschluss*; Bundesverfassungsgericht [Germany] BVerfGE 151, 202 *Europäische Bankenunion*; Bundesverfassungsgericht [Germany] BVerfGE 154, 17 *PSPP-Programm der EZB*.

[74] Bundesverfassungsgericht [Germany] BVerfGE 157, 332 *Eigenmittelbeschluss-Ratifizierungsgesetz*.

[75] Feichtner (n 69); Hilpold (n 70).

[76] Court Constitutionelle [Belgium] 33/2012.

[77] Werner Vandenbruwaene, *Constitutional Change through Eurocrisis Law: Belgium* (European University Institute 2014).

[78] Thierse (n 24).

[79] Bundesverfassungsgericht [Germany] 2 BvR 1219/10; Bundesverfassungsgericht [Germany] 2 BvR 1824/12; Bundesverfassungsgericht [Germany] 2 BvR 2731/13; Bundesverfassungsgericht [Germany] 2 BvR 980/16; Bundesverfassungsgericht [Germany] 2 BvR 71/20.

[80] Bundesverfassungsgericht [Germany] 2 BvR 1651/15.

[81] Bundesverfassungsgericht [Germany] 2 BvR 547/21.

[82] Bundesverfassungsgericht [Germany] 2 BvR 1438/12.

individuals to challenge the constitutionality of CETA, the EU's trade agreement with Canada.[83] A concurrent complaint by private activist Marianne Grimmenstein assembled another 68,000 complainants.[84] The complainants held that the CETA committee system, which has certain autonomous rule-setting powers, infringed on their right to vote.[85]

6.4 CONCLUSIONS

This chapter reviewed the role of national courts in a system of remedies against fundamental rights violations by the European Union. While the European legal hierarchy, based on the principle of primacy of EU law as envisaged by the CJEU, does not foresee an independent role for them, national courts can and do provide such remedies. However, the degree to which they do so is predicated both on opportunity structures, such as the availability of (national) rights to rely on, procedures that provide remedies, and access to courts for private litigants, as well as on more contingent factors such as the national judiciary's receptivity to fundamental rights claims against EU acts, litigant resources, and the existence of a support structure for rights claims, such as a well-qualified legal profession and organised civil society. Such conditions cluster in some regions more so than in others. The empirical overview of rights claims against EU acts has repeatedly focused on Germany and its constitutional court. Here, an active civil society meets with a broad interpretation of national fundamental rights by a well-respected and politically influential constitutional court that provides comparatively broad access in the form of constitutional complaints. In an earlier phase of EU market integration, German companies and their legal counsel claimed economic rights against EU trade regulation. Beginning with the Treaty of Maastricht, civil society actors, often a handful of repeat litigants, started claiming their right to vote, recast as a right to democracy, against virtually all major EU projects. Social rights, largely absent from the German constitution, played a significant role in litigation by individuals, trade unions, and professional associations in countries affected by bail-out conditionality during the sovereign debt crisis. 'Classic' civil liberties, on the other hand, hardly feature at all in rights claims against EU acts. Those affected by EU migration policy and external action face substantial barriers to legal remedies: they lack individual resources, access to courts, and judicial receptivity to their claims.

[83] Bundesverfassungsgericht [Germany] 2 BvR 1823/16.

[84] Bundesverfassungsgericht [Germany] 2 BvR 1444/16.

[85] Markus Krajewski, 'Vorläufig teilweise verfassungskonform: Zum CETA-Beschluss des Bundesverfassungsgerichts' (*Verfassungsblog*, 12 March 2022).

In recent years, a different set of courts has moved to the centre of the debate about national legal challenges to EU acts. The constitutional courts of Hungary and Poland have issued several judgments challenging the primacy of EU law over national constitutions.[86] In a number of cases since 2016, the Hungarian constitutional court has invoked the concept of constitutional identity, most prominently developed by the German constitutional court in its judgment on the Treaty of Lisbon, in order to defend the Hungarian government's refusal to accept relocated migrants from other EU countries and to push back migrants at the Serbian border.[87] In 2021, the Polish constitutional court, referencing the PSPP judgment of the German constitutional court, declared EU law on effective legal protection and judicial independence, as interpreted by the CJEU, incompatible with the Polish constitution.[88] Commentators have pointed out parallels to Danish and Italian cases that invoke the protection of national constitutional identity against EU acts.[89] Nonetheless, these cases stand out from those covered in this chapter. The Hungarian and Polish cases were initiated by government entities in abstract review proceedings to defend government policies. They were brought before courts where the majority of judges had been appointed by pro-government parliamentary majorities. They were not initiated by civil society actors and are not good faith efforts to safeguard the fundamental rights of such applicants against public authorities.

I will conclude with two observations about the limits of what this chapter has offered. First, the overview presented in this chapter is impressionistic. It can be seen as the beginning of an endeavour to more systematically map and classify fundamental rights–based litigation against EU acts in national courts. Existing literature largely covers prominent cases where litigants have had some success, giving cause to doctrinal and normative debate. Unsuccessful attempts receive little (if any) attention and, given restrictive publication practices of national courts,[90] may prove difficult to identify in the

86 Fabbrini and Sajó (n 13); Jakub Jaraczewski, 'Gazing into the Abyss: The K 3/21 decision of the Polish Constitutional Tribunal' (*Verfassungsblog*, 12 October 2021); Gábor Halmai, 'Abuse of constitutional identity: the Hungarian constitutional court on interpretation of article E) (2) of the fundamental law' (2018) 43 Review of Central and East European law 23.

87 Gábor Halmai, 'Coping Strategies of the Hungarian Constitutional Court since 2010' (*Verfassungsblog*, 27 September 2022).

88 Jaraczewski (n 86).

89 Fabbrini and Sajó (n 13).

90 For example, the German constitutional court does not publish constitutional complaints that it does not accept for decision – which amounts to 98% of all such complaints. German courts in general publish less than 1% of all judgments. Those that do get published are biased towards unusual or innovative outcomes: Hanjo Hamann, 'Der blinde Fleck der deutschen Rechtswissenschaft – Zur digitalen Verfügbarkeit instanzgerichtlicher Rechtsprechung' (2021) 76 JuristenZeitung 656.

first place. Finally, this chapter has not addressed the question of whether national remedies are normatively desirable. The previous paragraph has highlighted the pitfalls of a commitment to legal pluralism in the EU.[91] Any positive assessment relies strongly on efforts of national judiciaries to safeguard fundamental rights against intrusions by all public authorities, not a selective preference for national over European actors. As I have pointed out, this is not a given in all EU Member States today. Nonetheless, fundamental rights challenges against EU acts in national courts are an empirical reality that deserves both greater empirical attention and more nuanced normative debate.

[91] R. Daniel Kelemen, 'The Dangers of Constitutional Pluralism' in Gareth Davies and Matej Avbelj (eds), *Research Handbook on Legal Pluralism an EU Law* (Edward Elgar 2018).

7

EU Accession to the ECHR

Completing the Complete System of EU Remedies?

JASPER KROMMENDIJK*

7.1 INTRODUCTION

Accession of the EU to the European Convention for the Protection of Human Rights and Fundamental Freedoms (ECHR, the Convention) is back on the table and becoming a realistic prospect. Negotiations kickstarted in mid-2020 and have unfolded relatively smoothly, partly facilitated by Russia's recent exclusion from the Council of Europe.[1] The 46 + 1 Group reached a deal on 17 March 2023, prior to the Summit of Heads of State and Government of the Council of Europe in Reykjavik in May 2023.[2] Accession to the ECHR will obviously have consequences for fundamental rights accountability of the EU. While most of the chapters in this volume focus on internal EU procedures and remedies that provide for (or obstruct) access to justice, this chapter takes stock of this external fundamental rights system conducive to effective judicial protection.

Eventual accession will close more than forty years of discussion. This discussion was first launched at the end of the 1970s in the good old days of

* I would like to thank Kris van der Pas, Annick Pijnenburg, and Guus de Vries for their valuable comments on an earlier version. Many thanks also go to Melanie Fink for her truly admirable substantive comments.

1 'EU accession to the ECHR' (Council of Europe Portal) <www.coe.int/en/web/human-rights-intergovernmental-cooperation/accession-of-the-european-union-to-the-european-convention-on-human-rights#{%22301661 37%22:[0]}>.

2 Note that this deal is incomplete, because it does not include an agreement on CFSP (see Section 7.4). The CJEU, Parliamentary Assembly, and ECtHR also need to give their opinions. 'Geannoteerde agenda van de bijeenkomst van de Raad Justitie en Binnenlandse Zaken, 8 en 9 december' (*Openoverheid*, December 2022) <https://open.overheid.nl/documenten/ronl-8ef5c0285d2b43b46ecb7e93e42ad3985c4a911b/pdf>, 12.

the European Communities.[3] Accession and its advantages and consequences have been among the 'favourite topics of discussion' of academics.[4] It is well known that accession has been thwarted twice by the Court of Justice of the European Union (CJEU) with its *Opinion 2/94* and *Opinion 2/13*. The latter opinion from December 2014 has been especially criticised.[5] *Opinion 2/13* has been described as a 'problematic attitude of "European exceptionalism"' and reflective of 'an overconfident belief that the EU under the Court's own stewardship, has risen above the political and institutional defects that typically generate fundamental rights infringements'.[6] Following *Opinion 2/13*, it was long thought that accession would be difficult or of limited added value.[7] Since June 2020, thirteen negotiation meetings haven taken place with a total of forty-four days of discussions. It seems that most of the objections that were raised by the CJEU have been addressed in one way or another.

With accession, 'one of the last gaps in European fundamental rights protection will be overcome'.[8] After accession, individuals can turn to the European Court of Human Rights (ECtHR) and complain about fundamental rights violations of the EU. Strasbourg can thus critically examine from an ECHR perspective the gaps in legal protection identified in other parts of this volume. This includes the strict *locus standi* requirements, the high threshold for damage, and the limited judicial review of the Common Foreign and Security Policy (CFSP). In addition to ex post accountability, accession could potentially have a preventive function and influence the position of the CJEU and other EU institutions and agencies. Accession could, however, also contribute to a more formalistic complacency on the part of the CJEU in

3 Commission, 'Memorandum on the accession of the European Communities to the Convention for Protection of Human Rights and Fundamental Freedoms', Bulletin Supplement 2/79, COM (79) 210 final; Paul Gragl, 'A giant leap for European human rights? The final agreement on the European Union's accession to the European Convention on Human Rights' (2014) 51 Common Market Law Review 13, 14.

4 Jean Paul Jacqué, 'The accession of the European Union to the European Convention of Human Rights and Fundamental Freedoms' (2011) 48 Common Market Law Review 995.

5 Christoph Krenn, 'Autonomy and effectiveness as common concerns: A path to ECHR accession after Opinion 2/13' (2015) 16 German Law Journal 147; Steve Peers, 'The CJEU and the EU's accession to the ECHR: A clear and present danger to human rights protection' (*EU Law Analysis*, 18 December 2014) <http://eulawanalysis.blogspot.com/2014/12/the-cjeu-and-eus-accession-to-echr.html.>.

6 Turkiler Isiksel, 'European exceptionalism and the EU's accession to the ECHR' (2016) 27 The European Journal of International Law 565, 565–566.

7 See Jasper Krommendijk, 'Opinion 2/13 as a Game Changer in the Dialogue between the European Courts?' in Emmanuelle Bribosia and Isabelle Rorive (eds), *Human Rights Tectonics. Global Perspectives on Integration and Fragmentation* (Intersentia 2018).

8 Gragl (n 3).

line with its often-repeated mantra that there is a 'complete system of remedies', without any substantive changes in its approach to remedies.[9]

This chapter answers the question as to what the potential impact of EU accession to the ECHR is from the perspective of fundamental rights accountability and effective judicial protection vis-à-vis the EU. In order to answer this question, this chapter examines the most recent version of the negotiated Accession Agreement (AA).[10] The Section 7.2 delves into the added value of accession. It shows how accession fills two protection gaps (Section 7.2.1) while also contributing to coherence and legal certainty (Section 7.2.2). This section ends with a reflection on expected substantive effects (Section 7.2.3). Section 7.3 focuses on the procedural practicalities governing review by the ECtHR following accession, discussing admissibility (Section 7.3.1), the co-respondent mechanism in relation to shared responsibility of the EU and EU Member States (Section 7.3.2), and the prior involvement procedure (Section 7.3.3). Section 7.4 analyses the particular context of the CFSP, not least because most gains in terms of remedying existing gaps in judicial protection could surface in the context of the CFSP.

7.2 THE BENEFITS OF ACCESSION

Many commentators and experts have over the years written about the (legal) advantages of accession of the EU to the ECHR. Various overviews can be made. For the purpose of this edited volume focused on the access of individuals to fundamental rights accountability mechanisms, three main perspectives are relevant.[11] The first is the importance of external scrutiny and remedies outside the EU legal system (Section 7.2.1). A second advantage concerns the strengthening of coherence between the ECHR and the EU legal order with positive effects for legal certainty (Section 7.2.2). The last subsection discusses other substantive effects positive from the perspective of judicial protection, such as a possible relaxation of standing requirements or a development of positive obligations in relation to the EU (Section 7.2.3).

9 Case C-583/11 P *Inuit Tapiriit Kanatami and Others* v *Parliament and Council* [2013] ECLI:EU:C:2013:625, para 92.

10 'Final consolidated version of the draft accession instruments' (CDDH ad hoc negotiation group ('46+1'), 17 March 2023) <https://rm.coe.int/final-consolidated-version-of-the-draft-accession-instruments/1680aaaecd>. (hereafter: Accession Agreement or AA).

11 In addition, because the EU becomes a contracting party, the EU can also be directly involved in negotiations in relation to the ECHR. The duty of sincere cooperation in Consolidated Version of the Treaty on European Union (TEU) [2008] OJ C115/13 art 4(3) also obliges Member States to conduct these negotiations as a block; Gragl (n 3) 15.

Accession of the EU not only has concrete *legal* effects. It is also of political and symbolic value.[12] This relates very much to the credibility of the EU and its foreign policy.[13] Accession sends a strong signal to third countries that the EU itself is also willing to accept external scrutiny.[14] Hence, the EU is subject to external fundamental rights monitoring in the same way as it demands from others.[15] Accession, thus, does away with 'charges of double standards'.[16]

7.2.1 *External Remedies Filling Two Protection Gaps*

Accession obviously has the immediate effect of providing natural or legal persons with the possibility to complain before the ECtHR. Currently they experience a gap in the protection of their ECHR rights in two different ways: the inability to complain about acts or omissions of the EU as well as the (near) impossibility to address the implementation of EU law by EU Member States when the latter have no margin of discretion. Accession will remedy these deficiencies and enables individual complaints in both scenarios. Accession even allows applications in relation to EU primary law.[17] This is noteworthy because the CJEU itself cannot annul or declare primary EU law invalid.[18] With respect to the first scenario, it is currently impossible to complain about fundamental rights violations (allegedly) committed by the

[12] Noreen O'Meara, '"A more secure Europe of rights?" The European Court of Human Rights, the Court of Justice of the European Union and EU accession to the ECHR' (2011) 12 German Law Journal 1813, 1825.

[13] Leonard Besselink, 'The Protection of Fundamental Rights post-Lisbon. The Interaction between the EU Charter of Fundamental Rights, the European Convention on Human Rights (ECHR) and National Constitutions' (FIDE General Report 2013) 35.

[14] Martin Kuijer, 'The accession of the European Union to the ECHR: A gift for the ECHR's 60th anniversary or an unwelcome intruder at the party?' (2011) 3 Amsterdam Law Forum 17, 22.

[15] Paul Craig, 'EU accession to the ECHR: Competence, procedure and substance' (2013) 36 Fordham International Law Journal 1114.

[16] Sionaidh Douglas-Scott, 'The European Union and human rights after the Treaty of Lisbon' (2011) 11 Human Rights Law Review 645, 658.

[17] Article 3(3) AA refers to 'a provision of the Treaty on European Union, the Treaty on the Functioning of the European Union or any other provision having the same legal value pursuant to those instruments'. In this scenario, Member States may become co-respondents, as discussed in Section 7.3.2. 'Appendix 5: Draft explanatory report to the Agreement on the Accession of the European Union to the Convention for the Protection of Human Rights and Fundamental Freedoms' (17 March 2023) <https://rm.coe.int/final-consolidated-version-of-the-draft-accession-instruments/1680aaaecd> (hereafter: Draft explanatory report to the AA) paras 41 and 56–57.

[18] From the perspective of the ECHR, such an exclusion stands at odds with the current practice that does not give national constitutions a similar status. Gragl (n 3) 28–29.

EU and its institutions.[19] Without EU accession to the Convention, the EU cannot be held liable under the ECHR. One well-known example is *Connolly*. This was a case brought by a European Commission official challenging a disciplinary procedure resulting in suspension following the publication of a book. He criticised the reasons for his dismissal as infringing his freedom of expression. The ECtHR declared the case inadmissible *ratione personae*, which means that the alleged violation of the ECHR was not committed by (or to be attributed to) a contracting State Party.[20] Another example of the broadening of the possibility for accountability of the EU concerns civilian and military missions launched in the context of the CFSP (Section 7.4 will discuss this more extensively). Accession will make it possible to complain before the ECtHR about alleged fundamental rights violations in the context of such missions.

The inability to make a complaint against the EU before the ECtHR prior to accession does not preclude the possibility that the EU Member States themselves are held responsible for violations of the Convention arising from their EU law obligations. Connolly, for example, not only complained against the EU but also the fifteen EU Member States at that time. The ECtHR, however, noted that at no time did any of the EU Member States in question intervene, directly or indirectly, in this dispute. Hence, there was no action or omission by these States that would be such as to engage their responsibility under the Convention. Where no Member States are involved in an infringement, the ECtHR also has no jurisdiction.[21]

Connolly illustrates that the accountability deficit can in principle be overcome by targeting EU Member States when they are (in)directly involved. Aside from pure EU acts or omissions, in many situations there is such involvement, because EU law frequently depends on the implementation by national authorities. Nonetheless, it is currently impossible to complain against EU Member States when they implement EU law without any discretion.[22] This relates to the *Bosphorus* doctrine developed in a case

[19] *Confédération française démocratique du travail v the European Communities, alternatively: their Member States a) jointly and b) severally* (dec.), App no 8030/77 (ECtHR, 10 July 1978); *M. & Co v Germany* (dec.), App no 13258/8 (ECtHR, 9 February 1990).

[20] The Commission official earlier started cases before the CJEU. See Joined Cases T-34/96 and 163/96 *Bernard Connolly v Commission of the European Communities* [1999] ECLI:EU:T:1999:102; Case C-274/99 P *Bernard Connolly v Commission of the European Communities* [2001] ECLI:EU:C:2001:127; *Connolly v 15 Member States of the European Union* (dec.), App no 73274/01 (ECtHR, 9 December 2008).

[21] See *Connolly v 15 Member States* (n 20); Douglas-Scott (n 16) 659.

[22] Kuijer (n 14) 21.

dealing with an alleged violation of the right to property following the seizure of an aircraft by Ireland on the basis of a strict obligation contained in an EU regulation with no discretion.[23] On the basis of this doctrine, the ECtHR presumes that the ECHR is not violated when the Member State had no discretion on the basis of EU law and when the full potential of the EU's supervisory mechanism and system of legal protection had been employed. This presumption can be rebutted if the protection of ECHR rights was manifestly deficient.[24] The *Bosphorus* presumption reflects the difficult position of Member States in situations in which there is no room for manoeuvre for Member States and, hence, no possibility to reconcile or pragmatically weigh conflicting obligations.[25] The presumption is also seen as an illustration of the willingness of the ECtHR to show comity and respect for the CJEU.[26] The ECtHR has only once rebutted the presumption since its *Bosphorus* judgment of 2006. In *Bivolaru and Moldovan*, the ECtHR determined for the first time that the presumption did not apply even though it did not find a breach of Article 3 ECHR because the French judge had applied the EU legal framework correctly.[27]

There is a burgeoning discussion in the literature whether accession means an end to the *Bosphorus* presumption. Most commentators think this is the case.[28] They argue that there is no reason to extend a preferential treatment to the EU that diverges from other regular ECHR contracting parties.[29] The ECtHR is expected to apply a more rigorous review of EU action instead of

[23] This presumption is also based on the rationale that the ECHR does not prevent states from transferring powers to an international organisation such as the EU, provided that fundamental rights are respected. *Matthews v United Kingdom*, App no 24833/94 (ECtHR, 18 February 1999).

[24] *Bosphorus v Ireland*, App no 45036/98 (ECtHR, 30 June 2005) para 156.

[25] Christiaan Timmermans, 'Will the Accession of the EU to the European Convention on Human Rights fundamentally change the relationship between the Luxemburg and the Strasbourg courts?' [2014] EUI Distinguished Lectures (Speech delivered at the 'Judicial Cooperation in Private Law' of 15 and 16 April 2013).

[26] Tobias Lock, 'EU Accession to the ECHR: Implications for Judicial Review in Strasbourg' (2010) 35 European Law Review 777, 798.

[27] Note that the ECtHR concluded in the other case (*Moldovan*) that the *Bosphorus* presumption of equivalent protection was fulfilled but that there was a manifest deficiency and, thus, a violation of Article 3 ECHR; *Bivolaru and Moldovan v France*, App no 40324/16 and 12623/17 (ECtHR, 25 March 2021).

[28] Kuijer (n 14) 21; Francis Jacobs, 'The Lisbon Treaty and the Court of Justice' in Andrea Biondi, Piet Eeckhout, and Stefanie Ripley (eds), *EU law after Lisbon* (Oxford University Press 2012) 205; Lock (n 26) 798; O'Meara (n 12) 1828; Pedro Cruz Villalón, 'Rights in Europe: The crowded house' (2012) King's College London Working Paper 01/2012, 6; Gragl (n 3) 19; Besselink (n 13) 37.

[29] Timmermans (n 25).

the more deferential *Bosphorus* presumption.[30] Timmermans, however, notes that it is ironical that the presumption existing before accession is abandoned after accession. He also argues that the CJEU is not comparable to supreme courts of Member States.[31]

In sum, accession provides external remedies that close two protection gaps. One might wonder how big the gaps are and, thus, in how many cases fundamental rights accountability remains a dead letter. Answering these questions is obviously highly speculative. The few declarations of inadmissibility by the ECtHR tell very little, because complaints against the EU are by definition unsuccessful and thus probably only the tip of the iceberg. Based on the case law of the CJEU, one could argue that there are only a limited number of violations committed by EU institutions.[32] One competition law example is *Baustahlgewebe* in which the CJEU held that the proceedings before the Court of First Instance were excessively long. It, hence, lowered the fine for the respective company.[33] A similar tendency can be reported for declarations of invalidity of EU law. In the last decade, there have been less than a handful of cases such as *Digital Rights Ireland* and *Schrems* in the context of data protection and privacy.[34] Once again, these numbers tell very little. They are more a reflection of the high thresholds for the fulfillment of the conditions for non-contractual liability of the EU or the strict *locus standi* requirements for legal and natural persons in relation to the action for annulment.

7.2.2 *Greater Coherency between the EU and ECHR*

At a more abstract level, accession has the consequence that the ECtHR becomes the 'ultimate arbiter'. The CJEU will be – in hierarchical terms – subject to the jurisdiction of the ECtHR.[35] The judgments of the ECtHR are binding on all EU institutions including the CJEU, following Article 46

[30] Douglas-Scott (n 16) 668.

[31] Timmermans (n 25).

[32] Isiksel (n 6) 583.

[33] Case C-185/95 *Baustahlgewebe v Commission* [1998] ECLI:EU:C:1998:608. In a later case, the CJEU determined that applicants must bring a separate action before the Court of First Instance to obtain damages for losses stemming from long judicial proceedings. Case C-50/12 P *Kendrion v Commission* [2013] ECLI:EU:C:2013:771..

[34] Case C-293/12 *Digital Rights Ireland* [2014] ECLI:EU:C:2014:238; Case C-362/14 *Schrems v Data Protection Commissioner* [2015] ECLI:EU:C:2015:650.

[35] This also brings to an end the 'pluralist framework' whereby there does not exist a final arbiter of the protection of fundamental rights in Europe. Iris Canor, 'Primus inter pares. Who is the ultimate guardian of fundamental rights in Europe?'(2000) 25 European Law Review 3.

ECHR.[36] The ECtHR can thus 'correct' the CJEU when the latter provides more limited protection.[37] The ECtHR has the last word and could solve a conflict between case law of both courts.[38] A consequence is that the ECHR acts as a clear 'minimum benchmark'.[39] The EU will no longer be 'the ultimate repository of meaning' with respect to fundamental rights in relation to EU law, at least to the extent that these rights are covered by the ECHR.[40] Also, from a substantive perspective, the meaning of these rights and their balance with other interests will eventually be made by Strasbourg.[41] Accession might lead the CJEU to offer less relative weight to market objectives.[42]

The hierarchical relationship minimises the risks of conflicting case law.[43] Even though real conflicts have almost never occurred,[44] the threat has been 'ever present'.[45] Currently, there is a lot of debate within the literature as to the possibility of diverging standards of judicial independence.[46] It also remains to be seen whether the ECtHR will follow the two-step test that the CJEU

36 Consolidated Version of The Treaty on the Functioning of the European Union OJ C326/47 (TFEU) art 216(2); Case *Opinion 2/13 – Accession of the EU to the ECHR* [2014] ECLI:EU:C:2014:2454, paras 180-182; Draft explanatory report to the AA (n 17) para 30.

37 Besselink (n 13) 35.

38 Timmermans (n 25).

39 Johan Callewaert, 'No more common understanding of fundamental rights' (2022) 22 La revue des jurists de Sciences Po 25, 25.

40 Craig (n 15) 1145.

41 Ibid 1146.

42 Isiksel (n 6) 583.

43 Douglas-Scott (n 16) 658–659; Kuijer (n 14) 21; Adam Łazowski and Ramses Wessel, 'When caveats turn into locks: *Opinion 2/13* on accession of the European Union to the ECHR' (2015) 16 German Law Journal 179. Former CJEU Judge Arestis held that the CJEU is 'very concerned with the consistency of its judgments' with the case-law of the ECtHR. George Arestis, 'Fundamental rights in the EU: three years after Lisbon, the Luxembourg perspective' College of Europe research papers 02/2013, 13. The Joint Communication from Presidents Costa and Skouris pointed to the need to ensure 'the greatest coherence' between the ECHR and the Charter. 'Joint communication from Presidents Costa and Skouris' (24 January 2011) <http://curia.europa.eu/jcms/upload/docs/application/pdf/2011-02/cedh_cjue_english.pdf.>.

44 The CJEU did not follow the ECtHR in *Emesa Sugar*, where the CJEU denied parties a right to comment on the AG's Opinion. Case C-17/98 *Emesa Sugar* [2000] ECLI:EU:C:2000:70; Bruno de Witte, 'The use of the ECHR and Convention case law by the European Court of Justice' in Patricia Popelier, Catherine van de Heyning, and Piet van Nuffel (eds), *Human rights protection in the European legal order: the interaction between the European and the national courts* (Intersentia 2011) 25; Douglas-Scott (n 16) 648; Sara Iglesias Sánchez, 'The Court and the Charter: The impact of the entry into force of the Lisbon Treaty on the ECJ's approach to fundamental rights' (2012) 49 Common Market Law Review 1565, 1602.

45 Jacqué (n 4) 1001.

46 Ben Smulders, 'Increasing convergence between the European court of Human Rights and the Court of Justice of the European Union in their recent case law on judicial independence: The case of irregular judicial appointments' (2022) 59 Common Market Law Review 105.

developed in the context of criminal cooperation marked by mutual trust. In *Aranyosi*, the CJEU held that the execution of a European arrest warrant has to be postponed if a national court finds that there are, firstly, systemic or generalised deficiencies as to the detention conditions in the issuing Member State and, secondly, a real risk for the individual of inhuman or degrading treatment.[47] The CJEU has extended this two-step test to situations involving the fundamental right to a fair trial.[48] The CJEU has declined the possibility of postponement where an individual risk cannot be proven.[49] It also ruled out the possibility to examine such an individual risk without any systemic or generalised deficiencies.[50] It is unclear whether this approach is in line with the ECHR and the case law of the ECtHR.[51] Nothing precludes the ECtHR from finding an individual case when there are no structural problems. Such divergences are less likely to occur after accession.

Given the binding nature of ECtHR judgments, accession could also 'cement more firmly' the role of ECtHR judgments in the EU legal order.[52] Accession could lead to a more deliberative and substantive engagement and dialogue with the ECtHR replacing the current discretionary, selective, and instrumental engagement with Strasbourg.[53] The CJEU treats ECtHR judgments currently as 'mere' useful sources of inspiration that are regularly taken into consideration. After accession, the CJEU can apply the ECHR directly,

47 Joined Cases C-404/15 and C-659/15 PPU *Aranyosi and Căldăraru* [2016] ECLI:EU:C:2016:198, paras 86–91.

48 Case C-216/18 PPU *Minister for Justice and Equality (Deficiencies in the system of justice)* [2018] ECLI:EU:C:2018:586.

49 A Dutch district court challenged the restrictiveness of the test. Thomas Vandamme, '"The two-step can't be the quick step": The CJEU reaffirms its case law on the European Arrest Warrant and the rule of law backsliding' (*European Law Blog*, 10 February 2021) <https://europeanlawblog.eu/2021/02/10/the-two-step-cant-be-the-quick-step-the-cjeu-reaffirms-its-case-law-on-the-european-arrest-warrant-and-the-rule-of-law-backsliding/>.

50 Case C-158/21 *Puig Gordi and Others* [2023] ECLI:EU:C:2023:57.

51 Joined Cases C-404/15 and C-659/15 PPU *Aranyosi and Căldăraru* [2016] ECLI:EU:C:2016:198, paras 89–92; compare Johan Callewaert, 'Do we still need Article 6(2) TEU? Considerations on the absence of EU accession to the ECHR and its consequences' (2018) 55 Common Market Law Review 1685; Jasper Krommendijk and Guus de Vries, 'Do Luxembourg and Strasbourg trust each other? The interaction between the Court of Justice and the European Court of Human Rights in cases concerning mutual trust' (2021) 4/5 European journal of human rights 319.

52 Gragl (n 3) 15.

53 Isiksel noted in 2016 that the fundamental rights case law of the CJEU has been 'curt, stipulative and tacit' and reticent. Isiksel (n 6) 582; De Witte (n 44); Krommendijk 'Opinion 2/13 as a Game Changer in the Dialogue between the European Courts?' (n 8); see, however, recently Case C-203/21 *Delta Stroy 2003* [2022] ECLI:EU:C:2022:865; Case C-69/21 *Staatssecretaris van Justitie en Veiligheid (Éloignement – Cannabis thérapeutique)* [2022] ECLI:EU:C:2022:913.

without a 'detour' via general principles of EU law in the sense of Article 6(3) of the Treaty on European Union (TEU).[54] Nonetheless, the question remains whether the CJEU will indeed treat the ECHR and ECtHR case law in the way outlined above. An option could be that it treats the ECHR in the same way as all international agreements and hence places the ECHR below the EU Treaties, as some ECHR Member States do in relation to their own constitution.[55]

In conclusion, accession is beneficial from the perspective of legal certainty and coherence.[56] It reduces the current complexity in the operation of these two legal orders.[57] Gragl aptly observed that 'the adverse effects of two parallel and juxtaposed legal regimes will be overcome' after accession.[58] Accession thus has an 'anti-patchwork effect'.[59] This is also desirable for national courts who are sometimes struggling with differing standards.

7.2.3 *The Substantive Effects of Accession in Practice*

The foregoing leads to the question of what substantive effects accession will have on the level of fundamental rights protection. Several commentators doubt whether accession will have a substantive impact, in part because the level of protection in relation to several ECHR rights is more limited.[60]

[54] Consolidated Version of the Treaty on European Union [2016] OJ C202/13; Besselink (n 13) 35.

[55] Christina Eckes, 'EU Accession to the ECHR: Between Autonomy and Adaptation' (2013) 76 The Modern Law Review 254, 277.

[56] Jörg Polakiewicz, 'EU law and the ECHR: Will EU accession to the European Convention on Human Rights square the circle? The draft accession agreement of 5 April 2013' [2013] SSRN Electronic Journal, conclusion.

[57] Johan Callewaert, *The accession of the European Union to the European Convention on Human Rights* (Council of Europe 2014) 90.

[58] Gragl (n 3) 56.

[59] Callewaert 'No more common understanding of fundamental rights' (n 39) 25.

[60] Timmermans (n 25). See, however, Polakiewicz (n 56) conclusion. Leskinen notes that accession will have an impact on EU competition law. Charlotte Leskinen, 'An evaluation of rights of defense during antitrust inspections in the light of the case law of the ECtHR: would accession of the European Union to the ECHR bring about a significant change' [2010] Instituto de Empresa Business School Working Paper 10/04.

Another unresolved question concerns protocols not ratified by all EU Member States. According to Article 1(1) AA, the EU 'only' accedes to the Convention, to the Protocol to the Convention and to Protocol No. 6 to the Convention. AG Cruz Villalón proposed an autonomous interpretation of Charter rights corresponding to ECHR rights in protocols not ratified by all EU Member States. Opinion of AG Cruz Villalón in Case C-617/10 *Åkerberg Fransson* [2013] ECLI:EU:C:2012:340, paras 82–87.

Much depends on the way in which the ECtHR will proceed after accession with respect to its intensity of review. Four aspects can be discerned. First, to what extent will the ECtHR grant the EU a different or broader margin of appreciation than the margin for 'regular' ECHR Member States? Even though the *Bosphorus* presumption will probably disappear, this margin enables the ECHR to take the special sui generis nature of the EU into consideration, including, for example, the fact that EU legislation is the result of choices of twenty-seven Member States.[61] It could be that the ECtHR is more reluctant to thwart a particular balance between conflicting rights and public interests that are the result of a careful legislative process involving various EU institutions and twenty-seven Member States. If the EU enjoys the same margin as regular state parties, it remains to be seen whether the balance struck by the EU legislature and CJEU falls within the margin. The balance struck between trade union rights and the freedom of services by the CJEU in *Viking/ Laval* has, for example, been questioned.[62] It is also far from certain whether the CJEU has stayed within the margin with its decision in *Achbita* balancing freedom of religion in the workplace and the freedom to conduct a business.[63]

A second uncertainty related to the ECtHR's intensity of review concerns the doctrine of positive obligations. It is unclear to what extent and how the ECtHR will extend its case law on positive obligations under the ECHR to the EU and apply it to a failure on the part of the EU to take (legislative or executive) action.[64] If the ECtHR does not differentiate between the EU and 'regular' Member States, the substantive impact of accession is arguably bigger. Extending the doctrine of positive obligations to the EU is not entirely risk-free from an EU perspective, in part because the CJEU has not yet

61 Craig (n 15) 1141.

62 Hans Petter Graver, 'The *Holship* ruling of the ECtHR and the protection of fundamental rights in Europe' (2022) 23 ERA Forum 19; Case C-341/05 *Laval un Partneri* [2007] ECLI: EU:C:2007:809; Case C-438/05 *International Transport Workers' Federation and The Finnish Seamen's Union v Viking Line ABP and OÜ Viking Line Eesti* [2007] ECLI:EU:C:2007:772; *Case of Norwegian Confederation of Trade Unions (LO) and Norwegian Transport Workers' Union (Ntf) v Norway*, App no. 45487/17 (ECtHR, 10 June 2021).

63 Case C-157/15 *Samira Achbita v G4S Secure Solutions* [2017] ECLI:EU:C:2017:203, paras 38–39; *Eweida and Others v United Kingdom*, App nos 48420/10, 36516/10, 51671/10 et al. (ECtHR, 15 January 2013); José Rafael Marín Aís, 'Freedom of Religion in the Workplace v. Freedom to Conduct a Business, the Islamic Veil Before the Court of Justice: Ms. Samira Achbita Case' (2018) 3 European Papers 409.

64 For a discussion of the difficulties, see Catherine Stubberfield, 'Lifting the Organisational Veil: Positive Obligations of the European Union Following Accession to the European Convention on Human Rights' (2012) 19 Australian International Law Journal 117.

accepted in full the doctrine.[65] The only exception is the CJEU's judgment in *La Quadrature du Net* of 2020 that positive obligations under the Charter may justify national legislation that requires providers of electronic communications services to retain particular data about communications.[66] An all too expansive adoption of positive obligations could be in tension with the principle laid down in Article 51(2) of the Charter of Fundamental Rights of the European Union (CFR)[67] and Article 6(1) TEU. According to this principle, the Charter does not extend the field of application of Union law beyond the powers of the Union, does not establish any new power or task for the Union, and does not modify the powers and tasks as defined in the Treaties. The question is to what extent the ECtHR will extend its doctrine in situations in which the EU has no or very limited competences.[68]

A third aspect relating to the intensity of review by the ECtHR deals with the rather procedural *Dhahbi* case law.[69] There is an abundant body of ECtHR case law on the duty to state reasons for decisions of national courts not to refer a case for a preliminary ruling to the CJEU. On several occasions, the ECtHR has found a violation of Article 6 ECHR in cases where the highest national court –despite a sufficiently clear and substantiated request by one of the parties in the proceedings – failed to make a preliminary reference.[70] In these cases, the violation consists of a failure to comply with the duty to state reasons under Article 6(1) ECHR. This failure concerns in

65 See about the scope for the development of positive obligations under the Charter: Malu Beijer, *The Limits of Fundamental Rights Protection by the EU. The Scope for the Development of Positive Obligations* (Intersentia 2017).

66 The CJEU held that positive obligations of the public authorities may result from Article 7 CFR, requiring them to adopt legal measures to protect an individual's private and family life, home, and communications. It also held that such obligations may arise from Articles 3 and 4 CFR, as regards the protection of an individual's physical and mental integrity and the prohibition of torture and inhuman and degrading treatment. In this connection, the CJEU also referred to the ECtHR's case law about the positive obligations flowing from Articles 3 and 8 ECHR. Case C-511/18 *La Quadrature du Net and Others* [2020] ECLI:EU:C:2020:791, paras 126–128 and 145.

67 Charter of Fundamental Rights of the European Union [2016] OJ C202/389.

68 Vassilis Pergantis and Stian Øby Johansen, 'The EU accession to the ECHR and the responsibility question. Between a rock and a hard place' in Nicolas Levrat and Others (eds), *The EU and Its Member States' Joint Participation in International Agreements* (Hart 2022) 242.

69 *Dhahbi v Italy*, App no 17120/09 (ECtHR, 8 April 2014).

70 See most recently *Sanofi Pasteur v France*, App no 25137/16 (ECtHR, 13 February 2020); for an analysis of this case: Jasper Krommendijk, 'Tell me more, tell me more: the obligation for national courts to reason their refusals to refer to the CJEU in *Sanofi Pasteur*' (*Strasbourg Observers*, 20 February 2020)<https://strasbourgobservers.com/2020/02/20/tell-me-more-tell-me-more-the-obligation-for-national-courts-to-reason-their-refusals-to-refer-to-the-cjeu-in-sanofi-pasteur/.>.

essence a more formal or procedural violation of the right to effective judicial protection. The ECtHR underscored in these judgments:

> [I]t is not for the Court to examine any errors that might have been committed by the domestic courts in interpreting or applying the relevant law .... On that latter point, it has also pointed out that it is primarily for the national authorities, notably the courts, to interpret and apply domestic law, if necessary, in conformity with Community law, the Court's role being confined to ascertaining whether the effects of such adjudication are compatible with the Convention.[71]

Nonetheless, even prior to accession, the ECtHR adopted a more substantive analysis in *Dangeville* and – more recently – *Spasov*. In the latter Romanian case, the ECtHR for the first time held that there was a 'denial of justice' and thus a violation of Article 6(1) ECHR due to a manifest error of law by a national court regarding the interpretation and application of EU law.[72] One would expect that after accession the ECtHR will adopt this more substantive approach and also scrutinse the application of EU law by national courts in more depth, obviously subject to the earlier mentioned margin of appreciation.

A fourth question concerns whether the ECtHR will 'accept' the strict *locus standi* requirements in relation to the action for annulment (Article 263 TFEU) and action for failure to act (Article 265 TFEU).[73] It is well known that direct access to the CJEU is difficult. When an act is not addressed to them, natural or legal persons have to show that they are directly and individually concerned (see Chapter 1).[74] Ever since the 1963 *Plaumann* judgment, the CJEU requires persons to show that the 'decision affects them by reason of certain attributes which are peculiar to them or by reason of circumstances in which they are differentiated from all other persons and by virtue of these factors distinguishes them individually just as in the case of the person addressed'.[75] AG Jacobs, the Court of First Instance (currently the General Court), and several commentators have argued for a relaxation of the

[71] *Sanofi Pasteur v France* (n 70) para 68.

[72] The engagement with EU substantive law by the ECtHR in *Spasov* is thus not wholly unprecedented, as it bears some resemblance to the use of EU law in the *Dangeville* case. *Dangeville v France*, App no 36677/97 (ECtHR, 16 April 2002).

[73] Consolidated Version of the Treaty on the Functioning of the European Union [2016] OJ C202/47 (TFEU).

[74] The Lisbon Treaty relaxed the standing rules for non-privileged applicants in relation to regulatory acts that do not entail implementing measures. Following Article 263(4) TFEU, applicants do not have to prove individual concern.

[75] Case C-25/62 *Plaumann v Commission* [1963] ECLI:EU:C:1963:17.

CJEU's interpretation of individual concern because they were of the opinion that a strict reading violates Article 6 and/or Article 13 ECHR.[76] The CJEU has, however, consistently resisted the temptation to reconsider its case law on individual concern, especially with a reference to the entire system of EU remedies and the possibilities for individuals to indirectly access the CJEU via the preliminary reference procedure (Article 267 TFEU). It famously held: 'To that end, the FEU Treaty has established, by Articles 263 and 277, on the one hand, and Article 267, on the other, a complete system of legal remedies and procedures designed to ensure judicial review of the legality of European Union acts, and has entrusted such review to the Courts of the European Union.'[77] The CJEU has also explicitly ruled out that the possession of an individual right leads to the establishment of standing as such.[78] It is not unthinkable that individuals will turn to the ECtHR after an inadmissibility decision and claim a violation of Articles 6 and 13 ECHR. In *Posti and Rahko v Finland*, the ECtHR held:

> where a decree, decision or other measure, albeit not formally addressed to any individual natural or legal person, in substance does affect the 'civil rights' or 'obligations' of such a person or of a group of persons in a similar situation, whether by reason of certain attributes peculiar to them or by reason of a factual situation which differentiates them from all other persons, Article 6 § 1 may require that the substance of the decision or measure in question is capable of being challenged by that person or group before a "tribunal" meeting the requirements of that provision.[79]

In the earlier mentioned *Bosphorus* case, the ECtHR nonetheless concluded, after recognising that access of individuals to the CJEU is 'limited', that the protection of fundamental rights is equivalent to the ECHR.[80] Judge Ress, however, stressed in his concurring opinion that this determination does not mean that the limited access via Article 263 TFEU is necessarily in accordance with the ECHR.[81] The Aarhus Compliance Committee determined,

[76] The CFI came to 'the inevitable conclusion' that the action for annulment 'can no longer be regarded, in the light of Articles 6 and 13 of the ECHR and of Article 47 of the CFR, as guaranteeing persons the right to an effective remedy enabling them to contest the legality of Community measures of general application which directly affect their legal situation'. Case T-177/01, *Jégo-Quéré v Commission* [2002] EU:T:2002:112; Opinion of AG Jacobs in Case C-50/00 P *Unión de Pequeños Agricultores (UPA)* [2002] EU:C:2002:197; Craig (n 15) 1130–1131.

[77] *Inuit* (n 9) para 92.

[78] Ibid para 106; Case C-565/19 P *Carvalho and Others v Parliament and Council* [2021] ECLI:EU:C:2021:252, paras 48–49.

[79] *Posti and Rahko v Finland*, App no 27824/95 (ECtHR, 24 September 2002) para 53.

[80] *Bosphorus* v *Ireland* (n 24) paras 162 and 165.

[81] Concurring opinion Judge Ress, para 1.

albeit only with respect to environmental matters, that the standing requirements are too severe to comply with the Aarhus Convention.[82]

In sum, this subsection shows that the impact of accession from an effective judicial protection perspective depends on the approach taken by the ECtHR. The eventual substantive effects also depend on possible (internal) procedural rules to be decided by the EU as to the implementation of ECtHR judgments. ECtHR judgments are 'only' declaratory in nature and do not as such invalidate secondary EU law.[83] The question from the perspective of EU law is whether a separate CJEU judgment annulling the respective provision(s) of the EU law instrument is subsequently necessary or whether the EU legislature can amend legislation so that it is in conformity with the ECHR without such an intermediate step. There are no guidelines for the CJEU (yet) on how to deal with ECtHR judgments.[84]

7.3 PROCEDURAL PRACTICALITIES AFTER ACCESSION

Now that accession seems to be becoming a reality it is important to take stock of the most important procedural aspects, primarily from the perspective of potential individual applicants being the victims of fundamental rights violations committed by the EU and, to a lesser extent, EU Member States in the implementation of their EU law obligations. This section takes the most recent negotiation document of 17 March 2023 as the basis of analysis.[85] This leads to one important caveat, namely that some aspects might change in the future. It goes beyond the scope of this chapter to fully analyse all details of relevant procedural issues. The procedures are quite complicated as several commentators have already noted.[86]

7.3.1 *ECtHR Admissibility Requirements*

The most obvious starting point for a procedural overview of the consequences of accession is admissibility. Applicants must overcome two procedural

82 Findings and Recommendations of the Compliance Committee With Regard to Communication ACCC/C/2008/32 (Part II) Concerning Compliance by the European Union (17 Mar. 2017) ECE/MP.PP/C.1/2017/7, para 64.

83 Gragl (n 3) 20.

84 Eckes (n 55) 281.

85 'Final consolidated version of the draft accession instruments' (CDDH ad hoc negotiation group ('46+1'), 17 March 2023) < https://rm.coe.int/final-consolidated-version-of-the-draft-accession-instruments/1680aaaecd>.

86 Besselink (n 13) 35; Gragl (n 3) 57; Lock (n 26) 1054.

admissibility hurdles before the ECtHR delves into the merits of their case. First, following Article 34, only persons, non-governmental organisations, or groups of individuals may bring a complaint against the EU before the ECtHR.[87] Second is the requirement to exhaust all 'domestic' remedies under EU law, following Article 35 ECHR.[88] This reflects the subsidiary nature of the ECHR system, giving national courts the opportunity to first reflect on the compatibility of their national laws with the ECHR.[89] The ECtHR described the exhaustion rule as 'one that is golden rather than cast in stone'.[90] The rule is not applied, amongst others, when the applicants can show that a remedy was not available in practice or that the remedy was inappropriate, ineffective, or unreasonable.[91]

Applying this logic to the EU 'complete system of legal remedies', accession enables natural and legal persons to access the ECtHR after having started and exhausted an action for annulment (Article 263(4) TFEU), action for failure to act (Article 265(3) TFEU), or action for damages (Articles 268 jo. 340 TFEU). The same holds true for civil service disputes between the EU and its staff (Article 270 TFEU) and disputes in relation to arbitration clauses in contracts concluded by or on behalf of the Union (Article 272 TFEU). Since the General Court has jurisdiction to hear and determine these actions at first instance, persons should in theory have made it all the way up to the Court of Justice. This is obviously subject to the aforementioned caveat that an appropriate and effective remedy was available. One unresolved question in this context is whether the ECtHR will require an individual to start an action for annulment even though it is evident that he does not satisfy the earlier discussed strict *locus standi* requirements.[92] Third party interveners are also expected to benefit from accession. This could include persons who (unsuccessfully) appealed the substantive decision of the General Court before the Court of Justice but

[87] This means that a Member State cannot complain before the ECtHR following a liability action against the EU. The General Court ruled on the first damages action against the EU by a Member State. Case T-151/20 *Czech Republic v European Commission* [2022] ECLI:EU:T:2022:281.

[88] Callewaert, 'Do we still need Article 6(2) TEU?' (n 51) 85.

[89] *A, B and C v Ireland*, App no 25579/05 (ECtHR, 16 December 2010) para 142; Registry of the ECtHR, 'Practical Guide on Admissibility Criteria' (*Registry of the ECtHR*, 31 August 2022) <www.echr.coe.int/documents/admissibility_guide_eng.p> paras 86–88.

[90] Practical Guide on Admissibility Criteria (n 89) para 89.

[91] For example with references to particular precedents, Practical Guide on Admissibility Criteria (n 89) paras 95–112; *De Wilde, Ooms and Versyp v Belgium*, App nos 2832/66, 2835/66 and 2899/66 (ECtHR, 18 June 1971).

[92] Lock (n 26) 788.

also those who were refused leave to intervene by the General Court and Court of Justice.[93]

This overview indicates that persons cannot directly turn to the ECtHR in relation to CJEU judgments rendered in the context of the preliminary reference procedure (Article 267 TFEU), as the explanatory report to the AA makes clear as well.[94] Individuals can, however, complain before the ECtHR vis-à-vis the national court's judgment implementing the CJEU's preliminary ruling, obviously subject to the domestic exhaustion rule.[95] This means that where a reference was made by a lower court, the persons should appeal to the higher or highest court(s) before they can complain before the ECtHR. Note that the person concerned can in this way indirectly 'challenge' the underlying CJEU ruling including the CJEU's interpretation of EU law and its pronouncements on the validity of EU law before the ECtHR. The ECtHR is subsequently in a position to review whether EU law, as interpreted by the CJEU, is in conformity with the ECHR. The EU can become a co-respondent in such a situation, as will be discussed in Section 7.3.2. One question is whether the ECtHR will require the applicant, in a case in which a reference was made, to have put forward the fundamental rights violations in their submissions before the referring court and the CJEU in the same way as the ECtHR has required applicants in 'regular' cases against an ECHR contracting party. Is it enough that the applicant merely alluded to the EU Charter of Fundamental Rights, or should the claims also have been couched in ECHR terms? There are indications in the case law that the ECtHR might be(come) strict(er), albeit only in a few UK cases.[96] The applicant is not required to have requested a reference for a preliminary ruling before the national court. A reference is generally not seen as a domestic legal remedy that must be exhausted before an individual can turn to the ECtHR, because the individual does not enjoy a right to a reference.[97] This was also acknowledged by the Presidents of the CJEU and ECtHR in their Joint Communication.[98]

93 Third party interveners can only do so 'where the decision of the General Court directly affects them'. Consolidated Version of the Statute of the Court of Justice of the European Union (Statute) OJ C83/210 art 56, para 2; Statute art 57, para 1.

94 Draft explanatory report to the AA (n 17) para 74.

95 Callewaert, 'Do we still need Article 6(2) TEU?' (n 51) 86.

96 *Lee v the UK*, App no 18860/19 (ECtHR, 7 December 2021) paras 56 and 70; *Hickey v the UK*, App no 39492/07 (ECtHR, 4 May 2010). Lize Glas, 'The age of subsidiarity? The ECtHR's approach to the admissibility requirement that applicants raise their Convention complaint before domestic courts' (2023) 41(2) Netherlands Quarterly of Human Rights 75.

97 Draft explanatory report to the AA (n 17) para 74; Gragl (n 3); Craig (n 15) 1125.

98 'Joint communication from Presidents Costa and Skouris' (24 January 2011) <http://curia.europa.eu/jcms/upload/docs/application/pdf/2011-02/cedh_cjue_english.pdf.>.

7.3.2 *Shared or Concurrent Responsibility and the Co-respondent Mechanism*

In many instances, the EU is not solely responsible for an alleged breach of fundamental rights.[99] Since implementation of EU law happens primarily at the national level, EU Member States are almost always involved in one way or another.[100] Under EU law, such acts of Member States implementing EU law are attributed to the Member State(s) concerned.[101] Attribution to Member States does not preclude the EU from being concurrently responsible. The alleged unlawful conduct on the part of the EU could, for example, consist of an omission to act or a failure to provide proper oversight, thereby contributing to or facilitating a breach on the part of the Member State. The failure to exercise sufficient supervisory powers on the part of EU institutions may give rise to liability on the part of the EU.[102] The CJEU has also held the Commission liable for its wrongful authorisation of import licences by EU Member States.[103]

For situations of concurrent or shared responsibility, the Accession Agreement foresees a so-called co-respondent mechanism. Article 3(1) AA entails that a new fourth paragraph will be added to Article 36 ECHR:

> 4. The European Union or a member State of the European Union may become a correspondent to proceedings by decision of the Court in the circumstances set out in the Agreement on the Accession of the European Union to the Convention for the Protection of Human Rights and Fundamental Freedoms. A co-respondent is a party to the case. The admissibility of an application shall be assessed without regard to the participation of a co-respondent in the proceedings.

99 See more generally about shared responsibility the Articles on the Responsibility of States for Internationally Wrongful Acts (ARSIWA) and the Articles on the Responsibility of International Organizations (ARIO); André Nollkaemper and Others, 'Guiding Principles on Shared Responsibility in International Law' (2020) 31 European Journal of International Law 15.

100 Draft explanatory report to the AA (n 17) para 46.

101 Draft explanatory report to the AA (n 17) para 27. This also reflects the ECtHR's determination that 'a Convention Party is responsible under Article 1 of the Convention for all acts and omissions of its organs regardless of whether the act or omission in question was a consequence of domestic law or of the necessity to comply with international legal obligation'. *Bosphorus* v *Ireland* (n 24) para 153.

102 See, e.g., Case C-4/69 *Lütticke v Commission* [1971] ECLI:EU:C:1971:40, para 17 (the Commission was not held liable for lack of a serious breach). Melanie Fink, 'EU liability for contributions to Member States' breaches of EU law' (2019) 56 Common Market Law Review 1227.

103 See, e.g., Joined Cases C-5/66, 7/66, 13/66–24/66 *Kampffmeyer and Others v Commission* [1967] EU:C:1967:31; Case C-30/66 *Becher v Commission* [1967] ECLI:EU:C:1967:44.

The mechanism benefits the applicant as well as the potential co-respondent. From the perspective of effective judicial protection of the applicant, the co-respondent mechanism ensures that individual applications against the *wrong* entity are not declared inadmissible.[104] Individuals often do not know the ins and outs of EU law and implementation rules so it can be difficult for them to determine whether the respondent is a Member State or the EU.[105] It could happen that natural or legal persons start an action against EU Member States –when implementing EU law – in such cases of shared or concurrent responsibility while the EU also played its part. Article 3(2) AA enables the EU to become a party to the proceedings before the ECtHR alongside the respondent State(s). EU Member States have a more limited possibility under Article 3(3) AA when an application is brought against the EU. They can only become a co-respondent in cases where the conformity of EU primary law with the ECHR is contested.[106] The anticipated mechanism benefits the co-respondent in the sense that they become a party to the case and, hence, can take part in the proceedings.

The current Accession Agreement has made it easier for the EU and EU Member States to act as co-respondents before the ECtHR. The reason is the CJEU's objections to the way the mechanism was set up in the AA 2013 in *Opinion 2/13*. The CJEU was critical about the required review by the ECtHR in relation to requests to intervene as co-respondents in a case before the ECtHR. On the basis of the AA 2013, the ECtHR could examine whether it is plausible that the conditions were met. According to the CJEU, this would require the ECtHR to assess the rules of EU law governing the division of powers between the EU and its Member States as well as the criteria for the attribution of their acts or omissions. The revised AA no longer uses the term 'request' but merely stipulates that the EU and/or EU Member States may become a co-respondent 'upon their initiative'. Article 3(5) AA further adds that 'The Court shall admit a co-respondent by decision if a reasoned assessment by the European Union sets out that the conditions in paragraph 2 or 3 of this article are met'. This presupposes an almost mechanical automaticity. That is confirmed by the explanatory report to the AA that provides that the 'assessment by the EU will be considered as determinative and authoritative'.[107]

[104] Gragl (n 3) 32.

[105] Gragl (n 3) 32; Craig (n 15) 1122.

[106] The rationale is that EU Member States are the *Herren der Verträge* and should, thus, be able to pronounce themselves on primary EU law that is being contested before the ECtHR, while they are not in such a position in relation to other EU (secondary) acts and omissions.

[107] Draft explanatory report to the AA (n 17) para 61.

A second substantive change in the current Accession Agreement is the amendment of Article 3(8) AA.[108] The amended provision reads: 'If the violation in respect of which a High Contracting Party is a co-respondent to the proceedings is established, the Court in its judgment shall hold the respondent and the corespondent *jointly responsible* for that violation' (emphasis added). The original provision in the AA 2013 enabled the ECtHR to divert from this default rule and determine that only one of them is responsible on the basis of the reasons given by the respondent and the co-respondent. The reason for this amendment is *Opinion 2/13* in which the Full Court held:

> The question of the apportionment of responsibility must be resolved solely in accordance with the relevant rules of EU law and be subject to review, if necessary, by the Court of Justice, which has exclusive jurisdiction to ensure that any agreement between co-respondent and respondent respects those rules. To permit the ECtHR to confirm any agreement that may exist between the EU and its Member States on the sharing of responsibility would be tantamount to allowing it to take the place of the Court of Justice in order to settle a question that falls within the latter's exclusive jurisdiction.[109]

The amendment also addresses the earlier concerns in the literature as to the interference of the ECtHR with the EU competence division.[110] It seems that the current AA requires subsequent steps at the EU level to execute the ECtHR judgment. The CJEU probably needs to apportion responsibility by the EU and the Member State(s) concerned. Internal attribution rules might be a logical step. The question thus remains how the EU will proceed following a determination of a violation of the ECHR by the ECtHR in situations of concurrent responsibility.

The previous paragraphs create perhaps the impression that the EU and its Member States enjoy a special and more lucrative position in comparison with other ECHR contracting parties. It appears that the current AA is even more deferential to the EU than the original AA 2013.[111] This picture is not entirely true, as the explanatory report to the AA also emphasises: the

[108] Other smaller changes relate to the obligation on the part of the ECtHR to make available to the EU information concerning all such applications that are communicated to its Member States (and applications against the EU should be communicated to the Member States). The EctHR also communicates its decisions to the parties.

[109] *Opinion 2/13* (n 36) para 234.

[110] Pergantis and Johansen (n 68) 261 and 267; Jacqué (n 4) 1016.

[111] It has been pointed out that the original AA already gives too much power to the EU, thereby limiting the possibilities for control on the part of the EctHR (e.g., only a plausibility review).

mechanism is not 'a procedural privilege' for the EU or its Member States. The report mentioned that it is a way 'to avoid gaps in participation, accountability and enforceability' in the Convention system, while also serving 'the proper administration of justice'.[112] It is important in this context to underscore the advantages of the co-respondent mechanism from the perspective of effective judicial protection of potential applicants. First, individuals only have to exhaust the local remedies of one entity: the Member State or the EU.[113] In addition, a possible wrong decision by the applicant(s) as to the respondent does not affect the admissibility decision as can be derived from the last sentence of the earlier quoted future Article 36(4) ECHR.[114] Second, the co-respondent becomes a party to the case and is, hence, also bound by the ECtHR judgment.[115] Third, if Member States enjoy no discretion, that is, when they are in a situation – in the words of Article 3(2) AA – where a 'violation could have been avoided only by disregarding an obligation under European Union law', the EU can be held responsible as well alongside the EU Member State(s) in question.[116]

7.3.3 *The Prior Involvement Procedure*

Article 3(7) of the Accession Agreement also establishes a procedure to ensure that the CJEU can make an assessment of the compatibility of EU law with the ECHR before the ECtHR does so, when it has not had a chance to interpret or decide on the validity of EU law. This prevents the ECtHR from delivering its own original interpretation of EU law or from deciding a case on the basis of a wrong interpretation of EU law.[117] Such a scenario would breach the CJEU's exclusive jurisdiction over the definitive interpretation of EU law, as the CJEU underscored in *Opinion 2/13*.[118] This procedure is reflective of the subsidiary role of the ECtHR.[119] The revised AA does not fundamentally change the procedure, except for the clarification that the procedure is not limited to questions of validity of

The EU and/or EU Member States may become a co-respondent if it 'appears' that such allegation calls into question the compatibility with the rights. Jacqué (n 4) 1015.

[112] Draft explanatory report to the AA (n 17) para 47; Gragl (n 3) 32.

[113] Draft explanatory report to the AA (n 17) para 48.

[114] Besselink (n 13) 38.

[115] Draft explanatory report to the AA (n 17) para 47.

[116] Gragl discussed this in depth, (n 3) 33–45.

[117] Gragl (n 3) 20 and 46.

[118] *Opinion 2/13* (n 36) para 246.

[119] Draft explanatory report to the AA (n 17) para 77; Jacqué (n 4) 1018.

secondary EU law but also questions of interpretation.[120] The procedure is primarily relevant in relation to situations in which a request for a preliminary ruling was not made, as the explanatory report to the AA also suggests.[121] It seems at first sight not relevant for direct actions before the CJEU, such as the action for annulment, because the CJEU had an opportunity to pronounce itself. Nonetheless, as noted earlier, such actions frequently result in inadmissibility decisions for lack of *locus standi* without any discussion of the merits. The Accession Agreement does not preclude the CJEU's prior involvement in these cases.

The prior involvement procedure seems to give the CJEU a prominent role. Its (future) role should, however, not be overstated for three reasons. First, the CJEU is only given a chance after the application is declared admissible by the ECtHR.[122] It could be argued that this is too late, because the admissibility decision might already involve some reflection on EU law, as the discussion of the strict *locus standi* requirements in Section 7.2.3 shows.[123] Second, the assessment of the CJEU will not bind the ECtHR. Article 3(7) AA provides: 'The provisions of this paragraph shall not affect the powers of the Court.' In addition, the explanatory report to the AA also mentions explicitly that the CJEU's assessment will not bind the Court.[124] Third, it is often difficult to make a distinction between interpretation and application of EU law. Formally, national laws (including EU law) are treated by the ECtHR as being part of the facts of the case. The ECtHR will not substitute itself for national authorities and will thus not interpret EU law as such.[125] But, in practice, the task to give an interpretation of the ECHR can 'shade, sometimes unavoidably, into the interpretation of national norms'.[126] Authors have thus questioned the CJEU's conclusion that the EU and its institutions cannot be bound 'in the exercise of their internal powers, to a particular interpretation of the rules of EU law'.[127] According to them, such 'second-guessing' is precisely the rationale of accession.[128]

[120] Ibid para 77.

[121] The report expects this situation to arise 'rarely'. Draft explanatory report to the AA (n 17) para 75.

[122] The proposed Article 36(4) provides: 'The admissibility of an application shall be assessed without regard to the participation of a corespondent in the proceedings.'

[123] Jacqué (n 4) 1021.

[124] Draft explanatory report to the AA (n 17) para 78.

[125] Jacqué (n 4) 1017.

[126] Isiksel (n 6) 575.

[127] *Opinion 2/13* (n 36) para 184.

[128] 'Internal' mechanisms are 'prone to error and manipulation' and biases. Isiksel (n 6) 575–576 and 581.

7.4 THE COMMON FOREIGN AND SECURITY POLICY

This section starts with an explanation of the current gap in effective judicial protection within EU law in relation to the Common Foreign and Security Policy (CFSP) (Section 7.4.1). It will subsequently examine how the 2013 and current AA have dealt with the CFSP and the challenges involved (Section 7.4.2).

7.4.1 *CFSP: The Current Gap in Effective Protection*

One major protection gap prior to accession concerns fundamental rights violations by the EU in the context of the CFSP. This problem has become more pertinent in recent years, because of the increasing shift of powers from Member States to the EU, as illustrated by the growing number of civilian and military operations and restrictive measures or sanctions.[129]

The gap in effective judicial protection in the CFSP relates to the limited jurisdiction of the CJEU in this area and its evolvement in recent years. The jurisdiction of the CJEU is clearly circumscribed in the Treaties, even though the CJEU itself has interpreted its jurisdiction broadly. Because of the special and intergovernmental nature of the CFSP area, also reflected in the inability to adopt legislative acts, Article 24 TEU stipulates that the CJEU shall not have jurisdiction in relation to the CFSP with two exceptions. First, the CJEU can monitor compliance with Article 40(1) TEU and make sure that the implementation of the CFSP does not affect the application of the procedures and the extent of the powers of the institutions in relation to other EU competences. In practice, this boils down to ensuring that the correct legal basis is used in the adoption of EU secondary law and that the correct corresponding decision-making procedures are used. Second, and most relevant for the purpose of this chapter, is the ability of the CJEU to review the legality of decisions providing for restrictive measures against natural or legal persons following Article 275 TFEU.

The CJEU has stretched these exceptions in its case law and has tried to minimise the effective judicial protection gap.[130] The rationale is that the limitations to the CJEU's jurisdiction derogate from the rule of general

[129] Gragl (n 3) 15.

[130] For a recent discussion with reference to older literature, see Maria José Rangel de Mesquita, 'Judicial review of Common Foreign and Security Policy by the ECtHR and the (re) negotiation on the accession of the EU to the ECHR' (2021) 28 Maastricht Journal 356. The CJEU has been quite lenient with respect to access to CFSP documents as well. Case T-14/98 *Hautala v Council* [1999] ECLI:EU:T:1999:157.

jurisdiction in Article 19 TEU and must, therefore, be interpreted narrowly and in the light of the right and principle of effective judicial protection.[131] The CJEU has, for example, provided a strict interpretation of the acts excluded from review in Article 275 TFEU. According to the CJEU, this does not include measures adopted by *Eulex Kosovo* such as the awarding of a public contract giving rise to expenditures for the EU budget.[132] In *H*, the CJEU also accepted jurisdiction to assess the action for annulment in relation to a decision of the Chief of Personnel of the EU Policy Mission in Bosnia and Herzegovina to redeploy an Italian national seconded to another office.[133] The CJEU has also accepted the possibility of preliminary references in relation to the validity of CFSP acts in *Rosneft*.[134] There is currently a case pending before the CJEU dealing with the question of whether the CJEU can also handle questions on the *interpretation* of a CFSP decision concerning restrictive measures.[135] In addition, the CJEU accepted non-contractual liability in relation to individual CFSP restrictive measures adopted on the basis of Chapter 2 of Title V TEU in *Bank Refah Kargaran*.[136] The question is whether the CJEU has jurisdiction in relation to damages caused by other CFSP acts, measures, or omissions, such as CFSP missions. There is currently another damages case (*KS and KD*) pending before the CJEU against the Council, Commission, and EEAS for the mishandling of recommendations of the EU Human Rights Review Panel established to investigate and prosecute war crimes committed during the war in Kosovo in 1999. The General Court dismissed the action for lack of jurisdiction 'to review the legality of such acts or omissions, which relate to strategic choices and decisions concerning the mandate of a crisis management mission set up under the CSDP,

[131] Case C-455/14 P *H v Council and Commission* [2016] ECLI:EU:C:2016:569; Case C-658/11 *Parliament v Council* [2014] ECLI:EU:C:2014:2025, para 70; Case C-439/13 P *Elitaliana* v *Eulex Kosovo* [2015] EU:C:2015:753, para 42.

[132] *Elitaliana* v *Eulex Kosovo* (n 131).

[133] *H v Council and Commission* (n 131), paras 59–60; see also a subsequent staff management case in relation to the EU Satellite Centre: Case C-14/19 P *CSUE v KF* [2020] ECLI:EU:C:2020:492, para 66.

[134] See also Graham Butler, 'A question of jurisdiction: Art. 267 TFEU preliminary references of a CFSP nature' (2017) 2 European Papers 201.

[135] Reference from the Regional Court of Bucharest in relation to Decision 2014/512/CFSP concerning restrictive measures in view of Russia's actions destabilising the situation in Ukraine. Case C-351/22 *Neves 77 Solutions* [case in progress].

[136] Case C-134/19 P *Bank Refah Kargaran* [2020] ECLI:EU:C:2020:793, para 44; The possibility of damages in relation to restrictive measures adopted on the basis of Article 215 TFEU has been recognised earlier. For example, Case T-384/11 *Safa Nicu Sepahan v Counccil* [2014] EU:T:2014:986; Stella Thanou, 'Individual restrictive measures and actions for damages before the General Court of the European Union' (2020) 20 ERA Forum 599.

which is an integral part of the CFSP, nor can it award damages to applicants who claim to have suffered harm as a result of those acts or omissions'.[137] It held that the action does not concern restrictive measures in the sense of Article 275 TFEU or compliance with Article 40 TEU.[138] The Court also distinguished the case from the CJEU's public procurement (*Elitaliana*) and staff management (*H*) cases.[139]

In sum, the advancing CJEU case law in relation to the CFSP already minimises the gaps in the CJEU's jurisdiction at the time of *Opinion 2/13*. Nonetheless, several acts, actions, or omissions performed in the context of the CFSP are still excluded from review.[140]

7.4.2 *CFSP: Accession of the EU and Its Benefits*

The AA 2013 did not provide for any specific arrangements in relation to the CFSP. The AA simply empowered the ECtHR to review the compatibility with the ECHR of acts, actions, or omissions performed in the context of the CFSP. This was problematic for the CJEU since it would give the ECtHR jurisdiction in a policy area in which the CJEU itself does not have jurisdiction.[141] Entrusting exclusive review to a non-EU body 'outside the institutional and judicial framework of the EU' fails to have regard to the 'specific characteristics of EU law', as the CJEU concluded critically in *Opinion 2/13*.[142] The CJEU's position in relation to CFSP has received a lot of criticism in the literature. Łazowski and Wessel held: 'It is one thing to prevent judicial activism in that area; it is quite another thing to deliberately leave gaps in the protection of fundamental rights.'[143] The CJEU's concerns in relation to the CFSP are arguably the most controversial aspect of *Opinion 2/13*. It is therefore no surprise that the CFSP has been reserved to the end of the negotiations on the EU's accession to the ECHR as so-called basket 4.

It still remains to be seen how the new AA will solve the problem of the limited jurisdiction of the CJEU in the CFSP. The March 2023 deal of the 46 + 1 Group left this question to the EU to solve as an internal matter.

[137] Case T-771/20 *KS and KD v Council and Others* [2021] EU:T:2021:798, para 27.

[138] Ibid para 33.

[139] Ibid paras 35–36.

[140] Christian Breitler, 'Jurisdiction in CFSP Matters – Conquering the Gallic Village One Case at a Time?' (*European Law Blogpost*, 13 October 2022) <https://ELB-Blogpost-Christian-Breitler-October-202239-final.pdf> (europeanlawblog.eu).

[141] *Opinion 2/13* (n 36) para 254.

[142] Ibid paras 255–258.

[143] Łazowski and Wessel (n 44) 212.

The EU will keep the Council of Europe's Steering Committee for Human Rights informed.[144] One possible solution is a reattribution mechanism as proposed by the EU in February 2023. The proposed Article 4a AA re-attributes CFSP acts to EU Member States: an 'act, measure or omission shall be attributed to one or more member States of the European Union ... if the European Union has designated that member State or those member States of the European Union as responsible for that act, measure or omission by means of a reasoned declaration'.[145] An earlier version of the explanatory report to the AA mentions in relation to this proposal that the decision whether an act, action, or omission falls within the scope of the CFSP is a matter of internal EU law, 'which can only be decided definitively' by the CJEU. The ECtHR shall accept this 'final determination'.[146] This also means that the Member State(s) designated will become respondent(s) in the case of re-attribution of responsibility and the action shall be deemed to be directed against the designated Member State(s) instead of the EU. This also has implications for the applicant(s) if they have not exhausted remedies 'in at least one member State jurisdiction'. The proceedings before the ECtHR are to be stayed in order to allow the applicant to pursue domestic remedies in the designated Member State(s), if those remedies are still available. Article 4a AA and the explanatory report to the AA explicitly provide for the activation of the co-respondent mechanism and prior involvement procedure discussed earlier.[147]

Note that it remains unclear whether the EU will stick to its earlier proposed re-attribution mechanism. It is also unclear whether it is acceptable for non-EU contracting parties to the ECHR. These parties have been critical about the proposal.[148] This could explain why the EU is reflecting on a

[144] 'Meeting report of the 18th meeting of the CDDH ad hoc negotiation group ("46+1") on the accession of the European Union to the European Convention on Human Rights' (Meeting Report, 17 March 2023) <https://rm.coe.int/meeting-report-18th-meeting/1680aa9807>, paras 7–8.

[145] 'Consolidated version of the draft Accession Instrument (as of 2 February 2023)' (CDDH ad hoc negotiation group ('46+1'), 16 February 2023) <https://rm.coe.int/consolidated-version-of-the-draft-accession-instruments-as-of-2-februa/1680aa3443>.

[146] Draft explanatory report of 'Consolidated version of the draft Accession Instrument (as of 2 February 2023)' (CDDH ad hoc negotiation group ['46+1'], 16 February 2023) <https://rm.coe.int/consolidated-version-of-the-draft-accession-instruments-as-of-2-februa/1680aa3443>, paras 26b–c.

[147] Draft explanatory report of the draft Accession Instrument (n 146) para 26a.

[148] See 'Meeting report of the 13th meeting of the CDDH ad hoc negotiation group ("46+1") on the accession of the European Union to the European Convention on Human Rights' (Meeting Report, 13 May 2022) <https://rm.coe.int/cddh-46-1-2022-r13-fin-en/1680a6801c>, paras. 37–39.

possible alternative solution in the form of an interpretative declaration in relation to the CFSP.[149] From a legal perspective, one also wonders how this re-attribution mechanism applies to civilian missions that have an accepted distinct legal capacity under EU law as 'subsidiary organs' of the EU. From the perspective of the ECtHR and especially its *Behrami and Saramati* case law, conduct of subsidiary organs of international organisations is attributable to the organisation.[150] Re-attribution to the EU Member States seems only logical when they instead of the EU maintain 'effective control'.[151] According to Hillion and Wessel, there is a (rebuttable) presumption in favour of attributing wrongful conduct of such missions to the EU, rather than to the contributing EU Member States.[152] In the earlier mentioned *KS and KD* case, the English High Court also followed this logic and determined in an *obiter dictum* that the case would most likely fall within the CJEU's exclusive jurisdiction, agreeing with the submissions of the intervening European Commission that the 'nature of the claim is not itself concerned with a sovereign policy choice made by the Member States'.[153] It seems that in this scenario it becomes difficult, or at least far-fetched, to use the legal fiction of re-attribution to Member States. One could thus have doubts about the

[149] 'Geannoteerde agenda van de bijeenkomst van de Raad Justitie en Binnenlandse Zaken, 8 en 9 december' (*Openoverheid*, December 2022) <https://open.overheid.nl/documenten/ronl-8ef5c0285d2b43b46ecb7e93e42ad3985c4a911b/pdf>, 12.

[150] In *Behrami and Behrami v France*, the applicants challenged the failure of the Interim administration for Kosovo (UNMIK) to demine as a result of which a child was killed. The ECtHR determined that UNMIK is a subsidiary organ of the UN, institutionally directly and fully answerable to the UN Security Council. The impugned (in)action was thus attributable to the UN and not its Member States. *Behrami and Behrami v France and Saramati v France, Germany and Norway* (dec.), App no 71412/01 (ECtHR, 2 May 2007) para 142.

[151] In *Saramati v France, Germany and Norway*, the applicant challenged the unlawful detention by the NATO led international security force (KFOR) that was mandated by the UN Security Council. The ECtHR held that it has no jurisdiction *ratione personae*, because the UN Security Council retained 'ultimate authority and control', while KFOR was only exercising lawfully delegated powers of the UN Security Council. The impugned action was hence attributable to the UN and not to the troop-contributing countries. Ibid paras 133–135. In the case of *Al-Jedda*, the ECtHR attributed the unlawful detention of an Iraqi by the US/UK led Coalition Provisional Authority to the UK, because the Security Council had 'neither effective control nor ultimate authority and control'. *Al-Jedda v United Kingdom*, App no 27021/08 (ECtHR, 7 July 2011) para 26.

[152] Christophe Hillion and Ramses A. Wessel, '"The Good, the Bad and the Ugly": three levels of judicial control over the CFSP' in Steven Blockmans and Panos Koutrakos (eds), *Research Handbook on EU Common Foreign and Security Policy* (Edward Elgar 2018).

[153] England and Wales High Court [UK] *Tomanović et.al. v the European Union et.al.* [2019] EWHC 263 (QB), paras 58 and 81. For an analysis, see Stian Øby Johansen, 'Suing the European Union in the UK: *Tomanović et. al. v. The EU et. al.*' (2019) 4 European Papers 345.

mechanism from the perspective of effective judicial protection if it leads to a legal vacuum in which liability claims are not dealt with by a court.

7.5 CONCLUSION

This chapter took stock of the consequences of the accession of the EU to the ECHR from the perspective of fundamental rights accountability and effective judicial protection vis-à-vis the EU. It showed that accession fills a current protection gap in two ways: it enables complaints against the EU (currently declared inadmissible by the ECtHR) as well as against EU Member States when they implement EU law and have no margin of discretion (currently shielded from scrutiny on the basis of the rebuttable *Bosphorus* presumption). Accession is also beneficial for the coherence of the two legal systems of the EU and the ECHR, reducing the likelihood of conflicts between the two orders. This chapter argued that it is difficult to predict the actual impact of accession on the level of protection of fundamental rights. Much depends on the actual scrutiny or intensity of review of the ECtHR. While the ECtHR will most likely do away with its *Bosphorus* presumption, it could factor in the special sui generis nature of the EU by granting a wider margin of appreciation than to 'regular' states. Uncertainties also exist in relation to the extent to which the ECtHR will extend its doctrine of positive obligations to the EU.

In many instances, the EU is not solely responsible for an alleged breach of fundamental rights. The Accession Agreement provides for a co-respondent mechanism for this reason. This mechanism facilitates effective judicial protection before the ECtHR in three ways. First, individuals only have to exhaust the local remedies of one entity: the Member State or the EU. Second, the co-respondent becomes a party to the case and is, hence, also bound by the ECtHR judgment. Third, if Member States are under a strict obligation of EU law and enjoy no discretion, the EU may be held responsible alongside the EU Member State(s) in question. Noteworthy about the latest version of the Accession Agreement is that the ECtHR will not divide responsibility between the EU and EU Member States. That is left to the EU, but it is (still) unclear how that will function in practice.

While the Accession Agreement provides some answers, several questions as to the consequences of accession can only be answered by the ECtHR. This not only concerns the earlier mentioned width of margin of appreciation or the doctrine of positive obligations but also the question as to whether the strict *locus standi* requirements meet the ECHR test.

While accession will definitely improve the possibilities for holding the EU accountable, it remains to be seen how this will work in reality. Several commentators have been sceptical. Pergantis and Johansen held: 'Depriving the ECtHR of the opportunity to interpret Union law, allocate responsibility, and determine remedies for the execution of its judgments undermines the external control that it is meant to exercise.'[154] This chapter, nonetheless, showed that the co-respondent mechanism and the prior involvement procedure do not *only* grant the EU and its Member States a more lucrative position in comparison with 'regular' ECHR state parties. Both procedures also have several advantages from the perspective of effective judicial protection of prospective applicants and fundamental rights accountability.

[154] Pergantis and Johansen (n 68) 247.

PART III

Pushing the Boundaries

8

Strategic Litigation

KRIS VAN DER PAS

8.1 INTRODUCTION

In the context of fundamental rights violations, we can observe an increase in the use of litigation strategies to call responsible actors to account.[1] This 'strategic' litigation can be described as 'the (intention of) legal action through a judicial mechanism in order to secure an outcome, either by an affected party or on behalf of an affected party ... used as a means to reach objectives which consist of creating change (e.g. legal, political, social) beyond the individual case or individual interest'.[2] Thus, litigation is pursued as a strategy as opposed to or in combination with (for example) lobbying or protesting, in order to achieve certain goals that have a broader purpose than winning a case.[3] The phenomenon has become widely known in the European context over the last few years especially in relation to climate change.[4]

[1] Michael Ramsden and Kris Gledhill, 'Defining Strategic Litigation' (2019) 4 Civil Justice Quarterly 407; Helen Duffy, *Strategic Human Rights Litigation* (Hart 2018); Annick Pijnenburg and Kris van der Pas, 'Strategic Litigation against European Migration Control Policies: The Legal Battleground of the Central Mediterranean Migration Route' (2022) 24 European Journal of Migration and Law 402.

[2] Kris van der Pas 'Conceptualising Strategic Litigation' (2021) 11 Oñati Socio-Legal Series 116.

[3] Lisa Vanhala, 'Legal Mobilization under Neo-corporatist Governance: Environmental NGOs before the Conseil d'État in France, 1975–2010' (2016) 4 Journal of Law and Courts 103; Douglas NeJaime, 'Winning through Losing' (2011) 96 Iowa Law Review 941.

[4] This kickstarted with the first judgment in the *Urgenda* case: Rechtbank Den Haag [Netherlands] *Stichting Urgenda v State of the Netherlands* nr. 19/00135, ECLI:NL:RBDHA:2015:7145. See further Joana Setzer and Catherine Higham, 'Global trends in climate change litigation: 2021 snapshot' (2021) Grantham Research Institute on Climate Change and the Environment and Centre for Climate Change Economics and Policy,

However, also in the migration context, strategic litigation is broadly pursued.[5]

Strategic litigation can be seen as a form of legal mobilisation. Legal mobilisation entails 'any type of process by which individual or collective actors invoke legal norms, discourse, or symbols to influence policy, culture or behavior'.[6] Litigation, in that sense, is one of these processes. In legal mobilisation literature, different explanations have been offered for why social movements, organisations, or individuals 'turn to the courts'.[7] One of these explanatory theories focuses on legal opportunities that either encourage or discourage litigation. As has become clear from the previous chapters, the EU remedies system and especially the Court of Justice of the European Union (CJEU) does not offer many of these legal opportunities that enable strategic litigation. Nevertheless, the CJEU has become a forum where NGOs and other actors have taken their cases to attempt to achieve change beyond the individual.[8]

This begs the question: How are these actors (NGOs, lawyers, individuals) making use of this avenue and what lessons can be drawn therefrom? Relying on literature on legal mobilisation, this chapter first discusses how the EU remedies system enables or disables strategic litigation (Section 8.2). It then delves into several cases of mobilisation of the EU remedies system and describes the way in which the actors involved worked with or around the legal opportunities provided by this system (Section 8.3). This perspective contributes to a more bottom-up perspective (of the litigants) as opposed to the top-down approach taken in Part I of the book. The selection of cases is by no means exhaustive but rather serves to illustrate mobilisation of the EU remedies system in relation to different fundamental rights violations. Section 8.4 discusses actions that are not necessarily formal legal procedures but

London School of Economics and Political Science <www.lse.ac.uk/granthaminstitute/wp-content/uploads/2021/07/Global-trends-in-climate-change-litigation_2021-snapshot.pdf> .

5 See, for example, the special issue of the German Law Journal in 2020 on 'Border Justice: Migration and Accountability for Human Rights Violations' (2020) 21 (3) German Law Journal; Pijnenburg and van der Pas (n 1).

6 Lisa Vanhala, 'Legal Mobilization' (2021) Oxford Bibliographies <www.oxfordbibliographies.com/view/document/obo-9780199756223/obo-9780199756223-0031.xml>.

7 See, for example, Lisa Conant and Others, 'Mobilizing European Law' (2018) 25 Journal of European Public Policy 1376.

8 Case C-411/10 and C-493/10 *N.S. v Secretary of State for the Home Department and M.E. and Others v Refugee Applications Commissioner and Minister for Justice, Equality and Law Reform* [2011] ECLI:EU:C:2011:865; Case C-673/13 P *European Commission v Stichting Greenpeace Nederland & Pesticide Action Network Europe* [2016] ECLI:EU:C:2016:889; Marion Guerrero, *Strategic litigation in EU gender equality law* (2020) European Commission, Chapter 3.

nevertheless ways in which actors have tried to call the EU to account for fundamental rights violations. The lessons drawn from these actions can inform future action in this field (Section 8.5).

8.2 THE EU AS A SYSTEM WITH CLOSED LEGAL OPPORTUNITY STRUCTURES

As the other chapters in this volume have highlighted, it is not easy to address fundamental rights violations by the EU within the EU remedies system. Among other aspects, the dependency on the national judge in the preliminary reference procedure and the *Plaumann*[9] criteria in direct actions create a hostile environment for pursuing broad social and/or legal change through the available avenues.[10] Moreover, while the European Court of Human Rights (ECtHR) has a flourishing practice of third-party interventions, the CJEU does not easily allow access to interveners.[11] When discussing (im)possibilities of legal procedural rules and how these encourage or discourage strategic litigation, socio-legal scholars have referred to the concept of legal opportunity structures.[12] Legal opportunity structures find their origin in earlier theories on political opportunity structures that influence the choice of strategy of social movements.[13] Simply put: 'open' political opportunity structures entail access to political actors and these actors being receptive towards the claims of the social movement.[14] When this is the case, political strategies (such as lobbying) are turned to by a social movement. If political opportunity structures are closed, a different ('outside') strategy is much more attractive, such as protesting or litigation.[15] Legal opportunity structures, then, focus on the legal

9 Case C-25/62 *Plaumann v Commission* [1963] ECLI:EU:C:1963:17.

10 Virginia Passalacqua, 'Legal mobilization via preliminary reference: Insights from the case of migrant rights' (2021) 58 Common Market Law Review 751.

11 Jasper Krommendijk and Kris van der Pas, 'To intervene or not to intervene: intervention before the court of justice of the european union in environmental and migration law' (2022) 26 The International Journal of Human Rights 1394.

12 Chris Hilson 'New Social Movements: the Role of Legal Opportunity' (2002) 9 Journal of European Public Policy 238. See also Ellen Andersen, *Out of the Closets and into the Courts: Legal Opportunity Structure and Gay Rights Litigation* (University of Michigan Press 2006); Gianluca De Fazio, 'Legal opportunity structure and social movement strategy in Northern Ireland and southern United States' (2012) 53 International Journal of Comparative Sociology 3.

13 Hilson, 'New Social Movements' (n 12).

14 Hanspeter Kriesi, 'Political Context and Opportunity' in D Snow, S Soule, and H Kriesi (eds), *The Blackwell Companion to Social Movements* (Blackwell 2004) 70; Andersen (n 12) 7.

15 Cary Coglianese, 'Litigating within Relationships: Disputes and Disturbance in the Regulatory Process' (1996) 30 Law & Society Review 738.

factors that influence strategy choice. When 'open', legal opportunity structures enable litigation and therefore this strategy is used.[16]

These legal opportunities entail different dimensions according to different authors. Andersen distinguishes four different dimensions, including access to justice, the 'configuration of elites' (receptiveness of judges towards the claims made), 'alliance and conflict systems' (in the courtroom), and 'cultural and legal frames' (societal views that shape legal opportunity structures).[17] This approach has been criticised by Vanhala, who agrees to some extent with the first two dimensions but argues that the last two dimensions are not really 'structures'.[18] De Fazio argues for three dimensions: access to the courts, availability of justiciable rights, and receptivity of the judiciary.[19] Although it is not the purpose of this chapter to provide a definitive approach to legal opportunity structures, these dimensions identified and applied to the EU remedies help to see how 'open' or 'closed' the system is. It should also be emphasised that legal opportunity structures are not static: they can change over time and even be the target of instances of litigation, trying to 'loosen' rules on standing, for example.[20]

De Fazio's dimensions here are taken as point of departure, as they are most suitable to adapt to the EU.[21] The first, access to the courts, is severely limited in the EU context: accessing the CJEU (as described above) is difficult. The second and third dimension, on the other hand, are more favourable in the EU remedies system: EU law has (generally speaking) created a set of rights that can be invoked in court, some more justiciable than others (for example, the Charter of Fundamental Rights of the European Union,[22] in the following 'the Charter').[23] Moreover, EU judges have not always shied away from delivering judgments on politically salient issues.[24] This paints a mixed picture: on the one hand, the EU courts can be a valuable avenue for strategic litigation but, on the other hand, access is limited.

[16] Andersen (n 12); Gianluca De Fazio, 'Legal opportunity structure and social movement strategy in Northern Ireland and southern United States' (2012) 53 International Journal of Comparative Sociology 3.

[17] Andersen (n 12) 11–14.

[18] Lisa Vanhala, *Making Rights a Reality* (Cambridge University Press 2011) 15–18.

[19] De Fazio, 'Legal opportunity structure and social movement strategy' (n 16) 6.

[20] Lisa Vanhala, 'Legal Opportunity Structures and the Paradox of Legal Mobilization by the Environmental Movement in the UK' (2012) 46 Law & Society Review 523, 523.

[21] See also Passalacqua, 'Legal mobilization via preliminary reference' (n 10).

[22] Charter of Fundamental Rights of the European Union [2007] OJ C303/1.

[23] Tobias Lock, 'Rights and Principles in the EU Charter of Fundamental Rights' (2019) 56 Common Market Law Review 1201.

[24] See, for an overview, Mark Dawson, Bruno de Witte, and Elise Muir, *Judicial activism at the European Court of Justice: causes, responses and solutions* (Edward Elgar 2013).

8.3 EXAMPLES OF SUCCESSFULLY MOBILISING BEFORE THE CJEU

Despite the closed first dimension of EU legal opportunities (access to the EU courts), examples of successful mobilisation of this system can be found in practice: in the preliminary reference procedure, in some direct actions before the CJEU, and in third-party interventions. Next to that, the EU system offers more quasi-legal avenues, which have been explored by different actors in different fields of law as well. The following sections will explore these examples, focusing on the 'closed' aspects of EU legal opportunities and investigating how the litigants worked with or around these obstacles.

8.3.1 *Mobilising the Preliminary Reference Procedure*

In several instances, actors have mobilised by making use of Article 267 Treaty on the Functioning of the European Union (TFEU).[25] This procedure, primarily intended for resolving conflicts between national laws and policies and EU law or interpreting EU legislation, has the major downside of a dependency on national judges to pose a question to the CJEU. This has notably been explored by Passalacqua, who has researched how from the bottom up, focusing on the litigants, the decision to refer can be influenced with Euro-expertise (EU legal expertise) in the field of migration law.[26] By having better resources available (i.e., knowledge), litigants are more likely to succeed in their endeavours (i.e., getting a judge to refer to the CJEU).[27] Passalacqua focuses in her article on three instances of mobilisation against national laws and policies in the United Kingdom, the Netherlands, and Italy. Other such examples exist, for example, in the field of gender equality and non-discrimination law.[28] The procedure has also been used to challenge acts of EU institutions due to alleged fundamental rights violations.[29]. One field of law where this has been particularly successful is explored here, looking at the

[25] Consolidated Version of the Treaty on the Functioning of the European Union [2016] OJ C202/47.

[26] Passalacqua, 'Legal mobilization via preliminary reference' (n 10); see also Tommaso Pavone, *The Ghostwriters: Lawyers and the Politics behind the Judicial Construction of Europe* (Cambridge University Press 2022).

[27] Marc Galanter, 'Why the "haves" come out ahead: speculations on the limits of legal change' (1974) 9 Law & Society Review 95, 95.

[28] For example, the famous *Defrenne* cases brought by Belgian feminist lawyer Élaine Vogel-Polsky, see Éliane Gubin, 'Éliane Vogel-Polsky: a woman of conviction' (2018) Institute for the Equality of Women and Men, Belgium, 89–91.

[29] Jos Hoevenaars, *A People's Court? A bottom-up approach to litigation before the European Court of Justice* (Eleven 2018).

cases, the actors behind them, the procedural hurdles they have had to overcome, and how they did so. This field of law is data protection.

The first widely known example is the case of *Digital Rights Ireland*, decided by the CJEU in April 2014.[30] In that case, the EU Data Retention Directive was declared invalid due to non-compliance with Articles 7 and 8 of the Charter. The Directive required Internet Service Providers (ISPs) to retain internet data for a period of six months to two years.[31] The successful challenge was started in 2006 before an Irish court by the digital rights lobbying and advocacy NGO Digital Rights Ireland.[32] It challenged both the EU Directive and the Irish implementation thereof. Importantly, the NGO was allowed to conduct the proceedings in *actio popularis*, meaning that the organisation litigated for a public interest (namely the privacy rights of individuals).[33] This possibility is not present in all EU Member States, highlighting the importance of beneficial national procedural rules. Moreover, among the members of the NGO (which has no staff or office) are practicing lawyers and legal academics.[34] Digital Rights Ireland was supported by many other similar organisations, such as the Electronic Frontier Foundation and Privacy International.[35] This means that the level of (Euro-)expertise within the NGO and in its relations with others was high. Despite significant delays that were suffered by the NGO in the national proceedings, eventually a preliminary reference was sent to the CJEU by the Irish court, which led to the CJEU judgment.[36]

30 Case C-293/12 and C-594/12 *Digital Rights Ireland* [2014] ECLI:EU:C:2014:238.

31 Directive (EC) 24/2006 on the retention of data generated or processed in connection with the provision of publicly available electronic communications services or of public communications networks and amending Directive 2002/58/EC [2006] OJ L105/54, specifically arts 5 and 6.

32 See <www.digitalrights.ie/>; Digital Rights Ireland (DRI), 'DRI brings legal action over mass surveillance' (*Digital Rights Ireland*, 14 September 2006) <www.digitalrights.ie/dri-brings-legal-action-over-mass-surveillance/>.

33 Orla Lynskey, 'The role of collective actors in the enforcement of the right to data protection under EU law' in Elise Muir and others (eds), *How EU law shapes opportunities for preliminary references on fundamental rights: discrimination, data protection and asylum* (EUI Working Papers 2017/17).

34 See <www.digitalrights.ie/about/>; Electronic Frontier Foundation, 'How Digital Rights Ireland Litigated Against the EU Data Retention Directive and Won' <www.eff.org/nl/node/81899>.

35 DRI (n 32); Electronic Frontier Foundation (n 34).

36 For more information about the impact of the case, see Marie-Pierre Granger and Kristina Irion, 'The Court of Justice and the Data Retention Directive in *Digital Rights Ireland*: Telling Off the EU Legislator and Teaching a Lesson in Privacy and Data Protection' (2014) 6 European Law Review 6.

The second example from the field of data protection is a fraction of a multitude of legal challenges brought by activist Maximilian Schrems. A preliminary ruling decided by the CJEU in October 2015, in the case of *Schrems I*, had significant consequences for the transfer of personal data from companies in the EU to the United States.[37] The judgment invalidated the 'Safe Harbor' agreement between the EU and the United States, which allowed for the transfer of such data.[38] The CJEU found that there were not enough safeguards in this agreement in light of Articles 7 and 8 of the Charter. Maximilian Schrems, an Austrian citizen (then law student) and Facebook user, challenged the transfer of his personal data from Facebook's servers in Ireland to those in the United States (after the revelations made in 2013 by Edward Snowden).[39] The Irish High Court was uncertain about the validity of the underlying Safe Harbor decision and decided to pose a question about its validity to the CJEU. The CJEU largely followed the arguments made by Schrems and declared the Decision invalid. Notably, as a third-party intervener, Digital Rights Ireland was involved in the case. Schrems himself is now a privacy lawyer and founder of an organisation (noyb) fighting for digital rights.[40] *Schrems I* is one of the many legal challenges brought by the activist and his organisation.[41]

These cases tell us several things. Firstly, the NGO Digital Rights Ireland benefitted from the possibility of starting an *actio popularis* in an Irish court, which is not possible in every EU Member State. Secondly, all litigants described in this section benefitted from legal, and specifically EU law, expertise, either through their own resources or with the help of a coalition of other individuals and organisations (sometimes formally through a third-party intervention).[42] This is necessary at times to provide a counterweight to the power of the national government to delay a procedure, such as in the Irish proceedings leading up to *Digital Rights Ireland*. It should be

37 Case C-362/14 *Schrems v Data Protection Commissioner* [2015] ECLI:EU:C:2015:650.

38 See Global Freedom of Expression, 'Schrems v. Data Protection Commissioner' <https://globalfreedomofexpression.columbia.edu/cases/schrems-v-data-protection-commissioner/>.

39 See Global Freedom of Expression (n 38); NOYB, 'Data transfers' <https://noyb.eu/en/project/eu-us-transfers>.

40 See <https://noyb.eu/en>.

41 See, for example, Case C-311/18 *Data Protection Commissioner v Facebook Ireland Ltd & Maximilian Schrems* [2020] ECLI:EU:C:2020:559; Vincent Manancourt, 'Meta faces record EU privacy fines' (*Politico*, 4 December 2022) <www.politico.eu/article/eu-fines-meta-privacy-tech-security-facebook-whatsapp-instagram/>.

42 Antoine Vauchez has coined the term 'Euro-lawyers' in this regard. See Antoine Vauchez, *Brokering Europe: Euro-Lawyers and the Making of a Transnational Polity* (Cambridge University Press 2015).

emphasised that these instances of mobilisation are rather exceptional: national implementation is necessary as litigation against EU acts cannot be brought before national courts. Therefore, challenging EU legislation or EU complicity in fundamental rights violations needs to be combined with a Member State 'element', so to say.

8.3.2 *Direct Actions*

The second type of mobilisation before the CJEU addressed here are direct actions, based on Article 263, 265, or 340 TFEU. Addressing fundamental rights violations by the EU through these procedures is difficult for a variety of reasons. Most obviously, the plaintiffs in the action for annulment and failure to act run into the difficulties of the *Plaumann* criteria of direct and individual concern.[43] As emphasised in Chapter 2, the conditions under which compensation is granted in the action for damages are strict. Most likely related to these difficulties, only very few strategic procedures as direct actions before the CJEU have been initiated.[44] Many attempts have been made to overcome these criteria especially in the field of environmental law. This line of case law, and case law more generally before the CJEU on environmental issues, is set out first in this section. The second part of this section focuses on two cases brought against the European Border and Coast Guard Agency, Frontex. One is an action for annulment, brought on behalf of two individuals by the NGO *front*-LEX.[45] The other is an action for damages, brought on behalf of a Syrian family by Prakken d'Oliveira Human Rights Lawyers.[46]

The requirement of individual concern that follows from *Plaumann* is especially difficult to satisfy in environmental litigation: environmental

[43] Case C-25/62 *Plaumann v Commission* [1963] ECLI:EU:C:1963:17.

[44] Exceptions can be found in relation to EU legislation on pesticides and access to documents, where several actions are successful as there is no implementation decision required (Article 263(4) TFEU) and a decision to refuse to provide documents is given. See, for example, Case C-458/19 P *ClientEarth v Commission* [2021] ECLI:EU:C:2021:802 and Case C-612/18 P *ClientEarth v Commission* [2020] ECLI:EU:C:2020:223.

[45] Case T-282/21 *SS and ST v Frontex* [2021]; see also Statewatch, 'EU: Frontex asks court to reject human rights case, seeks legal costs from asylum seekers' (*Statewatch.org*, 5 January 2022) <www.statewatch.org/news/2022/january/eu-frontex-asks-court-to-reject-human-rights-case-seeks-legal-costs-from-asylum-seekers/>.

[46] Case T-600/21 *WS and Others v Frontex* [2023] ECLI:EU:T:2023:492; see also Prakken d'Oliveira, 'EU agency Frontex charged with illegal pushbacks' (*Prakken d'Oliveira*, News 2021) <www.prakkendoliveira.nl/en/news/news-2021/eu-agency-frontex-charged-with-illegal-pushbacks>; Statewatch, 'Frontex: the ongoing failure to implement human rights safeguards'(*Statewatch.org*, 25 January 2022) <www.statewatch.org/analyses/2022/frontex-the-ongoing-failure-to-implement-human-rights-safeguards/>.

measures are of a general nature and do not concern specific individuals.[47] The first case in which this was explicitly dealt with was a case initiated by Greenpeace before the General Court (then the Court of First Instance) and later the Court of Justice.[48] In relation to the procedural hurdle, Greenpeace defended the view that the environmental legal field is separate from other fields of law, as there is a particular type of public and shared interest at stake, unsuitable for a requirement such as individual concern.[49] If *locus standi* was not granted in the case, Greenpeace argued that a legal vacuum would come into being. This case did not succeed. Shortly thereafter, the Aarhus Convention was signed by the EU in 2005.[50] The third pillar of that Convention ensures access to justice in environmental matters, also (and specifically) for NGOs.[51] This led to a series of challenges to the strict *locus standi* rules in CJEU direct actions.[52] Still, no substantial change to the *Plaumann* criteria could be realised. Also attempts by individuals (together with an NGO) to overcome these criteria have proven unsuccessful.[53] A different strategy was adopted by ClientEarth, who questioned the EU's implementation of the Aarhus Convention before the Aarhus Convention Compliance Committee. This Committee found the EU to be incompliant with the Convention. This was subsequently used in litigation by the NGO Mellifera before the CJEU, but the Court rejected the Aarhus Committee's finding alleging it is non-binding (a 'draft version').[54] Environmental NGOs have not given up in this regard and continue to bring claims before the CJEU to overcome the *Plaumann* criteria. These cases form an example of the challenging of legal opportunity structures as part of strategic litigation: the NGOs in the cases purposefully litigate about procedural requirements to 'loosen' them.[55]

47 Mario Pagano, 'Overcoming Plaumann in EU environmental litigation: An analysis of ENGOs legal arguments in actions for annulment' (2019) Diritto e Processo 311.

48 Case C-321/95 P *Stichting Greenpeace Council and Others v Commission of the European Communities* [1998] ECLI:EU:C:1998:153.

49 Ibid para 18.

50 See the Convention on Access to Information, Public Participation in Decision-Making and Access to Justice in Environmental Matters (Aarhus Convention) 1998 <https://treaties.un.org/Pages/ViewDetails.aspx?src=IND&mtdsg_no=XXVII-13&chapter=27&clang=_en>.

51 Ibid art 11.

52 For example, Case C-404/12 P and C-405/12 P *Council and Commission v Stichting Natuur en Milieu and Pesticide Action Network Europe* [2015] ECLI:EU:C:2015:5.

53 Case C-565/19 P *Carvalho and Others v Parliament and Council* [2021] ECLI:EU:C:2021:252.

54 Case C-784/18 P *Mellifera v Commission* [2020] ECLI:EU:C:2020:630.

55 As also described in the UK context by Vanhala, 'Legal Opportunity Structures and the Paradox of Legal Mobilization by the Environmental Movement in the UK' (n 20).

The action for failure to act and the action for damages brought against Frontex are pending at the time of writing, and it is uncertain whether the use of these procedures will be successful, that is, whether the applicants will have their cases declared admissible by the CJEU. Nevertheless, it is interesting to look at these cases in more detail, as they are one of the few examples in which these actions have been purposefully mobilised to address fundamental rights violations by the EU. The failure to act brought by *front*-LEX alleges a failure by Frontex to terminate its operation in the Aegean Sea, in the context of which the applicants suffered fundamental rights violations on their journey to Greece.[56] Frontex argues that the complaint should be declared inadmissible as the actors that invited Frontex to act in the first place are the NGOs behind the complaint and not the applicants themselves.[57] Moreover, the argument of a lack of *locus standi* (once again based on the *Plaumann* criteria) is put forward by Frontex as well.[58] The second procedure, the action for damages initiated by human rights lawyers, is on behalf of a Syrian family who were allegedly victims of a 'pushback' by Frontex.[59] The family applied for asylum in Greece but were deported by Frontex and Greek authorities on a plane to Turkey, where they were subsequently imprisoned.[60] It is noteworthy that in both procedures, a more 'strategic' actor is acting on behalf of individuals, namely a human rights law firm and an NGO. The procedural reality of Articles 265 and 340 TFEU require this, as these actors (NGO and law firm) themselves cannot prove that they suffered damage or were directly harmed by a failure to act. Similar to the environmental field, these legal actions do not stand alone but are part of a multitude of political and legal efforts undertaken by different actors.[61] This shows the deployment of 'integrated advocacy', using a multitude of strategies simultaneously alongside litigation efforts.[62]

[56] Case T-282/21 *SS and ST v Frontex* [2022] ECLI:EU:T:2022:235; see also Statewatch, 'EU: Frontex asks court to reject human rights case' (n 44).

[57] See Formal Plea of Inadmissibility T-282/21 (*Statewatch.org*, 1 October 2021) <www.statewatch.org/media/3023/formal-plea-of-inadmissibility_redacted.pdf>.

[58] See Ibid.

[59] See Prakken d'Oliveira (n 46).

[60] See Ibid.

[61] See European Ombudsman, 'Ombudsman opens inquiry to assess European Border and Coast Guard Agency (Frontex) 'Complaints Mechanism'' (*Ombudsman.europa.eu*, 12 November 2020) <www.ombudsman.europa.eu/en/news-document/en/134739>; Bellingcat, 'Frontex at Fault: European Border Force Complicit in 'Illegal' Pushbacks' (*Bellingcat*, 23 October 2020) <www.bellingcat.com/news/2020/10/23/frontex-at-fault-european-border-force-complicit-in-illegal-pushbacks/>; Jacopo Barigazzi, 'EU watchdog opens investigation into border agency Frontex' (*Politico*, 11 January 2021) <www.politico.eu/article/olaf-opens-investigation-on-frontex-for-allegations-of-pushbacks-and-misconduct/>.

[62] David Scott FitzGerald, *Refuge beyond Reach: How Rich Democracies Repel Asylum Seekers* (Oxford University Press 2019) 257–258.

As can be seen from these examples, the procedural barriers in direct actions are high for strategic litigators. Direct access to the CJEU is limited, which requires legal action to overcome these barriers or legal action by making use of individual complainants. As stated in Section 8.2, EU legal opportunity structures are more 'open' when it comes to the availability of rights: an aspect that is used by the environmental NGOs to their advantage, by arguing for procedural flexibility due to strong substantive protection. EU legal expertise here is, once again, vital to successfully mobilise these procedures. Alongside this, relations need to be established with individuals on behalf of whom strategic litigation can be initiated. Moreover, a persistent strategy with multiple legal actions brought could increase the chances of success, but only time will tell. If the Frontex procedures prove unsuccessful, they can still provide a compelling argument for civil society in Europe that there is a lack of access to justice for fundamental rights violation by EU agencies.[63] This could feed into the discussion of accession to the European Convention on Human Rights as well (see also Chapter 7).

8.3.3 *Third-Party Interventions*

In both the preliminary reference procedure and direct actions, there is the possibility for actors to intervene as a third party. Third-party intervention can be compared to the practice of using an *amicus curiae*, 'friend of the court', who can provide information to the judges to help them decide on the case.[64] By providing the CJEU with arguments, the result of a court procedure can potentially be influenced. This is, therefore, a useful tool in strategic litigation. Moreover, as accessing the Court as a direct litigant is difficult, third-party intervention ensures participation in the proceedings.[65] Nevertheless, intervening in CJEU cases is not an easy feat either, as is described below. In any case, the third party must 'accept the case as he finds it', meaning that no new grounds can be put forward.[66] Still, this tool has been used by several actors before the CJEU. This section first delves into third-party intervention in the preliminary reference procedure, after which intervention in direct actions is discussed.

63 And in some ways, losing these procedures can be (more) effective. See NeJaime, 'Winning through Losing' (n 3).

64 Differing views on this exist, nevertheless, the two are used interchangeably in for example Astrid Wiik, *Amicus Curiae before International Courts and Tribunals* (Nomos 2018).

65 Krommendijk and van der Pas, 'To intervene or not to intervene' (n 11), 1395.

66 Rules of Procedure of the Court of Justice of the European Union [2012] OJ L 265/1, arts 97, 129.

According to Articles 96 and 97 of the Court's Rules of Procedure, only parties to the main proceedings can submit their observations to the CJEU in a reference for a preliminary ruling. In practice, this means that actors have to be involved at the national level already, otherwise the gates to intervene are closed.[67] In turn, national rules on third-party intervention or submitting amicus briefs differ greatly among the twenty-seven EU Member States.[68] This creates an uneven playing field. In the common law jurisdictions, submitting amicus briefs is relatively easy. This has resulted in some 'strategic' third-party interventions in important cases coming from UK and Irish preliminary references. Most notably, in the case of *N.S. and M.E.*, there were multiple NGOs who intervened, such as UNHCR, Amnesty, and the AIRE Centre.[69] The involvement of the NGOs in this case, a landmark case on the 'Dublin system' and the transfer of asylum seekers in the European Union, was the result of strategic involvement that started at the national level, otherwise intervention at CJEU level would not have been possible. The UK-based AIRE Centre has intervened in multiple CJEU cases in the field of migration and social policy.[70] UNHCR has also intervened in a few CJEU cases, but when formal access was closed, it has turned to informally submitting its views (see Section 8.4.3).[71] As well as these examples from the migration field, interventions are also common in the aforementioned data protection cases.[72] Similarly, these cases originate from a common law jurisdiction and it can be assumed that the actors keep one another involved. This procedural framework places a heavy burden on NGOs who want to be involved in preliminary reference procedures at CJEU level, as they need to be aware of cases at the national level and national rules need to allow for intervention.[73]

67 Krommendijk and van der Pas, 'To intervene or not to intervene' (n 11).

68 Sergio Carrera, Marie de Somer, and Bilyana Petkova, 'The Court of Justice of the European Union as a Fundamental Rights Tribunal: Challenges for the effective Delivery of Fundamental Rights in the Area of Freedom, Security and Justice', (2012) CEPS paper 49, 16.

69 Case C-411/10 and C-493/10 N.S. *v Secretary of State for the Home Department and* M.E. *and Others v Refugee Applications Commissioner and Minister for Justice, Equality and Law Reform* [2011] ECLI:EU:C:2011:865.

70 Krommendijk and van der Pas, 'To intervene or not to intervene' (n 11), 1400.

71 See UNHCR, 'UNHCR Interventions before the Court of Justice of the EU' <www.unhcr.org/protection/operations/5f9ab7d44/unhcr-interventions-court-justice-eu.html>.

72 Digital Rights Ireland intervened, for example, in the case of Schrems, Case C-362/14 *Schrems v Data Protection Commissioner* [2015] ECLI:EU:C:2015:650.

73 Jasper Krommendijk and Kris van der Pas, 'Third-party interventions before the Court of Justice in migration law cases', (*EU Migration Law Blog*, 29 November 2022) <https://eumigrationlawblog.eu/third-party-interventions-before-the-court-of-justice-in-migration-law-cases/>.

In direct actions, the possibilities to intervene are a bit broader, as any person that 'can establish an interest in the result of a case submitted to the Court' can intervene.[74] This interest is generally interpreted by the CJEU as meaning that the economic situation of the intervener is directly affected, but there has been a more flexible approach towards associations promoting collective interests.[75] Several environmental cases can be found before the CJEU where parties intervened; however, a problematic aspect for the interveners is that if the applicants in the main proceedings lack standing, there is no possibility to intervene on the merits.[76] Thus, the strict *locus standi* requirements in direct actions have an effect on third-party intervention as well. It is only exceptionally that third-party intervention in direct actions happens in practice.[77]

In sum, although third-party intervention could be a way for NGOs to be involved in strategic litigation, only a few successful examples can be found. A dependency on national rules and the strict requirements in direct procedures before the court form obstacles for this strategic litigation avenue. This makes this avenue resource-intensive: there needs to be awareness of cases brought at the national level for third-party intervention in preliminary rulings and intervening in direct actions is a waste of time if a case does not pass the admissibility stage. Moreover, relations among organisations seem to be of importance: keeping each other informed so that third-party interventions can be submitted.

8.4 OTHER (CREATIVE) WAYS OF USING THE EU REMEDIES SYSTEM

The sections above have elaborated on the most common and well-known form of strategic litigation within the EU remedies system: going to the CJEU. Nevertheless, other avenues are also thinkable and have been used by different actors already. This section elaborates on some of these.

8.4.1 *Petition to the European Court of Auditors*

One institution that has been called upon regarding alleged fundamental rights violations by the EU is the European Court of Auditors (ECA). The

[74] Protocol (No 3) on the Statute of the Court of Justice of the European Union, [2016] OJ C 202/210, art 40.

[75] Krommendijk and van der Pas, 'To intervene or not to intervene' (n 11), 1402; Koen Lenaerts, Ignace Maselis, and Kathleen Gutman, *EU Procedural Law* (Oxford University Press 2015), 787.

[76] Krommendijk and van der Pas, 'To intervene or not to intervene' (n 11), 1402.

[77] Case T-189/14 Deza v ECHA [2017] ECLI:EU:C:2017:4.

ECA is responsible for carrying out the EU's external audit, supervising control over the EU budget.[78] In April 2020, three NGOs submitted a complaint to the ECA about the mismanagement of EU funds through the 'Support to Integrated Border and Migration Management in Libya' (IBM) Programme.[79] These NGOs are repeat-players in strategic litigation, especially when it comes to the field of migration law.[80] In a novel way, the NGOs link fundamental rights obligations of the EU to the management of funds, alleging that the EU budget is used to violate fundamental rights (in Libya). The ECA responded in May 2020 that it would not initiate a review of the IBM programme at that time, partly due to its limited resources.[81] Still, this complaint presents an interesting case study of a route that could be used successfully. As a downside, the actors submitting such a complaint can do no more than that: submit information to the institution. There is no possibility of formal involvement in any procedure that follows.[82] Nonetheless, if a formal review is initiated by the ECA, this could lead to more accountability of the EU for possible fundamental rights violations and could become a useful avenue in fields other than migration as well.

8.4.2 *Calling upon Other (Non-Judicial) European Institutions*

The aforementioned strategies relate to the use of courts, but other EU institutions can also be called upon to challenge alleged fundamental rights violations by the EU. Under Article 227 TFEU, natural and legal persons

[78] TFEU, arts 285, 287; Nikos Vogiatzis, 'The Independence of the European Court of Auditors', (2019) 56 Common Market Law Review 667.

[79] GLAN, ASGI, ARCI, 'Complaint to the European Court of Auditors Concerning the Mismanagement of EU Funds by the EU Trust Fund for Africa's 'Support to Integrated Border and Migration Management in Libya' (IBM) Programme Submitted by Global Legal Action Network (GLAN), Association for Juridical Studies on Immigration (ASGI), and Italian Recreational and Cultural Association (ARCI)' (2020) <www.glanlaw.org/_files/ugd/14ee1a_ae6a20e6b5ea4b00b0aa0e77ece91241.pdf>.

[80] The NGOs are the Association for Juridical Studies on Immigration (ASGI), the Italian Recreational and Cultural Association (ARCI), and the Global Legal Action Network (GLAN). The latter is no longer involved in this complaint, but involvement has been taken over by the NGO De:Border Collective. See GLAN, 'EU Financial Complicity in Libyan Migrant Abuses' <www.glanlaw.org/eu-complicity-in-libyan-abuses>; see Pijnenburg and van der Pas (n 1).

[81] GLAN, 'Petition to European Parliament Challenging EU's Material Support to Libyan Abuses against Migrants' (2020) <www.glanlaw.org/single-post/2020/06/11/petition-to-european-parliament-challenges-eu-s-material-support-to-libyan-abuses-against>.

[82] This can be compared to complaints and information submitted to the International Criminal Court, Pijnenburg and van der Pas (n 1).

are given the right to address a petition to the European Parliament on EU activities that affect them directly. The same three organisations that submitted the complaint to the ECA have made use of this right of petition on the same topic, the mismanagement of EU funds leading to fundamental rights violations in Libya.[83] The argument made to use Article 227 TFEU is that the organisations consist of EU taxpayers, hence the mismanagement of funds affects them directly.[84] A Committee on Petitions of the European Parliament considers and can follow up on these petitions.[85] For strategic purposes, a downside is that the petition must be brought by the ones directly affected by the EU's activities. Therefore, a strategic litigator cannot send the petition on behalf of a large group of individuals who suffer from EU fundamental rights violations.

A second available route that makes use of an EU non-judicial institution is the submission of information to an EU body such as the European Data Protection Board (EDPB). The NGO noyb of privacy activist Maximilian Schrems has made use of this option, by submitting a complaint to multiple Data Protection Authorities (DPA) in May 2018 about the tech company Meta running personalised ads without user consent.[86] Four years later, in December 2022, news broke that Meta will have to pay a fine of almost 400 million euros.[87] Although the decision on the fine was taken by the Irish DPA, it was pushed by the EDPB to do so. The EDPB coordinates the consistent application of EU privacy rules throughout the EU.[88] Similar to the procedures mentioned before, the involvement of strategic actors stops after submitting a complaint and information. Nevertheless, if the consequent procedure has a positive outcome, the desired impact can become a reality.

A last avenue that is already elaborated on elsewhere in this volume (Chapter 5) is the submission of complaints to the EU Ombudsman. As the Ombudsman is responsible for investigating complaints about

83 See GLAN (n 81).
84 See ibid; GLAN, ASGI, ARCI (n 79).
85 See <www.europarl.europa.eu/committees/en/peti/about>.
86 See noyb, 'noby win: Personalized Ads on Facebook, Instagram and WhatsApp declared illegal' (6 December 2022) <https://noyb.eu/en/noyb-win-personalized-ads-facebook-instagram-and-whatsapp-declared-illegal>; noyb, 'noyb.eu filed complains of 'forced consent' against Google, Instagram, WhatsApp and Facebook' (25 May 2018) <https://noyb.eu/en/noybeu-filed-complaints-over-forced-consent-against-google-instagram-whatsapp-and-facebook>.
87 See Thomas Hill and AP, 'Meta fined 390m for privacy law breaches in the EU' (*Euronews*, 4 January 2023) <www.euronews.com/2023/01/04/meta-fined-390m-for-privacy-law-breaches-in-the-eu#:~:text=European%20Union%20regulators%20on%20Wednesday,based%20on%20their%20online%20activity>.
88 See <https://edpb.europa.eu/about-edpb/about-edpb/who-we-are_en>.

maladministration of the EU, fundamental rights issues have also been brought to the attention of the EU Ombudsman.[89] For example, several environmental NGOs have submitted a complaint on the European Investment Bank not disclosing information about the environmental impacts of financed projects.[90] This led to the Ombudsman issuing decisions on this topic in April 2022.[91] However, such decisions are non-binding, which poses limits to the effectiveness of this option (if decisions are positive for the strategic actors in the first place).

8.4.3 *Informal Involvement*

Strategic litigation is not always visible: at times, strategic involvement by actors is 'hidden', behind individual clients or other organisations. Such informal involvement can still be a way of influencing legal procedures, including within the EU remedies system, and therefore deserves attention here. For example, as described above, formal third-party intervention in the preliminary reference procedure before the CJEU is rather difficult. In that regard, it is interesting to note that UNHCR has resorted to informal third-party intervention submissions in the form of 'written observations' or 'public statements'.[92] Although the influence of such informal involvement is difficult to measure, it is a way for actors to have their voice heard in Luxembourg. Another way of being involved is through the provision of expert opinions or expertise to lawyers who have cases pending before the CJEU. This is the strategy deployed by the Dutch Council for Refugees (DCR). Due to their network with Dutch migration lawyers, the DCR and their Committee Strategic Litigation is able to (at times) provide arguments to lawyers in preliminary references before the CJEU that originate from the Netherlands.[93] Additionally, in their written submissions before Dutch courts, the Committee often pushes for preliminary questions to be asked.[94] Similarly

[89] It is specifically one of the areas of work of the Ombudsman, see <www.ombudsman.europa.eu/en/areas-of-work>.

[90] See ClientEarth, 'EU Ombudsman reprimands EIB for lack of transparency on funding's environmental impacts' (25 April 2022) <www.clientearth.org/latest/press-office/press/eu-ombudsman-reprimands-eib-for-lack-of-transparency-on-funding-s-environmental-impacts/>.

[91] See Ombudsman, 'Ombudman asks EIB to improve transparency around the projects it finances' (25 April 2022) <www.ombudsman.europa.eu/en/news-document/en/155122>.

[92] See UNHCR (n 71) .

[93] Hoevenaars (n 29); Kris van der Pas, 'All That Glitters Is Not Gold? Civil Society Organisations (non-)Mobilisation of European Union Law' (2024) 62 Journal of Common Market Studies 525.

[94] van der Pas, 'All That Glitters Is Not Gold?' (n 93).

from the Dutch context, the informal involvement of a law clinic can be pointed out. At the Vrije Universiteit Amsterdam, the Migration Law Clinic has been submitting 'expert opinions', which support the reasoning of the lawyers in the preliminary ruling procedure.[95] Through these lawyers' pleadings, the submissions of the DCR and the law clinic are brought into the case. Again, these types of involvement show the relevance of coalitions and networks, such as contact with national lawyers and knowledge of pending preliminary references and the importance of Euro-expertise.

8.5 CONCLUSION

The collection of examples above warrants several questions. Firstly, how did these actors manage to successfully mobilise or litigate? The answer to that question differs by procedure, but some common denominators can be found. Most importantly, all actors involved have a certain (high) level of EU legal expertise, also referred to as Euro-expertise. In his seminal 1974 article, Galanter already referred to the notion and importance of being a litigating 'repeat-player'.[96] The more resources, knowledge, and experience a litigant has, the higher the chances of success, according to Galanter. Applying this to the present chapter, the same seems to hold true within the EU context. This indicates that more investment into Euro-expertise is worth it. Substantively, Euro-expertise makes benefitting from the availability of rights within the EU remedies system possible. Procedurally, Euro-expertise helps litigants to access the rather closed system and make use of this substantive protection that the EU offers. This chapter has shown the relevance of relations, networks, and coalitions in this respect. A lack of Euro-expertise in one organisation can be compensated with the involvement of another.

Moreover, as litigants sometimes have to work through individual complainants, relations with communities and grassroots organisations seem of importance as well. There is no *actio popularis* possible before the EU courts, which makes clients all the more relevant. Nevertheless, as Section 8.4 has shown, other ways of involvement can circumvent possible difficulties in finding the 'perfect' case, by working around the EU courts in other parts of the EU remedies system.

Additionally, some applicants seem to have gone forum shopping, finding the national legal system most suitable and procedurally more favourable for

95 See Migration Law Clinic, 'CJEU: Judge must review legality of migration detention measure ex officio' (8 November 2022) <https://migrationlawclinic.org/2022/11/08/cjeu-judge-must-review-legality-of-detention-measure-ex-officio/>.

96 Galanter, 'Why the "haves" come out ahead' (n 27).

bringing a complaint about EU fundamental rights violations. This shows the unequal playing field among EU Member States when it comes to strategic litigation. Some systems are more 'open' in terms of legal opportunities than others. For example, in some countries judges might be more willing to pose a preliminary question to the CJEU than in others.[97] Or third-party intervention at the national level is easier. This makes EU legal opportunities dependent on the national level and opens access but not to everybody. Litigators seem to have made use of the available avenues in some Member States, where others are closed.

The second question that results from the current chapter is: How can access to the EU remedies system for strategic litigants be improved? Although a non-normative answer to this question is impossible to provide, the closedness of the EU system in terms of the first dimension of legal opportunity structures indicates that more access to the CJEU and other formal procedural options are desirable. In this regard, there are two different ways forward. The first is the creation of a new procedure, such as a form of collective action or *actio popularis* before the CJEU. Political support for something like this might be lacking.

There is also a (perhaps more feasible) second option: a more relaxed approach towards certain procedural requirements. The *Plaumann* criteria are the most telling example of this, but relaxing the requirements for third-party interventions before the CJEU is also possible (such as the approach of the ECtHR). This opens up EU legal opportunity structures and creates possibilities for strategic litigation. Moreover, what has been highlighted already are the differences between the EU Member States when it comes to procedural rules on access to courts, which in turn influences access to the CJEU. A more equal playing field in this regard is one of the ways in which the current availability of procedures can be streamlined as well. For example, the three EU non-discrimination Directives contain a provision that ensures standing for organisations wanting to tackle discrimination in an administrative or judicial procedure.[98] Such harmonisation on collective action or litigation for a public interest can be a way of securing a more 'open' EU remedies system.

97 Tommaso Pavone, 'From Marx to Market: Lawyers, European Law, and the Contentious Transformation of the Port of Genoa' (2018) 53 Law & Society Review 851.

98 Directive (EC) 54/2006 on the implementation of the principle of equal opportunities and equal treatment of men and women in matters of employment and occupation (recast) [2006] OJ L204/23, art 17; Council Directive (EC) 43/2000 implementing the principle of equal treatment between persons irrespective of racial or ethnic origin [2000] OJ L180/22, art 7; Council Directive 2000/78/EC of 27 November 2000 establishing a general framework for equal treatment in employment and occupation [2000] OJ L303/16, art 9.

9

Finding a New (Old?) Way Forward

International Arbitration as a Supplementary Tool for Fundamental Rights Violations

VERONIKA YEFREMOVA

9.1 INTRODUCTION

This chapter examines what legal space exists within the EU judicial system for arbitration to be used as a supplementary tool to remedy fundamental rights violations. This exercise is more creative and theoretical in nature since arbitration is not currently used to remedy violations by the EU. Moreover, arbitration exists outside the scope of the EU judicial system. However, since arbitration is a valuable dispute resolution mechanism, this chapter will assess whether it is possible to have more space to use such a tool in situations where an individual has had their rights violated and has no access to a court. The premise for this chapter primarily lies in the fact that the EU judicial system has been established and used for many years. In the eyes of the Court of Justice of the European Union (CJEU), there exists a full system of remedies.[1] The EU judicial system has been essential to the process of integration ever since the creation of the EU. The judicial system has been later enhanced through extensive treaty revision and case law of the CJEU. The use of arbitration in certain sectors has shown that parties prefer to opt for private dispute resolution mechanisms or private enforcement.[2] With the expanding competence of the EU and the far-reaching policies that can be found in the EU Treaties, a significant gap has emerged between EU policy objectives and provision of an effective remedy in practice. Against this background, this chapter will explore the legal room for using international arbitration where no access to court is available in practice in fundamental rights violations by

[1] Case C-294/83 *Les Verts v Parliament* [1986] ECLI:EU:C:1986:166, para 23.

[2] See, for example, fields of law such as the energy sector and competition law.

the EU. This analysis will provide a view of whether and to what extent international arbitration can be used to close the enforcement gap that has become apparent when dealing with fundamental rights violations by the EU.

This chapter is divided into three sections. Firstly, the chapter begins by outlining what international arbitration is, the strengths and weaknesses of the system, and how it is being used within the EU. Moreover, the relationship between the EU judicial system and private international law is highlighted. Secondly, the chapter assesses the constitutional limits imposed through the CJEU approach and Treaty provisions where arbitration is concerned. Finally, the chapter will analyse the constitutional potential and practical implications of introducing arbitration as a dispute resolution avenue. In doing so, this chapter uses inter-state arbitration and investment-treaty arbitration cases as examples; however, the framework for these is excluded from the discussion.

9.2 THE MODEL OF INTERNATIONAL ARBITRATION

9.2.1 *Defining International Arbitration*

International arbitration can be defined as an extra-judicial mechanism of dispute resolution, which is considered one of the alternative dispute resolution mechanisms.[3] The term *international commercial arbitration* refers to a procedure where disputes between private individuals or corporations are resolved.[4] Moreover, it can also be between a state acting in its private capacity and a private party. The mechanism is considered to be part of the adjudication system of any legal order.[5] There is a group of scholars who are of the opinion that all arbitration is private, even when it concerns a dispute between an investor and a state. This idea mainly stems from the fact that the arbitrators who adjudicate on the dispute are appointed by the parties, rather than belonging to a judicial institution. However, this is not always the case.

[3] Georgios Zekos, 'The Historical Appearance of Arbitration as a Dispute Mechanism' in Georgis Zekos *International Commercial and Marine arbitration* (Routledge-Cavendish 2008) 1. <www.lawcatalog.com/media/productattach/n/j/nj_arbitration_handbook_ch01_1.pdf>; Sarah Rudolph, 'Blackstone's Vision of Alternative Dispute Resolution' (1992) 22(2) Memphis University Law Review 279.

[4] John Merrils, *International Dispute Settlement* (4th edn, Cambridge University Press 2005) 117; Chukwudi Ojiegbe, *International Commercial Arbitration in the European Union* (1st edn, Edward Elgar 2020) 78.

[5] Gus van Harten, 'The public-private distinction in the international arbitration of individual claims against the state' (2007) 56(2) International and comparative corporate law quarterly 381; Burkhard Hess, *The Private-Public Divide in International Dispute Resolution* (Brill Nijhoff 2018) 192.

The fact that it may be a private dispute resolution system does not take away from the fact that it is a mechanism that guarantees access to justice and has final and binding arbitral awards. The author is of the opinion that private arbitration concerns disputes that are brought by private parties or between a private party and a state acting in its private capacity.

Private arbitration allows the parties to create their own arbitration process.[6] This is done through the principle of private autonomy, as it is an integral principle of arbitration. Hence, this also means that the elements of the arbitration process result from choices the parties make. For example, the seat of arbitration, which procedural rules apply, and the arbitrators are all choices that the parties make themselves. This means that there also has to be consent given by the parties to arbitration or it needs to be provided in an agreement. Therefore, arbitration is usually an agreed form of dispute settlement.

9.2.2 *Benefits of International Arbitration*

International arbitration has become the preferred mechanism for many cross-border commercial disputes due to three main benefits.[7] The first is the flexibility in proceedings. The parties to the arbitration agreement may choose the type of tribunal that will hear the dispute, the applicable law (*lex arbitri*), the seat of arbitration, and which conflict of laws to use. Hence, the parties are able to choose the evidence rules and the time limits since most of these rules are outlined in the applicable and chosen law. Therefore, the parties are able to design their own proceedings.

A second benefit of arbitration is the ability to choose one's arbitrators.[8] Since disputes that arise come from different fields, they require different types of expertise to resolve the dispute at hand. The parties to a dispute are free to choose arbitrators according to their expertise.[9] There are arbitrators who are

6 Ojiegbe (n 4) 2.

7 White & Case and Queen Mary University of London, '2018 International Arbitration Survey: The Evolution of International Arbitration' (*White & Case*, 2018), <www.whitecase.com/sites/whitecase/files/files/download/publications/qmul-international-arbitration-survey-2018-19.pdf> charts 1 and 2; Singapore Management University, School of Law, Singapore International Dispute Resolution Academy (SIDRA), SIDRA International Dispute Resolution Survey: 2020 Final Report (*Sidra*, 2020) <https://sidra.smu.edu.sg/sidra-international-dispute-resolution-survey-final-report-2020> exhibit 4.1. all; S Brekoulakis and G Dimitropoulos (eds), *International Commercial Courts: The Future of Transnational Adjudication* (Cambridge University Press 2022).

8 General Principles of Law in International Commercial Arbitration, (1988) 101(1) Harvard Law Review, 1817.

9 Ibid 1818.

either professors or practitioners in different fields of law and beyond. This is particularly advantageous when the resolution of a dispute hinges on specific technical expertise that judges may not always possess.

A third benefit of arbitration is that an arbitral award is final and binding.[10] The arbitral award has *res judicata* effects.[11] Unlike other private dispute resolution mechanisms, an arbitral award can and should be enforced in any national jurisdiction.[12] Since arbitral awards are recognised and enforced in national jurisdictions, this means that the arbitrators will do their utmost best to resolve the case, as any arbitral tribunal would strive for the award to be enforceable (depending especially on whether the state signed the New York Convention).[13] Therefore, although arbitration is considered a private dispute resolution mechanism, all the regulations that concern the protection of the weaker party or fundamental rights are still applied in arbitral proceedings. Hence, while doing their jobs, arbitral tribunalstend to apply, even if not obligated to, laws and norms that any national court would apply, in order to achieve enforceability of the arbitral award.[14]

9.2.3 *Limitations of International Arbitration*

As with any system, there are also a few limitations that can be attributed to using arbitration as a dispute resolution mechanism. The first limitation concerns the confidentiality of the dispute resolution process.[15] It poses a limit to commercial arbitration since awards are not always publicly available. It poses risks that decision-making in arbitration proceedings does not adhere to any sort of check and transparency. For EU law purposes, this is a limitation since it is not possible to check how EU law was interpreted in a dispute. Moreover, this translates into issues with legal certainty since it then becomes difficult to establish a common line taken in awards is in a certain situation.[16] Hence, it poses a limit to using arbitration.

[10] Zekos (n 3) 14.

[11] Allan Rosas, 'The EU and International Dispute Settlement' (2017) 1(1) Europe and the World Law Review 1, 14; Konstanze von Papp, *EU Law and International Arbitration: Managing Distrust Through Dialogue* (1st edn, Hart 2021) 58.

[12] Zekos (n 3) 14.

[13] Von Papp (n 11) 3.

[14] Christophe Hillion and Ramses Wessel, 'The European Union and International Dispute Settlement: Mapping Principles and Conditions' in Marise Cremona, Anne Thies, and Ramses A Wessel (eds), *The European Union and International Dispute Settlement* (Hart 2017) 8.

[15] Zekos (n 3) 5.

[16] Ibid 6.

A second limitation of arbitration, which ties into the previous one, concerns the issue of transparency and consistency.[17] Due to some arbitral awards not being made public, this raises the question of how disputes are in fact resolved by the arbitrators. This also plays into decision-making of arbitral tribunals not being public, hence not transparent. A limitation exists here in the sense that when a dispute deals with private and public interests and is not transparent, that is a problem. Since public interest can be violated when a private interest is decided, it becomes crucial for national courts who enforce the award to check this. This poses a risk that national courts when enforcing the award will want to carry out a full review.

A third limitation is that arbitration can form a limit to effective judicial protection within the EU. Given the fact that international arbitration exists outside the scope of the EU judicial mechanism, if a party to a dispute decides to take a dispute to arbitration, that party is in fact deciding to take the dispute out of the EU judicial system. From an EU perspective, practically this means that effective judicial protection as guaranteed under Article 47 Charter of Fundamental Rights of the European Union ('the Charter') is not achieved.[18] On the EU level, more specifically, Article 47 Charter recognises access to justice as a '*core fundamental right*'.[19] This means that arbitration undermines this fundamental principle of EU law. Secondly, if an arbitration clause in a contract or agreement exists, the dispute will go to arbitration, which means that a national court can only enforce or annul the arbitral award, hence a limited judicial review.[20] Although this does not mean that it is a breach of fundamental rights per se, it does mean that the EU threshold of effective judicial protection might not be met. Therefore, from an EU law perspective, the limited review stemming from the *res judicata* of arbitral awards may undermine effective judicial protection.

[17] Fabrizio Cafaggi, 'Private Regulation in European Private Law' EUI RSCAS WP 2009/31, 6; Julia Black, 'Constitutionalising Self-Regulation' (1996) 59 (1) Modern Law Review 24.

[18] Charter of Fundamental Rights of the European Union [2016] OJ C202/389 (CFR); Norbert Reich, 'More Clarity after "*Claro*"? Arbitration Clauses in Consumer Contracts as an ADR (Alternative Dispute Resolution) Mechanism for Effective and Speedy Conflict Resolution, or as "Deni de Justice"?' (2007) 1 European Review of Contract Law 41.

[19] CFR, art 47; Malik Dahlan, Rosa Lastra, and Gustavo Rochette, *Research Handbook on EU Energy Law and Policy* (1st edn, Edward Elgar 2022) 318.

[20] Anna van Duin, *Effective Judicial Protection in Consumer Litigation* (Intersentia 2022) 76; Norbert Reich, 'Party Autonomy and Consumer Arbitration in Conflict: A "Trojan Horse" in the Access to Justice in the E.U. ADR-Directive 2013/11?' (2015) Penn State Journal of Law & International Affairs 290, 320; Clare Ambrose, 'Arbitration and the Free Movement of Judgments' (2003) Arbitration International Law 3, 8.

9.3 SETTING THE SCENE: INTERNATIONAL ARBITRATION AND EU LAW

This section outlines where arbitration fits under the EU framework. Firstly, the development of private international law in the EU will be outlined. Secondly, an overview of the legal instruments on the EU level will allow an understanding of what room exists for arbitration.

9.3.1 *The EU's Competence and Arbitration*

International arbitration is considered to belong to a branch of private international law, which predominantly relies on party autonomy and expression of will from parties to a dispute. There is no fully-fledged European Private International Law, although it is becoming more regulated within the EU sphere.[21] Since arbitration mainly depends on private law and domestic procedural law, it is also dependent on private international law. Hence why this framework is relevant for using arbitration.

Even though the EU has expanded its regulation into numerous policy areas, private international law has been an area of law that was originally left untouched.[22] This is also evident from the EU's competences in matters of private international law. There is no specific field of 'EU arbitration law' that would be regulated in the Treaty on the Functioning of the European Union (TFEU).[23] Generally, there is no provision in the Treaties that explicitly refers to, or deals with, arbitration.[24] However, this was not always the case. A provision was inserted into the Treaty of European Economic Community (hereinafter, 'EEC'), under Article 220 EEC.[25] Here, the

[21] Case C-184/12 *United Antwerp Maritime Agencies (Unamar) NV v Navigation Maritime Bulgare* [2013] EU:C:2013:663; European Private International Law is imbedded in the Rome I Regulation, more specifically recital 11; Regulation (EC) No 593/2008 of the European Parliament and of the Council of 17 June 2008 on the law applicable to contractual obligations (Rome I) [2008] OJ L177; see interesting observations in Martina Mantovani, EU Private International Law before the ECJ: A Look into Empirical Data (The European Association of Private International Law, 19 September 2022) <https://eapil.org/2022/09/19/eu-private-international-law-before-the-ecj-a-look-into-empirical-data/>.

[22] Federico Ferretti, 'EU Internal Market Law and the Law of International Commercial Arbitration: Have the EU Chickens Come Home to Roost?' (2020) 20(1) Cambridge Yearbook of European Studies 141.

[23] Consolidated Version of the Treaty on the Functioning of the European Union [2016] OJ C202/47 (TFEU).

[24] Jürgen Basedow, 'EU Law in International Arbitration: Referrals to the European Court of Justice' (2015) 32(4) Journal of International Arbitration 368.

[25] Ibid 368.

following is established: 'Member States shall, in so far as necessary, engage in negotiations with each other with the view to securing to the benefit of their nationals: ... the simplification of the formalities governing the reciprocal recognition and enforcement of judgments of courts or tribunals and of arbitration awards.'[26]

The Maastricht Treaty did not include private international law, even though there were important legal architecture changes being made. A 'Three-Pillar Structure' was created and placed judicial cooperation into the third pillar.[27] This created important substantive changes for the Treaty. For private international law, this meant that the integration was less than in fields that found themselves in the first pillar. Through the pillar structure, Member States gained more room for cooperation.[28] This was seen as a compromise whereby Member States achieved more ways for cooperation within the Pillar Structure but were not subject to the supranational integration approach and the sensitivity of the fields was still respected.[29] This approach also allowed the European Council to still retain its powers. Therefore, a middle ground was found to address these more sensitive topics.

Only within the framework of Communitarisation, in the Treaty of Amsterdam, did private international law become part of the first pillar.[30] Ever since then, international arbitration and EU law have come into closer contact.[31] Though in practice, the interaction of arbitration and the EU legal order differs to varying degrees depending on the field of EU law and the competence that the EU and Member States have in the given fields.[32]

The inclusion of private international law in the first pillar created a shift in the competence divide between the EU and Member States. What was originally a matter for Member States to decide, given that the area contains private relations, now gave the EU competence.[33] The EU has competence to 'take measures in the field of judicial cooperation in civil matters having cross-border implications', as long as this relates to the proper functioning of the

[26] Treaty establishing the European Economic Community [1957] OJ C340/173 (TEC), art 220.

[27] Ojiegbe (n 4) 197.

[28] Catherine Barnard and Steve Peers, *European Law* (Oxford University Press 2018) 21.

[29] Ibid 21.

[30] Ojiegbe (n 4) 224.

[31] George Bermann, 'Reconciling European Union law demands with the demands of International Arbitration' (2011) 34(1) Fordham International Law Journal 1195.

[32] Sophie Nappert, 'International Arbitration as a Tool of Global Governance: The Use (and Abuse) of Discretion' in Eric Brousseau, Jean-Michel Glachant, and Jérôme Sgard (eds), *The Oxford Handbook of Institutions of International Economic Governance and Market Regulation* (Oxford University Press 2019) 14.

[33] Ferretti (n 22) 141.

internal market.[34] As stated under Article 3(2) Treaty on the European Union (TEU), a common area and the development of cooperation in civil matters having cross-border effects is possible with the legal basis under Articles 67 and 81 TFEU.[35]

Later, with the Treaty of Lisbon, the Union only gained powers to initiate development of alternative dispute settlement methods, which most of the time excludes arbitration as discussed in this chapter.[36] These powers are not absolute, but this explains why there has been more reference to alternative dispute settlement as a potential remedy in secondary legislation.

Treaty amendments meant that the EU and Member States now have a shared competence in the field of private international law. For arbitration, Member States still retain most powers since most arbitration is governed domestically.[37] The principles of conferral, subsidiarity, and proportionality apply.[38] As also stated under Article 3(2) TEU, what can be seen within the EU is that a common area and the development of cooperation in civil matters having cross-border effects is possible with the legal basis under Article 81 TFEU.[39] On the other hand, given the shared competence, EU institutions can enact legislation.[40]

9.3.2 *Legal Instruments That Regulate Arbitration*

On the international level, the New York Convention is an essential multilateral international treaty in the field of arbitration.[41] The Convention deals

34 Consolidated Version of the Treaty Establishing the European Community, arts 61 and 65.

35 Consolidated Version of the Treaty on European Union [2016] OJ C202/13 (TEU); TFEU, art 81; for more information on this, please see Herman-Josef Blake and Stelio Mangiameli, *Treaty on the Functioning of the European Union – A Commentary* (Springer Commentaries on International and European Law 2021).

36 Basedow (n 24) 369; TFEU, art 81(2)(g); Although the EU's conferred power for alternative dispute resolution is found under article 81, some of the legal instruments adopted on the EU level have been under article 114 TFEU. See Directive (EU) 2013/11 of the European Parliament and of the Council of 21 May 2013 on alternative dispute resolution for consumer disputes and amending Regulation 2005/2004 (EC) and Directive 2009/22/EC, 2013 OJ L165/63; Regulation 524/2013 (EU) of the European Parliament and of the Council of 21 May 2013 on online dispute resolution for consumer disputes and amending Regulation 2006/2004 (EC) and Directive 2009/22/EC ('Regulation on Consumer ODR') [2013] OJ L165/1.

37 Von Papp (n 11) 14.

38 TEU, arts 61 and 65; Kieran Bradley, 'Activities of the European Community in the Field of Private International Law in 2007' (2007) Yearbook of Private International Law 399, 401.

39 TFEU, art 81; for more information on this, please see Blake and Mangiameli(n 35).

40 Ojiegbe (n 4) 175.

41 Convention on the Recognition and Enforcement of Foreign Arbitral Awards, signed at New York 1958; Von Papp (n 11) 2.

with enforcement and recognition of arbitral awards and ensures that arbitral agreements are upheld. All Member States are also signatories to the New York Convention. The EU itself is not a signatory to the New York Convention and there is no equivalent that exists on the EU level. There is the Brussels I bis Regulation, the successor of the Brussels Convention, which deals with the free movement of judgments in cross-border situations.[42] The Brussels I bis Regulation covers all civil and commercial matters. The term 'civil and commercial matters' is not defined under the regulation itself; the concept has gained an autonomous interpretation under EU law.[43] The main aim of the Brussels I bis Regulation is ensuring the proper functioning of the internal market, judicial fairness, and international comity.[44] Arbitration is, however, excluded from the scope of the regulation. This is provided in recital 12 and Article 2(d) of the regulation.

The reasoning behind the arbitration exclusion was mainly due to prior existence of international conventions, specifically the New York Convention, which dealt with arbitration when the Regulation was enforced. This is why most issues of arbitration are left to the New York Convention and national legislation to deal with. This way EU legislation avoided overlap with existing international conventions.

On the national level, each jurisdiction has their own rules that regulate arbitration. It is only on this level that one can find codes of civil procedure and rules on how arbitral tribunals and courts should interact (together with the rules that exist on the international level).

9.4 CONSTITUTIONAL LIMITS TO ARBITRATION WITHIN THE EU JUDICIAL SYSTEM

9.4.1 *The CJEU Approach to International Arbitration*

Constitutional limits are crucial in assessing the legal space that exists for arbitration within the EU judicial system. The main limit has developed through the CJEU's approach to arbitration. Therefore, this section will

[42] Regulation (EU) No 1215/2012 of the European Parliament and of the Council of 12 December 2012 on jurisdiction and the recognition and enforcement of judgments in civil and commercial matters (recast) [2012] OJ L351/1 (Regulation (EU) No 1215/2012); Brussels Convention on jurisdiction and the enforcement of judgments in civil and commercial matters [1972] OJ L299/1.

[43] This interpretation can be found in case law, for example Case C-292/05 *Erini Lechouritou and Others v Dimosio tis Omospondiakis* [2007] ECLI:EU:C:2007:102.

[44] Regulation (EU) No 1215/2012, recitals 12 and 20.

outline the leading case law that deals with arbitration. The section is structured in a way that resembles the argumentation used by the CJEU when dealing with arbitration, namely in light of the autonomy of EU law and the uniform application of EU law.

9.4.1.1 The Principle of Autonomy and International Arbitration

The notion of the autonomy of EU law is central to the CJEU's approach to arbitration. It forms the main constitutional limit to the use of international arbitration where a dispute concerns an element of EU law. In the CJEU's case law, the type of relation between the CJEU and an international dispute settlement body and the type of dispute resolution body are the main aspects that determine whether a specific dispute resolution mechanism is contrary to the principle of autonomy. While relationships with commercial arbitration are not contrary to EU law, relationships of interaction, for example, in *Opinion 2/13*, have been declared contrary to EU law.[45]

One prominent example of when the EU and a dispute resolution body coexist can be seen in *Opinion 2/13*. This judgment concerned the question of whether EU law is compatible with the draft agreement for the accession to the European Convention on Human Rights. The Court stated that it would undermine the autonomy of EU law if the EU acceded to the Charter of Human Rights under the 'old' agreement that was in front of the Court.[46] As stated in *Opinion 2/13*, an agreement or dispute settlement mechanism outside the scope of EU law cannot affect the powers fixed by the Treaties and the autonomy of the EU legal system.[47] The Opinion also stated that Member States should not submit a dispute that deals with the Treaties to any 'other method of settlement other than those provided therein'.[48]

In the same vein, judgments such as *Achmea* and *Komstroy* show that the arbitration procedure under the arbitral agreement in the given case is contrary to EU law and undermines the autonomy of EU law.[49] The case in

[45] Case *Opinion 2/13 – Accession of the EU to the ECHR* [2014] ECLI:EU:C:2014:2454.

[46] Ibid.

[47] Ibid para 201.

[48] Ibid para 201; Case *Opinion 1/91 – Draft agreement between the Community, on the one hand, and the countries of the European Free Trade Association, on the other, relating to the creation of the European Economic Area* [1991] ECLI:EU:C:1991:490, para 35; Case *Opinion 1/00 – Proposed agreement between the European Community and non-Member States on the establishment of a European Common Aviation Area* [2002] ECLI:EU:C:2002:231, paras 11–12.

[49] Case C-284/16 *Slowakische Republik (Slovak Republic) v Achmea BV ('Achmea')* [2018] ECLI:EU:C:2018:158; Case C-741/19 *Republic of Moldova v Komstroy LLC ('Komstroy')* [2021] EU:C:2021:655.

Achmea concerned the question of whether Article 344 TFEU precluded the application of a bilateral investment protection agreement when the contracting state acceded to the EU.[50] The CJEU established that the intra-EU bilateral investment treaty would be against EU law since it would take the dispute outside the CJEU jurisdiction.[51] The CJEU relied on the principle of autonomy of the EU to state that international agreements cannot affect the powers laid down in the Treaties.[52] Relying on the ruling in *Opinion 2/13*, the Court reiterated that the legal system was designed to ensure the uniformity of the interpretation of EU law.[53] The Court went on to make a differentiation between investor-state arbitration and commercial arbitration. With commercial arbitration, since it is expressly based on the will of the parties, it does not have the same effect on the legal system as investor-state arbitration. Therefore, in these circumstances, there is more legal space provided to choose to go to commercial arbitration.

In *Komstroy*, the Court followed a similar logic.[54] The dispute arose because of a Moldovan investor and a Ukrainian investor having a dispute about the definition of 'investment'.[55] The dispute was referred to the CJEU by a preliminary ruling reference from the Paris Court of Appeal. The judgment confirmed the same distinction with regards to commercial arbitration, where the Court reasoned that since arbitral awards are reviewed by national courts, the principles of EU law can be examined in the process of that review.

In conclusion, when investor-state arbitration is concerned, autonomy is used as a limit. In situations of commercial arbitration, where the parties to a dispute choose to turn to arbitration, following the reasoning of the Court this is not barred by autonomy. On the other hand, in situations where arbitration affects the powers as envisaged by the Treaties, then the principle of autonomy is used as a bar. This distinction requires some attention. Although this may be a way for the CJEU to give commercial arbitration more space and accept it, it is still questionable whether that review will be accepted by the CJEU. Since this would mean that arbitral tribunals would interpret EU law without a review from the CJEU, it is hard to believe it will be accepted.

50 Ibid para 23.
51 Ibid.
52 Ibid para 32.
53 Ibid para 35; *Opinion 2/13* (n 45) para 174.
54 *Komstroy* (n 49) para 43.
55 Ibid para 15.

9.4.1.2 Argument of Uniform Application of EU Law and Arbitration

Ensuring effective and uniform application of EU law is another central argument used by the CJEU when it deals with limiting arbitration. It serves as a limit to arbitration when arbitral tribunals apply EU law and that application then needs to be checked. In the case of arbitration, this check is done by national courts in the post-award stage, which results either in the annulment or enforcement of the arbitral award. According to the CJEU's case law, when a case concerns the validity of an arbitration agreement or annulment of such an award that deals with EU law, national courts should have the possibility to review the application of EU law. However, this review is quite limited in practice.

Given the fact that arbitral awards enjoy *res judicata* effects, judicial review is limited to either enforcing the award or annulling it.[56] This means that if an error in law occurred, it is not possible to remedy the error in one part of the arbitral award.[57] The only remedy a national court would have would be to annul the arbitral award. This annulment is based on a violation of the uniform and effective application of EU law.

The limit on arbitration in the form of rendering it a violation of the uniform application of EU law is relevant when arbitration poses a risk to the effectiveness of any EU law norm. This is so when the balancing act between the benefits of arbitration and the potential violations it brings no longer favours the EU legal order. Hence, the uniform application of EU law argument becomes a bar to arbitration.

A good illustration of this is the *Mostaza Claro* judgment.[58] Although it is a case that stems from the field of consumer protection, which is quite specific and has a lot of secondary legislation for the protection of the weaker party, nevertheless it serves the purpose of showing how effective judicial protection is used by the Court. In general, the enforcement of consumer rights has been limited to the principles of effectiveness and equivalence by the case law of the CJEU.[59] However, the CJEU also made clear that domestic procedural rules should not make it extremely difficult for private parties, in this case consumers, to use their substantive rights under EU law. The Court went

[56] Manuel Penades Fons, 'The Effectiveness of EU law and Private Arbitration' (2020) 57(1) Common Market Law Review 1072.

[57] Ibid.

[58] Case C-168/05 *Mostaza Claro v Centro Móvil Milenium SL* [2006] ECLI:EU:C:2006:675.

[59] Pieter Jan Kuijper, Fabian Amtenbrink, Deirdre Curtin, Bruno De Witte, Alison McDonnell, Stefaan van den Bogaert, *The Law of the European Union* (5th edn, Wolters Kluwer International 2018) 1162.

further in stating that in order to ensure the effectiveness of the EU legal order, it is necessary to allow national courts to examine the validity of arbitration agreements in the post-award phase.[60] The CJEU justified this more intrusive approach as being 'necessary for ensuring that the consumer enjoys effective protection, in view of the real risk that he is unaware of his rights or encounters difficulties in enforcing them'.[61] The Court relied on the principle of equivalence, as it had previously also done in *Eco Swiss*, to rule that domestic public policy and EU public policy are complementary.[62]

Similar reasoning to *Mostaza Claro* can be found in the *Asturcom* judgment.[63] This case concerned a consumer who had not participated in the arbitration proceedings; however, the arbitral award was later issued and not annulled by the consumer. The arbitral award was enforced in Spain.[64] Firstly, it is clear from the case that the consumer was given the opportunity to annul the award in front of the Spanish courts.[65] Given this context, and once again relying on the principles of effectiveness and equivalence, the CJEU stated that if it were to put the obligation on the Spanish court to review and annul the award, this would go against the principle of *res judicata* and would impose 'an unjustifiable high price on the Member States'.[66]

9.4.2 *Interim Conclusion*

This section shows that the CJEU's approach limits arbitration based on autonomy and ensuring effective application of EU law. Although these arguments are quite reasonable from the point of view of ensuring and protecting the EU legal order from external influence, this cautious view may not be working in the CJEU's favour. Although this section has focused on the most integral cases while mapping out the legal room for arbitration, the discussion has also shown a broader 'cost' that would be incurred if international arbitration were used. This cost is twofold.

Firstly, for international arbitration to have room within the EU, a broader definition of autonomy needs to be applied. A softer definition of autonomy

60 Penades Fons (n 56) 1072.
61 *Mostaza Claro* (n 58) para 28.
62 Ibid para 35.
63 Case C-40/08 *Asturcom Telecomunicaciones SL v Cristina Rodríguez Nogueira* [2009] ECLI: EU:C:2009:615, para 52.
64 Ibid paras 39–46.
65 Ibid para 37.
66 Ibid paras 39–46.

would allow the EU to interact with external bodies, such as arbitral tribunals, without it posing a risk to constitutional norms of the EU. The 'cost' would be that arbitrators apply EU law in each case. This of course poses the risk that EU law would be interpreted incorrectly and would dilute the uniform application of EU law. However, as the system currently stands, arbitrators already apply EU law when dealing with an arbitration proceeding. Hence, it may be better for the EU to reduce the risks by opening up to the possibility of using arbitration as a dispute settlement mechanism.

Secondly, from the EU perspective, having more arbitration means a balancing act needs to be struck between effective judicial protection as enshrined under Article 47 Charter and having arbitration achieve access to justice from the international perspective. From the EU perspective, utilising arbitration comes at a cost of taking the dispute outside the scope of the EU judicial system, meaning that individuals would not receive the same guarantees as envisaged under Article 47 Charter. Paradoxically, though, on the flip side, this then means that using arbitration could resolve the problem individuals have in enforcing their rights.

From the international law perspective, these safeguards exist in the international domain within the arbitration practice. This, however, is not a gamble that the CJEU is willing to take, since there is no guarantee that these safeguards would be used. Therefore, it is necessary to perform a balancing act between the principles at stake.

9.5 CONSTITUTIONAL POTENTIAL FOR ARBITRATION WITHIN THE EU JUDICIAL SYSTEM

This section zooms in on how international arbitration could be utilised by the EU in order to guarantee individuals an opportunity to enforce their rights. This could take the form of a 'rights-compatible' process and a mechanism that would allow for access to court where a court is not available.[67] This section is divided into two sub-sections. Section 9.5.1 will discuss the ways forward in possibly using arbitration and Section 9.5.2 will analyse the practical implications of using arbitration alongside the EU judicial system. It will also draw together the whole discussion in order to see whether it is possible to use arbitration as a 'rights guarantor' mechanism and a supplementary tool to the EU judicial system and, if so, how this could be possible.

[67] The term rights-compatible is used in other fields, see, for example, Van Duin (n 20) 92.

9.5.1 *Way Forward for Potentially Using Arbitration in Fundamental Rights Violations*

A distinction should be made between law enforcement and rights enforcement in the EU when arbitration could potentially be used as a supplementary tool. Since the crux of using arbitration is to induce rights enforcement, this is the main focus. The reason for this distinction is twofold. Firstly, the main argument of the CJEU where arbitration is concerned has been that it needs to be limited mainly for the purposes of ensuring effective and uniform application of EU law; this can be related to law enforcement grounds.[68] This means that arbitration, as a consensual (commercial) dispute resolution mechanism, can be used since the parties know (or at least should) that they take the dispute out of the scope of the EU judicial system. Therefore, it comes down to a balancing act between application of EU law and party autonomy in order to guarantee rights enforcement.

It is not disputed that the EU judicial system operates on the idea that individuals derive rights from EU law, which should entail a possible remedy if such rights are infringed.[69] This presumption also operates on the basis that a right to an effective remedy should not be harmed by national procedural requirements that place grave burdens on the individual and possibly harm a claim to be lodged.[70] The CJEU has stated in numerous instances that an individual should not have their substantive rights hindered due to overburdensome procedural requirements of a Member State court system.[71] In precisely these situations, where strict national procedural rules hinder the possibility of access to court, for example, arbitration could be used to enforce rights. Since arbitration is predominantly made up of civil procedure, contract law, and private international law, it can be a fitting adjudication system to serve as a rights enforcement mechanism.[72] This way, an individual seeking to enforce their substantive rights would be able to do so with arbitration, avoiding the strict procedural hurdles of national courts or the limited standing before the CJEU.

68 *Mostaza Claro* (n 58); Van Duin (n 20) 58.

69 Opinion of AG Kokott in C-176/17 *Profi Credit Polska* [2018] ECLI:EU:C:2018:711, points 71–73.

70 Case C-176/17 *Profi Credit Polska* [2018] ECLI:EU:C:2018:71, paras 61 and 69; Case C-49/14 *Finanmadrid* [2016] ECLI:EU:C:2016:98, para 52.

71 In particular, this deals with time limits and costs, together with strict administrative requirements and other procedural rules. See, for example, Case C-433/11 *SKP k.s. v Kveta Polhošová* [2012] ECLI:EU:C:2012:702, para 34; *Credit Polska* (n 70) paras 63–64.

72 George Bermann, *International Arbitration and Private International Law* (Brill Nijhoff 2017).

If one were to extrapolate the reasoning of the CJEU in consumer protection cases where the Court deals with situations involving a restriction of rights of consumers to an effective remedy and an exercise of rights conferred by the Unfair Terms in Consumer Contracts Directive, much could be used as an inspiration for using arbitration.[73] Given the fact that EU competences are expanding, and with it more secondary legislation is being drafted, there are more rights that are derived and need a viable remedy available. The expanding competences also result in the EU having more room to potentially violate fundamental rights, since it has more involvement within various fields. This means that a judicial system is necessary to mirror this – this is where arbitration could come in.

The caveat here is that it comes at the price of taking a dispute outside the scope of the EU judicial system and EU law would be interpreted by arbitrators. Therefore, this becomes a balancing exercise where the balance needs to be struck between effectively interpreting EU law and ensuring that individuals have a venue to seek redress for fundamental rights violations. The argument put forward in this chapter is that international arbitration should in no way replace the EU judicial system. The thesis is that arbitration could be used as a supplementary mechanism for when there is an enforcement gap in the EU. In addition to being an alternative way to remedy fundamental rights violations by the EU, arbitration can serve as a tool for rights compliance, hence stepping in when no access to an effective remedy is possible.

9.5.2 *Practical Implications for Using Arbitration within the EU Judicial System*

It is quite a bold statement to say that international arbitration should be used in situations where the EU violates fundamental rights of individuals, since in practice this would mean that arbitrators would apply and interpret EU law in situations where the EU has violated fundamental rights and the EU would allow for this (one would need consent for this from both sides). However, if one follows the reasoning that an individual who derives rights from EU law should also have a remedy available when those rights are violated, it would be beneficial for the EU to use arbitration as a supplementary mechanism, instead of not having any possibility to enforce their rights. Simply put, the balancing act rests with the question of whether it is better to use international

[73] Van Duin (n 20) 92; Case C-266/18 *Aqua Med* [2019] ECLI:EU:C:2019:282, paras 50–51; Council Directive 93/13/EEC of 5 April 1993 on unfair terms in consumer contracts [1998] OJ L95/29.

arbitration and risk potentially diluting EU law than not having access to court available in situations of fundamental rights violation. This is because in practice arbitral tribunals apply EU law as developed by the CJEU because these tribunals want their arbitral awards enforced. Therefore, one could understand why the CJEU makes the argument of autonomy and uses a guarded approach in relation to arbitration, however, this approach harms the EU, especially as a global actor.

Institutionally speaking, the competence to act in this field is already established by the Treaties as discussed before, therefore no Treaty amendments would need to be made (neither are they desired). What is required, however, is a shift in approach. This is dependent on whether Member States could reach a common approach in how to treat arbitration, since most rules are still governed by domestic law. Moreover, it depends on the approach that the CJEU continues to develop towards arbitration. The question still stands whether commercial arbitration will keep being treated differently from investor-state arbitration or whether the lines will soon blur, depending on the cases that the Court receives.

The CJEU's approach also develops constitutional principles such as proportionality, subsidiarity, and conferral, which remain the principles at the EU's disposal to resolve questions that deal with arbitration.[74] Therefore, it is a matter of approach and using the principles in the EU's 'toolbox' in the relationship with arbitration. Practically speaking, at the time of writing, this may be hard to achieve since arbitration and the EU are not in a state of full cooperation as the two systems function independently. Taking this coexistence of systems together with the constitutionalisation of EU law, the abovementioned discussion shows the costs that come with using arbitration. With this said, the analysis has also shown openness and some space for arbitration within the EU legal order. This is something that both Member States and the EU should keep in mind.

9.6 CONCLUSION

In conclusion, the discussion on the relationship between EU law and international arbitration is left divided in practice. Although there are numerous benefits that can be derived from using arbitration as a dispute settlement mechanism, the fact that it exists outside the scope of the EU judicial system is an issue from the EU perspective. Given the growing EU competences and the rise in disputes that concern international trade matters, arbitration has

[74] Ferretti (n 22) 152.

become a favoured dispute resolution approach. Against this backdrop, the chapter has analysed how much legal space there actually is for international arbitration. This chapter has analysed what limits have emerged when arbitration enters the EU system. Reflecting on this, the concluding section has shown how international arbitration can be utilised within the EU judicial system in a way that would avoid diluting the EU's legal system but where the mechanism could be used in situations of rights enforcement for individuals.

Since one of the main objectives of the EU is to ensure proper access to justice, it is time to make more use of arbitration for EU law disputes. A way forward would be to allow more space for arbitration to provide a rights enforcement mechanism where no remedy is available on the EU level. What is required in order for this to be achieved at this stage mainly concerns a softer approach from the CJEU. This in no way means that international arbitration should replace the EU judicial system or undermine the autonomy and effectiveness of EU law. However, in situations where arbitration can and does serve as a dispute resolution mechanism in fundamental rights violations – here, the CJEU should be more understanding. Most importantly, this would guarantee individuals a chance to bring claims in situations of fundamental rights violations and therefore indeed fulfil the promise of a full system of remedies.

Given the benefits of using arbitration, it may be time to reconcile some of the tensions that arise in the relationship between arbitration and the EU. In no way does this chapter argue that arbitration should replace the existing judicial framework, but it may be time to ponder the question of how to move towards a more peaceful coexistence in order to allow a more welcoming use of arbitration. Given the costs that come with using this form of dispute settlement from the EU perspective, it may be time to perform a balancing act in trying to see how to utilise the adjudication method without hindering too many EU principles. In any case, this chapter has engaged in a more theoretical exercise on how the legal space could allow for arbitration to be used in fundamental rights violations.

10

Online Dispute Resolution

A Viable Avenue for Redressing Fundamental Rights Violations?

MARIA JOSÉ SCHMIDT-KESSEN

10.1 INTRODUCTION

This chapter looks beyond established mechanisms that could be used (creatively) to seek redress and explores if and how a new mechanism in the form of an EU online dispute resolution system could potentially improve access to redress for victims of fundamental rights violations by the EU. Online dispute resolution (ODR) systems are defined as 'mechanism[s] for resolving disputes through the use of electronic communications and other information and communication technology'.[1] In very basic terms, ODR is a form of alternative dispute resolution (ADR) that relies on a technology-based intermediary, or an ODR platform, to organise communication between the parties and, ultimately, to settle the parties' dispute. ODR systems have emerged together with the rise of the Internet and e-commerce to facilitate the settlement of cross-border disputes. Well-known examples of ODR platforms are eBay's Resolution Center[2] and the domain name dispute resolution system of the Internet Corporation for Assigned Names and Numbers (ICANN).[3]

The EU legal system is no stranger to ADR and ODR. ADR and ODR systems were first introduced as a form of redress mechanism in the field of consumer law. Now, ADR and ODR mechanisms can be found in a variety of

[1] UNCITRAL, *Technical Note on Online Dispute Resolution* (13 December 2016), pt. 24.

[2] Amy Schmitz and Colin Rule, *The New Handshake: Online Dispute Resolution and the Future of Consumer Protection* (American Bar Association 2017).

[3] ICANN Domain Name Dispute Resolution Policies <www.icann.org/resources/pages/dndr-2012-02-25-en>.

fields of EU law, including telecommunications law[4] and the recently passed Digital Services Act (DSA).[5] They have become a go-to tool for the EU legislator whenever there is a problem with the underenforcement of legal provisions protecting consumers and when access to justice and redress cannot be adequately provided through traditional court proceedings via the judicial system.

This raises the question of whether ODR mechanisms can be transferred outside the realm of private law. Could an ODR mechanism also be used in disputes where one of the parties is a public entity, like the EU, and the other is a victim of a (serious) fundamental rights violation? This chapter sheds light on this question by laying out the basic elements of ODR systems in Section 10.2 and by looking for inspiration among some examples of existing ODR mechanisms in Section 10.3. Finally, Section 10.4 of the chapter discusses design options for an EU ODR system that could function as a redress mechanism for fundamental rights violations by the EU and engages with possible benefits and shortcomings of such a system.

10.2 A BRIEF HISTORY AND BASIC ELEMENTS OF ODR

10.2.1 *A Brief History of ODR: From Private Actors to Public Sector*

To better understand the nature and capabilities of ODR, it is worth starting with a short history of ODR. ODR emerged in the mid-1990s as a response to the Internet becoming more widely available and accessible for commercial and private use. During this early period of the Web, the first online marketplaces like Amazon and eBay launched, and projects of collective content creation by internet users like Wikipedia emerged. With more and more online interactions and commercial transactions taking place around the globe, the number of conflicts originating from these interactions rose.

[4] In the event of B2C dispute settlement in the telecoms sector, see Article 25 of Directive 2018/1972 establishing the European Electronic Communications Code, which obliges national telecoms regulators to offer ADR services to consumers. Many national regulators implement this obligation in the form of an ODR mechanism, see, e.g., the Austrian ADR Body for Electronic Communications Services where the entire procedure takes place electronically. Directive (EU) 2018/1972 of the European Parliament and of the Council establishing the European Electronic Communications Code [2018] OJ L321/36, art 25; Austrian ADR Body for Electronic Communications Services <www.rtr.at/TKP/service/schlichtung_telekom/Webformular.de.html>.

[5] Regulation (EU) 2022/2065 of the European Parliament and of the Council on a Single Market For Digital Services and amending Directive 2000/31/EC [2022] OJ L211/1 (Digital Services Act), art 21.

It quickly became apparent that traditional court systems were not best suited to deal with conflicts originating from interactions on the Web. First, online transactions often had a cross-border dimension, which created a host of jurisdictional questions for national courts.[6] Second, the disputes were often of low value, making recourse to the traditional court system disproportionately costly.

Online intermediaries soon understood that they would have to find solutions for solving disputes between users if their business model were to succeed. In the case of online marketplaces, for example, promises of cheaper prices and greater convenience were insufficient to attract buyers and gain their loyalty. Buyers had to trust the platform. To build trust and prevent sham offers and fraudulent practices by buyers or sellers, platforms introduced rating and feedback mechanisms. These mechanisms, however, did not eliminate disputes between buyers and sellers. This is how eBay, for example, entered into a collaboration with researchers from the Massachusetts Amherst Center for Information Technology and Dispute Resolution to design an online dispute resolution system to settle disputes between buyers and sellers in 1999.[7] By 2010, eBay's dispute resolution system handled sixty million claims per year.[8] The eBay example is useful to highlight two features of ODR. First, ODR initially developed and grew in the private sector, for business reasons. Second, the early history of ODR and its handling of extremely large numbers of complaints have given ODR a reputation of being a fast, cheap, and effective mechanism for settling disputes.

Another example of an early ODR mechanism is ICANN's Uniform Domain Name Dispute Resolution Policy. In contrast to e-commerce platforms, ICANN performs a global internet governance function: it is a private, not-for-profit organisation that administers, among others, the Internet's global domain name system.[9] ICANN's ODR system is administered by various accredited arbitrators and deals in most part with claims from trademark owners that oppose the registration of domain names that use their trademarks without authorisation. As with e-commerce and other internet platforms, ICANN's ODR system allows the settling of disputes in the place where they originate: on the Internet.

[6] Ethan Katsh, 'ODR: A Look at History' in Mohamed S Abdel Wahab, Ethan Katsh, and Daniel Rainey (eds), *Online Dispute Resolution: Theory and Practice* (Eleven 2011) 24.

[7] Ibid 27.

[8] Pablo Cortes, 'Online Dispute Resolution Services: A Selected Number of Case Studies' (2014) 6 Computer and Telecommunications Law Review 172.

[9] ICANN also administers a global repository of IP addresses and helps remove any clashes or repetitions in this system and 13 root servers.

While ODR was initially conceived as a dispute resolution mechanism for disputes that arose *online*, its benefits like speed, accessibility, convenience, and expertise, as well as its trust-building function soon inspired various actors to pilot ODR mechanisms for *offline* disputes. The New York City Government, for example, started using the private ODR provider Cybersettle to allow individuals to settle their claims against the city relating to sidewalks, personal injury, or traffic vehicles.[10] Cybersettle was used in cases where the city's liability was not disputed and only the amount of monetary compensation had to be determined. The Cybersettle ODR tool is an automated negotiation process, which offers a blind-bidding process where software determines a negotiated outcome based on secret offers made by the parties. It should be noted, though, that automated negotiation processes are only useful if the only outstanding issue between the parties to a dispute is the amount of monetary compensation.[11]

The potential of ODR for offline disputes, however, goes further. Courts and administrative agencies have found various opportunities for using ODR in the public sector for disputes that go beyond the mere settlement of the amount of compensation. States and provinces in the United States and Canada, for example, have introduced ODR systems to decide appeals against property tax claims.[12] The ODR system for property tax appeals introduced in 2012 in British Columbia, for example, yielded an amicable solution in 75% of appeals submitted.[13] Overall, users of the system reported high satisfaction rates regarding the accessibility and convenience of the system.[14]

ODR has also been implemented in various jurisdictions at a pre-trial stage for a variety of civil law disputes. In the Netherlands, for example, the platform *Rechtwijzer* started operating in 2014 as an ODR tool for family separation and divorce disputes, which allowed the parties to engage in a structured dialogue to reach a divorce settlement agreement.[15] Agreements reached through the platform can be subsequently presented before court to make the settlement binding.

10 Cortes (n 8) 172.

11 Ibid.

12 Ethan Katsh and Colin Rule, 'What We Know and Need to Know about Online Dispute Resolution' (2016), 67 South Carolina Law Review 329.

13 Ibid.

14 Ibid.

15 Due to lack of continued public funding, the Rechtwijzer platform was wound down in 2017 and reopened as the platform Uitelkaar.nl in 2017 by a private for-profit entity. For more details, see Laura Kistemaker, 'Rechtwijzer and Uitelkaar.nl. Dutch Experiences with ODR for Divorce' (2021) 59 Family Court Review 232.

One of the most ambitious implementations of ODR systems connected to the judiciary is the English Civil Online Court (Online Civil Money Claims). The original plan for the English Civil Online Court was to handle most civil claims for sums below £25,000 through a three-stage process: at the first stage, software would assist parties in filling out claims and responses. At the second stage, online or telephone facilitation by court-provided case officers would be offered to the parties to reach a settlement. Lastly, if no settlement was reached at the second stage, the claim could be taken at a third stage to a judge who would decide the case based on the documents submitted during the prior stages. If required by the circumstances of specific cases, the judge could conduct hearings online, by telephone, or face-to-face. The Online Civil Money Claims project launched a pilot in 2017 for claims brought before County Courts for money claims of up to £10,000 brought by individuals or up to £25,000 brought by represented individuals.[16] More than 100,000 claims were issued in the first eighteen months of operation of the pilot.[17] Furthermore, the pilot was expanded during the Covid-19 pandemic due to increased demand.[18]

10.2.2 *The Technological Component of ODR*

To understand the potential of ODR, it is useful to start from its basic elements and various possible design choices. At the most basic level, ODR adds a 'fourth party'[19] to dispute resolution. Traditional dispute resolution involves three parties: applicant, defendant, and a neutral third party (a judge, a mediator, an arbiter). ODR adds to these three parties a fourth party: technology. In ODR, technology comes in the form of software, user interfaces, databases, electronic communication, etc. In contrast to offline ADR, which, in principle, only requires a neutral individual acting as third party and

[16] See UK Government Justice, Practice Direction 51R – Online Civil Money Claims Pilot <www.justice.gov.uk/courts/procedure-rules/civil/rules/practice-direction-51r-online-court-pilot>.

[17] UK Government Press Release, 'More than 100,000 Civil Money Claims Issued Online' (Gov.uk, 3 July 2020) <www.gov.uk/government/news/more-than-10000-civil-money-claims-issued-online#full-publication-update-history>.

[18] Practical Law Dispute Resolution, 'COVID-19: 119th Practice Direction Update on the Online Civil Money Claims Pilot (PD 51R)' (Practical Law UK, 15 April 2020) <https://uk.practicallaw.thomsonreuters.com/w-025-0230?originationContext=document&transitionType=DocumentItem&contextData=(sc.Default)&ppcid=b7c79252b7b54220b6dd90e1b27d8ecd&comp=pluk>.

[19] The term was coined by Ethan Katsh and Janet Rifkin, *Online Dispute Resolution: Resolving Conflicts in Cyberspace* (Jossey-Bass 2001).

can be set up ad hoc, ODR requires a more permanent infrastructure. It requires at least an electronic system or platform for 'generating, sending, receiving, storing, exchanging or otherwise processing communications in a manner that ensures data security'.[20] Technology can have an important role at the initiation, resolution, and enforcement stages of ODR procedures.

When initiating an ODR procedure, technology can enable a variety of functions. It can allow for asynchronous communication between parties and alert parties whenever a party has submitted a new communication. Technology can also streamline the completion of forms and documents, so that all relevant arguments and evidence are presented and structured in a way that allows the settlement to be conducted more smoothly. This is one of the important functions of the technological solutions in the examples of *Rechtwijzer* and the first stage of the UK Online Civil Money Claims. In a more sophisticated version, for example, with the help of Artificial Intelligence (AI) tools, technology can help to identify and name a legal issue for parties in the first place. In a pilot programme funded by PEW Charitable Trust, researchers from Stanford and Suffolk University, for example, are developing and testing natural language processing (NLP) algorithms to help ODR users identify and frame their legal issues.[21]

Software tools can also help in providing options for solving conflicts at the settlement stage of the procedure. At a very basic level, ODR can simply offer video conferencing and other communication tools that enable parties to negotiate or a third party to hear parties and to propose solutions. But technology itself can also help in guiding parties to find a solution. As the example of Cybersettle above shows, automated blind bidding can help parties to find common ground to agree on monetary compensation. In the context of e-commerce, some platforms have experimented with software solutions that enable crowd-judging. On Alibaba's Taobao platform, for example, disputes between buyers and sellers are solved by authorised users voting on the most appropriate solution for the dispute.[22] With the lightning speed at which AI solutions are developing, we can probably expect more and more automation of the solution of disputes with ever more complex questions involved, which

[20] UNCITRAL (n 1) 26.

[21] Amy Schmitz and Janet Martinez, 'ODR and Innovation in the United States' in Mohamed S. Abdel Wahab, Ethan Katsh, and Daniel Rainey (eds), *Online Dispute Resolution: Theory and Practice* (2nd edn, Eleven 2021).

[22] Alan Kwan, Alex S Yang, and Angela Huyue Zhang, 'Crowd-judging on Two-sided Platforms: An Analysis of In-group Bias', Management Science, published online in *Articles in Advance* 7 June 2023.

will be available not only to ODR mechanisms but to traditional ADR and court systems, too.

Lastly, technology solutions embedded in an ODR system can ensure the enforcement of settlements. In the case of online platforms that also control payments (e.g., through collaboration with a payment service provider), the outcomes of dispute resolution between buyers and sellers, or service providers and recipients, can be enforced through charge-back functions.[23] If the outcome of a dispute settlement between buyer and seller is that the buyer should have their money back, the chargeback mechanism will take care of implementing the remedy by reversing the payment transaction. In the case of transactions occurring via distributed ledger technologies (DLTs), like the Bitcoin blockchain, the software protocols used to record transactions could also implement automatic enforcement mechanisms for dispute settlement procedures.[24] This would be possible, for example, through the operation of smart contracts that have a pre-authorisation or escrow function, which only transfer the amount of a transaction after a human or algorithmic arbiter has verified that there is no dispute or once a dispute has been resolved in favour of the recipient.

10.2.3 *Designing ODR Mechanisms*

The design of ODR mechanisms, including technological choices, ultimately depends on several different factors. The UNCITRAL Technical Notes on Online Dispute Resolution suggest that ODR mechanisms can comprise one or more of the following three stages: a first stage of technology-enabled negotiation between the parties, a second stage of facilitated settlement by appointing a neutral third party that mediates between the parties, and a third stage that could be, for example, binding arbitration. The difference between the stages is the level of involvement of a third party in mediating the dispute and the bindingness of the outcome. This three-stage model is followed by the English Online Civil Money Claims platform. Other ODR mechanisms comprise only the first stage, as, for example, the Brazilian consumer ODR platform Consumidor.gov.br,[25] which enables consumers to file complaints against companies and companies to respond.[26]

23 Schmitz and Martinez (n 21); Pietro Ortolani, 'Self-Enforcing Online Dispute Resolution: Lessons from Bitcoin' (2016) 36 Oxford Journal of Legal Studies 595.

24 Ortolani, 'Self-Enforcing Online Dispute Resolution' (n 23).

25 Accessible via <https://consumidor.gov.br/pages/principal/?1683090534811>.

26 For a more detailed discussion of the establishment of Consumidor.gov.br, see Maria José Schmidt-Kessen, Rafaela Nogueira, and Marta Cantero Gamito, 'Success or Failure? –

Blomgren Amsler, Martinez, and Smith provide a more elaborate framework with six criteria to guide the design of dispute settlement systems,[27] which also apply to ODR mechanisms.[28] The six criteria are (i) goals, (ii) stakeholders, (iii) context and culture, (iv) structures and processes, (v) resources, and (vi) accountability. Before developing an ODR system, its goal(s) should be determined. At the most abstract level, the goal of an ODR system is to deliver justice in some of its normative forms, including justice in terms of outcome (substantive, distributive, utilitarian, social), process (access, voice, participation, accuracy, transparency, due process), and/or community (restorative, corrective, transitional, retributive, deterrent). In narrower terms, the goals of a specific ODR system will be tailored to a specific type of conflict that the system seeks to address. In e-commerce ODR systems, for example, such goals can be to enhance consumer trust or to encourage traders' participation by providing speedy settlements. In pre-trial ODR systems, the goal can be to unburden the court's docket while ensuring a fair and fast settlement of smaller claims between parties.

The second factor in designing an ODR system considers the stakeholders that create, use, and are affected by the ODR system, their background, power constellations, and respective resources. In the case of the EU ODR platform, for example, the stakeholders are consumers, companies, and national ODR bodies. Stakeholders should be consulted and actively involved in the process of designing an ODR system.

The third factor is context and culture. An ODR system has to be responsive to the context and culture in which it operates. An online marketplace's ODR system, for example, needs to consider that it might be used regularly for handling cross-border disputes, among anonymous parties, at a high volume, and for a low value. Family ODR systems will need to consider that they are dealing with conflicts usually taking place in geographic proximity, between parties that know each other well, with a strong emotional component, and with a life-altering impact of the outcome on the parties and their affected children.

Effectiveness of Consumer ODR Platforms in Brazil and in the EU' (2020) 43 Journal of Consumer Policy 659.

27 Lisa Blomgren Amsler, Janet Martinez, and Stephanie E Smith, *Dispute System Design* (Stanford University Press 2020).

28 Schmitz and Martinez (n 21). Along very similar lines to the six criteria for dispute system design, the International Council for Online Dispute Resolution (ICODR) has published a list to guide ODR platforms, systems, and tools. The principles are accessibility, accountability, competency, confidentiality, equality, fairness and impartiality, legality, security, and transparency. They are accessible via <https://icodr.org/standards/>.

The fourth factor, process and structure, refers to the ODR's procedural design to prevent, manage, and resolve disputes. They can involve one or more of the UNCITRAL ODR stages (negotiation, mediation, arbitration) mentioned above. The procedures should identify the ODR participants' interests (including their fundamental rights, economic, social, and political interests) and be designed so as to ensure that these interests are recognised and furthered in the procedure.[29]

The fifth factor is resources. For an ODR system, these resources refer to the expenditures for running the system and individual procedures, personnel costs and training, and, importantly, maintenance of the IT infrastructure of the ODR platform. In this context, it is also of central importance who pays for these costs. Depending on who finances the system, it might be perceived as biased.[30]

Lastly, the sixth factor of accountability refers to periodic evaluations as to the ODR system's functioning. Since an ODR system runs on an IT infrastructure, it will automatically generate a large volume of digital data that can be used for subsequent evaluation purposes if there are sufficient resources, cybersecurity, and privacy safeguards in place. The evaluation also entails asking whether stakeholders are actually making use of the system, whether neutral third parties (human or AI-based) involved are delivering unbiased and accurate services, and whether users of the system are satisfied with it. If the ODR system is sufficiently transparent, external parties will also be able to monitor and report on the effectiveness of the ODR system.

The six design criteria of Blomgren Amsler, Martinez, and Smith remain silent on how the remedies of dispute settlement systems or ODR should be designed, especially if procedures are not binding. Section 10.3 will present some examples of existing ODR systems to exemplify the choices made in relation to the six criteria as well as the types of remedies and redress that these various systems award.

29 It is important to note that this interest-based design differs from a rights-based or power-based design, which are considered as less desirable by Blomgren Amsler et al. See Blomgren Amsler, Martinez, and Smith (n 27). The original distinction between interest-, rights-, and power-based dispute resolution was made in the context of solving employment conflicts by Ury, Brett and Goldberg. See William L Ury, Jeanne M Brett, and Stephen B Goldberg, *Getting Disputes Resolved* (Jossey-Bass 1988).

30 This has been a critique levelled against ICANN's dispute resolution system, which appears to be biased towards trademark owners. See Michael Geist, 'Fair.com? An Examination of the Allegations of Systemic Unfairness in the ICANN UDRP' (2002) 27 Brooklyn Journal of International Law 903.

10.3 EXAMPLES OF ODR MECHANISMS

To date, there is no ODR mechanism to enable redress for victims of fundamental rights violations by EU institutions. Yet a panoply of ODR mechanisms exist that could each provide elements and ideas for such a mechanism. This section gives examples of three types of ODR mechanisms that offer insights and learnings for the design of an EU ODR mechanism to redress fundamental rights violations. First, the chapter looks at examples of ODR mechanisms set up by the judiciary, which perform court-like tasks within the judicial or administrative system of their respective jurisdictions when it comes to civil claims. Second, the chapter looks at a precedent of an ODR mechanism set up by the EU itself: the EU consumer ODR platform. Third, the chapter looks at ODR mechanisms that have been created to address fundamental rights violations occurring on the Internet. These are the out-of-court dispute settlement bodies to be set up in the framework of the Digital Services Act (DSA)[31] and the Oversight Board set up by the large US-based technology company Meta (formerly Facebook).[32] None of these ODR mechanisms offers a ready-to-copy precedent for an ODR mechanism to be used by the EU to redress fundamental rights violations, but each of the types of example can offer lessons for the design of an EU fundamental rights ODR mechanism.

10.3.1 *ODR Mechanisms Set up by the Judiciary*

As mentioned in the brief history of ODR above, one of the main examples of ODR mechanisms within the public sector is pre-trial ODR implemented by national judicial systems and administrative agencies. One of the most salient examples is the previously mentioned UK Online Civil Money Claims (OCMC) pilot, which is scheduled to run until November 2023.[33] The pilot was launched after Lord Justice Briggs set out his vision for an online court in his 2016 Report,[34] which followed the conclusion of the Civil Courts Structure Review. Given that accessing the justice system in the United Kingdom is unaffordable for many, the online court project aims at making litigation for small claims more accessible by reducing costs. Cost reductions

31 DSA, arts 20–21.

32 <www.oversightboard.com/>.

33 Practice Direction 51R (n 18) section 2.1(1).

34 Michael Briggs, 'Civil Courts Structure Review' (Judiciary of England and Wales, July 2016)< www.judiciary.uk/wp-content/uploads/2016/07/civil-courts-structure-review-final-report-jul-16-final-1.pdf>.

are achieved through eliminating mandatory representation and the use of ADR before a claim is heard by a judge. The goals of the OCMC pilot are, on the one hand, to enhance access to justice[35] and, on the other hand, to help in the modernisation of the English civil court system.[36]

One of the notable features of the OCMC pilot is its extensive stakeholder consultation and piloting phase. Lord Justice Briggs had already conducted several consultations with the general public, judges, and other stakeholders in the process of writing his final report.[37] The first phase of the OCMC pilot (August 2017 until March 2018)[38] was conducted with only 1,400 selected participants before opening it to the general public. Furthermore, OCMC users are polled after submitting their claims to understand their level of satisfaction[39] and to generate feedback for further improving the system.

As explained above, the OCMC platform offers in a first step an online interface to fill in the details of the claim, which can then be submitted via the platform. The fees for submitting a claim depend on the amount of the claim (between 4 to 8% of the amount claimed),[40] and there is the possibility for applying for legal aid to cover the fees for low-income claimants. It also allows the respondent to file a response via the platform. So far, 378,000 claims have been submitted.[41] In a second stage, the platform offers mediation, which has been used in 9,560 cases to date and has led to a settlement at this stage in 50.4% of cases within 24 days on average. Settlements reached through mediation result in an agreement between the parties that is legally binding. At any point in the procedure, the claim can be referred to a judge. Overall, the OCMC has yielded positive results in the form of faster settlements, higher

35 Michael Briggs, 'The Civil Online Court in England', in Rabeea Assy and Andrew Higgins (eds), *Principles, Procedure, and Justice: Essays in Honour of Adrian Zuckerman* (Oxford University Press 2020) 135–152; Mahar Abbasy, 'The Online Civil Money Claim: Litigation, ADR and ODR in One Single Dispute Resolution Process' (2020) 7 International Journal of Online Dispute Resolution 4.

36 Briggs, 'The Civil Online Court in England' (n 34).

37 Ibid.

38 HM Courts & Tribunals Service, 'Fact Sheet: New Online Civil Claims Pilot Rolled Out' (UK Parliament, 2018) <www.parliament.uk/globalassets/documents/commons-committees/Justice/correspondence/Lucy-Frazer-HMCTS-online-civil-claims-pilot.pdf>.

39 The HM Courts and Tribunals Service published a fact sheet that reports that the OCMC service achieved a 95% user satisfaction rating – however, without explaining specifically what users were satisfied with or which kinds of users answered the survey. See UK Government, 'Fact Sheet: Online Civil Money Claims' <www.gov.uk/government/publications/hmcts-reform-civil-fact-sheets/fact-sheet-online-civil-money-claims>.

40 HM Courts & Tribunals Service, 'Fact Sheet: New Online Civil Claims Pilot Rolled Out' (n 38)

41 These figures are as of 20 March 2023. See UK Government, 'Fact Sheet: Online Civil Money Claims' (n 39).

rates of mediation, and a faster procedure for judges to issue orders based on the digital file.[42]

The growth of pre-trial ODR has not only affected the United Kingdom but also other European states. In reaction to these developments, the Council of Europe issued a set of guidelines on online dispute resolution mechanisms in civil and administrative court proceedings in 2021.[43] The guidelines are not binding but give guidance to states on how to design national pre-trial ODR proceedings that are in line with Article 6 (right to a fair trial) and Article 13 (right to a remedy) of the European Convention on Human Rights.[44] The guidelines address a variety of issues around ODR procedures, including accessibility, due process, transparency, and cybersecurity. The guidelines would be a good reference for any potential ODR mechanism to offer redress to victims of fundamental rights violations by the EU.

10.3.2 *The EU Consumer ODR Platform*

When it comes to consumer law, the EU legislator has put a lot of emphasis on ADR and ODR as a solution to the widespread underenforcement of consumer law. The EU ODR Regulation,[45] which came into effect in 2016, sets out the rules for setting up a European online platform that offers easy and low-cost dispute resolution through electronic means to achieve a higher level of consumer protection in the EU.

The procedure via the ODR platform is set by EU law, and the ODR platform itself is financed by the EU. The ODR platform is only a first step that allows consumers to submit a complaint and a trader to react. Subsequently, the procedure foresees that consumer and trader will agree on an accredited ADR body that will ultimately settle the dispute. Under the EU ADR Directive, accredited ADR bodies must be able to provide comparable remedies to consumers as those provided by courts.[46] The goals of the EU

[42] UK Government, 'Fact Sheet: Online Civil Money Claims' (n 39).

[43] Council of Europe, 'Guidelines of the Committee of Ministers of the Council of Europe on online dispute resolution mechanisms in civil and administrative court proceedings – Explanatory Memorandum' (2021) CM(2021)36-add5-final <https://search.coe.int/cm/Pages/result_details.aspx?ObjectId=0900001680a2cf97>.

[44] Ibid.

[45] Regulation (EU) No 524/2013 of the European Parliament and of the Council of 21 May 2013 on online dispute resolution for consumer disputes and amending Regulation (EC) No 2006/2004 and Directive 2009/22/EC [2013] OJ L165/1 (ODR Regulation).

[46] Directive (EU) 2013/11 of the European Parliament and of the Council of 21 May 2013 on alternative dispute resolution for consumer disputes and amending Regulation (EC) No 2006/2004 and Directive 2009/22/EC [2013] OJ L165/63 (Directive on Consumer ADR), art 11.

ODR platform are to achieve a high level of consumer protection and to boost growth and integration of the EU's digital single market.[47] The ODR procedure is available to any consumer regarding complaints in respect of online purchases from a trader established in the EU.[48] It thus follows the logic of early ODR that disputes arising online would be best resolved online.

The initial years of operation suggest that the vision for the ODR platform did not materialise as expected. Traders rarely responded to consumer complaints via the platform (80% of complaints were closed thirty days after submission due to no response from the trader)[49] and only around 2% of claims submitted eventually reached an ADR body.[50] This suggests that consumers and especially traders were insufficiently involved in the process of designing the platform to achieve the desired goals.[51]

The Commission has published annual reports on the functioning of the ODR platforms and has run surveys among users of the platform. It eventually responded with a change to the platform's design in July 2019, which now first offers consumers a self-test.[52] The self-test allows consumers various options to proceed with their complaints: either bilaterally contacting a trader (and negotiating), contacting a European Consumer Center, or contacting an ADR body through the platform. As a result, actual complaints submitted to the platform decreased significantly – the procedure offered by the platform was simply not the preferred option for consumers. In 2020, again, only 1% of complaints submitted via the platform reached an ADR body, while 20% managed to resolve their complaint in bilateral talks with traders.[53] The EU Commission did react to the lack of engagement with the formal procedure offered by the ODR platform. It completely revised the design of the ODR platform and turned it more into an information portal that explains to consumers various options to proceed with their complaints. The ODR offer is now only a secondary feature of the website. This is an important example of

47 ODR Regulation, recs 1–4 and 8.

48 Ibid art 2.

49 EU Commission, '1st Report on the Functioning of the Online Dispute Resolution Platform' (2017) COM(2017) 744 final; EU Commission, '2nd Report on the Functioning of the Online Dispute Resolution Platform', (Commission, 6 December 2018) < https://commission.europa.eu/system/files/2018-12/2nd_report_on_the_functioning_of_the_odr_platform_3.pdf>.

50 Ibid.

51 Schmidt-Kessen, Nogueira, and Cantero Gamito (n 26).

52 EU Commission '3rd Report on the Functioning of the Online Dispute Resolution Platform' (Commission, 17 December 2020) <https://commission.europa.eu/system/files/2020-12/odr_report_2020_clean_final.pdf>.

53 EU Commission, '4th Report on the Functioning of the Online Dispute Resolution Platform' (Commission, 20 December 2021) <https://commission.europa.eu/system/files/2021-12/2021-report-final.pdf>.

an ODR mechanism that did not deliver on its promises. A more extensive stakeholder consultation, like that carried out for the OCMC, as well as a piloting phase could probably have helped design the EU consumer ODR platform in a more effective manner.

10.3.3 *ODR Mechanisms to Redress Fundamental Rights Violations*

The previous examples have shown that ODR has been used beyond a purely commercial setting: ODR has gained prominence in the judicial system and administrative agencies in various jurisdictions within and beyond the EU. Furthermore, the example of the EU ODR consumer platform is a precedent for an ODR platform that was set up by EU law. In both contexts, ODR has been used to settle small claims. In this section, I discuss two examples of ODR mechanisms that have been set up to address potential fundamental rights violations. One of these is mandated by EU law: the out-of-court dispute settlement systems to be set up in the framework of the DSA. The other has been set up as a self-regulatory measure: the Meta Oversight Board. Both deal with disputes that arise from fundamental rights violations occurring on the Internet, in particular in relation to freedom of speech.

The DSA is a regulatory framework that aims at reducing a variety of risks from illegal online content, including fundamental rights violations. It also regulates the procedures by which online platforms[54] themselves remove illegal online content, referred to as online content moderation.[55] The DSA foresees that online platforms should implement internal complaint mechanisms and allows for appeals to external dispute settlement bodies. The idea behind these mechanisms is that users will be better protected, and online platforms will have to take due regard of the rights and legitimate interests of users in their content moderation practices, including users' fundamental

[54] Online platforms are defined in Article 2(h) DSA as 'a provider of a hosting service which, at the request of a recipient of the service, stores and disseminates to the public information, unless that activity is a minor and purely ancillary feature of another service or a minor functionality of the principal service and, for objective and technical reasons, cannot be used without that other service, and the integration of the feature or functionality into the other service is not a means to circumvent the applicability of this Regulation'.

[55] The activity of content moderation has been framed by prior scholarship as a quasi-judicial activity by private actors, see Catalina Goanta and Pietro Ortolani, 'Unpacking Content Moderation: The Rise of Social Media Platforms as Online Civil Courts' in Xandra Kramer, Jos Hoevenaars, Betül Kas, and Erlis Themeli (eds), *Frontiers in Civil Justice* (Edward Elgar 2022). De Gregorio equates content moderation to an activity that, due to the power of dominant platforms, has an important constitutional dimension because of the inroads into fundamental rights it can have. See Giovanni de Gregorio, 'Democratising online content moderation: A constitutional framework' (2020) 36 Computer Law & Security Review 1.

rights. In particular, online platforms must explain how they will take due regard of the rights and legitimate interests of all parties in their content moderation activity, including users' fundamental rights 'such as the freedom of expression, freedom and pluralism of the media, and other fundamental rights and freedoms as enshrined in the Charter'.[56]

When a platform takes a decision to remove the content of a user, or refuses to remove content reported by a user, users must have access to an internal complaints mechanism to complain about the platform's decision.[57] In addition, users must have the possibility to appeal decisions made by a platform's internal complaint handling system to a certified out-of-court dispute settlement body or online mediation instance.[58] This can enhance access to justice, given that national court systems would be overburdened if they had to hear an appeal against every single content moderation decision and given that it might be too costly for most users to access a court in these cases.[59] The Digital Services Coordinators of each Member State will have the power to certify dispute settlement bodies.[60] In principle, these bodies will not have the power to impose binding solutions on the parties.[61]

The certified dispute settlement bodies need to be independent from platform providers, and members should be remunerated in ways that are not linked to the outcome of the procedure.[62] The members should have the necessary expertise in relation to one or more areas of illegal online content or in relation to the application or enforcement of the terms of service of one or more platforms.[63] This will likely also include expertise on fundamental rights, given that freedom of expression is often one interest at stake in content moderation decisions, and careful balancing against other interests is necessary. In terms of costs, the service of the out-of-court dispute settlement bodies should be free of charge for users.[64]

While the DSA out-of-court dispute settlement bodies are still in the process of being set up at the time of writing, there are some national precedents that show that such independent dispute settlement bodies can function without being perceived as biased towards platforms. In Germany, a similar ODR

56 DSA, art 14(4).
57 Ibid art 20.
58 Ibid art 21.
59 Pietro Ortolani, 'If You Build it, They will Come' (Verfassungsblog, 7 November 2022) <https://verfassungsblog.de/dsa-build-it/>.
60 DSA, art 21(2).
61 Ibid.
62 Ibid art 21(3)(c).
63 Ibid art 21(3)(b).
64 This applies unless the user was in bad faith, see DSA, art 21(4).

process was set up under the national law on illegal online content (Netzwerkdurchsetzungsgesetz – NetzDG) and is administered by an NGO, Freiwillige Selbstkontrolle Multimedia-Diensteanbieter (FSM). It is financed by a range of media and IT industry players, yet it has not been perceived as biased towards media players or online platforms.[65]

There is another example of an already functioning appeals body to review online content moderation by social media platforms: the Meta Oversight Board. In 2018 and 2019, Meta conducted a global consultation for setting up an independent appeals body, which would decide the most difficult issues and questions regarding its content moderation practices.[66] In 2019, the charter of the Oversight Board was published,[67] which lays down the relationship between Meta, the Oversight Board, and an independent trust that deals with the financing and staffing of the Oversight Board. Members are to be elected for a three-time renewable term of three years, and the trust decides on the compensation of the board members without the outcome of the decisions having an influence on the compensation. Furthermore, the charter of the Oversight Board lays down two procedures for appeals. On the one hand, the Board selects cases from appeals launched by users and. on the other, Meta can refer cases to the Board.[68] When taking decisions, the Board should review the content in light of Facebook's values and policies, as well as fundamental rights norms.[69] Lastly, the Board's decisions in relation to a specific piece of content are binding, while any policy recommendations are not binding on Facebook.[70]

According to the Charter of the Oversight Board, the size of the Board should be at least eleven members (likely to reach forty once fully staffed).[71] Article 1(2) of the Charter also specifies that members must have 'a broad range of knowledge, competencies, diversity, and expertise'. They should have no conflicts of interest and must have demonstrated 'experience at deliberating thoughtfully and as an open-minded contributor to a team'.[72] They should

65 Daniel Holznagel, 'A Self-Regulatory Race to the Bottom through Out-of-Court Dispute Settlement in the Digital Services Act' (Verfassungsblog, 16 March 2022) <https://verfassungsblog.de/a-self-regulatory-race-to-the-bottom-through-art-18-digital-services-act/>.

66 Kate Klonick, 'The Facebook Oversight Board: Creating an Independent Institution to Adjudicate Online Free Expression' (2020) 129 Yale Law Journal 2420.

67 Charter of the Oversight Board (Oversight Board, February 2023) <www.oversightboard.com/governance/>.

68 Ibid art 2(1).

69 Ibid art 2(2).

70 Ibid art 4.

71 Ibid art 1(1).

72 Ibid art 2.

also have the skills to deliver reasoned opinions on the application of rules or policies, and they need to have familiarity with matters relating to digital content and governance, including 'free expression, civic discourse, safety, privacy and technology'.[73] When looking at professional background, two-thirds of the members are lawyers.[74] Furthermore, two-thirds of the members have expertise in fundamental rights in general or in relation to specific fundamental rights fields (e.g., women's rights or freedom of speech). In its decision practice, the Meta Oversight Board regularly goes beyond analysing Meta's content moderation terms and uses international fundamental rights instruments in its interpretation.[75]

In June 2022, the Board published its first Annual Report, which gives insights into the kinds of fundamental rights violations that users seek remedy for or that pose particular challenges to content moderators.[76] According to the report, the Board received more than 1.1 million appeals submitted by users. Most of these related to the Community Standards on Bullying and Harassment (32.4%), Violence and Incitement (28.9%), and Hate Speech (24.8%).

10.4 ODR AS A REDRESS MECHANISM FOR FUNDAMENTAL RIGHTS VIOLATIONS BY THE EU

This section explores possible avenues to establish an ODR mechanism to redress fundamental rights violations by EU institutions. It starts by exploring which legal basis in the EU Treaties could potentially be used to establish such a mechanism. It then discusses possible design options for this ODR mechanism based on the examples discussed in Section 10.3.

10.4.1 *Legal Basis*

To discuss the possibility of establishing an ODR mechanism to provide some form of redress requires first establishing whether there would be any legal

73 Ibid.

74 Sixteen out of twenty-three members at the time of writing.

75 Lorenzo Gradoni, 'Constitutional Review via Facebook's Oversight Board: How platform governance had its Marbury v Madison' (Verfassungsblog, 10 February 2021) <https://verfassungsblog.de/fob-marbury-v-madison/>. See also the First Annual Report of the Oversight Board that gives examples of its references to international fundamental rights instruments in its decisional practice, Oversight Board, 'Oversight Board Publishes First Annual Report' (June 2022) <www.oversightboard.com/news/322324590080612-oversight-board-publishes-first-annual-report/>.

76 Oversight Board (n 75).

basis in the EU Treaties for having such an ODR mechanism. The legal basis for the two legal instruments that most prominently support the establishment of ODR mechanisms, the ODR Regulation and the DSA, both have Article 114 of the Treaty on the Functioning of the European Union (TFEU) as their legal basis.[77] Article 114 in conjunction with Article 26 TFEU gives the EU legislature the powers to enact legislation to further the function of the EU internal market. An ODR mechanism to redress the fundamental rights violations by EU bodies and agencies, however, would not have an internal market rationale. This means that Article 114 would not be an appropriate legal basis for establishing such a mechanism.

In general, there is no specific legal basis that would allow the EU to enact legislation to establish an ODR mechanism for addressing fundamental rights violations by its institutions. There are, however, some legal bases in the TFEU that could be used creatively to establish an ODR mechanism for violations of specific fundamental rights. One legal basis, for example, would be Article 19 TFEU, which allows the EU to enact legislation combatting discrimination. Another would be Article 16 TFEU on the right to data protection, which allows the EU to enact legislation regarding the processing of personal data by EU institutions. Such legislation could, in theory, also include a redress mechanism for victims of data protection violations. If we think about the type of fundamental rights violations by EU institutions that seem to be of most relevance at present, Article 78 TFEU might also be a starting point to initiate a legislative proposal. Article 78 TFEU is the legal basis for the EU's common asylum policy and protection of third country nationals in need of protection. Under Article 78 (2) (d) TFEU, the European Parliament and Council acting by ordinary legislative procedure can adopt measures on 'common procedures for the granting and withdrawing of uniform asylum or subsidiary protection status'. Potentially, an ODR mechanism could be implemented as a form of mechanism to address complaints by persons whose fundamental rights have been violated by the EU Agency for Asylum. As Schramm discusses in this volume,[78] there is already a complaints mechanism in place under the European Asylum Policy Regulation implemented by the Agency's Fundamental Rights Office.[79] A similar mechanism

[77] Consolidated Version of the Treaty on the Functioning of the European Union [2016] OJ C202/47.

[78] See Moritz Schramm in this volume, Chapter 5.

[79] Regulation (EU) 2021/2303 of the European Parliament and of the Council of 15 December 2021 on the European Union Agency for Asylum and repealing Regulation (EU) No 439/2010 [2021] OJ L468/1, art 51.

exists under the Frontex Regulation.[80] Neither of these mechanisms has been particularly visible or effective so far[81] but could potentially be enhanced through turning them into ODR mechanisms.

As an alternative, it could be possible to subsume a potential ODR mechanism under the umbrella of the European Ombudsman. Article 228 TFEU is the legal basis for the office of the Ombudsman and allows the Ombudsman to conduct inquiries into fundamental rights violations by EU institutions, bodies, and agencies upon her own motion or a complaint submitted to her. This would allow for one central ODR mechanism to complain about fundamental rights violations by any EU body, institution, or agency. The problem with Article 228 TFEU, however, is that only natural or legal persons residing in Europe can submit complaints. One would thus have to think of a network of NGOs that could submit complaints on behalf of third country citizens that have been victims of fundamental rights violations by EU bodies and agencies to the Ombudsman.

10.4.2 *Design Options for an EU ODR Fundamental Rights Redress Mechanism*

If the obstacles relating to the legal basis could be overcome, the process of designing an ODR mechanism subsumed under the Ombudsman's office or other specialised EU agencies could fruitfully draw on the six design criteria for dispute settlement systems and existing ODR mechanisms.

The first step would be to establish the goals of the ODR mechanism. These seem relatively clear: to enable some form of access to redress for victims of fundamental rights violations by EU agencies and bodies, as well as fostering and demonstrating the EU's commitment to international fundamental rights regimes.

The second step to establish such a mechanism would be to extensively engage with stakeholders. This could take the form of a stakeholder consultation, which involves victims of fundamental rights violations by the EU, as well as the organisations that give these individuals a voice, like civil society organisations. As seen in the examples above of the English OCMC and the Meta Oversight Board, several rounds of consultations with a variety of stakeholders helped to establish ODR mechanisms that

80 Regulation (EU) 2019/1896 of the European Parliament and of the Council of 13 November 2019 on the European Border and Coast Guard and repealing Regulations (EU) No 1052/2013 and (EU) 2016/1624 [2019] OJ L295/1, art 111.

81 See Schramm (n 78).

are being used by stakeholders and that enjoy a necessary level of trust to function.

Third, it is essential to consider the context and culture of an EU ODR mechanism to redress fundamental rights violations. One important part of context and culture would be to set up the ODR mechanism in a truly accessible way for victims. Especially when thinking about victims outside the EU borders, access becomes a challenge due to physical, economic, and language barriers. As a starting point, the ODR platform would need to be available in more languages than the current EU languages.[82] Furthermore, it should have a user interface that can be easily accessed through all types of electronic devices, including mobile devices. Especially when testing prototypes of the ODR mechanism, it should be ensured that the users that are involved in tests are in a comparable situation in terms of IT literacy,[83] literacy in general, language, and socio-economic background. This would avoid similar pitfalls as with the EU consumer ODR platform, which was not designed in a sufficiently user-centric manner to successfully take off.

Fourth, decisions regarding the structure and procedure of the ODR mechanism will need to be made. The procedural rules could be guided by the principles that can be found in the 2021 guidelines by the Council of Europe. In principle, the procedure would commence with the submission of a complaint – the simple registration of these complaints could already create a very important database on alleged fundamental rights violations by the EU bodies and agencies. In a second stage, a committee of members appointed by the Ombudsman or Fundamental Rights Officers could decide on the complaint and whether there has indeed been a fundamental rights violation attributable to EU agencies or bodies. This committee should be staffed by individuals that have a professional or academic background in fundamental rights law. The example of selection criteria for members sitting on the

82 For innovative ways of limiting language barriers for access to justice, see Margaret Hagan and Others, 'Design Report: Language Access Innovations in Court: How Can Courts Use Technology & Design to Support People in Court When They're Not Proficient in English?' (Stanford University Legal Design Lab, February 2019), <www.srln.org/system/files/attachments/Language_Access_Innovations_in_Court__design_report_from_Legal_Design_Lab__5_.pdf>.

83 There are some promising pilot programmes from the United States in the area of accessing social benefits, which showed how the user interface can really make a difference for people that come from a background where IT literacy and literacy in general can pose significant obstacles in accessing social benefits, see for example, Zack Quaintance 'Michigan Scales Back Massive Applications Process with Human-Centric Design' (Government Technology, 31 January 2018) <www.govtech.com/health/michigan-scales-back-massive-applications-process-with-human-centric-design.html>.

Article 21 DSA dispute settlement bodies and the Meta Oversight Board show that such criteria can be tailored to the specific context in which the ODR platform operates. Once a decision has been taken by the committee, the Ombudsman or Fundamental Rights Officers could resort to the forms of redress they can award, which are, admittedly, limited.

The complaints mechanisms administered by the Fundamental Rights Officers at the EU Asylum Agency and Frontex do not have any effective remedies available other than forwarding the message that there has been a fundamental rights violation to the executive director or national authorities.[84] The Ombudsman seems at least to have political influence to persuade other EU institutions.[85] She could address the agency or body that has committed the fundamental rights violation and ask for one of the internationally recognised forms of redress (cessation of the violation, damages, reparation, acceptance of responsibility, and preventing future violations) or try to influence the political process.[86]

As neither the Ombudsman nor the Fundamental Rights Officers have any enforcement powers, the entire ODR procedure would not be binding. The fact that the procedure is not binding, however, does not completely eliminate its effectiveness. In the case of the Meta Oversight Board, for example, decisions do not bind Meta regarding its overall policies but only in respect of the specific case. Nonetheless, the Oversight Board can make recommendations and has used its Annual Report to show whether Meta has made any progress on its recommendations. In this sense, even a non-binding mechanism can establish some form of accountability through transparency and reporting.

Fifth, there is the question of the resources for funding the ODR procedure. In the examples given in this chapter, all ODR platforms are funded by the fees paid by one or both parties. In the case of an EU ODR mechanism to address fundamental rights violations by EU Institutions, the mechanism would likely have to be funded by the EU. After all, it would be an accountability mechanism for its own institutions and agencies. Placing fees on the victims would not be equitable. As in several other ODR systems discussed above, the weaker party usually gets access for free to the ODR system. If the mechanism were to be administered by the Ombudsman's Office or the Fundamental Rights Officers, they should receive an additional budget for it.[87]

84 Schramm (n 78).

85 For a more detailed analysis of the Ombudsman's political soft power, see ibid.

86 See also ibid.

87 Ibid.

Lastly, to create a sustainable and well-functioning ODR system, periodic evaluations would be necessary. Periodic evaluations could be facilitated by the publication of an annual report by the Ombudsman or Fundamental Rights Officers, similar to the reports published by the EU Commission in relation to the consumer ODR platform, the Meta Oversight Board, or the future DSA out-of-court dispute settlement bodies. This would allow for public scrutiny and for drawing lessons from the operation of the mechanism and improving it in the future.

10.5 CONCLUSION

If the EU is to have any integrity regarding its commitment to fundamental rights, it will sooner or later have to find a way to hold its institutions, bodies, and agencies that violate fundamental rights accountable and to award redress to victims of these fundamental rights violations. As the current institutional set up does not yet allow for effective redress for victims of fundamental rights violations by the EU, this chapter explores the possibility of establishing an EU ODR mechanism to this effect.

While ODR was born in a private and commercial context, it has spread into the public realm and is used in the framework of judicial and administrative procedures at national level. Furthermore, ODR is being increasingly seen as a solution to help in preventing and solving disputes around fundamental rights violations by private actors, such as online platforms, for example, in the case of the DSA dispute settlement bodies and the Meta Oversight Board.

One of the most significant obstacles to establishing an EU ODR mechanism addressing complaints about fundamental rights violations by EU agencies and bodies is that we lack a clear legal basis that would allow for instituting such a mechanism. Nonetheless, as a starting point, this chapter explores the option to implement such a system under the EU Ombudsman's office or under the Fundamental Rights Officers of the EU Asylum Agency or Frontex. When it comes to the possibility of filing complaints, however, victims of fundamental rights violations would likely have to act with the help of EU-based NGOs or individuals to submit claims to an ODR mechanism administered by the Ombudsman, which is far from ideal but a pragmatic solution to the limitations imposed by Article 228 TFEU.

Furthermore, the design of an EU fundamental rights ODR mechanism could fruitfully draw from experiences of existing ODR mechanisms, as well as Guidelines by the Council of Europe on ODR. While the remedies or redress that such an ODR system could award at this point in time would not be extensive, the mechanism would at least allow for establishing an EU-wide database recording complaints and decisions on whether there was a fundamental rights violation in specific cases. Furthermore, the Ombudsman could use the advocacy powers she has to influence EU agencies and bodies to change their processes and working modes that lead to fundamental rights violations.

PART IV

Testing the Remedies System

11

EU Law Enforcement Authorities and Access to Justice

KOEN BOVEND'EERDT,* ARGYRO KARAGIANNI, AND MIROSLAVA SCHOLTEN

11.1 INTRODUCTION

In the context of enforcing the law, the rule of law makes demands, inter alia, on both *individuals* and *those who govern* or rule over them. In broad terms, the rule of law requires of individuals that they respect and abide by legal norms promulgated by those who govern. To prevent or to respond to (alleged) violations of a prescribed norm – or more generally, to ensure that a norm is effectively respected – those who govern rely on enforcement (i.e., 'the sword'). Enforcement consists of public action to prevent or respond to a violation of a prescribed norm.[1]

Of those who govern, the rule of law requires that, in enforcing the law, they themselves do not operate beyond, or place themselves above, the law and what this law deems permissible. That is where fundamental rights enter into play: to protect the individual against the arbitrary exercise of power by those who govern.[2] The role of the rule of law then, in which fundamental rights find their expression, is to concern itself with the way in which power is exercised and to cast it in a constraining harness of public norms that grant, delimit, and control the discretionary exercise of power ('the shield').[3]

* The views expressed are my own and do not reflect the official position of the Hoge Raad.

1 Volker Röben, 'The Enforcement Authority of International Institutions' (2008) 9 German Law Journal 1965, 1966. Note that this definition does not include enforcement by private actors which, though relevant, is outside the ambit of this contribution.

2 This is stated by the ECtHR, in the context of the right to privacy, in *Lozovyye v Russia*, App no 4587/09 (ECtHR, 24 April 2018) para 36; See also Koen Bovend'Eerdt, 'The Protection of Fundamental Rights in OLAF Composite Enforcement Procedures (and the EPPO's Ship Smoke on the Horizon)' (PhD thesis, Utrecht University 2023) ch 1.5.3.1.

3 Jeremy Waldron, 'The Concept and the Rule of Law' (2008) 43 Georgia Law Review 1, 6. While, in the literature, fundamental rights are often considered as both (or either) 'swords'

For an individual to have fundamental rights is one thing; to see them effectively enforced and protected is another. To ensure that their fundamental rights are enforceable, there is a duty incumbent on those who govern to put in place institutions that uphold the individual's rights and connected to that, to grant the individual whose rights have been infringed access to those institutions. It is this latter component that is generally referred to as 'access to justice'. As the name suggests, access to justice consists of two elements: 'access' and 'justice'. The first is procedural in nature and serves to ensure that those whose fundamental rights are violated have (equal) access to the means in place that can address these violations. The second element is substantive and more normative in nature; it demands that just outcomes are to be achieved (i.e., that the individual's rights are adequately protected), yet the definition and perception of what is just may vary in light of individuals' morality, context, and other pre-existing and emerging factors. The two elements are necessarily connected: the attainment of justice or of a just result presupposes access.[4] When it comes to 'access to justice', one of the core notions in this contribution, we focus primarily (though certainly not exclusively) on the procedural limb of 'access to justice'. In other words, we are interested in potential pathways or mechanisms for achieving justice, not in justice in the result.

In short, then, as a concept, access to justice takes on a functional role in the perennial rule of law debate and in this contribution is understood as an

and 'shields', we favour the latter. In the law enforcement/access to justice context, fundamental rights, as invoked by an individual, enter into play only *after* there has been an initial interference by enforcement authorities. This is reflected in, for instance, the European Convention on Human Rights (ECHR) Article 13, which states that everyone whose rights and freedoms as set forth in this Convention are violated shall have an effective remedy. We also find support for this position in the relevant law enforcement literature, among many others: John Vervaele, 'Special procedural measures and the protection of human rights: General Report' (2009) 80 International Review of Penal Law 75, 83; John Vervaele, 'Surveillance and Criminal Investigation: Blurring of Thresholds and Boundaries in the Criminal Justice System' in Serge Gutwirth, Ronald Leenes, and Paul De Hert (eds), *Reloading Data Protection. Multidisciplinary Insights and Contemporary Challenges* (Springer 2014). See also the recently published *liber amicorum* for John Vervaele in which the 'sword versus shield' matter is discussed in various contributions: Michiel Luchtman and Others (eds), *Of Swords and Shields: Due Process and Crime Control in Times of Globalization – Liber Amicorum prof. dr. J.A.E. Vervaele* (Eleven 2023).

4 Mauro Cappelletti and Bryant Garth, 'Access to Justice: The Newest Wave in the Worldwide Movement to Make Rights Effective' (1978) 27 Buffalo Law Review 181, 182; See also Salvo Nicolosi and Elmin Omičević, 'The Rise of EU Migration Agencies: Striking a Balance between Enforcement Needs and Access to Justice' (2022) Jean Monnet Network on EU Law Enforcement Working Paper Series 16/22, 1 <jmn-eulen.nl/wp-content/uploads/sites/575/2022/05/WP-Series-No.-16-22-THE-RISE-OF-EU-MIGRATION-AGENCIES-Striking-a-Balance-Between-Enforcement-Needs-and-Access-to-Justice-Nicolosi-Omicevic.pdf>.

instrument that allows for the effective protection of the individual's fundamental rights ('the shield') against violations by those who govern in the process of enforcement ('the sword').

Against this background, one development is that of an ever-evolving EU polity. The EU has become more than an international organisation where the addressees of international agreements have been predominantly the nation-states. Ever since *Van Gend & Loos*, individuals have been considered as important actors in enforcing (fundamental) rights with which Union law has endowed them particularly because the Member States have a 'natural aversion to controlling their own behaviour'.[5] This has become all the more important in the last two decades with the advent of EU law enforcement authorities: supranational actors created by EU law that have at their disposal enforcement powers and monitor compliance with its laws, investigate suspected violations, and/or sanction non-compliance with the view of stopping, deterring, and/or restoring after undesirable behaviour.[6]

In this contribution, we offer a critical appraisal of the individual's (in) access to justice when their fundamental rights have been violated during enforcement by EU law enforcement authorities. Direct enforcement by EU law enforcement authorities has been proliferating despite uncertainties that this novel type of public power has brought in terms of control mechanisms, both judicial and non-judicial.[7] Direct enforcement, and the shared activities and joint decisions of EU and national authorities it entails, have been 'squeezed' into the existing system of separated controls between the EU and the Member State legal orders. This brings with it challenges regarding the control over public power that may affect 'access to' and 'justice', not only from a strictly legal perspective but also from a normative conceptual perspective. To what extent can the law and the obligations that flow from it be foreseeable for the individuals subject to direct enforcement actions? To what extent have different substantive, procedural, and institutional issues been aligned between existing systems of control? What mechanisms of control could bring more 'justice' and satisfaction in such a setting and upon which conditions does this depend?

5 Olivier Linden, 'The Internal Market' in Miroslava Scholten (ed), *Research Handbook on EU Law Enforcement* (Edward Elgar 2023) 281.

6 Miroslava Scholten, Michiel Luchtman, and Elmar Schmidt, 'The Proliferation of EU Enforcement Authorities: A New Development in Law Enforcement in the EU' in Miroslava Scholten and Michiel Luchtman (eds), *Law Enforcement by EU Authorities: Implications for Political and Judicial Accountability* (Edward Elgar 2017) 4–5.

7 Miroslava Scholten and Michiel Luchtman, *Law Enforcement by EU Authorities: Implications for Political and Judicial Accountability* (Edward Elgar 2017).

For the remainder of this contribution, we proceed in the following fashion. In Section 11.2, we offer a – perhaps somewhat unorthodox – understanding of the notion of 'access to justice' in light of the EU's powers of direct enforcement by means of EU law enforcement authorities. Access to justice, or so we argue, is more than access to, or effective remedies before, a court that is to enforce the individual's fundamental rights and hold state authorities accountable (i.e., the judicial pathway), but also encompasses other, non-judicial, mechanisms – both at the national and the Union level and for each separate procedure of enforcement – which provide the individual with means to enforce their rights and ensure that those violating rights are held to account. We start by outlining which fundamental rights are at stake at the various stages of enforcement and how these rights may be interfered with and/or violated by EU law enforcement authorities (Section 11.2.1). Thereafter, in Section 11.2.2, we demonstrate how direct enforcement by EU law enforcement authorities has brought about a shift in the ways in which Union law in particular policy areas is enforced and how this shift has largely not been accompanied by a change in the way in which judicial control is offered in order to remedy violations of fundamental rights suffered by the individual subject to enforcement action. To substitute and/or complement the absence of judicial control, other mechanisms have been put in place that help achieve the individual's access to justice.[8] These non-judicial mechanisms are, or so we argue, better suited to ensuring that fundamental rights are effectively protected. This is reflected in socio-legal literature[9] in which it is established that access to court and a possible positive outcome does not necessarily equate to the attainment of justice. Enforcement's success is highly dependent on its preventive function, rather than sanctioning, as it can be more effective from both economic and policy goals perspectives.[10] In short, the point we wish to drive home is that, in the current EU constellation, courts are – contrary to what is generally assumed – not always, or in any case not necessarily, best-suited for remedying fundamental rights violations and providing the protection the individual needs.

In Section 11.3, we then examine the way in which 'access to justice' is given shape in the legal frameworks of three EU enforcement authorities: the European Securities and Markets Authority (ESMA), the European

8 Miroslava Scholten, Béla Strauss, and Alex Brenninkmeijer, 'Controlling EU Agencies: An Introduction' in Miroslava Scholten and Alex Brenninkmeijer (eds), *Controlling EU Agencies. The Rule of Law in a Multi-jurisdictional Legal Order* (Edward Elgar 2020) 5.

9 See, for instance, a thorough overview of relevant studies in Benjamin van Rooi and Adam Fine, *The Behavioral Code. The Hidden Ways That the Law Makes Us Better … or Worse* (Beacon Press 2021).

10 Miroslava Scholten, 'Challenges and successes of enforcement of EU law' in Miroslava Scholten (ed), *Research Handbook on the Enforcement of EU Law* (Edward Elgar 2023) 524.

Commission's Directorate General for Competition (DG COMP), and the European Anti-Fraud Office (OLAF). We look at these three EU enforcement authorities in particular because of the three different ways in which they share their functions with their national counterparts. The first is hierarchically positioned above national authorities (ESMA). The second acts in parallel with national authorities (DG COMP). The third acts mainly in support of national authorities (OLAF). In short, each of the authorities chosen represents one of three 'families' or 'flavours' of EU law enforcement authorities,[11] thereby offering a representative sample to discuss.

In Section 11.4, we evaluate the different ways in which the concept of 'access to justice' is implemented in the legal frameworks of the three authorities studied. In Section 11.5, we outline recommendations for ways in which the individual's access to justice can be improved in the legal frameworks of the three agencies subject to study and further (academic) research.

11.2 ACCESS TO JUSTICE IN ENFORCEMENT BY EU ENFORCEMENT AUTHORITIES

In the process of enforcement, three stages are normally distinguished: monitoring compliance with, investigating possible violations of, and sanctioning non-compliance with the applicable law.[12] In the socio-legal literature and in legislative practice (discussed in Sections 11.2.1 and 11.2.2), one can witness a development of theories and tools aimed at enhancing compliance of individuals with the applicable law. Therefore, such theories and tools aim at ensuring the preventive (rather than the responsive) function of enforcement.[13] From a law and economics perspective, enforcement can be seen as more effective, including time- and cost-efficient, if individuals' compliance with the law is achieved at the earliest possible stage of enforcement. In this connection, literature on compliance and better regulation shows the importance of investing in educating those who need to comply with the rules, rather than simply sanctioning

[11] Miroslava Scholten, 'Mind the Trend! Enforcement of EU Law Has Been Moving to Brussels' (2017) Journal of European Public Policy 1348, 1351; Miroslava Scholten, Martino Maggetti, and Esther Versluis, 'Political and Judicial Accountability in Shared Enforcement in the EU' in Miroslava Scholten and Michiel Luchtman (eds), *Law Enforcement by EU Authorities: Implications for Political and Judicial Accountability* (Edward Elgar 2017) 353.

[12] John Vervaele (ed), *Compliance and Enforcement of European Community Law* (Kluwer International 1999).

[13] Miroslava Scholten and Leander Stähler, 'Introduction to the Research Handbook on EU Law Enforcement' in Miroslava Scholten (ed), *Research Handbook on the Enforcement of EU Law* (Edward Elgar 2023) 2.

them.[14] Should sanctions ultimately prove necessary, the same literature shows the importance of using an enforcement ladder, that is, escalating from soft enforcement tools, like warnings and dialogues, to hard ones like punitive fines, to enhance effectiveness. We may notice that these theories find application in the existing laws and operation of EU enforcement authorities. For instance, EU enforcement authorities increasingly use soft law guidance whereby they explain how they ought to enforce laws, how certain ambiguous concepts are to be interpreted, and may hold (informal) dialogues as a tool to enhance compliance and thus prevent violations or as soft sanctioning mechanisms.

Access to justice by private actors – natural and legal persons – is of paramount importance when it comes to enforcement actions by public authorities. This is because regulation as such can restrict the rights and freedoms of private actors and in the process of enforcing substantive regulatory norms, such rights and freedoms can be affected further. Think, for instance, about obligations imposed by relevant EU legislation on financial market participants to provide specific information to enforcement authorities on a regular basis.[15] If an EU enforcement authority concludes that the financial market participant violated the relevant legislation and therefore imposes a fine or even withdraws the participant's authorisation, the freedom to conduct a business may be restricted even further. To ensure there is no abuse of public power, private actors must have access to justice to question and check the relevant authorities' enforcement actions and decisions. Access to justice is thus essential at all of the three enforcement stages: monitoring, investigating, and sanctioning. In this section, we distinguish which fundamental rights are relevant at each enforcement stage (Section 11.2.1). Then, in Section 11.2.2, we discuss the evolution of the concept of access to justice in relation to enforcement and the evolution of its meaning to encompass more possibilities to promote fundamental rights than just 'access to the court'.

11.2.1 *Enforcement Stages and Applicable Fundamental Rights*

11.2.1.1 Monitoring

Monitoring compliance with substantive norms is an essential first step in the enforcement process. Private parties as such may have an active role in the

[14] Robert Baldwin, Martin Cave, and Martin Lodge, 'Responsive Regulation' in Baldwin and Others (eds), *Understanding Regulation: Theory, Strategy, and Practice* (2nd edn, Oxford University Press 2011).

[15] See, for example, Directive (EU) 2014/65 of the European Parliament and of the Council of 15 May 2014 on markets in financial instruments and amending Directive 2002/92/EC and Directive 2011/61/EU [2014] OJ L173/349.

monitoring stage. For instance, a company that operates in a competitive market may notice wrongdoing by another company and file a complaint with the relevant supervisory authority or even go directly to court. Depending on the legislative setup, an EU enforcement authority may have responsibility to monitor compliance with laws too, without depending on individual complaints. To that effect, relevant legislation may bestow upon an EU enforcement authority such powers as monitoring the proper functioning of financial markets; requesting from market participants information on a regular or ad hoc basis; conducting ad hoc, planned, or risk-based designed on-site inspections; holding (ad hoc) dialogues to promote and ensure compliance; and issuing (soft law) guidance to educate relevant parties and incentivise compliance. For this, an EU enforcement authority needs to have sufficient resources. If resources are limited, the authority may adopt prioritisation policies and conduct risk-based inspections. Often, the monitoring of compliance is organised in a mixed way (private actors' complaints and public authorities' public supervision).

At the monitoring stage, the following procedural safeguards are relevant to consider as their affordance will ensure that the fundamental right to good administration and the right to judicial protection will be observed should any dispute arise as a result of the monitoring stage. First, the power of enforcement authorities to ask for (more) information needs to be balanced with the obligation to have a legal basis and state reasons for issuing such requests, which in turn allows supervised entities to assess the scope of the obligation to cooperate. Then, a grey area concerns informal information requests and the issuance of non-binding instruments, like guidance, notices, and recommendations. These have to be done professionally and private parties need to have protection against possible abuses of power in the course of such informal contacts, otherwise disputes based on informal contacts may lead to subsequent legal actions. One such instance is the uncertainty surrounding the formal force and further judicial reviewability of soft law guidance that can be used for ensuring compliance. More specifically, parties may question the binding force of such documents and disagree on their content and the procedure preceding their adoption. Yet such soft law documents could form the basis of enforcement decisions vis-à-vis private actors, including the imposition of fines. While an addressee may question the decision imposing the fine, soft law instruments as such cannot be challenged through an action for annulment (Article 263 of the Treaty on the Functioning of the European Union (TFEU)) (see Chapter 14). In any case, to question the controversial soft law guidance, a private party would need to go through all three stages of the enforcement process, which requires time and resources. Against this background, other channels seem necessary to make sure that the relevant parties are not denied access to justice. Think, for instance, of the right to participate and to be consulted ex ante, when soft law instruments are being adopted. In light of the aforementioned better compliance studies, perhaps even the right to request helpful guidance and/or be educated (by the EU authority) as to how to comply with such documents is required.

11.2.1.2 Investigation

The investigation of potential violations of laws, rules, or norms is the next stage of enforcement after monitoring, though in some cases there may be no public authority role in monitoring as such. When monitoring does take place, 'day-to-day' supervision can give rise to a suspicion that a substantive norm has been infringed, which, as a result, can function as a prelude to a subsequent investigation. Investigations are there to gather information/evidence on the basis of which proof can be established that can (help) justify the imposition of a subsequent (punitive) sanction against those to which the substantive norm in question is addressed by either the European law enforcement authority in question or by another EU or national authority.[16]

The fundamental rights that are most often – though by no means exclusively – interfered with during investigations are the right to privacy and the right to a fair trial. According to Article 7 of the Charter of Fundamental Rights of the European Union (CFR), everyone has the right to respect for, among other things, their private and family life, home, and communications.[17] It is particularly this right's dimensions of 'home' and 'communications' that are at issue during investigations. The reason for including the right to a fair trial is that the investigation phase in many ways determines the conditions that allow for or inhibit a future trial from being fair.[18] An illustrative example in this regard, drawn from the well of case law of the European Court of Human Rights (ECtHR), is not being able to consult with a lawyer during an interrogation by police authorities and the subsequent admissibility of that evidence at trial.[19] Another example, of particular

[16] Which authority is responsible for the imposition of a sanction depends very much on each and every European law enforcement authority's legal framework. This will be discussed in greater detail below.

[17] Charter of Fundamental Rights of the European Union [2012] OJ C326/02 (CFR) art 7.

[18] *Ibrahim and Others v the United Kingdom*, App nos 50541/08, 50571/08, 50573/08 and 40351/09 (ECtHR, 13 September 2016) para 253.

[19] See, among many others dealing with this particular issue, *Imbrioscia v Switzerland*, App no 13972/88 (ECtHR, 24 November 1993) para 38.

importance at the interface of non-punitive (EU) and parallel or subsequent punitive proceedings (EU or national), is where an individual is under a duty to cooperate during administrative investigations and this information is later used against them in punitive proceedings, thereby breaching the privilege against self-incrimination.[20]

All in all, in the investigation of potential violations of EU law, EU enforcement authorities may have directly or via relevant national authorities the powers to enter premises, to request information/interview, and to make a production order/require access to information. To ensure that the fundamental rights at stake are adequately protected, investigatory powers must have a 'sound basis in law'[21] and investigations must respect defence rights and safeguards such as, among others, the right to have access to a lawyer, the privilege against self-incrimination, the legal professional privilege, the right to be informed, and the right to translation.[22]

11.2.1.3 Sanctioning

If the investigation leads to the conclusion that there is a violation of the law, the sanctioning stage may follow. Sanctions vary greatly across sectors: warnings, fines, periodic penalty payments and interim measures, suspension of voting rights, withdrawals of licences, recommendations, and public notices, to name but a few. There seems to be a development in legislation and in enforcement practice resembling the scholarly ideas of the usefulness of 'responsive regulation' and of the 'enforcement pyramid'.[23] These theories support the idea that to respond to non-compliance in the most proportionate way, depending on the severity of the violation, the enforcement authority should gradually escalate its enforcement response from the lighter tools (e.g., informal warnings) to the heftier ones (e.g., fines and withdrawal of licences).

As the sanctioning stage has the most intrusive effect upon the ability to exercise certain rights and freedoms, like the right to property or the freedom to conduct a business, it is essential to have in place mechanisms to control

[20] *Saunders v United Kingdom*, App no 19187/91 (ECtHR, 17 December 1996) para 67.

[21] *Kruslin v France*, App no 11801/85 (ECtHR, 24 April 1990) para 30.

[22] Michiel Luchtman, 'Pertinent Issues of Punitive Enforcement in a Composite Legal Order' in Michiel Luchtman, Katalin Ligeti, and John Vervaele (eds), *EU Enforcement Authorities. Punitive Law Enforcement in a Composite Legal Order* (Hart 2023) 277–279.

[23] Ian Ayres and John Braithwaite, *Responsive Regulation: Transcending the Deregulation Debate* (Oxford University Press 1992); Robert Baldwin, Martin Cave, and Martin Lodge, *Understanding Regulation: Theory, Strategy, and Practice* (2nd edn, Oxford University Press 2011), ch 11.

potential abuses of enforcement authorities' sanctioning powers. In the first instance, before the imposition of measures adversely affecting their interests, the relevant private parties must be granted the right to have access to the file and be informed of the allegations against them and be put in a position to respond to such allegations through the effective exercise of their right to be heard. Secondly, addressees of a sanctioning decision must be able to challenge it before a court. Thirdly, the existence of other safeguards and principles, such as the principles of legality and proportionality are essential. Montaldo elaborates in this respect the principle of proportionality, 'the more intense a public power and its effects on individuals are, the more demanding this principle becomes. This is why proportionality is of a particular significance in the domain of sanctions, where the magnitude of public coercive powers reaches its peak'.[24] Therefore, as a fourth point, it is important to ensure that the decision-making processes and the bodies determining the type and severity of a sanction are independent, impartial, and transparent. For this, the enforcement authority needs to have its independent operation secured de jure and de facto. Finally, political controls over sanctioning policies and choices of a supervisor may be seen as mechanisms complementing access to justice.

11.2.2 *The Evolution of the Concept of Access to Justice in Enforcement Matters: Beyond the Nation-State and beyond the 'Judge'*

Thus far we have looked at the function of fundamental rights within the nation-state and subsequently highlighted the fundamental rights that are at risk of being violated during the three different enforcement stages. In this section, we aim to show that even though an increasing number of EU policy areas are enforced directly at the EU level, this development has largely not been accompanied by a change in which judicial control is offered. In other words, while tasks are shared, controls remain separated.[25]

The traditional method of enforcing EU norms has been that of 'indirect' or 'decentralised' enforcement: the EU legislator sets out substantive norms and the EU Member States enforce them.[26] In enforcing EU norms, Member

[24] Stefano Montaldo, 'EU Sanctioning Power and the Principle of Proportionality' in Stefano Montaldo, Francesco Costamagna, and Alberto Miglio (eds), *EU Law Enforcement. The Evolution of Sanctioning Powers* (Routledge 2021) 115–117.

[25] Miroslava Scholten, 'Shared Tasks, but Separated Controls: Building the System of Control for Shared Administration in an EU Multi-Jurisdictional Setting' (2019) 10 European Journal of Risk Regulation 538.

[26] Mario Chiti, 'Forms of European Administrative Action' (2004) 68 Law and Contemporary Problems 37, 47.

States enjoy enforcement autonomy, a term meant to indicate that where Union law does not lay down enforcement specificities, Member States remain free to lay down national procedural rules for the enforcement of EU rights.[27] However, indirect enforcement does not always bring about the envisaged results. Relevant literature has attributed problems of non-implementation of and non-compliance with EU policies to such causes as political unwillingness at the Member State level and lack of national resources.[28]

One way of addressing the aforementioned (indirect) enforcement deficit has been the shift towards direct modes of enforcing EU law, notably through the creation of EU law enforcement authorities: supranational actors created by EU law that have at their disposal enforcement powers and monitor compliance, investigate suspected violations, and/or sanction non-compliance with EU law.[29] In the context of direct enforcement of EU law, various new modes of interaction between the EU and the national level have been instituted. These novel modes of EU administration have been characterised as shared, mixed, multilevel, multijurisdictional, composite, and integrated.[30] Their common denominator is that, under the umbrella of an EU actor, the different national legal orders of the Member State are brought together.[31] EU actors are in constant liaison with national counterparts and operate in a functional EU territory.[32] Direct enforcement of EU law by EU law enforcement authorities challenges the traditional understanding of fundamental rights,[33] including the right of access to a court and to remedies. We shall illustrate this point by means of three examples.

[27] It is worth noting that enforcement autonomy is delimited by the principles of effectiveness and equivalence. The former means that national rules for the implementation of Union law must not render virtually impossible or excessively difficult the exercise of rights conferred by EU law. The latter means that national rules governing an issue with an EU dimension should not be less favourable than rules governing a similar domestic issue. See, in that respect, Rob Widdershoven, 'National Procedural Autonomy and General EU Law Limits' (2019) 12 Review of European Administrative Law 5.

[28] Scholten, 'Mind the Trend!' (n 11).

[29] Scholten, Luchtman, and Schmidt (n 6).

[30] Mariavittoria Catanzariti and Alexander H. Türk, 'EU agencies and the rise of a mixed administration in the EU multi-jurisdictional setting: facing the challenges of the rule of law' in Miroslava Scholten and Alex Brenninkmeijer (eds), *Controlling EU Agencies: The Rule of Law in a Multi-Jurisdictional Legal Order* (Edward Elgar 2020).

[31] Michiel Luchtman, 'The rise of EU law enforcement authorities' in Michiel Luchtman, Katalin Ligeti, and John Vervaele (eds), *EU Enforcement Authorities – Punitive Law Enforcement in a Composite Legal Order* (Hart 2023).

[32] Argyro Karagianni, *The protection of fundamental rights in composite banking supervision procedures* (Europa Law 2022) 30.

[33] Frank Meyer, 'Protection of fundamental rights in a multi-jurisdictional setting of the EU' in Miroslava Scholten and Alex Brenninkmeijer (eds), *Controlling EU Agencies: The Rule of Law in a Multi-Jurisdictional Legal Order* (Edward Elgar 2020) 145.

The first example concerns difficulties pertaining to effectuation of the right of access to a court when an EU binding measure culminates in a national sanction: in the investigative stage of enforcement, an EU authority carries out an on-site inspection at the business premises of a private party and obtains important evidence suggesting that the investigated person violated substantive legal provisions. However, given that the EU authority is not competent to sanction on its own motion, it requests that its national counterpart opens sanctioning proceedings vis-à-vis the aforementioned private party. A sanction is indeed imposed by the EU authority's national counterpart. The affected party appeals the decision before the competent national court arguing inter alia that the EU authority engaged in a fishing expedition thereby violating their right to privacy. In light of the well-known *Foto-Frost* doctrine,[34] national courts are not allowed to invalidate acts of EU organs. The only possibility then left to the reviewing national court is to make use of the preliminary reference procedure (see Chapter 4) and refer a question to the Court of Justice.

A second example concerns national enforcement action leading to EU sanctions and the difficulties surrounding the review – by EU courts – of the national part of such a shared procedure. Think of the following example. A national enforcement authority obtains evidence in the context of an on-site inspection. That evidence is thereafter transferred to the EU authority. Subsequently, based on that evidence, the EU actor imposes on the investigated person a punitive sanction. However, the addressee of the EU sanction argues that, in obtaining the critical piece of evidence, the national authority acted unlawfully. Can the Court of Justice of the European Union (CJEU), which will be called upon to review the final EU decision in accordance with Article 263 TFEU, also review the legality of the acts of the national organs? The CJEU has asserted in that respect that the principle of 'single judicial review',[35] which emanates from the principle of sincere cooperation (Article 4(3) Treaty on European Union (TEU)), demands that the EU courts alone carry out judicial review, that is, they are exclusively competent to review the legality of the acts of national organs. While the reasoning behind the court's view, namely that single judicial review rules out the possibility of contradictory rulings, is compelling, at the same time, the court has not yet explained on the basis of which standards – EU or national – such national acts shall be reviewed.[36]

[34] Case C-314/85 *Foto-Frost v Hauptzollamt Lübeck-Ost* [1987] ECLI:EU:C:1987:452, para 15.

[35] Case C-219/17 *Berlusconi and Fininvest* [2018] ECLI:EU:C:2018:1023, para 49.

[36] Filipe Brito Bastos, 'Derivative illegality in European Composite Administrative Procedures' (2018) 55 Common Market Law Review 101.

A third example concerns the situation in which an EU authority carries out (non- binding) preparatory work that forms the basis for the opening of a national sanctioning procedure. However, according to the CJEU, given that the action of the EU authority was merely preparatory, and therefore did not affect the legal position of the individual, that individual is now unable to question the legality of the act of the EU authority through an action for annulment.[37]

All three examples demonstrate that while we witness a shift in the ways in which Union law in particular policy areas is enforced, this shift has largely not been accompanied by a change in the way in which judicial control is offered to remedy violations of rights suffered by the individual subject to enforcement action. While procedures for the enforcement of EU law are increasingly hybrid/ shared between EU and national actors, judicial review seems to be stuck to dogmas developed within the nation state, according to which a court is only competent to review acts emanating from organs within that court's own jurisdiction. As a result, effective access to a court might in fact become illusory, seeing as the mechanisms currently foreseen, like the preliminary reference procedure, may be quite lengthy and cumbersome for an individual to seek. After all, as has been rightly noted in that respect – 'justice delayed is justice denied'.[38] Furthermore, EU courts reviewing the legality of national measures may not always be well placed to carry out a full review of national questions of law and fact.[39] In other circumstances, decisive preparatory acts of EU authorities are not subject to any review as they do not change the legal position of the concerned party. This is precisely the reason why the main argument that we wish to bring forward in this contribution is that access to justice is (or must be) more than access to a court. As access to a court may – in the multijurisdictional EU law enforcement setting – know certain limitations, it is essential that judicial mechanisms are complemented or accompanied by sufficient non-judicial control mechanisms.

The other important argument here is that enforcement features certain characteristics that necessitate other forms of control, from a functional perspective. Establishing enforcement priorities as to how to allocate scarce human, financial, and technological resources and equipment in enforcement, which clearly can affect private parties' access to justice, is an area where political accountability normally plays an essential role. Access to

[37] Case T-193/04 *Tillack v Commission* [2006] ECLI:EU:T:2006:292, para 68.

[38] Katalin Ligeti and Gavin Robinson, 'Composite Enforcement and Comprehensive Judicial Protection' in Michiel Luchtman, Katalin Ligeti, and John Vervaele (eds), *EU Enforcement Authorities – Punitive Law Enforcement in a Composite Legal Order* (Hart 2023) 71.

[39] Karagianni (n 32) 247.

non-judicial control mechanisms may then allow many more possibilities, actors, and procedures to make sure that rights and freedoms are being ensured. At the end of the day, justice means solving the problem at stake and ensuring the effectiveness of policies in a legitimate way, including with the protection of fundamental rights. Achieving 'justice beyond the judge' could be done, for instance, through the availability of mechanisms of direct complaint procedures before public authorities (administrative bodies and other dispute resolution tools), contacting members of parliament (political accountability), quasi-legal routes (Ombudsman), mechanisms of external review, or even informal channels. This is especially the case if the enforcement authority lacks independence in its enforcement operations, that is, the ability to withstand pressures from the political sphere and the supervised sector. How could one ensure their fundamental rights if the enforcement authority were dependent on a political will or an industry lobby when making such essential and far-reaching choices as whether to investigate a case or not or to impose a sanction or not? Enforcement action can only ensure fundamental rights and be legitimate if the enforcer (institution, staff, procedures) can be organised in an impartial way. To do this, independence should be guaranteed. In light of rich academic literature on this concept, one can distil the necessity of having relevant de jure obligations (institutional, personnel, financial dimensions to protect functional discretion)[40] brought to life de facto, thanks to having relevant institutional and contextual culture.

In Section 11.3, we will follow the distinction between the judicial and non-judicial remedies for the enforcement actions of the three selected EU law enforcement authorities and touch upon the question of independence of relevant authorities and their staff.

11.3 IMPLEMENTATION OF ACCESS TO JUSTICE IN THE LEGAL FRAMEWORKS OF EU LAW ENFORCEMENT AUTHORITIES: THE CASE OF ESMA, DG COMP, AND OLAF

In this section, we look at the legal frameworks of three EU enforcement authorities – ESMA, DG COMP, and OLAF. These three have been selected in light of the three types of division of competences between EU and national authorities distinguished earlier – hierarchical, parallel, and supportive.[41] The

[40] Miroslava Scholten, 'Independence vs. Accountability: Proving the Negative Correlation' (2014) 21 Maastricht Journal of European and Comparative Law 1.

[41] Scholten and Luchtman, *Law Enforcement by EU Authorities* (n 7).

first refers to a hierarchical positioning of the EU enforcement authority above the national authority. This is so for ESMA. The second division of competences exists where the EU and national authorities operate in parallel. That is the case for DG COMP. The third and last division of competences, which applies to OLAF, is where the EU authority acts mainly in support of national authorities.[42] The aim of this section is to explore which of these types of division of enforcement competences may be more or less likely to ensure access to justice.

11.3.1 *ESMA*

ESMA enjoys direct powers in all three stages of enforcement. ESMA contributes to ensuring stability and safety of financial markets by regulating and supervising private actors like credit rating agencies (CRAs) and trade repositories (TRs). At the same time, as ESMA activities interfere with the freedoms of private parties, it has to respect these parties' fundamental rights and freedoms. How does ESMA do this? First of all, to be able to operate on the EU financial markets, supervised private entities, for example, CRAs, shall receive an authorisation/licence from ESMA. For instance, CRAs assign credit ratings to individual companies and countries. Such ratings may be used by investors to decide whether they wish to invest in debt securities, therefore ESMA supervises these entities together with relevant national counterparts and it ensures that ratings are not based on falsified information. ESMA can delegate some powers to its national counterparts, however, it normally does not do so. The main reason why ESMA carries out supervisory and enforcement tasks by itself is that – by virtue of EU law – it has at its disposal all necessary direct supervisory and enforcement powers. In that sense, unlike other EU enforcement authorities, it does not rely on the powers of national counterparts. For many years, ESMA has had a dedicated supervision department that monitors these entities' performance and ensures compliance with relevant laws in various ways.

To be specific about its enforcement powers, ESMA can issue a great number of soft law documents clarifying how relevant sectoral laws are to be implemented. For instance, ESMA often issues technical standards that are to be endorsed by the Commission (for instance, Commission Delegated Regulation (EU) No 449/2012 where the terms of application for registration licence for CRAs are clarified, including which information needs to be

[42] See Section 11.1.

submitted and through which forms). ESMA can address requests for information to supervised entities and carry out inspections, which are 'risk-based, proportionate, forward looking and action oriented'.[43] Finally, financial market participants have the opportunity to pose questions to ESMA through its webpage and ESMA's answers form additional guidance, the so-called Q&As.

Once the selected private actors are registered/licensed, ESMA monitors them, can investigate possible suspicions of non-compliant behaviour, and can sanction violations via public notices and fines. The law is clear as to the sole responsibility of ESMA over these participants of financial markets. ESMA does not have to share any powers with the relevant authorities at the national level, unless it chooses to delegate some tasks or requires assistance at the national level.

Information gathering is crucial for enforcement in the financial sector. In that respect, ESMA has set a number of requirements as to the information that has to be submitted to its supervisory section on a regular basis. For instance, CRAs have to report rating data to ESMA, which ESMA then analyses. In 2013, ESMA issued Recommendations and Guidelines on the scope of Credit Rating Agency Regulation (CRAR)[44] addressed to, among others, CRAs. In addition, ESMA can perform on-site inspections to get more evidence-based information in addition to its desk-based analysis and it can also receive complaints to check an element concerning CRAs and their reporting. Article 23 (b–e) CRAR sets detailed rules as to how and when ESMA can request information when it supervises and when an Independent Investigator may investigate issues that have given rise to suspicion of violating the law and lead to sanctioning.

11.3.1.1 ESMA and the Person Concerned's Judicial Remedies: 'Access to Court'

Generally speaking, the fact that ESMA is solely responsible for overseeing the relevant private actors and for sanctioning non-compliance makes access to the court a clear-cut issue. ESMA is an EU agency, and its decisions are

[43] European Securities and Markets Authority, 'Investigations and Inspections' <www.esma.europa.eu/esmas-activities/supervision-and-convergence/investigations-and-inspections>.

[44] Regulation (EU) 513/2011 of the European Parliament and of the Council of 11 May 2011 amending Regulation (EC) No 1060/2009 on credit rating agencies Text with EEA relevance [2011] OJ L145/30.

legally binding for the addressees; the latter can appeal final decisions to ESMA's Board of Appeal and to the CJEU. Concerning the respect of fundamental rights in relation to CRAs, the relevant legislation (such as CRAR) provides relevant procedural safeguards for all the stages of enforcement. There are rules on how to submit questions for the Q&A guidelines. At the monitoring stage, when ESMA addresses information requests to supervised entities, it must abide by a list of requirements, including the obligation to state reasons and an indication of the possibility to request information (Article 23b). The same applies to general investigations and on-site inspections. Article 23e CRAR provides specific procedures for deciding on a fine, including the observation of the right to be heard, which shall be granted during the investigation by the Independent Investigation Officer (IIO) and before the Board adopts the final decision and determines the amount of the fine, if relevant. The fines are specified in Article 36a and relevant annex III and vary depending on the violation and whether it happened 'intentionally or negligently', where the latter would lead to a lower fine. As the enforcement has the most detrimental effect upon the rights and freedoms of private actors, the final decisions and fines can be subject to appeal before the Board of Appeal (BoA), which is a joint BoA for three EU supervisory agencies, and then before the CJEU. Article 36e CRAR states, among others, that the CJEU 'may annul, reduce or increase the fine or periodic penalty payment imposed'.

There are three instances where one may question the clarity of procedural safeguards and the availability of judicial review. First, ESMA's guidelines and Q&As fall within the category of so-called soft law (see Chapter 14). The adoption of soft law has been regulated by ESMA's founding regulation (Articles 10–16 Regulation 1095/2010, as amended in 2019), yet the adoption procedure gives ESMA some discretion whether or not to hold a public consultation. There may be instances where the public and the financial market participants are not consulted. As there is no normative framework regarding the question of the extent to which a public consultation and participatory rights should be there, the CJEU's restricted possibility to review soft law may be seen as problematic. It seems debatable whether private parties should be under an obligation to comply with soft law de jure if they have not been consulted ex ante as regards the adoption of soft law potentially affecting their operation and supervision over them. This is in part because ESMA is an independent agency lacking fully-fledged input legitimacy itself. If the court is so strict as to the status and review of soft law, one may need to have an obligation to enhance the ex ante participation of private actors in adopting soft law.

This comes from the idea of having a more comprehensive system of control.[45]

Secondly, the legal status of the applicable soft law is unclear. Even though recent case-law (*FBF*) clarifies the possibility to question the validity of soft law through the preliminary reference procedure, the initiation of action against soft law by the addressee is unclear still.[46]

Finally, as recent research shows,[47] the legislative language of acts regulating ESMA's enforcement powers and procedures is not always clear and may raise questions. More specifically, it is not clear how terms such as 'intentional' or 'negligent' violations by private actors shall be interpreted. This includes, for instance, the question as to where to look for guidance – EU and/or national legal systems and in which areas (public, criminal, private, etc.) when one has to respect procedural safeguards and interpret EU law that lacks clarity as to which law should apply. Furthermore, CRAR allows national procedural differences to be part of ESMA's procedures when it states that ESMA has to respect national laws when going on-site. This may lead to different procedural guarantees, which are defined nationally, for private parties in similar situations. For instance, if ESMA decides to inspect a private actor in a country where a judicial authorisation is required before the inspection, the private actor may experience more protection (judicial check on the inspection decision), than if no such national requirement is imposed on ESMA. The question is whether there is enough of a safeguard to ensure that ESMA is prevented from potential forum shopping among the jurisdictions when choosing where to inspect and, further, whether such divergent standards are allowed.[48]

11.3.1.2 ESMA and the Person Concerned's Non-judicial Remedies: 'Access to Justice'

The recently amended 2019 founding regulation of ESMA (Regulation (EU) 2019/2175) includes a new article, a so far unprecedented clause that can be seen

[45] Miroslava Scholten and Alex Brenninkmeijer (eds), *Controlling EU Agencies: The Rule of Law in a Multi-Jurisdictional Legal Order* (Edward Elgar 2020).

[46] Case C-911/19 *Fédération bancaire française (FBF) v Autorité de contrôle prudentiel et de résolution (ACPR)* [2021] ECLI:EU:C:2021:599; Opinion of AG Bobek [2021] ECLI:EU:C:2021:294.

[47] Jonathan Foster, 'A power to fine: Establishing negligence and intent in infringements by credit rating agencies and trade repositories' in Miroslava Scholten (ed), *Research Handbook on the Enforcement of EU Law* (Edward Elgar 2023) 265.

[48] Marloes van Rijsbergen and Miroslava Scholten, 'ESMA Inspecting: The Implications for Judicial Control under Shared Enforcement' (2016) 7 European Journal of Risk Regulation 3.

as an additional tool to seek 'justice'. Article 60a establishes a new procedure on how to address acts exceeding ESMA's competence: 'Any natural or legal person may send reasoned advice to the Commission if that person is of the opinion that the Authority has exceeded its competence.' The operation of this provision is as yet unclear. Furthermore, this policy area is one where many private actors, their associations, and lobby organisations operate. Clearly, all these actors and citizens can address relevant MEPs with their concerns about ESMA's operation, and the European Parliament can exercise political accountability (Article 3 of the founding regulation) through ad hoc hearings and through the submission of annual reports. The EU Ombudsman is available, too, as this is an institution that can be approached by anyone who has experienced maladministration by EU institutions and agencies.

11.3.1.3 The Degree of Independence of ESMA

As mentioned, the protection of fundamental rights in enforcement is tightly interconnected with independence of the supervisor. For this reason, the independence of ESMA has been regulated in secondary law (Articles 42, 46, 49, 52, 59, 62 of the founding regulation) and internal policies and documents available online.[49] The de jure organisation of independence seems quite advanced. The personnel independence is regulated for both the top-level functions, staff and non-staff, and is based on legal requirements for appointment, sophisticated appointment and removal procedures for the top-level official, and considerations of ethical behaviour and subsequent positions. The set-up of ESMA respects institutional and financial independence (Article 5 – legal personality, Article 62 – independence for contributions to the budget and a mixed composition of the budget). For the enforcement as such, an element of independence is seen in delineating the supervisory, investigation, and sanctioning stages, each of which is exercised by different sections/personnel of ESMA with the possibility to be heard when it comes to investigations and sanctioning.

11.3.2 *DG COMP and the European Competition Network*

Enshrined in Articles 101 and 102 TFEU, EU antitrust rules are addressed to economic operators. They prohibit agreements between competitors that

[49] Regulation (EU) No 1095/2010 of the European Parliament and of the Council of 24 November 2010 as amended by Regulation (EU) 2019/2175; European Securities and Markets Authority, 'Ethichs and Conflicts Interest' <www.esma.europa.eu/about-esma/governance-structure/ethics-and-conflicts-interest>.

harm competition and anticompetitive unilateral conduct by dominant firms. In that sense, the individuals whose rights may be interfered with in the course of antitrust proceedings are first and foremost economic operators, commonly known as 'undertakings'. However, the fundamental rights of other parties, like those of complainants, may also be at stake.[50] Indeed, third-party complaints play a key role in the public enforcement of antitrust rules, in view of the fact that, through third-party complaints, competition authorities may often become aware of alleged irregularities in the markets.

Regulation 1/2003[51] has introduced a system of parallel enforcement, meaning that DG COMP and the national competition authorities (NCAs) enforce Articles 101 and 102 TFEU in tandem. To that effect, they are enabled to exchange with each other information and use in evidence any matter of fact or of law.[52] Given that a system of parallel competences may give rise to parallel proceedings, which is problematic not only from an efficiency perspective but also from a fundamental rights perspective (*ne bis in idem*), duplication of effort is avoided in at least two ways. First, Article 11(6) of Regulation 1/2003 foresees that the initiation by DG COMP of antitrust proceedings shall relieve the NCAs of their competence to enforce Articles 101 and 102 TFEU. Secondly, the European Competition Network (ECN),[53] a network that brings together DG COMP and the twenty-seven NCAs, functions as a forum for case allocation[54] and information exchange, which ultimately contributes to avoiding duplication of efforts and proceedings. The ECN does not, however, possess legal personality, therefore its allocation decisions may not be appealed before a court, which raises important questions concerning the (non-judicial) remedies that concerned undertakings are able to seek vis-à-vis ECN case allocation that may be affecting their legal position. This will be further discussed below.

[50] See, critically, Malgorzata Kozak and Jacek Mainardi, 'Rights of Complainants before the European Commission – a Critical Analysis' (2023) 14 Journal of European Competition Law & Practice 3.

[51] Council Regulation (EC) 1/2003 of 16 December 2002 on the implementation of the rules on competition laid down in Articles 81 and 82 of the Treaty [2003] OJ L1/1 (Regulation 1/2003).

[52] Ibid art 12.

[53] EC, 'European Competition Network' (competition-policy.ec) <competition-policy.ec.europa.eu/european-competition-network_en>.

[54] The rules for case allocation within the ECN are included in the Commission Notice on cooperation within the Network of Competition Authorities [2004] OJ C101/43 (ECN Notice). In short, the overarching principle is that the authority receiving a complaint or starting an ex officio investigation will remain in charge of the case. Reallocation will occur only if the initial authority is not well-placed to act or other authorities are better placed to act. A 'well-placed' authority is one on whose territory an agreement or anticompetitive practice is implemented, who can gather the evidence required to prove the infringement, and who is able to bring an infringement to an end.

DG COMP has a plethora of investigative and sanctioning powers. More specifically, it may carry out investigations into sectors of the economy (sector inquiries),[55] request information from undertakings by simple request or by decision,[56] interview legal or natural persons who consent to be interviewed,[57] and carry out on-site inspections at business premises[58] and other premises, land, and means of transport.[59] It is important to note that, with the exception of information requests ordered by simple request, and requests for interviews, all of DG COMP's powers are of a coercive nature, as refusal to cooperate could result in the imposition of punitive sanctions.[60] As to sanctioning powers,[61] where substantive antitrust rules have been violated, DG COMP has the power to impose punitive fines[62] and periodic penalty payments.[63]

The fundamental rights that are primarily at stake during antitrust investigations are the obligation to state reasons, the right to privacy – particularly during on-site inspections and fair trial rights, such as access to a lawyer, the legal professional privilege, and the privilege against self- incrimination. During the *inter partes* stage, which follows the investigative stage, the right to good administration (Article 41 CFR) and more specifically the right to have access to the file and the right to be heard are of paramount importance. Regarding the sanctioning stage, the principle of legality, the proportionality of the sanction, and the prohibition against double jeopardy (*ne bis in idem*) come into play.

11.3.2.1 Safeguards and Defence Rights in DG COMP's Legal Framework

DG COMP's legal framework contains various procedural safeguards. Some of these are included in Regulation 1/2003 and in Regulation 773/2004,[64]

55 Regulation 1/2003 (n 51) art 17.

56 Ibid art 18.

57 Ibid art 19.

58 Ibid art 20.

59 Ibid art 21.

60 Ibid art 23(1).

61 It is important to note that alongside punitive administrative fines, DG COMP may also terminate an investigation through a settlement procedure or through a decision to accept commitments on the part of investigated parties. However, due to space constraints and seeing as the imposition of punitive administrative fines and penalties, as a traditional 'command and control' enforcement tool, interferes with various fundamental rights, it is for this reason that our discussion revolves only around punitive administrative fines and periodic penalty payments.

62 Regulation 1/2003 (n 51) art 23(2).

63 Ibid 24(1).

64 Commission Regulation (EC) 773/2004 of 7 April 2004 relating to the conduct of proceedings by the Commission pursuant to Articles 81 and 82 of the EC Treaty [2004] OJ L123/18 (Regulation 773/2004).

while others were initially developed in the case law of the CJEU and were subsequently included in DG COMP's internal manual of procedures[65] and in European Commission soft law instruments.[66] More specifically, if DG COMP rejects a complaint, they must respect the duty to state reasons.[67] Information requests ordered pursuant to a decision must also respect the obligation to state reasons, by specifying as a minimum the legal basis, the purpose of the request, and the required information and by fixing time-limits.[68] Likewise, on-site inspections must be ordered on the basis of a decision specifying the subject matter and purpose of the inspection. If, for the performance of an inspection, national law requires ex ante authorisation by a judicial authority,[69] national courts are competent to review the arbitrariness and excessiveness of the envisaged coercive measures, while the CJEU is competent to carry out a lawfulness check.[70] During an investigation, undertakings are allowed to consult their lawyer[71] and are entitled to a (limited) right to remain silent.[72] Furthermore, undertakings may invoke the confidentiality of communications between lawyer and client (legal professional privilege).[73] Following the investigation phase, if DG COMP considers that there are grounds to continue the proceedings, they may either proceed towards the adoption of a statement of objections (SO) or engage in discussion with an eye to a commitment decision.[74] If an SO is adopted, undertakings must be granted the right to be heard[75] and to have access to the file.[76] When imposing sanctions and setting the amount of fines, DG COMP must respect the principle of proportionality.[77] To that effect, the Commission has published Guidelines on the method of setting fines.[78]

[65] EC, 'Antitrust Manual of Procedures' (Competitionpolicy.ec, November 2019) <competition-policy.ec.europa.eu/system/files/2023-02/antitrust_manproc_11_2019_en.pdf>.

[66] Commission notice on best practices for the conduct of proceedings concerning Articles 101 and 102 TFEU [2011] OJ C308/6 (Commission Notice Articles 101 and 102 TFEU).

[67] Regulation 773/2004 (n 64) art 7.

[68] See Regulation 1/2003 (n 51) arts 18(3) and 20(4).

[69] Ibid art 20(7).

[70] Case C-94/00 *Roquette Frères* [2002] ECLI:EU:C:2002:603.

[71] Case C-136/79 *National Panasonic v Commission* [1980] ECLI:EU:C:1980:169.

[72] *Case C-374/87 Orkem v Commission [1989]* ECLI:EU:C:1989:387.

[73] Case C-550/07 P *Akzo Nobel Chemicals and Akcros Chemicals v Commission* [2010] ECLI:EU:C:2010:512; Case C-155/79 *AM & S v Commission* [1982] ECLI:EU:C:1982:157.

[74] Commission Notice Articles 101 and 102 TFEU (n 66) para 75.

[75] Regulation 1/2003 (n 51) art 27(1).

[76] Ibid art 27(2).

[77] Case T704/14- *Marine Harvest v Commission* [2017] ECLI:EU:T:2017:753, para 580.

[78] Guidelines on the method of setting fines imposed pursuant to Article 23(2)(a) of Regulation No 1/2003 [2006] OJ C210/2.

The NCAs' powers are laid down in national law. Directive ECN+ seeks to harmonise the minimum investigative and sanctioning powers that NCAs must have at their disposal,[79] admissibility of evidence,[80] and safeguards.[81] However, seeing as the ECN+ Directive is a minimum harmonisation instrument, the national standards regarding the protection of defence rights in investigations for the enforcement of EU competition law still differ to a significant extent.[82]

11.3.2.2 DG COMP and the Person Concerned's Judicial Remedies: 'Access to Court'

The addressees of final European Commission decisions can appeal them directly before the CJEU by means of an action for annulment.[83] Final decisions are understood as those that bring about a distinct change in the legal position of their addressee,[84] such as a decision to perform an on-site inspection, information requests by decision, settlement and commitment decisions, decisions to impose fines and periodic penalty payments, and decisions to reject a complaint.

More problematic in light of judicial accountability is the issue of the ECN's allocation decisions. Given that the ECN lacks legal personality, such decisions are not open to judicial review. Yet if one considers allocation decisions tantamount to a choice of forum, which may in turn significantly affect the legal position and the content of the defence rights that are available to investigated individuals, the question arises as to how persons affected by allocation decisions can seek effective remedies. Furthermore, DG COMP's broad margin of discretion in cartel investigations to choose to end a procedure by means of a settlement and not through the imposition of a fine, as well as its discretion to conclude a procedure by means of commitments, also raise questions from the perspective of access to a court. We do not, therefore, refer to the final decision as such, which is subject to the review of the CJEU in any

79 Directive (EU) 2019/1 of the European Parliament and of the Council of 11 December 2018 to empower the competition authorities of the Member States to be more effective enforcers and to ensure the proper functioning of the internal market [2019] OJ L11/3, chs IV and V.

80 Ibid art 32.

81 Ibid art 3.

82 Malgorzata Kozak, 'ECN+ Directive – A missed opportunity for strengthening the rights of parties?' in Catalin S. Rusu and Others (eds), *New Directions of Antitrust Enforcement* (Wolf Legal 2020).

83 Consolidated Version of the Treaty on the Functioning of the European Union [2016] OJ C202/47, art 263.

84 *Tillack v Commission* (n 37) para 67.

case, but rather to the (interim) decision to choose one path and not another. These discretionary choices and the lack of judicial control thereof should therefore be offset by other non-judicial remedies, which we shall examine below.

11.3.2.3 DG COMP and the Person Concerned's Non-judicial Remedies: 'Access to Justice'

POLITICAL ACCOUNTABILITY Seeing as DG COMP is a European Commission Directorate, the rules regarding the Commission's political accountability vis-à-vis the European Parliament (EP)[85] are applicable. More specifically, the Commission's president is elected by the EP upon the Council's proposal.[86] The Commission must submit to the EP an annual general report, which shall be discussed by the latter in open session.[87] In terms of rectification, under Article 17(8) TEU, the EP has the power to dismiss the Commission. Furthermore, under Article 226 TFEU, following the request of a quarter of its members, the EP may set up a temporary Committee of Inquiry to investigate alleged contraventions in the implementation of Union law. The European Commission and the EP have concluded a Framework Agreement that governs their relations[88] and contains modalities to 'strengthen the political responsibility and legitimacy of the Commission'.[89] The picture that emerges if one studies relevant documents of the past decade, such as EP reports and debates regarding Commission annual reports on competition policy is one where the EP repeatedly voices concerns regarding the lengthiness of antitrust investigations;[90] the lack of involvement of the EP when designing soft law instruments;[91] the independence of DG COMP; and, more specifically, the need for a strict separation between the internal divisions that draft guidelines and those that enforce them,[92] the lack of binding legal provisions concerning the setting of fines,[93] and the lack of

85 Consolidated Version of the Treaty on European Union [2016] OJ C202/13, arts 14(1) and 17 (7).

86 Ibid art 17(7).

87 TFEU (n 83) art 233.

88 Framework Agreement on relations between the European Parliament and the European Commission [2010] OJ L304/47.

89 Ibid art 1.

90 European Parliament resolution of 18 June 2020 on competition policy – annual report 2019 [2021] OJ C362/22, para 40.

91 Ibid para 88.

92 Ibid para 155.

93 Ibid para 159.

comprehensive feedback on DG COMP's part concerning specific requests made by the EP in the latter's annual competition report.[94] All of this shows that the adoption and enforcement of soft law instruments may not be as transparent.

In addition to the EP, the Commission and thus DG COMP are subject to the checks of the ECA. Pursuant to Articles 285–287 TFEU, the ECA checks whether the EU budget was raised and spent lawfully and whether financial management was sound.[95]

The NCAs are accountable vis-à-vis national parliaments with a recital in the ECN+ Directive merely stating that Member States may require NCAs to publish periodic reports on their activities to national parliaments, while the monitoring of their financial expenditure might also be foreseen.[96]

Due to lack of legal personality, the ECN cannot be held accountable vis-à-vis the EP or national parliaments regarding its (allocation) decisions. Interestingly, even though information concerning the ECN's activities may be indirectly provided to the EP through the Commission's annual report, it has been noted that 'the EP's debates and resolutions on the Commission annual reports reflect a very low level of accountability concerning the ECN',[97] with the EP generally endorsing the functioning of the ECN and not raising any concerns regarding transparency and accountability within the ECN.[98]

THE HEARING OFFICERS A Hearing Officer is an independent person whose tasks revolve around safeguarding the effective exercise of procedural rights in DG COMP antitrust proceedings. Hearing Officers are not part of DG COMP but – for administrative purposes – are attached to the Competition Commissioner.[99] More specifically, undertakings may ask the Hearing Officer to examine claims that a document is covered by the legal professional

94 Ibid para 156.

95 TFEU (n 83) art 287(2).

96 Directive (EU) 2019/1 of the European Parliament and of the Council of 11 December 2018 to empower the competition authorities of the Member States to be more effective enforcers and to ensure the proper functioning of the internal market [2019] OJ L11/3, recital 22.

97 Katalin Cseres and Annalies Outhuijse, 'Parallel enforcement and accountability: EU competition law' in Miroslava Scholten and Michiel Luchtman (eds), *Law Enforcement by EU Authorities: Implications for Political and Judicial Accountability* (Edward Elgar 2017) 107.

98 Ibid 108.

99 Decision 2011/695 of the President of the European Commission of 13 October 2011 on the function and terms of reference of the hearing officer in certain competition proceedings [2011] OJ L275/29, art 2.

privilege,[100] to examine requests related to the applicability of the privilege against self-incrimination,[101] to grant extension of time-limits,[102] and – where they find that undertakings have not been properly informed whether they are subject to the investigation, including its purpose and subject matter – to compel DG COMP to inform undertakings of their procedural status.[103] Moreover, Hearing Officers decide on whether the right to be heard – including an oral hearing – and the right to have access to the file can be granted to third parties, that is, persons other than those to whom the SO is addressed.[104]

11.3.2.4 Independence

In the context of EU antitrust law enforcement, the independence of the European Commission/DG COMP, the NCAs, and the ECN is critical for at least two reasons. First, given that competition authorities are empowered to impose fines of a criminal nature, within the meaning of Article 6 of European Convention on Human Rights (ECHR), it is logically expected that they must also meet the requirements of an 'independent and impartial tribunal'.[105] Secondly, it has rightly been noted that, as various Member States may have an interest in national companies, through for instance the holding of shares, having an independent competition authority is instrumental in ensuring that the enforcement authority will not be captured by the industry/State interests.[106] Additionally, one should not forget that the need for independence transcends the authority to also reach the judiciary. Indeed, assuming that a competition authority is not an 'independent and impartial tribunal' within the meaning of Article 6 ECHR, it is of paramount importance that the judiciary reviewing the decisions of the competition authority is independent. Independence is then key for an individual's access to justice, as the degree of

[100] Ibid art 4(2)(a).
[101] Ibid art 4(2)(b).
[102] Ibid arts 4(2)I and 9.
[103] Ibid art 4(2)(d).
[104] Ibid arts 5–7.
[105] It is worth noting, however, that the ECtHR has recognised that even if the administrative authority is not independent in itself, that does not amount to a violation of the right to a fair trial, so far as the decision of the administrative authority is later reviewed by a judicial authority that has 'full jurisdiction', namely 'the power to quash in all respects, on questions of fact and law, the decision of the body below', see *Menarini Diagnostics S.r.l. v Italy*, App no 43509/08 (ECtHR, 27 September 2011).
[106] Rubén Perea Molleda, 'The Ecn+ Directive and the Next Steps for Independence in Competition Law Enforcement' (2020) 12 Journal of European Competition Law & Practice 167.

independence of a competition authority may affect the overall fairness of antitrust enforcement proceedings.

With respect to DG Comp's independence, pursuant to Article 245 TFEU, the members of the Commission shall be independent. In addition, a number of checks and balances aim at ensuring the independence of the decision-making process. More specifically, an Advisory Committee is established, which consists of members of the twenty-seven NCAs, the Hearing Officer, the Commission's legal service, and a Chief Economist. That committee must always be consulted prior to the adoption of a decision.[107] As far as the NCAs are concerned, independence requirements are set out in Article 4 of the ECN+ Directive.

Lately, the de facto independence of the Commission, the NCAs, and the ECN have been questioned. As far as the Commission is concerned, it has been noted that, notwithstanding the control exerted by the Advisory Committee, the fact remains that decisions are taken by the College of Commissioners, a decision-making body consisting of twenty-seven politicians prone to political lobbying and external influences.[108] As regards the NCAs, it is yet to be seen whether and, if so, to what extent the inclusion of quite broadly formulated independence requirements in the ECN+ Directive will bring about the envisaged results. One thing is for sure: at the moment, the rule of law crisis in various EU Member States places the independence of competition authorities and of the courts subsequently reviewing their decision in a state of flux. Considering that the Commission is allowed to reject complaints on the grounds that an NCA is better placed to examine a complaint,[109] combined with the fact that allocation decisions that take place within the ECN are not subject to any (judicial) control, it becomes evident that some cases may end up being dealt with by NCAs whose independence can be strongly questioned, without the individual having at their disposal any judicial avenue to attain justice.

11.3.3 *OLAF*

OLAF's mission is to step up the fight against fraud, corruption, and any other illegal activity affecting the financial interests of the Union.[110] To that end,

[107] Regulation 1/2003 (n 51) art 14(1).

[108] Perea Molleda (n 106).

[109] Case T-791/19 *Sped-Pro S.A. v Commission* [2022] ECLI:EU:T:2022:67.

[110] Regulation (EU, Euratom) 883/2013 of the European Parliament and of the Council of 11 September 2013 concerning investigations conducted by the European Anti-Fraud Office (OLAF) and repealing Regulation (EC) No 1073/1999 of the European Parliament and of the

OLAF carries out administrative investigations in the Member States (i.e., 'external investigations') and in the Union's institutions, bodies, offices, and agencies (i.e., 'internal investigations').[111] For reasons of clarity, we consider only the first – external – type of investigations. OLAF investigates so-called persons concerned: any natural or legal person suspected of having committed any act that falls within OLAF's mandate. To be sure, this mandate is very broad and covers potentially any act where Union money is involved, irrespective of the policy area affected and irrespective of where – at the EU or Member State level – the alleged infringement has taken place.

OLAF, as should be clear by now, is an investigatory body. It does not monitor nor does it impose sanctions. OLAF's Director-General opens an investigation when there is a 'sufficient suspicion', which is often based on information that derives from third parties, that may or may not have monitoring functions or anonymous information.[112] At the end of an investigation, when OLAF wishes to see follow-up to its work – in the form of sanctions or otherwise – its Director-General draws up a report (often) accompanied by recommendations that indicate the action to be taken by the Member State concerned: disciplinary, administrative, financial, or judicial (i.e., punitive) action.[113] OLAF's reports are admissible as evidence in national proceedings.[114]

The fundamental rights that may be interfered with or violated, considering OLAF's restricted investigatory task, are limited to those outlined in Section 11.2.1: the right to privacy and the right to a fair trial. With respect to the first, as indicated earlier, OLAF's on-the-spot checks and inspections interfere with the natural or legal person's right to respect for the home and their communications, as protected by Article 7 CFR.[115] The right to a fair trial is not directly at risk in OLAF's investigations. After all, the (potential) trial before a Member State court only takes place *after* OLAF has concluded its work. Nevertheless, the way in which OLAF obtains evidence during its

Council and Council Regulation (Euratom) No 1074/1999 [2013] OJ L248/1 (Regulation (EU, Euratom) 883/2013), art 1(1).

[111] Ibid arts 2(4), 3, and 4.

[112] Regulation (EU, Euratom) 883/2013 (n 110) art 5.

[113] Regulation (EU, Euratom) 883/2013 (n 110) arts 11(1) and (2). The distinction as drawn here is not so strict in reality. It is also possible that OLAF, in an external investigation, finds sufficient reasons to (also) transmit its investigation report and accompanying recommendations to EU institutions, bodies, offices, and agencies (i.e., not only to the Member State concerned).

[114] Though the conditions under which they are admissible differ, depending on the nature of the proceedings (punitive or other). See Regulation (EU, Euratom) 883/2013 (n 110) art 11(2).

[115] Section 11.2.1.

investigations – by means of its on-the-spot checks and its interviews – is of importance for the trial and sanctioning phase and what OLAF does 'often determines the framework in which the offence charged will be considered at the trial'.[116] OLAF's legal framework recognises this and, accordingly, provides the person concerned with the necessary procedural guarantees.[117] The person concerned has the right to avoid self-incrimination even though OLAF exercises no compulsion. In addition, they have the right to be assisted by a 'person of choice'; a broad denominator that includes lawyers. Once the investigation has been completed and before conclusions referring to a person concerned by name are drawn up, that person shall be given the opportunity to comment on the facts concerning them.[118] In other words, while OLAF's legal framework does not say so explicitly, the person concerned has a right to be heard before the report is transmitted for follow-up proceedings. Beyond that, to make the exercise of procedural safeguards effective, the person concerned also has the right to be informed of the safeguards with which OLAF must comply.[119]

11.3.3.1 Safeguards and Defence Rights in OLAF's Legal Framework

While OLAF's legal framework offers a host of safeguards, some are notably absent. The legal professional privilege is awarded no particular status in OLAF's legal framework and is mentioned only in passing in internal guidelines. If during digital forensics operations in the context of an on-the-spot check the person concerned claims that the device in question contains data of a legally privileged nature, the data shall be acquired and placed in a sealed envelope. The representative of the economic operator shall be told that they will be invited for a meeting to resolve the issue before OLAF opens the sealed envelope.[120] The internal guidelines do not dictate whether the information,

[116] *Ibrahim and Others v the United Kingdom* (n 18) para 253.

[117] For an in-depth overview, see Katalin Ligeti, 'The Protection of the Procedural Rights of the Person Concerned by OLAF Administrative Investigations and the Admissibility of OLAF Final Reports as Criminal Evidence' (2017) <www.europarl.europa.eu/RegData/etudes/IDAN/2017/603790/IPOL_IDA(2017)603790_EN.pdf>.

[118] Regulation (EU, Euratom) 883/2013 (n 110) art 9(4). Note, however, that, in duly justified cases, where necessary to preserve the confidentiality of the investigation or an ongoing or future criminal investigation by the EPPO or a national judicial authority, the Director-General may, where appropriate after consulting the European Public Prosecutor's Office or the national judicial authority concerned, decide to defer the fulfilment of the obligation to invite the person concerned to comment.

[119] Regulation (EU, Euratom) 883/2013 (n 110) art 9(2).

[120] Guidelines on Digital Forensic Proceedings for OLAF Staff 2016, art 6.3.

if indeed it falls under the scope of the legal professional privilege, may still be used or whether it must be excluded from the case file if OLAF and the person concerned do not come to a resolution on the issue. Additionally, it seems to regulate only those situations in which privileged information is stored digitally; 'physical' privileged information – letters and the like – are not accorded protection.

Another safeguard that, until recently, was notably absent is the right to have access to the file. Contrary to other fields of law, such as competition law enforcement by DG COMP, the CJEU refused for a long time to extend the protection of the right to have access to the file to the OLAF. The reasoning that underpinned the Court's judgment was that no obligation under EU (fundamental rights) law existed to grant the person concerned access to the file, because (i) OLAF's report – that is, the end-product of its work – does not bind the Member State authorities to which it is addressed; and/or (ii) it is these national authorities that, ultimately, bring about a 'distinct change' in the concerned person's legal position. According to the CJEU, it is incumbent on the authority initiating the follow-up to OLAF's investigative work to grant access to the file.[121] In the last few years, the CJEU seemingly has backed down, ever so slightly, from this position. In *Homoki v Commission*, the CJEU held that OLAF cannot refuse the person concerned access to the investigation report after an investigation has been closed and when such disclosure would no longer prejudice OLAF or its investigations.[122] In a similar application in *Vendrame v Commission*, yet to be decided on, Vendrame lodged an action before the CJEU complaining of OLAF's refusal to grant access to the investigation report.[123]

Because of OLAF's limited (investigatory) task and the consequent need for national authorities to jump in when follow-up, by means of further investigations and/or ultimately sanctioning, is necessary, there is a division of responsibility (and of labour) when it comes to ensuring access to justice in the case of fundamental rights interferences and violations. In Sections

[121] Case T-215/02 *Gomez Reino* [2003] ECLI:EU:T:2003:352 para 65; Case T-259/03 *Nikolaou v Commission* [2007] ECLI:EU:T:2007:254; Case T-48/05 *Franchet and Byk v Commission* [2008] ECLI:EU:T:2008:257; Case T-447/11 *Catinis v Commission* [2014] ECLI:EU:T:2014:267 paras 63–64. This reasoning has been criticised in the literature. See, among others, Jan Inghelram, 'Fundamental Rights, the European Anti-Fraud Office (OLAF) and a European Public Prosecutor's Office (EPPO): Some Selected Issues' (2012) 1 Kritische Vierteljahresschrift für Gesetzgebung und Rechtswissenschaft 67, 73–74; Simone White, 'Rights of Defence in Administrative Investigations: Access to the File in EC Investigations' (2009) 1 Review of European Law 57, 63.

[122] Case T-517/19 *Homoki v Commission* [2021] ECLI:EU:T:2021:529.

[123] Case T-379/21 *Vendrame v Commission* [2021] ECLI:EU:T:2023:399.

11.3.3.2 and 11.3.3.3, we highlight how this division features in the person concerned's quest for access to judicial remedies and non-judicial remedies.

11.3.3.2 OLAF and the Person Concerned's Judicial Remedies: 'Access to Court'

OLAF's investigative acts can interfere with or violate the person concerned's fundamental rights. Because these acts are imputable to the EU legal order, judicial control – at least in theory – is available at the EU level. The CJEU controls OLAF's investigations by means of the action for annulment and the action for damages.[124] Beyond these two direct forms of review before the EU court, a person can indirectly have an OLAF act reviewed when a national court refers a preliminary question on the validity of an OLAF act to the Court of Justice. Our discussion here will focus on the first two forms of (direct) review.

The Court of Justice has consistently qualified whatever OLAF does – its investigative acts as well as its investigation reports – as preparatory in nature, that is, measures that pave the way for a final decision at the national level and that, in and of themselves, do not bring about a distinct change in the legal position of the person concerned.[125] Such preparatory measures are, according to *IBM v Commission*, only open to an action for annulment where they themselves are the 'culmination of a procedure distinct' from a national decision on the liability of the person concerned.[126] Because OLAF, at least in external investigations, necessarily depends on national authorities for follow-up on its investigations, the 'distinct procedure' criterion poses, in the current OLAF framework, an almost insurmountable hurdle to persons concerned wishing to annul an act attributable to OLAF.[127]

Because actions for annulment are essentially closed off to the person concerned, the only pathway still left open to them is an action for contractual or non-contractual damages because neither of these poses admissibility requirements. Actions for damages have thus far shown poor returns for the

[124] This Section borrows heavily from Bovend'Eerdt, 'The Protection of Fundamental Rights in OLAF Composite Enforcement Procedures' (n 2) ch 2.6.

[125] Case C-60/81 *IBM v Commission* [1981] ECLI:EU:T:1981:264, para 10.

[126] Ibid para 11.

[127] See, in greater detail, Katalin Ligeti and Gavin Robinson, 'Composite Enforcement and Judicial Protection' in Michiel Luchtman, Katalin Ligeti, and John Vervaele (eds), *EU Enforcement Authorities. Punitive Law Enforcement in a Composite Legal Order* (Hart 2023) 88–92.

person concerned.[128] The main issue lies in establishing causality between the unlawful act in question and the damage incurred, the latter of which is in most cases ultimately felt at the domestic level.

11.3.3.3 OLAF and the Person Concerned's Non-judicial Remedies: 'Access to Justice'

To make up for or complement the individual's lack of access to court, the EU legislator has put in place non-judicial mechanisms to try and hold OLAF accountable. Many of these mechanisms, put in place before the 2020 revision of OLAF's legal framework, try to attain a degree of political accountability. The purpose of these political mechanisms is to provide a sense of ex post accountability that 'helps promote transparency and to avoid arbitrariness in the exercise of OLAF's functions. It provides for a forum to identify and discuss possible loopholes in the framework for investigations'.[129] These mechanisms do not, however, provide the person concerned with a pathway to justice because they do not relate to OLAF's investigations *in concreto*, but – on the contrary – operate on an 'investigation-overarching' level and concern OLAF's fulfilment of its investigative task in general. Moreover, the person concerned whose rights have been interfered with or violated in the context of an OLAF investigation is not placed in the driving seat and cannot by their own motion initiate actions before or in these fora. In other words, the person concerned is completely at the mercy of OLAF or other institutions. OLAF's legal framework puts in place the following mechanisms to ensure political accountability: the duty to report to, and exchange views with, EU institutions; the European Court of Auditor's audits; and supervision by OLAF's Supervisory Committee.[130]

In addition to forms of political accountability, OLAF's legal framework has in place a number of internal and external review mechanisms that allow for some means of controlling the legality of OLAF's investigations: (i) OLAF's Review Team, (ii) the controller of procedural guarantees, and (iii), the Ombudsman. We discuss each in turn.

[128] In fact, damages have only been awarded in internal investigations.

[129] European Union Committee, *Strengthening OLAF, the European Anti-Fraud Office. Report with Evidence* (Hour of Lords 2003–2004, 139) 18–20; Michiel Luchtman and Martin Wasmeier, 'The Political and Judicial Accountability of OLAF' in Miroslava Scholten and Michiel Luchtman (eds), *Law Enforcement by EU Authorities: Implications for Political and Judicial Accountability* (Edward Elgar 2017) 232–233.

[130] Luchtman and Wasmeier (n 129) 230–236.

INTERNAL REVIEW

OLAF's Review Team

OLAF's legal framework obliges the Director-General to put in place an internal advisory and control procedure. This procedure includes a legality check relating, inter alia, to the respect of procedural guarantees and fundamental rights of the persons concerned and of the national law of the Member States concerned.[131] This legality check is to be carried out by OLAF's Review Team, which consists of experts in law and investigative procedures.[132] The end product of a review – both ex ante and ex post – is an opinion that the Review Team provides to OLAF's DG. The DG, in turn, uses this opinion as a basis for decision-making.

While praiseworthy, there are notable caveats. The first and foremost is that it does not give the person concerned whose fundamental rights have been interfered with or have been violated a means to have their voice heard. The person concerned cannot request that the Review Team assess the legality of a particular investigative act or evaluate interferences with their fundamental rights. Secondly, the Review Team is not independent. The team, while not involved in carrying out investigative acts or writing the report, is part of OLAF's staff and, in that guise, operates under the authority of the DG.[133] Thirdly, and already mentioned above, the Review Team does not have decision-making power. Its opinions are advisory only and the DG may deviate from these opinions if they wish to do so.[134] Fourth, one can question the effectiveness of the review. OLAF's SC issued an opinion in which it found that that the Review Team's opinions were not systematically followed-up on.[135]

EXTERNAL REVIEW

The Controller of Procedural Guarantees

OLAF's legal framework quite recently established the Controller of Procedural Guarantees.[136] The Controller is appointed by the Commission

[131] The purpose of the latter, of course, is to ensure the admissibility of OLAF's investigation report in national (punitive) proceedings.

[132] Regulation (EU, Euratom) 883/2013 (n 110) art 17(7).

[133] Jan Inghelram, 'Fundamental Rights, the European Anti-Fraud Office (OLAF) and a European Public Prosecutor's Office (EPPO): Some Selected Issues' (2012) 1 Kritische Vierteljahresschrift für Gesetzgebung und Rechtswissenschaft 67, 70.

[134] Ibid.

[135] OLAF Supervisory Committee, 'Opinion No 2/2015. Legality Check and Review in OLAF' 14.

[136] The Controller of Procedural Guarantees was introduced by way of Regulation (EU, Euratom) 2020/2223 of the European Parliament and of the Council of 23 December 2020 amending Regulation (EU, Euratom) No 883/2013, as regards cooperation with the European

and is administratively attached to OLAF's SC.[137] The Controller's purpose, as the name already suggests, is to ensure that the person concerned's procedural guarantees and fundamental rights are protected and complied with.[138] To that end, OLAF's legal framework provides for a complaints mechanism that allows the person concerned to lodge a complaint with the Controller regarding OLAF's compliance with procedural guarantees as well as on the grounds of an infringement of the rules applicable to investigations by the OLAF, in particular, infringements of procedural requirements and fundamental rights.[139] The Controller, when dealing with complaints, does not interfere with OLAF's investigation but has access to the necessary case-related documents and may organise and conduct hearings.[140] The complaint mechanism is adversarial in nature: both OLAF and the person concerned can state their case and have the right to be heard before the Controller completes the assessment.[141] Where a breach is established, the Controller invites OLAF to take action to resolve the complaint. If the Controller finds the solution provided by OLAF satisfactory, the Controller closes the case; if the Controller does not find the solution satisfactory, they issue a recommendation on how to resolve the complaint.[142] OLAF's DG takes appropriate action as warranted by the recommendation. If the DG decides not to follow the Controller's recommendation, the DG shall communicate to the complainant and to the Controller the main reasons for that decision.[143]

The Controller, in contrast to the Review Team, is completely independent both from OLAF and from the SC to which it is attached. The Controller neither seeks nor takes instructions from anyone in the performance of their duties.[144] Moreover, the Controller is concerned with inter alia the legality of specific investigative acts. Importantly, the person concerned can *motu proprio* lodge a complaint before the Controller. The person concerned does not depend on OLAF or other bodies or authorities in their quest to access justice.

Public Prosecutor's Office and the effectiveness of the European Anti-Fraud Office investigations [2020] OJ L437/49 (Regulation (EU, Euratom) 2020/2223).

[137] Regulation (Eu, Euratom) 883/2013 (n 110) art 9a(1).

[138] Regulation (EU, Euratom) 2020/2223 (n 136) recital (32).

[139] Ibid recital (32) and art 9b.

[140] Decision of the Controller of Procedural Guarantees Adopting Implementing Provisions for the Handling of Complaints [2022] OJ C494/17 (Decision 494/17) arts 8 and 9.

[141] Ibid art 7(1).

[142] Ibid arts 10 and 11.

[143] Regulation (Eu, Euratom) 883/2013 (n 110) art 9b(7); Decision 494/17 (n 140) art 13(2).

[144] Regulation (EU, Euratom) 883/2013 (n 110) art 9a(6).

Notwithstanding all the above, the Controller – when push comes to shove – only has the power to issue recommendations. Although the DG must state reasons if they consider deviation justified, they can decide not to follow the Controller's recommendation.

The Ombudsman

The European Ombudsman can receive complaints from the person concerned in relation to instances of maladministration by OLAF like it does for all Union institutions, bodies, offices, and agencies in accordance with its constitutional mandate.[145] Maladministration can include, among other things, the violation of fundamental rights of the person concerned.[146] On the basis of a complaint – or on their own initiative – the Ombudsman conducts inquiries into the alleged maladministration.[147] Where the Ombudsman establishes instances of maladministration, they make recommendations to OLAF to address these instances. In relation to OLAF the Ombudsman has, on a number of occasions, dealt with complaints. Many of these complaints have concerned OLAF's refusal to provide access to the case file or the investigation report by persons concerned and third parties.[148] Other complaints concerned OLAF's failure to follow the applicable investigative formalities and not affording the person concerned a reasonable opportunity to respond to the findings.[149]

While the Ombudsman, in a similar fashion to the Controller of Procedural Guarantees, allows the person to file a complaint on their own initiative before an independent authority concerning interferences and violations of fundamental rights, the complaint also suffers from the same defects. At the end of its inquiry, when the Ombudsman closes a case by way of decision, they can only recommend remedial action to OLAF. These recommendations, as the name suggests, are just that: non-binding recommendations.

145 TFEU (n 83) art 228(1); see also Regulation (EU, Euratom) 2021/1163 of the European Parliament of 24 June 2021 laying down the regulations and general conditions governing the performance of the Ombudsman's duties (Statute of the European Ombudsman) and repealing Decision 94/262/ECSC, EC, Euratom [2021] OJ L253/1 (Regulation (EU, Euratom) 2021/1163), art 2(1).

146 European Ombudsman, Fundamental Rights (ombudsman.europa.eu) <www.ombudsman.europa.eu/en/areas-of-work/fundamental-rights>.

147 Statute of the European Ombudsman (n 145) art 3.

148 See, for instance, European Ombudsman Case 598/2013/OV European Anti-Fraud Office (16 December 2013) <europa.eu/!7XrxPP>.

149 See, for instance, European Ombudsman Case 1560/2010/FOR European Anti-Fraud Office (6 September 2010) <europa.eu/!PHngCh>; European Ombudsman Cases 723/2005/OV and 790/2005/OV *European Anti-Fraud Office* (18 December 2009) <europa.eu/!q3C9Px>.

11.4 DISCUSSION

The aim of this edited volume is to investigate whether private parties have remedies (judicial and non-judicial) available when their fundamental rights are violated by the EU (here: by an EU enforcement authority). From our analysis, we can identify three key, cross-cutting themes where concerns exist in relation to access to remedies when fundamental rights have been violated by EU law enforcement authorities. These are:

1. the limits of judicial review of non-binding preparatory acts and soft law instruments. As a corollary, the right to access to the court can be undermined;
2. the principle of national procedural autonomy may lead to different degrees of protection of fundamental rights, which can affect legal certainty and fairness; and
3. the limits of ex ante judicial remedies and of non-judicial remedies, like political accountability, which could mitigate gaps stemming from the limits of ex post judicial control and hence ensure more comprehensive control over executive discretion.

We briefly discuss these themes here and outline potential solutions to rectify the possible gaps in the protection of fundamental rights.

First, it is important to reiterate the following. During enforcement processes, EU law enforcement authorities, often together with national counterparts, may license private parties, monitor compliance, and investigate and/or sanction violations of the law. As such powers affect the rights and freedoms of private actors, EU law enforcement authorities are bound by the law to respect fundamental rights, such as the right to good administration (Article 41 CFR), the right to privacy (Article 7 CFR), fair trial rights (Articles 47/48 CFR), and the right of access to the court (Article 47 CFR). More specifically, the right to good administration includes the obligation to state reasons, the right to be informed, the right to be heard, and the right to have access to the file. The defence rights include, among others, the right to have access to a lawyer, the privilege against self-incrimination, and the legal professional privilege. In addition to that, sanctions must respect the principles of legality and proportionality of offences and penalties law (Article 49 CFR).

Going back to the first point of the list above, our analysis shows that enforcement by EU enforcement authorities can – by necessity or by design – allow for actions not easily amenable to judicial review, such as soft law and investigations that can (ultimately) result in punitive follow-up at the Member State level, which can nonetheless interfere with, and even violate, fundamental rights of the natural or legal person in question. In many of these instances, there is no possibility to obtain legal protection or to remedy these violations through the judicial avenue leading to Luxembourg. Think, for instance, about ESMA supervising private actors on a daily basis, including through informal conversations and guidance. From an effective enforcement perspective, the deployment of such informal tools seems essential to achieve compliance yet may lead to possible disagreements with the private actors. The private actors may have difficulties in having standing before the court if no de jure binding decision has been issued by ESMA against them or if soft law instruments have no legal force.

Furthermore, when various enforcement stages (monitoring, investigating, sanctioning) are exercised by the EU authority and its national counterparts, this can result in procedural hurdles in ensuring access to the court. A good example is OLAF. Because OLAF merely draws up a report accompanied by recommendations on the punitive follow-up to be taken at the Member State level and does not have the competence to impose sanctions, the CJEU has consistently held that the action for annulment is closed off for the person concerned as OLAF's work is considered as preparatory and does not bring about change in the legal position of the person concerned (a standing requirement under TFEU Article 263). All the while, national courts do not possess the competence to rule on the validity of OLAF's investigative acts or the report established as a result thereof, as doing so would violate the heavily guarded division of jurisdictional competences laid down in *Foto-Frost*. OLAF can, however, interfere with or violate the fundamental rights of the person concerned in the context of its investigations. The multi-jurisdictional legal order of the EU poses similar challenges in the field of enforcement of competition law. Here, too, some decisions by bodies lacking legal personality, like the ECN, seem to be subject to judicial scrutiny. Yet the ECN's allocation decisions determine the content of the procedural rights that will ultimately be available to the parties subject to EU competition law enforcement proceedings.

The fact that the EU consists of multiple legal orders leads to the challenge of ensuring the protection of fundamental rights in the same fashion. The principle of national procedural autonomy shields national sovereignty and accommodates procedural differences and divergent fundamental rights' standards across the Union. At the same time, this may come at the expense of legal certainty especially when the legal framework is designed in such a way as to allow EU law enforcement authorities to choose to carry out enforcement actions and obtain evidence in jurisdictions offering the least protection. A good example in that respect is ESMA and on-site inspections.

EU law allows ESMA to seek ex ante judicial authorisation before the performance of an on-site inspection only if national law so requires. In the absence of EU law harmonising mandatory ex ante judicial authorisation, an EU enforcement authority may decide to carry out investigative activities in Member States that provide for lesser ex ante legal protection. In a similar vein, the fact that the twenty-seven Member States protect fundamental rights differently, yet evidence obtained on the basis of divergent standards can be exchanged freely between competition authorities and be used for sanctioning in various Member States, may come at the expense of procedural fairness.

To what extent can there be non-judicial remedies to address possible violations of fundamental rights by EU enforcement authorities (EEAs)? Our third point on the list above indicates that while non-judicial remedies may exist, they cannot possibly offer the same kind of protection that judicial remedies can. We have identified the following non-judicial remedies: political accountability, the availability of hearing officers (DG COMP), controllers of procedural guarantees (OLAF), Ombudsman, special mechanisms like a request to the Commission (ESMA), and ex ante forms of control via, for instance, consultation and participation of private parties in certain procedures. These remedies are important and can help those who seek justice for violation of their specific rights. The mechanisms of political accountability and the Ombudsman may address such violations from a structural perspective via, for instance, adjusting the law, which could stop such violations in the future and give the satisfaction of being heard and having one's complaint taken into consideration. However, the limits of such non-judicial remedies are twofold. For one, unless a recommendation or advice is given by internal mechanisms of review, like the ESMA Board of Appeals or the DG COMP's hearing officer, non-judicial mechanisms cannot rectify immediately the violation of one's rights in a specific case. This is because EU enforcement authorities are required by law to carry out supervision and enforcement in an independent manner. No politician should be able to influence the EU authority when they enforce the law against private actors. Hence, we discussed the issue of independence and its importance at the institutional and personnel levels in enforcement. For two, non-judicial remedies do not and cannot possibly offer the same kind of protection that judicial remedies can as they often lack certain qualities that go part and parcel with the judicial authorities and remedies: taking binding decisions, availability of remedies *in concreto* and not merely *in abstracto*, and independence within the meaning of Article 6 ECHR/ 47 CFR. At the same time, it may also be the case that the legislative design of non-judicial remedies may not have yet been developed. These are often rather recent changes; future empirical research will hopefully show to what extent these can be effective means to find justice.

11.4.1 *What Are the Lessons That We Can Draw from Our Analysis?*

First of all, the three types of EEAs that we have considered in our analysis are useful for analytical purposes to see and assess the sources of potential violations of fundamental rights. The clearer the division of competences among EU and national authorities and the lesser the degree of possible de jure joint enforcement action, the clearer the judicial remedy becomes. For instance, if ESMA carries out all the enforcement actions on its own, the private party has only one authority to address and the private party can do so according to the EU standards of fundamental rights and via other non-judicial remedies at the EU level. At the same time, the more divided the enforcement process between EU and national jurisdictions and the greater the degree of mixing supervisors, the more challenges there can be in seeking judicial redress: Which court? Which standard of fundamental rights? Is there a check on an action or decision of an EEA? etc.

Secondly, the legislative design of enforcement responsibilities, tasks, powers, fundamental rights, and controls is of paramount importance to prevent violations of fundamental rights and redress if the violation has happened. However, at the moment of writing, the legislative design of direct EU law enforcement often results in an allocation of responsibility that may not be matched with accompanying (judicial or non-judicial) remedies at the respective national or EU level. While it is true that we are discussing a relatively new development, such a mismatch must be prevented. Relevant procedural guarantees and procedures need to be developed and be clear for both the EU authorities and the supervised parties. For instance, requests for information need to be based on good reasons, especially if they are issued informally. Supervised parties should be heard, especially if ex post controls, such as judicial review, do not cover specific types of acts, which can limit or affect fundamental rights. Judicial dialogue between EU and national courts should be enhanced in order to overcome the strict dichotomy between the EU and the national level when it comes to judicial review of EU law enforcement authorities' actions.

Finally, as part and parcel of the previous lesson, the coexistence of judicial and non-judicial remedies can complement each other's gaps and ultimately ensure a fully-fledged protection of fundamental rights if designed properly and aligned with one another, including EU-national alignment. For instance, if effective enforcement in the field of financial markets requires informal supervisory practices, mediation procedures could be envisaged to ensure a mechanism of redress of possible violations of fundamental rights during such informal supervision. If soft law guidance is crucial to enhance compliance, private actors need to be able to ensure they are being heard when the guidance is developed. If the legislator is setting novel types of cooperation, such as shared enforcement, it should be clear which standard of fundamental rights protection should apply, what key terms on the basis of which enforcement authorities base their decisions mean (e.g., violation with intent or negligently), and which jurisdiction(s) should be responsible for the review of all stages of enforcement. Lastly, it is essential that the EU legislator does not attempt to use (non-judicial) remedies, such as internal mechanisms of review by internal units, to fill the gaps in judicial protection in the domain of direct enforcement by EU authorities, but rather seeks to complement the existence of judicial remedies.

11.5 CONCLUSION

This chapter has discussed the question of the access to justice by private parties during enforcement procedures in the EU, especially EEAs. We have argued that enforcement activities have characteristics showing the necessity of both judicial and non-judicial remedies if one's fundamental rights have been violated. Enforcement is a process that aims at ensuring policy goals and ensuring core values, where non-compliance should be better prevented, rather than responded to. This implies the importance of having informal, preparatory, ex ante as well as legally binding actions and decisions. These actions and decisions can, however, lead to violations of fundamental rights: rights to good administration, access to the court, privacy, due process, etc. These violations can be challenging to address for a number of reasons, including the multi-jurisdictional legal order of the EU at times lacking legislative clarity as to the scope of certain fundamental rights standards and enforcement responsibilities and the importance of informal actions and guidance enhancing compliance. In this context, we have argued for the importance of developing an alignment between judicial and non-judicial remedies to address violations of fundamental rights in a comprehensive and proportionate way.

12

Legal Protection against Fundamental Rights Breaches through Factual Conduct by the European Union

FLORIN COMAN-KUND*

12.1 INTRODUCTION

Starting from the premise that factual conduct by European Union (EU) institutions, agencies, and bodies (hereafter referred to generically as 'EU bodies' in line with the consistent terminology adopted in this volume) may breach fundamental rights of individuals, this chapter examines what appears to be rather a 'blind spot' in EU law and scholarship, namely the legal protection against factual conduct by the EU. In doing so, the chapter engages first with some conceptual clarifications of the term 'factual conduct' by reference to the concepts of 'legally binding act' and 'legally non-binding act' (or soft law) and provides some illustrations of EU factual conduct potentially infringing fundamental rights. Second, the chapter looks at the system of EU legal remedies (both judicial and non-judicial remedies are included within the scope of this investigation) as enshrined in the Treaty on the Functioning of the European Union (TFEU)[1] and the jurisprudence of the Court of Justice of the European Union (CJEU), as well as in relevant EU secondary legislation, with a view to establishing their potential to address fundamental rights breaches by EU factual conduct. Third, the chapter ends with an assessment of the overall system of legal protection against fundamental rights breaches through factual conduct by the EU, revealing strengths, gaps, and challenges, and suggesting some solutions for improvement, in

* This chapter is dedicated to the memory of my father, Dr Liviu Coman-Kund. The author would like to thank Melanie Fink for the feedback and suggestions on this chapter; the usual disclaimer applies. All websites and electronic sources were last accessed on 25 August 2023.

[1] Consolidated Version of the Treaty on the Functioning of the European Union [2016] OJ C202/47 (TFEU).

particular in the form of enhancing, in light of Articles 41 and 47 of the Charter of Fundamental Rights of the EU (CFR),[2] the array of EU administrative/non-judicial mechanisms and remedies with judicially reviewable outcomes.

12.2 EU FACTUAL CONDUCT AND FUNDAMENTAL RIGHTS

12.2.1 *Conceptual Reflections on EU Factual Conduct*

Public administration features as the most prominent form of action legally binding acts, be they of a general or individual application. Yet the bulk of daily public administration also entails a lot of human actions, acts, activities, or conduct that do not amount to formal legally binding acts.[3] Such administrative acts or conduct, though not intended to produce legal effects like a binding legal act, entail nevertheless (sometimes significant) factual and legal consequences; as such, they may also arguably infringe fundamental rights.[4]

The range of administrative forms of action outside the category of formal legally binding acts is broad and diverse. It includes various acts and operations that lead to the adoption[5] or ensure the implementation/enforcement[6]

[2] Charter of Fundamental Rights of the European Union [2016] OJ C202/389.

[3] The term 'formal legally binding act' refers in this context to legal instruments that are explicitly enshrined as acts with binding effects in the relevant legal framework and that normally must meet specific procedural and formal criteria to come into being and produce their binding effects (e.g., regulations, directives, and decisions enshrined in Article 288 TFEU are illustrative of this category); this allows drawing a distinction between such formal binding acts, whereby their form and substance are in principle fully consistent in indicating their binding nature, and genuine legally binding acts identified on the basis of the 'substance prevails over form' test used by the Court of Justice of the European Union (CJEU) since *ERTA* to determine whether a certain action, no matter the label and form, is in fact genuinely producing legal effects vis-à-vis third parties, see Case 22/70 *Commission v Council. European Agreement on Road Transport (ERTA)* [1971] EU:C:1971:32, para. 42. In the latter case, administrative actions, including factual conduct (as discussed later in this chapter), that meet the criteria of the *ERTA* test would amount to genuine legally binding acts even if their form does not correspond to that of a legally binding act; if this is the case, such 'factual conduct' qua form expressing a legally binding act qua nature would be subject to the system of legal review and remedies put in place for legally binding acts.

[4] See Timo Rademacher, 'Factual Administrative Conduct and Judicial Review in EU Law' (2017) 29 (2) European Review of Public Law 399, 401.

[5] E.g., various preparatory documents, proposals, draft rules, reports, and opinions.

[6] E.g., the concrete actions to enter the premises of an undertaking, as well as searching and collecting relevant information and documents following a formal inspection decision adopted by the European Commission under the EU competition rules according to Council Regulation (EC) No 1/2003 of 16 December 2002 on the implementation of the rules on competition laid down in Articles 81 and 82 of the Treaty [2003] OJ L1/1; checking identity of

of a formal legally binding act. It also arguably includes more free-standing acts and factual conduct such as legally non-binding or 'soft law' acts[7] as well as various concrete actions and operations.[8]

From a conceptual point of view, the term 'factual conduct' can be understood in two different ways.[9] In one sense, it can be construed as an act of conduct or as a legal fact in the shape of human behaviour that is not intended per se to produce legally binding effects, but which nevertheless may entail certain legal and practical consequences according to law.[10] According to this understanding, 'factual conduct' would broadly encompass all administrative acts (forms of action) outside the category of formal legally binding acts. In a second sense, 'factual conduct' is to be understood as a specific form of administrative action. According to this second, more specific, understanding, it encompasses administrative actions and operations that amount broadly speaking to 'physical acts'[11] or measures of a factual nature. Such acts express the conduct of a public authority or its servants in the outside world in a factual manner, their legal relevance (as legally binding acts or mere acts of conduct having some legal relevance) being determined by the applicable legal framework.[12] Factual conduct can thus

persons, body searches, confiscation of goods/items in the implementation of an operational decision during a joint operation at the Union's external borders.

7 E.g., recommendations and opinions based on Article 288 TFEU, communications, white papers, green papers, letters, resolutions, guidelines, codes of conduct, etc.

8 E.g., data collection and processing operations, accessing and searching an EU database, drawing up the agenda and minutes of an official meeting, publication of notices of information, questions and answers, 'naming and shaming' practices, for instance, by the so-called European Supervisory Authorities (ESAs) in the context of the implementation and enforcement of the EU financial governance framework (for a recent example of such practices regarding the European Banking Authority, see European Banking Authority, Regulatory Technical Standards on a central database on AML/CFT in the EU (European Banking Authority, 20 December 2021) <www.eba.europa.eu/regulation-and-policy/anti-money-laundering-and-countering-financing-terrorism/regulatory-technical-standards-central-database-amlcft-eu#pane-new-ed8f3c99-9589-454a-a87e-37f2578a1783>; and The Compliance Lady, European Banking Authority's "Name & Shame" Database To Be Operational In January 2022 (Compliance Lady, 21 December 2021) <https://thecompliancelady.com/2021/12/21/european-banking-authoritys-name-shame-database-to-be-operational-in-january-2022/>.

9 For an interesting conceptual framework regarding EU factual conduct and its potential legal effects, see Napoleon Xanthoulis, 'Administrative Factual Conduct: Legal Effects and Judicial Control in EU Law' (2019) 12 Review of European Administrative Law 39, 45–56.

10 Rademacher (n 4) 399–400; see also Herwig C H Hofmann, Gerard C Rowe, and Alexander H Türk, *Administrative Law and Policy of the European Union* (Oxford University Press 2011) 667–672.

11 See Case 53/85 *AKZO Chemie BV and AKZO Chemie UK Ltd v Commission* [1986] ECLI:EU:C:1986:256, para 17.

12 Hence, factual conduct does not cover formal legally binding acts or formal non-binding acts and instruments adopted by the EU administration according to prescribed procedures and

include various physical acts and operations, either free-standing or connected to the adoption and implementation/enforcement of a formal legal act (binding or non-binding). Examples include: publishing/handling information, collecting and processing personal data, feeding a database with information or extracting information therefrom, providing an answer to a request or a petition, preparing a draft legal act, preparing and submitting a report or letter, publishing a legal act in the official journal/communicating the legal act to interested persons, entering business premises, searching for information, collecting and sealing documents and other items during an inspection/investigation, and using police executive powers.[13]

Relying mainly on the second sense of the term for the purpose of this chapter, as in our view it analytically depicts more accurately the phenomenon under consideration, we note that factual conduct is very much present in the activity of the EU public administration. All EU bodies handle personal and non-personal data and information, publish and exchange information and various documents, undertake preparatory operations and actions for the purpose of adopting a formal legal act, and carry out various operations and actions for ensuring their implementation. It is less common for EU bodies to carry out physical implementation and enforcement of EU law, as these matters are normally reserved for the Member States' administrations. Yet there are notable examples of EU bodies doing this (see also Chapter 11). These include the European Commission in competition law[14] and, more recently, the European Central Bank (ECB) in its supervisory role within the Single Supervisory Mechanism (SSM),[15] the European Border and Coast

formats (the latter being also called 'soft law'). As to the latter, though they have no binding force, formal recommendations and opinions adopted by the EU institutions (in particular the Council and the Commission) based on Article 288 TFEU are technically included in the category of 'legal acts of the Union'; the same seems to apply, at least according to scholarly and some official sources, for communications, guidelines, notices, resolutions, etc. that are not listed under Article 288 TFEU, and therefore are labelled as 'atypical acts', see Florin Coman-Kund and Corina Andone, 'Persuasive Rather than 'Binding' EU Soft Law? Towards an Argumentative Template for European Commission's Recommendations' in Petra Láncos, Napoleon Xanthoulis, and Luis Arroyo Jiménez (eds), *The Legal Effects of EU Soft Law: Theory, Language and Sectoral Insights into EU Multi-level Governance* (Edward Elgar 2023) 150; and Opinion of Advocate-General Bobek in Case C-16/16P *Belgium v Commission* [2017] ECLI:EU:C:2017:959, paras 55–62.

[13] E.g., operating an arrest, use of firearms, body and identity checks, placing a visa stamp in a passport, operating a patrol vessel during a joint operation at EU external borders, using physical force to prevent crossing of borders, etc.

[14] See Regulation 1/2003.

[15] Council Regulation (EU) No 1024/2013 of 15 October 2013 conferring specific tasks on the European Central Bank concerning policies relating to the prudential supervision of credit institutions [2013] OJ L287/63 (SSM Regulation).

Guard Agency (Frontex) with its new direct operational powers in joint operations at the Union's external borders,[16] and the European Public Prosecutor's Office (EPPO) with its wide-ranging investigation powers.[17] This trend is likely to continue in view of the ongoing phenomenon of EU administrative integration and hybridisation, with more EU bodies being granted (gradually increasing) direct enforcement and implementing powers, often exercised within rather intricate composite (EU and national) legal frameworks and in complex relationship with national competent authorities.[18]

12.2.2 *Risks for Fundamental Rights from EU Factual Conduct*

EU factual conduct (understood as acts of 'physical' conduct by EU institutions, agencies and bodies, and their staff) may directly or indirectly affect fundamental rights of natural and legal persons. Examples are abundant in this respect. For instance, personal data processing operations by EU bodies may breach directly or indirectly the data protection rights (enshrined in Article 8 CFR and further given substance in Regulation 2018/1725)[19] as well as the right to respect for private and family life (Article 7 CFR) of the individual. Abusive or inappropriate personal data processing by Europol as regards persons suspected of being involved in serious crime might ultimately result in unlawful arrests and home searches by enforcement authorities in the Member States, in breach of the right to liberty and security of the person (Article 6 CFR) and/or the right to respect for private and family life (Article 7 CFR). Disseminating/publishing abusive defamatory information about individuals and legal persons may affect their reputation and consequently result

[16] Regulation (EU) 2019/1896 of the European Parliament and of the Council of 13 November 2019 on the European Border and Coast Guard and repealing Regulations (EU) No 1052/2013 and (EU) 2016/1624 [2019] OJ L295/1 (EBCG Regulation).

[17] Council Regulation (EU) 2017/1939 of 12 October 2017 implementing enhanced cooperation on the establishment of the European Public Prosecutor's Office ('the EPPO') [2017] OJ L283/1 (EPPO Regulation).

[18] See generally Deirdre Curtin, *Executive Power of the European Union. Law, Practices and the Living Constitution* (Oxford University Press 2009) 65–66; regarding EU law enforcement, see Miroslava Scholten and Michiel Luchtman (eds), *Law Enforcement by EU Authorities. Implications for Political and Judicial Accountability* (Edward Elgar 2017) 19; regarding specifically physical conduct in EU composite procedures, see Xanthoulis (n 9) 69–71.

[19] Regulation (EU) 2018/1725 of the European Parliament and of the Council of 23 October 2018 on the protection of natural persons with regard to the processing of personal data by the Union institutions, bodies, offices and agencies and on the free movement of such data, and repealing Regulation (EC) No 45/2001 and Decision No 1247/2002/EC [2018] OJ L295/39.

in a breach of human dignity (Article 1 CFR)[20] or the freedom to conduct a business (Article 16 CFR).[21] Irregularities committed by Commission officials implementing EU competition law, officials of the European Anti-Fraud Office (OLAF) under Regulation 883/2013,[22] or ECB officials in the implementation of the SSM Regulation during an inspection at the premises of an undertaking, might result in a breach of Article 7 CFR (protection of 'home', including business premises)[23] or a breach of the right to property (Article 17 CFR).[24] Last but not least, the exercise of executive powers by Frontex operational staff during joint operations at sea and/or land borders[25] could amount to a breach of the right to life (Article 2 CFR), the right to the integrity of the person (Article 3 CFR), prohibition of torture and inhuman or degrading treatment or punishment (Article 4 CFR), or the right to asylum (Article 18 CFR) and non-refoulement (Article 19 CFR).

The ability of EU factual conduct to directly and indirectly breach fundamental rights raises in turn the issue of ensuring adequate legal protection and remedies against such conduct. Are legal safeguards and remedies necessary and, if so, sufficiently available to address fundamental rights breaches by EU factual conduct?

[20] See, for instance, the so-called *Tillack* judgments, Case T-193/04 *Tillack v Commission* [2006] ECLI:EU:T:2006:292; and Case C-521/04 PR *Tillack v Commission* [2005] ECLI:EU:C:2005:240.

[21] For instance, EBA's 'naming and shaming' register in the AML/CFT database, see European Banking Authority, Final report on draft regulatory technical standards under Article 9a (1) and (3) of Regulation (EU) No 1093/2010 setting up an AML/CFT central database and specifying the materiality of weaknesses, the type of information collected, the practical implementation of the information collection and the analysis and dissemination of the information contained therein (European Banking Authority, 20 December 2021).

[22] Regulation (EU, Euratom) No 883/2013 of the European Parliament and of the Council of 11 September 2013 concerning investigations conducted by the European Anti-Fraud Office (OLAF) and repealing Regulation (EC) No 1073/1999 of the European Parliament and of the Council and Council Regulation (Euratom) No 1074/1999 as amended by Regulation (EU, Euratom) 2016/2030 of the European Parliament and of the Council of 26 October 2016 amending Regulation (EU, Euratom) No 883/2013, as regards the secretariat of the Supervisory Committee of the European Anti-Fraud Office (OLAF) [2016] OJ L317/1.

[23] See Case C-94/00 *Roquette Frères SA v Directeur général de la concurrence, de la consommation et de la répression des fraudes, and Commission of the European Communities* [2002] ECLI:EU:C:2002:603; and Case C-583/13 P *Deutsche Bahn AG and Others v Commission* [2015] ECLI:EU:C:2015:404.

[24] E.g., if during the inspection certain belongings (e.g., computers, hardware, furniture, etc.) of the company investigated are damaged.

[25] E.g., use of firearms, the use of force with a view to immobilising persons crossing the Union's external borders or to preclude persons from entering the EU territory, the forced confinement of a person within a specific area, or the refusal to offer support to persons in distress.

12.3 LEGAL PROTECTION AGAINST FUNDAMENTAL RIGHTS BREACHES BY EU FACTUAL CONDUCT

Factual conduct by EU bodies is prescribed and confined by law. The relevant legal framework provides rules and principles establishing when, how, under what conditions, and by whom factual conduct can occur in order to conduce to the legal effects assigned to it by legal norms.[26] In other words, factual conduct, just like formal legal acts, needs to abide by the principle of legality of administrative action[27] as a specific reflection of the rule of law underpinning the EU legal order.[28] According to some, 'the test of the legality of factual conduct should not differ from that applicable to formal measures taken by the administration'.[29] In this respect, EU factual conduct must occur within the boundaries of the competence of the relevant EU actor and it must observe all relevant substantive and procedural rules applicable. Moreover, it should meet 'the standards of the general principles of law which generally govern the legality of EU acts, such as the principles of good administration, proportionality, and the protection of fundamental rights'.[30] EU factual conduct meeting these legality standards should not in principle result by itself in breaches of fundamental rights. On the contrary, EU factual conduct that does not meet the legality standards mentioned previously could entail breaches of fundamental rights, as already shown earlier in this chapter. In this context, legitimate questions arise as to how legal review of such conduct can be ensured and whether there is adequate legal protection for

[26] E.g., Regulation 1/2003 provides detailed rules according to which the Commission's investigations and inspections of undertakings suspected of breaches of Articles 101–102 TFEU are to take place; similarly, Regulation 2018/1725, and more specific legal acts, such as the EPPO Regulation, Regulation (EU) 2016/794 of the European Parliament and of the Council of 11 May 2016 on the European Union Agency for Law Enforcement Cooperation (Europol) and replacing and repealing Council Decisions 2009/371/JHA, 2009/934/JHA, 2009/935/JHA, 2009/936/JHA and 2009/968/JHA [2016] OJ L135/53 (Europol Regulation); and Regulation (EU) 2018/1862 of the European Parliament and of the Council of 28 November 2018 on the establishment, operation and use of the Schengen Information System (SIS) in the field of police cooperation and judicial cooperation in criminal matters, amending and repealing Council Decision 2007/533/JHA, and repealing Regulation (EC) No 1986/2006 of the European Parliament and of the Council and Commission Decision 2010/261/EU [2018] OJ L312/56 (SIS Regulation), as regards, for instance, access by Europol to the 'SIS' database (Article 48), lay down detailed rules and safeguards pertaining to the exercise of processing data operations by EU bodies as controllers and processors.

[27] See Hofmann, Rowe, and Türk (n 10) 151–153; and Xanthoulis (n 9) 72–73.

[28] Case C-294/83 *Les Verts v Parliament* [1986] ECLI:EU:C:1986:166, para 23.

[29] Hofmann, Rowe, and Türk (n 10) 672.

[30] Ibid; see also Case C-583/11 P. *Inuit Tapiriit Kanatami and Others v Parliament and Council* [2013] ECLI:EU:C:2013:625, para 91.

the person affected against such breaches in light inter alia of the rights to an effective legal remedy enshrined in Article 47 CFR.[31]

The legal protection, and, in this context, also the legal review of EU factual conduct affecting fundamental rights is examined in a more overarching fashion in Sections 12.4 and 12.5, by looking first at available judicial remedies in light of Article 47 CFR and, second, by considering additional EU administrative/non-judicial mechanisms and remedies that might offer redress for fundamental rights breaches.

12.4 JUDICIAL REMEDIES

12.4.1 *The Right to an Effective Judicial Remedy for Fundamental Rights Breaches*

Article 47 CFR proclaims the right to an effective remedy before a tribunal for 'everyone whose rights and freedoms guaranteed by the law of the Union are violated'. This provision does not expressly specify or limit the ways in which rights and freedoms could be violated, which would imply that any type of violation, be it through a formal legal act or factual conduct, should be covered by the right to an effective (judicial) remedy. The view that factual conduct comes within the scope of Article 47 CFR and that, as a result, it should be matched by full legal protection in the form of appropriate judicial remedies, finds support in legal scholarship.[32] As for the Court of Justice, one may wonder whether its rather restrictive 'dependent approach'[33] to Article 47 CFR could entail limitations on judicial review of factual conduct and, implicitly, on the remedies the individual whose fundamental rights have been breached might effectively rely on. More specifically, drawing on the non-binding Explanations relating to the Charter of Fundamental Rights,[34] the Court affirmed in its landmark *Inuit* judgment,[35] that Article 47 CFR 'is not intended to change the system of judicial review laid down by the Treaties, and particularly the rules relating to the admissibility of direct actions brought

[31] Though legal review of EU administrative action (focusing on the question of whether the conduct of administration takes place in accordance with applicable law, without being necessary per se that that conduct also results in breaches of fundamental rights) is an important means to ensure effective protection of fundamental rights, it is not to be equated, however, with legal protection/remedies enabling a person to prevent or remedy a breach of his/her rights.

[32] Rademacher (n 4) 419–421.

[33] Ibid 412–413.

[34] Explanations relating to the Charter of Fundamental Rights [2007] OJ C303/17, 29.

[35] *Inuit* (n 30) para 97.

before the Courts of the European Union'. As a result, it appears that Article 47 CFR cannot be relied upon to establish new judicial remedies/review avenues or to amend those enshrined in the TFEU.[36]

However, within these confines, it is argued that Article 47 TFEU, giving expression to the principle of effective judicial protection and enshrining it as a fundamental right, could be used creatively by EU courts. It should be relied upon as a canon of interpretation regarding access to the judicial remedies laid down in the Treaties for persons invoking breaches of their fundamental rights by EU acts and measures. Such an approach could arguably offer a quick fix to the potential gaps within the current EU system of judicial remedies regarding violations of fundamental rights, until the more far-reaching solutions suggested by the Court – that is, the use of the formal amendment procedure of the Founding Treaties,[37] and the Member States' duties 'to establish a system of legal remedies and procedures which ensure respect for the fundamental right to effective judicial protection'[38] – have fully addressed the issue.

Against this background, one needs to consider how far the judicial remedies available for individuals enshrined in the Treaties and carved out through CJEU jurisprudence are effective in addressing the breaches of fundamental rights caused by EU factual conduct. The following judicial remedies are briefly examined for the purpose of this query: action for annulment (Article 263 TFEU), failure to act (Article 265 TFEU), preliminary reference procedure (Article 267 TFEU), action for damages (Article 268 *juncto* Article 340 TFEU), and plea of illegality (Article 277 TFEU).

12.4.2 *The Action for Annulment*

The action for annulment appears to raise particular challenges with regard to EU factual conduct in view of its admissibility conditions. Especially the fact

[36] In particular, TFEU arts 263 (action for annulment), 265 (action for failure to act), 267 (preliminary reference), 277 (plea of illegality), and 268 *juncto* 340 (action for damages); for a view criticising the Court's reading of Article 47 CFR, and further suggesting creative judicial remedies and review mechanisms with regard to the factual conduct by EU administration, see Rademacher (n 4) 421–424.

[37] Case C-50/00 P *Unión de Pequeños Agricultores (UPA)* [2002] ECLI:EU:C:2002:462, para 45.

[38] *Inuit* (n 30) paras 100–104. Regarding the Member States' duty to ensure respect for the fundamental right to effective judicial protection, Rademacher carefully concluded, based on a comparative overview of four national legal systems (Germany, France, Austria, and the UK, as a former EU Member State) that there is a trend in the EU Member States to increasingly extend judicial protection to factual conduct, see Rademacher (n 4) 426–428. Yet it is difficult to see how legal remedies in the Member States could be effective against factual conduct by EU bodies, whose actions can in principle be reviewed only by EU courts.

that only acts of EU bodies that are 'intended to produce legal effects *vis-à-vis* third parties' are judicially reviewable arguably creates a considerable hurdle for persons willing to challenge before the CJEU EU factual conduct infringing their rights. As recently reconfirmed by the CJEU, 'it is settled case-law of the Court that actions for annulment, provided for under Article 263 TFEU, are available in the case of all measures adopted by the institutions, bodies, offices and agencies of the European Union, whatever their form, *which are intended to have binding legal effects*' (emphasis added).[39] This means that unless EU factual conduct qualifies as an act or measure intended to have binding legal effects, it cannot be directly challenged under Article 263 TFEU. This observation raises two questions: (1) Could EU factual conduct qualify under certain circumstances as 'an act or measure intended to have binding legal effects'? and (2) Is there any (indirect) way to review the legality of EU factual conduct that does not qualify as 'an act or measure intended to have binding legal effects' under Article 263 TFEU?

The answer to the first question could be positive, especially if Article 263 TFEU is read in light of Article 47 CFR, as suggested earlier. After all, the Court considers reviewable under Article 263 TFEU any EU measures intended to have binding legal effects, *whatever their form* (emphasis added). In this respect, the Court was quite creative in the past in inferring from a physical act directly affecting the situation of the applicant the existence of a tacit administrative decision that could be reviewed under the annulment procedure.[40] In such a case, one may wonder whether factual conduct is in itself the expression of the challengeable tacit or implicit legal act or whether it is a mere indication of the existence of a previous tacit administrative decision that is being implemented via the physical act. By referring in *Akzo and Akcros* to 'the tacit rejection decision *expressed through* (emphasis added) the physical act of seizing and placing those documents on the file without placing them in a sealed envelope',[41] the CJEU seems to show a slight preference for the first scenario. In this vein, one could consider the factual conduct directly affecting the legal situation of the individual, similarly to a formal legal binding act, as some sort of '*instant*' implicit decision, whereby

[39] Case C-911/19 *Fédération bancaire française (FBF) v Autorité de contrôle prudentiel et de résolution (ACPR)* [2021] ECLI:EU:C:2021:599, para 36; this judgment largely confirms the CJEU's long-standing view on acts challengeable under the annulment procedure, see, for instance, Joined Cases T-125/03 and T-253/03 *Akzo Nobel Chemicals Ltd, and Akcros Chemicals Ltd v Commission* [2007] ECLI:EU:T:2007:287, para 45; and Case C-60/81 *IBM v Commission* [1981] ECLI:EU:C:1981:264, para 9.

[40] See *Akzo and Akcros* (n 39) paras 49 and 52.

[41] Ibid para 52.

the physical act itself amounts to a legally binding act. Such a legal construct, reflecting a more extensive understanding of the concept of 'act intended to produce legal effects *vis-à-vis* third parties' read in light of Article 47 CFR, could capture various situations in which free-standing EU factual conduct directly breaches fundamental rights.[42] While the concept of 'instant implicit decision' might still need to gain ground, EU legal scholars highlight, more in line with the second scenario, that the notion of a tacit or implicit decision '*underpinning* [emphasis added] a physical act or factual measure is common in the administrative law of the Member States', and they argue for its extended application to ensure more effective protection of fundamental rights against EU factual conduct.[43] In any case, if free-standing factual conduct does not amount somehow to an act intended to have binding legal effects, it cannot be reviewed under Article 263 TFEU.

This brings us to the second question: Is there any (indirect) way to review the legality of EU factual conduct that does not qualify as 'an act or measure intended to have binding legal effects'? Legal review of factual conduct could in principle be ensured incidentally, in view of the relationship of such conduct with a legal act reviewable under Article 263 TFEU. Most obviously, factual conduct that can be qualified as 'preparatory acts' of a legally reviewable act can be reviewed by the Court in the context of the challenge brought to the latter act.[44] This, however, raises the question whether such legal review does not sometimes come too late, as the relevant factual conduct might have produced legal and practical consequences well before the adoption of the legal act.[45] Furthermore, if no legally binding act is finally adopted, then any 'preparatory' factual conduct carried out prior to that will not be in principle judicially reviewable,[46] unless such factual conduct represents 'the culmination of a special procedure … and which produce binding legal effects such as to affect the interests of an applicant, by bringing about a distinct change in his legal position'.[47] As for the factual conduct that *implements* legally binding

[42] In Rademacher's view, the CJEU's *AKZO* line of case law – *AKZO* (n 11) and *Akzo and Akcros* (n 39) – marks a more flexible approach to the admissibility conditions for annulment, underpinned by the concern to offer judicial protection against breaches of fundamental rights and legal interests by EU actions, and entailing that 'any act capable of violating an applicant's right or legally protected interest was considered to be – for this very reason – binding on him or her or it', see Rademacher (n 4) 407.

[43] Hofmann, Rowe, and Türk (n 10) 669.

[44] *IBM* (n 39) para 12; see also Koen Lenaerts and Others, *EU Procedural Law* (Oxford University Press 2014) 273–274.

[45] See Rademacher (n 4) 423–424.

[46] See Hofmann, Rowe, and Türk (n 10) 667–668.

[47] See *Akzo and Akcros* (n 39) para 45.

acts, legal review is reserved in principle only to the legally binding act, on the ground that 'the validity of a decision cannot be affected by acts subsequent to its adoption'.[48] The only apparent exception seems to be in the case of factual conduct entailing or underpinning an implicit or tacit legal act, but even in that case it is questionable whether the Court actually reviews the implementing physical act itself or rather exclusively the underlying implicit/tacit legally binding act. In this regard, the concept of '*instant*' implicit decision could perhaps bring some added explanatory value with respect to the legal review of such 'factual conduct' by conceptually equating the physical act with a reviewable act under Article 263 TFEU (not with the mere implementation thereof).[49]

12.4.3 *Failure to Act*

Failure to act is to some extent the mirror image of the action for annulment,[50] and it could also be of relevance as far as breaches of fundamental rights via EU factual conduct are concerned. Article 265 TFEU, third paragraph enables individuals to go to the CJEU for failure of an EU institution, body, office, or agency to address to them 'any act', except for recommendations and opinions. Yet it becomes apparent that individuals can rely on this judicial remedy only where the relevant EU body failed to adopt a legally binding act concerning them,[51] while being under an obligation to do so.[52] Hence, similarly to the action for annulment, failure to act does not seem a particularly suitable legal remedy against EU factual conduct, except for those instances in which the factual conduct that should have been enacted by the defaulting EU body would amount to an implicit decision impacting on the legal situation of the individual.[53] Additionally, for a potential action under Article 265 TFEU to be admissible, the relevant EU body must have 'been

[48] Case 85/87 *Dow Benelux NV v Commission* [1989] ECLI:EU:C:1989:379, para 49; see also Lenaerts and Others (n 44) 277.

[49] This would bring us back to the scenario discussed earlier under the first question, i.e., free-standing factual conduct that amounts to an act intended to have binding legal effects.

[50] Some call the two actions 'two sides of the same coin', Lenaerts and Others (n 44) 426.

[51] Ibid 425 and 430–431, and the case law cited there.

[52] Ibid 422–424.

[53] Examples of such 'failures' could be, e.g.: the failure to rectify within a reasonable deadline personal data in an EU database at the legitimate request of the data subject; failure by an EU official to remove from the website of the relevant EU body personal data posted there in breach of the relevant EU data protection legislation; failure by a Frontex official to intervene to stop an ongoing infringement of fundamental rights of an individual during a joint operation; failure of an EU Commission official to take specific actions to ensure appropriate protection of the documents and items collected during an investigation taking place at the

called upon to act' by the individual and, furthermore, not defined its position on the matter after being called to act.[54] As a final point, if successful, the action for failure to act results in a court judgment with a rather limited impact: declaring that the failure to act was illegal but without the possibility to impose on the EU body the type, content, and form of the act that should have been taken.[55]

12.4.4 *Preliminary Reference Procedure*

Arguably, some of the gaps resulting from the limited judicial review of factual conduct under Article 263 TFEU could be covered by the preliminary reference procedure under Article 267 TFEU (see also Chapter 4). As is well known from the CJEU's jurisprudence, the admissibility of a question for preliminary ruling extends to the interpretation and validity of *any acts* of EU institutions, bodies, offices, or agencies.[56] This clearly covers formal acts, be they legally binding or not, but it is less clear if EU factual conduct in the form of a mere physical act also qualifies as an 'act' under Article 267 TFEU.[57] A reading of Article 267 TFEU in light of the fundamental right to an effective legal remedy enshrined in Article 47 CFR offers support for the view that the category of acts of EU bodies 'without any exception'[58] encompasses also physical acts representing factual conduct.[59]

Yet, even if this is the case, there are several difficulties with judicial review of EU factual conduct under Article 267 TFEU. First, for a preliminary question on EU factual conduct to be raised before a national court, there must be a decision or measure adopted by a national authority that the person

premises of an undertaking, potentially leading to the loss or destruction of the respective documents and items.

54 TFEU art 265, second paragraph; for a detailed analysis, see Lenaerts and Others (n 44) 432–435.

55 See Lenaerts and Others (n 44) 439–440.

56 See Case C-322/88 *Salvatore Grimaldi v Fonds des maladies professionnelles* [1989] ECLI:EU:C:1989:646, paras 8–9, and subsequent confirmatory CJEU jurisprudence, most recently, Case C-16/16P *Belgium v Commission* [2018] ECLI:EU:C:2018:79, para 44; *FBF v ACPR* (n 39) paras 56–57; and Case C-501/18 *BT v Balgarska Narodna Banka* [2021] ECLI:EU:C:2021:249, para 82; see also Lenaerts and Others (n 44) 464.

57 Unless, of course, it expresses a tacit/implicit decision.

58 *BT* (n 56) para 82.

59 See, in this vein, Hofmann, Rowe, and Türk (n 10) 668. Further support for such a conclusion is provided by the *Tillack* case, in which the General Court highlighted the possibility for the applicant to ask the competent national court to refer a preliminary question to the CJEU on the validity of an 'act' of forwarding information to national authorities by OLAF, *Tillack* (n 20) para 80.

who claims their fundamental rights are being breached by that EU conduct could challenge.[60] Second, the national measure/act challenged before the national court should be sufficiently linked to the EU factual conduct in such a way that establishing the validity of the latter would enable the national court to decide on the matter.[61] If the national court does not find the relevant EU factual conduct 'necessary' to judge the case before it, the matter will not in principle reach the CJEU.[62] Third, even if a question for a preliminary ruling regarding the validity of EU factual conduct reaches the CJEU, it has been emphasised that judicial review might often come too late to ensure effective protection of the fundamental rights affected by that conduct.[63]

12.4.5 *Action for Damages*

In view of the shortcomings highlighted earlier, the action for damages enshrined in Articles 268 *juncto* 340 TFEU could in principle offer a more reliable remedy against breaches of fundamental rights caused by EU factual conduct.[64] In any case, prima facie the action for damages has a generous scope as it covers '*any damage* (emphasis added) caused by its institutions or by servants in the performance of their duties'. It thus covers both material and non-material damage[65] caused by any acts (both formal legal binding acts as well as factual conduct) of the EU 'institutions'[66] or EU servants. However, this judicial remedy also displays several shortcomings and difficulties.

First, in spite of the apparently generous, though slightly vague,[67] formulation in the Founding Treaties, the standards for EU liability are in reality quite

[60] If there is no identifiable national conduct, Article 267 TFEU cannot be triggered, TFEU art 267; see also Rademacher (n 4) 410.

[61] According to Article 267 TFEU, second paragraph, the national court considers that a decision on the preliminary question 'is necessary' to judge on the matter before it, TFEU art 267.

[62] See Rademacher (n 4) 410.

[63] See Hofmann, Rowe, and Türk (n 10) 668.

[64] See also Melanie Fink, 'EU Liability for Contributions to Member States' Breaches of EU Law' (2019) 56 (5) Common Market Law Review 1227, 1233.

[65] See Paul Craig and Grainne de Burca, *EU Law. Text, Cases and Materials* (7th edn, Oxford University Press 2020) 633, and the case law cited there.

[66] To be read broadly, in light of Article 47 CFR, as encompassing also EU bodies, offices, and agencies; such a broad reading is also confirmed in the CJEU's jurisprudence – see, for instance, *Tillack* (n 20) para 97 restating that 'an action to establish liability seeks compensation for damage resulting from a measure or from unlawful conduct, attributable to a *Community institution or body* (emphasis added)'.

[67] I.e., the generic reference to 'the general principles common to the laws of the Member States' entails a lot of leeway for the CJEU in identifying and shaping the conditions and criteria for establishing the existence and extent of the Union's liability for damages.

high,[68] as they are interpreted and applied quite strictly by EU courts.[69] While a breach of fundamental rights via EU factual conduct could relatively easily meet the condition that 'the rule of law infringed must be intended to confer rights on the individual', things become more difficult with the requirement that 'the breach must be sufficiently serious', as well as with the 'damage' and the 'causal link'. Proving a sufficiently serious breach is in principle easier in the case of an EU measure that does not entail discretionary choices,[70] and it proves particularly difficult where the EU measure entails the exercise of some degree of discretionary power; in this respect, even an illegal EU measure annulled under Article 263 TFEU is not per se sufficient to meet the threshold for a sufficiently serious breach under Article 340 TFEU.[71] In our view, Article 47 CFR requires a more lenient reading of the CJEU's 'sufficiently serious breach' condition under Article 340 TFEU, so that EU legally binding acts, including here factual conduct amounting to an instant implicit decision, as well as genuine factual conduct in the form of self-standing physical acts that directly breach fundamental rights, meet the threshold as a matter of principle.[72] As to the damage suffered as a result of EU factual

[68] See Landmark Case C-352/98 P *Bergaderm and Goupil v Commission* [2000] ECLI:EU:C:2000:361, and subsequent relevant jurisprudence in the footprints of '*Bergaderm*'.

[69] See Melanie Fink, 'The Action for Damages as a Fundamental Rights Remedy: Holding Frontex Liable' (2020) 21 German Law Journal 532, 547; one obvious consequence of the CJEU's restrictive approach to EU liability is that, in practice, the likelihood that actions for damages by individuals claiming fundamental rights breaches are successful is fairly small.

[70] 'Where … the institution in question has only considerably reduced, or even no, discretion, the mere infringement of Community law *may* (emphasis added) be sufficient to establish the existence of a sufficiently serious breach' *Bergaderm* (n 68) para 44.

[71] See Case T-212/03 *My Travel Group v Commission* [2008] ELCI:EU:T:2008:315, paras 41–43; specifically with regard to the situation in which the illegal EU measure annulled by the CJEU does not amount to a sufficiently serious breach, though it also entails a breach of the fundamental rights of the individual, see Case T-341/07 *Sison v Council* [2011] ECLI:EU:T:2011:687, paras 73–80; and Fink, 'The Action for Damages' (n 69) 542. Whereas the annulment action and the action for damages follow a different rationale and, therefore, feature different criteria and conditions, a reading of Article 340 TFEU in light of Article 47 CFR should entail closer equivalence between an infringement of EU law under Article 263 TFEU and a sufficiently serious breach under Article 340 TFEU, in particular when breaches of fundamental rights are at stake; as a result, the main concern in an action for damages for fundamental rights breaches should be on establishing the damage and the causal link between the breach and the damage.

[72] See also Rademacher (n 4) 434; this author calls for the 'modernisation' of Article 340 TFEU, basically in the form of a more lenient reading of the conditions for damages, in particular the sufficiently serious breach (to be understood as any breach of EU law conferring rights on the individual) and the damage (when an injunction or mere symbolic compensation is requested); for a similar view supporting more generally the lowering of the EU liability threshold in case of fundamental rights breaches, see Fink, 'The Action for Damages' (n 69) 543.

conduct breaching fundamental rights, this might be difficult to establish and quantify,[73] especially in view of the non-pecuniary consequences that the breach of some fundamental rights entails.[74] Last but not least, the causal link between the EU factual conduct and the damage might be difficult to establish, especially when it is embedded into a broader complex framework entailing concomitant or subsequent actions by EU and Member State actors that might interfere with the causation chain.[75]

Second, the monetary compensation that is usually provided within the framework of the action for damages might not fully remedy the situation where redressing a breach of fundamental rights by EU factual conduct would require positive administrative action to end the breach and re-establish the situation before the breach occurred.[76] Yet this point of critique seems to be at least partly addressed by the fact that EU courts acknowledge that Article 340 TFEU does not in principle exclude compensation in kind 'if necessary in the form of an injunction to do or not to do something' if this is in line with the general principles of non-contractual liability common to the laws of the Member States.[77] However, one may wonder how far EU courts are willing to have recourse to such types of compensation more extensively and especially

[73] According to CJEU jurisprudence, 'actual damage' must have been suffered entailing that the applicant must prove before the court a 'real and certain' loss, see, for instance, Case T-88/09 *Idromacchine Srl, Alessandro Capuzzo and Roberto Capuzzo v European Commission* [2011] ECLI:EU:T:2011:641, para 25.

[74] For instance, breaches of human dignity or the right to liberty and security by factual conduct of Frontex staff during joint operations, breaches of privacy and data protection rights by personal data processing operations, etc. While Article 340 TFEU enshrines the obligation for the EU to 'make good any damage', in practice it appears that the CJEU awards damages for non-material damage only exceptionally; and see Craig and de Burca (n 65) 633; for an instance in which compensation for non-material damage has been awarded, see *Idromacchine* (n 73) paras 29–80.

[75] Hybrid, composite, or shared administrative procedures/frameworks entailing complex interactions between EU and Member State actors are a case in point; for an example illustrating this point as far as liability for fundamental rights breaches through processing/dissemination of personal data by an EU body is concerned, see *Tillack* (n 20) and Rademacher (n 4) 411; for examples raising the same issue in the context of EU external border management, see Melanie Fink, *Frontex and Human Rights: Responsibility in 'Multi-actor Situations' under the ECHR and EU Public Liability Law* (Oxford University Press 2019) 180–316.

[76] Some examples illustrating this are the need to compel the relevant EU body to withdraw, rectify, or delete inaccurate personal data made public and harming the privacy, reputation, or other fundamental rights of the individual; the need to put an end to a 'pushback' operation and allow the people subject to such physical actions to cross the EU border and submit an asylum application; and the need to compel the relevant EU body not to use for any purpose and to return documents and information seized illegally during an investigation.

[77] See *Idromacchine* (n 73) para 81; see also Case T-279/03 *Galileo International Technology and Others v Commission* [2006] ECLI:EU:T:2006:121, para 63, in which the Court exceptionally

in cases of fundamental rights breaches by EU factual conduct.[78] A reading of Article 340 TFEU in light of the right to an effective judicial remedy in Article 47 CFR would, in our view, justify such an approach.

12.4.6 *Plea of Illegality*

Another judicial remedy provided in the Founding Treaties is the more indirect plea of illegality under Article 277 TFEU. This remedy is limited in three ways: (1) it can be invoked only against an act of general application; (2) only the four grounds for annulment laid down in the second paragraph of Article 263 TFEU may be invoked to establish the illegality of the act; and (3) the illegality of the act only triggers the inapplicability of that act within the direct action before the EU court in which the plea of illegality has been raised.[79] This remedy seems prima facie of limited relevance in the case of EU factual conduct causing breaches of fundamental rights. Only in the rather unlikely scenario in which EU factual conduct would express an (instant) implicit binding legal act of general application, and on the basis of which individual acts or measures are enacted directly affecting the legal situation of the individual, could Article 277 TFEU be invoked within a direct action against such individual acts or measures.[80]

12.4.7 *Incomplete Judicial Protection for Fundamental Rights Breaches by EU Factual Conduct*

One may question whether the paradigm of 'a complete system of legal remedies and procedures designed to ensure judicial review of the legality of European Union acts' announced by the CJEU in *Les Verts*[81] and reaffirmed in *Inuit*[82] withstands a reality check, as far as EU factual conduct breaching

granted such compensation in kind in the form of an injunction against the Commission, by prohibiting it from using a trademark (paras 64–73).

78 This seems particularly relevant in the case of factual conduct, as full restitution and compensation might often be more difficult to obtain because of the material consequences deriving from physical acts, as compared to formal legal acts; lacking such compensatory intervention, the victim will be left with financial or symbolic compensation as the sole remedy for the violation of their fundamental rights through EU factual conduct.

79 Lenaerts and Others (n 44) 453.

80 See, for an instance in which notices for an invitation to tender were qualified as 'general acts' reviewable under Article 277 TFEU, Case C-92/78 *Simmenthal v Commission* [1979] ECLI: EU:C:1979:53.

81 *Les Verts* (n 28) para 23.

82 *Inuit* (n 30) para 92.

fundamental rights is concerned. Especially if this paradigm is read in light of Article 47 CFR asserting a judicially effective remedy for 'everyone whose rights and freedoms guaranteed by the law of the Union are violated'. Based on the previous analysis, one may argue that the judicial remedies available in the Founding Treaties reveal shortcomings as to the completeness and effectiveness of judicial protection in such instances.[83] Solutions to address this could be: (1) an extensive understanding of the concept of 'reviewable act' in line with *AKZO* jurisprudence whereby factual conduct directly affecting the legal situation and fundamental rights of the individual would amount to implicit reviewable legal acts[84] and (2) a far-reaching interpretation of the action for damages encompassing extensive ways of compensation and a more flexible reading of the conditions for damages that could cover, at least in part, the blind spots of current judicial review of EU factual conduct.[85] It remains to be seen how far EU Courts will be willing to consider such solutions in their future jurisprudence, but even if they do, gaps will arguably remain in the EU system of judicial remedies (especially as regards the lack of preventive judicial protection against potentially harmful EU factual conduct).[86]

[83] See also Jens-Peter Schneider, 'Information Exchange and Its Problems' in Carol Harlow, Päivi Leino, and Giacinto della Cananea (eds), *Research Handbook on EU Administrative Law* (Edward Elgar 2017) 104–105. The fact that, pending a direct action before the CJEU, the Court may suspend the act contested (Article 278 TFEU) and prescribe any interim measures (Article 279 TFEU) does not alter this observation: first, suspension and other interim measures are ancillary to a direct action before the CJEU and normally are granted only after a direct action was brought before the CJEU – see Lenaerts and Others (n 44) 569 – but bringing such an action against EU factual conduct remains quite difficult to begin with (especially under Article 263 TFEU), TFEU arts 263 and 278–279; second, the principle remains that actions before EU courts do not have suspensory effect, meaning that EU judges will only exceptionally order the suspension of the contested measure or prescribe interim relief measures, Lenaerts and Others (n 44) 563; third, while Article 279 TFEU refers to 'any necessary interim measures', which may also include appropriate injunctions against EU institutions, bodies, offices, and agencies, EU courts seem to be particularly cautious with granting such measures, guided by the concern to avoid exercising powers vested with other EU institutions and thereby disturbing the principle of institutional balance, see Lenaerts and Others (n 44) 565–566 and 569.

[84] See Herwig, C H Hofmann, and Morgane Tidghi 'Rights and Remedies in Implementation of EU Policies by Multi-Jurisdictional Networks' (2014) 20(1) European Public Law 147, 155.

[85] See Rademacher (n 4) 430–435 and Fink 'The Action for Damages' (n 69) 543. Rademacher in particular maintains that EU courts should consider granting more extensively non-monetary compensation (including in the form of declaratory and injunctive measures) for breaches of fundamental rights by EU factual conduct, see Rademacher (n 4) 432.

[86] This gap has been acknowledged more broadly also by EU courts as far as potentially harmful EU actions that do not amount to legally binding acts are concerned: 'although it may seem desirable that individuals should have, in addition to the possibility of an action for damages, a remedy under which actions of the Community institutions liable to prejudice their interests but which do not amount to decisions may be prevented or brought to an end, it is clear that a

Therefore, it may be opportune to look further afield and also consider other (non-judicial) remedies available in EU law to assess whether they may or could, alone or in combination with available EU judicial remedies, address some of the gaps and shortcomings highlighted earlier

12.5 NON-JUDICIAL REMEDIES

12.5.1 *Non-judicial Remedies and the Right/Principle of Good Administration*

While discussions on legal review and legal protection usually focus on the availability and sufficiency of judicial remedies, one should not forget that, in a broad sense, the system of legal remedies is not limited to that. While judicial remedies, in view of their importance, could be placed at the forefront of the Union's system of legal protection, non-judicial remedies also play a role in ensuring review of and redress against EU administrative action. In fact, under certain conditions, non-judicial remedies (i.e., actions and procedures against administrative actions that do not directly involve courts) could arguably be more accessible and effective in addressing fundamental rights breaches of individuals, be they natural or legal persons. Thus, compared to costly, time-consuming, and restrictive judicial remedies, non-judicial internal and external remedies and review mechanisms in the form of complaints,[87] referrals,[88] and appeals procedures[89] could provide easier access, comprehensive scrutiny, and relatively timely redress against potentially harmful EU administrative measures, including factual conduct.[90] After all, in light of the commandment of an 'open, efficient and independent

remedy of that nature, which would necessarily involve the Community judicature issuing directions to the institutions, is not provided for by the Treaty', Joined Cases T-377/00, 379/00, 380/00, T-260/01 and 272/01 *Philip Morris and Others v Commission* [2003] ECLI:EU:T:2003:6, para 124; see also Rademacher (n 4) 434.

87 E.g., complaints to the European Ombudsman, Frontex complaint procedure against fundamental rights breaches.

88 E.g., the referral of 'any act of an executive agency which injures a third party' to the Commission for a legality review, Council Regulation (EC) No 58/2003 of 19 December 2002 laying down the statute for executive agencies to be entrusted with certain tasks in the management of Community programmes [2003] OJ L11/1, art 22.

89 E.g., the procedure before the boards of appeal of EU agencies, see for a comprehensive work on this topic, Merijn Chamon, Annalisa Volpato, and Mariolina Eliantonio (eds), *Boards of Appeal of EU Agencies: Towards Judicialization of Administrative Review?* (Oxford University Press 2022).

90 Especially if such administrative remedies/procedures also provide for possibilities to quickly suspend the application of the measure challenged and/or to impose interim measures.

European administration' in Article 298 (1) TFEU, giving the public administration a chance first to repair its own mistakes and to offer redress via easily accessible non-judicial remedies could largely alleviate the need to have recourse to judicial review.

While access to judicial remedies is enshrined both as a common principle of EU law in CJEU jurisprudence and as a fundamental right under Article 47 CFR, there is no similar explicit constitutional recognition for non-judicial remedies against EU action.[91] Arguably, access to non-judicial remedies could be considered as a dimension of the multi-sided good or sound administration laid down as a fundamental right in Article 41 CFR and also established as a general principle of law by EU courts.[92] Following this line of reasoning, the set-up of effective administrative remedies could be seen as an inherent guarantee for the enforcement of the specific rights encompassed within 'good' or 'sound' administration. It could be arguably incorporated within the scope of 'the right to have his or her affairs handled impartially, fairly and within a reasonable time' under Article 41 (1) CFR. To be sure, availability of an administrative remedy against EU measures affecting individuals is not mentioned in the list of specific rights under Article 41 (2) CFR. Yet it has been maintained that Article 41 CFR only provides 'examples of procedural rights to good administration', and that it 'serves to establish a minimum protection of certain elements generally accepted in the existing case law of the European courts as principles of good administration and rights of defence'.[93] As a result, EU courts could in principle go beyond the rights explicitly listed in Article 41 CFR, though they also warn that 'the principle of sound administration, does not, in itself, confer rights upon individuals ... except where it constitutes the expression of specific rights' like those enshrined in Article 41 CFR.[94] Alternatively, the availability of effective administrative remedies could be regarded as an element of the general principle of good/sound administration continuously developed by EU courts. As mentioned previously, it could function as a guarantee for the exercise and enforcement of the specific rights included within the scope of good

[91] One should note, however, that the EU Ombudsman, as an administrative remedy against maladministration by EU bodies, is enshrined in Article 228 TFEU and Article 43 CFR, TFEU art 228; Charter of Fundamental Rights of the European Union [2016] OJ C202/389 (CFR), art 43.

[92] On the use of 'principle of sound administration' terminology, see *Tillack* (n 20) para 127; on the interchangeable use between 'sound' and 'good' administration, see Hofmann, Rowe, and Türk (n 10) 194.

[93] Hofmann, Rowe, and Türk (n 10) 203; see also the explanations of Article 41 CFR in the Explanations relating to the Charter of Fundamental Rights (n 34) 28.

[94] *Tillack* (n 20) para 127.

administration and enshrined in Article 41 CFR; additionally, it would also be an enabling element for the right to claim damages provided in Article 41 (3) CFR, especially if this is seen, separately from Article 340 TFEU, as a right to claim damages directly from the EU administration at fault (without necessarily ending up before the EU courts).[95]

Since there is a lack of clarity in EU primary law and case law regarding the availability and requirements of non-judicial remedies, the landscape of such remedies is quite diverse and eclectic (see also Chapter 5).[96] In what follows, a few selected non-judicial remedies will be discussed as cases in point as to their applicability to fundamental rights breaches by EU factual conduct. A general observation regarding the mechanisms discussed here is that they are not designed solely to serve as remedies for the individual but to also fulfil other functions pertaining to legal review, scrutiny, and overall accountability of EU public administration (see also Chapter 5).

12.5.2 *EU Ombudsman*

One obvious horizontal non-judicial remedy available against EU acts and measures consists of the possibility, as well as the fundamental right according to Article 43 CFR, for individuals (natural and legal persons) to lodge complaints with the European Ombudsman.[97] This remedy is very generous in terms of accessibility and scope. It is open to all EU citizens as well as any natural and legal person residing or having its registered office in a Member State, and it covers any instance of 'maladministration' in the activities of EU bodies (except for the CJEU).[98] Instances or cases (as enshrined in Article 43

[95] In such a case, the availability of an administrative procedure to claim compensation for the damages incurred as a result of an EU administrative measure would be essential. Article 19 of the European Code of Good Administrative Behaviour seems to imply the availability of non-judicial remedies within the scope of Article 41 CFR: 'A decision of the institution which may adversely affect the rights or interests of a private person shall contain *an indication of the appeal possibilities available for challenging the decision* (emphasis added). It shall in particular indicate the *nature of the remedies, the bodies before which they can be exercised, and the time-limits for exercising them* (emphasis added).' Yet, for the time being, a specific right to an effective administrative remedy cannot be easily spelled out from Article 41 CFR; it will be for the EU courts and/or the EU legislator to do so.

[96] For an observation, in the context of legal protection regarding information exchanges, that supervisory mechanisms are organised 'in very sector specific ways', see Schneider (n 83) 111.

[97] For comprehensive studies on the EU Ombudsman, see Herwig C H Hofmann and Jacques Ziller (eds), *Accountability in the EU: the Role of the European Ombudsman* (Edward Elgar 2017); and Michał Krajewski, *Relative Authority of Judicial and Extra-Judicial Review: EU Courts, Boards of Appeal, Ombudsman* (Hart 2021).

[98] TFEU, art 228(1).

CFR) of maladministration are to be interpreted broadly, including legally binding and non-binding acts, formal acts and measures, as well as factual conduct.[99] This administrative remedy can thus be used by individuals claiming breaches of their fundamental rights by EU factual conduct, such as improper collection or handling of personal data of an individual by an EU body infringing their reputation or privacy and data protection rights, negligent or malevolent physical acts during an investigation resulting in illegal seizure and further disclosure of sensitive documents affecting the legal situation of an individual, or the improper use of physical force by Frontex staff during joint operations at the Union's external borders endangering the life, physical integrity, or liberty of a person.[100]

While the Ombudsman has a broad competence and is easily accessible for individuals alleging breaches of fundamental rights by EU factual conduct, its major limitation consists of the fact that its findings are not binding on the EU administration. The finding of an instance of maladministration in the examples mentioned above is followed by proposed solutions, suggestions, and recommendations for addressing the act of maladministration, but the EU body concerned remains entirely free to accept or reject them.[101] Moreover, the CJEU emphasised in *Tillack* the nature of the Ombudsman as an 'alternative non-judicial remedy' and made clear that the classification as an 'act of maladministration' by the Ombudsman does not, in itself, interfere with the judicial determination of whether the conduct of an EU body is 'a sufficiently serious breach of a rule of law' for the purpose of Article 340 TFEU.[102] However, the prestige of the EU Ombudsman as a moral figure and epistemic authority, supported by sufficient resources and an adequate framework of dialogue and peer pressure in relation to the EU administration, could make it quite an influential and effective actor in successfully addressing instances of

[99] Maladministration by EU bodies may include (but is not limited to) lack of transparency in decision-making, refusal of access to documents and information, violations of fundamental rights, improper use of discretion, etc., see European Ombudsman, Annual Report 2022 (European Ombudsman, 25 April 2023), 5 and 19.

[100] The European Ombudsman may also start an inquiry on its own initiative in such instances, see ibid 11–12.

[101] See TFEU art 228(2) second paragraph and Regulation (EU, Euratom) 2021/1163 of the European Parliament of 24 June 2021 laying down the regulations and general conditions governing the performance of the Ombudsman's duties (Statute of the European Ombudsman) and repealing Decision 94/262/ECSC, EC, Euratom [2021] OJ L 253/1, arts1–3. Since they are non-binding, EU Ombudsman's decisions cannot be challenged in principle before the CJEU under Article 263 TFEU.

[102] *Tillack* (n 20) para 128.

maladministration, including breaches of fundamental rights by EU factual conduct (see also Chapter 5).[103]

12.5.3 *Legal Review of EU Executive Agencies' Acts*

Another interesting non-judicial remedy is provided by Regulation 58/2003 regarding specifically the legal review of the acts of EU executive agencies.[104] Article 22 of Regulation 58/2003 enables any person directly and individually concerned by 'any act of an executive agency which injures a third party' to refer that act to the Commission for a review of its legality. While the requirement that the person is directly and individually concerned by the act mirrors the strict standing conditions for non-privileged applicants under Article 263 TFEU, the reference to 'any act' of the agency arguably encompasses not only formal legally binding acts but also factual conduct in the form of physical acts liable to directly affect the legal situation of the individual.[105] Examples of such 'acts' in the form of factual conduct could be the provision by the European Research Council Executive Agency (ERCEA) or the European Research Executive Agency (REA) of incorrect information and guidelines regarding calls for proposals under EU research grant programmes that misleads some potential applicants and ultimately precludes them from submitting a grant proposal or the compiling and subsequent dissemination by an EU executive agency of a list of potential applicants for EU grant programmes that are considered 'undesirable' because of their perceived 'problematic' political views. Pending the review of the act, the Commission 'may suspend the implementation of the act at issue or prescribe interim measures'.[106] Finally, the Commission may either 'uphold the executive agency's act or decide that the agency must modify it in whole or in part',[107] the respective executive agency being under a duty to comply with the Commission's decision.[108] Quite importantly in this context, according to Article 22 (5), the explicit or implicit decision of the Commission to reject the administrative appeal filed by the individual against the act of the

103 This would be the case where EU administration largely accepts and follows the solutions and recommendations of the EU Ombudsman in practice; positive signs that this is indeed the case transpire from the Ombudsman's annual reports, see, for instance, European Ombudsman, Annual Report 2022 (n 99) 21.

104 Regulation 58/2003.

105 See, for this argument, Hofmann, Rowe, and Türk (n 10) 668.

106 Regulation 58/2003, art 22 (3).

107 Ibid. In our view the modification 'in whole' of the act also covers the possibility to revoke or withdraw the act.

108 Ibid art 22(4).

executive agency[109] is subject to judicial review by the CJEU under Article 263 TFEU. In this way, the agency's act in the form of factual conduct directly breaching the fundamental rights of the applicant could be reviewed indirectly (in the context of the review of the Commission's decision to reject the appeal against the act) by the CJEU.

12.5.4 *Boards of Appeal*

Another rather overarching non-judicial remedy available in EU law is the so-called board of appeal (BoA) featured quite prominently within various EU offices and agencies.[110] Characterised by some as a 'quasi-judicial' remedy,[111] the BoAs are in fact administrative remedies within the structure of the respective EU office or agency that bear certain similarities to courts and court proceedings.[112] In this respect, they enjoy in principle a high degree of independence within the respective office or agency and the procedures before them are generally of an adversarial nature.[113] What is more, it appears that overall the EU legal acts establishing BoAs within various offices and agencies followed the model of EU Courts regarding standing and challengeable acts.[114] Accordingly, in general only decisions of the office or agency that are of direct and individual concern to the individual may be appealed before a BoA.[115] As administrative review bodies, BoAs in principle can exercise

[109] This would normally be coupled with a decision to uphold the agency's act or to modify it differently from what is requested in the applicant's administrative appeal.

[110] E.g., Community Plant Variety Office (CPVO), European Union Intellectual Property Office (EUIPO), European Union Aviation Safety Agency (EASA), European Chemicals Agency (ECHA).

[111] See Case T-133/08 *Schräder v CPVO* [2012] ECLI:EU:T:2012:430, para 137, and Case C-546/12 P *Schräder v CPVO* [2015] ECLI:EU:C:2015:332, paras 73–76; see also Marco Lamandini, 'The ESAs' Board of Appeal as a Blueprint for the Quasi-Judicial Review of European Financial Supervision' (2014) 6 European Company Law 290; and Dominique Ritleng, 'Boards of Appeal of EU Agencies and Article 47 of the Charter: Uneasy Bedfellows?' in Merijn Chamon, Annalisa Volpato, and Mariolina Eliantonio (eds), *Boards of Appeal of EU Agencies: Towards Judicialization of Administrative Review?* (Oxford University Press 2022) 305.

[112] See Ritleng (n 111) 301–306.

[113] Ibid 305.

[114] Merijn Chamon, Annalisa Volpato, and Mariolina Eliantonio, 'Conclusion' in Merijn Chamon, Annalisa Volpato, and Mariolina Eliantonio (eds), *Boards of Appeal of EU Agencies: Towards Judicialization of Administrative Review?* (Oxford University Press 2022) 328–329.

[115] See, for an example, Regulation (EU) 2018/1139 of the European Parliament and of the Council of 4 July 2018 on common rules in the field of civil aviation and establishing a European Union Aviation Safety Agency, and amending Regulations (EC) No 2111/2005, (EC) No 1008/2008, (EU) No 996/2010, (EU) No 376/2014 and Directives 2014/30/EU and 2014/53/EU of the European Parliament and of the Council, and repealing Regulations (EC)

more intensive scrutiny and have more extensive review powers over the contested decision as compared to judicial review, and their binding decisions may be ultimately challenged before EU courts under Article 263 TFEU.[116] However, in view of its admissibility standards, this quite far-reaching administrative remedy seems to be of little relevance as regards factual conduct breaching fundamental rights, except, just like in the case of judicial review under Article 263 TFEU, for those instances in which such factual conduct could qualify as an (instant) tacit or implicit administrative act directly affecting the fundamental rights and legitimate interests of the individual. However, in view of its apparent advantages both as a legal review mechanism and as a potential legal remedy, one may consider further extending the scope of BoAs review in the future, similarly to the legal review model of EU executive agencies' acts, to any acts (including factual conduct) of the EU body affecting the legal situation of the individual and making such a BoA model an entrenched feature of the overall EU institutional framework.

12.5.5 *Frontex Fundamental Rights Complaint Mechanism*

Staying within the sphere of EU agencies, the European Border and Coast Guard Agency (EBCG Agency, Frontex, or 'the Agency') features a specific administrative review mechanism, particularly tailored for breaches of fundamental rights by EU factual conduct. This is the (in)famous complaints mechanism[117] set up on the basis of Article 111 of the EBCG Regulation[118] for addressing alleged breaches of fundamental rights caused by staff involved in the Agency's (operational) activities.[119] Being available free of charge for

No 552/2004 and (EC) No 216/2008 of the European Parliament and of the Council and Council Regulation (EEC) No 3922/91[2018] OJ L212/1 (EASA Regulation) art 109.

[116] See Ritleng (n 111) 301–304.

[117] See, for a harsh critique of the Frontex complaint mechanism, Sergio Carrera and Marco Stefan, 'Complaint Mechanisms in Border Management and Expulsion Operations in Europe. Effective Remedies for Victims of Human Rights Violations?' (2018) Centre for European Policy Studies (CEPS) Brussels, 22–27 <www.ceps.eu/ceps-publications/complaint-mechanisms-border-management-and-expulsion-operations-europe-effective/>.

[118] EBCG Regulation.

[119] EBCG Regulation art 111 (2) seems to indicate that the complaints mechanism concerns the operational activities of the Agency (joint operations, pilot projects, rapid border interventions, migration management support team deployment, return operations, return interventions, or an operational activity of the Agency in a third country); yet the recent Management Board Decision 19/2022 revising the Agency's rules on the complaints mechanism appears to extend the availability of the mechanism more generally to 'the actions or a failure to act on the part of staff involved in *an Agency activity*' (emphasis added), see Frontex – European Border and Coast Guard Agency Management Board Decision 19/2022 of 16 March 2022 adopting the Agency's rules on the complaints mechanism art 3 (1). However, the fact that the Frontex

any person (no matter the age)[120] directly affected by any actions or failure to act on the part of staff involved in Frontex's activities,[121] the complaints mechanism looks prima facie like a remedy genuinely intended to bridge the gap concerning review of as well as redress for potentially harmful factual conduct of the Agency and its staff during external border management operations.[122]

However, the complaints mechanism also features some alleged shortcomings and limitations that have triggered criticism regarding its legal design and practical operation.[123]

First, while the extensive involvement of the Frontex Fundamental Rights Officer (FRO) in handling individual complaints is to be welcomed, questions pertaining to the genuine independence of the FRO vis-à-vis the management of the Agency as well as to the limited powers of the FRO regarding the outcome of the procedure leave a mixed impression as to its effectiveness in addressing fundamental right breaches.[124] Thus, in the instances in which the FRO finds the existence of concrete fundamental rights violations, for instance in the form of excessive use of force by Frontex staff against individuals attempting to cross the EU external border by land, it draws up a report that includes recommendations for appropriate follow-up by the Frontex Executive Director (ED).[125] Next, although the EBCG Regulation and the Agency's rules on the complaints mechanism provide that the ED 'shall ensure the appropriate follow-up'[126] … 'to FRO's recommendation through

Management Board decision merely implements Article 111 EBCG Regulation and considering that the Frontex Fundamental Rights Officer (FRO) assesses the admissibility of complaints based on Article 111 (2)–(3) EBCG Regulation, one may conclude that the recently updated complaints mechanism is still aimed at addressing fundamental rights breaches within the framework of the Agency's operational activities.

[120] Frontex Management Board Decision 19/2022 art 3 (1).

[121] EBCG Regulation art 111 (2); Frontex Management Board Decision 19/2022 art 3 (1).

[122] E.g., 'pushbacks' and physical expulsions in the area of the Union's sea and land borders, body searches, use of force to contain inflows of migrants, apprehension of personal belongings of individuals crossing EU external borders, etc.

[123] See, for instance, Marco Stefan and Leonhard den Hertog, 'Frontex: Great Powers But No Appeals' in Merijn Chamon, Annalisa Volpato, and Mariolina Eliantonio (eds), *Boards of Appeal of EU Agencies: Towards Judicialization of Administrative Review?* (Oxford University Press 2022) 151–165; and European Ombudsman Case OI/5/2020/MHZ on the functioning of the European Border and Coast Guard Agency's (Frontex) complaints mechanism for alleged breaches of fundamental rights and the role of the Fundamental Rights Officer (15 June 2021); this led to the recent revision of the Agency's complaints mechanism by Frontex Management Board Decision 19/2022.

[124] See Stefan and Hertog (n 123) 162.

[125] Frontex Management Board Decision 19/2022 art 7 (4).

[126] EBCG Regulation art 111 (6).

measures provided for by the applicable rules',[127] the fact remains that the ED has broad discretion in establishing the 'appropriate follow-up' and is not formally bound by the FRO's findings and recommendations.[128] The obligation stipulated for the ED to report back to the FRO as to 'the findings, the implementation of disciplinary measures, and follow-up by the Agency in response to a complaint' does not change this;[129] in fact, the Agency's rules on the complaints mechanism provide clearly that a complaint may be declared unfounded by the ED.[130]

Second, it remains unclear what the 'follow-up' by the ED may consist of. Both the EBCG Regulation[131] and the Agency's rules on the complaints mechanism[132] merely refer more explicitly to disciplinary measures and referral for initiation of civil and criminal proceedings; for the rest, formulations remain rather vague, such as 'any follow-up measure'[133] or 'undertaking immediate action' in case of an imminent risk of irreparable harm to the complainant or to the Agency.[134] One may thus wonder whether the follow-up measures decided by the ED should also include redress for the individual whose rights have been breached by the Agency's factual conduct, such as putting an end to the infringement, where applicable, and/or various compensatory measures for the harm suffered. If this mechanism and its follow-up are not aimed at properly addressing the breaches of the complainant's fundamental rights caused by the Agency's operational activities, one may seriously question whether this procedure represents a genuine remedy for the individual.[135]

Third, one may wonder whether the affected individual can legally challenge the outcome of the complaint procedure; one may consider in particular a decision by the ED to declare a complaint unfounded or an ED decision

[127] Frontex Management Board Decision 19/2022 art 10 (1).

[128] As such, the FRO's powers within the complaints procedure resemble those of the EU Ombudsman: making non-binding recommendations and suggestions for improvement.

[129] EBCG Regulation art 111 (6).

[130] Frontex Management Board Decision 19/2022 art 10 (5).

[131] EBCG Regulation art 111 (6).

[132] Frontex Management Board Decision 19/2022 art 10 (1).

[133] Ibid art 10 (3).

[134] Ibid art 11 (1).

[135] Some take the view that since the complaint mechanism 'focuses primarily on internal measures' pertaining 'to actions in relation to the staff or national authorities involved, and not to the complainant', it 'offers no administrative remedy to the affected individual', Stefan and Hertog (n 123) 163 and 171. Against this background, the only option left to the individual whose rights have been infringed by factual conduct of the Agency or its staff seems to be the judicial remedy of action for damages, explicitly encompassing, according to Article 97 (3) EBCG Regulation, damages caused by the use of the Agency's executive powers.

by which inappropriate follow-up by the Agency is taken on the complaint. Somewhat paradoxically, the legal review of such ED decisions is not clearly stipulated in the EBCG Regulation, prompting the remark that 'the complaint mechanism is by design not fit to contest decisions of the agency'.[136] In our view, to the extent that such decisions represent acts of the Agency that directly affect the legal situation of the complainant (and in our view this is the case where they do not properly address complainants' breaches of fundamental rights), they are covered by Article 98 EBCG Regulation and, as a result, should be challengeable before the CJEU under Article 263 TFEU.[137] In this respect, the revised Agency rules on the complaints mechanism arguably bring more clarity on this matter as they now stipulate that the 'decisions adopted by the Executive Director … in relation to an admissible complaint shall contain an indication of the appeal possibilities provided under EU … law available for challenging the decision'.[138]

Last but not least, the effectiveness in practice of the complaints mechanism has been called into question. With a low number of complaints being registered over the years, and no complaints recorded until June 2021 regarding the activities of Agency staff members,[139] concerns (followed by recommendations for improvement) have been raised inter alia regarding the accessibility, transparency, and proper functioning of this procedure.[140]

12.5.6 *The European Data Protection Supervisor (EDPS)*

Finally, a horizontal but rather specific non-judicial remedy available in the area of personal data processing by EU institutions, bodies, offices, and agencies deserves closer attention. Regulation 2018/1725 (the so-called General Data Protection Regulation for EU institutions and bodies) entrusts the European Data Protection Supervisor (EDPS) both with an overarching

[136] Stefan and Hertog (n 123) 163–164.

[137] According to Article 98 (1) EBCG, 'Proceedings may be brought before the Court of Justice for the annulment of acts of the Agency that are intended to produce legal effects vis-à-vis third parties, in accordance with Article 263 TFEU.'

[138] Frontex Management Board Decision 19/2022 art 15 (2). In our view, such 'appeal possibilities' should include both follow-up non-judicial review mechanisms (if available) and the possibility to challenge the ED decision before the CJEU under Article 263 TFEU.

[139] 'Between 2016 and January 2021, the FRO had received 69 complaints of which 22 were admissible', European Ombudsman, Decision in OI/5/2020/MHZ (n 123) 4.

[140] See, in this respect, European Ombudsman, Decision in OI/5/2020/MHZ (n 123), and the suggestions for improvement listed there. The Agency's revised rules on the complaints mechanism (2022) can be seen as an attempt to address these shortcomings in light of the increased probability for Frontex's staff actions to breach fundamental rights in the exercise of the significant operational and executive powers entrusted to the Agency since 2019.

supervisory function regarding the processing of personal data by EU institutions and bodies and with the function of an administrative remedy for data subjects whose rights have allegedly been breached by unlawful data processing.[141] For certain, unlawful data processing by EU institutions and bodies may entail formal legal acts but also (perhaps in particular) factual conduct in the form of various physical operations (e.g., inadvertent collecting, recording, retrieving, consulting, altering, or deleting personal data in a database such as EURODAC or Europol Information System (EIS); combining, structuring, or analysing personal data for profiling purposes; prohibited disclosure by transmission of personal data to a third party,[142] including, for instance, exchanges of personal data with third countries by Frontex within the EUROSUR framework; unauthorised dissemination of personal data to the public,[143] etc.).[144] The right to lodge a complaint with the EDPS is granted broadly to any data subject who considers that the processing of his/her personal data infringes Regulation 2018/1725.[145]

Further, clear obligations are established for the EDPS in dealing with the complaint. First, the EDPS has a duty of information to the complainant as to the progress and outcome of the complaint, as well as to the availability of a judicial remedy.[146] Second, the EDPS is under a duty to handle the complaint or inform the data subject about the progress/outcome of the complaint within three months; failure to do so equates to an implicit negative decision by the EDPS.[147]

Next, unlike the EU Ombudsman and the Frontex FRO, the EDPS has quite extensive formal powers vis-à-vis EU institutions and bodies at fault. Within the realm of its so-called corrective powers, the EDPS may inter alia order the controller or the processor to: 'comply with the data subject's requests to exercise his or her rights',[148] or 'bring processing operations into compliance [with Regulation 2018/1725] … where appropriate, in a specified manner and within a specified period',[149] or further to ensure 'the rectification

[141] Regulation 2018/1725 arts 52 and 57 (1) (a) and (e).
[142] E.g., sensitive personal data collected during an EPPO coordinated criminal investigation being transmitted by the EPPO to private persons with whom the suspects entertain close relationships, resulting in the damaging of their reputation.
[143] In this respect, the *Tillack* affair provides an excellent example of a press release published by OLAF, containing allegations of criminal acts having been committed by an identifiable individual, *Tillack* (n 20) paras 7–24.
[144] Regulation 2018/1725 art 3 (3).
[145] Regulation 2018/1725 art 63 (1). In our view, the data processing that can be subjected to the complaint procedure can cover both formal legal binding acts and factual conduct.
[146] Ibid art 63 (2).
[147] Ibid art 63 (3).
[148] Ibid art 58 (2) (d).
[149] Ibid art 58 (2) (e).

or erasure of personal data or restriction of processing' pursuant to the data subject's rights under Regulation 2018/1725.[150] Additionally, and quite notably, the EDPS can effectively enforce the measures mentioned previously by imposing administrative fines for non-compliance by the relevant EU institution or body.[151] The EDPS seems thus to have effective legal means to properly address breaches of fundamental rights by EU personal data processing operations.

Finally, but quite importantly, the decision of the EDPS concerning a data subject's complaint, including the implicit negative decision where the EDPS fails to handle the complaint or inform the data subject about the progress or outcome of the complaint, can be challenged before the CJEU by the data subject.[152] Hence, in the area of personal data processing, the synergy between a strong administrative remedy provided by the EDPS and the judicial review of EDPS ensuing decisions bears the promise, at least on paper, of offering quite effective legal protection as concerns breaches of data subjects' fundamental rights by EU factual conduct in the form of various physical data processing operations.[153]

12.6 OVERALL ASSESSMENT AND THE WAY FORWARD: DEPLOYING EFFECTIVE EU ADMINISTRATIVE REMEDIES WITH JUDICIALLY REVIEWABLE OUTCOMES

A number of observations are put forward based on the previous analysis in this chapter with regard to the current legal protection landscape regarding breaches of fundamental rights through EU factual conduct. First, the system of judicial remedies in the EU Founding Treaties does not seem to fully

[150] Ibid art 58 (2) (h).

[151] Ibid art 58 (2) (i).

[152] Ibid art 64 (2).

[153] Ibid arts 63 (1) and 64 (1) suggest that data subjects can also go directly before the CJEU, without filing a complaint first with the EDPS, for breaches of their rights by EU data processing operations; however, in this scenario, the admissibility requirements pertaining to the actions before the CJEU (action for annulment or actions for damages) must be met; this will likely raise insurmountable obstacles to the action for annulment where the fundamental rights of the individual have been infringed by physical data processing operations, unless the CJEU qualifies them as implicit binding legal acts. Therefore, relying first on the remedy provided by the EDPS with a 'last resort' prospect of a judicial challenge against the EDPS decision has several advantages: (1) it would strengthen, through the involvement of the EDPS, the position of the data subject against the faulty EU body; (2) it may lead to timely and proper redress, without a need to have recourse to judicial review; (3) it ensures extensive, indirect, judicial review over any EU data processing operations, through the possibility to challenge the EDPS decisions before the CJEU.

ensure the right to an effective judicial remedy for 'everyone whose rights and freedoms guaranteed by the law of the Union are violated' through EU factual conduct. Access to EU courts remains quite challenging as far as the admissibility of an annulment action under Article 263 TFEU against EU factual conduct breaching fundamental rights is concerned. Moreover, the high restrictive thresholds regarding the EU liability conditions under Article 340 TFEU arguably entail low chances of success for the individual affected by EU factual conduct to obtain proper compensation. The long delays between the occurrence of the harmful factual conduct and the possibility for judicial intervention under Article 267 TFEU, as well as the uncertainties surrounding this procedure, do not offer an optimistic picture either. A more extensive and flexible approach regarding the concept of 'reviewable act' under Article 263 TFEU as well as regarding the EU non-contractual liability under Article 340 TFEU could arguably address these shortcomings to some extent.[154] But even if this were the case, judicial review still may not offer full satisfaction because of the limited powers of EU Courts, which, besides the possibility of awarding compensation for damages,[155] are confined to merely annulling or declaring invalid the contested EU measure without being able to by and large issue orders or injunctions against the EU actor at fault.[156]

Second, the brief overview of the diverse non-judicial remedies discussed here also reveals some limitations and shortcomings regarding the capacity to address fundamental rights breaches by EU factual conduct.[157] Some of these (e.g., EU agency BoAs) do not seem well-suited for challenges against EU factual conduct. Others display problematic legal design and practical operation as regards access, transparency, independence, fair and speedy handling,

[154] Some provisions in EU secondary legislation arguably could be seen as an attempt to broaden judicial review with regard to EU factual conduct; such an example is Regulation 2018/1725 art 64 (1) providing that 'the Court of Justice shall have jurisdiction to hear *all disputes relating to the provisions of this Regulation* (emphasis added), including claims for damages'. Yet one may question the validity of such interpretation, entailing that a provision of EU secondary legislation would extend judicial review beyond the scope of the judicial remedies in EU primary law, as interpreted by the CJEU in its jurisprudence (in particular in its *Inuit* case law), see also Rademacher (n 4) 428–430.

[155] Even if compensation were awarded more generously by EU courts, the fact remains that such compensation might often offer only rather belated and partial redress for the harm incurred by the individual as a result of EU factual conduct that might have produced sometimes irreversible and long-standing consequences, especially if its effects have continued for a long time before being discontinued by proper intervention.

[156] See Lenaerts and Others (n 44) 411–412 and 475.

[157] Such limitations could partly be explained by the multi-purpose design of these mechanisms, serving simultaneously the need for legal review, scrutiny, and accountability of EU administrative action and the need to offer a legal remedy to the individual against harmful measures by EU administration.

and offering appropriate redress (e.g., Frontex's complaints mechanism). Furthermore, the interplay between non-judicial remedies and judicial remedies is not always fully addressed in EU secondary legislation; this might not always be necessary in view of the specific role and features of the non-judicial remedy, such as the EU Ombudsman, but it is striking with respect to Frontex's complaints mechanism for fundamental rights breaches. On the positive side, it must be noted that non-judicial remedies generally allow for more timely, comprehensive, and insightful review of the relevant EU measures, including redress possibilities, as compared to the limited legal review carried out by EU courts. What is more, EU law features a few non-judicial remedies (e.g., EDPS and the legality review of the acts of EU executive agencies) that seem capable (at least on paper) of offering effective redress for fundamental rights breaches through EU factual conduct and, on top of that, the final outcome of such remedies can be challenged before the EU Courts.

We therefore put forward a number of reflections and recommendations with a view to addressing this apparent blind spot in legal protection concerning fundamental rights breaches through EU factual conduct.

First, in our view, upholding sound administration both as a general principle of EU law and as a right of the individual (Article 41 CFR) requires having in place effective administrative remedies against EU measures. Only in this way may one hope to enforce in a timely manner, if need be, 'the right to have his or her affairs handled impartially, fairly and within a reasonable time' laid down in Article 41 (1) CFR. After all, for the individual, it is most important to have a quick, accessible, and effective remedy or mechanism to put an end to the breach and obtain appropriate redress for the harm incurred as soon as possible. This can best be ensured by the EU administration in the first instance. From this viewpoint, judicial review can be seen rather as the 'last resort' remedy,[158] not being particularly advantageous for the individual in view of the high costs involved, time incurred between the breach and the possibility for the court to address it, and difficulty accessing the EU courts, as well as the rather limited review and redress EU courts may be able or willing to offer. In order to be fully effective, such administrative remedies should abide by certain procedural and substantive benchmarks ensuring that they are sufficiently accessible to the individual, independent, prompt, transparent, comprehensive, and thorough,[159] as well as capable of offering appropriate redress. Therefore, serious consideration should be given in EU administrative

[158] I.e., when the EU administration fails to address and redress properly fundamental rights breaches.

[159] For the listing of these standards in the context of the EU Ombudsman's assessment of Frontex's complaints mechanism, see Decision in OI/5/2020/MHZ (n 123) para 16.

law to further developing underlying principles and criteria, as well as to designing effective administrative remedies addressing fundamental rights breaches by any form of EU action, including factual conduct.[160] Moreover, a more systemic perspective should be taken, by also looking at and clarifying the synergies and complementarity between various non-judicial remedies with a view to avoiding gaps or overlaps in legal protection and bearing in mind the fact that an optimal combination of administrative remedies could better address the situation.[161]

Second, we suggest that a combined reading of the principle of sound administration (enshrined as a right in Article 41 CFR) and the principle of an effective remedy (enshrined as a right in Article 47 CFR) could support a more complete system of legal protection against EU action, featuring easily accessible, comprehensive, and strong administrative remedies with, in principle, judicially reviewable outcomes. This entails that, as a rule, administrative remedies should result in final legally binding decisions that can then be challenged before EU courts under Article 263 TFEU. In this respect, we suggest, as a default approach, extending and adapting, where appropriate, the model of the EDPS when designing administrative remedies against EU action.[162] In this way, the individual should in principle have the chance to obtain appropriate redress the easier way (via the administrative remedy), with the safeguard that their rights will be ultimately protected by the EU courts if the relevant EU body fails to do so.[163] Ensuring by default judicial review concerning the final outcomes of administrative remedies could also fulfil a preventive function, in that it would increase the pressure on the EU administration to address properly fundamental rights infringements, once the 'sword of Damocles' of judicial review is hanging there. Along the same lines, we also support the idea of the opening up of judicial protection offered by the CJEU,

[160] The Research Network on EU Administrative Law (ReNEUAL) project could be an appropriate forum to achieve this, in particular in view of its previous work on the ReNEUAL Model Rules on EU Administrative Procedure <www.reneual.eu/>.

[161] For instance, one should consider the complementarity relationship between the EU Ombudsman and other administrative remedies with different features, such as suspensory effects and legally binding outcomes.

[162] For a similar suggestion on the establishment of a centralised EU supervisory authority whose decisions could be challenged by individuals before the CJEU, though limited to the specific sector of information management and exchange within highly complex and integrated hybrid networks and information systems involving EU and Member States' actors, see ReNEUAL Model Rules on EU Administrative Procedure (2014), Book VI – Administrative Information Management, 258 and 302–306; see also Schneider (n 83) 109–111; and Hofmann and Tidghi (n 84) 160–163.

[163] In this respect, EU agencies' BoAs could be aligned to the EDPS model, by extending their jurisdiction to EU factual conduct affecting the legal situation of the individual.

and in particular Rademacher's view that EU Courts should more generously trigger EU non-contractual liability for damages, in instances of fundamental rights breaches through EU factual conduct.[164] In this way, one may hope to close the gap of legal protection against harmful EU factual conduct.

12.7 CONCLUSION

With the focus of inquiry on the legal protection against breaches of fundamental rights through EU factual conduct, this chapter first attempted to provide some clarification on the concept of 'factual conduct' and illustrate concretely how such factual conduct may infringe fundamental rights. Favouring an understanding of factual conduct as 'physical acts and operations' by EU bodies (and their staff), the chapter looked next into the available legal review and legal protection avenues regarding such EU conduct, in particular when it allegedly breaches fundamental rights of individuals. After examining both judicial and selected non-judicial remedies as elements of an overarching EU system of legal protection premised on the constitutional parameters of sound administration and effective judicial remedies, it highlighted the potential as well as the shortcomings of existing legal remedies to address fundamental rights breaches by EU factual conduct. It detected 'blind spots' in legal protection, in particular in the form of insufficient and ineffective judicial review of factual conduct as well as in the form of problematic legal design and practical operation of some of the currently available administrative remedies. To close the gap of legal protection against harmful EU factual conduct, the chapter suggests focusing more on designing a coherent system of strong and effective administrative remedies with final outcomes that can be challenged before the CJEU, along with more opening up of judicial protection by EU courts, in particular under Articles 263 and 340 TFEU.

[164] See Rademacher (n 4) 430–435.

13

Composite Procedures, the Violation of Fundamental Rights, and the Availability of Sufficient Remedies in the Multi-level EU Judicial Architecture

MARIOLINA ELIANTONIO

13.1 INTRODUCTION

In contemporary European law, it has become increasingly evident that EU law is not implemented according to the traditional distinction between direct and indirect administration but through various systems and patterns of cooperation between national and EU authorities, as well as between national authorities themselves. These cooperative mechanisms generate so-called composite procedures, that is, administrative decision-making processes that involve administrative authorities belonging to more than one legal system for the implementation of EU law.[1] While this form of procedural cooperation is now a prevalent mechanism in EU administrative governance, composite procedures lack both an 'official' definition and a clear conceptualisation.

This phenomenon has generated increasing scholarly attention and attempts at providing taxonomies, labels, and detailed analyses of composite procedures in ever-growing EU policy fields.[2] At the same time, because of the separation of jurisdictions both horizontally and vertically (excluding – at least in principle – the possibility for EU courts to review national administrative measures and for national courts to review measures stemming from either

[1] The term was famously coined by Herwig Hofmann. See Herwig C Hofmann, 'Composite decision-making procedures in EU administrative law' in Herwig C Hofmann and Alexander H Türk (eds), *Legal Challenges in EU Administrative Law – Towards an Integrated Administration* (Edward Elgar 2009) 136.

[2] The literature has grown so much in recent years that providing a full account of the scholarly debate would exceed the remit of this chapter. For an up-to-date overview of the phenomenon of composite procedures and an account of the strands of literature examining it, see Mariolina Eliantonio 'Access to Justice in Composite Procedures for the Implementation of EU Law: The Story so Far' (2023) <https://papers.ssrn.com/sol3/papers.cfm?abstract_id=4373333>.

another national legal system or the EU legal order), the literature has specifically discussed the question of access to justice in the framework of these composite procedures.[3] This question has also been tackled by the Court of Justice of the European Union (CJEU) on several occasions, and a body of case law is increasingly emerging on the question of the competent court and the reviewable acts adopted in the context of the composite procedures.[4]

A less explored angle in this debate, however, is the question of the remedies available to redress possible fundamental rights violations occurring in the context of the composite procedures. In light of the above-mentioned separation of jurisdictions between national and EU courts and the partial gap-filling case law of the CJEU, is the current system of remedies sufficient to ensure that, if national or European authorities violate fundamental rights in the context of composite procedures, there is access to a court to control such alleged violations? In turn, this question is linked to the need for the EU multi-level system of protection to ensure respect for the right to an effective remedy enshrined in Article 47 of the Charter of Fundamental Rights ('the Charter') whenever rights guaranteed by EU law are allegedly violated.[5]

In order to tackle this question, this chapter proceeds as follows. In Section 13.2, a categorisation of composite procedures is provided together with an examination of possible fundamental rights that might be violated in their context. Far from providing an exhaustive taxonomy of these procedures, the categories discussed in this section have been selected because they give rise to different problems in terms of possible violations of fundamental rights. In this regard, it should also be noted that, for the purposes of this chapter (and in line with the focus of this volume on the *EU* system of remedies), only those procedures entailing cooperation between EU and national authorities will be examined (so-called vertical composite procedures), to the exclusion of 'purely' horizontal procedures, that is, scenarios in which only national authorities cooperate with each other for the implementation of EU law

[3] See, in general, Mariolina Eliantonio, 'Judicial Review in an Integrated Administration: The Case of "Composite Procedures"' (2014) 7 Review of European Administrative Law 65; Filipe Brito Bastos, 'Derivative Illegality in the European Composite Administrative Procedures' (2018) 55 Common Market Law Review 101.

[4] See, e.g., Case C-97/91 *Oleificio Borelli SpA v Commission* [1992] ECLI:EU:C:1992:491; Case C-219/17 *Berlusconi and Fininvest* [2018] ECLI:EU:C:2018:1023; Case C-785/18 *GAEC Jeanningros v Institut national de l'origine et de la qualité (INAO) and Others* [2020] ECLI:EU:C:2020:46.

[5] Charter of Fundamental Rights of the European Union [2016] OJ C202/389.

without the involvement of the EU level of administration.[6] Finally, it is important to note that the focus of the chapter is on situations in which (EU or national) administrative authorities infringe EU fundamental rights, to the exclusion of situations in which these authorities correctly execute laws that, in turn, violate those fundamental rights. This question relates to the review of EU or national legislation against higher parameters and falls outside the scope of this chapter, which is centred around the control of administrative action.

After providing a categorisation of composite procedures and the fundamental rights possibly engaged therein, in Section 13.3, the available remedies in the scenarios outlined in the earlier section will be presented and their possible gaps will be examined. Section 13.4 concludes. The chapter will show that, while composite procedures are capable of violating both substantive and procedural EU fundamental rights, the current system of remedies seems to be ill-suited to provide effective remedies in multi-jurisdictional decision-making processes.

13.2 VERTICAL COMPOSITE PROCEDURES AND THE VIOLATION OF FUNDAMENTAL RIGHTS

13.2.1 *The Universe of Vertical Composite Procedures: A Proposed Division*

The universe of composite procedures (and, within it, the galaxy of vertical procedures entailing the cooperation of EU and Member State authorities) is extremely varied and in continuous evolution and, as a consequence, multiple categorisations are possible.[7] For the purposes of this chapter and in light of the focus of this volume on remedies for fundamental rights violations, in the following, it is submitted that the more or less 'formalised' and decisional

6 On this distinction, as well as the peculiar problems of access to justice in horizontal composite procedures, see Paolo Mazzotti and Mariolina Eliantonio, 'Transnational Judicial Review in Horizontal Composite Procedures: *Berlioz*, *Donnellan*, and the Constitutional Law of the Union' (2020) 5 European Papers 41; and Paolo Mazzotti and Mariolina Eliantonio, 'Towards a Theory of Transnational Judicial Review in European Administrative Law' (2021) 13 Italian Journal of Public Law 350 <www.ijpl.eu/wp-content/uploads/2022/10/3.Eliantonio_Mazzotti.pdf>.

7 See, for earlier attempts at categorisations, Sergio Alonso de León, 'Composite Administrative Procedures in the European Union' (Doctoral thesis, Universidad Carlos III de Madrid, 2016); Brito Bastos, 'Derivative Illegality in the European Composite Administrative Procedures' (n 3); Giacinto Della Cananea, 'The European Union's Mixed Administrative Proceedings' (2005) 68 Law and Contemporary Problems 197; Eliantonio, 'Judicial Review in an Integrated Administration' (n 3). The most recent one is in Eliantonio, 'Access to Justice in Composite Procedures for the Implementation of EU Law: The Story so Far' (n 2).

nature of an administrative action represents a suitable criterion to distinguish different types of composite procedures. From this perspective, one can draw a distinction between procedures that entail various types of factual acts and procedures that instead comprise measures that are not factual in nature (whether binding or not). This distinction is relevant for the purposes of this chapter for two reasons. First, because of the different types of fundamental rights that may be at stake in the course of the decision-making process. In particular, factual conduct is capable of infringing specific fundamental rights regarding domicile and correspondence. Second, because, as will be shown below, the more or less formal nature of the administrative action at stake has implications for the identification of the appropriate judicial forum.

In Section 13.2.2, possible factual conduct scenarios identifiable in the framework of vertical composite procedures will be considered, with a discussion of the fundamental rights that might come into play in those situations. In Section 13.2.3, within the very diverse universe of composite procedures that do not entail factual conduct on the part of the authorities, examples will be provided of different fundamental rights that might be relevant in these procedures. They are not specifically linked to the 'type' of procedure (e.g., whether they culminate in limiting the legal sphere of an individual, such as the ban on the import of a product or an order of repatriation, or entail the expansion of the individual's legal sphere, such as the granting of an authorisation to carry out a certain activity) but on the subject matter of the procedure. Furthermore, fundamental rights that might be relevant in all types of composite procedure (whether decisional or not in nature, or entailing more or less 'formalised' administrative measures) are 'procedural' in nature (e.g., the right to be heard). These will be examined in Section 13.2.4. As will be shown, these rights display peculiar features in the context of composite procedures and have been subject to fairly extensive scrutiny by the CJEU.

13.2.2 *Factual Action, Composite Procedures, and the Infringement of Fundamental Rights*

The notion of 'factual action' is not a dogmatic category known at the EU level, unlike several national systems.[8] Yet it is beyond doubt that both national and EU authorities carry out factual actions in the framework of

8 For a comparative overview, see Chris Backes and Mariolina Eliantonio (eds), *Cases, Materials and Text on Judicial Review of Administrative Action* (Hart 2019), ch 4; for an examination of factual conduct at the EU level in general, see Timo Rademacher, 'Factual Administrative Conduct and Judicial Review in EU Law' (2017) 29 European Review of Public Law 399.

composite procedures for the implementation of EU law and that these actions can have a severe impact on individuals' fundamental rights (see also Chapter 12).[9]

This can happen, for example, in the framework of inspection procedures: in increasingly more policy fields, composite procedures entail enforcement actions, including inspections.[10] For example, in the fields of competition law, fisheries, and aviation safety, EU authorities (be it the Commission or the competent European agencies) can carry out inspection activities, including, for example, seizure of documents, confiscation of computer systems, and interrogation of witnesses.[11] These inspection activities may be part of composite procedures when a subsequent act of the enforcement process, such as the imposition of a sanction, is adopted at the national level. Cooperation in enforcement tasks may also take place at the inspection step itself, when national and EU authorities cooperate in various ways in carrying out an inspection.[12] Inspections and the actions they entail may be in conflict with Article 7 of the Charter, protecting the right to private life, home, and communications, which corresponds to the first paragraph of Article 8 of the ECHR. That these fundamental rights might be at stake in such cases has also been confirmed by the case law of the CJEU.[13]

Factual action can also go beyond inspection activities and includes the performance of other types of acts. For example, Frontex has been carrying out factual activities (such as the detention or transfer of individuals from one location to another) in support of search and rescue activities performed by national authorities at the EU borders, which may conflict (and indeed have been considered as conflicting) with, amongst others, the fundamental right to asylum and the prohibition of refoulement contained in Articles 18 and 19 of the Charter.[14] Other fundamental rights contained in the Charter, such as the prohibition of torture contained in Article 4 or the right to liberty enshrined in

[9] Napoleon Xanthoulis, 'Administrative factual conduct: Legal effects and judicial control in EU law' (2019) 12 Review of European Administrative Law 39.

[10] For an examination of shared enforcement activities between national and EU authorities, see Miroslava Scholten and Michiel Luchtman (eds), *Law Enforcement by EU Authorities: Implications for Political and Judicial Accountability* (Edward Elgar 2017).

[11] Maurizia De Bellis, 'Multi-level Administration, Inspections and Fundamental Rights: Is Judicial Protection Full and Effective?' (2021) 22 German Law Journal 416; and extensively Maurizia De Bellis, *I poteri ispettivi dell'amministrazione europea* (Giappichelli 2021).

[12] See further with examples and references to legislation, Eliantonio, 'Access to Justice in Composite Procedures for the Implementation of EU Law: The Story so Far' (n 2).

[13] In the pre-Charter times, see Case C-94/00 *Roquette Frères* [2002] ECLI:EU:C:2002:603.

[14] See the EP Briefing 'Addressing pushbacks at the EU's external borders' <www.europarl.europa.eu/RegData/etudes/BRIE/2022/738191/EPRS_BRI(2022)738191_EN.pdf>.

Article 6, can also be of relevance in this context. The same fundamental rights can be violated in the framework of the cooperation between the national competent authorities and the European Union Agency for Asylum, in the context of which the Agency is tasked with, amongst others, conducting admissibility interviews with migrants.[15]

13.2.3 *Other Composite Procedures and 'Substantive' Fundamental Rights*

Composite procedures of a decisional nature, and which do not involve factual conduct, are present in very diverse policy fields, ranging from competition law to the Common Agricultural Policy, asylum, risk regulation, environmental policy, and data protection. It is therefore fairly straightforward to conclude that a large range of possible fundamental rights can come into play in these very diverse situations. Without any attempt at completeness, in this section, examples of types of composite procedure will be provided to show how and why EU fundamental rights might be violated.

An increasingly common type of composite procedure entails the sharing of data between EU and national authorities.[16] At the outset, it should be mentioned, with respect to these procedures and the proposed categorisation based on the presence of factual conduct in a vertical composite procedure, that these acts of information, as has been appropriately argued, 'sit uneasily within [the] legal/factual dichotomy'.[17]

These data sharing procedures often take place through various databases, in which national authorities enter information that, in turn, may be used by other national authorities. In some cases, the role of the EU level of

[15] See EASO Special Operating Plan To Greece <https://euaa.europa.eu/sites/default/files/easo%20special%20operating%20plan%20to%20greece%202017_%2014122016.pdf>; for the framing of the phenomenon as a composite procedure, see Evangelia L Tsourdi, 'Bottom-up Salvation? From Practical Cooperation Towards Joint Implementation Through the European Asylum Support Office' (2016) 3 European Papers 997; Gaia Lisi and Mariolina Eliantonio, 'The Gaps in Judicial Accountability of EASO in the processing of asylum requests in Hotspots' (2019) 4 European Papers 589.

[16] On these types of procedure, see, amongst others, Deidre M Curtin and Filipe Brito Bastos, 'Interoperable Information Sharing and the Five Novel Frontiers of EU Governance: A Special Issue' (2020) 26 European Public Law 59; Diana-Urania Galetta, Herwig C H Hofmann, and Jens-Peter Schneider, 'Information Exchange in the European Administrative Union: An Introduction' (2014) 20 European Public Law 65; Mariolina Eliantonio, 'Information Exchange in European Administrative Law: A Threat to Effective Judicial Protection?' (2016) 23 Maastricht Journal of European and Comparative Law 531.

[17] Simona Demková, *Automated Decision-Making and Effective Remedies: The New Dynamics in the Protection of EU Fundamental Rights in the Area of Freedom, Security and Justice* (Edward Elgar 2023) 23.

administration can materialise in the facilitation of the sharing of information between authorities of different legal systems. This is the case for the Rapid Exchange of Information System (RAPEX). This is an alert system for unsafe consumer products, established by the General Product Safety Directive.[18] In this system, Member States share information concerning dangerous products with the Commission. After validation by the Commission, the information is made available to the competent authorities throughout the EU, which can take measures to prevent the circulation of the product, such as a ban on sales or withdrawal from the market. Potentially, in such cases, the composite procedure thereby generated might come into conflict with the freedom to conduct a business protected by Article 16 of the Charter.

In other cases, the EU presence can relate to the creation and management of a database, such as the Schengen Information System (SIS), through which competent national authorities, such as the police and border guards, are able to enter alerts on people and objects in the database, which can be consulted by the competent authorities of all Member States, and which can form the basis of restrictive measures such as removal from the national territory. The involvement of the EU legal system is, however, 'silent' in that it is limited, through the EU Agency for large-scale IT systems (eu-LISA), to the operational management of the central IT system and the network on which the system operates. This has implications for the accountability of the EU administrative authorities, and hence for access to justice, since their participation in the decision-making process is unclear.[19] Regardless of the more or less 'explicit' role of the Agency in the procedure, like in the cases of Frontex and the European Union Agency for Asylum examined above, the fundamental right to asylum and the prohibition of refoulement contained in Articles 18 and 19 of the Charter might be violated as a consequence of the actions of public authorities taken on the basis of alerts entered in the SIS system, as well

[18] Directive 2001/95/EC of the European Parliament and of the Council of 3 December 2001 on general product safety [2002] OJ L11/4.

[19] See further on this Niovi Vavoula, 'Information Sharing in the Dublin System: Remedies for Asylum Seekers In-Between Gaps in Judicial Protection and Interstate Trust' (2021) 22 German Law Journal 391; Jens-Peter Schneider, 'Basic Structures of Information Management in the European Administrative Union' (2014) 20(1) European Public Law 89; Morgane Tidghi and Herwig C H Hofmann, 'Rights and Remedies in Implementation of EU Policies by Multi-Jurisdictional Networks' (2014) 20 European Public Law 147; Ferdinand Wollenschläger, 'Informationssysteme als Herausforderung für den Rechtsschutz im Europäischen Verwaltungsverbund: Das EU-Schnellwarnsystem für Lebens- und Futtermittel (RASFF)' (2019) 52 Die Verwaltung 1.

as the right to respect for family life and the rights of the child, as enshrined in Articles 7 and 24 of the Charter.[20]

At the same time, in the examples of both the RAPEX- and the SIS-generated procedures, it is clear that, as certain personal data are shared, the right to data protection contained in Article 8 of the Charter might also come into play.[21]

Other sets of composite procedures entail the authorisation or denial thereof to place on the market a product or a substance. Various types of composite procedures are indeed foreseen for the authorisation to place on the market genetically modified organisms, medicines, pesticides, and so on, entailing the cooperation in various forms and at various stages between national and EU authorities.[22] In such cases, one could imagine that the freedom to conduct a business protected by Article 16 of the Charter as well as the prohibition of discrimination contained in Article 21 might come into play.

13.2.4 *Composite Procedures and Fundamental 'Procedural' Rights*

All composite procedures, whether entailing enforcement measures or leading to an authorisation or the drafting of a plan or the ban of a product or person from the European administrative space, whether taken in economic or non-economic fields, whether comprising only two or multiple cooperative steps, need to respect several procedural fundamental rights. The starting point here

[20] See, on this point, Case C-193/19 *A v Migrationsverket* [2021] ECLI:EU:C:2021:168; and Opinion of AG De La Tour [2020] ECLI:EU:C:2020:594.

[21] Indeed, in Recital 56, Regulation (EU) 2018/1861 of the European Parliament and of the Council of 28 November 2018 on the establishment, operation and use of the Schengen Information System (SIS) in the field of border checks, and amending the Convention implementing the Schengen Agreement, and amending and repealing Regulation (EC) 1987/2006 [2018] OJ L312/56 makes explicit reference to Article 8.

[22] See on these procedures, on medical authorisations, Mariolina Eliantonio and Sabrina Röttger-Wirtz, 'From Integration to Exclusion: EU Composite Administration and Gaps in Judicial Accountability in the Authorisation of Pharmaceuticals' (2019) 10 European Journal of Risk Regulation 393; on GMOs, Rui Lanceiro and Mariolina Eliantonio, 'The Genetically Modified Organisms' Regime: A Playground for Multi-Level Administration and a Nightmare for Effective Judicial Protection?' (2021) 22 German Law Journal 371; in general on product authorisations: Luca De Lucia, 'Autorizzazioni transnazionali e cooperazione amministrativa nell'ordinamento europeo' (2010) 3 Rivista Italiana di Diritto Pubblico Comunitario 759. For a comparison covering composite procedures in the field of chemicals, pesticides, medicines, and food safety, see Emilie Chevalier, 'Administrative Cooperation in the field of Risk Regulation', in Emilie Chevalier, Mariolina Eliantonio, and Rui Lanceiro (eds), *Administrative Cooperation in the European Union* (Bruylant, forthcoming 2024).

is Article 41 of the Charter, referring to the right to good administration, including the right to be heard and the duty to give reasons. Article 41 is closely linked to the right to an effective remedy under Article 47 of the Charter, because judicial protection cannot be considered effective if the person concerned is unable to ascertain the reasons upon which the decision relating to them is taken.[23] The obligation to give reasons aims to enable the person concerned to 'defend his rights in the best possible conditions and to decide, with full knowledge of the relevant facts, whether there is any point in his applying to the court with jurisdiction'.[24]

Early in the case law, it was established that the right to be heard applies to individual decisions, which is a typical outcome of composite procedures (e.g., in the case of authorisation to place a product on the market or the imposition of a sanction).[25] However, the exercise of this right can be particularly arduous in the case of composite procedures: *Quid iuris* indeed if the right to be heard was not exercised in one step of the procedure? Can this omission be 'compensated' down the line of the decision-making chain, although the following decisional steps might be taken by authorities pertaining to a different legal system from that of the authority that violated the right to be heard in the first place? Can the omission of the authority of one legal system 'contaminate' the actions of the authorities belonging to a different legal system? What is the relevant level of administration before which the right to be heard can or must be exercised?[26]

These issues came to the attention of the CJEU in the context of the structural funds in the *Lisrestal* case, in which the Court considered a cooperative mechanism between the national authorities and the Commission leading to the reduction of the financial assistance received by the applicant.[27] The right to be heard was considered violated by the Court, and this circumstance led to the invalidity of the final Commission decision. However, interestingly, in the absence of a clear indication in the underlying legislation, the Court did not specify whether the right to be heard had to be afforded by the national or EU authorities, although the national authorities

[23] Case C-300/11 *ZZ v Secretary of State for the Home Department* [2013] ECLI:EU:C:2013:363, para 53.

[24] Ibid para 53 and the case law cited.

[25] Case C-17/74 *Transocean Marine Paint v Commission* [1974] ECLI:EU:C:1974:106; Case C-86/76 *Hoffmann-La Roche v Commission* [1979] ECLI:EU:C:1979:36.

[26] Alonso de León (n 7); Filipe Brito Bastos, 'Beyond executive federalism: the judicial crafting of the law of composite administrative decision-making' (PhD thesis, European University Institute 2018).

[27] Case C-32/95 P *Commission v Lisrestal* [1996] ECLI:EU:C:1996:402.

had no discretion to decide on the recovery of the funds. In a later case, *Mediocurso*, the applicants had been heard by the national authorities but there were indications that the right to be heard could have been infringed as the applicants had been given too little time to submit their observations. The Court of Justice on appeal, reversing the decision of the (then) Court of First Instance, invalidated the final Commission decision.[28]

Also the later case law[29] confirms that, while the right to be heard needs to be respected regardless of whether it is specifically mentioned in the applicable rules, it is not required that it be granted before the authority making the 'real' determination in the composite procedure.[30] This line of case law, however, seems to stand in contradiction with another strand of decisions that the CJEU handed down in the field of the repayment of import duties. After confirming the earlier position in *France-Aviation*,[31] in a long line of subsequent case law, it held that a person vis-à-vis whom an unfavourable decision is to be adopted must be heard by the authority who has the discretion to take the decision (in the cases at stake, the Commission).[32]

This contradiction in case law of the CJEU did not go unnoticed, with Alonso de León stating that the European courts 'fail to see the connection between some of the cases', possibly because they do not recognise composite procedures as a category of their own.[33] While he proposes that the right to be heard in composite procedures must be afforded before the authority 'in the driving seat' of the procedure (i.e., holding the discretionary power with respect to the final decision), he acknowledges that this very solution might present additional complexities in procedures with more complex collaborative structures, such as in the case of authorisation of pesticides or genetically modified organisms, where national and EU authorities intervene at several

28 Case C-462/98 P *Mediocurso v Commission* [2000] ECLI:EU:C:2000:480.

29 Case T-189/02 *Ente per le Ville vesuviane v Commission* [2009] ECLI:EU:C:2009:529; Case T-102/00 *Vlaams Fonds v Commission* [2003] ECLI:EU:T:2003:192; Case T-158/07 *Cofac v Commission* [2009] ECLI:EU:T:2009:489.

30 Alonso de León (n 7) 271.

31 Case T-346/94 *France-Aviation v Commission* [1995] ECLI:EU:T:1995:187.

32 Case T-42/96 *Eyckeler & Malt AG v Commission* [1998] ECLI:EU:T:1998:40; Case T-50/96 *Primex Produkte Import-Export GmbH & Co. KG, Gebr. Kruse GmbH, Interporc Im- und Export GmbH v Commission* [1998] ECLI:EU:T:1998:223; Case T-290/97 *Mehibas Dordtselaan BV v Commission* [2000] ECLI:EU:T:2000:8. As noted by Alonso de Leon (n 7), this line of case law culminated in the *Wilson Holland* case, in which the CJEU stated that the right to be heard had to be guaranteed before the Commission even if the applicants 'made a declaration that the file which the national authorities transmitted to the Commission was complete and they had nothing to add'. Case T-186/97 *Wilson Holland and Others v Commission* [2001] ECLI:EU:T:2001:133, para 160.

33 Alonso de León (n 7) 267.

points of the procedure.[34] What is however clear from this case law is that, whenever a composite procedure is concluded with an EU measure on which the 'main' decision-making power is held by an EU administrative authority, the violation of the right to be heard at the national level is able to 'contaminate' the validity of the final EU law. This finding is in line with the division of jurisdictions between the national and EU courts, which will be discussed in Section 13.3.

The duty to give reasons, which undoubtedly also applies to acts of individual scope, resembles to some extent the broader *problématique* discussed with respect to the challenges of the right to be heard in composite procedures: Which governance level must discharge the duty to give reasons in composite procedures? Can the shortcomings of one authority be compensated by an authority belonging to a different legal system?

While the duty to give reasons, like the right to be heard, is sometimes enshrined in the legislation creating a composite procedure,[35] the case law has revolved around situations in which this duty is not precisely stated. In particular, as highlighted by Brito Bastos, two situations have been brought to the attention of the Court, both relating to composite procedures where a national preparatory measure is followed by a final EU measure: first, whether EU authorities must include the reasons contained in the relevant national preparatory acts in their statements of reasons; second, whether EU authorities may discharge their duty to give reasons simply by *per relationem* (i.e., merely by referring back to the national preparatory measures).[36]

With respect to the first point, the ruling in *Sweden v Commission* (which was confirmed in later case law)[37] allows the conclusion that if the statement of reasons contained in the preparatory measure contains facts and

[34] Alonso de León (n 7) 290–291. For a way to read more coherence in the case law, and the idea that it shows a departure from the notion of 'executive federalism' towards a more unitary vision of the European administrative space, see Filipe Brito Bastos, 'Beyond executive federalism' (n 26) ch 4.

[35] See, for example, Regulation (EC) No 1829/2003 of the European Parliament and of the Council of 22 September 2003 on genetically modified food and feed [2003] OJ L268/1, art 6 (6), which binds the European Food Safety Authority to a duty to substantiate the opinions it issues in the procedures for the authorisation of genetically modified food or feed. The European Medicines Agency is under the same duty when issuing opinions concerning the approval of pharmaceuticals (see Parliament and Directive 2001/83/EC of the European Parliament and of the Council of 6 November 2001 on the Community code relating to medicinal products for human use [2001] OJ L311/67, art 32 (5)).

[36] Filipe Brito Bastos, 'Beyond executive federalism' (n 26) 174–175.

[37] Case T-344/15 *France v Commission* [2017] ECLI:EU:T:2017:250; Case T-653/16 R *Malta v Commission* [2018] ECLI:EU:T:2018:241; Case C-135/11 P, *Internationaler Tierschutz-Fonds gGmbH* [2012] ECLI:EU:C:2012:376.

circumstances that are decisive for the final decision then the EU authority issuing the final measure should include them in its own statement of reasons.[38]

Regarding the possibility for EU authorities to refer to the statement of reasons of the national preparatory measure, the CJEU has been consistent since the *Branco* ruling that this is possible, provided that the EU measure confirms the preparatory measure adopted by national authorities, which should themselves have issued a sufficiently clear statement of reasons, and that the addressee has been able to take cognisance of the measure.[39]

While this case law solves some of the issues connected to the extent of the duty to give reasons in composite procedures, as with respect for the right to be heard, several doubts still remain: What is the extent of the duty to give reasons if the procedure is reversed and it is the EU authority taking the preparatory measure? To what extent should national preparatory measures be subject to a duty to give reasons? What about composite procedures involving more than two steps or two legal systems?

These questions are not only relevant with respect to the decision-making process itself but also for the question of the competent judicial instance when any of those (procedural or substantive) fundamental rights are violated. It is to this question that the chapter now turns.

13.3 FINDING THE COMPETENT COURT IN COMPOSITE PROCEDURES: MISSION IMPOSSIBLE?[40]

13.3.1 *The Separation of Jurisdiction as the Cornerstone of the European Judicial Architecture*

As the examples presented above have shown, the variegated universe of composite procedures, as the regulatory manifestation of the increasingly intense cooperation between national and European authorities for the implementation of EU law, are present in virtually all EU policy fields. Despite their capacity to violate fundamental rights protected by the EU legal order, the

[38] Case C-64/05 P *Sweden v Commission*, [2007] ECLI:EU:C:2007:802.

[39] Case T-85/94 *Branco I* [1995] ECLI:EU:T:1995:4. See, for later case law, e.g., Case T-199/99 *Sgaravatti v Commission* [2002] ECLI:EU:T:2002:228; Case T-241/00 *Azienda Agricola "Le Canne" Srl v Commission* [2002] ECLI:EU:T:2002:57; Case T-182/96 *Partex v Commission* [1999] ECLI:EU:T:1999:171.

[40] The arguments made in this section draw from the author's earlier work, and in particular Eliantonio, 'Access to Justice in Composite Procedures for the Implementation of EU Law: The Story so Far' (n 2).

current judicial framework seems ill-suited to cater for their comprehensive judicial control.

This is because of the traditional approach to the judicial review of administrative action, which is based on the principle of territoriality. On this basis, the jurisdiction of courts is limited to the review of the administrative action stemming from the authorities belonging to the domestic legal system. This approach would make judicial review of a national court on an EU measure, or vice versa of the CJEU on a measure adopted by a national authority, in principle, impossible.

This strict separation of judicial control of administrative action (with the only avenue of procedural integration represented by the preliminary question of validity under Article 267 TFEU,[41] see Chapter 4) creates difficulties in access to justice. These are likely to arise for two main reasons. First, because the actions of the several national and EU authorities participating in a composite procedure might be so intertwined that it could be difficult to trace the contribution of each authority in the process and, consequently, the attributability of a conduct to a specific level of administrative governance. Second, because, even if an action could be 'isolated' and attributed to a specific administrative authority, the several preliminary steps leading to a final decision within a composite procedure might not be reviewable in any legal system. They might not constitute a reviewable act in the legal system to which these steps, acts, or actions belong (in light of their preparatory nature), and, at the same time, they might not be subject to judicial control in the court of the legal system adopting the final decision because of the limitations generated by the principle of territoriality. In Section 13.3.2, the access to justice issues arising from composite procedures entailing factual conduct will be examined. As Section 13.3.2 will show, these issues mostly revolve around the question of attributability of a conduct to a specific level of governance. Section 13.3.3 will then consider the case law of the Court of Justice concerning procedures of a decisional nature. This division mirrors the distinction made in Section 13.2 and is warranted by the different problems arising from these two types of vertical composite procedure. Section 13.3.3 will show that the CJEU has been asked on a number of occasions to determine the extent of its own jurisdiction as well of that of the national courts in composite procedures. However, many questions are still left unanswered and possible gaps in judicial protection might persist.

[41] Consolidated Version of the Treaty on the Functioning of the European Union [2016] OJ C202/47.

13.3.2 *Factual Action in Composite Procedures and the Problem of Attributability*

As introduced in Section 13.2, composite procedures can entail a variety of actions of a factual nature, such as the removal of individuals from the EU territory, the carrying out of interviews, the seizing of documents, and the like. When these acts are carried out in the context of composite procedures, and in particular when the factual action is itself cooperative in nature, it is very difficult to attribute a specific conduct to one or other administrative authority. If, for example, a national inspector and an inspector of the European Central Bank, working together in the so-called Joint Inspection Teams, perform a number of actions on the premises of a financial institution, the actions will be so intertwined as to render attributability of conduct to the national or European level of governance next to impossible.[42]

If this problem is solved and disentangling the EU action from the national action is somehow possible, access to justice will nevertheless not be fully ensured per se in cases of fundamental rights violations.

Where the procedure is concluded with a national measure, the national competent court will be able to send a question concerning the validity of the EU conduct to the CJEU. The latter is, according to its *Foto-Frost* ruling,[43] the sole judicial authority in the case of doubt on the validity of acts or actions stemming from an EU authority, able to control it. Furthermore, according to the *Grimaldi* ruling, preliminary questions of validity are admitted with respect to all measures of EU law.[44] Hence, for a factual action of an EU authority, the preliminary question of validity seems to be available.[45]

However, even in this – seemingly easy – case, the fact that the use of the preliminary question of validity presupposes the capacity of the national court to 'discern' the EU contribution to the national measure might place the

[42] On this, see Laura Vissink, *Effective Legal Protection in Banking Supervision* (Europa Law 2021), esp. ch 5. For similar problems raised by the 'hotspots', see Agostina Pirrello, 'The European Union Agency for Asylum: legal remedies and national articulations in composite border procedures' (forthcoming 2024) European Law Journal; similar considerations are expressed in Salvo Nicolosi, 'Frontex and Migrants' Access to Justice: Drifting Effective Judicial Protection?' (Verfassungsblog, 7 September 2022) <https://verfassungsblog.de/frontex-and-migrants-access-to-justice/>; see also Melanie Fink, *Frontex and Human Rights: Responsibility in 'Multi-Actor Situations' under the ECHR and EU Public Liability Law* (Oxford University Press 2018) 97–141, 232–274.

[43] Case C-314/85 *Foto-Frost v Hauptzollamt Lübeck-Ost* [1987] ECLI:EU:C:1987:452.

[44] Case C-322/88 *Salvatore Grimaldi v Fonds des maladies professionnelles* [1989] ECLI:EU:C:1989:646.

[45] For the same conclusion, see De Bellis, 'Multi-level Administration, Inspections and Fundamental Rights: Is Judicial Protection Full and Effective?' (n 11) 436.

national court in a conundrum: Should it – in doubt concerning the attributability of conduct to the EU authority – send a preliminary question of validity, even though the contribution of the EU administrative authority might not be discernible (incurring a risk of the preliminary question being declared inadmissible), or should it accept the indiscernibility of EU and national action and review the measure, possibly in breach of its *Foto-Frost* obligation?

Furthermore, if the procedure concludes with an EU measure, the competent EU court will be faced with the lack of a 'reverse' preliminary ruling, whereby the CJEU could ask a national court to review the validity of the factual conduct of a national authority.[46] In this situation, the applicant might need to access a national court to have the conduct of the national authorities reviewed. However, whether this claim will be admissible remains to be seen, and it is equally not clear whether the case law concerning composite procedures concluded with an EU measure and entailing 'formalised' preliminary national measures (i.e., the *Borelli/Berlusconi* line of case law examined in Section 13.3.3) can also be applied when factual conduct is at stake.

13.3.3 *Composite Procedures, Discretion, and the Quest for the Competent Court*

For the myriads of composite procedures where no factual conduct is involved, and the preliminary measures adopted by the competent national and EU authorities materialise in more 'formalised' measures (such as an opinion, a plan, an objection, etc.), it is again helpful to differentiate the situations in which the final measure of the decision-making process is adopted by the national or the EU level of administration.

As in the scenarios discussed above with respect to factual conduct, in the case of a composite procedure concluded by a national measure, the preliminary measures of the EU authorities can be challenged through a preliminary question of validity under Article 267 TFEU. For the opposite situation, when a composite procedure ends with an EU measure, the hurdle to access to justice arises from the combined absence of a 'reverse' preliminary ruling and the preliminary nature of national measures, which would, in most legal systems, lead to the inadmissibility of a claim against these measures.

[46] For a thorough discussion on how the introduction of such a mechanism would solve the gaps in judicial protection in such situations, see Torben Ellerbrok, 'Das umgekehrte Vorabentscheidungsverfahren als Schlussstein im europäischen Rechtsschutzverbund' (2022) 113 Verwaltungsarchiv 202.

In order to ensure access to justice in these situations, the Court has intervened with two landmark rulings that require national preliminary measures to be either autonomously reviewed before the national courts or to be reviewed by the CJEU in the context of a claim against the final EU measure. The first solution was proposed in the *Borelli* ruling, in which the Court held first that it was not entitled to review acts of national authorities but also, second, that national courts had to admit claims against national preparatory measures, regardless of the limitation posed to that review by the applicable national procedural rules.[47] After *Borelli*, the same approach was repeated in a number of cases relating to the field of protected denomination of origins and geographical indications under the applicable EU legislation. In these cases, the Court confirmed, on the basis of *Borelli*, that national preparatory measures should be reviewed by national courts but only when such a measure 'constitutes a necessary step in the procedure for the adoption of a[n] [EU] measure, [and in regard to which] the [EU] institutions have only a limited or non-existent discretion'.[48]

The solution envisaged in *Borelli* therefore only applies if the EU authorities adopting the final measure retain little or no margin of discretion vis-à-vis the preparatory national measure. If, instead, the EU authority retains a margin of discretion in respect of the final measure to be issued vis-à-vis the preparatory measure of the national authorities, the system of judicial protection afforded in such cases is the one proposed by the *Berlusconi* ruling. In this case, the Court ruled that, for composite procedures where the final decision-making power lies with the EU authorities, the CJEU has jurisdiction to review the entirety of the decision-making chain, including its national component.[49] Advocating a form of 'integrated' judicial review, the CJEU has, at the same time, and in an established line of case law (though limited to date to the banking sector), stripped national courts of their jurisdiction to review certain national preparatory measures that are part of composite procedures.[50]

47 See, for an extensive discussion of this case law and its implication for EU administrative law, Filipe Brito Bastos, 'The *Borelli* Doctrine revisited: three issues of coherence in a landmark ruling for EU administrative justice' (2015) 8 Review of European Administrative law 269.

48 Case C-269/99 *Carl Kühne GmbH & Co. KG and Others v Jütro Konservenfabrik GmbH & Co. KG* [2001] ECLI:EU:C:2001:659. See more recently also Case C-343/07 *Bavaria NV and Bavaria Italia Srl v Bayerischer Brauerbund eV* [2009] ECLI:EU:C:2009:415.

49 *Berlusconi and Fininvest* (n 4).

50 E.g., Case T-698/16 *Trasta Komercbanka and Others v ECB* [2022] ECLI:EU:T:2022:737; Case T-330/19 *PNB Banka AS* [2022] ECLI:EU:T:2022:775; Cases T-351/18 and T-584/18 *Ukrselhosprom PCF LLC and Versobank AS, established in Tallinn (Estonia) v European Central Bank (ECB)* [2021] ECLI:EU:T:2021:669. See also the Opinion of AG Kokott in Cases C-750/21 P and C-256/22 P *Pilatus Bank plc v ECB* [2023] ECLI:EU:C:2023:431, in

The combined reading of *Borelli* and *Berlusconi* entails that the determining criterion to vest national courts with the jurisdiction (and the duty) to review national preparatory measures is that of the margin of discretion afforded to the final EU decision-maker.[51]

However, the criterion established by the CJEU, based on the margin of discretion afforded to the final EU decision-maker is not without difficulties for those who need to apply it. In *Berlusconi*, the CJEU uses the notion of 'discretion' to refer to the margin of manoeuvre of the EU authorities to decide on the *content* of a decision (as opposed to a situation in which this content is pre-determined by the content of the national preparatory measure). However, the notion of discretion can also relate, for example, to the question of *whether* to exercise a power or to *which form* a decision can take. Furthermore, discretion can relate to policy choices but also the assessment of facts.[52] This somewhat oversimplified view of discretion is not realistic in light of the variety of legislative scenarios through which composite procedures can be generated. It is also liable to generate further preliminary references and legal uncertainty: Who is to assess whether the legal framework is such to grant 'exclusive jurisdiction' to the CJEU or conversely whether a national court must be seized of the review of a preliminary measure? *Quid iuris* of time limits if the CJEU eventually decides that the preliminary measure needs to be reviewed by the national courts?

The *Borelli* and *Berlusconi* rulings also leave a number of further questions unanswered. In particular, the solution proposed by the *Borelli* ruling still remains unclear from a practical point of view and has only been partially clarified by the *Jeanningros* ruling.[53] Indeed, while the obligation for national

which the AG reiterates this point in connection with the infringement of the right to be heard by a national preparatory measure.

51 For a discussion of the coherence between Borelli and Berlusconi, see Brito Bastos 'Derivative Illegality in the European Composite Administrative Procedures' (n 3) 110–113, who argues that in *Borelli* a number of constitutional arguments speak against the possibility of derivative illegality (i.e., the capacity of national measures to contaminate final EU measures), which in turn limits the possibility to 'centralise' judicial control in the hands of the CJEU over the entirety of the process. See also Paul Dermine and Mariolina Eliantonio, 'Case Note: CJEU (Grand Chamber), Judgment of 19 December 2018, C-219/17, Silvio Berlusconi and Finanziaria d'investimento Fininvest SpA (Fininvest) v Banca d'Italia and Istituto per la Vigilanza Sulle Assicurazioni (IVASS)' (2019) 12 Review of European Administrative Law 237.

52 Herwig C H Hofmann, 'Multi-Jurisdictional Composite Procedures. The Backbone to the EU's Single Regulatory Space' (2019) 3 University of Luxembourg Law Working Paper Series 12.

53 *Jeanningros* (n 4).

courts to review national preparatory measures binding on the EU authority taking the final decision was clear after *Borelli*, the question remained open as to what would happen if a final decision is taken by the Union administration before the national court has had the opportunity to review the binding national preparatory act upon which it is based.

In *Jeanningros*, the Court clarified that, on the one hand, any pending proceedings against the national preparatory act should continue and, on the other, a national ruling holding that act invalid should lead the EU authority to revoke a decision taken on that basis (upon the assumption that the time limits under Article 263 would be long expired). While this confirms for potential applicants that the national route must remain open even when the EU authority has taken a final decision, it still does not clarify the remedies at their disposal if the Commission were to refuse to or simply does not revoke its final measure after the national proceedings are concluded. Is an action for failure to act under Article 265 TFEU then open to applicants? Given the lack of formalised communication channels between national courts and the Commission, what if the Commission is simply unaware of the fact that the relevant national proceedings are concluded?[54]

If one considers specifically the *Berlusconi* scenario, the review of the national measure permitted by the CJEU seems to be limited to errors of EU law, to the exclusion, therefore, of flaws in the national preparatory act based on domestic procedural law.[55] A different solution would entail the CJEU applying national law and would make the determination of the validity of an EU measure indirectly dependent on varying national procedural arrangements. However, the exclusion from the scope of judicial control of these national preparatory measures of errors stemming from national law inevitably creates what has been referred to as an 'administrative crack in the EU's rule of law'.[56]

Furthermore, it is unclear how the combined reading of *Borelli* and *Berlusconi* can be applied in composite procedures that entail more than two steps. This difficulty is exemplified in the *Association Greenpeace France* ruling, which concerned the authorisation scheme in the field of

[54] See, on these points, Filipe Brito Bastos 'Judicial Annulment of National Preparatory Acts and the Effects on Final Union Administrative Decisions: Comments on the Judgment of 29 January 2020, Case C-785/18 Jeanningros, EU:C:2020:46' (2021) 14(2) Review of European Administrative Law 109, 115 et seq.

[55] Dermine and Eliantonio, 'Case Note: CJEU (Grand Chamber), Judgment of 19 December 2018, C-219/17' (n 51) 249–250.

[56] Filipe Brito Bastos, 'An Administrative Crack in the EU's Rule of Law: Composite Decision-making and Nonjusticiable National Law' (2020) 16 European Constitutional Law Review 63.

GMOs.[57] In this case, the applicant complained that the actions of the national authority where the procedure had started were irregular and therefore rendered the final Commission decision irregular. The Court could thus still implicitly rely on the *Borelli* ruling and find that national courts are competent for the review of that preliminary national measure.[58] However, it is not clear which would be the competent court to review the input of *another* national authority in the process (e.g., in the form of an objection to the assessment made by the first authority).

A separate and final reflection should be dedicated to the emerging case law concerning a special type of composite procedure that is based on information sharing between the EU and national authorities, such as in the above-mentioned cases of the SIS and RAPEX databases.[59] The *Borelli* and *Berlusconi* cases do not seem to fit the schemes of composite procedures in these scenarios as the final decision-making process does not lie with the EU level, and the existence of the preliminary question of validity does not solve the problem of access to justice. This is because these procedures involve the EU authorities and more than one national authority: they are thus 'triangular' in nature in that they are started at one national level, with an intermediate participation of the EU authorities, and concluded at another national level.

The case law in this framework is rather limited and leaves many questions unanswered. Two cases, *Malagutti*[60] and *Bowland*,[61] dismissing an action for damages against the EU for sharing allegedly incorrect information (on the basis of which national measures had been adopted), seem to indicate that, according to the CJEU, the EU action within these systems is limited to 'passing on' the information, which remains within the full responsibility of the Member State that shared the information in the first place. The 'triangularity' in these procedures seems therefore, according to this case law, merely formal.

[57] Case C-6/99 *Association Greenpeace France and Others v Ministère de l'Agriculture et de la Pêche and Others* [1999] ECLI:EU:C:1999:587.

[58] On the point of the coherence between *Borelli* and *Greenpeace*, see Filipe Brito Bastos, 'The *Borelli* Doctrine revisited: three issues of coherence in a landmark ruling for EU administrative justice' (2015) 8 Review of European Administrative law 269, 277 et seq.

[59] See further on this point, Demková, *Automated Decision-Making and Effective Remedies* (n 17); Benjamin Jan, 'Safeguarding the Right to an Effective Remedy in Algorithmic Multi-Governance Systems: An Inquiry in Artificial Intelligence-Powered Informational Cooperation in the EU Administrative Space' (2023) 16 Review of European Administrative Law 9; Niovi Vavoula 'Information Sharing in the Dublin System: Remedies for Asylum Seekers In-Between Gaps in Judicial Protection and Interstate Trust' (n 19).

[60] Case T-177/02 *Malagutti-Vezinhet v Commission* [2004] ECLI:EU:T:2004:72.

[61] Case T-212/06 *Bowland Dairy Products v Commission* [2009] ECLI:EU:T:2009:419.

If these procedures are then to be considered horizontal *in substance*, where can or should national preparatory measures in these cases be reviewed? The recent *Funke* ruling seems to indicate that preparatory measures in which the information is shared (in this case, within the RAPEX system) must at least be open to judicial control in the legal system where the measure was taken.[62] However, in this case, there had not yet been any national measure taken after the alert was shared by the Commission to the Member States. If a subsequent national measure (e.g., determining that a product be banned from the market) is taken by the authority of another Member State, should an applicant initiate two separate proceedings in the course of both legal systems involved in the procedure?[63]

13.4 CONCLUSIONS

This contribution has sought to examine the question of the availability of a sufficient system of remedies against fundamental rights violations possibly occurring in the context of the so-called vertical composite procedures, that is, administrative decision-making processes in which national and EU authorities collaborate in the implementation of EU law.

The chapter has shown, first, that the complex web of interactions between national and EU administrative levels, intervening at different moments of administrative procedures, taking a variety of – more or less formalised – forms is capable of affecting a number of EU fundamental rights, both substantive and procedural in nature. In this context, further research should examine the universe of composite procedures, by discovering possible common patterns and notable differences.[64]

Second, the contribution has demonstrated that procedural integration at the level of the decision-making sits uncomfortably with the traditional approach to the judicial review of administrative action, which is based on the principle of territoriality and on the separation of jurisdictions between national and EU courts. As a consequence, there may well be situations in which private parties might be denied the right to challenge acts emanating from composite procedures.

This is notably the case in composite procedures including factual conduct for which it might be extremely difficult to attribute conduct to a specific level

62 Case C-626/21 *Funke Sp. z o.o. v Landespolizeidirektion Wien* [2023] ECLI:EU:C:2023:412.

63 Further on this, see Eliantonio, 'Information Exchange in European Administrative Law: A Threat to Effective Judicial Protection?' (n 16).

64 For an attempt, see Emilie Chevalier, Mariolina Eliantonio, and Rui Lanceiro, *Administrative Cooperation in the European Space* (Bruylant, forthcoming 2024).

of governance. However, even where the contribution of national and EU authorities materialises in more 'formalised' measure, the patchwork solution currently in place through the preliminary question of validity, on the one hand, and the combined reading of *Borelli* and *Berlusconi*, on the other hand, leaves many questions unanswered and possible gaps in judicial protection open. Even more questions seem to arise in the increasingly more frequent composite procedures entailing the sharing of data between national and EU authorities.

Already since the *Les Verts* ruling, the CJEU has held that the EU is 'based on the rule of law, inasmuch as neither its Member States nor its institutions can avoid a review of the question whether the measures adopted by them are in conformity with the basic constitutional charter, the Treaty'.[65] This statement is embodied in Article 47 of the Charter guaranteeing the right to an effective remedy. The picture described above with respect to access to justice in composite procedures shows that this right does not seem currently to be fully ensured. Further research should be devoted to a comparative analysis of national case law where composite procedures have been at stake, to assess whether and to what extent the *Borelli* and *Berlusconi* rulings have been correctly understood and applied at the national level.

While several gaps in access to justice within composite procedures seem to persist, and the CJEU has failed to clarify a number of essential aspects of judicial review in this respect, there are also structural shortcomings that ought to be mentioned. In the absence of a 'reverse' preliminary question, which admittedly is not for the CJEU to create, the Court was unable to tackle some of the fundamental shortcomings of access to justice in composite procedures. It is therefore to be hoped that a fundamental reconsideration of how to ensure access to justice in an increasingly 'integrated' administration will soon be placed on the agenda of the EU legislator. This reconsideration would not only require that sufficient multi-level procedural mechanisms are in place, such as the creation of the above-mentioned system of 'reverse' preliminary questions, but also ideally a truly integrated system of judicial control whereby one judicial instance (in a straightforward fashion the one currently controlling the act which concludes a composite procedure) would be empowered to review the entirety of the decisional chain.[66]

[65] Case C-294/83 *Les Verts v Parliament* [1986] ECLI:EU:C:1986:166, para 23.

[66] Mariolina Eliantonio, 'Judicial Review in an Integrated Administration' (n 3).

14

Soft Law and Challenges to Access to Justice

MERIJN CHAMON*

14.1 INTRODUCTION

This chapter explores the challenges that the informalisation of EU governance, through the reliance on soft law, poses for the possibilities for private parties to challenge EU conduct that may be in violation of their fundamental rights. First, this main research question will be situated in the broader debate on reliance on soft law in EU law. Subsequently, the ontological question of how soft law, given its non-binding nature, may constitute an interference with a fundamental right will be addressed and different examples of the increased reliance on soft law will be used to illustrate recent developments. Having sketched the state of play and the challenges that soft law may pose for fundamental rights, the chapter will then turn to the EU's system of remedies. The latter has been crafted with a view to providing legal protection against binding governmental action. Soft law undermines that assumption and the difficulty in challenging it through conventional mechanisms of legal protection may itself become a possible interference, this time with the right to an effective legal protection as enshrined in Article 47 of the Charter of Fundamental Rights of the EU (CFR, 'the Charter').[1] After having identified the (conventional) remedies available, the chapter will make some suggestions to adapt the system of remedies addressing the specific challenge posed by soft law.

* I would like to thank the editor and Dr Joyce De Coninck for comments on an earlier draft. All errors or omissions remain mine.

[1] Charter of Fundamental Rights of the European Union [2016] OJ C202/389 (CFR), art 47.

14.2 SOFT LAW: WHAT'S IN A NAME

The final part of this second section of the chapter is devoted to illustrating, through a series of examples, how, in practice, soft law could interfere with fundamental rights. Before presenting these examples, however, some preliminary clarifications need to be made. First, Senden's definition of soft law will be presented together with a discussion of the different functions that soft law may fulfil, before dealing with the question of how, in theory, soft law may interfere with fundamental rights.

14.2.1 *What Is Soft Law and What Makes It Soft?*

The study of soft law in the EU legal order is already well established. A seminal work, and one that has advanced an often relied on definition of the notion, was that of Senden. She qualifies soft law as 'rules of conduct which are laid down in instruments which have not been attributed legally binding force as such, but nevertheless may have certain (indirect) legal effects, and that are aimed at and may produce practical effects'.[2] This definition remains rather vague, however, and a lot of intellectual effort has since gone into attempts to better understand what kind of practical and/or indirect legal effects are *sufficiently* relevant in order for non-binding acts to be considered legally significant enough to constitute soft *law*.[3] Further research has therefore looked into the question of which precise features makes soft law *soft* and the types of soft law that exist.

On what makes soft law soft and trying to better capture the notion of soft law, Terpan proposed to understand the phenomenon as a function of two criteria, those being obligation and enforcement. A norm can then be qualified as hard law when it cumulatively prescribes a sufficiently clear obligation that can also be enforced. Conversely, norms that do not prescribe sufficiently clear obligations would constitute soft law as would norms that do prescribe obligations but that are not enforceable. To determine whether a sufficiently clear obligation is being prescribed, Terpan considers the source and the content of the norm in question and, in terms of enforcement, he distinguishes between norms that are subject to judicial (or at least very

[2] Linda Senden, *Soft law in European Community Law* (Hart 2004) 112; See also Linda Senden and Ton van den Brink, *Checks and Balances of Soft EU Rule-Making*, European Parliament Directorate General for Internal Policies, PE 462.433, 11.

[3] In their standard work, Hofmann, Rowe, and Türk even avoid the term soft law as they find it misleading to describe a plethora of administrative rules. See Herwig Hofmann, Gerald Rowe, and Alexander Türk, *EU Administrative Law* (Oxford University Press 2011) 536.

constraining) control, those subject to non-coercive control (such as mere monitoring), and those subject to no control.[4]

14.2.2 *Soft Law's Different Functions*

To better appreciate the dynamics (and interference with fundamental rights) that may flow from soft law, it is useful to distinguish the different functions that soft law acts may fulfil. Here, different authors have elaborated different typologies. Senden and Van den Brink, for instance, distinguish between soft regulatory rule-making and soft administrative rule making. The first has a para-law policy-steering function while the purpose of the other is to give post-legislative guidance.[5] The classification of soft law adopted specifically for EU agencies as proposed by Rocca and Eliantonio also categorises soft law in light of its position in the policy cycle and can also be integrated in that of Senden and Van den Brink. Rocca and Eliantonio distinguish four types: where soft law is adopted in the form of acceptable means of compliance or technical guidance (categories one and two of Rocca and Eliantonio), it will typically fulfil the function of post-legislative guidance; conversely, technical documents and high quality information (categories four and three of Rocca and Eliantonio) typically fulfil a para-law function.[6] Just like the origin of a norm's soft nature above, the conceptual distinction between these two main categories is important because it feeds into the constitutional assessment of the informalisation of EU governance through soft law.

On the one hand, post-legislative soft law may be beneficial to clarify the meaning and scope of legislative provisions. On the other hand, there also exists a risk that in the post-legislative phase, through the soft law guidance, a binding norm is given (slightly) different meaning, thereby also possibly altering fundamental rights interferences flowing from that binding norm. In that case, however, a binding norm still exists that might meet the requirements of Article 52(1) of the Charter. In contrast, soft law fulfilling a para-legislative function does not have such a binding norm to fall back on, raising the question of whether any fundamental rights interferences by such soft law would be 'prescribed by law' or whether they would be ipso facto violations.

4 Fabien Terpan, 'Soft Law in the European Union – The Changing Nature of EU Law' (2015) 21 European Law Journal 68.

5 Senden and Van den Brink (n 2) 12.

6 See Penelope Rocca and Mariolina Eliantonio, 'European Union soft law by agencies: An analysis of the legitimacy of their procedural frameworks' in Maurizia de Bellis, Giacinto della Cananea, Martina Conticelli (eds), *EU executive governance: Agencies and procedures* (Giappichelli 2020) 185–186.

A final consideration to present at this point is the dual question of the author and the addressee of the soft law. In EU law, perhaps the archetypical form of soft law are the Commission's guidelines in the field of competition law where the Commission set out its view on how EU competition law is to be applied. This soft law has no specific addressees but helps private parties anticipate the Commission's practice, since the soft law has self-binding effect on the Commission as the (main) actor responsible for the enforcement of EU competition law.[7] More recently, a different trend can be seen, as will be further illustrated below, whereby a proliferation in the authors of soft law can be witnessed. In this fairly new constellation,[8] the rather straightforward link between the author adopting the soft law and the enforcement actor has also been severed, meaning there is no *self*-binding effect anymore either. Often EU agencies or bodies are called on to adopt soft law, fleshing out legislative provisions that are to be applied by national authorities. While such soft law may still fulfil the clarification function of post-legislative soft law noted above, the fact remains that the fiction of an authority limiting its own (enforcement) discretion can no longer be upheld in these cases. That would mean that the position of private parties is weakened, and the possible interferences with their fundamental rights may become more acute. This since the soft law will still carry in it an expectation of compliance but without being balanced by the legitimate expectation that the enforcement actor has limited its own discretion.

This feature is exacerbated by a further feature of the typical composition of EU agencies or bodies adopting soft law. Unlike the main EU executive (the Commission), the main decision-making entities of EU agencies and bodies are the national authorities responsible for the implementation of EU law. The further risk this poses is illustrated nicely by the recent *ThyssenKrupp* cases. At issue here was a composite procedure whereby the EU customs expert group (composed of national authorities) could not agree on whether certain conditions to grant an exceptional authorisation to one of ThyssenKrupp's competitors were met. Still, a majority in the expert group was in favour of granting the authorisation and the Commission concluded that the conditions to do so were indeed met. The Dutch customs authority

7 See Joined Cases C-189/02 P, C-202/02 P, C-205/02 P to C-208/02 P and C-213/02 P *Dansk Rørindustri and Others v Commission* [2005] ECLI:EU:C:2005:408, para 211.

8 This constellation is not entirely new since precursors to it can be found in EU law decades back. See, for instance, the Administrative Commission for the coordination of social security regimes which was criticised early on by Maas, see Herman Maas, 'La Commission administrative pour la sécurité sociale des travailleurs migrants' (1966) 2 Cahiers de droit européen 343. The new aspect to it is that it is becoming a standard feature in EU governance, e.g. through an increasing number of 'Boards' that wield soft law powers.

subsequently formally granted the authorisation and claimed that it was *obliged* to do so in light of the Commission's conclusion.[9] This because a further soft law act adopted by the expert group, 'the new administrative practice', provided that such Commission conclusions are binding on the national authorities.[10] The General Court (GC) ruled that the Commission's conclusion was not challengeable pursuant to Article 263 TFEU[11] since the relevant legislation merely prescribed that national authorities 'shall take it' into account.[12] The GC's findings were upheld by the Court of Justice, which furthermore remarked that the 'fact that ... the competent customs authority took its decision in the belief that it was bound by the contested conclusion does not ... have the effect of making that conclusion an act which is legally binding'.[13] For readers versed in the admissibility requirements of Article 263 TFEU procedures, the Courts' findings will appear logical and sound. However, a troubling dynamic at play here is that national authorities come together at EU level and de facto limit their own discretion through soft law, obfuscating the available remedies available to private parties. As Eliantonio explains in Chapter 13, where the EU adopts preliminary measures and national authorities adopt the final act, a disentangling of who does what becomes paramount.

14.2.3 *Soft Law Interferences with Fundamental Rights in Theory*

Having further clarified what makes soft law *soft* and how soft law may occupy different positions in the policy cycle, it is now possible to look into the implications of soft law from a fundamental rights perspective. Two questions are especially relevant here: First, if soft law is soft because it does not prescribe a hard obligation and/or because any possible obligation prescribed will not be enforced through a 'constraining' enforcement mechanism, can it become sufficiently relevant for its fundamental rights implications? Secondly, if a limitation or restriction may result from soft law, under which conditions may those limitations or restrictions be said to be 'prescribed by law'? Under the Convention, this requirement first refers back to the domestic law of a party but that domestic law must itself also be in conformity with the

9 See Order in Case T-577/17 *ThyssenKrupp v Commission* [2018] ECLI:EU:T:2018:411, para 8.

10 Ibid para 65.

11 Consolidated Version of the Treaty on the Functioning of the European Union [2016] OJ C202/47 (TFEU), art 263.

12 See Order in *ThyssenKrupp* (n 9) para 68.

13 Ibid para 72.

Convention. While the domestic law need not formally be law, and can be enactments of lower rank than statutes and even unwritten law, it must meet qualitative requirements, including those of accessibility and foreseeability.[14] While this seems to provide sufficient flexibility to encompass soft law, the flexibility is arguably aimed at accommodating the different legal systems of parties to the Convention.[15] Given the risks that soft law poses for executive overreach in the EU,[16] limitations flowing exclusively from soft law might have to be ruled out as being 'prescribed by law' regardless of whether the soft law was accessible and its application foreseeable. Most of the time, however, a limitation will not flow *exclusively* from soft law, the latter instead fulfilling a mediating function. Where soft law is tolerated in such scenarios it becomes crucial to ensure proper remedies, as discussed in Section 14.3.

Returning to the first question, the relevance arguably lies in the practical and indirect effects that soft law may produce. After all, from a fundamental rights perspective, the question is not so much whether the norm prescribing (in)action on the part of the government is valid and/or binding but if and how such (in)action impacts the fundamental rights position of the individual.

The constitutional relevance of soft law is still obscured, however, since the notion of a limitation or restriction (of a fundamental right) has arguably not been properly clarified by either the European Court of Human Rights (ECtHR) or the Court of Justice of the EU (CJEU). For the ECtHR, this might not come as a surprise since the cornerstone of the Convention is the right of individual petition.[17] The ECtHR thus addresses specific (individual) complaints of concrete (alleged) violations of fundamental rights and not abstract questions relating to possible dubious legislative acts or government policy.[18] Such a constellation provides less opportunity for theory-crafting compared to the system in which the CJEU operates of which the purpose is not to protect fundamental rights but to oversee the construction of an internal market. In its system of remedies, the cornerstone is the preliminary reference procedure[19] and an independent Commission can bring infringement actions against Member States. Returning to the ECtHR, Letsas notes that its diagnostic test has five main

[14] See *Kafkaris v Cyprus*, Application no. 21906/04 (ECtHR, 12 February 2018), paras 139–140.

[15] Villiger notes that the inclusion of 'unwritten law' results from the need to accommodate common law systems. See Mark Eugen Villiger, *Handbook on the European Convention on Human Rights* (Brill 2022) 417.

[16] Margrit Cohn, *A Theory of the Executive Branch* (Oxford University Press 2021) 62–64.

[17] Mark Eugen Villiger, *Handbook on the European Convention on Human Rights* (Brill 2022) 19.

[18] See *Le Mailloux v France*, App no 18108/20 (ECtHR, 5 November 2020).

[19] Case *Opinion 2/13 – Accession of the EU to the ECHR* [2014] ECLI:EU:C:2014:2454, para 176.

stages, those being: (i) whether the facts come within the ECHR's scope, (ii) whether there is an interference with a right, (iii) whether the interference is prescribed by law, (iv) whether a legitimate is aim pursued, and (v) whether the interference is necessary in a democratic society.[20] While the second stage is conceptually distinct from the others,[21] in practice it is often subsumed under the fifth stage, which has also meant that the ECtHR has not developed a horizontal approach to the question of which types of governmental action or inaction may amount to an interference.[22] Since such an approach is lacking, the ECtHR has not articulated a general approach to the potential fundamental rights implications of soft law either.

When the interference question is explicitly addressed by the ECtHR, it is necessarily done in a case-by-case manner. In those cases, it is not exceptional for the ECtHR to simply postulate that there has been no restriction, without elaborating any reasoning in this regard. It thus, for instance, held that 'in themselves, the security checks to which passengers are subject in airports prior to departure do not constitute a restriction on freedom of movement'.[23] On other occasions, the finding of a lack of a restriction is more reasoned. In *Cha'are Shalom Ve Tsedek v France*, the ECtHR held that while ritual slaughter was protected under Article 9 of the Convention, 'there would be interference with the freedom to manifest one's religion only if the illegality of performing ritual slaughter made it impossible for ultra-orthodox Jews to eat meat from animals slaughtered in accordance with the religious prescriptions they considered applicable'.[24] Similarly, in *A, B and C v Ireland*, the Grand Chamber of the ECtHR ruled that there was no interference with a woman's right to life by a party's anti-abortion legislation when the woman in question could go abroad to receive treatment.[25] As Gerards notes, if the Court were to

[20] George Letsas, 'The scope and balancing of rights – Diagnostic or constitutive?' in Eva Brems and Janneke Gerards (eds), *Shaping Rights in the ECHR: The Role of the European Court of Human Rights in Determining the Scope of Human Rights* (Cambridge University Press 2014) 54.

[21] In this regard, it is telling that the Practical Guide on Admissibility Criteria remarks that the existence of an interference is a separate issue to be tested as part of the admissibility. It does so, however, in a section devoted to the cases where there is 'no lack of proportionality between the aims and the means'. As Letsas' test shows, however, it is nonsensical to discuss proportionality before the existence of an interference is found. See Registry of the ECtHR, Practical Guide on Admissibility Criteria, 31 August 2022, para 305.

[22] Noting there is little to no jurisprudence on the notions of limitation or restrictions, see Yves Haeck and Clara Burbano Herrera, *Procederen voor het Europees Hof voor de Rechten van de Mens* (Intersentia 2011) 55 at fn 241.

[23] *Phull v France*, App no 35753/03 (ECtHR, 11 January 2005).

[24] *Cha'are Shalom Ve Tsedek v France*, App no 27417/95 (ECtHR, 27 June 2000) para 80.

[25] *A, B and C v Ireland*, App no 25579/05 (ECtHR, 16 December 2010) paras 158–159.

follow this approach consistently, not many interferences would be found,[26] since an interference could only be qualified as such when it resulted in the impossibility to enjoy the protection of the right concerned. Linking back to soft law, that threshold might never be met since its soft nature means that non-compliant behaviour remains entirely possible.

On the other hand, in a greater number of cases, the Court links the degree of interference with the intensity of the proportionality review.[27] As a result, 'although in some cases the Court pays express attention to the phase of interference, in other cases it implicitly accepts or assumes the existence of an interference, or it merges the test of interference with the test of applicability or that of jurisdiction [or that of the justification of an interference]'.[28] Linking back again to soft law, this would mean that the existence of an interference will be accepted but that the proportionality review might be lenient. The lack of a clear position on the possible interfering effects flowing from soft law contrasts with the approach of the CJEU, at least in the area of the internal market.[29] As noted, this can arguably be explained by the different purposes of both Courts and the different procedural avenues to reach them.

In its internal market jurisprudence, it is firmly established case law that where national measures 'are capable of hindering or rendering less attractive the exercise of the fundamental freedoms guaranteed by the Treaty' they will constitute interferences.[30] That non-binding measures may also constitute restrictions on free movement is explicitly established in case law of the CJEU, since the restrictive *effect* of non-binding measures may be comparable to that of binding measures.[31] The degree of interference will then only be relevant in the possible assessment of the proportionality of the (national) measure. Of course, this 'internal market' logic might not be transposable to the fundamental rights protection offered by the Charter. While the CJEU itself has created a bridge between the two, that bridge does not connect the internal market freedoms with the full scope of material rights in the Charter. Instead, the Court held that where there are interferences with the

26 Janneke Gerards, *General Principles of the European Convention on Human Rights* (Cambridge University Press 2019) 17.

27 Ibid 17–18.

28 Ibid 18.

29 In its review of limitations on Charter rights the CJEU links its review to the approach of the ECtHR. See Joined Cases C-293/12 and C-594/12 *Digital Rights Ireland* [2014] ECLI:EU:C:2014:238, para 47.

30 Case C-212/06 *Flemish care insurance* [2008] ECLI:EU:C:2008:178, para 45; see also Joined Cases 177/82 and 178/82 *Van de Haar* [1984] ECLI:EU:C:1984:144, para 13.

31 See Case C-227/06 *Commission v Belgium* [2008] ECLI:EU:C:2008:160, paras 54–55; Case 249/81 *Commission v Ireland* [1982] ECLI:EU:C:1982:402, para 27.

fundamental freedoms of the internal market, these automatically cover interferences with only a limited subset of Charter rights (notably those laid down in Articles 15 to 17),[32] amalgamating the assessment of both. Going back to soft law's effects and as AG Bobek explained, soft law as an imperfect norm may not be coercively enforced but still have the 'normative ambition of inducing compliance'.[33] In the law of the internal market, such an ambition is sufficient for the measures to be caught by the free movement rules. Applying the same logic, the possibility of soft law constituting an interference with fundamental rights should be accepted.

The more concrete question of whether this means that the Charter applies to EU soft law further falls apart in two sub-questions, in light of the Charter's field of application. As Kenner and Peake note, the first is whether EU institutions are bound by the Charter when adopting soft law. For those authors, 'ideally, when it adopts non-binding policies, it should also be regarded as constrained and empowered by fundamental rights. However, in those contexts, as its output is not legally binding, it would be difficult to enforce this commitment in the courts'.[34] The second question is whether EU Member States are to be considered as implementing EU law when they adopt binding measures in the wake of EU soft law. As the law currently stands, Kenner and Peake answer this question in the negative but again call for a de facto respect for the Charter in order not to erode the protection offered by the latter.[35] At this point, it is useful to make a distinction between the different ways in which EU soft law may be followed upon or implemented. Thus, once an EU institution or body adopts soft law, generally four scenarios are possible: (i) the soft law is addressed to private parties (or has no addressee) and is acted upon by them; (ii) a governmental body (EU or national) adopts a binding act further to the EU soft law; (iii) a national body adopts soft law further to the EU soft law; (iv) the EU soft law is acted upon through factual conduct of a governmental body (EU or national). Evidently, the possibility for parties to bring a potential fundamental rights interference before a court will be influenced by which of the four scenarios is at issue.

While the Court has not addressed the first scenario explicitly yet, the dynamics that would be in play have popped up in cases before it. In *Bevándorlási és Állgmpolgársági Hivatal*, the Court noted that asylum seekers

32 Case C-322/16 *Global Starnet* [2017] ECLI:EU:C:2017:985, para 50.

33 See Opinion of AG Bobek in Case C-16/16 P *Belgium v Commission* [2017] ECLI:EU:C:2017:959, para 86.

34 Jeff Kenner and Katrina Peake, 'Art 33 – Family and Professional Life' in Steve Peers and Others (eds), *The EU Charter of Fundamental Rights: A Commentary* (Hart 2021) 946–947.

35 Ibid 947.

cannot be required to undergo a personality test, since their consent to do so would be required. However, it explicitly accepted that 'that consent is not necessarily given freely, being de facto imposed under the pressure of the circumstances in which applicants for international protection find themselves'.[36] The Court thus recognised that an applicant might be indirectly or practically forced, in which case there is an interference with the right to respect for a private life that needs to be justified. In the separate context of EU-induced national austerity programmes, which come under the second of the four scenarios noted above, AG Saugmandsgaard Øe in *Associação Sindical dos Juízes Portugueses* held that the Council recommendation based on Article 126(7) TFEU at issue 'did not fix sufficiently specific and precise objectives to support the view that the Portuguese State implemented on the basis of that recommendation requirements of EU law within the meaning of Article 51 of the Charter'.[37] This suggests, however, that, on the more fundamental preliminary point, the AG did not per se rule out that a Member State could be said to be implementing EU law in the sense of Article 51 of the Charter when acting on EU soft law.

14.2.4 *Soft Law Interferences with Fundamental Rights in Practice*

To make things more concrete, the present section will look into three distinct areas to illustrate how soft law may result in fundamental rights interferences. The first is the area of economic coordination and the Euro crisis response. To assist Eurozone Member States that are cut off from the international financial markets, the Eurozone Member States established the European Stability Mechanism (ESM) as an international organisation distinct from the EU. The ESM Treaty[38] confers a number of important tasks on the European Commission and the European Central Bank, which the CJEU accepted in the *Pringle* case.[39] The ESM funds made available to the Eurozone Member States are conditional on the negotiation and conclusion of a Memorandum of Understanding (MoU) between the ESM and the Member State concerned. These MoUs, while negotiated and signed by the Commission, follow from the ESM Treaty and therefore do not constitute challengeable acts

[36] Case C-473/16 *F v Bevándorlási és Állampolgársági Hivatal* [2018] ECLI:EU:C:2018:36, para 53.

[37] Opinion of AG Saugmandsgaard Øe in Case C-64/16 *Associação Sindical dos Juízes Portugueses* [2017] ECLI:EU:C:2017:395, para 51

[38] Treaty Establishing the European Stability Mechanism [2012] T/ESM 2012-LT/en 1 (ESM).

[39] Case C-370/12 *Pringle* [2012] ECLI:EU:C:2012:756, paras 155–169.

under Article 263 TFEU.[40] At the same time, the EU can still be held liable for the Commission's wrongful acts or omissions, specifically under the Charter (and the right to property, notably of those people affected by the austerity or restructuring measures taken in execution of the MoU), as confirmed by the Court in *Ledra Advertising*.[41]

The legal nature of the MoUs, negotiated by the Commission under the ESM, is highly disputed. The analogous MoUs agreed between the Commission and non-Eurozone Member States, under EU law, were considered to be 'mandatory' by the CJEU,[42] against the findings of the AG,[43] but it is unclear whether this can be transposed to the ESM MoUs. AG Wathelet in *Mallis* suggested they are non-binding,[44] as does Repasi,[45] while Poulou suggests they are binding.[46] The Court in *Ledra Advertising* did not address this question and focuses on the Commission's conduct in negotiating the MoU. Distinguishing the negotiation by the Commission from the MoU itself is in part built on a legal fiction however, and it seems difficult to see how the Commission's conduct as such would constitute an interference in the absence of the MoU itself constituting such an interference. The Court of Justice indeed seems to assume that the MoU (as negotiated by the Commission) interfered with the right to property of the deposit holders at the banks that were put under resolution. *Ledra* would thus imply either that the CJEU accepts that a non-binding act may have such constraining practical or indirect legal effects that a fundamental rights interference may result from it or, alternatively, that it believed the MoU was binding. While *Ledra* concerned the right to property of deposit holders (of Cypriot banks), it is

[40] Joined Cases C-8/15 P to C-10/15 P *Ledra Advertising e.a. v Commission & ECB* [2016] ECLI:EU:C:2016:701, para 54. See also Joined Cases C-105/15 P to C-109/15 P *Mallis e.a. v Commission & ECB* [2016] ECLI:EU:C:2016:702.

[41] Anastasia Poulou, 'The Liability of the EU in the ESM framework' (2017) 24 Maastricht Journal of European and Comparative Law 137; See also the decisions of national courts cited by Poulou, where the Greek Supreme Administrative Court held the MoU to be non-binding while the Portuguese Constitutional Court confirmed that the MoU constitutes a binding act.

[42] Case C-258/14 *Florescu* [2017] ECLI:EU:C:2017:448, para 41.

[43] Opinion of AG Bot in Case C-258/14 *Florescu* [2016] ECLI:EU:C:2016:995, para 53.

[44] Opinion of AG Wathelet in Joined Cases C-105/15 P to C-109/15 P *Mallis e.a. v Commission & ECB* [2016] ECLI:EU:C:2016:294, para 85. In contrast, in his Opinion in the *Ledra* case, AG Wahl qualified the MoU as an international agreement, see Opinion of AG Wahl in Joined Cases C-8/15 P to C-10/15 P *Ledra Advertising e.a. v Commission & ECB* [2016] ECLI:EU:C:2016:290, para 98.

[45] René Repasi, 'Judicial protection against austerity measures in the euro area: Ledra and Mallis' (2017) Common Market Law Review 1123, 1141–1142.

[46] Anastasia Poulou, 'Financial assistance conditionality and human rights protection: What is the role of the EU Charter of Fundamental Rights?' (2017) 54 Common Market Law Review 991, 1019–1022.

useful to flag that the MoU also prescribed an austerity programme with significant fundamental rights implications. For instance, the Cyprus MoU foresaw that Cyprus would reform its pension system, increasing the minimum age for pension entitlements and reducing pensions.[47]

A second set of examples can be seen in the soft law adopted in the Area of Freedom, Security and Justice (AFSJ), for instance, by the EU Agency for Asylum (EUAA). Article 13 of its establishing Regulation provides that its Management Board can adopt operational standards, indicators, guidelines, and best practices to ensure a correct and effective implementation of Union law on asylum.[48] The agency thus adopts post-legislative guidance fleshing out different provisions of the EU asylum acquis, such as the Asylum Procedures Directive. In its Articles 14 and 15, the latter sets out the rule that applicants are entitled to a personal interview before a decision on their application is made as well as setting out the requirements that such a personal interview must meet.[49] Under Article 15(3)(c) of the Directive, the 'communication shall take place in the language preferred by the applicant unless there is another language which he or she understands and in which he or she is able to communicate clearly'. In the EUAA's Guidance on asylum procedure: operational standards and indicators of September 2019, however, Standard 30 prescribes that 'the personal interview takes place in a language the applicant understands'.[50] The 'good practice' listed under that standard provides that if no interpreter is available in the language that the applicant understands, another language 'that the applicant is reasonably expected to understand' can be used. The guidance that is provided to national authorities to comply with the Directive thus effectively sets a lower (or at least less detailed) standard than the Directive itself. Since the latter is explicitly intended to promote inter alia the right to human dignity and the right to asylum,[51] it cannot be excluded that the guidance might set the actual standard for the administrative practice of Member States and thereby

[47] See points 2.11 and 3.1 of the Memorandum of Understanding on Specific Economic Policy Conditionality annexed to European Commission, The Economic Adjustment Programme for Cyprus (2013) *European Economy Occasional Papers* 149.

[48] See Regulation (EU) 2021/2303 of the European Parliament and of the Council of 15 December 2021 on the European Union Agency for Asylum and repealing Regulation (EU) No 439/2010 [2021] OJ L468/1 (EUAA), art 13.

[49] See Directive (EU) 2013/32 of the European Parliament and of the Council of 26 June 2013 on common procedures for granting and withdrawing international protection [2013] OJ L180/60 (Recast Asylum Procedures Directive), arts 14–15.

[50] EASO Guidance on asylum procedure: operational standards and indicators, EASO Practical Guides Series, September 2019, 19.

[51] Recast Asylum Procedures Directive (n 49) recital 60.

interfere with these fundamental rights. This despite the Court in *Addis* ruling that the personal interview is of fundamental importance in the asylum procedure.[52]

A further example in the AFSJ can be found in the EU's response to Russia's invasion of Ukraine. Quite quickly this led to calls within the EU of banning Russian tourists from acquiring Schengen visas, although the Schengen Visa Code[53] does not explicitly provide for such a ban. Following the EU Council's suspension of the EU-Russia visa facilitation agreement,[54] Russian citizens are to be given the default treatment under the Visa Code regulation when applying for visas. When it comes to refusing Russian citizens' applications, the main relevant provision in the Visa Code on which Member States would rely is Article 21(3)(d), which requires Member States to verify that 'the applicant is not considered to be a threat to public policy, internal security or public … or to the international relations of any of the Member States'. While the regulation has not been amended, in September 2022 the European Commission did adopt guidance specifically for the issuance of visas to Russian citizens.[55] These guidelines seem to lower the bar for Member States to refuse applications from Russians: 'As far as Russian nationals travelling for tourism are concerned, having a very strict approach is justified as it is more difficult to assess the justification for the journey.'[56] The Commission in its guidance also seems to lower the bar by introducing the notion of a '*potential* threat', a concept that does not as such appear in the Visa Code or the (general) Visa Handbook.[57] While there is evidently no fundamental right of Russians to visit the EU, one may well argue that there is a fundamental right for Russian citizens, pursuant to Articles 20 and 21 of the Charter, not to be treated differently from, for example, Kazakh citizens (i.e., citizens of states other than Russia that are also listed in

52 Case C-517/17 *Addis* [2020] ECLI:EU:C:2020:579, paras 59 and 66.

53 Regulation (EC) 810/2009 of the European Parliament and of the Council of 13 July 2009 establishing a Community Code on Visas (Visa Code) [2009] OJ L243/1.

54 Council Decision (EU) 2022/1500 of 9 September 2022 on the suspension in whole of the application of the Agreement between the European Community and the Russian Federation on the facilitation of the issuance of visas to the citizens of the European Union and the Russian Federation [2022] OJ L234I/1 (Council Decision 2022/1500).

55 European Commission, Providing guidelines on general visa issuance in relation to Russian applicants following Council Decision 1500/2022 C (2022) 7111 final.

56 Council Decision 1500/2022 (n 54) para 23.

57 European Commission, ANNEX to the Commission Implementing Decision amending Commission Decision C (2010) 1620 final as regards the replacement of the Handbook for the processing of visa applications and the modification of issued visas (Visa Code Handbook I), C (2020) 395 final.

Annex I of Regulation 2018/1806[58] with which the EU has not concluded a facilitation agreement).[59] Arguably, the result of the guidance is that Member States are given a basis to routinely reject applications from Russians requesting a visa for touristic purposes.

A third illustration may be found in the digital sphere where the EU has adopted ambitious legislative packages in recent years. Although the General Data Protection Regulation[60] is not limited in scope to the processing of data through digital means, its importance for the digital information society is self-evident. In 2022, the EU legislator also adopted the Digital Services Act (DSA) and a Data Governance Act (DGA).[61] Aside from their special relevance for the digital provision of services and the digital processing of data, two further features of these three different legislative instruments are noteworthy for the purposes of this chapter: they contain important enabling clauses foreseeing the adoption of soft law to ensure the proper application of the legislative acts and they rely on a new type of governance mechanism by setting up so-called Boards (the European Data Protection Board [EDPB], the European Board for Digital Services [EBDS], and the European Data Innovation Board [EDIB]) that are to adopt such soft law. While these Boards are heterogeneous in their nature, structure, and functioning,[62] they have in common that they bring together representatives of the national authorities and that they are given the power to adopt soft law (guidance) on any issue coming under the scope of their respective legislative acts. This is very similar to the constellation at issue in the *ThyssenKrupp* cases discussed

[58] Regulation (EU) 2018/1806 of the European Parliament and of the Council of 14 November 2018 listing the third countries whose nationals must be in possession of visas when crossing the external borders and those whose nationals are exempt from that requirement [2018] OJ L303/39 (Visa Requirement Regulation).

[59] While the Court has ruled that third countries do not come within the scope of Article 20 of the Charter, this is different from the citizens of those third countries. See Case C-272/15 *Swiss International Air Lines* [2016] ECLI:EU:C:2016:993, para 29.

[60] Regulation (EU) 679/2016 of the European Parliament and of the Council of 27 April 2016 on the protection of natural persons with regard to the processing of personal data and on the free movement of such data, and repealing Directive 95/46/EC [2016] OJ L119/1 (GDPR).

[61] Regulation (EU) 2022/868 of the European Parliament and of the Council of 30 May 2022 on European data governance [2022] OJ L152/1 (Data Governance Act); Regulation (EU) 2022/2065 of the European Parliament and of the Council of 19 October 2022 on a Single Market For Digital Services [2022] OJ L277/1 (DSA).

[62] The EDPB, for instance, strongly resembles a proper EU agency since it has legal personality and brings together *exclusively* representatives of the EU Member States. The EBDS and the EDIB have no legal personality and the latter is also composed of representatives of stakeholders. Only the DGA explicitly prescribes that the EDIB is to be a Commission expert group (in the sense of European Commission, establishing horizontal rules on the creation and operation of Commission expert groups, C (2016) 3301 final).

above. When it comes to the actual application of these legislative packages, different fundamental rights are evidently in play. The DSA is especially clear on this as it provides in its Article 34 that providers must make an assessment of how their services and the way they are offered may negatively affect rights, in particular the fundamental rights to human dignity enshrined in Article 1 of the Charter; to respect for private and family life enshrined in Article 7 of the Charter; to the protection of personal data enshrined in Article 8 of the Charter; to freedom of expression and information, including the freedom and pluralism of the media, enshrined in Article 11 of the Charter; to non-discrimination enshrined in Article 21 of the Charter; to respect for the rights of the child enshrined in Article 24 of the Charter; and to a high-level of consumer protection enshrined in Article 38 of the Charter.[63]

How providers are concretely meant to mitigate risks is initially left to self-regulation, but Article 35(3) provides that the Commission 'may issue guidelines ... in relation to specific risks, in particular to present best practices and recommend possible measures, having due regard to the possible consequences of the measures on fundamental rights enshrined in the Charter of all parties involved'. In short, it may be expected that soft law will de facto determine the limits within which fundamental rights may be impacted by providers of very large online platforms and very large online search engines.[64] Generally, for these three acts, their actual implementation will be significantly steered by acts of soft law, adopted by either the Commission, the Boards, or the regulated entities themselves.

What the examples in these three very diverse policy fields show is, first, a seemingly insatiable appetite for soft law, not just on the part of the executive branch and, second, the very real possibilities for soft law to affect the legal position of natural and legal persons.

14.3 REMEDIES AND SOFT LAW

The argument was made above that the scope of the Charter could, and in light of soft law's practical effects should, extend to soft law. If that is indeed the case, the question becomes which remedies are available to challenge soft law's interferences with fundamental rights. This section will highlight the two

[63] DSA, art 34(1)(b).

[64] As highlighted by Mantelero, the DSA's focus on risk mitigation rather than prevention implies that interferences with fundamental rights are accepted, under the legislative framework, as inevitable costs to access potential technological benefits brought by digital services. See Alessandro Mantelero, 'Fundamental rights impact assessments in the DSA' (Verfassungsblog, 1 November 2022) <https://verfassungsblog.de/dsa-impact-assessment/>.

main existing judicial mechanisms that are available, as well as one administrative mechanism. The backdrop of this discussion is that soft law, by its nature, precludes the remedy of the action for annulment under Article 263 TFEU.

14.3.1 *Unavailability of the Action for Annulment*

The Court of Justice shut this door firmly in 2018 in *Belgium v Commission*,[65] despite suggestions by AG Bobek to take a more flexible approach. The Court of Justice thereby endorsed the findings of the General Court, which, at first instance, observed that the recommendation does not have and is not intended to have binding legal effects with the result that it cannot be classified as a challengeable act for the purposes of Article 263 TFEU.[66] The problematic repercussions of *Belgium v Commission* for effective judicial protection were decried by Arnull in strong terms: '[I]n direct actions the Court of Justice and the General Court now sometimes seem content to collude with other institutions to evade the requirements laid down by the Treaty.'[67] What therefore remains is the action for damages and the preliminary reference procedure, before the Courts, and the different forms of review by administrative bodies as a non-judicial remedy.

14.3.2 *The Action for Damages*

As the *Ledra* case discussed above suggests (assuming the CJEU found the MoU to constitute soft law), it is in principle possible to challenge the fundamental rights interferences of soft law through an action for damages. It is established case law of the EU Courts to require three cumulative conditions for the EU to incur non-contractual liability, those being the unlawfulness of the EU's conduct, the fact of damage, and the existence of a causal link between the conduct and the damage.[68] In *Ledra*, the Court dismissed the claim for damages on the first of these conditions by finding that

65 Case C-16/16 P *Belgium v Commission* [2018] ECLI:EU:C:2018:79. For a broader discussion of the problem of challenging soft law through the action for annulment, see Giulia Gentile, 'Ensuring effective judicial review of EU soft law via the action for annulment before the EU courts: A plea for a liberal-constitutional approach' (2020) 16 European Constitutional Law Review 466.

66 Case T-721/14 *Belgium v Commission* [2015] ECLI:EU:T:2015:829, para 37.

67 Anthony Arnull, 'EU Recommendations and Judicial Review' (2018) 14 European Constitutional Law Review 609, 621.

68 See Joined Cases C-447/17 P and C-479/17 P *EU v Guardian Europe & Guardian Europe v EU* [2019] ECLI:EU:C:2019:672, para 147.

the Commission had not committed a sufficiently serious violation of the fundamental right involved because the restriction of the fundamental right could be justified pursuant to Article 52(1) of the Charter.[69] Specifically for soft law, the third cumulative condition appears to be the most problematic, however. Under the Court's established case law, a sufficiently direct causal link means that the conduct must be the *determining* cause of the damage.[70] Yet, given its non-binding nature, the indirect legal and practical effects of soft law seem incapable of ever constituting such a *determining* cause.[71] This is clear where EU soft law is subsequently implemented by further decisions (binding or non-binding) but also when it results in the first and fourth scenarios noted above in Section 14.2.3. The threshold to show that soft law itself *determined* a private party's behaviour or the factual conduct of a government body lies exceptionally high. Where the action for annulment against soft law will be inadmissible, an action for damages might be admissible but would then always fail on the merits.

14.3.3 *The Preliminary Reference Procedure*

The only judicial remedy practically available will then be the preliminary reference procedure, as evidenced by the *FBF* case.[72] In that case, the Court followed up on *Belgium v Commission* mentioned earlier where it refused to review soft law in an action for annulment but where it noted that 'Article 267 TFEU confers on the Court jurisdiction to deliver a preliminary ruling on the validity and interpretation of all acts of the EU institutions without exception'.[73] From a more institutional perspective, the Court's decision, as also predicted by AG Bobek in his Opinion in *FBF*,[74] goes against the current evolution of the judicial system at EU level. In terms of workload, it would have made more sense to allow for a direct review of soft law measures, given the recent expansion of the General Court. That the Court confirmed that

[69] The general threshold is therefore high, since even a non-justifiable restriction of a fundamental right may not be sufficiently serious. See, e.g., Case T-341/07 *Sison v Council* [2011] ECLI:EU:T:2011:687, para 75; Joyce De Coninck, 'Effective Remedies for Human Rights Violations in EU CSDP Military Missions: Smoke and Mirrors in Human Rights Adjudication?' (2023) 24 German Law Journal 353-359.

[70] *Guardian Europe* (n 68) para 32.

[71] See Case T-193/04 *Tillack v Commission* [2006] ECLI:EU:T:2006:292, paras 122–124.

[72] Case C-911/19 *Fédération bancaire française (FBF) v Autorité de contrôle prudentiel et de résolution (ACPR)* [2021] ECLI:EU:C:2021:599.

[73] *Belgium v Commission* (n 65) para 44.

[74] Opinion of AG Bobek in Case C-911/19 *Fédération bancaire française (FBF) v Autorité de contrôle prudentiel et de résolution (ACPR)* [2021] ECLI:EU:C:2021:294, para 148.

there would be a possibility to seize it in order to challenge the validity of soft law was still welcomed by Gündel,[75] but there are at least three important constraints, inherent to the preliminary reference procedure, that require pointing out. First, the preliminary reference procedure requires a reference point in the national legal order that can be relied on to seize a national judge; second, a procedure must also be available at national level (which may not be self-evident in the realm of soft law); and third, the preliminary reference procedure is not a self-standing remedy but instead depends on the national judge referring questions.

The first two of these constraints are intertwined: concretely, a natural or legal person taking issue with an EU soft law measure will only be able to indirectly challenge this measure before a national judge if there is a national measure or conduct that is challengeable pursuant to a procedure available in national law. In the first scenario noted above in Section 14.2.3, such a reference point may not be available. This puts an acute challenge to the right of natural and legal persons to effective legal protection. The avenue to which the Court directs applicants revives the same problems that resulted from *Plaumann* and the Court's response in cases like *UPA* and *Jégo Quéré*,[76] as well as revealing a further challenge to the principle of procedural autonomy.

In the scenario where EU soft law will be followed up on or implemented at national level through further (national) soft law, this may prove problematic. While different national legal systems seem increasingly open to allow such challenges,[77] this option still does not seem to exist in the majority of national legal systems. In addition, the requirements to be fulfilled by applicants may vary greatly between Member States. Should these differences simply be accepted in light of national procedural autonomy? That is doubtful. While national procedural autonomy should be considered a legal principle, rather than a temporary state of affairs in EU law, it is still to be balanced with other principles such as that to effective legal protection.[78] In this regard, Arnull has

[75] See Jörg Gundel, 'Rechtsschutz gegen Empfehlungen der EU-Kommission?' (2018) Europarecht 605.

[76] Case C-25/62 *Plaumann v Commission* [1963] ECLI:EU:C:1963:17; Case C-50/00 P *Unión de Pequeños Agricultores (UPA)* [2002] ECLI:EU:C:2002:462; Case 263/02 *Jégo Quéré* [2004] ECLI:EU:C:2004:210.

[77] Mariolina Eliantonio, 'Judicial Review of Soft Law before the European and the National Courts A Wind of Change Blowing from the Member States?' in Mariolina Eliantonio, Emilia Korkea-aho, Oana Ştefan (eds), *EU Soft Law in the Member States Theoretical Findings and Empirical Evidence* (Hart 2021) 286.

[78] See Markus Ludwigs, 'Die Verfahrensautonomie der Mitgliedstaaten' (2018) Neue Zeitschrift für Verwaltungsrecht 1420.

noted that in the post-Lisbon era 'the venerable principles of national procedural autonomy, equivalence and effectiveness seem to have been absorbed into a more complex matrix of rules and principles which represent a considerable intrusion into fields formerly considered the prerogative of the Member States'.[79] In line with *UPA*, *Unibet*,[80] and Article 19(1) TEU,[81] it would instead be up to the Member States to provide adequate remedies. Assuming that the Court will refuse to revisit its *Belgium v Commission* ruling, it will be up to the Member States courts to fix any resulting lacunae. This is already a significant requirement imposed on those legal systems that have not (yet) accepted the reviewability of national soft law endogenously. However, it will be most acute in those cases under a second scenario, in the vein of *Jégo-Quéré*, where there is no national measure (not even a soft law measure) to be contested to begin with.

The third constraint of the Court's solution in *FBF* is that, under the established case law of the Court of Justice,[82] the preliminary reference procedure is not a self-standing remedy offered to (private) parties. It is rather an instrument through which national courts may enter into dialogue with the Court of Justice and whether preliminary references are sent to the Court ultimately depends on those national judges, not on the parties appearing before them. *FBF* therefore means that a *genuine* remedy against soft law will depend on national judges referring questions on validity to the Court of Justice.

14.3.4 *Subjecting Soft Law to Administrative Review*

In light of the constraints that come with the preliminary reference procedure identified in Section 14.3.3, it is important to draw attention to other possible remedies. As Jääskinen observed, there are indeed 'alternative ways of constitutionally legitimised control structures of the use of public powers' and 'judicial protection is a societally and economically scarce resource which cannot be light-heartedly allocated to cases that are better dealt with [by] other

79 Anthony Arnull, 'Article 47 CFR and national procedural autonomy' (2020) 45 European Law Review 690.

80 While not at issue as such in that case, the Court did clarify in *Unibet* that EU law does not create new remedies in the national legal orders unless 'in the national legal system in question no legal remedy exists which makes it possible to (possibly indirectly) ensure respect for an individual's rights under EU law'. See Case C-432/05 *Unibet* [2007] ECLI:EU:C:2007:163, paras 40–41.

81 Consolidated Version of the Treaty on European Union [2016] OJ C202/13 (TEU), art 19.

82 Case 283/81 *Cilfit* [1982] ECLI:EU:C:1982:335, para 9.

types of remedies or that do not deserve the attention of courts'.[83] While the possibility to seize an independent judicial tribunal would appear to be a requirement under Article 47 of the Charter, there may indeed be other (administrative) remedies available that may be more effective. Apart from the general possibility to seize the Ombudsman (when a soft law act is alleged to be vitiated by an instance of maladministration), such administrative remedies arguably ought to bear the brunt of ensuring adequate legal protection, with the judicial remedy acting as a safety valve.

The EU legislator has in the past already experimented with administrative review procedures that potentially allow soft law to be challenged. The typical constellation in which such review procedures have been established is one where an EU agency has been granted certain powers and where the Commission has been identified as the body competent to review its acts at the request of a private party. Pre-Lisbon, such clauses were included to ensure the possibility of at least some review of agency decisions, given the agencies' unclear passive legal standing in the action for annulment.[84] Post-Lisbon, such clauses are not strictly needed anymore, which explains why they were deleted in the 2019 revisions of the Eurofound, Cedefop, and EU-OSHA Regulations and in the 2017 European Union Intellectual Property Office Regulation.[85] Remarkably, the revision in 2022 of the establishing regulation of the European Centre for Disease Prevention and Control (ECDC) revamped this procedure, rather than deleting it from the regulation all together.[86] Article 28 of the ECDC Regulation now provides:

Article 28

Examination of legality

1. Member States, members of the Management Board and third parties directly and individually concerned may refer any act of the Centre, whether express or implied, to the Commission for examination of the legality of that act ('administrative appeal').

[83] Niilo Jääskinen, 'Final Thoughts' in Mariolina Eliantonio, Emilia Korkea-aho, Oana Ştefan (eds), *EU Soft Law in the Member States Theoretical Findings and Empirical Evidence* (Hart 2021) 361.

[84] See Merijn Chamon, *EU Agencies – Legal and Political Limits to the Transformation of the EU Administration* (Oxford University Press 2016) 334–336.

[85] See Regulation (EC) on the Community trade mark (codified version) 207/2009, [2009] OJ L78/1, art 122 (not taken over in Regulation 2017/1001, OJ 2017 L 154/1).

[86] See Regulation (EU) 2022/2370 of the European Parliament and of the Council of 23 November 2022 amending Regulation (EC) No 851/2004 establishing a European centre for disease prevention and control [2022] OJ L314/1, art 1(30).

2. Any administrative appeal shall be made to the Commission within 15 days of the day on which the party concerned first became aware of the act in question.
3. The Commission shall take a decision within one month. If no decision has been taken within that period, the administrative appeal shall be deemed to have been dismissed.
4. An action for annulment of the Commission's explicit or implicit decision referred to in paragraph 3 of this Article to dismiss the administrative appeal may be brought before the Court of Justice of the European Union in accordance with Article 263 TFEU.

Similar mechanisms are still in place for the Community Plant Variety Office (CPVO)[87] and for the European Food Safety Authority (EFSA).[88] While part of the administrative appeal is modelled on Article 263 TFEU, notably the requirement that private parties need to be directly and individually concerned, the scope of the appeal seems to be broader, since *any* act of the agency may be referred to the Commission.[89]

In 2019, the EU legislator further experimented with this type of review mechanism by introducing Article 60a in the three Regulations establishing the European Supervisory Authorities (ESAs) in the financial sector.[90] The new provision was introduced specifically to allow for a review of some of the soft law that the ESAs adopt.[91] Article 60a provides: 'Any natural or legal person may send reasoned advice to the Commission if that person is of the opinion that the Authority has exceeded its competence, including by failing to respect the principle of proportionality referred to in Article 1(5), when acting under Articles 16 and 16b, and that is of direct and individual concern

87 See Regulation (EC) 2100/94 on Community plant variety rights [1994] OJ L227/1, art 44.

88 See Regulation (EC) 1829/2003 of the European Parliament and of the Council on genetically modified food and feed [2003] OJ L268/1, art 36; Regulation (EC) 1935/2004 of the European Parliament and of the Council on materials and articles intended to come into contact with food and repealing Directives 80/590/EEC and 89/109/EEC [2004] OJ L338/4, art 14.

89 The relevant provisions setting out the administrative appeals against the CPVO and EFSA refer to any acts or any decisions. Furthermore, the administrative appeals against the EFSA also extend to the agency's failure to act.

90 See Regulations 1093/2010, 1094/2010, and 1095/2010 establishing the European Banking Authority, the European Insurance and Occupational Pensions Authority and the European Securities and Markets Authority [2010] OJ L 331/12-48-84 (ESA Regulations).

91 More concretely against the guidelines, recommendations, and Q&As adopted by the ESAs pursuant to Articles 16 and 16b of their establishing Regulations. The opinions that the ESAs may also adopt pursuant to Article 16a are therefore excluded from the scope of the review mechanism.

to that person.'[92] Although it has already been in force for a couple of years, this administrative review procedure has not actually been relied on yet.

For a number of reasons, it is also doubtful whether that procedure offers any genuine *remedy* against the ESAs exceeding their competences through the adoption of soft law. First, only individually and directly concerned persons may communicate reasoned advice to the Commission per Article 60a. This arguably makes the remedy dependent on similar standing requirements as those under Article 263 TFEU and the earlier administrative review procedures, but it is unclear how these would apply in the given context, as soft law acts cannot in principle be of direct concern to a person. After all, in the Courts' established case law, direct concern means that a measure 'must directly affect the legal situation of the individual and, second, it must leave no discretion to its addressees who are entrusted with the task of implementing it, such implementation being purely automatic and resulting from the EU rules alone without the application of other intermediate rules'.[93] Since the effects of soft law are merely of a practical nature or, at the most, indirect legal effects, it seems a priori impossible for soft law to ever be of 'direct concern'. In addition, if the *Plaumann* criteria would also apply mutatis mutandis, it would be almost impossible for a party to demonstrate that they are individually concerned by the ESAs' guidelines and Q&As since these will be general in scope.[94] This may be different for the ESAs' recommendations, as Article 16 of the ESA Regulations provides that they may be addressed 'to one or more [national] competent authorities or to one or more financial institutions'. Still, since direct and individual concern are cumulative conditions, the standing requirement will never be met for soft law. Unless, of course, 'direct and individual concern' is not to be understood in the same way as the analogous notions in Article 263 TFEU.

Second, Article 60a does not provide an actual remedy. Even if an admissible complaint were to be lodged, the Commission cannot, under Article 60a or any other provision of the ESAs Regulations, provide an *actual* remedy where it finds that an ESA has exceeded its competences. Only ESAs can issue

[92] Regulation (EU) 2019/2175 of the European Parliament and of the Council of 18 December 2019 amending Regulation (EU) No 1093/2010 establishing a European Supervisory Authority (European Banking Authority), Regulation (EU) No 1094/2010 establishing a European Supervisory Authority (European Insurance and Occupational Pensions Authority), Regulation (EU) No 1095/2010 establishing a European Supervisory Authority (European Securities and Markets Authority) [2019] OJ L334/1.

[93] See, e.g., Joined Cases C-622/16 P to C-624/16 P *Scuola Elementare Maria Montessori Srl v Commission* [2018] ECLI:EU:C:2018:873, para 42.

[94] ESA Regulations, arts 16 and 16b.

and, in turn, repeal guidelines, recommendations, and Q&As and the Commission cannot give instructions to the ESAs or override the soft law, except where it has been specifically empowered to adopt delegated or implementing acts. Article 60a therefore at best represents an alert mechanism. While the attempt of the legislator to afford private parties protection against the effects of the ESAs' soft law should be lauded, the effectiveness of Article 60a of the ESAs Regulations will be undermined by the legislator's failure to recognise that the challenges posed by soft law represent a paradigm shift for the system of remedies. Transplanting admissibility requirements from procedures that aim at the review of hard law ignores the fundamental features characterising soft law. While administrative review of soft law seems an appropriate way forward (see below), it would have to be devised mindful of the specific features of soft law.

14.3.5 *A Possible Way Forward*

Building on the legislator's recognition, in the 2019 ESAs Regulations, of the importance of a possibility to review soft law, complementing the existing EU system of remedies with a dedicated administrative review mechanism appears to be the way forward. Special attention should thereby be devoted to three issues: access to the mechanism, the nature of the adjudicating body, and the remedy provided.

As noted in the discussion of Article 60a of the ESAs Regulations, the mechanism's admissibility requirements should take proper account of soft law's non-binding nature and therefore not replicate those applicable under Article 263 TFEU. Instead, the mechanism could be open to parties showing an interest.

As regards the body made responsible to review soft law, the 2019 revision of the ESAs Regulations also provides interesting clues. During the legislative negotiations, the European Parliament had proposed to extend the mandate of the ESAs' Joint Board of Appeal, making it competent to hear challenges to the ESAs' soft law.[95] The Parliament's suggestion did not make it in the end, but it is interesting, nonetheless. Within decision-making EU agencies, there are already specialised and independent boards of appeal that are competent to review (individual) binding decisions.[96] The 2019 revision thus constituted

[95] See Merijn Chamon, 'The joint board of appeal as an accountability mechanism for the ESAs' in Carl Fredrik Bergström and Magnus Strand (eds), *Legal Accountability in EU Markets for Financial Instruments: The Dual Role of Investment Firms* (Edward Elgar 2021) 76.

[96] On the Boards of Appeal, see Merijn Chamon, Annalisa Volpato, and Mariolina Eliantonio (eds), *Boards of Appeal of EU Agencies – Towards Judicialization of Administrative Review?*

a missed opportunity to tap this potential and it would be worthwhile to revisit this possibility. For those EU agencies adopting soft law and who are already equipped with a Board of Appeal, the latter's mandate could be broadened.[97] Where soft law is adopted by other agencies or bodies of the EU or by the Commission itself, a variant of Article 60a of the ESAs Regulations could be envisaged where the review is entrusted to a functionally independent entity within the Commission. Just like the independent Regulatory Scrutiny Board (unilaterally established by the Commission) double-checks the soundness of the Commission's proposals and impact assessment, so could an independent review board be entrusted with scrutinising soft law.[98]

Lastly, any mechanism should provide for a clear remedy. Given soft law's non-binding nature, that remedy need not mimic the remedy under Article 263 TFEU, just like the admissibility requirements need not be mimicked. Instead, a requirement for the original author to reconsider the soft law in light of the reviewing authority's remarks could also be sufficient.

14.4 CONCLUSION

The present chapter looked into how the informalisation of governance through the adoption of soft law can affect the fundamental rights position of private parties. After briefly exploring the nature and function of soft law, the primordial question for this chapter to address was how soft law, given its formally non-constraining nature, is relevant from a fundamental rights perspective.

Although the jurisprudence of the ECtHR and the CJEU is not explicit on this point, the chapter argued that the possibility of fundamental rights

(Oxford University Press 2022); Paola Chirulli and Luca de Lucia, 'Specialised adjudication in EU administrative law: the Boards of Appeal of EU agencies' (2015) 40 European Law Review 832.

97 As the law stands, Boards of Appeal of EU agencies can only review binding measures. This is contrary to the suggestion of AG Campos Sánchez-Bordona in his Opinion in Case C-501/18 *BT v Balgarska Narodna Banka* [2020] ECLI:EU:C:2020:729, para 81; for a failed attempt to have a Board of Appeal review an act of soft law (*in casu* an opinion of the European Agency for Energy Regulators), see Case T-63/16 *E-Control v ACER* [2017] ECLI:EU:T:2017:456, para 37; for arguments in favour of such a broadening, see Carlo Tovo, 'The Boards of Appeal of Networked Services Agencies: Specialized Arbitrators of Transnational Regulatory Conflicts?' in Merijn Chamon, Annalisa Volpato, and Mariolina Eliantonio (eds), *Boards of Appeal of EU Agencies – Towards Judicialization of Administrative Review?* (Oxford University Press 2022) 34; Marco Lamandini, 'The ESAs' Board of Appeal as a Blueprint for the Quasi-Judicial Review of European Financial Supervision' (2014) 11 European Company Law 293.

98 See, for an earlier suggestion, Oliver Streckert, *Verwaltungsinterner Unionsrechtsschutz – Kohärenter Rechtsschutz durch Einführung eines Widerspruchskammermodells für die Europäische Kommission* (Mohr Siebeck 2016).

interferences by soft law (and concomitantly the need for review) should be accepted by drawing an analogy to the CJEU's case law on the fundamental freedoms in the internal market. To further bring this point home, four examples from three very different policy areas were presented to illustrate possible soft law interferences with fundamental rights.

Subsequently, the chapter looked into the remedies available in the EU in relation to soft law, starting with the judicial remedies. Since the latter are premised on the idea that government acts through binding measures, they do not cater to the review of soft law. Only with the recent *FBF* case has the Court of Justice left open one avenue to assess the legality of soft law, albeit that the preliminary reference procedure on its own cannot secure a watertight system. As a result, a further fundamental rights interference could result, since the right to an effective remedy may not be guaranteed for all instances where soft law is adopted at EU level.

The chapter then looked into the possibility of relying on non-judicial remedies for challenging soft law, highlighting how the EU legislator has already experimented with this approach. While the legislator's attempts do not seem to have been fully thought through, they should be supported and built upon, since extra-judicial administrative review of soft law seems more attuned to challenging soft law than going through the judicial avenue of the preliminary reference procedure.

15

The EU's Artificial Intelligence Laboratory and Fundamental Rights

SIMONA DEMKOVá

15.1 INTRODUCTION

This contribution examines the possibilities for individuals to access remedies against potential violations of their fundamental rights by EU actors, specifically the EU agencies' deployment of artificial intelligence (AI). Presenting the intricate landscape of the EU's border surveillance, Section 15.2 sheds light on the prominent role of Frontex in developing and managing AI systems, including automated risk assessments and drone-based aerial surveillance. These two examples are used to illustrate how the EU's AI-powered conduct endangers fundamental rights protected under the EU Charter of Fundamental Rights (CFR).[1] These risks emerge for privacy and data protection rights, non-discrimination, and other substantive rights, such as the right to asylum. In light of these concerns, Section 15.3 examines the possibilities to access remedies by first considering the impact of AI uses on the procedural rights to good administration and effective judicial protection, before clarifying the emerging remedial system under the proposed AI Act[2] in its interplay

[1] Charter of Fundamental Rights of the European Union [2016] OJ C202/389 (CFR).

[2] Commission, 'Proposal for a Regulation of the European Parliament and of the Council laying down harmonised rules on artificial intelligence (Artificial Intelligence Act) and amending certain Union legislative acts' COM (2021) 206 final, (AI Act Proposal). This chapter was finalised in September 2023, and revised in May 2024. Therefore, this contribution takes into account the latest available draft of 16.4.2024 – the Corrigendum to the position of the European Parliament adopted at first reading on 13 March 2024 with a view to the adoption of Regulation (EU) 2024/[...] of the European Parliament and of the Council laying down harmonised rules on artificial intelligence (Artificial Intelligence Act) P9_TA(2024)0138 (COM(2021)0206 – C9-0146/2021 – 2021/0106(COD)).

with the EU's existing data protection framework. Lastly, the chapter sketches the evolving role of the European Data Protection Supervisor (EDPS) in this context, pointing out the key areas demanding further clarifications in order to fill the remedial gaps (Section 15.4).

15.2 EU BORDER SURVEILLANCE AND THE RISKS TO FUNDAMENTAL RIGHTS

As European integration deepens, the need for enhanced security measures has led to modernising the EU's information systems and other border surveillance capabilities, increasingly involving tools that can be classified as AI systems. The latter refers to '*a machine-based system that is designed to operate with varying levels of autonomy and that may exhibit adaptiveness after deployment, and that, for explicit or implicit objectives, infers, from the input it receives, how to* generate outputs such as *predictions, content*, recommendations, or decisions *that can influence physical or virtual* environments.'.[3] Among the AI tools explored for use in the EU's border surveillance are tools to support the detection of forged travel documents and automated pre-processing of long-stay and residence permit applications for the Schengen Area, as well as the use of AI for risk assessments by way of identification of irregular travelling patterns, high-security risks, or epidemic risks. The design, testing, deployment, and evaluation of these systems is principally entrusted to eu-LISA – the agency responsible for the operational management of the systems in the area of freedom, security, and justice.[4] This task comes with a not-unimportant caveat that the design of the AI tools to be used in border control is delegated – with expensive tenders – to private developers.[5] For instance, a €300 million contract was agreed in 2020 with Idemia and Sopra Steria for the implementation of the new, sensitive data processing Biometric Matching System (BMS).[6] Similarly, EU agencies, such as the EU's Border

[3] AI Act, art 3(1).

[4] Regulation (EU) 2018/1726 of 14 November 2018 and amending Regulation (EC) No 1987/2006 and Council Decision 2007/533/JHA and repealing Regulation (EU) No 1077/2011 [2018] OJ L295/99.

[5] Chris Jones, Ana Valdivia, and Jane Kilpatrick, 'Funds for Fortress Europe: Spending by Frontex and Eu-LISA' (*Statewatch*, 28 January 2022) <www.statewatch.org/analyses/2022/funds-for-fortress-europe-spending-by-frontex-and-eu-lisa/>. As the authors report, the total amount spent by eu-LISA on contracts with the private sector between 2014–2020 alone was €1.5 billion.

[6] Ibid. Another contract worth €140 million was agreed with a consortium made up of Atos, IBM, and Leonardo (formerly Finmeccanica) for the additional work on the BMS.

and Coast Guard Agency – Frontex,[7] invest heavily in developing AI-powered border surveillance systems, including aerial and other hardware tools.[8]

Frontex is among the key EU actors whose tasks and powers are pointedly enhanced by the use of AI systems. Several factors are driving the increasing interest in using AI in the EU's border security context. These include the need to process large amounts of data, the longing for cost and resource efficiency, coupled with the decreasing costs of data storage and processing power, the political democratisation of AI technology, and the resulting influence of EU initiatives embracing the development and deployment of AI.[9] To illustrate the risks that AI uses pose to fundamental rights, the following discussion zooms in on the Frontex's AI-powered conduct (Section 15.2.1) before depicting the risks posed by these uses to fundamental rights (Section 15.2.2).

15.2.1 *Frontex at the Forefront of Border Surveillance*

Frontex is rapidly expanding its AI capabilities. Among those currently explored are AI tools for automated border control (e.g., e-gate hardware), document scanning tools, facial recognition and other biometric verification tools, maritime domain awareness capabilities, unmanned surveillance tools (i.e., 'towers' planted in border regions to detect illegal border crossings), and other forms of unmanned autonomous aerial surveillance systems.[10] Two examples deserve closer inspection to illustrate how the AI uses by EU actors give rise to fundamental rights violations: automated risk assessments and AI-powered aerial surveillance.

15.2.1.1 Automated Risk Assessments

Automated risk assessment (ARA) refers to a process of identifying potential risks by using computer systems, algorithms, or data analysis techniques to evaluate risks in a given context. The ARA relies on extensive datasets that are

7 Regulation (EU) 2019/1896 of the European Parliament and of the Council of 13 November 2019 on the European Border and Coast Guard and repealing Regulations (EU) No 1052/2013 and (EU) 2016/1624 [2019] OJ L295/1.

8 Jones, Valdivia, and Kilpatrick (n 5).

9 Frontex, 'Artificial Intelligence-Based Capabilities for the European Border and Coast Guard: Final Report' (European Border and Coast Guard Agency 2021) <https://frontex.europa.eu/publications/artificial-intelligence-based-capabilities-for-the-european-border-and-coast-guard-final-report-CYyjoe> s 2.2.

10 Ibid annex C.

widely available in the digital age.[11] Increasing reliance on automated risk assessments in the EU's border security is not new. It emerges from a long-standing practice of informational cooperation in the EU's area freedom, security, and justice based on large-scale automated matching of personal data.[12] Among others, the exchange of detailed alert files occurs among the national competent authorities and the EU agencies via the Schengen Information System (SIS), the Visa Information System (VIS), and Eurodac, and soon also the Entry/Exit System (EES), the EU Travel Information and Authorisation System (ETIAS), and the European Criminal Records Information System (ECRIS-TCN).[13] In addition, automated exchanges of personal data take place among the national authorities, EU agencies, and third parties, such as airline companies or online communication services, under specially set up frameworks, such as the PNR scheme.[14] These information exchange frameworks provide for automated assessments of gathered information in order to identify and locate potential security threats. The identification may rely on matches between the alerts containing purely alphanumeric data concerning a specific individual. Generally, however, the data collected within the alerts also include sensitive and genetic data,[15] such as DNA, fingerprints, or facial images, enabling advanced identification based on pre-defined algorithms embodying the characteristics of AI tools.[16]

[11] Giovanni De Gregorio and Sofia Ranchordás, 'Breaking down Information Silos with Big Data: A Legal Analysis of Data Sharing' in Joe Cannataci, Valeria Falce, and Oresto Pollicino (eds), *Legal Challenges of Big Data* (Edward Elgar 2020).

[12] Simona Demková, *Automated Decision-Making and Effective Remedies: The New Dynamics in the Protection of EU Fundamental Rights in the Area of Freedom, Security and Justice* (Edward Elgar 2023) ch 2.

[13] Niovi Vavoula, Immigration and Privacy in the Law of the European Union: The Case of Information Systems (Brill Nijhoff 2022) <https://brill.com/view/title/35886>.

[14] The PNR Scheme refers to the EU regime set up by Directive (EU) 2016/681 enabling national law enforcement authorities to process and automatically analyse potential security risks among the passengers on the EU's external and/or internal flights. Directive (EU) 2016/681 of the European Parliament and of the Council of 27 April 2016 on the use of passenger name record (PNR) data for the prevention, detection, investigation and prosecution of terrorist offences and serious crime [2016] OJ L119/132; see also Julien Jeandesboz, 'Ceci n'est Pas Un Contrôle: PNR Data Processing and the Reshaping of Borderless Travel in the Schengen Area' (2021) 23 European Journal of Migration and Law 431.

[15] Paul Quinn and Gianclaudio Malgieri, 'The Difficulty of Defining Sensitive Data – The Concept of Sensitive Data in the EU Data Protection Framework' (2021) 22 German Law Journal 1583.

[16] Laurent Beslay and Javier Galbally, 'Fingerprint Identification Technology for Its Implementation in the Schengen Information System II (SIS-II)' [2015] JRC Science for Policy Report EUR 27473, <https://publications.jrc.ec.europa.eu/repository/handle/JRC97779> 100; Joint Research Centre, *Study on Fingermark and Palmmark Identification Technologies for Their Implementation in the Schengen Information System* (Publications

EU agencies, including Frontex, employ a range of automated risk assessment tools in the performance of their tasks. Specifically, Frontex will host the ETIAS Central Unit, managing the automated risk analyses in the ETIAS – the European Travel Information and Authorisation System.[17] From mid-2025, the system will undertake pre-screening of about 1.4 billion people from sixty visa-exempt countries for their travel to the Schengen states.[18] The pre-screening aims to contribute to a high level of security, prevent illegal immigration, prevent, detect, and investigate terrorist offences or other serious crimes, as well as protect public health.[19] Beyond the ETIAS Central Unit hosted by Frontex, the ETIAS will operate on the National Units of the thirty European countries and the system itself, which is developed and maintained by eu-LISA.[20] The fast processing of future travel applications will be guaranteed by an automated risk assessment performed by this ETIAS Central System.[21]

The risk assessment will entail a threefold comparison of travel application data. First, the Central System automatically compares the information submitted by the travel applicant against the alerts stored within the abovementioned EU information systems, namely the SIS, VIS, Eurodac, and EES, as well as against Europol data and Interpol databases.[22] Second, the traveller's application will be compared against a set of risk criteria predetermined by the ETIAS Central Unit – that is, Frontex.[23] Lastly, the comparisons will be done against the ETIAS 'Watchlist' of persons suspected of involvement in terrorist offences or other serious crimes.[24] While the first category of ARA in the ETIAS process places the responsibility on the

Office of the EU 2019) <http://publications.europa.eu/publication/manifestation_identifier/PUB_KJNA29755ENN>; Niovi Vavoula, 'Artificial Intelligence (AI) at Schengen Borders: Automated Processing, Algorithmic Profiling and Facial Recognition in the Era of Techno-Solutionism' (2021) 23 European Journal of Migration and Law 457.

17 Regulation (EU) 2018/1240 of the European Parliament and of the Council of 12 September 2018 establishing a European Travel Information and Authorisation System (ETIAS) and amending Regulations (EU) No 1077/2011, (EU) No 515/2014, (EU) 2016/399, (EU) 2016/1624 and (EU) 2017/2226, OJ L236/1 (ETIAS Regulation).

18 'What Is ETIAS' (Travel-europe.europa.eu) <https://travel-europe.europa.eu/etias/what-etias_en> .

19 ETIAS Regulation, art 4.

20 Ibid arts 5–7; See also 'Eu-LISA – Core Activities' (eulisa.europa.eu) <www.eulisa.europa.eu/Activities>.

21 ETIAS Regulation, art 20.

22 The latter include the ETIAS Central System, the Interpol Stolen and Lost Travel Document database (SLTD), and the Interpol Travel Documents Associated with Notices database (TDAWN).

23 ETIAS Regulation, art 33.

24 Ibid art 34.

Member States (as primarily responsible for entering alerts into the EU large-scale databases), the latter two categories also directly involve EU agencies, namely Frontex and Europol (due to their role in setting up the ARA criteria or the 'watchlist'). Given the focus on AI uses by EU actors in this chapter, only the Frontex-defined risk criteria encompassed within the pre-screening algorithm will be further discussed.

The Frontex-operated Central Unit should construe the risk criteria on the basis of risks identified by the EU Commission in corresponding implementing acts. The latter could be drawn from the EES and ETIAS statistics on abnormal rates of overstaying and refusals of entry for a specific group of travellers due to a security, illegal immigration, or high epidemic risk based on the information provided by Member States as well as by the WHO.[25] Based on this information, the ETIAS Central Unit will define the final screening rules underlying the ETIAS Central System's algorithm.[26] Pursuant to Article 33(1) ETIAS Regulation, 'these screening rules shall be an algorithm enabling profiling' based on a comparison of the application data with specific risk indicators.

The algorithm will be built on a combination of data concerning the age range, sex, nationality, country and city of residence, level of education (primary, secondary, higher, or none), and current occupation.[27] These data will serve to evaluate a person's behaviour, location, or movements based on a detailed history of one's travels, submitted in the ETIAS application form. This type of practice thus corresponds to the practice of profiling, which, pursuant to the EU data protection rules,[28] should be prohibited, unless accompanied by strict safeguards.[29] Pursuant to the jurisprudence of the Court of Justice of the European Union (CJEU), the safeguards must ensure that the criteria used for profiling are targeted, proportionate, specific, and

[25] Ibid art 33(2) and (3).

[26] Paulina Jo Pesch, Diana Dimitrova, and Franziska Boehm, 'Data Protection and Machine-Learning-Supported Decision-Making at the EU Border: ETIAS Profiling Under Scrutiny' in Agnieszka Gryszczyńska and Others (eds), *Privacy Technologies and Policy* (Springer International 2022).

[27] ETIAS Regulation, art 33(4).

[28] GDPR, art 4(4) defines profiling as 'any form of automated processing of personal data consisting of the use of personal data to evaluate certain personal aspects relating to a natural person, in particular to analyse or predict aspects concerning that natural person's performance at work, economic situation, health, personal preferences, interests, reliability, behaviour, location or movements'. Regulation (EU) 2016/679 of the European Parliament and of the Council of 27 April 2016 on the protection of natural persons with regard to the processing of personal data and on the free movement of such data, and repealing Directive 95/46/EC (General Data Protection Regulation) [2016] OJ L119/1 (GDPR).

[29] GDPR, art 22; and its equivalent Regulation (EU) 2018/1725, art 24.

regularly reviewed, as well as not be based solely on the protected categories of age, sex, and others.[30] The ETIAS algorithm may however be targeting specific country of origin or nationality, which can give rise to concerns of discrimination, as discussed further below. In this respect, it is worth highlighting that ETIAS automated risk assessments will serve to select a rather small group of potential security threats from an ocean of otherwise innocent, law-abiding citizens. As the ETIAS explanatory website states, it is expected that about 97% of applications will be automatically approved. It is expected that the remaining 3% will require further manual verification by the ETIAS Central Unit in cooperation with the National Units.[31]

Every refusal of travel authorisation in ETIAS will have to be notified to the applicant, explaining the reasons for the decision.[32] The notice email should include information on how the applicant may appeal this decision and details of the competent authorities and the relevant time limits.[33] The appeals will be handled by the Member State refusing the entry and hence in accordance with that state's national law.[34] Individuals without an ETIAS authorisation will be refused boarding at international airports or will be stopped when trying to cross Schengen's external borders by land. Accordingly, it is of the utmost importance that the system's AI component embodied within the algorithmic risk assessments does not lead to disproportionate interferences with individuals' fundamental rights, including the rights to privacy, data protection, and protection from discrimination. Equally, the ETIAS National Unit authorities must be sufficiently trained and equipped to ensure that refusal decisions are not based solely on the automated hit in the system.[35]

15.2.1.2 Aerial Surveillance

In another vein, Frontex employs AI tools to improve situational awareness and early response in pre-frontier areas. This activity is essentially facilitated through the European Border Surveillance System (EUROSUR).[36] The

[30] Case C-817/19 *Ligue des droits humains v Conseil des ministers* [2022] ECLI:EU:C:2022:491, para 189 and 196.

[31] 'ETIAS' (Frontex.europa.eu) <https://frontex.europa.eu/what-we-do/etias/>.

[32] ETIAS Regulation, arts 32 and 37.

[33] Ibid art 38(2).

[34] Ibid art 32(3).

[35] Ibid recital (25).

[36] Originally Regulation (EU) No 1052/2013 of the European Parliament and of the Council of 22 October 2013 establishing the European Border Surveillance System (EUROSUR) [2013] OJ L295/11, which was repealed by Regulation (EU) 2019/1896 of the European Parliament and of the Council of 13 November 2019 on the European Border and Coast Guard and

system is a crucial information resource enabling Frontex to establish situational pictures of the land, sea, and air to identify potential illegal crossings and vessels in distress.[37] The system contains information collected through aerial (including unmanned drones) surveillance, automated vessel tracking and detection capabilities, software functionalities allowing complex calculations for detecting anomalies and predicting vessel positions, as well as precise weather and oceanographic forecasts enabled by the so-called EUROSUR fusion services deployed by Frontex.[38] With the help of the most advanced technology, Frontex is thus responsible for establishing the 'European situational pictures' and 'specific situational pictures' aimed at assisting the national coast guards of the EU and EU-associated states in the performance of border tasks.[39]

The collection of information to be shared via EUROSUR increasingly relies on AI tools. Notably, in recent years, Frontex has significantly expanded its aerial surveillance arsenal.[40] This expansion required significant investments in advanced technology developed by private companies.[41] AI-powered drones or satellites enabling monitoring of the situation on land or sea do not directly pose risks to fundamental rights. However, reliance on such AI-powered surveillance tools gives the EU's border authorities unmatched knowledge about the border situation, permitting the authorities to take actions that may put certain fundamental rights at risk, such as the right to asylum.

Furthermore, as the EU Fundamental Rights Agency states, ongoing development of these technologies and the sharing of the gathered intelligence through EUROSUR is likely to employ algorithms used to track suspicious vessels or extend to the processing of photographs and videos of ships with migrants by maritime surveillance aircraft.[42] In other words, the AI-powered information exchange will also directly implicate privacy and data protection rights. Therefore, the Frontex AI-powered border surveillance tools must also

repealing Regulations (EU) No 1052/2013 and (EU) 2016/1624 [2019] OJ L295/1 (EBCG Regulation), section 3. The use of EUROSUR is governed under the Commission Implementing Regulation (EU) 2021/581 of 9 April 2021 on the situational pictures of the European Border Surveillance System (EUROSUR), C/2021/2361 [2021] OJ L124/3 (EUROSUR Implementing Regulation).

37 EUROSUR Implementing Regulation, arts 1 and 2.

38 EBCG Regulation, art 28.

39 Ibid art 69.

40 Raluca Csernatoni, 'Constructing the EU's High-Tech Borders: FRONTEX and Dual-Use Drones for Border Management' (2018) 27 European Security 175.

41 Ibid.

42 European Union Agency for Fundamental Rights, 'How the Eurosur Regulation Affects Fundamental Rights' <https://fra.europa.eu/sites/default/files/fra_uploads/fra-2018-eurosur-regulation-fundamental-rights-impact_en.pdf> 4.

be subject to close legal scrutiny by independent supervisory authorities and potentially courts when risks to fundamental rights materialise.

The two examples of AI-powered information exchange frameworks examined here facilitate distinct types of border control conduct. On the one hand, the ETIAS automated risk assessments support decision-making by national authorities on whether or not to let someone into the Schengen area.[43] On the other hand, EUROSUR, accompanied by AI-powered land, sea, and air surveillance equipment, create detailed situational pictures with clear instructions for actions to be taken in the context of joint operations between the Frontex teams and national border guard authorities concerning identified vessels carrying individuals, primarily refugees in need of international protection. The two examples pose distinct risks to the fundamental rights of the individuals concerned.

15.2.2 *The Diverse Nature of the Risks to Fundamental Rights*

EU law requires that any use of AI, including by EU actors, must comply with fundamental rights enshrined in the EU Charter of Fundamental Rights and protected as general principles of EU law, irrespective of the area of AI use concerned.[44] This emerges from the requirements of the Union as a legal order based on the rule of law, which, under Article 2 TEU, declares, among others, respect for human dignity and human rights, including the rights of persons belonging to minorities.[45] With rapid technological progress, the use of AI as a system technology[46] brings about an ever greater potential for misuse, which broadly impacts human dignity and various fundamental rights deeply connected to the inviolability of a human being.[47] This concern is broadly acknowledged within the international community and the EU,[48] asserting that protection of human values, including fundamental freedoms,

43 Simona Demková, 'The Decisional Value of Information in European Semi-Automated Decision-Making' (2021) 14 Review of European Administrative Law 29.

44 AI Act, Preamble (1) and art (1)(1).

45 Consolidated Version of the Treaty on European Union [2016] OJ C202/13 (TEU).

46 Haroon Sheikh, Corien Prins, and Erik Schrijvers, *Mission AI: The New System Technology* (Springer International 2023) <https://link.springer.com/10.1007/978-3-031-21448-6>.

47 Article 1 of the Charter. See, Paola Inverardi, 'The Challenge of Human Dignity in the Era of Autonomous Systems' in Hannes Werthner and Others (eds), *Perspectives on Digital Humanism* (Springer International 2022) <https://doi.org/10.1007/978-3-030-86144-5_4>; Sean Kanuck, 'Humor, Ethics, and Dignity: Being Human in the Age of Artificial Intelligence' (2019) 33 Ethics & International Affairs 3.

48 High-Level Expert Group on Artificial Intelligence, Ethics Guidelines for Trustworthy AI, 2019, 39; Closely mirroring the OECD, Recommendation of the Council on Artificial Intelligence, OECD/LEGAL/0449, 2022, 7; and Organisation of Economic Cooperation and

equality, fairness, the rule of law, social justice, data protection, and privacy, shall remain at the centre of placing AI into use in modern democratic societies.

Preserving human dignity in the age of AI requires that individuals retain control over their lives, including when and how they are being subjected, without knowledge or informed consent, to the use of AI. Putting humans and human dignity at the centre of the use of AI is necessary to ensure full respect for fundamental rights. It should thus be the starting point in every discussion on the development, deployment, and reliance on AI where human lives are at stake. However, as the Court of Justice repeats, fundamental rights 'do not constitute unfettered prerogatives'.[49] They must be viewed in light of their function within society, and, if necessary, they may be limited as long as any interferences with the rights are duly justified.[50] Accordingly, the deployment of and reliance on AI shall be reviewed with the same set of considerations in mind: it must be legally authorised, respect the essence of specific rights, and be proportionate and necessary under the objectives of general interest recognised by the Union or the need to protect the rights and freedoms of others (Article 52(1) CFR).

The examples of AI use by Frontex examined above exhibit the breadth of cross-cutting fundamental rights concerns occurring in AI-powered border surveillance. Three key concerns can be highlighted: the risks to privacy and data protection (Articles 7 and 8 CFR), discrimination (Article 21 CFR), and risks to other substantive rights, such as the right to asylum (Article 18 CFR).

15.2.2.1 Privacy and Data Protection

Given that the functionality of AI relies on the wide availability of (personal) data, the discussions on the use of AI tend to revolve around the rights of privacy and personal data protection, enshrined in Articles 7 and 8 of the Charter. Although deeply interconnected, these rights are separate, embodying the more traditional right to privacy and the modern right to data protection.[51] They share a common goal of safeguarding individual autonomy

Development, 'OECD Principles on Artificial Intelligence' <https://legalinstruments.oecd.org/en/instruments/OECD-LEGAL-0449> accessed 29 November 2021.

49 Case C-4/73 *Nold* [1977] ECLI:EU:C:1974:51, para 14.

50 Takis Tridimas and Giulia Gentile, 'The Essence of Rights: An Unreliable Boundary?' (2019) 20 German Law Journal 794.

51 Plixavra Vogiatzoglou and Peggy Valcke, 'Two Decades of Article 8 CFR: A Critical Exploration of the Fundamental Right to Personal Data Protection in EU Law' [2022] Research Handbook on EU Data Protection Law 11; see also Opinion of AG Sharpston in

and dignity by providing a personal space to freely develop their identities and thoughts, thus laying the foundation for exercising other fundamental rights, such as freedom of thought, expression, information, and association.[52]

Privacy and data protection will generally be implicated in the examined uses of AI in border surveillance. On the one hand, data protection concerns arise extensively in the context of the large-scale processing of personal data for automated risk assessments. Far beyond the scope of this chapter to examine all,[53] two risks are particularly worth mentioning. ARAs, such as those envisioned under the ETIAS, risk circumventing fundamental data protection principles, especially the purpose limitation and the related requirements of necessity and proportionality, as well as the prohibition on profiling, including based on discriminatory grounds.[54] As explained above, the AI-powered ETIAS assessments will be based on a threefold comparison of personal data, including sensitive data, against existing EU databases, against risk criteria predefined by the ETIAS Central Unit operated by Frontex, and against the ETIAS Watchlist.

The EU systems' interoperability will facilitate the comparisons against the EU large-scale databases.[55] Effectively, interoperability[56] will transform the

Cases C-92/09 and C-93/02, *Volker und Markus Schecke GbR v Land Hessen* [2010] ECLI: EU:C:2010:353, para 71.

[52] European Union Agency for Fundamental Rights, 'Getting the Future Right – Artificial Intelligence and Fundamental Rights' (14 December 2020) <https://fra.europa.eu/en/publication/2020/artificial-intelligence-and-fundamental-rights> 61; Orla Lynskey, 'Deconstructing Data Protection: The "Added Value" Of A Right To Data Protection In The EU Legal Order' (2014) 63 International & Comparative Law Quarterly 569.

[53] As the secondary rules of EU data protection law that put the right enshrined in Article 8 CFR into use expand the rights of data subjects beyond those explicitly listed in Article 8 CFR (Chapter 3 of the GDPR), Charter of Fundamental Rights of the European Union [2012] OJ C326/02 (CFR) art 8.

[54] Evelien Brouwer, 'Legality and Data Protection Law: The Forgotten Purpose of Purpose Limitation' in Leonard FM Besselink, F Pennings and Sacha Prechal (eds), *The eclipse of the legality principle in the European Union* (Kluwer Law International 2011).

[55] Interoperability means 'the ability of information systems to exchange data and to enable the sharing of information. It is about a targeted and intelligent way of using existing data to best effect, without creating new databases or changing the access rights to the existing information systems'. European Commission, 'Security Union: Closing the Information Gap' <https://home-affairs.ec.europa.eu/system/files_en?file=2019-04/20190416_agenda-security-factsheet-closing-information-gaps_en.pdf>.

[56] Regulation (EU) 2019/817 of the European Parliament and of the Council of 20 May 2019 on establishing a framework for interoperability between EU information systems in the field of borders and visa [2019] OJ L135/27; and Regulation (EU) 2019/818 of the European Parliament and of the Council of 20 May 2019 on establishing a framework for interoperability between EU information systems in the field of police and judicial cooperation, asylum and migration [2019] OJ L135/85 (the Interoperability Regulations). The systems are foreseen to become interoperable in 2024.

border surveillance architecture by enabling far-reaching linking of personal information stored in silo-based alerts.[57] The interlinking of databases will blur the boundaries between law enforcement and intelligence services and between the tasks of the EU and national law enforcement and migration authorities, undermining data protection safeguards.[58] Specifically, in the ETIAS authorisation process, the purpose limitation principle as a critical data protection safeguard seems to disappear completely, for instance, due to the requirement that the ETIAS Central Unit, hosted by Frontex, shall have access to 'any linked application files, as well as to all the hits triggered during automated processing'.[59]

Furthermore, the comparison against screening criteria defined by Frontex will employ algorithms to evaluate the risk factor of a specific individual, akin to a practice of profiling, to facilitate decisions about individuals' lives. According to Article 22(3) of the GDPR, such automated decisions should, in principle, be prohibited unless accompanied by sufficient safeguards, including meaningful human intervention.[60] Since ETIAS assessments will lead to automatic authorisations[61] and quasi-automated refusals of entry,[62] these decisions will have significant consequences for individuals. Automated risk assessments will not only interfere with the data protection right but also pose a distinct threat of discrimination while making access to remedies ever more difficult, as discussed below.

On the other hand, privacy concerns will feature, for instance, wherever surveillance measures are employed in public places. Aerial surveillance, such as with the help of aircraft or drones that record the situational pictures on the land or seas, is increasingly being used by Frontex and can interfere with individuals' privacy by closely monitoring their location, behaviour, movements, and other aspects of personal activities without their knowledge or consent. The use of aerial surveillance technologies allows for gathering visual and sometimes audio information from above, which can capture private moments and sensitive

57 De Gregorio and Ranchordás (n 11).

58 Francesca Galli, 'Interoperable Databases: New Cooperation Dynamics in the EU AFSJ?' (2020) 26 European Public Law 109; Statewatch, 'Frontex and Interoperable Databases: Knowledge as Power?' (Statewatch 2023) <www.statewatch.org/frontex-and-interoperable-databases-knowledge-as-power/>.

59 ETIAS Regulation art 22.

60 Article 29 Data Protection Working Party, 'Guidelines on Automated Individual Decision-Making and Profiling for the Purposes of Regulation 2016/679, Adopted on 3 October 2017, as Last Revised and Adopted on 6 February 2018, 17/EN WP251rev.01' <https://ec.europa.eu/newsroom/article29/items/612053>.

61 ETIAS Regulation art 21(1).

62 Ibid art 22.

information.[63] This intrusion can violate individuals' right to privacy and data protection and potentially expose vulnerable persons to unwarranted conduct by surveillance authorities. It is of the utmost importance that whenever such technologies evolve to increasingly sophisticated people-monitoring tools, their deployment is limited to their original purposes with strict legal safeguards in place and effective opportunities to seek redress in case of misconduct.

15.2.2.2 Risk of Discrimination

Article 21 of the Charter guarantees individuals protection against any form of discrimination based on the protected grounds, such as sex, race, colour, ethnic or social origin, genetic features, language, religion or belief, political or any other opinion, and others. Discrimination concerns are fundamental to the discussions on subjecting human lives to the uses of artificial intelligence. This is because the very purpose of any computational analysis through algorithmic data processing is to evaluate, categorise, or otherwise discover patterns in the analysed data, including personal data. However, human or machine bias may affect the algorithmic output in many ways.[64]

Risk assessment systems, such as the ETIAS, rely on an algorithmic model, which processes large amounts of personal data to make decisions about individual lives. Pursuant to Article 14 of the ETIAS Regulation, any processing of personal data 'shall not result in discrimination against third-country nationals'. However, these assessment algorithms are designed and trained on personal data, which includes the protected grounds under the right to non-discrimination, such as sex, age, place of birth, or nationality.[65] Therefore, to guarantee the right to non-discrimination, the criteria used to train the ETIAS algorithm to evaluate a certain risk behaviour of a specific individual need to be carefully designed to avoid perpetuating or even amplifying existing societal biases.[66] Indeed, discriminatory misconduct has been found to occur in other administrative contexts, such as in the infamous welfare allocation

[63] Luisa Marin and Kamila Krajčíková, 'Deploying Drones in Policing Southern European Borders: Constraints and Challenges for Data Protection and Human Rights' in Aleš Završnik (ed), *Drones and Unmanned Aerial Systems: Legal and Social Implications for Security and Surveillance* (Springer International Publishing 2016) <https://doi.org/10.1007/978-3-319-23760-2_6>; Csernatoni (n 40).

[64] Gianclaudio Malgieri, 'Automated Decision-Making and Data Protection in Europe' (2022) Research Handbook on Privacy and Data Protection Law 433.

[65] ETIAS Regulation, art 17(2).

[66] Malgieri (n 64).

scandal in the Netherlands.[67] The data quality and lawfulness of the data stored in the EU large-scale systems used for ETIAS comparisons and the design of the risk criteria to be used in the ETIAS ARA-based authorisations must cautiously balance the non-discrimination requirements of EU data protection rules with the requirements of the Charter right. Namely, the algorithm must be built to ensure that any AI-driven decision-making is not based solely on special categories of data, reflecting the protective grounds under Article 21 of the Charter.[68] The safeguards, including meaningful transparency for the manual human review following an automated match, must be effective in practice. This includes effective enforcement of compliance with these safeguards, given that such AI tools are powerful in nudging the national competent authorities to decide in a certain way, which may lead to other violations.[69]

Recently, the Court of Justice enumerated the essential guidelines for designing the risk criteria for algorithmic assessments in the security context. In the *Ligue des droits humains* judgment,[70] the Court interpreted the EU's PNR Scheme as requiring that any comparison of passengers' name records against pre-determined risk criteria demands that such criteria are defined in a way that keeps incorrect identifications to a minimum.[71] To achieve this aim, any match must be individually reviewed by non-automated means to highlight any false positives and identify discriminatory results.[72] Furthermore, such review will be effective only where it is clearly established as a requirement in the rules of conduct in the specific context, is well documented, and the officials are sufficiently trained, including to 'give preference to the result of the individual review conducted by non-automated means'.[73]

This requirement of manual review is especially crucial since confronting direct or indirect discriminatory effects in AI-driven decision-making in legal proceedings is rather difficult for the affected individuals.[74] Indeed, in this

[67] Melissa Heikkila, 'Dutch Scandal Serves as a Warning for Europe over Risks of Using Algorithms' (politico.eu, 29 March 2022) <www.politico.eu/article/dutch-scandal-serves-as-a-warning-for-europe-over-risks-of-using-algorithms/>; 'Boete Belastingdienst voor zwarte lijst FSV' (Autoriteit Persoonsgegevens, 12 April 2022) <https://autoriteitpersoonsgegevens.nl/actueel/boete-belastingdienst-voor-zwarte-lijst-fsv>.

[68] GDPR, art 22(4) in conjunction with art 9.

[69] Demková, Automated Decision-Making and Effective Remedies (n 12) 34–36.

[70] Case C-817/19 *Ligue des droits humains v Conseil des ministers* [2022] ECLI:EU:C:2022:491.

[71] Ibid para 204.

[72] Ibid para 203.

[73] Ibid paras 205–208.

[74] European Union Agency for Fundamental Rights, 'Getting the Future Right' (n 52) 69.

respect, the Court also demands that the affected individuals are informed about the pre-determined assessment criteria so as to enable them to understand and defend themselves,[75] as discussed in the next section.

15.2.2.3 Risks to Other Substantive Rights

Beyond the rights to privacy, data protection, and non-discrimination, the AI uses in border surveillance might directly or indirectly implicate other substantive fundamental rights. For instance, AI-powered border surveillance may lead to detention of individuals presenting themselves at the land borders without a valid ETIAS authorisation in interference with their liberty and security (Article 6 CFR). In another vein, AI-powered aerial surveillance enabling identification of migrants on the sea might lead to wrongful actions being taken by the Frontex-led operations, possibly leading to violations of individuals' right to life (Article 2 CFR). Recent investigations by human rights organisations revealed evidence that information gathered from Frontex-operated aerial surveillance has been utilised in facilitating illegal pushbacks of refugees that may contract their right to asylum (Article 18 CFR).[76]

In conjunction with the use of drones, EU Member States have engaged in cooperative agreements with southern Mediterranean countries, such as Libya and Turkey, to intercept and return migrants, thereby externalising the responsibility for these actions.[77] This approach prevents other vessels from intervening or disembarking rescued individuals in supposedly safe harbours. EU Member States have justified these measures by claiming that search and rescue activities act as a 'pull factor' for migrants coming to EU countries. Frontex has often been viewed as a passive bystander in this context, given the division of responsibilities in the EU's integrated border management (EIBM).[78] Under the EIBM, the final responsibility still lies with the

[75] *Ligue des droits humains* (n 70) para 210.

[76] 'MEPs to Grill Frontex Director on Agency's Role in Pushbacks of Asylum-Seekers' (European Parliament, 30 November 2020) <www.europarl.europa.eu/news/en/press-room/20201126IPR92509/meps-to-grill-frontex-director-on-agency-s-role-in-pushbacks-of-asylum-seekers>; Judith Sunderland and Lorenzo Pezzani, 'Airborne Complicity: Frontex Aerial Surveillance Enables Abuse' (Human Rights Watch, 12 August 2022) <www.hrw.org/node/383557>.

[77] Abbas Azimi and Others, 'The Crotone Cover Up' (*Lighthouse Reports*, 2 June 2023) <www.lighthousereports.com/investigation/the-crotone-cover-up/>.

[78] Frontex, 'Technical and Operational Strategy for European Integrated Border Management' <http://op.europa.eu/en/publication-detail/-/publication/2123579d-f151–11e9-a32c-01aa75ed71a1>; see also the collections in Miroslava Scholten and Michiel Luchtman (eds), *Law Enforcement by EU Authorities Implications for Political and Judicial Accountability* (Edward Elgar 2017).

Member States. Lately, this division has been criticised as it transpired from a classified EU report[79] that Frontex knowingly contributed to illegal pushback practices.[80] These practices violate the right to asylum under Article 18 CFR and the cornerstone of international human rights law – the principle of non-refoulment.[81]

And, as already mentioned above, with the continuing development of aerial surveillance, new risks to fundamental rights will emerge. These risks might arise from the processing of photographs and videos of vessels with migrants on board as well as the potential implications of the algorithms that will be used to track the vessels flagged as suspicious. All these types of AI-powered capacities of the EU's Frontex-led border surveillance will expand the above risks to privacy, data protection, and discrimination and may continue to indirectly support unlawful practices, such as decisions on whether or not to save the lives of individuals in distress on the seas and those in need of international protection.[82]

15.3 EXPLORING THE POSSIBILITIES FOR ACCESS TO REMEDIES

In the EU legal order, when a person considers that the EU actors have violated their rights, they have the right to seek an effective remedy (Article 47 CFR). The use of AI, however, brings considerable challenges to ensuring that AI-powered conduct is both non-arbitrary and sufficiently reviewable to fulfil the requirements of this constitutional guarantee, which constitutes 'the essence of the rule of law'.[83] To assess the properties of the EU remedial architecture, it is therefore necessary to also consider the interrelated impacts

79 The 123 page report was published in full by the German freedom of information newspapers *Frag Den Staat*, *Lighthouse Reports*, and *Der Spiegel*, to whom the report was first leaked, available at <https://cdn.prod.www.spiegel.de/media/00847a5e-8604-45dc-a0fe-37d920056673/Directorate_A_redacted-2.pdf>.

80 'Frontex Failing to Protect People at EU Borders' (Human Rights Watch, 23 June 2021) <www.hrw.org/news/2021/06/23/frontex-failing-protect-people-eu-borders>; 'EU: Frontex Complicit in Abuse in Libya' (Human Rights Watch, 12 December 2022) <www.hrw.org/news/2022/12/12/eu-frontex-complicit-abuse-libya>.

81 See also Sir Elihu Lauterpacht and Daniel Bethlehem, 'The Scope and Content of the Principle of Non-Refoulement: Opinion' in Erika Feller, Volker Türk, and Frances Nicholson (eds), *Refugee Protection in International Law* (Cambridge University Press 2003); Rebecca M M Wallace, 'The Principle of Non-Refoulement in International Refugee Law' in Vincent Chetail and Céline Bauloz (eds), *Research Handbook on International Law and Migration* (Edward Elgar 2014).

82 European Union Agency for Fundamental Rights, 'How the Eurosur Regulation Affects Fundamental Rights' (n 42).

83 Case C-72/15 *Rosneft* [2017] ECLI:EU:C:2017:236, para 73; Case C-216/18 PPU *Minister for Justice and Equality v LM* [2018] ECLI:EU:C:2018:586, para 51.

of the AI on the exercise of procedural requirements under the rights to good administration and effective judicial protection (Section 15.3.1). The discussion then turns to the construction of remedies based on the scope and interplay of the upcoming AI Act with the EU's existing data protection framework (Section 15.3.2).

15.3.1 *The Impact of AI Use on Individuals' Access to Remedies*

Article 41 CFR guarantees to everyone the right to good administration in decisions or other legal acts adopted by EU actors. Historically, the CJEU interpreted this right as a general principle of EU law,[84] which expanded its application wherever EU law applies. Under its umbrella,[85] the right to good administration enshrines rights and obligations, which hold at their core the enabling role for legal accountability in public conduct. On the one hand, the right demands that the authorities act fairly, impartially, and within a reasonable time. On the other hand, it obliges the authorities to present sufficient reasons substantiating their acts vis-à-vis the affected persons. In *TUM*, the Court formulated the interplay of good administration requirements as 'the duty of the competent institution to examine carefully and impartially all the relevant aspects of the individual case' prior to decision-making.[86] In *Nölle*, the Court further recognised this duty of care as an individual right arising from the clear, precise, and unconditional obligation in Article 41 CFR.[87] The authorities' compliance with their duty of care obligations ensures that the affected person understands the evidentiary basis of the decision in order to decide whether or not to seek remedies against it. As an essential procedural requirement,[88] failure to comply with the duty of care obligations may lead to the annulment of the decision.[89]

84 See Case C-166/13 *Mukarubega v Seine-Saint-Denis* [2014] ECLI:EU:C:2014:2336, paras 43–49; Case C-521/15 *Spain v Council* [2017] ECLI:EU:C:2017:982, para 89; Case C-604/12 N [2014] ECLI:EU:C:2014:302, para 49; or the more recent Joined Cases C-225/19 and C-226/19 *R.N.N.S., K.A. v Minister van Buitenlandse Zaken* [2020] ECLI:EU:C:2020:951, para 34.

85 Herwig C H Hofmann and Bucura Catalina Mihaescu-Evans, 'The Relation between the Charter's Fundamental Rights and the Unwritten General Principles of EU Law: Good Administration as the Test Case' (2013) 9 European Constitutional Law Review 73.

86 Case C-269/90 *TUM* [1991] ECLI:EU:C:1991:438, para 14.

87 Case C-16/90 *Nölle v Hauptzollamt Bremen-Freihafen* [1991] ECLI:EU:C:1991:402, para 29.

88 Herwig C H Hofmann, 'The Duty of Care in EU Public Law – A Principle between Discretion and Proportionality' (2020) 13 Review of European Administrative Law 87; Demková, *Automated Decision-Making and Effective Remedies* (n 12) ch 6.

89 Simona Demková and Herwig C H Hofmann, 'General Principles of Procedural Justice' in Katja Ziegler, Päivi Neuvonen, and Violeta Moreno-Lax (eds), *Research Handbook on General Principles of EU Law: Constructing Legal Orders in Europe* (Edward Elgar 2022).

It is in its defence-enabling function that the right to good administration also becomes central to remedial possibilities against the AI-driven EU conduct. In this context, compliance with the good administration requirements faces significant obstacles. The opacity of algorithmic risk assessments, exemplified in the ETIAS authorisation process, poses substantial challenges to the authorities' ability to reason their decisions and ensure that these are based on factually correct, relevant, and complete information. As explained above, any of the 1.4 billion visa-exempt citizens that apply through the ETIAS website will be automatically screened for any suspicion of posing serious threat to public security. This suspicion will be found to exist whenever an automated processing of the traveller's application results in a hit against pre-determined risk criteria in conjunction with an automatic comparison with millions of alerts stored in other EU information systems. If the process results in a hit, the competent authorities will have to manually review the data, ensuring the possibility to contradict the automated result, in view of their duty of care obligations. This requirement of human intervention ensures that each rejection of travel authorisation is not a decision based solely on automated processing of personal data (Article 22(3) GDPR).

However, to what extent will the manual review verify the correctness, relevance, and completeness of the information so as to uncover whether or not the hit was, for instance, due to discriminatory profiling by the prescreening algorithm? This question does not permit an easy answer,[90] especially considering the context in which the manual reviews will take place: namely, time-pressured (the ETIAS rules estimate a response within a few days where manual verification is required), without sufficient AI expertise of the officials, and facing other constraints, such as well-documented automation and confirmation biases in manual reviews,[91] coupled with a limited access to the training data underpinning the risk assessment algorithm.

The diminished potential to meet the requirements of good administration in the AI-powered decision-making will have direct implications for the individuals' access to effective remedies. In fact, in its jurisprudence, the CJEU often equates the requirements of reasoning under the right to good administration to the requirements of an effective remedy under Article 47 CFR.[92] Their interplay, according to the Court, lies in enabling the person to ascertain the reasons upon which the decision is based, 'so as to make it possible for him or her to

[90] Demková, Automated Decision-Making and Effective Remedies (n 12) 175–178.

[91] Saar Alon-Barkat and Madalina Busuioc, 'Human–AI Interactions in Public Sector Decision Making: "Automation Bias" and "Selective Adherence" to Algorithmic Advice' (2023) 33 Journal of Public Administration Research and Theory 153.

[92] Demková and Hofmann (n 89).

defend his or her rights in the best possible conditions'.[93] Individuals will only be able to defend themselves when it is indeed possible to understand the relevant decision and the process under which it was taken. Additionally, the Court recognises the significance of reasoning for ability of judges and other supervisory authorities to exercise effective review. Indeed, these concerns are reflected in the regulation of AI – the AI Act, which brings about specific transparency requirements intended to facilitate the AI users' ability to act with a meaningful human control over AI-generated outputs.

Before turning to the AI Act, it remains to be stressed that judicial remedies are rather limited in the context of AI-powered conduct based on composite administrative procedures involving actors at EU and Member State levels.[94] The courts' jurisdiction to review AI-driven decision-making is territorially limited and constrained by the narrow notion of what constitutes a reviewable act.[95] On the one hand, the former prevents individuals from challenging the conduct of the EU actors directly before the Court of Justice when the responsibility lies with the national authorities, such as in case of refusals to ETIAS applications or illegal pushbacks of migrants.[96] The staff of the competent ETIAS National Unit will need to manually review the automated refusals, hence exercise final discretion.[97] Also, where an ETIAS ARA results in a hit with the information entered by Europol, the ETIAS Regulation only establishes a consultation procedure between the Europol and the responsible Member State.[98] Under this procedure, Europol must provide the responsible Member State with a 'reasoned opinion on the application'.[99] Nonetheless, the final decision – hence final discretion – lies with the Member State concerned. Accordingly, complaints against potential discriminatory effects of the ETIAS algorithm in these circumstances might thus only be raised before the courts of

93 *R.N.N.S., K.A. v Minister van Buitenlandse Zaken* (n 84) para 43.

94 Gloria González Fuster and Others, 'The Right to Lodge a Data Protection Complaint: OK, but Then What? An Empirical Study of Current Practices under the GDPR' (Data Protection Law Scholars Network and Access Now, 2022) <www.accessnow.org/cms/assets/uploads/2022/06/Complaint-study-Final-version-before-design-June-15.pdf>.

95 Simona Demková, 'Enforcing Remedies: The Challenges of Automatisation for Effective Oversight' in Katalin Ligeti and Kei Hannah Brodersen (eds), *Studies on enforcement in multi-regulatory systems* (Nomos 2022). See also Eliantonio in this volume, Chapter 13.

96 Case T-600/21 *WS and Others v Frontex* ECLI:EU:T:2023:492 and the comment by Melanie Fink and Jorrit Rijpma, 'The EU General Court's Judgment in the Case of WS and Others v Frontex: Human Rights Violations at EU External Borders Going Unpunished' (EU Law Analysis, 22 September 2023) <https://eulawanalysis.blogspot.com/2023/09/the-eu-general-courts-judgment-in-case.html> accessed 2 October 2023. For discussion on access to damages, see Fink, Rauchegger, and De Coninck in this volume, Chapter 2.

97 ETIAS Regulation, arts 25 and 26.

98 Ibid art 29.

99 Ibid art 29(4).

that State, without the possibility of uncovering the factual basis of the information supplied by Europol and relied on in the refusal decision.

On the other hand, these *potential* discriminatory effects of the underlying risk criteria might not be deemed to produce legal effects to trigger justiciability of the ARA. Indeed, pursuant to the requirement of 'direct and individual concern,' the impact of the discriminatory effect might not occur for each person whose application had been refused by the ETIAS ARA.[100] Accordingly, as argued elsewhere,[101] construing reviewability in a similar context needs to reflect the underlying automation and output biases if we expect EU law to guarantee sufficient legal protection to the affected individuals. Yet, for now, EU law does not recognise the impact of the screening algorithm on the final decisions taken by the Member States.[102] As such, for now, there seems to be no possibility of direct judicial remedy against the Frontex-based ETIAS Central Unit for its role in the development and deployment of the ETIAS risk criteria algorithm.

15.3.2 *Unwrapping the Remedial Possibilities under the Upcoming AI Act*

In 2018, EU legislators embarked on the process of designing specific rules governing develoment and use of artificial intelligence systems in the EU, that would ensure, inter alia, full respect for fundamental rights.[103] The efforts culminated in the proposal for a horizontal regulation of AI – the AI Act.[104] Central to this is the EU's self-proclaimed 'human-centric approach to AI', which shall 'strive to ensure that human values are central to the way in which AI systems are developed, deployed, used and monitored, by ensuring respect for fundamental rights'.[105]

That the human-centric Act will mitigate the above-identified risks to fundamental rights should, however, not be taken for granted. With the legal basis set in Article 114 TFEU,[106] the AI Act will first and foremost ensure safe operation of AI systems on the EU's internal market (Article 1). The Act's pledge to guarantee respect for fundamental rights is arguably manifested in its 'risk-based approach'. On the most basic level, the Act differentiates between

[100] Napoleon Xanthoulis, 'Administrative Factual Conduct: Legal Effects and Judicial Control in EU Law' (2019) 12 Review of European Administrative Law 39.

[101] Demková, 'The Decisional Value of Information in European Semi-Automated Decision-Making' (n 43) 48.

[102] Ibid.

[103] Commission, 'Artificial Intelligence for Europe' COM (2018) 237 final.

[104] AI Act (n 2).

[105] AI HLEG, Ethics Guidelines for Trustworthy AI, 2019, available at <https://digital-strategy.ec.europa.eu/en/library/ethics-guidelines-trustworthy-ai> 39.

[106] Consolidated Version of the Treaty on the Functioning of the European Union [2016] OJ C202/47 (TFEU).

'prohibitions of certain [AI] practices' and 'specific requirements for high-risk AI systems' (Article 1(2)). The former include systems using subliminal techniques beyond a person's consciousness (manipulation), uses of AI that may exploit vulnerable individuals (Article 5 (a) and (b)), or the real-time biometric identification systems in publicly accessible spaces for law enforcement purposes, except where duly authorised (Article 5(c)).[107] According to the latest text, the list of high-risk systems in Annex III should be amended to consider the impact of the AI use on the relevant action or a decision to be taken.[108] Ultimately, the concept of risk to fundamental rights underpinning the AI Act's approach is defined as 'the combination of the probability of an occurrence of harm and the severity of that harm'.[109]

Although far from settled, the final elaboration of the prohibited and high-risk AI uses will determine the extent to which the AI Act can provide some form of fundamental rights protection also in the context of AI uses by the EU actors. Yet, as we await clarity on the AI Act's final shape, one aspect is clear: the AI Act will need to be applied in conjunction with the existing EU law, including the rules on remedies and existing data protection rules, wherever the system relies on, among others, processing of personal data. Accordingly, the following discussion highlights two key aspects, which will be determinative for the protection of fundamental rights from the risks posed by the EU's AI uses: first, the scope of application of the AI Act to the EU actors' use of AI and, second, the interplay and main discrepancies between the AI Act's substantive rules and the data protection rules.

15.3.2.1 The Scope of Application of the AI Act to Border Surveillance

The Act emerges as the EU's effort to establish general rules on the development, authorisation, and deployment of AI systems in the Union. Accordingly,

[107] Generally, the list used is defined in Article 2(2) of Council Framework Decision 2002/584/JHA or in reference to crimes that are punishable by a custodial sentence or a detention order for a maximum period of at least three years. The classification of high-risk AI uses is provided in Annex III. Council Framework Decision of 13 June 2002 on the European arrest warrant and the surrender procedures between Member States [2002] OJ L190/1 (Council Framework Decision 190/1).

[108] *AI Act art 6(3) states: '[...] an AI system referred to in Annex III shall not be considered to be high-risk where it does not pose a significant risk of harm to the health, safety or fundamental rights of natural persons, including by not materially influencing the outcome of decision making.'*

[109] AI Act art 3(2). Luca Bertuzzi, 'AI Act: EU Parliament's Crunch Time on High-Risk Categorisation, Prohibited Practices' (www.euractiv.com, 7 February 2023) <www.euractiv.com/section/artificial-intelligence/news/ai-act-eu-parliaments-crunch-time-on-high-risk-categorisation-prohibited-practices/>; see also Council Framework Decision 190/1, preamble (14).

its provisions will need to be complied with in their entirety. Pursuant to Article 2 of the AI Act, the rules apply to both 'providers' placing on the market or putting into service AI systems, irrespective of their location, and 'deployers' of AI systems with the establishment in the Union.[110] The AI Act will also apply to EU actors when acting as a provider or deployer of an AI system. There are some exceptions, however. For instance, the AI Act will not apply to AI systems developed or used exclusively for military purposes or for purely research purposes.[111]

More worryingly, the initial Commission Proposal excluded from its scope the AI systems that are 'components of the large-scale IT systems', such as the SIS, EES, or ETIAS, before the entry into force of this regulation.[112] This has been revised to require that these systems comply with the AI Act *by 31 December 2030*.[113] Nevertheless, both solutions leave out the expansive use of AI systems in the EU border surveillance without immediate rules that could address the above-identified risks of AI uses. As the EDPS and the European Data Protection Board (EDPB) highlighted in their joint opinion, such exclusion 'risks circumventing the safeguards enshrined in the AI Act'.[114] It also undermines the broader exercise of powers by the competent supervisory authorities, such as the EDPS, when presented with complaints regarding AI uses and claims of violations of the data protection rules.

15.3.2.2 The Interplay between the AI Act and the EU Data Protection Rules

The new safeguards introduced under the AI Act might only contribute to enhanced fundamental rights protection if crafted carefully on the basis of their interaction with the existing data protection rules is properly considered.[115]

[110] AI Act art. 2.

[111] AI Act arts 2(3) and (4).

[112] AI Act Proposal, art 83(1).

[113] AI Act 111(1).

[114] European Data Protection Supervisor, 'EDPS – EDPB Joint Opinion on the Proposal for a Regulation of the European Parliament and of the Council Laying down Harmonised Rules on Artificial Intelligence (Artificial Intelligence Act)' (EDPS.eu, 2021) <https://edps.europa.eu/node/7140_en>.

[115] Lilian Edwards, 'Expert Opinion: Regulating AI in Europe: Four Problems and Four Solutions' (Ada Lovelace Institute 2022) <www.adalovelaceinstitute.org/report/regulating-ai-in-europe/>. As Lilian Edwards points out, the Proposal takes an 'essentially individualistic approach to fundamental rights' lacking instead a more 'systematic concern for groups' rights and interests'. The latter, according to Edwards, may differ from the traditional categories of groups under anti-discrimination law. Indeed, algorithmic processing of personal data may lead to new algorithmically constituted categories of groups that deserve greater attention. But see AI Act Proposal, art 10(3) on training data in datasets.

However, a number of discrepancies appear between the two legal frameworks, which may pose difficulties for the EDPS that acts as the first instance avenue for addressing potential fundamental rights violations by EU actors. Three aspects of this interplay specifically affect individuals' access to remedies.

First, the EU data protection framework is far from homogeneous. The framework essentially consists of the GDPR, Regulation (EU) 2018/1725 (the 'EU DPR') governing the processing of personal data by Union institutions, bodies, offices, and agencies, and the so-called Law Enforcement Directive (EU) 2016/680 (the 'LED') governing the processing of personal data by national law enforcement authorities.[116] While it is the EU DPR that governs the use of AI by the EU actors examined in this chapter, we also see that the final legal responsibility in the EU's integrated border control rests with the national border authorities or law enforcement authorities.[117] The data processing activities of the EU agencies, such as Frontex, are furthermore governed by the agencies' own founding regulations. These specialised legal instruments thus embody both the exceptions to the EU DPR and the *lex specialis* rules of LED.[118] Accordingly, while the EU DPR/in conjunction with the Frontex and ETIAS Regulations will apply to the AI-powered ETIAS system and the development of its algorithm by eu-LISA and Frontex in their distinct capacities, the LED and/or GDPR will govern the ETIAS searches and reliance on the generated output by the national border and law enforcement authorities.

Second, this fragmentation is problematic for access to remedies in view of against potential violations of fundamental rights in AI-driven conduct of the EU actors, considering the remedial system under the EU data protection framework. The latter is essentially a twofold system. Individuals may lodge a complaint with an independent supervisory authority of the Member State/EDPS.[119] Furthermore, affected individuals enjoy the right to an effective

[116] Other legal instruments governing personal data processing composing the EU data protection framework include for instance the e-Privacy Directive 2002/58/EC of the European Parliament and of the Council of 12 July 2002 concerning the processing of personal data and the protection of privacy in the electronic communications sector (Directive on privacy and electronic communications) [2002] OJ L201/37 (e-Privacy Directive).

[117] Diana Dimitrova, 'Data Protection within Police and Judicial Cooperation' in Herwig C H Hofmann, Gerard C Rowe, and Alexander H Türk (eds), *Specialized Administrative Law of the European Union: A Sectoral Review* (Oxford University Press 2018). As the author reminds, Article 87(2)(a) TFEU laying down the legal basis for police cooperation between the EU Member States mandated the EU to establish rules on 'relevant information' processing.

[118] Teresa Quintel, *Data Protection, Migration and Border Control: The GDPR, the Law Enforcement Directive and Beyond* (Bloomsbury 2022) <www.bloomsbury.com/uk/data-protection-migration-and-border-control-9781509959648/>.

[119] GDPR, art 77; EU DPR, art 63; Directive (EU) 2016/680 of the European Parliament and of the Council of 27 April 2016 on the protection of natural persons with regard to the processing of personal data by competent authorities for the purposes of the prevention, investigation,

judicial remedy against a decision of that supervisory authority/EDPS or against a decision of the controller or processor.[120] The GDPR also provides for the possibility of representative action by civil society organisations on behalf of the data subjects.[121] Research, however, shows that direct remedies are often not utilised, especially in the security context where collection of personal data within the alerts entered in the EU information systems is rarely known to the data subjects.[122]

Instead, a person that is refused travel authorisation will in most cases be able to appeal the only final refusal decision before the supervisory authority of the refusing Member State. In this context, they will, for instance, be able to file a complaint against the Member State authority for non-compliance with the obligation to manually review the automated hit, pursuant to the requirements of Articles 22 GDPR/11 LED. The Member State authority will, however, lack jurisdiction to review the development and deployment of the ETIAS risk algorithm. Accordingly, the affected person will have to lodge a separate complaint with the EDPS, which is competent to review the acts of the ETIAS Central Unit based in the Frontex agency.

Lastly, in their complaint to the EDPS, the affected person will only be able to invoke their rights as the data subject.[123] The list of data subjects' rights develops the substance of the autonomous fundamental right to personal data protection (Article 8 CFR). Via the remedial avenues under EU data protection law, individuals might however be able to bring claims concerning potential violations of other fundamental rights, including, for instance, non-discrimination or the right to an effective remedy. In other words, where the EU data protection rules provides specific safeguards regarding non-discrimination, such as in the context of processing special categories of data,[124] they integrate many of the Charter rights relevant to the digital context.[125]

detection or prosecution of criminal offences or the execution of criminal penalties, and on the free movement of such data, and repealing Council Framework Decision 2008/977/JHA [2016] OJ L119/89 (LED) art 52.

[120] GDPR, arts 78–79; EU DPR, art 64; LED, arts 53–54.

[121] GDPR, art 80; EU DPR, art 67; LED, art 55.

[122] Sergio Carrera and Marco Stefan, 'Complaint Mechanisms in Border Management and Expulsion Operations in Europe: Effective Remedies For Victims of Human Rights Violations?' (Centre for European Policy Studies 2018) <www.ceps.eu/ceps-publications/complaint-mechanisms-border-management-and-expulsion-operations-europe-effective/>; Fuster and Others (n 93); Demková, Automated Decision-Making and Effective Remedies (n 12).

[123] GDPR, arts 15–22; EU DPR, arts 14–24; LED, arts 12–18.

[124] See, for instance, GDPR, recitals (75) and (85) and arts 9 and 22(4).

[125] As the Court reminds us, an act under EU law should 'be interpreted, as far as possible, in such a way as not to affect its validity and conformity with primary law as a whole, and in particular, with the provisions of the Charter'. See *Ligue des droits humains* (n 70) para 86 with reference to Case C-481/19 *Consob* [2021] ECLI:EU:C:2021:84, para 50 and the case law cited.

Overall, integrating the Charter's rights in the secondary data subject rights could, however, lead to an inferior legal protection. This is because data protection law guarantees data subjects' rights with substantial number of exceptions and limitations, which is evident from the long list of exceptions to the general prohibition on processing special categories of personal data in Article 9(2) GDPR. Such a priori exceptions might not be subject to the same proportionality and necessity test as permissible limits to fundamental rights are under Article 52(1) CFR.[126] Although the Court of Justice does apply a strict review of proportionality and necessity in similar high-risk AI uses as demonstrated in the PNR case, subjecting the safeguards under the PNR to a very strict scrutiny, the same may not be the case for complaints addressed by national supervisory authorities. A strict proportionality review is especially necessary, given that the affected persons might often not have sufficient possibilities to bring claims of violations of the Charter's rights before the courts, since, as explaine above, enforcement of data-specific rights primarily rests with independent data protection authorities (DPAs). The DPAs' remedial competence, however, differs substantially from judicial competence. Yet, given their primary role in the digital age, these authorities, increasingly perform quasi-judicial review of claims, which implicate Charter rights, beyond the requirements guaranteed under EU data protection framework.

The last, and key concern arising from the interplay between the AI Act and existing data protection remedies, concerns precisely the designation and cooperation among the variety of supervisory authorities with competences over different parts of an AI-driven conduct that may lead to potential fundamental rights violations. As a product safety regulation, the Commission's original AI Act Proposal did not include any rights and remedies for the affected persons in relation to the uses of AI systems. Critics found this lacuna highly problematic,[127] given that the Act's risk-based approach was envisioned to ensure full respect of fundamental rights and freedoms. Without a right to complain against the AI risks, individuals may be able to subsume their claims under their rights as data subjects. This would, however, prove to be only a partial remedy against the diverse and serious risks posed by the use of AI systems, as demonstrated in this chapter. It is therefore essential that individuals have meaningful access to redress mechanisms. The European Parliament proposed to fill this vacuum with the introduction of Chapter 3a to the AI Act Proposal.[128] The effort culminated in the addition of Section 4

[126] Any such limits must be established in law, respect the essence of the right, and be necessary and proportionate to the objectives sought.

[127] Edwards (n 115).

[128] For an in-depth analysis of the remedial set up under the AI Act from a comparative perspective, see De Gregorio, Giovanni and Demková, Simona, The Constitutional Right to

in the final version of the Act, which provides however only provides a limited consolidation of the calls for enhancing access to justice against the risks of AI. Namely, the remedies under the AI Act are essentially two-fold: (a) a product-related complaint mechanisms before the designated market surveillance authorities; (b) the right to an explanation of individual decision-making when the latter is made on the basis of a high-risk AI output.

Furthermore, the effective enforcement of remedies under the AI Act will be contingent on more substantive discrepancies between the two legal frameworks which are however beyond the scope of this chapter.[129] For instance, such discrepancies surface with respect to the definitions. The original proposal lacked any recognition of the position of the affected private persons under the AI Act legal framework. Notably, the original notion of the 'user' within the AI Act Proposal has been changed to denote the 'deployer', meaning any natural or legal person, public authority, agency, or other body using an AI system under its authority, except where the AI system is used in the course of a personal non-professional activity.[130] The AI 'users', now called 'deployers' thus indicate the data controllers or processors in the GDPR sense.[131] In another vein, discrepancies arise from the formulations of the scope of various corresponding rules within the two legal frameworks. For instance, pursuant to recital 63 of the AI Act Proposal, classification of an AI system as high-risk, and hence permitting its use, does not automatically mean that the use of that system is lawful under 'other Union law', including data protection rules. The Proposal further clarifies that 'any such use should continue to occur solely in accordance with the applicable requirements resulting from the Charter and from the applicable acts of secondary Union law and national law'. Yet the AI Act provides its own legal basis, for instance, for the processing of special categories of personal data, which shall however not contradict the general prohibition under the data protection rules.[132] Assuming that these discrepancies will eventually be resolved, the access to effective remedies against the AI-driven conduct of EU actors, such as Frontex, requires specific attention on the role and powers of the EDPS. In

an Effective Remedy in the Digital Age: A Perspective from Europe (January 31, 2024). In van Oirsouw, Ch., de Poorter, J.; Leijten, I.; van der Schyff, G.; Stremler, M.; de Visser, M. (eds), European Yearbook of Constitutional Law (forthcoming, 2024), Available at SSRN: https://ssrn.com/abstract=4712096 or http://dx.doi.org/10.2139/ssrn.4712096

[129] Drawing on links and discrepancies between the GDPR and the AI Act identified in the study by Artur Bogucki and Others, 'The AI Act and Emerging EU Digital Acquis: Overlaps, Gaps and Inconsistencies' (Centre for European Policy Studies, 2022) CEPS In-Depth Analysis s 2.1.1. <www.ceps.eu/ceps-publications/the-ai-act-and-emerging-eu-digital-acquis/>.

[130] AI Act, art 3(4).

[131] Bogucki and Others (n 128) 8.

[132] AI Act, art. 10(5).

order to effectively safeguard fundamental rights of individuals affected by the EU uses of AI, the EDPS will need to divert its role and powers by carefully crafting requirements under EU data protection rules in light of their potential interplay with AI Act requirements.

15.4 DOUBLE-HATTING THE EDPS

The AI Act envisions a central role for the EDPS to oversee AI uses by the EU actors, including Frontex. To appraise the potentials of this role, this section explores how the AI Act, in conjunction with the EU DPR, construe the EDPS' competence and whether they do so with sufficient clarity so as to contribute to mitigating the above-identified risks to fundamental rights.

As explained above, under the EU DPR, the EDPS is responsible for ensuring that any processing of personal data by EU institutions, bodies, offices, and agencies respects the fundamental rights and freedoms of natural persons (Article 52(2)). To that end, the Supervisor, among others, receives and handles complaints from the data subjects (Article 63 EU DPR). Through this redress mechanism, individuals are given the possibility to take control over their data and seek remedies for any breaches of their rights as data subjects.[133] However, the mere existence of the possibility to complain about potential breaches of data subjects' rights under the EU DPR does not necessarily guarantee the EU actors' compliance with fundamental rights more broadly. Indeed, to that end, pursuant to Article 64 EU DPR, individuals also enjoy the right to an effective judicial remedy before the Court of Justice of the EU, including through direct claims for damages and appeals against the decision of the EDPS.[134]

Under the AI Act, the EDPS' role in remedying potential violations of fundamental rights is, however, less clear. The definition of 'national competent authority' under Article 3(3), specifies that for AI development and uses by EU actors, '*references to national competent authorities or market surveillance authorities in this Regulation shall be construed as references to the European Data Protection Supervisor.*'. For the latter, Article 74(9) further specified that wherever the AI Act applies to the EU actors, the EDPS shall be the designated supervisory authority, '*except in relation to the [CJEU]acting in its judicial capacity.*'. This opens up the question, however: what are the powers and competences of the EDPS as a market surveillace authority in respect of the AI Act as a product safety regulation and what does that mean for the individuals' access to effective remedies?

[133] Pieter T J Wolters, 'The Control by and Rights of the Data Subject Under the GDPR' (2018) 22 (1) Journal of Internet Law 6.

[134] EU DPR, art 64(3).

Under the AI Act, the EDPS will assume diverse tasks with respect to the enforcement of the AI Act's obligations. There is at the moment, however, no clear gap in the procedural possibility to lodge complaints with the EDPS under the AI Act. In contrast to the envisioned right to lodge a complaint with the national market surveillance authority under Article 85 AI Act, the AI Act does not afford the same right to lodge a complaint with the EDPS, akin to Article 63 EU DPR. Nor, therefore, does the AI Act grant the right to an effective judicial remedy against the decisions of the EDPS concerning EU actors' deployment of AI systems with the requirements of the AI Act., akin to Article 64 EU DPR (and in light of the requirements of Article 47 of the Charter). Without a direct procedural access to remedies, individuals will thus have to rely on their rights as data subjects under the EU DPR in seeking protection against the potential violations by the EU actors' use of AI, despite the existence of clear obligations falling on the latter.

Instead, under the AI Act framework, the EDPS will assume a threefold role, as (a) 'a market surveillance authority' (Article 74(9)), (b) an "observer" within the new European AI Board (Article 65(2)), and (c) the designer of regulatory sandboxes for EU actors (Article 57(3).).

First, in its capacity as a market surveillance authority, the EDPS will undertake conformity assessments (a form of ex ante compliance mechanism) for the EU actors' uses of AI and notify the outcomes of these assessments to the Commission.[135] While on the face of it a clear task, the AI Act requires that *deployers of highrisk AI systems that are bodies governed by public law, or private entities providing public services and deployers of certain high-risk AI systems, such as banking or insurance entities, should carry out a fundamental rights impact assessment prior to putting it into use, according to Article 27.* without clearly encompassing this within the mandate of the EDPS. As a whole, the conformity assessment procedure with respect to the EU actors' development and deployment of AI is rather underspecified. This perhaps calls into question the EU legislators' choice of a single regulatory instrument as opposed to, for instance, a separate, more targeted regulation governing the EU actors' obligations, akin to the EU DPR.

Second, the EDPS will play a further role within the newly established European Artificial Intelligence Board (hearafter the AI Board).[136] The AI Board should *advise and assist the Commission and the Member States to facilitate the consistent and effective application (Article 66)*, including by facilitating coordination and harmonisation of practices of national competent

[135] AI Act as per the obligations falling upon national market surveillance authorities under articles 43 and 70.

[136] Ibid art 65.

authorities, *collecting and sharing technical and* regulatory *expertise and best practices; issuing* recommendations *and* written *opinions on any relevant* matters related to the implementation of the AI Act; and other advisory and coordinating tasks aimed at improving the implementation of the AI Act as a whole.[137] Perhaps akin to the role of the European Data Protection Board in its advisory capacity,[138] by itself this role will not constitute a remedial avenue for individuals to ask for an effective review of EU actors' uses of AI systems, as the Board will not possess any direct enforcement powers.[139]

Lastly, the EDPS will also participate in the organisation of regulatory sandboxes for the development, testing and validation of innovative AI systems at the Union level, before they are deployed. The policy option of regulatory sandboxes has emerged as experimental regulatory method aim to address the uncertainty of the AI industry and its associated knowledge gaps, with the intention to enable smaller companies to prepare for the necessary conformity assessments.[140] Pursuant to Article 57, the sandboxes shall provide a, '*controlled environment that fosters innovation and facilitates the development, training, testing and validation of innovative AI systems for a limited time before their being placed on the market or put into service pursuant to a specific sandbox plan agreed between the providers or prospective providers and the competent authority*' Research in the field of AI and ethics has compared the reliance on regulatory sandboxes to 'nurturing moral imaginations'.[141] Pursuant to the third paragraph of Article 53, the AI regulatory sandboxes 'shall not affect the supervisory and corrective powers of the competent authorities' and 'any significant risks to fundamental rights, democracy and rule of law, health and safety or the environment identified during the development and testing of such AI systems shall result in immediate and adequate mitigation'. (Article 57(11)). The EDPS will be tasked with organising such sandboxes at the EU level (Article 57(3)). In this context, the EDPS shall provide guidance and supervision within the sandbox with respect to identifying risks, in particular to fundamental rights, among others, and to demonstrating mitigation measures

[137] Ibid art 66.

[138] Doubts as to this role have also been expressed by the EDPB-EDPS, 'Joint Opinion 5/2021 on the proposal for a Regulation of the European Parliament and of the Council laying down harmonised rules on artificial intelligence (Artificial Intelligence Act)' (Edpb.eu, 18 June 2021) <https://edpb.europa.eu/our-work-tools/our-documents/edpbedps-joint-opinion/edpb-edps-joint-opinion-52021-proposal_en>.

[139] AI Act art 66.

[140] Jon Truby and Others, 'A Sandbox Approach to Regulating High-Risk Artificial Intelligence Applications' (2022) 13 European Journal of Risk Regulation 270.

[141] Kristin Undheim, Truls Erikson, and Bram Timmermans, 'True Uncertainty and Ethical AI: Regulatory Sandboxes as a Policy Tool for Moral Imagination' (AI and Ethics, 24 November 2022) <https://doi.org/10.1007/s43681–022-00240-x>.

and their effectiveness to mitigate the identified risks. A relative novelty in EU law, regulatory sandboxes emerge as a form of 'experimental legal regime', which, according to Ranchordas, can 'waive [or] modify national regulatory requirements (or implementation)' as a way of offering 'safe testbeds for innovative products and services without putting the whole system at risk'.[142] As a relatively new legal phenomenon, there is a lack of empirical knowledge about their potential usefulness to improve fundamental rights protection.

In view of the many difficulties in lodging complaints in the digital context,[143] the fundamental rights–protecting role of the EDPS is much wider under the EU DPR rules.[144] Beyond ensuring the EU actors' compliance with the data subjects' rights, the EDPS' role entails promoting public awareness, conducting investigations, advising the EU institutions, adopting soft-law guidelines and clarifying the data protection requirements, authorising contractual clauses, and many others. In this respect, the supervisory role of the EDPS is likely to continue in its existing fashion with respect to the EU's uses of AI applications, making a direct reference to the new AI-specific requirements enumerated under the AI Act in tandem with the data protection requirements. Indeed, for instance, the current EDPS has taken a firm stance on the AI-driven data processing activities of the EU agencies, including Frontex and Europol.[145]

Navigating the landscape of exceptions and derogations with respect to data uses, especially in the law enforcement context, will, however, continue to undermine the EU's efforts to ensure a human-centred use and deployment of AI meant to ensure full respect for fundamental rights. In light of the ongoing technological empowerment of the EU agencies, as exemplified by the expanding role of Frontex,[146] more structural adjustments of the EDPS'

[142] Sofia Ranchordás, 'Experimental Lawmaking in the EU: Regulatory Sandboxes' (Social Science Research Network, 22 October 2021) SSRN Scholarly Paper ID 3963810 2 <https://papers.ssrn.com/abstract=3963810>.

[143] Fuster and Others (n 94).

[144] EU DPR, ch VI.

[145] European Data Protection Supervisor, 'EDPS Takes Legal Action as New Europol Regulation Puts Rule of Law and EDPS Independence under Threat' (Edps.eu, 22 September 2022) <https://edps.europa.eu/press-publications/press-news/press-releases/2022/edps-takes-legal-action-new-europol-regulation-puts-rule-law-and-edps-independence-under-threat>. See also the EDPS Supervisory Opinion on the Rules on Processing of Operational Personal Data by the European Border and Coast Guard Agency (Frontex), (Case 2022-0147) (Edps.eu, 7 June 2022) <https://edps.europa.eu/data-protection/our-work/publications/supervisory-opinions/edps-supervisory-opinion-rules_en>.

[146] Anneliese Baldaccini, 'Counter-Terrorism and the EU Strategy for Border Security: Framing Suspects with Biometric Documents and Databases' (2008) 10 European Journal of Migration and Law 31; Sergio Carrera and Valsamis Mitsilegas, 'Constitutionalising the Security Union' in Sergio Carrera and Valsamis Mitsilegas (eds), *Constitutionalising the Security Union: Effectiveness, rule of law and rights in countering terrorism and crime* (Centre for European Policy Studies 2017).

powers and tasks vis-a-vis AI-powered EU conduct might be necessary for the effective enforcement of rights under the fragmented legal frameworks, instead of merely introducing more rights and obligations.[147] For now, direct protection of fundamental rights against the uses of AI by EU actors will remain primarily within the power of the EDPS under the remedial avenues stemming from the EU DPR. Accordingly, the way the Supervisor will apply the new AI-specific rules in conjunction with the individuals' rights as data subjects will be crucial to furthering the protection of fundamental rights in the AI-driven conduct of the EU actors, such as Frontex.

15.5 CONCLUSION

Illustrated with the case of EU agencies like Frontex, which have spearheaded the development and deployment of AI for border surveillance purposes, the chapter assessed their risks to fundamental rights and the affected persons' possibilities to remedy the likely violations. By examining two examples of AI uses by Frontex – automated risk assessments under the new ETIAS system and AI-powered aerial surveillance for border response – the chapter demonstrates diverse risks to fundamental rights, including privacy, personal data protection, non-discrimination, and the right to asylum.

In light of these concerns, the chapter highlighted the challenges for access to remedies against AI uses by the EU actors, including to procedural rights to good administration and effective judicial remedy and in the current remedial set up under the emerging framework for regulating AI – the AI Act. Examining the limis of the AI Act in determining a concrete role of the European Data Protection Supervisor (EDPS) the chapter calls for further restructuring of the EDPS powers with respect to fundamental rights protection in view of its combined mandate under the EU's data protection and AI frameworks. With the identified gaps still in place, including the lack of a direct remedy against the EU actors' use of AI under the AI Act, the EDPS will play a central role in guaranteeing the legal protection of fundamental rights in the emerging AI-powered conduct. To undertake this role effectively, the gaps identified in this chapter will need to be carefully addressed.

[147] Herwig C H Hofmann, Gerard C Rowe, and Alexander H Türk (eds), *Specialized Administrative Law of the European Union: A Sectoral Review* (Oxford University Press 2018).

Conclusion

MELANIE FINK

This book critically examined the EU's remedies system from a fundamental rights perspective, focusing on the EU's activities outside the realm of law-making. How can private parties vindicate their fundamental rights against the EU? Is there untapped potential within the remedies system to accommodate fundamental rights complaints? Does the EU remedies system live up to the promises of effectiveness and completeness?

The chapters show a complex and nuanced picture. This conclusion draws together some of the recurring strands of argumentation presented in this book. In broad strokes, it discusses, first, the limits of the EU remedies system and, second, its potential, closing with an overall reflection.

C.1 THE LIMITS OF THE EU REMEDIES SYSTEM

C.1.1 *Judicial Remedies and the Outdated Vision of the EU as a Lawmaker*

In line with the traditional distribution of tasks between the Union and its Member States, challenging EU conduct often means challenging EU laws. The centrepiece of the remedies system, the action for annulment, allows individuals to challenge EU laws. But it is well known just how restrictive access to this procedure is (Chapter 1 – Gentile), which can be explained to some extent by a presumption of lawfulness – the EU legislator 'can do no wrong' (Chapter 3 – Grozdanovski). Even once that hurdle is cleared, fundamental rights challenges to EU laws predominantly concern procedure, with substantive contestation remaining the exception (Chapter 1 – Gentile).

The bigger challenge is conduct that does not neatly fall within the category of 'law', strictly speaking. As we learn from Chapter 14 (Chamon), judicial mechanisms in the EU Treaties are premised on the idea that government acts through binding measures. Even though this principle has been somewhat relaxed in the context of the preliminary reference procedure, ultimately there is no watertight system of remedies for harm done through soft law. Chapter 12 (Coman-Kund) comes to a similar conclusion, arguing that in relation to factual conduct, the judicial remedies available are neither complete nor effective. These conclusions are echoed in Chapters 11 (Bovend'Eerdt, Karagianni, Scholten) and 15 (Demková) regarding law enforcement and the use of artificial intelligence, respectively. In short, the EU's remedies system has not been designed with these types of conduct in mind and struggles to accommodate them.

Part IV of this volume (Bovend'Eerdt, Karagianni, Scholten; Coman-Kund; Eliantonio; Chamon; Demková) highlights two points. First, many of the EU's 'non-legal' activities have always been part of the EU's toolbox. However, as the scale on which the EU exercises these types of powers increases, so too does the gap in the remedies system. With this in mind, it is important that future conferrals of 'executive' powers go hand in hand with the setting up of remedial procedures, at least until broader reform can be achieved. Second, many of the activities the EU remedies system fails to capture are inherently fundamental rights sensitive. This is especially true of law enforcement (Chapter 11 – Bovend'Eerdt, Karagianni, Scholten), factual conduct (Chapter 12 – Coman-Kund), and the use of Artificial Intelligence (Chapter 15 – Demková). This makes the need for establishing remedies outside the possibilities of challenging 'legal acts' even greater.

C.1.2 *The Reluctance to Engage in Fundamental Rights Reasoning*

One of the 'great benefits' of the incorporation of the Charter of Fundamental Rights of the EU (CFR, 'the Charter') into EU primary law is that the EU's remedies system can be relied upon to vindicate Charter rights.[1] For the Working Group that advised the drafters of the (failed) Constitutional Treaty, this seems to have been one of the reasons why they did not find the inclusion of a fundamental rights complaints procedure into EU law necessary.[2] However, the chapters in this book found that the adoption of the Charter seems to have provided little momentum to the further development of the remedies system from a fundamental rights perspective.

[1] Charter of Fundamental Rights of the European Union [2016] OJ C202/389 (CFR); The European Convention, Final Report of Working Group II, 22 October 2002, CONV 354/02, 15.

[2] The European Convention, Final Report of Working Group II, 22 October 2002, CONV 354/02, 15.

First, while Article 47 CFR has been relied on to make some improvements to the remedies system, for instance, in relation to the Common Foreign and Security Policy, it has overall been of limited relevance in shaping the mechanisms available to individuals to enforce their rights against the EU. This is, according to the Court of Justice of the EU (CJEU, the Court), because 'Article 47 of the Charter … is not intended to change the system of judicial review laid down by the Treaties, and particularly the rules relating to the admissibility of direct actions brought before the Courts of the European Union'.[3] Chapters 1 (Gentile) and 3 (Grozdanovski) illustrate how this line of reasoning seems to apply not only to the restrictions set out in the Treaties but also to the interpretation of its components, especially the notions of 'direct and individual concern' and 'legal act', in the Court's own case law. Also, in relation to the action for damages, Article 47 CFR has not been significantly relied upon by the Court to shape the strict conditions under which liability arises (Chapter 2 – Fink, Rauchegger, De Coninck). Given the flexibility the Treaties provide (see Section C.2), this restrictive stance seems unnecessary. It also stands in stark contrast to the impact Article 47 CFR has had on the Member States' remedies systems, creating – as Chapter 3 (Grozdanovski) points out – a 'two-speed effective judicial protection'.

Second, the Court does not engage in any fundamental rights reasoning to justify its restrictive stance on the need and possibilities for modifying the remedies system. Specifically, the argument that the remedies system is 'complete' is never substantiated by reference to Article 47 CFR. There is no in-depth discussion of what Article 47 CFR requires from the EU and how the remedies system complies with that. Rather than a persuasive argument, the 'completeness' of the remedies system is a claim or – more generously – a promise. Ultimately, this approach by the Court is facilitated by the lack of any external control of the CJEU itself and once more underlines the need for accession of the EU to the European Convention on Human Rights (ECHR) (Chapter 7 – Krommendijk).

C.1.3 *The Over-reliance on National Courts*

The argument surrounding the 'completeness' of the EU's remedies system builds on the idea that the CJEU and national courts share the responsibility

3 Case C-583/11 P *Inuit Tapiriit Kanatami and Others v Parliament and Council* [2013] ECLI: EU:C:2013:625, para 97.

to provide remedies (Chapter 3 – Grozdanovski; Chapter 4 – López Zurita). The CJEU has repeatedly held that the restrictions for private parties to bring actions for annulment do not create a lacuna in judicial protection because private parties are still able to file actions before national courts, which in turn refer questions regarding the validity of EU acts to the CJEU under the preliminary reference procedure.[4] This possibility, the Court has stressed, 'constitutes the very essence of the Community system of judicial protection'.[5] If a gap does arise, 'it is for the Member States to establish a system of legal remedies and procedures which ensure respect for the right to effective judicial protection'.[6]

Where national implementation measures have been taken, individuals can indeed use the preliminary reference procedure to challenge the validity of EU acts and – as Chapter 4 (López Zurita) argues – fundamental rights have for a long time been 'a favourite ground' to do so. Chapter 6 (Hofmann) shows that national courts may also play a role outside the narrow context of the preliminary reference procedure, even though their function in this respect is understudied and needs more empirical attention as well as a more nuanced normative debate.

One of the limits of this approach is the dependency it creates on national law. Chapters 4 (López Zurita), 6 (Hofmann), 8 (van der Pas), 11 (Bovend'Eerdt, Karagianni, Scholten), and 14 (Chamon) illustrate that relying on national courts carries the risk that the effectiveness and fairness of the EU's remedies system is dependent on national rules of procedure and national (litigation) culture. In addition, national courts are not suitable to resolve the challenges that the EU's shared administration poses. Chapter 13 (Eliantonio) shows how the strict division of responsibilities between the EU and Member State courts cannot do justice to the administrative reality in the EU, in which the activities of the EU and its Member States are closely intertwined. The nature of fundamental rights commitments often requires a joint effort. Yet joint fundamental rights responsibility is difficult to implement under the current judicial framework (Chapter 13 – Eliantonio; Chapter 2 – Fink, Rauchegger, De Coninck). An additionally complicating factor is that in its cooperation with the Member States, the EU often takes on a preparatory, supportive, or assisting function. Leaving ultimate responsibility

4 Ibid para 92; very clearly also Opinion of AG Bobek in Case C-911/19 *FBF* [2021] ECLI:EU:C:2021:294, para 138.

5 Case C-300/99 P *Area Cova and Others v Council* [2001] ECLI:EU:C:2001:71, para 54.

6 Case C-50/00 P *Unión de Pequeños Agricultores v Council* [2002] ECLI:EU:C:2002:462, para 41.

for wrongdoing in this context with the Member States might be pragmatic, but it also reduces the EU's own responsibility to a minimum that is not reconcilable with the rule of law (Chapter 2 – Fink, Rauchegger, De Coninck). These challenges cannot be resolved by national courts, not only for lack of competence but also due to the need for uniformity. They require a stronger role by the CJEU.

C.2 THE POTENTIAL OF THE EU REMEDIES SYSTEM

C.2.1 *Looking beyond the Action for Annulment*

One of the most significant strengths of the remedies system is that many of the limitations exposed in this book are only sketched out in very general terms in the Treaties and ultimately stem from the strict interpretation thereof by the CJEU. This opens up space to better accommodate fundamental rights complaints without a risk that this would require changes in the system of judicial review laid down by the Treaties.

While the Charter cannot displace the Treaties, it can guide their interpretation. As Chapters 1 (Gentile), 3 (Grozdanovski), and 12 (Coman-Kund) show, the admissibility of actions for annulment could very well be interpreted less restrictively, possibly using Article 47 CFR. But other actions might harbour even greater untapped potential. As Chapters 2 (Fink, Rauchegger, De Coninck) and 12 (Coman-Kund) concluded, the action for damages is flexible enough to allow the Court to rely on Article 47 CFR for a less restrictive stance on the conditions under which compensation is awarded in the fundamental rights context.

C.2.2 *Looking beyond the CJEU*

Staying within the framework provided for by the Treaties also means there is an outer limit to reforming judicial remedies. But there is plenty of room to develop mechanisms outside the court system. This volume shows just how varied the non-judicial mechanisms are that have been set up under the Treaties or EU secondary law to provide ex ante control or deal with complaints against EU bodies by private parties. Beyond the well-known European Ombudsman, there are review bodies that deal with specific rights (such as the European Data Protection Supervisor) or specific EU bodies (Boards of Appeal, Fundamental Rights Officers). These lack the type of authority we usually associate with the effective vindication of rights and the guarantees of independence we know from courts. But Chapters 5 (Schramm), 11

(Bovend'Eerdt, Karagianni, Scholten), 12 (Coman-Kund), 14 (Chamon), and 15 (Demková) all show how these mechanisms have considerable potential to improve access to justice in the EU, especially due to their expertise and capacity to address structural root causes of fundamental rights violations.

Chapter 5 (Schramm) presents a compelling argument that review bodies should 'team up' with courts so that their respective strengths can be combined. With the judicial authority of the courts and the capacity of review bodies to address structural root causes of fundamental rights violations, they could together deliver more comprehensive protection than each of them alone. Chapters 11 (Bovend'Eerdt, Karagianni, Scholten), 12 (Coman-Kund), 14 (Chamon), and 15 (Demková) echo the argument that such review mechanisms are a way forward, especially when the EU does not act through traditional 'legal acts'. This requires reform. But as Chapter 5 (Schramm) argues, the burden to place themselves more firmly on the 'remedies map' is also on the review bodies themselves, who may want to increase their impact through more direct and powerful public messaging.

What seems important is a thorough discussion on how best to integrate review bodies into the remedies system in practice. Establishing review bodies without fully equipping them with the necessary powers and funds might do more harm than good because they may then, as Chapter 5 (Schramm) argues, risk becoming 'ceremonial legitimation of otherwise structurally flawed practices'. Especially the early versions of the Fundamental Rights Complaints Procedure established for the EU agency Frontex is a cautionary tale in that respect.

C.2.3 *Looking beyond EU Law*

While the EU may be unique, this is not necessarily the case for all the questions concerning the design of its remedies system. Part of the problem lies in the fact that the EU has developed a range of 'state-like' functions and powers that were not foreseen when it was set up. The necessary 'updates' to the remedies system can be inspired by national regimes, which have to provide for remedies against similar types of powers.

However, the EU is not a state. Crucially, its legal system consists of multiple levels that complement and depend on each other but also retain their independent functions. The EU fulfils its tasks within a shared administration where EU bodies and Member State authorities cooperate and interact. As Chapter 13 (Eliantonio) shows, this legal reality forms a particular challenge to the creation of an effective remedies system. Since no state has to deal with a multi-level system of this nature, it might be worth looking at international law, especially the law of international responsibility, for inspiration on how to address some of these challenges.

As noted above, the Court has not yet developed a clear line of fundamental rights reasoning either to remove or to justify the limits in the remedies system. In this respect, the Court might draw on the case law of the European Court of Human Rights (ECtHR). As Chapter 7 (Krommendijk) argues, it is hard to anticipate whether, in the event of accession, the ECtHR would consider the remedies system, especially the standing requirements under the action for annulment, compliant with the ECHR, but greater coherence between the ECHR and the CFR is in any case beneficial for legal certainty.

Less obvious possibilities for inspiration lie in international arbitration. As Chapter 9 (Yefremova) argues, arbitration as a fundamental rights enforcement mechanism might be incorporated at EU level to a greater degree, at least as a 'gap-filler' where no other remedies exist. While this would require caution, so as not to undermine the uniform interpretation of EU law, it is worth exploring where this could be useful, especially in light of the expertise, flexibility, and authority arbitration could bring to the table.

C.2.4 *Technology as Opportunity*

New technologies pose significant risks to fundamental rights. Chapter 15 (Demková) shows how diverse these risks are, both substantively but also procedurally. The challenges to the requirements of transparency and good administration posed by decision-making informed by artificial intelligence have direct implications for individuals' access to effective remedies.

At the same time, Chapter 10 (Schmidt-Kessen) illustrates the potential new technologies hold to strengthen access to remedial mechanisms. Online Dispute Resolution is increasingly used in the context of fundamental rights disputes by private actors, such as online platforms, and has spread into the public realm in a number of national jurisdictions. While we lack a clear legal basis to incorporate a fundamental rights–specific Online Dispute Resolution mechanism in the context of which individuals could hold EU bodies to account, it might be implemented under the umbrella of existing administrative mechanisms, such as the EU Ombudsman's office.

C.2.5 *Applicants with Agency*

Many suggestions advanced in this book require some form of intervention by the EU legislator or courts. At the same time, the book carries a more empowering message. The empirical study in Chapter 4 (López Zurita) found some indications that framing a complaint more clearly in fundamental rights terms might increase its chances of success. While not systematically studied, Chapter 2 (Fink, Rauchegger, De Coninck) found that of all the successful damages cases since 2015, 80% included references to the Charter in the grounds of judgment. Similarly striking, Chapter 1 (Gentile) found that at first instance 64% of successful actions for annulment involved fundamental rights. These findings suggest that the applicants themselves might have more power than it may seem at first sight to push the boundaries of the remedies system, simply by relying more strongly on their Charter rights.

Chapter 8 (van der Pas) provides a look at how that could be done. Access to 'Euro-expertise', that is, a high level of EU legal expertise, is crucial and can be provided by specialised NGOs, coalitions, networks, and also individual experts. While the formal judicial proceedings route may not always be feasible, petitions and complaints to other (administrative) bodies or even informal involvement may equally allow litigants to open up avenues to be heard and shape EU law in an otherwise rather closed system of remedies.

C.3 FINAL REMARKS

Clearly, and understandably, the drafters of the EU's remedies system could not anticipate how EU power would evolve and what this would require in terms of remedies. As a consequence, today, more than six decades later, the remedies system is simply outdated.

What this means for the protection of fundamental rights and the possibilities for victims of violations thereof to seek justice came to the fore in *WS and Others v Frontex*, decided by the General Court in September 2023.[7] The applicants in the case were a Syrian family escaping Aleppo at the height of the war in 2016 to seek international protection in the EU, in the course of which they suffered what they argued were gross violations of their fundamental rights. They turned to the EU courts to hold the EU agency Frontex accountable for its role therein. The action was unsuccessful. More worrying than the outcome as such is the lack of any engagement whatsoever by the General Court with the fundamental rights dimension of the case. The Court not only failed to provide effective judicial protection to the applicants but also ignored the broader rule of law implications of allowing EU public power to escape accountability.

[7] Case T-600/21 *WS and Others v Frontex* [2023] ECLI:EU:T:2023:492.

The 'complete system of remedies' is not a claim, it is a promise. But it is not a promise that the EU currently lives up to. Without any external source of authority that could sound the alarm, it falls on the CJEU to take a stronger role as a fundamental rights court and on the EU legislator to develop additional judicial and non-judicial mechanisms that can fill the gaps. For 'without mechanisms for their effective vindication', 'the possession of rights is meaningless'.[8]

[8] Mauro Cappelletti and Bryant Garth, *Access to Justice: Vol. I A World Survey* (Book I, Sijthoff; Giuffrè 1978) 8.

Bibliography

Aalto P, *Public Liability in EU Law: Brasserie, Bergaderm and Beyond* (Hart 2011).

Abbasy M, 'The Online Civil Money Claim: Litigation, ADR and ODR in One Single Dispute Resolution Process' (2020) 7 International Journal of Online Dispute Resolution 4.

Ackermann B, 'Good-Bye, Montesquieu' in Susan Rose-Ackerman, Blake Emerson, and Peter Lindseth (eds), *Comparative Administrative Law* (2nd edn, Edward Elgar 2017).

Adam C and Others, *Taking the EU to Court. Annulment Proceedings and Multilevel Judicial Conflict* (Palgrave 2020).

Alberti J, 'The Position of Boards of Appeal: Between Functional Continuity and Independence' in Merijn Chamon and Mariolina Eliantonio (eds), *Boards of Appeal of EU Agencies* (Oxford University Press 2022).

Alonso de León S, 'Composite Administrative Procedures in the European Union' (PhD thesis, Universidad Carlos III de Madrid 2016).

Alter K, *Establishing the Supremacy of European Law: The Making of an International Rule of Law in Europe* (Oxford University Press 2001).

Ambrose C, 'Arbitration and the Free Movement of Judgments' (2003) 19(1) Arbitration International Law 3.

Anderson D and Demetriou M, *References to the European Court* (2nd edn, Sweet & Maxwell 2002).

Andersen E, *Out of the Closets and into the Courts: Legal Opportunity Structure and Gay Rights Litigation* (University of Michigan Press 2006).

Anderson T, Schum D, and Twining W, *Analysis of Evidence* (Cambridge University Press 2005).

Andone C and Coman-Kund F, 'A Legal-Argumentative Framework for Persuasive EU Soft Law: The Case of the European Commission's Recommendations', in Petra Láncos, Napoleon Xanthoulis, and Luis Arroyo Jiménez (eds), *The Legal Effects of EU Soft Law: Theory, Language and Sectoral Insights into EU Multi-level Governance* (Edward Elgar 2023).

Arestis G, 'Fundamental rights in the EU: three years after Lisbon, the Luxembourg perspective' (Cooperative Research Paper 02/2013, College of Europe).

Aristova E and Grusic U, 'Introduction: Civil Remedies and Human Rights in Flux' in Ekaterina Aristova and Ugljesa Grusic (eds), *Civil Remedies and Human Rights in Flux: Key Legal Developments in Selected Jurisdictions* (1st edn, Hart 2022).

Arnull A, 'EU Recommendations and Judicial Review' (2018) 14 European Constitutional Law Review 609.

'Article 47 CFR and national procedural autonomy' (2020) 45 European Law Review 681.

Arrigioni M, 'The Administrative Board of Review of the European Central Bank: A Critical Analysis' [2020] Rivista Orizzonti del Diritto Commerciale 519.

Arroyo Jiménez L, 'Effective Judicial Protection and Mutual Recognition in the European Administrative Space' (2021) 22 German Law Journal 344.

Asimov M, 'Five Models of Administrative Adjudication' (2015) 63 The American Journal of Comparative Law 3.

Ayres I and Braithwaite J, *Responsive Regulation: Transcending the Deregulation Debate* (Oxford University Press 1992).

Azimi A and Others, 'The Crotone Cover Up' (*Lighthouse Reports*, 2 June 2023) <www.lighthousereports.com/investigation/the-crotone-cover-up/>.

Azoulai L and Vries K M de (eds), *EU Migration Law: Legal Complexities and Political Rationales* (Oxford University Press 2014).

Backes C and Eliantonio M (eds), *Cases, Materials and Text on Judicial Review of Administrative Action* (Hart 2019).

Baldaccini A, 'Counter-Terrorism and the EU Strategy for Border Security: Framing Suspects with Biometric Documents and Databases' (2008) 10 European Journal of Migration and Law 31.

Baldwin R, Cave M, and Lodge M, 'Responsive Regulation' in Robert Baldwin and Others (eds), *Understanding Regulation: Theory, Strategy, and Practice* (2nd edn, Oxford University Press 2011).

Bardutzky S, 'Constitutional Courts, Preliminary Rulings and the "New Form of Law": The Adjudication of the European Stability Mechanism' (2016) 16 German Law Journal 1771.

Barents R, 'EU Procedural Law and Effective Legal Protection' (2014) 51 Common Market Law Review 1437.

Bagińska E (ed), *Damages for Violations of Human Rights: A Comparative Study of Domestic Legal Systems* (Springer 2016).

Barnard C and Peers S, *European Law* (Oxford University Press 2014).

Basedow J, 'EU Law in International Arbitration: Referrals to the European Court of Justice' (2015) 32(4) Journal of International Arbitration 367.

Baude W, 'Adjudication Outside Article III' (2020) 133 Harvard Law Review 1511.

Beijer M, *The Limits of Fundamental Rights Protection by the EU. The Scope for the Development of Positive Obligations* (Intersentia 2017).

'Procedural Fundamental Rights Review by the Court of Justice of the European Union' in Janneke Gerards and Eva Brems (eds), *Procedural Review in European Fundamental Rights Cases* (Cambridge University Press 2017).

Bell E, 'An Introduction to Judicial Fact-Finding' (2013) 39 Commonwealth Law Bulletin 519.

Bell J and Lichère F, *Contemporary French Administrative Law* (Cambridge University Press 2022).

Bentham J, A *Treatise on Judicial Evidence* (Baldwin 1825).

Bermann G, 'Reconciling European Union law demands with the demands of International Arbitration' (2011) 34(1) Fordham International Law Journal 1193.

Bernard E, *La spécificité du standard juridique en droit communautaire* (Bruylant 2010).

Bertea S, 'Looking for Coherence within the European Community' (2005) 11 European Law Journal 154.

Bertuzzi L, 'AI Act: EU Parliament's Crunch Time on High-Risk Categorisation, Prohibited Practices' (www.euractiv.com, 7 February 2023) <www.euractiv.com/section/artificial-intelligence/news/ai-act-eu-parliaments-crunch-time-on-high-risk-categorisation-prohibited-practices/>.

Beslay L and Galbally J, 'Fingerprint Identification Technology for Its Implementation in the Schengen Information System II (SIS-II)' [2015] JRC Science for Policy Report EUR 27473, <https://publications.jrc.ec.europa.eu/repository/handle/JRC97779> 100.

Besselink L, 'The Protection of Fundamental Rights Post-Lisbon. The Interaction between the EU Charter of Fundamental Rights, the European Convention on Human Rights (ECHR) and National Constitutions' (FIDE General Report 2013).

Beukers T, de Witte B, and Kilpatrick C (eds), *Constitutional Change through Euro-Crisis Law* (Cambridge University Press 2017).

Bilchitz D, *Poverty and Fundamental Rights: The Justification and Enforcement of Socio-economic Rights* (Oxford University Press 2007).

Black J, 'Constitutionalising Self-Regulation' (1996) 59(1) Modern Law Review 1468.

Blake H J and Mangiameli S, *Treaty on the Functioning of the European Union – A Commentary* (Springer Commentaries on International and European Law 2021).

Blomgren Amsler L, Martinez J, and Smith S E, *Dispute System Design* (Stanford University Press 2020).

Bobek M, 'What Are Grand Chambers For?' (2021) 23 Cambridge Yearbook of European Legal Studies 1.

Bogucki A and Others, 'The AI Act and Emerging EU Digital Acquis: Overlaps, Gaps and Inconsistencies', CEPS In-Depth Analysis, 2022 <www.ceps.eu/ceps-publications/the-ai-act-and-emerging-eu-digital-acquis/>.

Bos K van den, Wilke H A M, and Lind E A, 'When Do We Need Procedural Fairness? The Role of Trust in Authority' (1998) 75(6) Journal of Personality and Social Psychology 1449.

Bourdieu P, *Outline of a Theory of Practice* (Cambridge University Press 1977).

Bovend'Eerdt K, 'The Protection of Fundamental Rights in OLAF Composite Enforcement Procedures (and the EPPO's Ship Smoke on the Horizon)' (PhD thesis, Utrecht University 2023).

Bradley K, 'Activities of the European Community in the Field of Private International Law in 2007' (2007) Yearbook of Private International Law 399.

Breitler C, 'Jurisdiction in CFSP Matters – Conquering the Gallic Village One Case at a Time?' (European Law Blog, 13 October 2022) <ELB-Blogpost-Christian-Breitler-October-202239-final.pdf (europeanlawblog.eu)>.

Brekke SA and Others, 'The CJEU Database Platform: Decisions and Decisions-Makers' (2023) *Journal of Law and Courts* 1.

Brekoulakis S and Dimitropoulos G, *International Commercial Courts: The Future of Transnational Adjudication* (Cambridge University Press 2022).

Brescia Morra C, Smits R, and Magliari A, 'The Administrative Board of Review of the European Central Bank: Experience after 2 Years' (2017) 18 European Business Organization Law Review 567.

Briggs M, 'Civil Courts Structure Review' (Judiciary of England and Wales, July 2016) <www.judiciary.uk/wp-content/uploads/2016/07/civil-courts-structure-review-final-report-jul-16-final-1.pdf>.

'The Civil Online Court in England' in Rabeea Assy and Andrew Higgins (eds), *Principles, Procedure, and Justice: Essays in honour of Adrian Zuckerman* (Oxford University Press 2020).

Brito Bastos F, 'The *Borelli* Doctrine revisited: three issues of coherence in a landmark ruling for EU administrative justice' (2015) 8 Review of European Administrative Law 269.

'Beyond executive federalism: the judicial crafting of the law of composite administrative decision-making' (PhD thesis, European University Institute 2018).

'Derivative Illegality in the European Composite Administrative Procedures' (2018) 55 Common Market Law Review 101.

'An Administrative Crack in the EU's Rule of Law: Composite Decision-making and Nonjusticiable National Law' (2020) 16 European Constitutional Law Review 63.

'Judicial Annulment of National Preparatory Acts and the Effects on Final Union Administrative Decisions: Comments on the Judgment of 29 January 2020, Case C-785/18 Jeanningros, EU:C:2020:46' (2021) 14(2) Review of European Administrative Law 109.

Broberg M, 'Preliminary References as a Means for Enforcing EU Law' in Andras Jakab and Dimitry Kochenov (eds), *The Enforcement of EU Law and Values: Ensuring Member States' Compliance* (Oxford University Press 2017).

Broberg M and Fenger N, *Preliminary References to the European Court of Justice* (2nd edn, Oxford University Press 2014).

The Procedure before the Court of Justice (Oxford University Press 2021).

Brockner J and Others, 'Culture and Procedural Fairness: When the Effects of What You Do Depend on How You Do It' (2000) 45(1) Administrative Science Quarterly 138.

Brouwer E, 'Legality and Data Protection Law: The Forgotten Purpose of Purpose Limitation' in Leonard F M Besselink, F Pennings, and Sacha Prechal (eds), *The eclipse of the legality principle in the European Union* (Kluwer Law International 2011).

Burson B, 'Refugee Status Determination' in Cathryn Costello, Michelle Foster, and Jane McAdam (eds), *The Oxford Handbook of International Refugee Law* (Oxford University Press 2021).

Bussani M and Infantino M, 'The Many Cultures of Tort Liability' in Mauro Bussani and Anthony J Sebok (eds), *Comparative Tort Law: Global Perspectives* (Edward Elgar 2015).

Butler G, 'A question of jurisdiction: Art. 267 TFEU preliminary references of a CFSP nature' (2017) 2 European Papers 201.

Cafaggi F, 'Private Regulation in European Private Law' EUI RSCAS Working Paper 2009/31.

Callewaert J, *The accession of the European Union to the European Convention on Human Rights* (Council of Europe 2014).

'Do we still need Article 6(2) TEU? Considerations on the absence of EU accession to the ECHR and its consequences' (2018) 55 Common Market Law Review 1685.

'No more common understanding of fundamental rights' (2022) 22 La revue des jurists de Sciences Po 25.

Cane P, *Administrative Tribunals and Adjudication* (Hart 2010).

Controlling Administrative Power: An Historical Comparison (Cambridge University Press 2016).

Canor I, 'Primus inter pares. Who is the ultimate guardian of fundamental rights in Europe?' (2000) 25 European Law Review 3.

Cappelletti M, *The Judicial Process in Comparative Perspective* (Clarendon Press 1989).

Cappelletti M and Garth B, *Access to Justice: Vol. I A World Survey* (Book I, Sijthoff; Giuffrè 1978).

'Access to Justice: The Newest Wave in the Worldwide Movement to Make Rights Effective' (1978) 27 Buffalo Law Review 181.

Carrera S and Mitsilegas V, 'Constitutionalising the Security Union' in Sergio Carrera and Valsamis Mitsilegas (eds), *Constitutionalising the Security Union: Effectiveness, rule of law and rights in countering terrorism and crime* (Centre for European Policy Studies 2017).

Carrera S, Somer M de and Petkova B, 'The Court of Justice of the European Union as a Fundamental Rights Tribunal: Challenges for the effective Delivery of Fundamental Rights in the Area of Freedom, Security and Justice' (2012) Centre for European Policy Studies paper 49.

Carrera S and Stefan M, 'Complaint Mechanisms in Border Management and Expulsion Operations in Europe: Effective Remedies For Victims of Human Rights Violations?' (Centre for European Policy Studies, 26 March 2018) <www.ceps.eu/ceps-publications/complaint-mechanisms-border-management-and-expulsion-operations-europe-effective/>.

Catanzariti M and Türk A, 'EU agencies and the rise of a mixed administration in the EU multi-jurisdictional setting: facing the challenges of the rule of law' in Miroslava Scholten and Alex Brenninkmeijer (eds), *Controlling EU Agencies. The Rule of Law in a Multi-Jurisdictional Legal Order* (Edward Elgar 2020).

Chalmers D and Chaves M, 'The Reference Points of EU Judicial Politics' (2012) 19 Journal of European Public Policy 25.

Chamon M, *EU Agencies – Legal and Political Limits to the Transformation of the EU Administration* (Oxford University Press 2016).

'The joint board of appeal as an accountability mechanism for the ESAs' in Carl Fredrik Bergström and Magnus Strand (eds), *Legal Accountability in EU Markets for Financial Instruments: The Dual Role of Investment Firms* (Edward Elgar 2021).

Chamon M, Volpato A, and Eliantonio M (eds), *Boards of Appeal of EU Agencies: Towards Judicialization of Administrative Review?* (Oxford University Press 2022).

Chayes A, 'The Role of the Judge in Public Law Litigation' (1976) 89 Harvard Law Review 1281.

Chevalier E, 'Administrative Cooperation in the field of Risk Regulation', in Chevalier E, Eliantonio M, and Lanceiro R (eds), *Administrative Cooperation in the European Union* (Bruylant, forthcoming 2024).

Chevalier E, Eliantonio M, and Lanceiro R, *Administrative Cooperation in the European Space* (Bruylant, forthcoming 2024).

Chirulli P and De Lucia L, 'Specialised adjudication in EU administrative law: the Boards of Appeal of EU agencies 39' (2015) 40 European Law Review 832.

Non-Judicial Remedies and EU Administration: Protection of Rights versus Preservation of Autonomy (Routledge 2021).

Chiti M, 'Forms of European administrative action' (2004) 68 Law & Contemporary Problems 37.

Chiti E, 'The Agencification Process and the Evolution of the EU Administrative System' in Paul Craig and Gràinne de Búrca (eds), *The Evolution of EU Law* (Oxford University Press 2021).

Cisotta R and Gallo D, 'The Portuguese Constitutional Court Case Law on Austerity Measures: A Reappraisal' in Claire Kilpatrick and Bruno de Witte (eds), *Social Rights in Times of Crisis in the Eurozone: The Role of Fundamental Rights' Challenges* (EUI Working papers LAW 05/2014)

Coglianese C, 'Litigating within Relationships: Disputes and Disturbance in the Regulatory Process' (1996) 30 Law & Society Review 738.

Cohen A and Vauchez A, 'The Social Construction of Law: The European Court of Justice and Its Legal Revolution Revisited' (2011) 7 Annual Review of Law and Social Science 417.

Conant L and Others, 'Mobilizing European Law' (2018) 25 Journal of European Public Policy 1376.

Constantinesco L J, *L'applicabilité directe dans le droit de la CEE* (Bruylant 2006).

Craig P, 'EU accession to the ECHR: Competence, procedure and substance' (2013) 36 Fordham International Law Journal 1114.

Craig P and Búrca G de, *EU Law: Text, Cases, and Materials* (7th edn, Oxford University Press 2020).

'Article 41: The Right to Good Administration' in Steve Peers and Others (eds), *The EU Charter of Fundamental Rights: A Commentary* (2nd edn, Hart 2021).

Cruz Villalón P, 'Rights in Europe: The crowded house' (2012) King's College London Working Paper 01/2012.

Cseres K and Outhuijse A, 'Parallel enforcement and accountability: EU competition law' in Miroslava Scholten and Michiel Luchtman (eds), *Law Enforcement by EU Authorities* (Edward Elgar 2017).

Csernatoni R, 'Constructing the EU's High-Tech Borders: FRONTEX and Dual-Use Drones for Border Management' (2018) 27 European Security 175.

Curtin D, *Executive Power of the European Union: Law, Practices, and the Living Constitution* (Oxford University Press 2009).

'From a Europe of Bits and Pieces to a Union of Variegated Differentiation' in P P Craig and G De Búrca (eds), *The Evolution of EU Law* (Oxford University Press 2021).

Curtin DM and Brito Bastos F, 'Interoperable Information Sharing and the Five Novel Frontiers of EU Governance: A Special Issue' (2020) 26 European Public Law 59.

Curtin D and Senden L, 'Public Accountability of Transnational Private Regulation: Chimera or Reality?' (2011) 38 Journal of Law and Society 163.

Dahlan M, Lastra R, and Rochette G, *Research Handbook on EU Energy Law and Policy* (1st edn, Edward Elgar 2022).

Dam C van, *European Tort Law* (Oxford University Press 2013).

Dannemann G, 'Constitutional Complaints: The European Perspective' (1994) 43 The International and Comparative Law Quarterly 142.

Davies B, *Resisting the European Court of Justice: West Germany's Confrontation with European Law, 1949–1979* (Cambridge University Press 2012).

'Internationale Handelsgesellschaft and the Miscalculation at the Inception of the ECJ's Human Rights Jurisprudence' in Bill Davies and Fernanda Nicola (eds), *EU Law Stories: Contextual and Critical Histories of European Jurisprudence* (Cambridge University Press 2017).

Davis D M, 'Socio-Economic Rights' in Michel Rosenfeld and András Sajó (eds), *The Oxford Handbook of Comparative Constitutional Law* (Oxford University Press 2012).

Davies G, 'Legislative Control of the European Court of Justice' (2014) 51 Common Market Law Review 1579.

Dawson M, Enderlein H, and Joerges C (eds), *Beyond the Crisis: The Governance of Europe's Economic, Political and Legal Transformation* (Oxford University Press 2015).

Dawson M, Witte B de, and Muir E, *Judicial activism at the European Court of Justice: causes, responses and solutions* (Edward Elgar 2013).

De Bellis M, 'Multi-level Administration, Inspections and Fundamental Rights: Is Judicial Protection Full and Effective?' (2021) 22 German Law Journal 416.

I poteri ispettivi dell'amministrazione europea (Giappichelli 2021).

De Coninck J, 'Catch-22 in the Law of Responsibility of International Organizations: Systemic Deficiencies in the EU Responsibility Paradigm for Unlawful Human Rights Conduct in Integrated Border Management' (PhD thesis, Ghent University 2020).

'Effective Remedies for Human Rights Violations in EU CSDP Military Missions: Smoke and Mirrors in Human Rights Adjudication?' (2023) 24 German Law Journal 342.

De Gregorio G, 'Democratising online content moderation: A constitutional framework' (2020) 36 Computer Law & Security Review 1.

De Gregorio G and Ranchordás S, 'Breaking down Information Silos with Big Data: A Legal Analysis of Data Sharing' in Joe Cannataci, Valeria Falce, and Oresto Pollicino (eds), *Legal Challenges of Big Data* (Edward Elgar 2020).

De Lucia L, 'Autorizzazioni transnazionali e cooperazione amministrativa nell'ordinamento europeo' (2010) 3 Rivista Italiana di Diritto Pubblico Comunitario 759.

Della Cananea G, 'The European Union's Mixed Administrative Proceedings' (2005) 68 Law and Contemporary Problems 197.

Demková S, 'The Decisional Value of Information in European Semi-Automated Decision-Making' (2021) 14 Review of European Administrative Law 29.

'Enforcing Remedies: The Challenges of Automatisation for Effective Oversight' in Katalin Ligeti and Kei Hannah Brodersen (eds), *Studies on enforcement in multi-regulatory systems* (Nomos 2022).

Automated Decision-Making and Effective Remedies: The New Dynamics in the Protection of EU Fundamental Rights in the Area of Freedom, Security and Justice (Edward Elgar 2023).

Demková S and Hofmann H C H, 'General Principles of Procedural Justice' in Katja Ziegler, Päivi Neuvonen, and Violeta Moreno-Lax (eds), *Research Handbook on General Principles of EU Law: Constructing Legal Orders in Europe* (Edward Elgar 2022).

Dermine P and Eliantonio M, 'Case Note: CJEU (Grand Chamber), Judgment of 19 December 2018, C-219/17, Silvio Berlusconi and Finanziaria d'investimento Fininvest SpA (Fininvest) v Banca d'Italia and Istituto per la Vigilanza Sulle Assicurazioni (IVASS)' (2019) 12 Review of European Administrative Law 237.

Dimitrova D, 'Data Protection within Police and Judicial Cooperation' in Herwig C H Hofmann, Gerard C Rowe and Alexander H Türk (eds), *Specialized Administrative Law of the European Union: A Sectoral Review* (Oxford University Press 2018).

Douglas-Scott S, 'The European Union and human rights after the Treaty of Lisbon' (2011) 11 Human Rights Law Review 645.

'The European Union and Fundamental Rights' in Robert Schütze and Takis Tridimas (eds), *Oxford Principles Of European Union Law: The European Union Legal Order: Volume I* (Oxford University Press 2018).

Duffy H, *Strategic Human Rights Litigation* (Hart 2018).

Duin A van, *Effective Judicial Protection in Consumer Litigation* (Intersentia 2022).

Eckes C, 'EU Accession to the ECHR: Between Autonomy and Adaptation' (2013) 76 The Modern Law Review 254.

Edwards L, 'Expert Opinion: Regulating AI in Europe: Four Problems and Four Solutions' (Ada Lovelace Institute, 31 March 2022) <www.adalovelaceinstitute.org/report/regulating-ai-in-europe/>.

Eliantonio M, 'Judicial Review in an Integrated Administration: The Case of "Composite Procedures"' (2014) 7 Review of European Administrative Law 65.

'Information Exchange in European Administrative Law: A Threat to Effective Judicial Protection?' (2016) 23 Maastricht Journal of European and Comparative Law 531.

'Judicial Review of Soft Law before the European and the National Courts a Wind of Change Blowing from the Member States?' in Mariolina Eliantonio, Emilia Korkea-aho, and Oana Ştefan (eds), *EU Soft Law in the Member States Theoretical Findings and Empirical Evidence* (Hart 2021).

'Access to Justice in Composite Procedures for the Implementation of EU Law: The Story so Far' (2023) <https://papers.ssrn.com/sol3/papers.cfm?abstract_id=4373333>.

Eliantonio M and Röttger-Wirtz S, 'From Integration to Exclusion: EU Composite Administration and Gaps in Judicial Accountability in the Authorisation of Pharmaceuticals' (2019) 10 European Journal of Risk Regulation 393.

Ellerbrok T, 'Das umgekehrte Vorabentscheidungsverfahren als Schlussstein im europäischen Rechtsschutzverbund' (2022) 113 Verwaltungsarchiv 202.

Epp C R, *The Rights Revolution: Lawyers, Activists, and Supreme Courts in Comparative Perspective* (University of Chicago Press 1998).

Fabbrini F and Sajó A, 'The dangers of constitutional identity' (2019) 25 European Law Journal 457.
Fallon R H, 'Of Legislative Courts, Administrative Agencies, and Article III' (1988) 101 Harvard Law Review 915.
Fartunova M, *La preuve dans le droit de l'Union européenne* (Bruylant 2013).
Fasone C, 'Constitutional Courts Facing the Euro Crisis. Italy, Portugal and Spain in a Comparative Perspective' (EUI Working Papers MWP 25/2014).
Fazio G de, 'Legal opportunity structure and social movement strategy in Northern Ireland and southern United States' (2012) 53 International Journal of Comparative Sociology 3.
Feichtner I, 'The German Constitutional Court's PSPP Judgment: Impediment and Impetus for the Democratization of Europe' (2020) 21 German Law Journal 1090.
Ferejohn J and Pasquino P, 'Constitutional Adjudication: Lessons from Europe' (2004) 82 Texas Law Review 1671.
Ferretti F, 'EU Internal Market Law and the Law of International Commercial Arbitration: Have the EU Chickens Come Home to Roost?' (2020) 20(1) Cambridge Yearbook of European Studies 133.
Fikfak V, 'Compliance and Compensation: Money as a Currency of Human Rights' in Rachel Murray and Debra Long (eds), *Research Handbook on Implementation of Human Rights in Practice* (Edward Elgar 2022).
Fines F, 'A General Analytical Perspective on Community Liability' in Ton Heukels and Alison McDonnell (eds), *The Action for Damages in Community Law* (Kluwer Law International 1997).
Fink M, *Frontex and Human Rights: Responsibility in 'Multi-Actor Situations' under the ECHR and EU Public Liability Law* (Oxford University Press 2018).
'EU liability for contributions to Member States' breaches of EU law' (2019) 56(5) Common Market Law Review 1227.
'The Action for Damages as a Fundamental Rights Remedy: Holding Frontex Liable' (2020) 21 German Law Journal 532.
Fink M and Idriz N, 'Effective Judicial Protection in the External Dimension of the EU's Migration and Asylum Policies?' in Eva Kassoti and Narin Idriz (eds), *The Informalisation of the EU's External Action in the Field of Migration and Asylum* (Edward Elgar 2022).
Fink M and Rijpma J J, 'The Management of the European Union's External Borders' in Evangelina Tsourdi and Philippe De Bruycker (eds), *Research Handbook on EU Migration and Asylum Law* (Edward Elgar 2022).
Fiss O M, 'The Bureaucratization of the Judiciary' (1983) 92 Yale Law Journal 1442.
FitzGerald D, *Refuge Beyond Reach: How Rich Democracies Repel Asylum Seekers* (Oxford University Press 2019).
Fons M P, 'The Effectiveness of EU law and Private Arbitration' (2020) 57(1) Common Market Law Review 1069.
Foster J, 'A power to fine: Establishing negligence and intent in infringements by credit rating agencies and trade repositories' in Miroslava Scholten (ed), *Research Handbook on the Enforcement of EU Law* (Edward Elgar 2023).
Fuster G G and Others, 'The Right to Lodge a Data Protection Complaint: OK, but Then What? An Empirical Study of Current Practices under the GDPR' (Data

Protection Law Scholars Network, June 2022) <www.accessnow.org/cms/assets/uploads/2022/06/Complaint-study-Final-version-before-design-June-15.pdf>.

Galanter M, 'Why the "haves" come out ahead: speculations on the limits of legal change' (1974) 9 Law & Society Review 95.

Galetta D U, Hofmann H C H and Schneider J P, 'Information Exchange in the European Administrative Union: An Introduction' (2014) 20 European Public Law 65.

Galli F, 'Interoperable Databases: New Cooperation Dynamics in the EU AFSJ?' (2020) 26 European Public Law 109.

Gammeltoft-Hansen T and Hathaway J C, 'Non-Refoulement in a World of Cooperative Deterrence' (2015) 53 Columbia Journal of Transnational Law 235.

Garben S, 'Sky-High Controversy and High-Flying Claims? The *Sturgeon* Case Law in Light of Judicial Activism, Euroscepticism and Eurolegalism' (2013) 50 Common Market Law Review 15.

García Antón R, *La Cuestión Prejudicial y La Fiscalidad Directa* (European University Institute 2015).

'The Reformulation of the Questions Referred to the CJEU for a Preliminary Ruling in Direct Taxation: Towards a Constructive Cooperation Model' (2015) 24 EC Tax Review 258.

Geist M, 'Fair.com? An Examination of the Allegations of Systemic Unfairness in the ICANN UDRP' (2002) 27 Brooklyn Journal of International Law 903.

Gentile G, 'The ECJ as the EU Court of Appeal' (2020) 13(1) Review of European Administrative Law 73.

'Ensuring effective judicial review of EU soft law via the action for annulment before the EU courts: A plea for a liberal-constitutional approach' (2020) 16 European Constitutional Law Review, 466.

Gerards J, *General Principles of the European Convention on Human Rights* (Cambridge University Press 2019).

Gerven W van, Lever J, and Larouche P, *Cases, Materials and Text on National, Supranational and International Tort Law* (Hart 2000).

Gestel R van and Poorter J de, *In the Court We Trust: Cooperation, Coordination and Collaboration between the ECJ and Supreme Administrative Courts* (Cambridge University Press 2019).

Gkliati M, 'The Application of the EU-Turkey Agreement: A Critical Analysis of the Decisions of the Greek Appeals Committees' (2017) 10 European Journal of Legal Studies 81.

Glas L, 'The age of subsidiarity? The ECtHR's approach to the admissibility requirement that applicants raise their Convention complaint before domestic courts' (2023) 41(2) Netherlands Quarterly of Human Rights 75.

Goanta C and Ortolani P, 'Unpacking Content Moderation: The Rise of Social Media Platforms as Online Civil Courts' in Xandra Kramer, Jos Hoevenaars, Betül Kas, and Erlis Themeli (eds), *Frontiers in Civil Justice* (Edward Elgar 2022).

Gradoni L, 'Constitutional Review via Facebook's Oversight Board: How platform governance had its Marbury v Madison' (Verfassungsblog, 10 February 2021) <https://verfassungsblog.de/fob-marbury-v-madison/>.

Gragl P, 'A giant leap for European human rights? The final agreement on the European Union's accession to the European Convention on Human Rights' (2014) 51 Common Market Law Review 13.

Grando M, *Evidence, Proof, and Fact-Finding in WTO Dispute Settlement* (Oxford University Press 2009).

Granger M P and Irion K, 'The Court of Justice and the Data Retention Directive in *Digital Rights Ireland*: Telling Off the EU Legislator and Teaching a Lesson in Privacy and Data Protection' (2014) 6 European Law Review 835.

Graver H P, 'The Holship ruling of the ECtHR and the protection of fundamental rights in Europe' (2022) 23 ERA Forum 19.

Grozdanovski L, *La présomption en droit de l'Union européenne* (Anthémis 2019).

Gubin E, *Éliane Vogel-Polsky: a woman of conviction* (Institute for the Equality of Women and Men 2018).

Guerrero M, 'Strategic litigation in EU gender equality law' (Publications office European Commission, 7 May 2020) <https://data.europa.eu/doi/10.2838/458994>.

Guinier L, 'From Racial Liberalism to Racial Literacy: Brown v. Board of Education and the Interest-Divergence Dilemma' (2004) 91 Journal of American History 92.

Gundel J, 'Rechtsschutz gegen Empfehlungen der EU-Kommission?' (2018) 53(5) Europarecht 593.

Gutman K, 'The Non-contractual Liability of the European Union: Principle, Practice and Promise' in Paula Giliker (ed), *Research Handbook on EU Tort Law* (Edward Elgar 2017).

'The Essence of the Fundamental Right to an Effective Remedy and to a Fair Trial in the Case-Law of the Court of Justice of the European Union: The Best Is Yet to Come' (2019) 20 German Law Journal 884.

Hagan M and Others, 'Design Report: Language Access Innovations in Court: How Can Courts Use Technology & Design to Support People in Court When They're Not Proficient in English?' (Legal Design Lab, February 2019) <https://justiceinnovation.law.stanford.edu/courses/language-access/>.

Halberstam D and von der Boegart S, 'A Fresh Look at Judicial Remedies in EU Equality Law and Beyond: The Untapped Possibility of Structural Injunctions' [2023] Michigan Law Public Law and Legal Theory Research Paper Series 23/012.

Halmai G, 'Abuse of constitutional identity: the Hungarian constitutional court on interpretation of article E) (2) of the fundamental law' (2018) 43 Review of Central and East European law 23.

'Coping Strategies of the Hungarian Constitutional Court since 2010' (Verfassungsblog, 27 September 2022) <https://verfassungsblog.de/coping-strategies-of-the-hungarian-constitutional-court-since-2010/>.

Hamann H, 'Der blinde Fleck der deutschen Rechtswissenschaft – Zur digitalen Verfügbarkeit instanzgerichtlicher Rechtsprechung' (2021) 76 Juristen Zeitung 656.

Hanf D, 'EU Liability Actions' in Robert Schütze and Takis Tridimas (eds), *Oxford Principles Of European Union Law: The European Union Legal Order: Volume I* (Oxford University Press 2018).

'The Trailblazers: The Boards of Appeal of EUIPO and CPVO' in Merijn Chamon, Annalisa Volpato, and Mariolina Eliantonio (eds), *Boards of Appeal of EU Agencies: Towards Judicialization of Administrative Review?* (Oxford University Press 2022).

Haraksim R, Galbally J, and Beslay L, 'Study on Fingermark and Palmmark Identification Technologies for Their Implementation in the Schengen Information System' (Joint Research Centre EC, 2019) <http://publications.europa.eu/publication/manifestation_identifier/PUB_KJNA29755ENN>.

Harding C, 'The Choice of Court Problem in Cases of Non-Contractual Liability under E.E.C. Law' (1979) 16 Common Market Law Review 389.

Harlow C, *State Liability: Tort Law and Beyond* (Oxford University Press 2004).

Harten G van, 'The public-private distinction in the international arbitration of individual claims against the state' (2007) 56(2) International and comparative corporate law quarterly 371.

Harvey D, 'Process-oriented federalism in the EU: A (partial) response to critiques of process review advocacy in the EU' (2021) 46(4) European Law Review 460.

Havu K A, 'Damages Liability for Non-Material Harm in EU Case Law' (2019) 44 European Law Review 492.

Heikkila M, 'Dutch Scandal Serves as a Warning for Europe over Risks of Using Algorithms' (Politico, 29 March 2022) <www.politico.eu/article/dutch-scandal-serves-as-a-warning-for-europe-over-risks-of-using-algorithms/>.

Hermansen S S L, 'Building Legitimacy: Strategic Case Allocations in the Court of Justice of the European Union' (2020) 27 Journal of European Public Policy 1127.

Hertogh M, 'A "European" conception of legal consciousness: rediscovering Eugen Ehrlich (2004) 31 Journal of Law and Society 457.

Hess B, *The Private-Public Divide in International Dispute Resolution* (1st edn, Brill Nijhoff 2018).

Hickman T R, 'Tort Law, Public Authorities, and the Human Rights Act 1998' in Duncan Fairgrieve, Mads Andenas, and John Bell (eds), *Tort Liability of Public Authorities in Comparative Perspective* (The British Institute of International and Comparative Law 2002).

Hillion C and Wessel R, 'The European Union and International Dispute Settlement: Mapping Principles and Conditions' in Marise Cremona, Anne Thies, and Ramses A Wessel (eds), *The European Union and International Dispute Settlement* (Hart 2017).

"The Good, the Bad and the Ugly': three levels of judicial control over the CFSP' in Steven Blockmans and Panos Koutrakos (eds), *Research Handbook on EU Common Foreign and Security Policy* (Edward Elgar 2018).

Hilpold P, 'So Long Solange? The PSPP Judgment of the German Constitutional Court and the Conflict between the German and the European "Popular Spirit"' (2021) 23 Cambridge Yearbook of European Legal Studies 159.

Hilson C, 'New Social Movements: the Role of Legal Opportunity' (2002) 9 Journal of European Public Policy 238.

Hinarejos A, *The Euro Area Crisis in Constitutional Perspective* (Oxford University Press 2015).

Hoevenaars J, *A People's Court? A bottom-up approach to litigation before the European Court of Justice* (Eleven 2018).

Hoevenaars J and Krommendijk J, 'Black Box in Luxembourg the Bewildering Experience of National Judges and Lawyers in the Context of the Preliminary Reference Procedure' (2021) 46 European Law Review 61.

Hofmann A and Naurin D, 'Explaining interest group litigation in Europe: Evidence from the comparative interest group survey' (2020) 34 Governance 1235.

Hofmann H C H, 'Composite decision-making procedures in EU administrative law' in Herwig C Hofmann and Alexander H Türk (eds), *Legal Challenges in EU Administrative Law – Towards an Integrated Administration* (Edward Elgar 2009) 136.

'Multi-Jurisdictional Composite Procedures. The Backbone to the EU's Single Regulatory Space' (2019) 3 University of Luxembourg Law Working Paper Series 12.

'The Duty of Care in EU Public Law - A Principle between Discretion and Proportionality' (2020) 13 Review of European Administrative Law 87.

'Article 47: Specific Provisions (Meaning)' in Steve Peers and Others (eds), *The EU Charter of Fundamental Rights: A Commentary* (2nd edn, Hart 2021).

Hofmann H C H and Mihaescu-Evans B C, 'The Relation between the Charter's Fundamental Rights and the Unwritten General Principles of EU Law: Good Administration as the Test Case' (2013) 9 European Constitutional Law Review 73.

Hofmann H C H, Rowe G C, and Türk A H, *EU Administrative Law* (Oxford University Press 2011).

Hofmann H C H, Rowe G C, and Türk A H (eds), *Specialized Administrative Law of the European Union: A Sectoral Review* (Oxford University Press 2018).

Hofmann H C H and Tidghi M, 'Rights and Remedies in Implementation of EU Policies by Multi-Jurisdictional Networks' (2014) 20(1) European Public Law 147.

Hofmann H C H and Ziller J (eds), *Accountability in the EU: the Role of the European Ombudsman* (Edward Elgar 2017).

Holznagel D, 'A Self-Regulatory Race to the Bottom through Out-of-Court Dispute Settlement in the Digital Services Act' (Verfassungsblog, 16 March 2022) <https://verfassungsblog.de/a-self-regulatory-race-to-the-bottom-through-art-18-digital-services-act/>.

Iglesias Sánchez S, 'The Court and the Charter: The impact of the entry into force of the Lisbon Treaty on the ECJ's approach to fundamental rights' (2012) 49 Common Market Law Review 1565.

Inghelram I, 'Fundamental Rights, the European Anti-Fraud Office (OLAF) and a European Public Prosecutor's Office (EPPO): Some Selected Issues' (2012) 1 Kritische Vierteljahresschrift für Gesetzgebung und Rechtswissenschaft 67.

Inverardi P, 'The Challenge of Human Dignity in the Era of Autonomous Systems' in Hannes Werthner and Others (eds), *Perspectives on Digital Humanism* (Springer 2022).

Isiksel T, 'European exceptionalism and the EU's accession to the ECHR' (2016) 27 The European Journal of International Law 565.

Jääskinen N, 'Final Thoughts', in Mariolina Eliantonio, Emilia Korkea-aho, Oana Ştefan (eds), *EU Soft Law in the Member States Theoretical Findings and Empirical Evidence* (Hart 2021).

Jacobs F, 'The Lisbon Treaty and the Court of Justice' in Andrea Biondi, Piet Eeckhout, and Stefanie Ripley (eds), *EU law after Lisbon* (Oxford University Press 2012).

Jacqué J P, 'The accession of the European Union to the European Convention of Human Rights and Fundamental Freedoms' (2011) 48 Common Market Law Review 995.

Jan B, 'Safeguarding the Right to an Effective Remedy in Algorithmic Multi-Governance Systems: An Inquiry in Artificial Intelligence-Powered Informational Cooperation in the EU Administrative Space' (2023) 16 Review of European Administrative Law 9.

Jaraczewski J, 'Gazing into the Abyss: The K 3/21 decision of the Polish Constitutional Tribunal' (Verfassungsblog, 12 October 2021) <https://verfassungsblog.de/gazing-into-the-abyss/>.

Jeandesboz J, 'Ceci n'est Pas Un Contrôle: PNR Data Processing and the Reshaping of Borderless Travel in the Schengen Area' (2021) 23 European Journal of Migration and Law 431.

Johansen S Ø, 'Suing the European Union in the UK: *Tomanović et. al. v. The EU et. al.*' (2019) 4 European Papers 345.

Jones C, Valdivia A, and Kilpatrick J, 'Funds for Fortress Europe: Spending by Frontex and Eu-LISA' (Statewatch, 28 January 2022) <www.statewatch.org/analyses/2022/funds-for-fortress-europe-spending-by-frontex-and-eu-lisa/>.

Kanuck S, 'Humor, Ethics, and Dignity: Being Human in the Age of Artificial Intelligence' (2019) 33 Ethics & International Affairs 3.

Kaplow J, 'Burden of Proof' (2012) 121 The Yale Law Journal 738.

Karagianni A, *The protection of fundamental rights in composite banking supervision procedures* (Europa Law 2022).

Kassoti E and Idriz N (eds), *The Informalisation of the EU's External Action in the Field of Migration and Asylum* (Springer 2022).

Katsh E, 'ODR: A Look at History' in Mohamed S Abdel Wahab, Ethan Katsh, and Daniel Rainey (eds), *Online Dispute Resolution: Theory and Practice* (1st edn, Eleven 2011).

Katsh E, and Rifkin J, *Online Dispute Resolution: Resolving Conflicts in Cyberspace* (Jossey-Bass 2001).

Katsh E and Rule C, 'What We Know and Need to Know about Online Dispute Resolution' (2016) 67 South Carolina Law Review 329.

Kelemen D, *Eurolegalism: The Transformation of Law and Regulation in the European Union* (Harvard University Press 2011).

Kenner J and Peake K, 'Art 33 – Family and Professional Life', in Steve Peers, Tamara Hervey, Jeff Kenner, and Angela Ward (eds), *The EU Charter of Fundamental Rights: A Commentary* (Hart 2021).

Kenny D, 'Proportionality, the burden of proof, and some signs of reconsideration' (2014) 52 Irish Jurist 141.

Khaitan T, 'Guarantor Institutions' (2021) 16 Asian Journal of Comparative Law 1.

Kilpatrick C, 'Are the Bailouts Immune to EU Social Challenge Because They Are Not EU Law?' (2014) 10 European Constitutional Law Review 393.

'Constitutions, Social Rights and Sovereign Debt States in Europe: A Challenging New Area of Constitutional Inquiry' in Bruno de Witte, Claire Kilpatrick, and Thomas Beukers (eds), *Constitutional Change through Euro-Crisis Law* (Cambridge University Press 2017).

Kitschelt H P, 'Political Opportunity Structures and Political Protest: Anti-Nuclear Movements in Four Democracies' (2009) 16 British Journal of Political Science 57.

Kistemaker L, 'Rechtwijzer and Uitelkaar.nl. Dutch Experiences with ODR for Divorce' (2021) 59 Family Court Review 232.
Klonick K, 'The Facebook Oversight Board: Creating an Independent Institution to Adjudicate Online Free Expression' (2020) 129 Yale Law Journal 2420.
Kornhauser L A, 'Incentives, Compensation, and Irreparable Harm' in André Nollkaemper, Dov Jacobs, and Jessica N M Schechinger (eds), *Distribution of Responsibilities in International Law* (Cambridge University Press 2015).
Koskenniemi M, 'Performing Legal Expertise: Reflections on the Construction of Transnational Authority' in Emilia Korkea-aho and Päivi Leino-Sandberg (eds), *Law, Legal Expertise and EU Policy-Making* (Cambridge University Press 2022).
Kozak M, 'ECN+ Directive – A missed opportunity for strengthening the rights of parties?' in Catalin S Rusu and Others (eds), *New Directions of Antitrust Enforcement* (Wolf Legal 2020).
Kozak M and Mainardi J, 'Rights of Complainants Before the European Commission – a Critical Analysis' (2023) 14(3) Journal of European Competition Law & Practice 152.
Krajewski M, *Relative Authority of Judicial and Extra-Judicial Review: EU Courts, Boards of Appeal, Ombudsman* (Hart 2021).
'Judicial and Extra-Judicial Review: The Quest for Epistemic Certainty' in Merijn Chamon, Mariolina Eliantonio, and Annalisa Volpato (eds), *Boards of Appeal of EU Agencies* (Oxford University Press 2022).
Krämer H, *Rechtsschutz im EG-Eigenverwaltungsrecht zwischen Einheitlichkeit und sektorieller Ausdifferenzierung: eine Untersuchung unter besonderer Berücksichtigung des Gemeinschaftsmarkenrechts* (Duncker & Humblot 2007).
Krenn C, 'Autonomy and effectiveness as common concerns: A path to ECHR accession after Opinion 2/13' (2015) 16 German Law Journal 147.
The Procedural and Organisational Law of the European Court of Justice: An Incomplete Transformation (Cambridge University Press 2022).
'A Sense of Common Purpose: On the Role of Case Assignment and the Judge-Rapporteur at the European Court of Justice' in Mikael Rask Madsen, Fernanda Nicola, and Antoine Vauchez (eds), *Researching the European Court of Justice: methodological shifts and law's embeddedness* (Cambridge University Press 2022).
Kriesi H, 'Political Context and Opportunity' in David Snow, Sarah Soule, and Hanspeter Kriesi (eds), *The Blackwell Companion to Social Movements* (Blackwell 2004).
Krommendijk J, 'Opinion 2/13 as a Game Changer in the Dialogue between the European Courts?' in Emmanuelle Bribosia, and Isabelle Rorive (eds), *Human Rights Tectonics. Global Perspectives on Integration and Fragmentation* (Intersentia 2018).
'Tell me more, tell me more: the obligation for national courts to reason their refusals to refer to the CJEU in Sanofi Pasteur' (Strasbourg Observers, 20 February 2020) <https://strasbourgobservers.com/2020/02/20/tell-me-more-tell-me-more-the-obligation-for-national-courts-to-reason-their-refusals-to-refer-to-the-cjeu-in-sanofi-pasteur/>.
Krommendijk J and Pas K van der, 'To intervene or not to intervene: intervention before the court of justice of the european union in environmental and migration law' (2022) 26 The International Journal of Human Rights 1394.

'Third-party interventions before the Court of Justice in migration law cases' (EU Migration Law Blog, 29 November 2022) <https://eumigrationlawblog.eu/third-party-interventions-before-the-court-of-justice-in-migration-law-cases/>.

Krommendijk J and Vries G de, 'Do Luxembourg and Strasbourg trust each other? The interaction between the Court of Justice and the European Court of Human Rights in cases concerning mutual trust' (2021) 4(5) European Journal of Human Rights 319.

Küçüksu A, 'Adjudicating Asylum as a Technical Matter at the Court of Justice of the European Union: Neglecting Human Rights When the CEAS Appears to Be in Jeopardy?' in Eva Kassoti and Narin Idriz (eds), *The Informalisation of the EU's External Action in the Field of Migration and Asylum* (Springer 2022).

Kuijer M, 'The accession of the European Union to the ECHR: A gift for the ECHR's 60th anniversary or an unwelcome intruder at the party?' (2011) 3 Amsterdam Law Forum 17.

Kuijper P J, Amtenbrink F, Curtin D, Witte B de, McDonnell A, and Bogaert S van den, *The Law of the European Union* (5th edn, Wouters Kluwer International 2018).

Kwan A, Yang S A, and Zhang A H, 'Crowd-judging on Two-sided Platforms: An Analysis of In-group Bias' (Management Science, 9 February 2023) <https://pubsonline.informs.org/doi/full/10.1287/mnsc.2023.4818>.

Lamandini M, 'The ESAs' Board of Appeal as a Blueprint for the Quasi-Judicial Review of European Financial Supervision' (2014) 11(6) European Company Law 290.

Lamandini M and Muñoz D R, 'Law and Practice of Financial Appeal Bodies (ESAs' Board of Appeal, SRB Appeal Panel): A View from the Inside' (2020) 57 Common Market Law Review 119.

Lanceiro R and Eliantonio M, 'The Genetically Modified Organisms' Regime: A Playground for Multi-Level Administration and a Nightmare for Effective Judicial Protection?' (2021) 22 German Law Journal 371.

Lasok P, *Lasok's European Court Practice and Procedure* (3rd edn, Bloomsbury Professional 2017).

Lauterpacht S E and Bethlehem D, 'The Scope and Content of the Principle of Non-Refoulement: Opinion' in Erika Feller, Volker Türk, and Frances Nicholson (eds), *Refugee Protection in International Law* (Cambridge University Press 2003).

Łazowski A and Wessel R, 'When caveats turn into locks: Opinion 2/13 on accession of the European Union to the ECHR' (2015) 16 German Law Journal 179.

Leczykiewicz D, 'Compensatory Remedies in EU law: The Relationship between EU Law and National Law' in Paula Giliker (ed), *Research Handbook on EU Tort Law* (Edward Elgar 2017).

Lenaerts K, 'Some Reflections on the Separation of Powers in the European Community' (1991) 28 Common Market Law Review 11.

'The Rule of Law and the Coherence of the Judicial System of the European Union' (2007) 44 Common Market Law Review 1625.

and Others, *EU Procedural Law* (Oxford University Press 2014).

Leskinen C, 'An evaluation of rights of defense during antitrust inspections in the light of the case law of the ECtHR: would accession of the European Union to the

ECHR bring about a significant change' Instituto de Empresa Business School Working Paper 10/04.

Letsas G, 'The scope and balancing of rights – Diagnostic or constitutive?', in Eva Brems and Janneke Gerards (eds), *Shaping Rights in the ECHR: The Role of the European Court of Human Rights in Determining the Scope of Human Rights* (Cambridge University Press 2014).

Levidis S and Others, 'Drift-Backs in the Aegean Sea' (Forensic Architecture, 15 July 2022) <https://forensic-architecture.org/investigation/drift-backs-in-the-aegean-sea>.

Ligeti K and Robinson G, 'Composite Enforcement and Comprehensive Judicial Protection' in Michiel Luchtman, Katalin Ligeti, and John Vervaele (eds), *EU Enforcement Authorities – Punitive Law Enforcement in a Composite Legal Order* (Hart 2023).

Linden O, 'The Internal Market' in Miroslava Scholten (ed), *Research Handbook on the Enforcement of EU Law* (Edward Elgar 2023).

Lindseth P L, *Power and Legitimacy: Reconciling Europe and the Nation-State* (Oxford University Press 2010).

Lisi G and Eliantonio M, 'The Gaps in Judicial Accountability of EASO in the Processing of Asylum Requests in Hotspots' (2019) 4 European Papers 589.

Lock T, 'EU Accession to the ECHR: Implications for Judicial Review in Strasbourg' (2010) 35 European Law Review 777.

'Rights and Principles in the EU Charter of Fundamental Rights' (2019) 56 Common Market Law Review 1201.

López Zurita L, 'The Survival of the Fitted? Individual Protection in the European Court of Justice's Preliminary Ruling Procedure' (PhD thesis, European University Institute 2021).

'Responding to What? Reformulated Questions, Useful Answers and Party Observations in the CJEU's Case Law' (The Court of Justice as a Relational Actor, University of Gothenburg, September 2022).

Lucía López Zurita and Stein Arne Brekke, A Spoonful of Sugar: Deference at the Court of Justice' (2023) *Journal of Common Market Studies*, available at https://doi.org/10.1111/jcms.13547.

Luchtman L and Wasmeier M, 'The Political and Judicial Accountability of OLAF' in Miroslava Scholten and Michiel Luchtman (eds), *Law Enforcement by EU Authorities. Implications for Political and Judicial Accountability* (Edward Elgar 2017).

Luchtman M, 'Pertinent Issues of Punitive Enforcement in a Composite Legal Order' in Michiel Luchtman, Katalin Ligeti, and John Vervaele (eds), *EU Enforcement Authorities. Punitive Law Enforcement in a Composite Legal Order* (Hart 2023).

'The rise of EU law enforcement authorities' in Michiel Luchtman, Katalin Ligeti, and John Vervaele (eds), *EU Enforcement Authorities. Punitive Law Enforcement in a Composite Legal Order* (Hart 2023).

and Others (eds), *Of Swords and Shields: Due Process and Crime Control in Times of Globalization – Liber Amicorum prof. dr. J.A.E. Vervaele* (Eleven 2023).

Ludwigs M, 'Die Verfahrensautonomie der Mitgliedstaaten' (2018) 19 Neue Zeitschrift für Verwaltungsrecht 1417.

Lustig D and Weiler J H H, 'Judicial review in the contemporary world – retrospective and prospective' (2018) 16(2) International Journal of Constitutional Law 316.

Lynskey O, 'Deconstructing Data Protection: The "Added Value" of a Right to Data Protection in the EU Legal Order' (2014) 63 International & Comparative Law Quarterly 569.

'The role of collective actors in the enforcement of the right to data protection under EU law' in Elise Muir and Others (eds), *How EU law shapes opportunities for preliminary references on fundamental rights: discriminationa, data protection and asylum* (EUI Working Papers 2017/17).

Maas H, 'La Commission administrative pour la sécurité sociale des travailleurs migrants' (1966) 2 Cahiers de droit européen 343.

MacCormick N, *Institutions of Law: An Essay in Legal Theory* (Oxford University Press 2007).

Machnikowski P, 'European Union' in Ken Oliphant (ed), *The Liability of Public Authorities in Comparative Perspective* (Intersentia 2017).

Malgieri G, 'Automated Decision-Making and Data Protection in Europe' in Gloria González, Rosamunde Van Brakel, and Paul De Hert (eds), *Research Handbook on Privacy and Data Protection Law* (Edward Elgar 2022).

Malleghem P A van and Baeten N, 'Before the laws stands a gatekeeper – Or, what is a 'regulatory act' in Article 263(4) TFEU?' (2014) 51 Common Market Law Review 1187.

Mantelero A, 'Fundamental rights impact assessments in the DSA' (Verfassungsblog, 1 November 2022) <https://verfassungsblog.de/dsa-impact-assessment/>.

Mare T de la and Donnelly C, 'Preliminary Rulings and EU Legal Integration: Evolution and Stasis' in Paul Craig and Grainne de Búrca (eds), *The evolution of EU law* (Oxford University Press 2011).

Mańko R, 'Action for Damages Against the EU: European Parliament Briefing' (2018) <www.europarl.europa.eu/RegData/etudes/BRIE/2018/630333/EPRS_BRI(2018)630333_EN.pdf>.

Marín Aís J R, 'Freedom of Religion in the Workplace v. Freedom to Conduct a Business, the Islamic Veil Before the Court of Justice: Ms. Samira Achbita Case' (2018) 3 European Papers 409.

Marin L and Krajčíková K, 'Deploying Drones in Policing Southern European Borders: Constraints and Challenges for Data Protection and Human Rights' in Aleš Završnik (ed), *Drones and Unmanned Aerial Systems: Legal and Social Implications for Security and Surveillance* (Springer 2016)

Mashaw J L, *Bureaucratic Justice: Managing Social Security Disability Claims* (Yale University Press 1983).

Mazzotti P and Eliantonio M, 'Transnational Judicial Review in Horizontal Composite Procedures: *Berlioz*, *Donnellan*, and the Constitutional Law of the Union' (2020) 5 European Papers 41.

'Towards a Theory of Transnational Judicial Review in European Administrative Law' (2021) 13 Italian Journal of Public Law 350 <ww.ijpl.eu/wp-content/uploads/2022/10/3.Eliantonio_Mazzotti.pdf>.

Mbongo P and Vauchez A, *Dans La Fabrique Du Droit Européen: Scènes, Acteurs et Publics de La Cour de Justice Des Communautés Européennes* (Bruylant 2009).

McHard A, 'Reconciling Human Rights and the Public interest' (1999) 62 Modern Law Review 671.

Mendes J and Venzke I (eds), *Allocating Authority: Who Should Do What in European and International Law?* (Hart 2018).

Merrils J, *International Dispute Settlement* (4th edn, Cambridge University Press 2005).

Meyer F, 'Protection of fundamental rights in a multi-jurisdictional setting of the EU' in Miroslava Scholten and Alex Brenninkmeijer (eds), *Controlling EU Agencies. The Rule of Law in a Multi-Jurisdictional Legal Order* (Edward Elgar 2020).

Meyer J W and Rowan B, 'Institutionalized Organizations: Formal Structure as Myth and Ceremony' (1977) 83 American Journal of Sociology 340.

Meyerson D, 'Why Courts Should not Balance Rights against the Public Interest' (2007) Melbourne University Law Review 873.

Möllers C, 'European Governance: Meaning and Value of a Concept' (2006) 43 Common Market Law Review 313.

The Three Branches: A Comparative Model of Separation of Powers (Oxford University Press 2013).

Morano-Foadi S and Andreadakis S, 'Reflections on the Architecture of the EU after the Treaty of Lisbon: The European Judicial Approach to Fundamental Rights' (2011) 17 European Law Journal 595.

Moreno Lax V, *Accessing Asylum in Europe: Extraterritorial Border Controls and Refugee Rights under EU Law* (Oxford University Press 2017).

Mot J de and Faure M, 'The Liability of Public Authorities: An Economic Analysis' in Ken Oliphant (ed), *The Liability of Public Authorities in Comparative Perspective* (Intersentia 2017).

Nappert S, 'International Arbitration as a Tool of Global Governance: The Use (and Abuse) of Discretion' in Eric Brousseau, Jean-Michel Glachant, and Jérôme Sgard (eds), *The Oxford Handbook of Institutions of International Economic Governance and Market Regulation* (Oxford University Press 2019).

Narrillos E, 'MEPs to Grill Frontex Director on Agency's Role in Pushbacks of Asylum-Seekers' (European Parliament Press Releases, 30 November 2020) <www.europarl.europa.eu/news/en/press-room/20201126IPR92509/meps-to-grill-frontex-director-on-agency-s-role-in-pushbacks-of-asylum-seekers>.

Nelken D, 'Using the Concept of Legal Culture' (2004) 29 Australian Journal of Legal Philosophy 1.

NeJaime D, 'Winning through Losing' (2011) 96 Iowa Law Review 941.

Neuwahl N A, 'The Treaty on European Union: A Step Forward in the Protection of Human Rights?' in Nanette A Neuwahl and Allan Rosas (eds), *The European Union and human rights* (Martinus Nijhoff 1995).

Nicolosi S and Omičević E, 'The Rise of EU Migration Agencies: Striking a Balance between Enforcement Needs and Access to Justice' (2022) *Jean Monnet Network on EU Law Enforcement Working Paper* 16/22, 1.

Nogueira de Brito M, 'Putting Social Rights in Brackets? The Portuguese Experience with Welfare Challenges in Times of Crisis' in Claire Kilpatrick and Bruno de Witte (eds), *Social Rights in Times of Crisis in the Eurozone: The Role of Fundamental Rights' Challenges* (EUI Working papers LAW 05/2014).

Nolan A, 'Welfare Rights in Crisis in the Eurozone: Ireland' in Claire Kilpatrick and Bruno de Witte (eds), *Social Rights in Times of Crisis in the Eurozone: The Role of Fundamental Rights' Challenges* (EUI Working papers LAW 05/2014).

Nollkaemper A and Others, 'Guiding Principles on Shared Responsibility in International Law' (2020) 31 European Journal of International Law 15.

Nussbaum M, *Women and human development: The capabilities approach* (Cambridge University Press 2000).

Creating Capabilities. The Human Development Approach (Harvard University Press 2013).

Nyikos S, 'Strategic Interaction among Courts within the Preliminary Reference Process – Stage 1: National Court Preemptive Opinions' (2006) 45 European Journal of Political Research 527.

Ojiegbe C, *International Commercial Arbitration in the European Union* (1st edn, Edward Elgar 2020).

O'Leary S, *Employment Law at the European Court of Justice: Judicial Structures, Policies and Processes* (Hart 2002).

Oliphant K, 'The Liability of Public Authorities in Comparative Perspective' in Ken Oliphant (ed), *The Liability of Public Authorities in Comparative Perspective* (Intersentia 2017).

Oliver P, 'Joint Liability of the Community and the Member States' in Ton Heukels and Alison McDonnell (eds), *The Action for Damages in Community Law* (Kluwer Law International 1997).

O'Meara N, '"A more secure Europe of rights?" The European Court of Human Rights, the Court of Justice of the European Union and EU accession to the ECHR' (2011) 12 German Law Journal 1813.

Ortolani P, 'Self-Enforcing Online Dispute Resolution: Lessons from Bitcoin' (2016) 36 Oxford Journal of Legal Studies 595.

'If You Build it, They will Come' (Verfassungsblog, 7 November 2022) <https://verfassungsblog.de/dsa-build-it/>.

Owusu-Bempah A, 'The interpretation and application of the right to effective participation' (2018) 22 The International Journal of Evidence and Proof 321.

Pagano M, 'Overcoming Plaumann in EU environmental litigation: an analysis of NGOs legal arguments in actions for annulment' (2019) Diritto e Processo 311.

Papp K von, *EU Law and International Arbitration: Managing Distrust Through Dialogue* (1st edn, Hart 2021).

Pas K van der, 'Conceptualising Strategic Litigation' (2021) 11 Oñati Socio-Legal Series 116.

Passalacqua V, 'Legal mobilization via preliminary reference: Insights from the case of migrant rights' (2021) 58 Common Market Law Review 751.

Pauwelyn J and Pelc K, 'Who Guards the "Guardians of the System"? The Role of the Secretariat in WTO Dispute Settlement' (2022) 116 American Journal of International Law 534.

Pavone T, 'From Marx to Market: Lawyers, European Law, and the Contentious Transformation of the Port of Genoa' (2018) 53 Law & Society Review 851.

The Ghostwriters: Lawyers and the Politics behind the Judicial Construction of Europe (Cambridge University Press 2022).

Peers S, 'The CJEU and the EU's accession to the ECHR: A clear and present danger to human rights protection' (EU Law Analysis, 18 December 2014) <http://eulawanalysis.blogspot.com/2014/12/the-cjeu-and-eus-accession-to-echr.html.>.

Perea Molleda R, 'The Ecn+ Directive and the Next Steps for Independence in Competition Law Enforcement' (2020) 12 Journal of European Competition Law & Practice 167.

Pergantis V and Johansen S Ø, 'The EU accession to the ECHR and the responsibility question. Between a rock and a hard place' in Nicolas Levrat and Others (eds), *The EU and Its Member States' Joint Participation in International Agreements* (Hart 2022).

Pescatore P, 'Les Travaux Du "Groupe Juridique" Dans La Négociation Des Traités de Rome' (1981) 34 Studia Diplomatica 159.

Etudes de droit européen 1962–2007 (Bruylant 2008).

'Van Gend En Loos, 3 February 1963 – A View from Within' in Miguel Poiares Maduro and Loïc Azoulai (eds), *The Past and Future of EU Law: The Classics of EU Law Revisited on the 50th Anniversary of the Rome Treaty* (Hart 2010).

Pesch P J, Dimitrova D, and Boehm F, 'Data Protection and Machine-Learning-Supported Decision-Making at the EU Border: ETIAS Profiling Under Scrutiny' in Agnieszka Gryszczyńska and Others (eds), *Privacy Technologies and Policy* (Springer 2022).

Peters A, 'The European Ombudsman and the European Constitution' (2006) 43 Common Market Law Review 697.

Beyond Human Rights: The Legal Status of the Individual in International Law (Cambridge University Press 2016).

Pfander J E, 'Article I Tribunals, Article III Courts, and the Judicial Power of the United States' (2004) 118 Harvard Law Review 643.

Pijnenburg A and Pas K van der, 'Strategic Litigation against European Migration Control Policies: the Legal Battleground of the Central Mediterranean Migration Route' (2022) 24 European Journal of Migration and Law 401.

Pirrello A, 'The European Union Agency for Asylum: legal remedies and national articulations in composite border procedures' (forthcoming 2024) European Law Journal.

Pócza K, Dobos G, and Gyulai A, 'How to Measure the Strength of Judicial Decisions: A Methodological Framework' (2017) 18 German Law Journal 1557.

Polakiewicz J, 'EU law and the ECHR: Will EU accession to the European Convention on Human Rights square the circle? The draft accession agreement of 5 April 2013' [2013] SSRN Electronic Journal.

Poli S, 'The right to effective judicial protection with respect to acts imposing restrictive measures and its transformative force for the Common Foreign and Security Policy' (2022) 59(4) Common Market Law Review 1045.

Półtorak N, 'Action for Damages in the Case of Infringement of Fundamental Rights by the European Union' in Ewa Bagińska (ed), *Damages for Violations of Human Rights: A Comparative Study of Domestic Legal Systems* (Springer 2016).

Poulou A, 'The Liability of the EU in the ESM framework' (2017) 24(1) Maastricht Journal of European and Comparative Law 127.

'Financial assistance conditionality and human rights protection: What is the role of the EU Charter of Fundamental Rights?' (2017) 54 Common Market Law Review 991.

Prechal S and Widdershoven R, 'Redefining the Relationship between Rewe-effectiveness and Effective Judicial Protection' (2011) 4 Review of European Administrative Law 31.

Prechal S, 'Individuals Challenging Directives in EU Courts' (2022) 59 Common Market Law Review 41.

Prieur M, Complaints and appeals in the area of environment in the member states of the European Union (Study for the Commission of the European Community, DGXI 1998).

Psychogiopoulou E, 'Welfare rights in crisis in Greece: The role of fundamental rights challenges' in Claire Kilpatrick and Bruno de Witte (eds), *Social Rights in Times of Crisis in the Eurozone: The Role of Fundamental Rights' Challenges* (EUI Working papers LAW 05/2014).

Quaintance Z, 'Michigan Scales Back Massive Applications Process with Human-Centric Design' (GovernmentTechnology, 31 January 2018), <www.govtech.com/health/michigan-scales-back-massive-applications-process-with-human-centric-design.html>.

Quinn P and Malgieri G, 'The Difficulty of Defining Sensitive Data – The Concept of Sensitive Data in the EU Data Protection Framework' (2021) 22 German Law Journal 1583.

Quintel T, *Data Protection, Migration and Border Control: The GDPR, the Law Enforcement Directive and Beyond* (Bloomsbury 2022).

Rademacher T, 'Factual Administrative Conduct and Judicial Review in EU Law' (2017) 29(2) European Review of Public Law 399.

Ramsden M and Gledhill K, 'Defining Strategic Litigation' (2019) 4 Civil Justice Quarterly 407.

Ranchordas S, Experimental lawmaking in the EU: Regulatory Sandboxes (Social Science Research Network, 22 October 2021) SSRN Scholarly Paper ID 3963810 2 <https://papers.ssrn.com/abstract=3963810>.

Rangel de Mesquita MJ, 'Judicial review of Common Foreign and Security Policy by the ECtHR and the (re)negotiation on the accession of the EU to the ECHR' (2021) 28 Maastricht Journal of European and Comparative Law 356.

Rasmussen H, 'Why Is Article 173 Interpreted against Private Plaintiffs?' (1980) 5 European Law Review 112.

Rasnača Z, *Constitutional Change through Eurocrisis Law: Latvia* (European University Institute 2014).

Rauchegger C, 'Article 47: Damages for Breach of the Charter as a Remedy under the First Paragraph of Article 47' in Steve Peers and Others (eds), *The EU Charter of Fundamental Rights: A Commentary* (2nd edn, Hart 2021).

Raz J, *The morality of freedom* (Claredon Press 1986).

Redondon MC, 'Legal Reasons: between Universalism and Particularism' (2005) 2(1) Journal of Moral Philosophy 47.

Reich N, 'More Clarity after "*Claro*"? Arbitration Clauses in Consumer Contracts as an ADR (Alternative Dispute Resolution) Mechanism for Effective and Speedy Conflict Resolution, or as "Deni de Justice"?' (2007) 3(1) European Review of Contract Law 41.

'Party Autonomy and Consumer Arbitration in Conflict: A "Trojan Horse" in the Access to Justice in the E.U. ADR-Directive 2013/11?' (2015) Penn State Journal of Law & International Affairs 258.

Renzenbrink U F, *Gemeinschaftshaftung und Mitgliedstaatliche Rechtsbehelfe: Vorrang, Subsidiarität oder Gleichstufigkeit?* (Peter Lang 2000).

Repasi R, 'Judicial protection against austerity measures in the euro area: Ledra and Mallis' (2017) 54(4) Common Market Law Review 1123.

Resnik J, 'Managerial Judges' (1982) 96 Harvard Law Review 374.

Rijsbergen M van and Scholten M, 'ESMA Inspecting: The Implications for Judicial Control under Shared Enforcement' (2016) 7 European Journal of Risk Regulation 569.

Ritleng D, 'Boards of Appeal of EU Agencies and Article 47 of the Charter: Uneasy Bedfellows?' in Merijn Chamon, Annalisa Volpato, and Mariolina Eliantonio (eds), *Boards of Appeal of EU Agencies: Towards Judicialization of Administrative Review?* (Oxford University Press 2022).

Röben V, 'The Enforcement Authority of International Institutions' (2008) 9 German Law Journal 1965.

Rocca P and Eliantonio M, 'European Union soft law by agencies: An analysis of the legitimacy of their procedural frameworks' in Maurizia de Bellis, Giacinto della Cananea, and Martina Conticelli (eds), *EU executive governance: Agencies and procedures* (Giappichelli 2020).

Rooi B van and Fine A, *The Behavioral Code. The Hidden Ways That the Law Makes Us Better . . . or Worse* (Beacon Press 2021).

Rosas A, 'The EU and International Dispute Settlement' (2017) 1(1) Europe and the World Law Review 1.

Rudolph S, 'Blackstone's Vision of Alternative Dispute Resolution' (1992) 22(2) Memphis University Law Review 279.

Ruffert M, *Law of Administrative Organization of the EU: A Comparative Approach* (Edward Elgar 2020).

Šadl U and Others, 'Law and Orders: The Orders of the European Court of Justice as a Window in the Judicial Process and Institutional Transformations' (2022) 1 European Law Open 549.

Šadl U, López Zurita L, and Piccolo S, 'Route 66. Mutations of the Internal Market Explored through the Prism of Citation Networks' (2023) 21 International Journal of Constitutional Law 826.

Šadl U and Wallerman Ghavanini A, '"The Referring Court Asks, in Essence": Is Reformulation of Preliminary Questions by the Court of Justice a Decision Writing Fixture or a Decision-Making Approach?' (2019) 25 European Law Journal 416.

Sadurski W, '*Solange, Chapter 3*': *Constitutional Courts in Central Europe* (EUI LAW Working Paper 40/2006).

Santos Vara J and Matellán L P, 'The Informalization of EU Return Policy: A Change of Paradigm in Migration Cooperation with Third Countries?' in Eva Kassoti and Narin Idriz (eds), *The Informalisation of the EU's External Action in the Field of Migration and Asylum* (Springer 2022).

Sarmiento D, 'Amending the Preliminary Reference Procedure for the Administrative Judge' (2009) 2 Review of European Administrative Law 29.

Säuberlich U, *Die Außervertragliche Haftung im Gemeinschaftsrecht: Eine Untersuchung der Mehrpersonenverhältnisse* (Springer 2005).

Scheingold SA, *The Politics of Rights: Lawyers, Public Policy, and Political Change* (Yale University Press 1974).

Schermers H and Waelbroeck D, *Judicial Protection in the European Union* (Kluwer Law International 2001).

Schmidt-Kessen M J, Nogueira R, and Cantero Gamito M, 'Success or Failure? – Effectiveness of Consumer ODR Platforms in Brazil and in the EU' (2020) 43 Journal of Consumer Policy 659.

Schmitz A and Martinez J, 'ODR and Innovation in the United States', in Mohamed S Abdel Wahab, Ethan Katsh, and Daniel Rainey (eds), *Online Dispute Resolution: Theory and Practice* (2nd edn, Eleven 2021).

Schneider J P, 'Basic Structures of Information Management in the European Administrative Union' (2014) 20(1) European Public Law 89.

'Information Exchange and Its Problems' in Carol Harlow, Päivi Leino, and Giacinto della Cananea (eds), *Research Handbook on EU Administrative Law* (Edward Elgar 2017).

Scholten M, 'Independence vs. Accountability: Proving the negative correlation' (2013) 21 Maastricht Journal of European and Comparative Law 197.

'Mind the Trend! Enforcement of EU Law Has Been Moving to Brussels' (2017) Journal of European Public Policy 1348.

Scholten M and Brenninkmeijer A, *Controlling EU Agencies. The Rule of Law in a Multi-jurisdictional Legal Order* (Edward Elgar 2020).

'Shared Tasks, but Separated Controls: Building the System of Control for Shared Administration in an EU Multi-Jurisdictional Setting' (2019) 10 European Journal of Risk Regulation 538.

Scholten M and Luchtman M (eds), *Law Enforcement by EU Authorities: Implications for Political and Judicial Accountability* (Edward Elgar 2017).

Scholten M, Strauss B, and Brenninkmeijer A, 'Controlling EU Agencies: an Introduction' in Miroslava Scholten and Alex Brenninkmeijer (eds), *Controlling EU Agencies. The Rule of Law in a Multi-jurisdictional Legal Order* (Edward Elgar 2020).

'Challenges and successes of enforcement of EU law' in Miroslava Scholten (ed), *Research Handbook on the Enforcement of EU Law* (Edward Elgar 2023).

Schramm M, 'Emulated Guardians: Practice, Politics, and Performativity of the DSA and the Oversight Board' (PhD Thesis, HU Berlin, June 2023).

Schuppert G F, 'Public Law: Towards a Post-National Model' in Kenneth Dyson and Klaus Goetz (eds), *Germany, Europe, and the Politics of Constraint* (Oxford University Press 2003).

Senden L, *Soft law in European Community Law* (Hart 2004).

Senden L and Brink T van den, 'Checks and Balances of Soft EU Rule-Making', Study for the European Parliament Directorate General for Internal Policies (2012) PE 462.433.

Setzer J and Higham C, 'Global trends in climate change litigation: 2021 snapshot' (2021) London: Grantham Research Institute on Climate Change and the Environment and Centre for Climate Change Economics and Policy, London School of Economics and Political Science.

Setzer J and Vanhala L C, 'Climate change litigation: A review of research on courts and litigants in climate governance' (2019) 10(3) WIREs Climate Change e580.

Shapiro M M, *Courts, a Comparative and Political Analysis* (University of Chicago Press 1981).

Shelton D, *Remedies in International Human Rights Law* (3rd edn, Oxford University Press 2015).

'Reparations in Human Rights Law' in Rachel Murray and Debra Long (eds), *Research Handbook on Implementation of Human Rights in Practice* (Edward Elgar 2022).

Shipan C R and Volden C, 'The Mechanisms of Policy Diffusion' (2008) 52 American Journal of Political Science 840.

Simmons B A, Dobbin F, and Garrett G (eds), *The Global Diffusion of Markets and Democracy* (Cambridge University Press 2008).

Singapore Management University, School of Law, Singapore International Dispute Resolution Academy (SIDRA), SIDRA International Dispute Resolution Survey: 2020 Final Report (*Sidra*, 2020) <https://sidra.smu.edu.sg/sidra-international-dispute-resolution-survey-final-report-2020>.

Sheikh H, Prins C, and Schrijvers E, *Mission AI: The New System Technology* (Springer 2023).

Silbey S S, 'After legal consciousness' (2005) 1 Annual Review of Law and Social Science 323.

Slaughter A M, Stone Sweet A, and Weiler J H H (eds), *The European Court and National Courts Doctrine & Jurisprudence: Legal Change in its Social Context* (Hart 1998).

Smulders B, 'Increasing convergence between the European court of Human Rights and the Court of Justice of the European Union in their recent case law on judicial independence: The case of irregular judicial appointments' (2022) 59 Common Market Law Review 105.

Solum L B, 'Procedural Justice' (2004) 67 Southern California Law Review 181.

Stancil P, 'Substantive Equality and Procedural Justice' (2016) 102 Iowa Law Review 1633.

Statewatch, 'Frontex and Interoperable Databases: Knowledge as Power?' (Statewatch 2023) < www.statewatch.org/frontex-and-interoperable-databases-knowledge-as-power/>.

Stefan M and Hertog L den, 'Frontex: Great Powers but No Appeals' in Merijn Chamon, Annalisa Volpato, and Mariolina Eliantonio (eds), *Boards of Appeal of EU Agencies: Towards Judicialization of Administrative Review?* (Oxford University Press 2022).

Stein E, 'Lawyers, Judges, and the Making of a Transnational Constitution' (1981) 75 American Journal of International Law 1.

Streckert O, *Verwaltungsinterner Unionsrechtsschutz – Kohärenter Rechtsschutz durch Einführung eines Widerspruchskammermodells für die Europäische Kommission* (Mohr Siebeck 2016).

Stronks M, *Grasping Legal Time: Temporality and European Migration Law* (Cambridge University Press 2022).

Stubberfield C, 'Lifting the Organisational Veil: Positive Obligations of the European Union Following Accession to the European Convention on Human Rights' (2012) 19 Australian International Law Journal 117.

Sugarman SD, 'Tort Damages for Non-Economic Loss: Personal Injury' in Mauro Bussani and Anthony J Sebok (eds), *Comparative Tort Law: Global Perspectives* (Edward Elgar 2015).

Sunderland J and Pezzani L, 'Airborne Complicity: Frontex Aerial Surveillance Enables Abuse' (Human Rights Watch, 12 August 2022) <www.hrw.org/node/383557>.

Syrpis P, 'The Relationship between Primary and Secondary Law in the EU' (2015) 52 Common Market Law Review 461.

Tas S, 'Frontex Actions: Out of Control?' [2020] TARN Working Paper 03/2020.

Thanou S, 'Individual restrictive measures and actions for damages before the General Court of the European Union' (2020) 20 ERA Forum 599.

Thierse S, 'Mobilisierung des Rechts: Organisierte Interessen und Verfassungsbeschwerden vor dem Bundesverfassungsgericht' (2020) 61 Politische Vierteljahresschrift 553.

Tidghi M and Hofmann H C H, 'Rights and Remedies in Implementation of EU Policies by Multi-Jurisdictional Networks' (2014) 20 European Public Law 147.

Timmermans C, 'Will the Accession of the EU to the European Convention on Human Rights fundamentally change the relationship between the Luxemburg and the Strasbourg courts?' [2014] EUI Distinguished Lectures (Speech delivered at the 'Judicial Cooperation in Private Law' of 15 and 16 April 2013).

Toth A G, 'The Concepts of Damage and Causality as Elements of Non-contractual Liability' in Ton Heukels and Alison McDonnell (eds), *The Action for Damages in Community Law* (Kluwer Law International 1997).

Tovo C, 'The Boards of Appeal of Networked Services Agencies: Specialized Arbitrators of Transnational Regulatory Conflicts?' in Merijn Chamon, Annalisa Volpato, and Mariolina Eliantonio (eds), *Boards of Appeal of EU Agencies – Towards Judicialization of Administrative Review?* (Oxford University Press 2022).

Travel Europe, 'What Is ETIAS' (Travel-europe.europa.eu) <https://travel-europe.europa.eu/etias/what-etias_en>.

Tridimas T and Gentile G, 'The Essence of Rights: An Unreliable Boundary?' (2019) 20 German Law Journal 794.

Truby J and Others, 'A Sandbox Approach to Regulating High-Risk Artificial Intelligence Applications' (2022) 13 European Journal of Risk Regulation 270.

Tsourdi EL, 'Bottom-up Salvation? From Practical Cooperation Towards Joint Implementation Through the European Asylum Support Office' (2016) 3 European Papers 997.

Türk A, *Judicial review in EU law* (Edward Elgar 2009).

Tushnet M V, *The New Fourth Branch: Institutions for Protecting Constitutional Democracy* (Cambridge University Press 2021).

Twining W, 'Moving Beyond Law: Interdisciplinarity and the Study of Evidence' in Philip Dawid, William Twining, and Mimi Vasilaki (eds), *Evidence, Inference and Enquiry* (Oxford University Press / British Academy 2011).

Undheim K, Erikson T, and Timmermans B, 'True Uncertainty and Ethical AI: Regulatory Sandboxes as a Policy Tool for Moral Imagination' (2023) 3(3) AI and Ethics 997.

Ury W L, Brett J M, and Goldberg S B, *Getting Disputes Resolved* (Jossey-Bass 1988).

Vandamme T, '"The two-step can't be the quick step': The CJEU reaffirms its case law on the European Arrest Warrant and the rule of law backsliding', (European Law Blog, 10 February 2021) <https://europeanlawblog.eu/2021/02/10/the-two-step-

cant-be-the-quick-step-the-cjeu-reaffirms-its-case-law-on-the-european-arrest-warrant-and-the-rule-of-law-backsliding/>.

Vandenbruwaene W, *Constitutional Change through Eurocrisis Law: Belgium* (European University Institute 2014).

Vanhala L, *Making Rights a Reality* (Cambridge University Press 2011).

'Legal Opportunity Structures and the Paradox of Legal Mobilization by the Environmental Movement in the UK' (2012) 46 Law & Society Review 523.

'Legal Mobilization under Neo-corporatist Governance: Environmental NGOs before the Conseil d'État in France, 1975–2010' (2016) 4 Journal of Law and Courts 103.

'Is Legal Mobilization for the Birds? Legal Opportunity Structures and Environmental Nongovernmental Organizations in the United Kingdom, France, Finland, and Italy' (2018) 51 Comparative Political Studies 380.

'Legal Mobilization' (Oxford Bibliographies, 23 November 2021) <www.oxfordbibliographies.com/view/document/obo-9780199756223/obo-9780199756223-0031.xml>.

Varuhas J N E, *Damages and Human Rights* (Hart 2016).

Vauchez A, 'The Force of a Weak Field: Law and Lawyers in the Government of the European Union (For a Renewed Research Agenda)' (2008) 2 International Political Sociology 128.

Brokering Europe: Euro-Lawyers and the Making of a Transnational Polity (Cambridge University Press 2015).

'The Genie of Independence and the European Bottle: How Independence Became Europe's Most Contentious Legal and Political Category' (2022) International Journal of Constitutional Law 1.

Vavoula N, 'Artificial Intelligence (AI) at Schengen Borders: Automated Processing, Algorithmic Profiling and Facial Recognition in the Era of Techno-Solutionism' (2021) 23 European Journal of Migration and Law 457.

'Information Sharing in the Dublin System: Remedies for Asylum Seekers In-Between Gaps in Judicial Protection and Interstate Trust' (2021) 22 German Law Journal 391.

Immigration and Privacy in the Law of the European Union: The Case of Information Systems (Brill Nijhoff 2022).

Venzke I, *How Interpretation Makes International Law* (Oxford University Press 2012).

Venzke I and Mendes J, 'The Idea of Relative Authority in European and International Law' (2018) 16 International Journal of Constitutional Law 75.

Vervaele J (ed), *Compliance and Enforcement of European Community Law* (Kluwer International 1999).

'Special procedural measures and the protection of human rights: General Report' (2009) 80 International Review of Penal Law 75.

'Surveillance and Criminal Investigation: Blurring of Thresholds and Boundaries in the Criminal Justice System' in Serge Gutwirth, Ronald Leenes, and Paul De Hert (eds), *Reloading Data Protection. Multidisciplinary Insights and Contemporary Challenges* (Springer 2014).

Vezzani S, 'The International Responsibility of the European Union and of Its Member States for Breaches of Obligations Arising from Investment Agreements:: Lex Specialis or European Exceptionalism?' in Mads Adenas and

Others (eds), *EU External Action in International Economical Law: Recent Trends and Developements* (T.M.C. Asser Press/Springer 2020).

Vissink L, *Effective Legal Protection in Banking Supervision* (Europa Law Publishing 2021).

Vogiatzis N, 'The Independence Of The European Court Of Auditors' (2019) 56 Common Market Law Review 667.

Vogiatzoglou P and Valcke P, 'Two Decades of Article 8 CFR: A Critical Exploration of the Fundamental Right to Personal Data Protection in EU Law' in Eleni Kosta, Ronald Leenes, and Irene Kamara (eds), *Research Handbook on EU Data Protection* (Edward Elgar 2022).

Vossen K, *Rechtsschutz in Der Europäischen Bankenaufsicht* (Mohr Siebeck 2020).

Waldron J, 'The Concept and the Rule of Law' (2008) 43 Georgia Law Review 1.

Wallace R M M, 'The Principle of Non-Refoulement in International Refugee Law' in Vincent Chetail and Céline Bauloz (eds), *Research Handbook on International Law and Migration* (Edward Elgar 2014).

Wallerman Ghavanini A, 'Mostly Harmless: The Referring Court in the Preliminary Reference Procedure' (2022) 47 European Law Review 310.

Ward A, 'Damages under the EU Charter of Fundamental Rights' (2012) 12 ERA Forum 589.

'Article 47: Interrelationship with Other Provisions of the Charter' in Steve Peers and Others (eds), *The EU Charter of Fundamental Rights: A Commentary* (2nd edn, Hart 2021).

'Article 47: The Right to an Effective Remedy under the First Paragraph of Article 47 and Challenge to EU Measure' in Steve Peers and Others (eds), *The EU Charter of Fundamental Rights: A Commentary* (2nd edn, Hart 2021).

'Article 51 – Field of Application' in Steve Peers and Others (eds), *The EU Charter of Fundamental Rights: a commentary* (2nd edn, Hart 2021).

Waters N, Freudenthal E and Williams L, 'Frontex at Fault: European Border Force Complicit in "Illegal" Pushbacks' (Bellingcat, 23 October 2020) <www.bellingcat.com/news/2020/10/23/frontex-at-fault-european-border-force-complicit-in-illegal-pushbacks/>.

Weiler J H H, 'The Transformation of Europe' (1991) 100 Yale Law Journal 2403.

Werkmeister C, Pötters S, and Traut J, 'Regulatory Acts within Article 263(4) TFEU – A Dissonant Extension of Locus Standi for Private Applicants' (2010–2011) 13 Cambridge Yearbook of European Legal Studies 311.

Westney D E, *Imitation and Innovation The Transfer of Western Organizational Patterns to Meiji Japan* (Harvard University Press 1987).

White & Case and Queen Mary University of London, '2018 International Arbitration Survey: The Evolution of International Arbitration' (White & Case, 2018) <www.whitecase.com/sites/whitecase/files/files/download/publications/qmul-international-arbitration-survey-2018-19.pdf>.

White S, 'Rights of Defence in Administrative Investigations: Access to the File in EC Investigations' (2009) 1 Review of European Law 57.

Widdershoven R, 'National Procedural Autonomy and General EU Law Limits' (2019) 12 Review of European Administrative Law 5.

Wigmore J H, A *Treaties on the Anglo-American System of Evidence in Trials at Common Law* (Brown 1923).

Wiik A, *Amicus Curiae before International Courts and Tribunals* (Nomos 2018).
Wildemeersch J, *Contentieux de la légalité des actes de l'Union européenne: le mythe du droit à un recours effectif* (Bruylant 2019).
Wille A and Bovens M, 'Watching EU Watchdogs Assessing the Accountability Powers of the European Court of Auditors and the European Ombudsman' (2022) 44 Journal of European Integration 183.
Wils W, 'Concurrent Liability of the Community and a Member State' (1992) 17 European Law Review 191.
Wind M, 'The Nordics, the EU and the Reluctance towards Supranational Judicial Review' (2010) 48 Journal of Common Market Studies 1039.
Witte B de, 'The use of the ECHR and Convention case law by the European Court of Justice' in Patricia Popelier, Catherine van de Heyning, and Piet van Nuffel (eds), *Human rights protection in the European legal order: the interaction between the European and the national courts* (Intersentia 2011).
Witte F de, 'Here Be Dragons: Legal Geography and EU Law' (2022) 1 European Law Open 113.
Wollenschläger F, 'Informationssysteme als Herausforderung für den Rechtsschutz im Europäischen Verwaltungsverbund: Das EU-Schnellwarnsystem für Lebens- und Futtermittel (RASFF)' (2019) 52 Die Verwaltung 1.
Wolters P T J, 'The Control by and Rights of the Data Subject Under the GDPR' (2018) 22 Journal of Internet Law 7.
Wright J, 'The Retreat from Osman: Z v United Kingdom in the European Court of Human Rights and Beyond' (2002) International & Comparative Law Quarterly 55.
Wróblewski J, 'La preuve juridique: axiologie, logique et argumentation' in Chaïm Perelman and Paul Foriers (eds), *La preuve en droit: études* (Bruylant 1981).
Xanthoulis N, 'Administrative Factual Conduct: Legal Effects and Judicial Control in EU Law' (2019) 12 Review of European Administrative Law 39.
Yannakourou M, 'Challenging austerity measures affecting work rights at domestic and international level. The case of Greece' in Claire Kilpatrick and Bruno de Witte (eds), *Social Rights in Times of Crisis in the Eurozone: The Role of Fundamental Rights' Challenges* (EUI Working papers LAW 05/2014).
Zamboni M, 'Legislative Policy and Effectiveness: A (Small) Contribution from Legal Theory' (2018) 9 European Journal Of Risk Regulation 416.
Zarbiyev F, 'On the Judge Centredness of the International Legal Self' (2021) 32 European Journal of International Law 1139.
Zekos G, 'The Historical Appearance of Arbitration as a Dispute Mechanism' in Georgis Zekos (ed), *International Commercial and Marine arbitration* (1st edn, Routledge-Cavendish 2008).
Zglinski J, 'The Rise of Deference: The Margin of Appreciation and Decentralized Judicial Review in EU Free Movement Law' (2018) 55 Common Market Law Review 1341.

Index

Page numbers: **bold** = table, *italics* = figure.

For EU product safety concerns, contact us at Calle de José Abascal, 56–1°, 28003 Madrid, Spain or eugpsr@cambridge.org.

www.ingramcontent.com/pod-product-compliance
Lightning Source LLC
LaVergne TN
LVHW011655200926
848484LV00004B/947
* 9 7 8 1 0 0 9 3 7 3 8 0 7 *